ICSE Exams 2026

AF819960

All in One

GEOGRAPHY

Class 10

ICSE Exams 2026

All in One®

GEOGRAPHY

Class 10

Author
Farah Sultan

arihant
SUCCESS AND NOTHING LESS

arihant
SUCCESS AND NOTHING LESS

ARIHANT PRAKASHAN
(School Division Series)

卐 ADMINISTRATIVE & PRODUCTION OFFICES

Regd. Office

'Ramchhaya' 4577/15, Agarwal Road, Darya Ganj, New Delhi -110002
Tele: 011- 47630600, 43518550; Fax: 011- 23280316

卐 Head Office

Kalindi, TP Nagar, Meerut (UP) - 250002, Tel: 0121-7156203, 7156204

卐 SALES & SUPPORT OFFICES

Agra, Ahmedabad, Bengaluru, Bareilly, Chennai, Delhi, Guwahati, Hyderabad, Jaipur, Jhansi, Kolkata, Lucknow, Nagpur & Pune.

PO No : TXT-XX-XXXXXXX-X-XX

Published By Arihant Publications (India) Ltd.

For further information about the books published by Arihant, log on to www.arihantbooks.com or e-mail at info@arihantbooks.com

Follow us on

卐 PRICE ₹ 330.00

PRODUCTION TEAM

Publishing Managers	Cover Designer	Inner Designer
Mahendra Singh Rawat & Keshav Mohan	Salman Shaikh	Ankit Tyagi
Project Head	**Page Layouting**	**Proof Reader**
Shivam Gupta	Jashoda	Ayushi

Index *cum* Study Planner

One Book- Endless Features

to Help you Succeed

CHAPTER 01

Interpretation of Topographical Maps

SYLLABUS

Interpretation of Topographical Maps

- Locating features with the help of a four figure or a six-figure grid reference.
- Definition of contour and contour interval. Identification of landforms marked by contours (steep slope, gentle slope, hill, valley, ridge / water divide, escarpment), triangulated height, spot height, bench mark, relative height/ depth.
- Interpretation of colour tints and conventional symbols used on a topographical survey of India map. Identification and definition of types of scale given on the map. Measuring distances and calculating area using the scale given therein.
- Marking directions between different locations, using eight cardinal points.
- Identify: Site of prominent villages and/or towns, types of land use / land cover and means of communication with the help of the index given at the bottom of the sheet.
- Identification of drainage (direction of flow and pattern) and settlement patterns.
- Identification of natural and man-made features.

Chapter Outlines

At the start of each chapter, all the topics of the chapter have been listed, so that students may know what they are going to study.

Quick Revision

At the end of each chapter, Quick Revision is given. It contains crux of the chapter in pointer form that provides the quick revision of the whole chapter.

Complete Theory in Each Chapter

Each chapter has Complete, Easy to Understand and Simplified theory covering latest syllabus. Theory is developed in such a way that it suitable for all types of learners.

QUiCK Revision

- The term 'climate' refers to the atmospheric conditions, which prevails in a large area over a long period of time.
- Generally, the climate of India belongs to the tropical monsoon type. The Tropic of Cancer, which passes through the centre of the country, divides it into sub-tropical climate zone (Northern part) and tropical zone (Southern part).
- Different parts of the country can experience different types of climate. So the regional variation in the climate is one of the major characteristics of India.
- Climate of India is affected by various factors such as latitude, altitude, Himalayan mountains, pressure and surface winds, Western disturbances, distance from the sea, tropical cyclones, by relief features, Monsoon wind, jet stream and El-Nino.

Definition and Significance of Map

A map is a symbolic representation of selected characteristics of a place, usually drawn on a flat surface. They teach about the world by showing sizes and shapes of countries, locations of features, and distances between places. Maps can show distributions of things over Earth, such as settlement patterns.

Check Your LEARNING...

1. Which type of climate India has?
2. Which regions of India experience - 45°C temperature?
3. Which regions of India faces low rainfall?
4. The Arabian sea lies in which direction?

Check Your Learning

A set of 3-5 Questions given in between the text, helps students to remain connected with the text while studying. They can instantly assess themselves for their understanding.

One Book- Endless Features
to Help you Succeed

Chapter Practice

Chapter Practice have all types of questions that are asked in the examinations such as Multiple Choice Questions, Short Questions and Structured Questions.

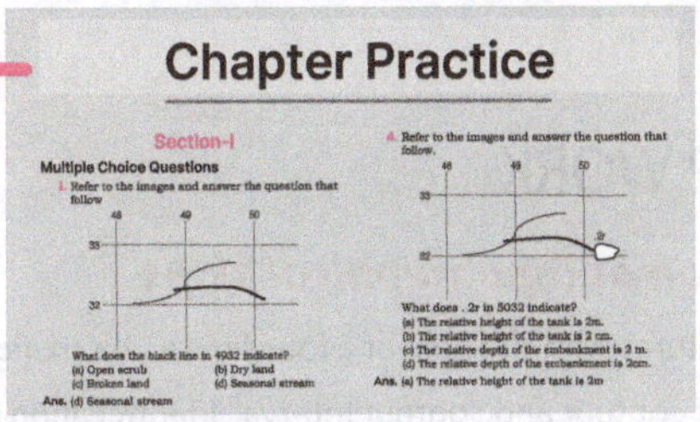
Chapter Practice

Section-I

Multiple Choice Questions

1. Refer to the images and answer the question that follow

What does the black line in 4932 indicate?
(a) Open scrub (b) Dry land
(c) Broken land (d) Seasonal stream

Ans. (d) Seasonal stream

4. Refer to the images and answer the question that follow.

What does . 2r in 5032 indicate?
(a) The relative height of the tank is 2m.
(b) The relative height of the tank is 2 cm.
(c) The relative depth of the embankment is 2 m.
(d) The relative depth of the embankment is 2cm.

Ans. (a) The relative height of the tank is 2m

Sample Question Papers

To make students practice of examination in real sense, there are 5 Sample Question Papers at the end. All these Sample Questions Papers are exactly prepared on the latest syllabus & pattern of examination.

Chapter Assessment

It is the Assessment exercise for the complete chapter. With this exercise, students can access their understanding of the chapter and can prepare for it accordingly.

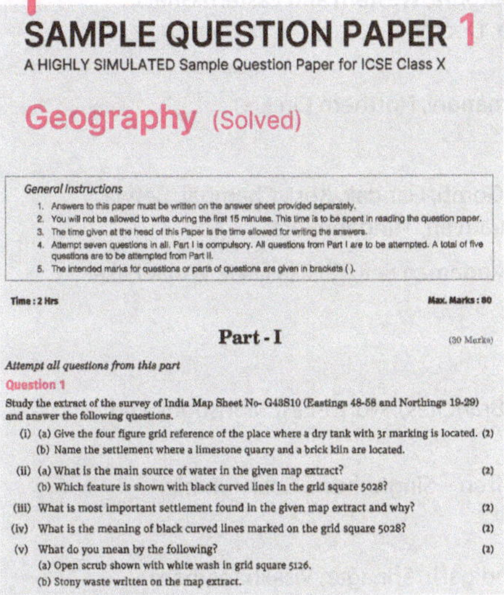
SAMPLE QUESTION PAPER 1
A HIGHLY SIMULATED Sample Question Paper for ICSE Class X

Geography (Solved)

General Instructions
1. Answers to this paper must be written on the answer sheet provided separately.
2. You will not be allowed to write during the first 15 minutes. This time is to be spent in reading the question paper.
3. The time given at the head of this Paper is the time allowed for writing the answers.
4. Attempt seven questions in all. Part I is compulsory. All questions from Part I are to be attempted. A total of five questions are to be attempted from Part II.
5. The intended marks for questions or parts of questions are given in brackets ( ).

Time : 2 Hrs **Max. Marks : 80**

Part - I
(30 Marks)

Attempt all questions from this part

Question 1

Study the extract of the survey of India Map Sheet No- G43S10 (Eastings 48-58 and Northings 19-29) and answer the following questions.

(i) (a) Give the four figure grid reference of the place where a dry tank with 3r marking is located. (2)
(b) Name the settlement where a limestone quarry and a brick kiln are located.

(ii) (a) What is the main source of water in the given map extract? (2)
(b) Which feature is shown with black curved lines in the grid square 5028?

(iii) What is most important settlement found in the given map extract and why? (2)

(iv) What is the meaning of black curved lines marked on the grid square 5028? (2)

(v) What do you mean by the following? (2)
(a) Open scrub shown with white wash in grid square 5126.
(b) Stony waste written on the map extract.

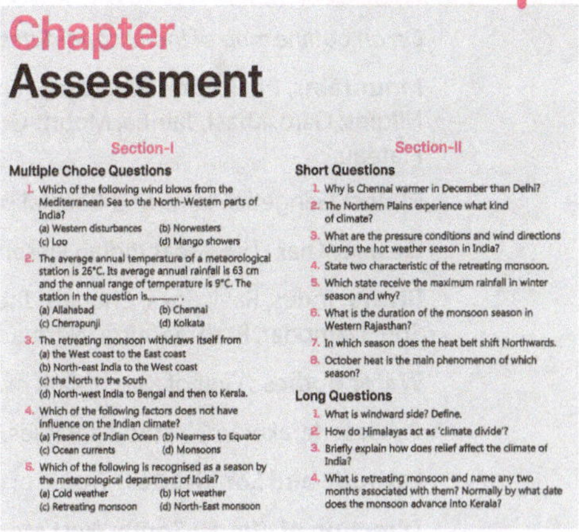
Chapter Assessment

Section-I

Multiple Choice Questions

1. Which of the following wind blows from the Mediterranean Sea to the North-Western parts of India?
(a) Western disturbances (b) Norwesters
(c) Loo (d) Mango showers
2. The average annual temperature of a meteorological station is 26°C. Its average annual rainfall is 63 cm and the annual range of temperature is 9°C. The station in the question is.......... .
(a) Allahabad (b) Chennai
(c) Cherrapunji (d) Kolkata
3. The retreating monsoon withdraws itself from
(a) the West coast to the East coast
(b) North-east India to the West coast
(c) the North to the South
(d) North-west India to Bengal and then to Kerala.
4. Which of the following factors does not have influence on the Indian climate?
(a) Presence of Indian Ocean (b) Nearness to Equator
(c) Ocean currents (d) Monsoons
5. Which of the following is recognised as a season by the meteorological department of India?
(a) Cold weather (b) Hot weather
(c) Retreating monsoon (d) North-East monsoon

Section-II

Short Questions

1. Why is Chennai warmer in December than Delhi?
2. The Northern Plains experience what kind of climate?
3. What are the pressure conditions and wind directions during the hot weather season in India?
4. State two characteristic of the retreating monsoon.
5. Which state receive the maximum rainfall in winter season and why?
6. What is the duration of the monsoon season in Western Rajasthan?
7. In which season does the heat belt shift Northwards.
8. October heat is the main phenomenon of which season?

Long Questions

1. What is windward side? Define.
2. How do Himalayas act as 'climate divide'?
3. Briefly explain how does relief affect the climate of India?
4. What is retreating monsoon and name any two months associated with them? Normally by what date does the monsoon advance into Kerala?

Latest Course *Structure*

There will be one paper of two hours duration carrying 80 marks and Internal Assessment of 20 marks.

PART I MAP WORK

1. *Interpretation of Topographical Maps*

a. Locating features with the help of a four-figure or a six-figure grid reference.

b. Definition of contour and contour interval. Identification of landforms marked by contours (steep slope, gentle slope, hill, valley, ridge / water divide, escarpment), triangulated height, spot height, bench mark, relative height/ depth.

c. Interpretation of colour tints and conventional symbols used on a topographical survey of India map.

d. Identification and definition of types of scale given on the map.
Measuring distances and calculating area using the scale given therein.

e. Marking directions between different locations, using eight cardinal points.

f. Identify: Site of prominent villages and/or towns, types of land use / land cover and means of communication with the help of the index given at the bottom of the sheet.

g. Identification of drainage (direction of flow and pattern) and settlement patterns.

h. Identification of natural and man-made features.

2. *Map of India*

On an outline map of India, candidates will be required to locate, mark and name the following

Mountains, Peaks and Plateaus: Himalayas, Karakoram, Aravali, Vindhyas, Satpura, Western and Eastern Ghats, Nilgiris, Garo, Khasi, Jaintia, Mount Godwin Austin (K2), Mount Kanchenjunga. Deccan Plateau, Chota Nagpur Plateau.

Plains: Gangetic Plains and Coastal plains – (Konkan, Kanara, Malabar, Coromandel, Northern Circars).

Desert: Thar (The Great Indian Desert)

Rivers: Indus, Ravi, Beas, Chenab, Jhelum, Satluj, Ganga, Yamuna, Ghaghra, Gomti, Gandak, Kosi, Chambal, Betwa, Son, Damodar, Brahmaputra, Narmada, Tapti, Mahanadi, Godavari, Krishna, Cauveri, Tungabhadra.

Water Bodies : Gulf of Kutch, Gulf of Khambhat, Gulf of Mannar, Palk Strait, Andaman Sea, Chilika Lake, Wular Lake.

Passes: Karakoram, Nathu-La Passes.

Latitude and Longitudes: Tropic of Cancer, Standard Meridian (82° 30′E).

Direction of Winds: South-West Monsoons (Arabian Sea and Bay of Bengal Branches), North-East Monsoons and Western Disturbances.

Distribution of Minerals: Oil-Mumbai High (Offshore Oil Field) and Digboi. Iron – Singhbhum, Coal – Jharia.

Soil Distribution : Alluvial, Laterite, Black and Red Soil.

Cities : Delhi, Mumbai, Kolkata, Chennai, Hyderabad, Bengaluru, Kochi, Chandigarh, Srinagar, Visakhapatnam, Allahabad.

Population : Distribution of Population (Dense and sparse).

PART II GEOGRAPHY OF INDIA

3. Location, Extent and Physical features

- Position and Extent of India. (through Map only).
- The physical features of India – mountains, plateaus, plains and rivers (through Map only).

4. Climate

- Distribution of Temperature, Rainfall, Winds in Summer and Winter and factors affecting the climate of the area.
- Monsoon and its mechanism. Seasons –March to May – Summer; June to September – Monsoon; October to November - Retreating Monsoon. December to February –Winter.

5. Soil Resources

- Types of soil (alluvial, black, red and laterite) distribution, composition and characteristics such as colour, texture, minerals and crops associated.
- Soil Erosion – causes, prevention and conservation.

6. Natural Vegetation

- Importance of forests.
- Types of vegetation (tropical evergreen, tropical deciduous, tropical desert, littoral and mountain), distribution and correlation with their environment.
- Forest conservation.

7. Water Resources

- Sources (Surface water and ground water).
- Need for conservation and conservation practices (Rain water harvesting and its importance).
- Irrigation: Importance and methods.

8. Mineral and Energy Resources

- Iron ore, Manganese, Copper, Bauxite – uses and their distribution.
- Conventional Sources: Coal, Petroleum, Natural gas (distribution, advantages and disadvantages). Hydel power (Bhakra Nangal Dam and Hirakud).
- Non-conventional Sources: Solar, wind, tidal, geo-thermal, nuclear and bio-gas (generation and advantages).

9. Agriculture

- Indian Agriculture – importance, problems and reforms.
- Types of farming in India: Subsistence and commercial: shifting, intensive, extensive, plantation and mixed.
- Agricultural seasons (rabi, kharif, zaid).

- Climatic conditions, soil requirements, methods of cultivation, processing and distribution of the following crops
  - rice, wheat, millets and pulses.
  - sugarcane, oilseeds (groundnut, mustard and soybean).
  - cotton, jute, tea and coffee.

10. Manufacturing Industries

- Importance and classification.
- Agro-based Industry - Sugar, Textile (Cotton and Silk).
- Mineral-based Industry – Iron & Steel (TISCO, Bhilai, Rourkela, Visakhapatnam) Petro-Chemical and Electronics.

11. Transport

- Importance and Modes – Roadways, Railways, Airways and Waterways – Advantages and disadvantages.

12. Waste Management

- Impact of waste accumulation - spoilage of landscape, pollution, health hazards, effect on terrestrial, aquatic (fresh water and marine) life.
- Need for waste management.
- Methods of safe disposal - segregation, dumping and composting.
- Need and methods for reducing, reusing and recycling waste.

Some Excerpts from

'Analysis of Pupils' Performance'

ICSE Geography Class 10

The document 'Analysis of Pupils' Performance, 2019' in ICSE Class 10 Examination, is prepared by Research Development and Consultancy Division (RDCD) of the Council for the Indian School Certificate Examination (CISCE).

The purpose of this document is to provide feedback to schools in terms of strengths and weaknesses of the candidates in handling the examination.

TOPICS FOUND DIFFICULT BY STUDENTS

- Toposheet: six figure reference, reason for presence of causeway, main means of irrigation and transport and significance of water body found in 2221.
- Map pointing: area of laterite soil in North, Gangetic plain and Digboi.
- Identifying the type of wind, calculation of total annual rainfall and reasoning related to factors affecting climate of India.
- Identifying vegetation belt in Nilgiri Hills, reasons for deepening of river bed helping in preventing soil erosion, benefits of modern means of irrigation, how transport helps in industrial growth, usefulness of segregation of waste before disposal.
- Man-made and natural features.
- Identifying most important settlement.
- Physical characteristic of laterite soil.
- Soil formed by weathering of basic lava rocks.
- Conditions for littoral forests.
- Mixed farming.
- Cropping seasons.
- Mining areas of minerals.
- Climatic requirement of crops.
- Cottage industry and cotton textile industry.
- Location of petro-chemical industries.

SUGGESTIONS FOR STUDENTS

- Study the chapters thoroughly. Avoid selective studies.
- Prepare tables/charts/notes etc. to revise before examination.
- Study the subject for acquiring knowledge and understanding of the subject and not for marks alone.
- Understand the concepts instead of merely cramming the concepts.
- Practice topographic sheet and map-based questions regularly.
- Concentrate on acquiring accuracy in map pointing by practicing it regularly.
- Master the technique to take note of key words.
- Learn to answer critical and analytical questions.
- Read books, newspapers and periodicals regularly.
- Solve past years' question papers.
- Read the instructions given on the question paper attentively.
- Use the 15 minutes reading time judiciously to make a proper choice of questions by reading the requirements of the question carefully.
- Choose the questions in which you are sure of answering all the parts.
- Do not answer extra questions unnecessarily. Concentrate on the questions you need to attempt.
- Read through the paper on completion to avoid mistakes.

List of Important Topics

from each chapter

On the basis of analysis of last 6 Years' Board Examination Papers, we have identified Important Topics from each chapter.

Chapter 1: Interpretation of Topographical Maps

- Grid References (four or six)
  (Average Marks in last 5 Yrs; 2023- 1 Mark, 2020- 2 Marks, 2019- 2 Marks, 2018-2 Marks)
- Scale of a Topographical Map and Measurement of Distances, Area and Direction
  (Average Marks in last 5 Yrs; 2023- 2 Marks, 2020- 2 Marks, 2019- 2 Marks, 2018- 3 Marks)
- Contours and Survey Marks and their interpretation and Conventional colours
  (Average Marks in last 5 Yrs; 2023- 2 Marks, 2020- 3 Marks, 2019- 2 Marks, 2018- 6 Marks)
- Identification of Drainage Patterns
  (Average Marks in last 5 Yrs; 2023- 1 Mark, 2020- 1 Mark, 2019- 1 Mark)
- Identification of Natural and Man-made features
  (Average Marks in last 5 Yrs; 2023- 1 Mark, 2020- 3 Marks, 2019- 3 Marks, 2018- 3 Marks)

Chapter 2: Map of India

- Mountains, Peaks, Plateaus and Passes
  (Average Marks in last 5 Yrs; 2023- 1 Mark, 2020- 1 Mark, 2019- 1 Mark, 2018-1 Mark, 2017- 1 Mark)
- Plains and Desert
  (Average Marks in last 5 Yrs; 2023- 1 Mark, 2020- 1 Mark, 2019- 1 Mark, 2018-1 Mark, 2017- 1 Mark)
- Rivers and water Bodies
  (Average Marks in last 5 Yrs; 2023- 1 Mark, 2020- 1 Mark, 2019- 1 Mark, 2018-1 Mark, 2017- 1 Mark)
- Latitude and Longitude and Direction of Winds
  (Average Marks in last 5 Yrs; 2023- 1 Mark, 2020- 1 Mark, 2018-1 Mark, 2017- 1 Mark)
- Distribution of Minerals, Soils
  (Average Marks in last 5 Yrs; 2023- 1 Mark, 2020- 1 Mark, 2019- 1 Mark, 2018-1 Mark, 2017- 1 Mark)
- Cities & Population
  (Average Marks in last 5 Yrs; 2023- 1 Mark, 2020- 1 Mark, 2019- 1 Mark, 2018-1 Mark, 2017- 1 Mark)

Chapter 4: The Climate of India

- Distribution of Temperature and Rainfall
  (Average Marks in last 5 Yrs; 2023- 1 Mark, 2019- 3 Marks, 2018-1 Mark, 2017 - 3 Marks)
- Factors affecting the Climate of an Area
  (Average Marks in last 5 Yrs; 2023 - 2 Marks)

- Monsoon & its Mechanism
  (Average Marks in last 5 Yrs; 2023- 2Marks, 2020- 3Marks, 2019- 2Marks, 2018-2 Marks, 2017-3 Marks)
- Seasons
  (Average Marks in last 5 Yrs; 2023- 6 Marks, 2020- 2 Marks, 2019- 5 Marks, 2018- 5 Marks, 2017- 2 Marks)

Chapter 5: Soils Resources

- Formation and Types of Soils
  (Average Marks in last 5 Yrs; 2023- 6 Marks, 2020- 5 Marks, 2018-3 Marks, 2017-5 Marks)
- Soil Erosion and Conservation
  (Average Marks in last 5 Yrs; 2023- 4 Marks, 2019- 3 Marks, 2018-3 Marks, 2017- 5 Marks)

Chapter 6: Natural Vegetation of India

- Importance and Types of Forests
  (Average Marks in last 5 Yrs; 2023- 6 Marks, 2020- 3 Marks, 2019- 3 Marks, 2018-3 Marks, 2017- 2 Marks)
- Deforestation and Forest Conservation
  (Average Marks in last 5 Yrs; 2023- 3 Marks, 2018-3 Marks)

Chapter 7: Water Resources

- Water Resources
  (Average Marks in last 5 Yrs; 2023- 2 Marks, 2020- 2 Marks, 2018-3 Marks)
- Irrigation : Methods
  (Average Marks in last 5 Yrs; 2023- 5 Marks, 2020- 5 Marks, 2019- 5 Marks, 2018- 3 Marks, 2017- 2 Marks)
- Need for Conservation and Conservation Practices
  (Average Marks in last 5 Yrs; 2023- 3 Marks, 2019- 1 Mark, 2018- 3 Marks)

Chapter 8: Minerals and Energy Resources

- Minerals
  (Average Marks in last 5 Yrs; 2023- 2 Marks, 2020- 2 Marks, 2019- 5 Marks, 2018-3 Marks, 2017-5 Marks)
- Conventional Sources of Energy
  (Average Marks in last 5 Yrs; 2023- 6 Marks, 2019- 3 Marks, 2018-2 Marks, 2017- 2 Marks)
- Non-Conventional Sources of Energy
  (Average Marks in last 5 Yrs; 2023- 3 Marks, 2020- 3 Marks, 2019- 2 Marks, 2018-2 Marks)

Chapter 9, 10 & 11: Agriculture in India, Food and Fiber Crops of India and Cash Crops of India

- Indian Agriculture (Importance, Problem, Reforms)
  (Average Marks in last 5 Yrs; 2023- 2 Marks, 2019- 2 Marks)
- Types of Farming
  (Average Marks in last 5 Yrs; 2023- 3 Marks, 2020- 2 Marks, 2018-2 Marks, 2017-2 Marks)
- Agricultural Seasons
  (Average Marks in last 5 Yrs; 2018-1 Mark)
- Major Crops
  (Average Marks in last 5 Yrs; 2023- 3 Marks, 2020- 5 Marks, 2019- 3 Marks, 2018-5 Marks, 2017-5 Marks)

Chapter 12: Manufacturing Industries

- Importance of Manufacturing Industries and Classification
  (Average Marks in last 5 Yrs; 2023- 3 Marks, 2020- 2 Marks)
- Agro - Based Industries
  (Average Marks in last 5 Yrs; 2023- 2 Marks, 2020- 5 Marks, 2019- 5 Marks, 2018- 6 Marks, 2017- 5 Marks)
- Mineral-Based Industries
  (Average Marks in last 5 Yrs; 2023- 4 Marks, 2020- 3 Marks, 2019- 1 Mark, 2018-2 Marks, 2017- 2 Marks)

Chapter 13: Transport

- Importance and Modes of Transport : (Roadways)
  (Average Marks in last 5 Yrs; 2023- 6 Marks, 2020- 2 Marks, 2019- 3 Marks, 2018- 3 Marks)
- Railways
  (Average Marks in last 5 Yrs; 2023- 2 Marks, 2020- 1 Mark, 2019- 3 Marks, 2018-2 Marks, 2017- 2 Marks)
- Airways
  (Average Marks in last 5 Yrs; 2023- 1 Mark, 2020 - 3 Marks, 2019- 1 Mark, 2018 - 3 Marks)
- Waterways
  (Average Marks in last 5 Yrs; 2020- 2 Marks, 2019- 3 Marks, 2018- 2 Marks, 2017-2 Marks)

Chapter 14: Waste Management

- Impact of Waste Accumulation
  (Average Marks in last 5 Yrs; 2023- 1 Mark)
- Need for Waste Management and Methods of Safe Disposal
  (Average Marks in last 5 Yrs; 2023- 6 Marks, 2020- 5 Marks, 2019- 3 Marks, 2018- 5 Marks)

CHAPTER 01

Interpretation of Topographical Maps

SYLLABUS

Interpretation of Topographical Maps

- Locating features with the help of a four figure or a six-figure grid reference.
- Definition of contour and contour interval. Identification of landforms marked by contours (steep slope, gentle slope, hill, valley, ridge / water divide, escarpment), triangulated height, spot height, bench mark, relative height/ depth.
- Interpretation of colour tints and conventional symbols used on a topographical survey of India map. Identification and definition of types of scale given on the map. Measuring distances and calculating area using the scale given therein.
- Marking directions between different locations, using eight cardinal points.
- Identify: Site of prominent villages and/or towns, types of land use / land cover and means of communication with the help of the index given at the bottom of the sheet.
- Identification of drainage (direction of flow and pattern) and settlement patterns.
- Identification of natural and man-made features.

Definition and Significance of Map

A map is a symbolic representation of selected characteristics of a place, usually drawn on a flat surface. They teach about the world by showing sizes and shapes of countries, locations of features, and distances between places. Maps can show distributions of things over Earth, such as settlement patterns.

A map is important because it is used to predict and figure out where things are located. Maps can show where streets run in a city. They can show where certain physical features such as mountains and rivers are located. They can show the location of territories of the various countries.

Elements of Map

The **title** and **sub-title** are the basic elements of a map. The title of the map indicates the place for which the map is drawn, example-India.

Sub-title gives information about the purpose of the map-example-physical or political.

- Direction as per the international convention indicates that every map identifies the North direction with the help of an arrow pointing to the North or with the alphabet 'N'.
- Some object like mountains, buildings or forests etc. are represented on a map by using signs, symbols, pictures or letters due to limited space. These are called conventional signs and symbols.
- Particularly topographical maps contain symbols, signs and pictures. In India such maps show the standard symbols set by the Indian survey department. For example, A plus sign (+) indicates spring. A symbol of two parallel horizontal lines (=) indicates a metal road.
- The scale of a map is the ratio or proportion between the distances on the ground. Maps represents the surface of the Earth on a small scale on a piece of paper.

- Small scale maps like wall maps and atlas maps show relief features through colours.

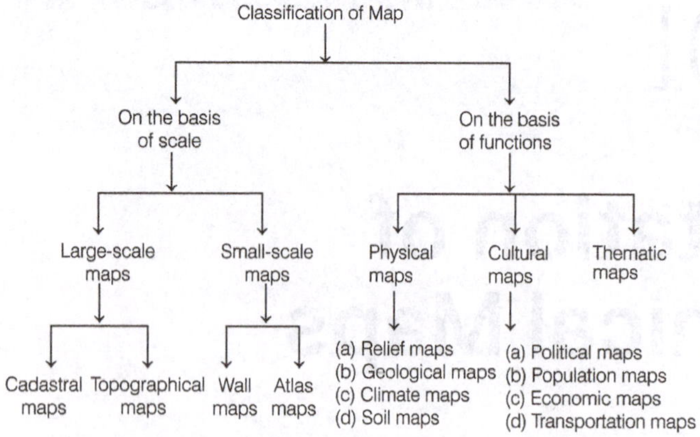

Topographical Maps

A map of a small area drawn on a relatively large-scale depicting detailed surface features both natural and man-made is called as 'Topographical map' or 'general purpose map'. These maps are used as basic tools for planning and executing projects like planning settlements, airports, highways, dams, pipelines, transmission lines, industrial plants, water bodies, relief, vegetation, cultivated land and countless other types of construction.

These maps also contain other specific information like names of towns, villages, rivers, forests, hills etc., besides symbols denoting buildings with specific functions like temples, post offices, railway stations etc. These maps are prepared and published by the National Mapping Organisation of each country e.g. in India, these maps are brought out by the Survey of India Department under the Ministry of Science and Technology.

Identification of Topographical Maps

If a part of India is being depicted in the map it can be deduced from the sheet number, which consists of a number and a fraction with a letter ('A' onwards up to Q, except I) in the numerator and another number in the denominator e.g. 45 D/7.

The first number indicates the serial number of the 4° (latitude) × 4° (longitude) square (India has been divided into many such squares for the purpose of survey).

This square is further divided into 16 squares (they are identified by letters), which are again divided into 16 squares (they are identified by numbers 1 to 16). Thus, the 45 D/7 sheet depicts an area corresponding to 1/4° × 1/4° (or 15' × 15') of latitude and longitude.

Grid References

Topographical maps show the specific details of surface features of a relatively small area on the ground. Topographical maps often feature area and **grid**[1] references, since, it is an ideal way to systematically and accurately locate specific points. The given topographical maps 45D/7 and 45D/10 have a grid of square marked on them, with each side of the square representing 1 km on the ground (2 cm = 1 km). Vertical lines of these squares are called **Easting**[2] (as they are numbered going from West to East) and horizontal lines which run from South to North are called **Northings**[3].

These vertical (longitude) and horizontal (latitude) parallel lines form a network which is called the 'Grid' and also identified as the 'grid reference'.

Grid lines are shown in red colour on the topographic sheets. Along the margins of a toposheet, the values of the Easting and Northings are indicated.

Rules for Reading a Grid Reference

There are some important rules to be followed while measuring Eastings and Northings on a topographical map

- Always start reading of grid reference from the bottom left hand corner (South-West corner) of the **grid squares**[4].
- The Easting always comes before the Northing when stating a location. One should always take the readings to the left of the Easting and to the North or the Northings.

1 **Grid** An imaginary network of equidistant lines e.g. parallels of latitudes and meridians of longitudes, which enables in locating the position of a place to be accurately defined in a simple way.

2 **Easting** It is the distance which is East in longitude from the preceding points of measurement. It is running vertically and shown by red lines on the toposheets.

3 **Northings** It is the distance which is North in latitude from the preceding points of measurement. It is running horizontally and shown by red colour.

4 **Grid Square** It is an area of 1 sq km demarcated on the toposheet on the intersection of grid lines. Each grid square measures 2 sq km distance of map.

Ways of Reading a Grid Reference

There are two ways through which a grid can be read out

(i) Four-Figure Grid Reference

In four-figure grid reference the approximate location of any objects is shown. In this method, the intersecting point of Eastings and Northings is taken as originating point.

For example in the figure given below the four-figure grid reference of the school (marked as S) is in the square with its centre at the Easting marked 17 and again its centre at the Northing marked 03.

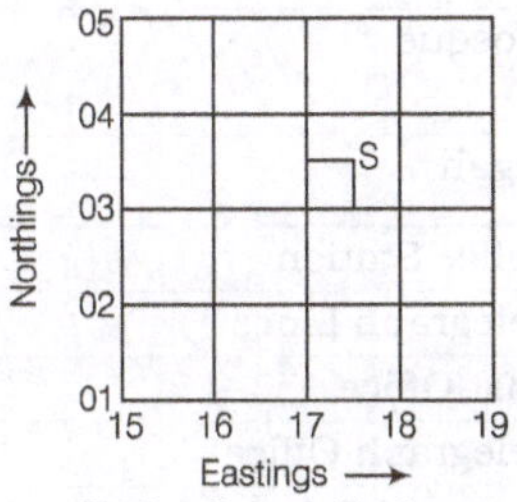

The four-figure grid reference of school is 1703

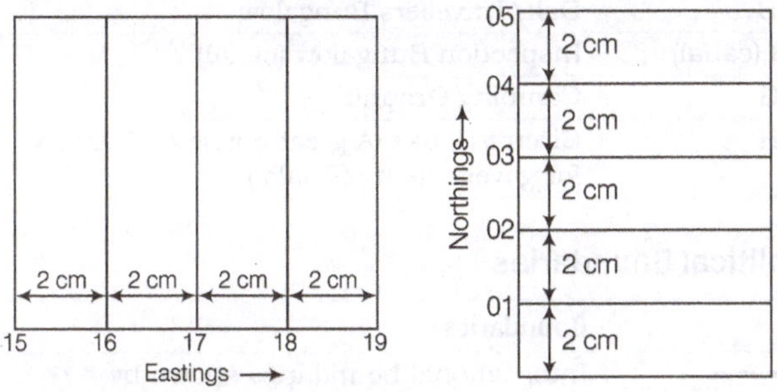

Thus, the four-figure grid reference will be 1703 i.e. the first-two numbers give the Easting and the next two numbers give the Northing.

(ii) Six-Figure Grid Reference

It is used to find the exact location or pinpoint location of any object like temple, school, railway station, spot height etc.

First, divide the 2 cm box (1km) or the co-ordinates on QQ ′ YY′ axis as LMNO square into ten equal parts, vertically and horizontally. Then 1 km × 1 km square is divided into 10 × 10 parts (each tiny square represents 100 m × 100 m, or 0.1 km × 0.1 km).

Hence, we can see that the 5th part of the Easting 17 and 6th part of the Northing 03 intersect each other and point T (Triangulated station). So, the six-figure grid reference of point T is 175036.

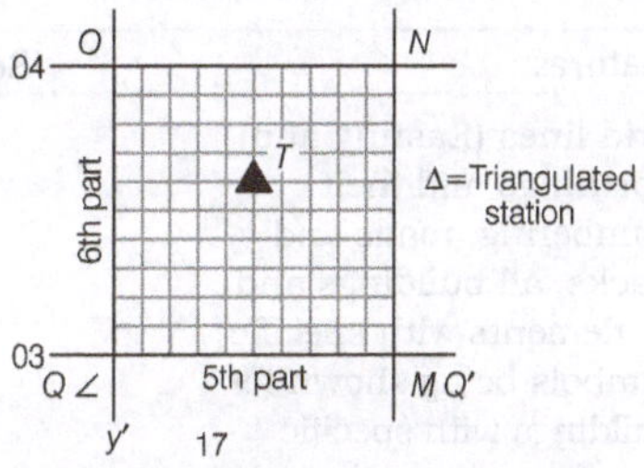

The Six-Figure Grid Reference of T is T 175036

Importance of Grid References

The four-figure grid references are applied to locate large areas like lakes, relief features, etc. while the six-figure grid reference are applied to locate the exact position of a particular place or feature like police station, spot height, wells, causeways, temple, etc.

National Grid Reference

Grid lines are imaginary lines drawn on a survey map in red colour. The origin of the grid is a point South-West of the map. The 'National Grid Reference' is used for indicating the correct position of a particular feature on the map.

Significance of Colours in Topographical Maps

Several natural and man-made features are represented by coloured area and by a set of standard symbols on all topographical maps. These colours are known as 'Conventional colours' such as

Colours	Features	Remarks
Black	All name, heights and their numbering, latitude and longitude lines, railway lines, telephone or telegraph lines, dry streams and river banks, surveyed trees and broken ground.	Surveyed trees are numbered and not allowed to be cut.
Blue	Perennial rivers, ponds, lakes, tanks, wells and other water bodies.	Seasonal rivers are shown as speckled.
Green	All forested areas, orchards, scattered trees and scrubs.	
Yellow	Cultivated areas or land.	
White	Uncultivable land, badlands or rocky area.	
Brown	Contour lines and their numbering, sand hills and dunes.	The symbol size as well as the size and style in which its name is written decide the size of the settlement.

Colours	Features	Remarks
Red	Grid lines (Easting and Northings and their numbering, roads and tracks, all buildings and settlements with specific symbols being shown for buildings with specific functions, permanent huts.	

Significance of Conventional Signs and Symbols in Topographical Maps

In **cartography**[5] symbols are everything. When we first think of symbols, we tend to think of graphics representing elements that appear points, like bridges and houses.

Symbols can be point like bridges, house and like roods, railways and rivers. Map itself is Nothing, but a symbol. The purpose of a map is to permit one to visualise an area of the Earth's surface with suitable features properly positioned.

These symbols or signs are called **conventional signs** or symbols. A group to conventional signs depicting natural and man-made features are called **Legend**[6]. Every map has its own legend without this topographic map cannot be read.

Conventional Signs and Symbols Used in Survey Maps

Urban or Man-Made Features

Settlements

	Permanent hut
	Temporary hut
	Settlement type
	**Nucleated** These settlements can be found into grouped or clustered form close to a railway station, a confluence, a mine or an industrials site.
	**Linear** Settlements which usually develop on either side of main road or along the coast with a view to provide services e.g. dhabas, hotels and shops.
	**Scattered** or **Dispersed** In these, the permanent huts are isolated or scattered. These hamlets spread over fertile farmland.

Structural Features

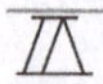	Tower
	Antiquities
	Fort
	Chhatri
	Mandir (temple)
	Church
	Tomb
	Graves
	Mosque
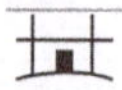	Idgah
PS	Police Station
....	Telegraph Lines
PO	Post Office
TO	Telegraph Office
PTO	Post and Telegraph Office (combined)
RH (forest)	Rest House
DB	Dak/Travellers Bungalow
IB (canal)	Inspection Bungalow (canal)
CG	Camping Ground
CH	Circuit House (A great house exclusively for government officials.)

Political Boundaries

	Boundaries
•—•—•	International boundaries shown by bold dash and dot. It indicates the borders between the countries.
—·—	State boundaries (demarcated) by single dash and dot line.
—×—×	State boundaries (undemarcated)
– – –	Districts (sub-divisions) It is a series of dashes forms the border between the districts with a state.
• • • •	Teshil/taluka is represented by a series of dots.
	Boundary pillars
••• ••	Forest boundary
□	Unlocated
■	Surveyed

5 **Cartography** It is an art, science and technology of making maps, charts plans and other modes of graphical expression as well as their study and use.

6 **Legend** An explanation or key to the symbols uses on a map or diagram.

Transport and Communication

Roads

Metalled (Pucca) Roads These roads shown in red double lines. Symbol of development of trade in the region. A number written beside the road shows a milestone.

Unmetalled (Kutch) Roads These roads are not tarred. Indicates an undeveloped area or village.

Cart Track It is a path little broader than pack-track made by bullock carts.

Pack Track (Pagdandi) It is a path for constant use by men or animals to travel. It is shown in red broken line.

Footpath with a Bridge It is for temporary use to cross a region. It is shown by a single line of dots in red colour.

Railways

Broad Gauge It is the distance between two rails i.e. 1.69 m.

Metre Gauge 1 m distance between the rails.

Narrow Gauge 0.7 m distance a railway line crossing a road.

It shows railway line with a station.

Light railway or tramway.

Cutting with a Tunnel It is an open vertical cut in high ground to enable a road or railway to pass through.

Level Gossing It indicates a railway line crossing a road.

Bridges

A bridges is a structure constructed across a road, river or railway to carry the traffic.

A ridge without a causeway.

Bridge with Piers The bridge supported by pillars.

Tunnel A passage for a railway line through a hill.

Ford or Ferry Ford is a shallow place where a river may be crossed wading. Ferry is a boat to carry people across a river where it is narrow.

Causeway A road that is raised above water, marshland, sand or stream. Its presence shows that the area of scanty rainfall. It is motorable only in dry season.

Features Connected with River, Drainage and Irrigation

Drainage System

Stream (nallah)

River River is larger than a stream, if speckled shows dry river and if coloured blue, shows a perennial river

Stream with track in bed.

Stream Undefined

River, dry with water channel shown in blue

River with Island and Rocks Specially in lower course the river load deposited is indicated by islands and rocks. It is more prominent if the river is dry.

Disappearing Stream Its water is absorbed in the soil (porous in nature) before it joints the main river.

Seasonal Streams These dry up in summer and occur only in rainy season, specially in arid or limestone regions.

Confluence It is a bend in the river flowing through a plain.

Falls It is shown by contours and written as falls along with heights (in metre) in a hilly region.

Broken Ground It is found along the banks of a stream or river in arid regions where the top soil gets easily eroded due to flooding during rainy season. This is not fit for cultivation.

This sign in blue shows river bank selving

River bank steep (3 to 6 metres)

River bank (over 6 metres)

Means of Irrigation and Other Water Features

Canal A long and narrow strip of water made for navigation or for irrigation during dry period.

Tank is the major source of irrigation, especially in hilly regions during dry periods. An embankment is built to keep the water flowing out.

A perennial tank having water throughout the year is shown in blue.

Tank (dry) It is speckled with black dots indicating area of seasonal rainfall.

Man-made tank = with embankment

Natural tank = without embankment

	Perennial lined well is a pucca well lined with bricks and cement with water. It is shown as a blue dot.
	Unlined well is shown as a blue circle if it contains water. The relative depth is indicated by a number beside it e.g. 40 r. It is a Kutch well.
	Brackish water is unfit for drinking and cultivation as it is salty. It is found in dry or arid areas with salt content in water due to evaporation.
	Shoal (submerged rock) is an area of shallow water.
	Swamp It is a low land that is seasonally flooded. Mostly found along the coastal areas.
	Dam (masonry) It is a man-made structure built across a river to control the overflow of water. It serves to irrigate, control flood and produce hydro electricity. It may be masonry or rock filled.
	Aqueduct is an artifical channel usually elevated and built of masonry.
	Reservoir (talao/table) is a man-made artificial tank with embankment to store water.
	It is an Earthen dam.
	Weir is a low dam across a river.
	Island is a landmass that is surrounded by water. If an island is uncultivable it is shown in white colour.

Vegetation Cover

	Vine on trellis
open scnub	**Open Scrub** Shows arid or desert condition. Here main occupation is animal husbandry.
	Plantain
	Palmyra It is a type of plant of desert of coastal vegetation.
	Grass This indicates grazing ground.
	Conifers are found mainly in colder highlands.
	Bamboos found in areas of scanty or less rainfall. There kikar and babul are main species.
	Surveyed tree is a Survey point shown in black colours. An open jungle is the characteristic of moderate rainfall.

PF	**Protected Forest** These are planted as shelter belts to prevent soil erosion in deserts.
	Deciduous forest
Fire line	**Fire line** It is a clearing or gap made in the forest to prevent the spread of forest fires.

Other Important Features

Stony waste	**Stony Waste** A land which is mostly covered with rock boulders and stones is called **Stony Waste.** This area is unfit for agriculture. It is shown as a white.
Sheet rock	**Sheet Rock** A land which is mainly covered by layer or sheet of rocks is known as 'Sheet Rock'.
Rock out crop	**Rock Out Crop** There top soil is removed by erosion and subsoil is exposed. Therefore, cultivation is not possible.
	Sand Dunes Heaps or mounds of sands are generally called 'Sand Dunes'. These features are shown in brown colour.
Brick kiln	**Kiln** (bricks) A furnace for firing or burning or drying bricks, limestone etc. It shows main occupation of the people who reside around there.
Lime kiln	**Kiln** (lime) It also shows employment source.
Stone quarry	**Stone Quarry** It shows the main occupation of the people where it Stone qusrryStone qusrryStone qusrrys found.
	Telegraph line

	Legend
8	Roads, metalled : accroding to importance, distance stone.
	Roads unmetalled : according to importance, bridge.
	Cart track Pack track and Pass. Footpath with bridge....
	Bridges; with piers, without causeway. Ford or Ferry.....
	Streams with track in bed; undefined. Canal.....
	Dams: masonry or rock-filled; Earth work, Weir.......
	River banks shelvings: steep 3 to 6 metres; over 6 metres....
	River dry with water channel: with island and rocks. .Tidal river....

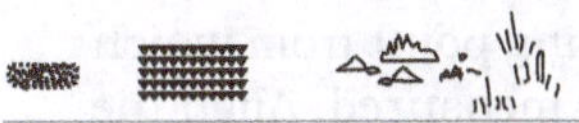	Submerged rocks. Shoal, Swamp, Reeds....
	Wells lined unlined. Tube-well. Spring Tanks: pernnial:dry
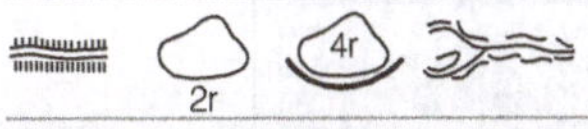	Embankments: road or rail: tank. Broken ground.....
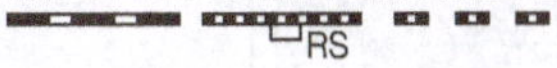	Railways, broad gauge: double: single with station:under construction.
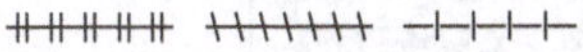	Railways other gauges double single, distance stone, under construction..
	Light railway or tramway, Telegraph line, Cutting with tunnel.
	Contours with sub-features, from-line, Rocky slopes, Cliffs..
	Sand features : (1) Flat, (2) Sand-hills (permanent), (3) Dunes (shifting)...
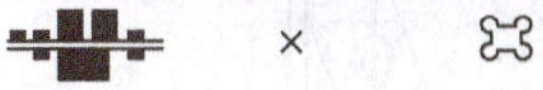	Towns or villages: inhabited; deserted, Fort....
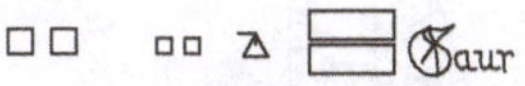	Huts: Permanent temporary, Tower, Antiquites
	Temple, Chhatri, Church, Mosque, Idgah, Tomb, Graves
	Lighthouse, Lightship, Buoys, lighted, unlighted Anchorage....
	Mine, Vine on trellis, Grass, Scrub....
	Falms palmyra; other, Plantain: Conifer, Bamboo, Other trees
	Boundary international.....
	Boundary state: demarcated; undemarcated...
	Boundary district; sub-divn, tashil or taluk, village, forest....
	Boundary pillars: surveyed; unlocated; village trijunction....
△200 •200 •63	Heights, triangulated: station: point......
BM 63.3 BM63.3 .63	Bench-mark geodetic: tertiary: canal.....
PO TO PTO PS	Post Office, Telegraph Office, Combined Office, Police Station....
DB IB (Canal) RH (Forest)	Bungalows Dak or travellers: inspection Rest-House.....
CH CG RF PF	Circuit house, Camping Ground, Forest Reserved, protected....
KIKRI DUAR NAGA	Spaced names administrative; locality: tribal....

Scale

The scale of a map is the ratio of a distance on the map of the corresponding distance on the ground. A map is a scaled graphic representation of a portion or whole of the Earth's surface. Scales are used to reduce the whole or part of the Earth's surface. There are three common types of scales given

(i) **Simple Statement or Verbal Scale** It expresses the units of the map as well as the ground e.g. 1 centimetre =10 kilometres.

It has the following characteristics

(i) The numerator refers to map distance and the denominator refers to ground distance.

(ii) If the numerator is in centimetres, then the denominator is in metres and kilometres.

(ii) **The Representative Fraction (RF)** The numerical scale of a map indicates the relationship of distance measured on a map and the corresponding distance on the ground.

The RF is always written with the map distance as 1 and is independent of any unit of measure. It could be yards, metres inches and so forth e.g. In the given reference map no 45D/10, 1:50000 is the RF of the map, which means that one unit of measure on the map is equal to 50000 units of the same measure on the ground. It is expressed in this way

$$RF = \frac{\text{Distance on the map}}{\text{Distance on the ground}} \Rightarrow RF = 1:50000$$

(iii) **Graphic (Bar) or Linear Scale** A graphic scale is a ruler printed on the map and is used to convert distances on the map to actual ground distances. In figure 1.8, the graphic scale is divided into two parts. To the right of the zero, the scale is marked in full units of measure and is called the 'Primary Scale'. To the left of the zero, the scale is divided into Secondary Scale and is called the 'Extension Scale'. This enables the map reader to measure distance in fractions also.

If we want to measure full units, we will begin with zero and use the right side or the primary scale.

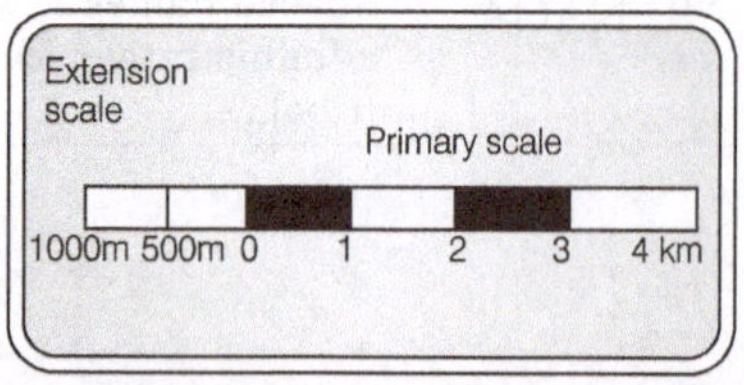

Measuring Distances on a Map

Measurement of Straight Distances

To determine straight-line distance between two points on a map, we can use a scale or a piece of paper

(i) Lay a straight-edged piece of paper or a scale on the map so that the edge of the paper or scale touches both points and extends past them. Make a tick mark on the edge of the paper at each point.

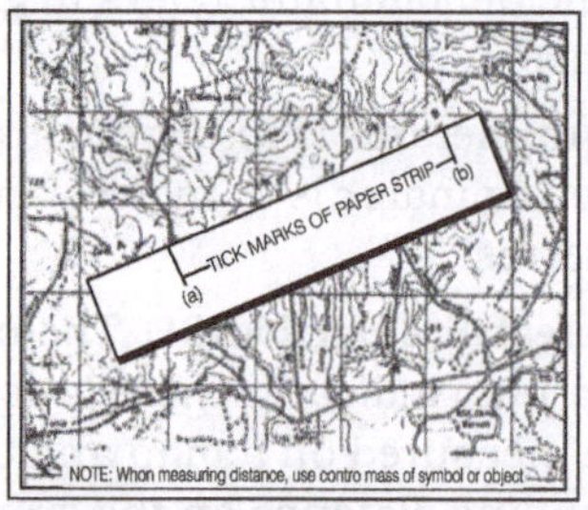

(ii) To convert the map distance to ground distance, move the paper/scale down to the graphic bar scale and align the right tick mark (b) with a printed number in the primary scale so that the left tick mark (a) is in the extension scale.

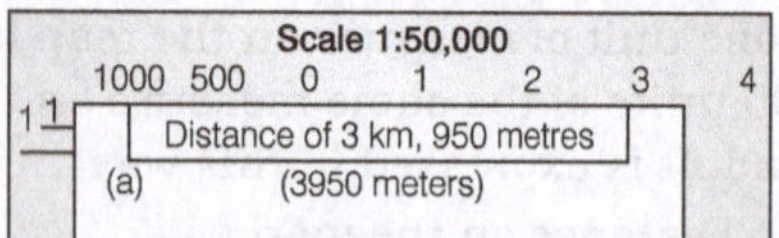

(iii) Now place the divider or strip of paper on the linear scale drawn on the map. This will directly give the distance on the ground between the two point.

Measurement of an Indirect or Curved Distance

To determine curved-lines (like course of a river or winding roads etc) distance between two points on a map, we use the following steps

(i) To measure distance along a road, stream or other curved line, the straight edge of a piece of paper is used. Place a tick mark on the paper and map at the beginning point from which the curved line is to be measured. Align the edge of the paper along a straight portion and make a tick mark on both map.

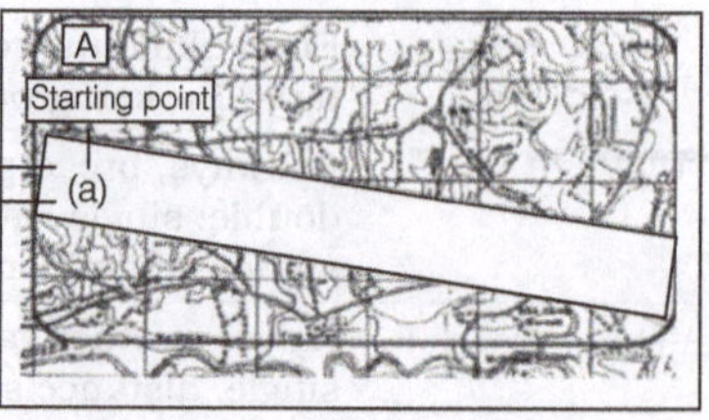

(ii) Keeping both tick marks together (on paper and map) place the point of the pencil close to the edge of the paper on the tick mark to hold it in place and pivot the paper until another straight portion of the curved line aligned with the edge of the paper.

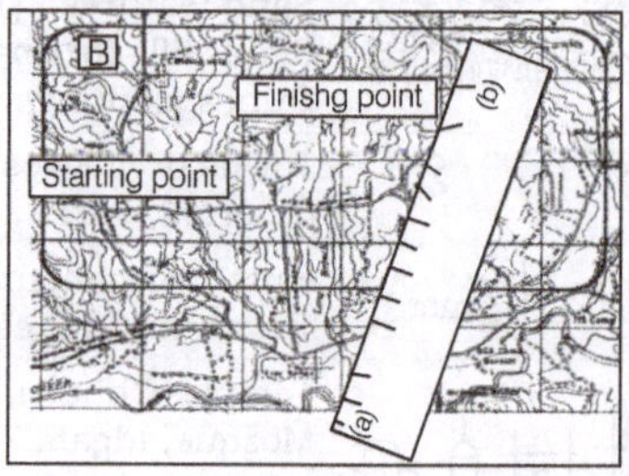

(iii) When you have completed measuring the distance, move the paper to the graphic scale to determine the ground distance as said in the previous example.

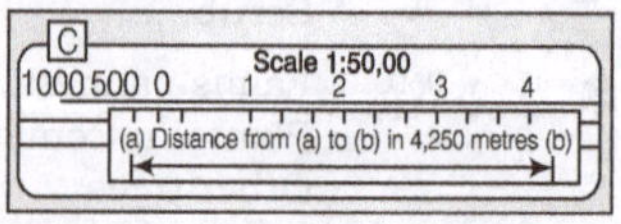

Note To measure an indirect distance thread and opisometre can also be used.

Measurement of Area by Grid Square Method

In topographical maps, each grid square measures 2 sq. cms (2 cm × 2 cm) or (1 km × 1 km). Since, 2 cm is equal to 1km. Hence, area of each square is 1 sq km. To calculate a certain area of topographical map, we need to follow some steps

1. Count the number of complete grid squares within the area.
2. The number of remaining square which covered more than half take them as 2/3.
3. If some squares covered half take them as 1/2.

4. If the squares covered are less than half take them as 1/3 squares and count (shown in figure below). Now, all these estimated squares are added together and then sum is multiplied by the scale of the map.

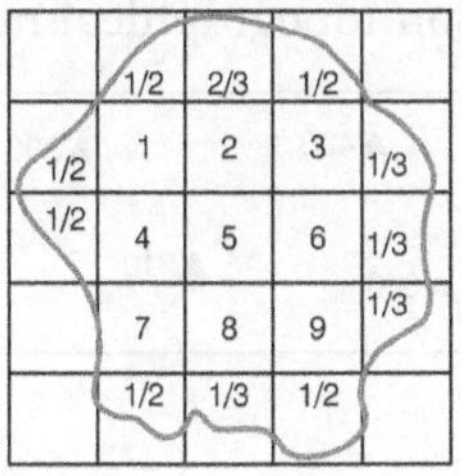

Marking Directions

There are the four cardinal points e.g. North-West, South-West, North-East and South-East figure given below. These are useful for indicating the flow of rivers and streams as well as the location of one town from another.

In the case of location of any town far from another, the word to and from are used e.g. if we want to go 'to' Mumbai 'from' Delhi, we will go SW i.e. South-West. However, if we want to go 'to' Delhi 'from' Mumbai, we will go NE i.e. North-East.

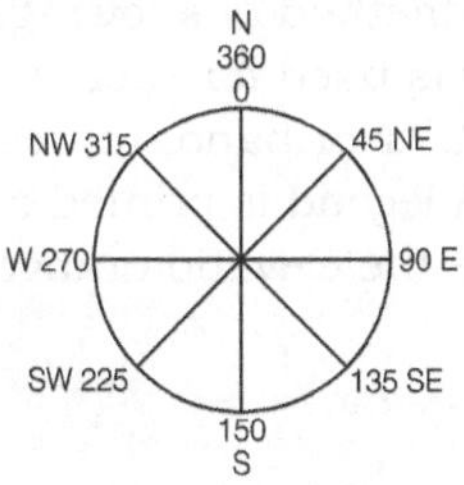

Bearing

A bearing is a measurement of direction between two points. It is the horizontal angle between the North and line joining the position of the observer and the object or feature in a clockwise direction. In figure given below x is the position of the observer.

The line x A connects the landmark A with x and makes a clockwise angle of 320° with the North-South line (NS) passing through the observer. Hence, we get the bearing of the landmark feature A with reference to the observer x i.e. 320°.

We can find out the position of an object by two ways of bearing such as

- **Forward Bearing** i.e. bearing from observer to the object.
- **Backward Bearing** i.e. bearing from the object to the observer.

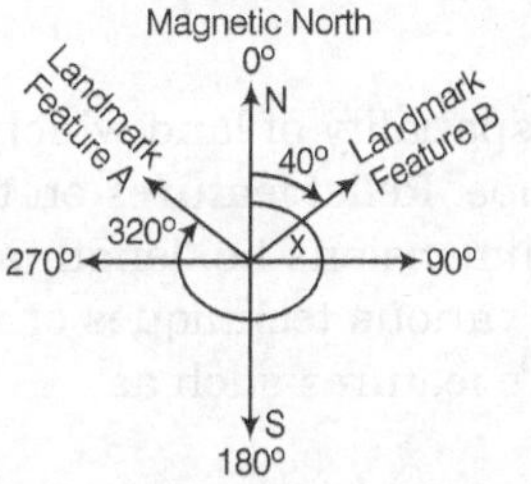

There are two other types of bearing such as

(i) **Magnetic Bearing** A bearing with reference to magentic North-South line is known as 'Magnetic Bearing'.

(ii) **Geographic or True Bearing** A bearing measured with reference to geographic North-South line is known as 'True Bearing'.

Magnetic North and True North

At present a simple device called Magnetic Compass is used to find directions. 'Magnetic field' of a compass needle always points towards the 'North', that is called 'Magnetic North'. But it is marginally deviated from the true or Geographical North by a few degrees, this deviation is called 'Magnetic Declination'.

True North or Geographical North is based on position of the North pole/North star. The declination or variation is caused by the magnetic North which is not fixed and moves slowly from time-to-time.

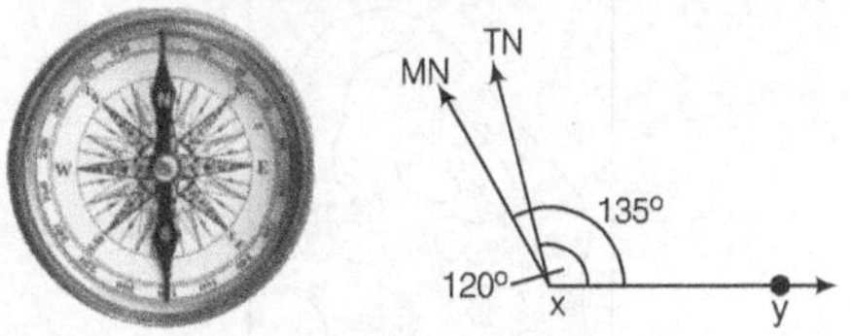

Identification of Natural and Man-Made Features

- **Natural Physical Features** These include various landforms, relief features i.e. plains, plateaus, hills, mountains, waterfalls, passes etc. These are depicted by various techniques like, contour, hachures, hill shading, layer tinting/colouring etc.
- **Man-Made or Cultural Features** These are villages, towns, types of land use, means of communication, settlement pattern, canals, bridge etc. These are depicted by symbols called 'conventional signs'.

Representation of Natural Relief Features

Relief refers to spatiality of land which includes its altitude and slope. Relief features on toposheet are shown by two dimensions i.e. length and breadth only. There are various techniques or methods to show the Earth's features such as

Hachures

These are short, broken lines used to show relief. Hachures are sometimes used with contour lines. They do not represent exact elevations, but are mainly used to show large, rocky outcrop areas.

Hachures are used extensively on small-scale maps to show mountain ranges, plateaus and mountain peaks.

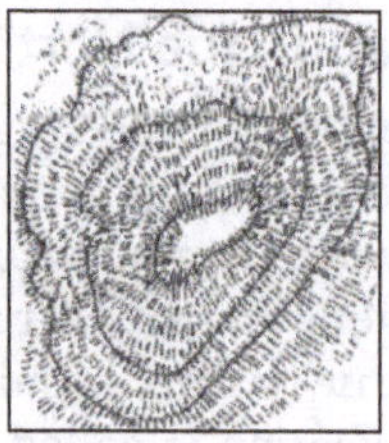

Hill Shading

These indicate relief by a shadow effect by tone and colour that results in the darkening of one side of terrain features such as hills and ridges. The darker the shading, the steeper the slope.

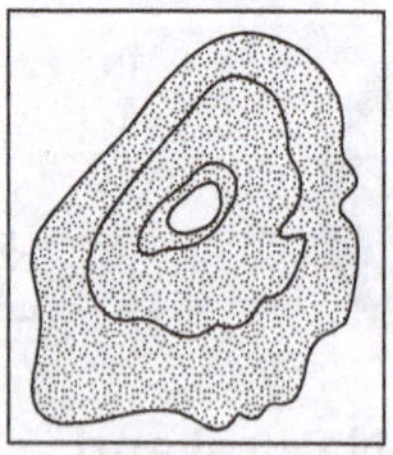

Form Lines

These are broken contour lines joining places with same height above the sea level. These lines help specially to bring out the minor details of the topography which are not easily shown by contours in an area of low relief and with large contour interval.

Triangulated Heights

When a point is accurately surveyed and shown with a triangle is called 'triangulated' height e.g. Δ340. It is determined trigonometrically. e.g. mountain peaks are indicated by triangulation points or heights on topographical maps.

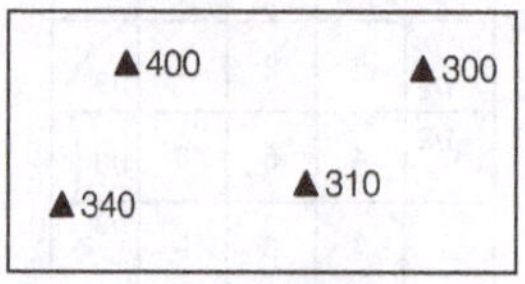

Spot Heights

It is a height of a point above the mean sea level. It is indicated by a dot followed by a number on the map e.g.•300. The number only gives information of a specific point not about the relief features, like plateaus, plains ridges, mountains, valleys etc.

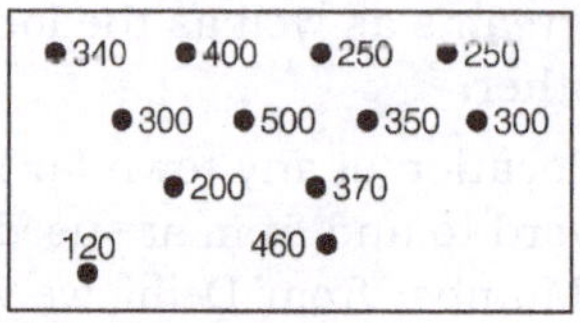

Layer Tinting/Colouring

Layer tinting is a method of showing relief by colour. A different colour is used for each band of elevation. Each shade of colour or band, represents a definite elevation range. A legend is printed on the map margin to indicate the elevation range represented by each colour.

Bench Mark

These are surveyed marks or permanent marks on a stone or a building to indicate the accurate height of that object above mean sea level. It is written on survey maps as BM 200, BM300 and so on.

Relative Height

In areas of steep slope, the difference between maximum and minimum is represented by the letter 'r' which indicated relative height of that area. So, if there is written on a toposheet 4r or 4r, it means that the relevant place is higher by 4 metres than its natural lowest place.

Surveyed Trees

These are those specific trees which are surveyed for a specific purpose. The goal of the survey is to provide useful information on the trees to the government, property owners or managers so, that they may decide what to do with the trees.

In some regions, a tree survey is mandatory in order to prevent a protected tree from being cut down accidentally by each colour.

Contours

These are imaginary lines joining places having same elevation above **mean sea level**[7]. The method of showing relief features through contour is very useful and versatile, because this provides a useful insight into the **topography**[8] of an area.

Contours are drawn at different Vertical Intervals (VI) such as 20, 40, 100, 120 m above mean sea level. It is known as **Contour Interval**[9].

This horizontal distance, also known as 'Horizontal Equivalent' (HE), is large when the slopes is gentler and decreases with increasing slope gradient.

Basic Principles of Contours

- A contour line is drawn to show places of equal heights.
- Contour lines and their shapes represent the height and slope or gradient of the landform.
- Closely spaced contour lines mean steep slope.
- Contour lines that are far apart mean gentle slope or flat land.
- Two contours of different elevation usually do not cross each other.
- When two or more contour lines merge with each other, they represent features of vertical slopes such as cliffs or waterfalls.
- Depressions are marked with short straight-lines inside the circle.

Identification of Simple Landforms by Contours

First of all, we will focus on drawing of contours and their cross-sections. Generally, all the topographical features show varying degrees of slopes, such as a flat plain shows gentle slopes and the cliffs and gorges are associated with steep slopes. Therefore, the spacing of contours is important as it indicates the slope of a feature.

Contour Interval

A contour interval is the vertical distance or difference in elevation between contour lines. Index contours are bold or thicker lines that appear at every fifth contour line. If the numbers associated with specific contour lines are increasing, the elevation of the terrain is also increasing. There are two types of contour interval:

(i) **Vertical Interval** The vertical distance on the ground which separates adjacent contour lines on a map.

(ii) **Horizontal Equivalent** It is the actual distance between two points on two contour lines.

Gradient

Gradient is a mathematical formula usually used to measure how steep or gentle a slope is. It measures how much the elevation of a slope changes as one moves horizontally over the surface. In other words, it measures the rate at which the slope is rising or falling. Gradient is typically expressed as a ratio.

To determine gradient, simply divide the change in elevation between the two points found on your topographic map by their horizontal distance. Gradient Vertical interval /horizontal equivalent.

Principle of Contour

- **Rule 1** - every point of a contour line has the same elevation.
- **Rule 2** - contour lines separate uphill from downhill.
- **Rule 3** - contour lines do not touch or cross each other except at a cliff.
- **Rule 4** - every 5th contour line is darker in colour.

Types of Landforms with Representation of Contours

Slopes

A slope is the upward or downward inclination of a natural or artificial surface or a deviation from the perpendicular or horizontal surface. There are various types of slope such as

(i) **Flat Low-Lying Land** Its elevation is varying between 20 m to 40 m above sea level. Due to gentle slopes it is fit for agriculture.

7. **Mean Sea Level** It is the average level of the surface of the sea (which varies slightly from place to place). Calculated from a series of continous record of tidal oscillation over a long period. It is the standard level from which all heights are calculated.
8. **Topography** All the surface features whether natural e.g. landfroms and other phenomena as well as features produced by human activities are including in it.
9. **Contour Interval** Interval between two successive contours. It is constant for a given map and also known as vertical interval.

(ii) **Undulating Slope** Undulating slope changes after short distances. Due to its concave and convex like shape it forms a wavy structure.

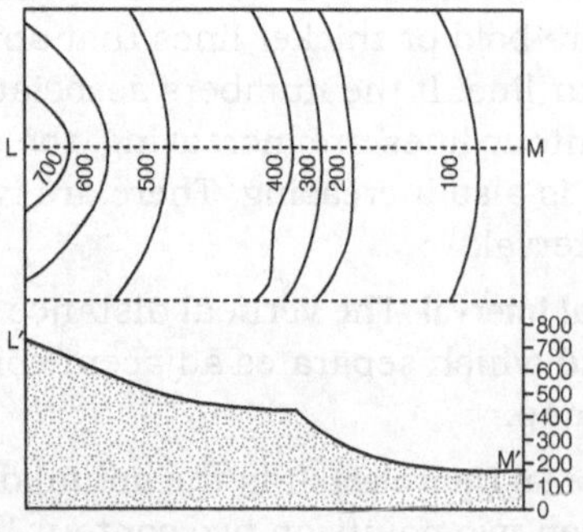

(iii) **Stepped (Terraced) Slope** In this feature two contour lines are found closer and two wide apart, which show that its slope first rises gently, then steeply, then gently again and so on.

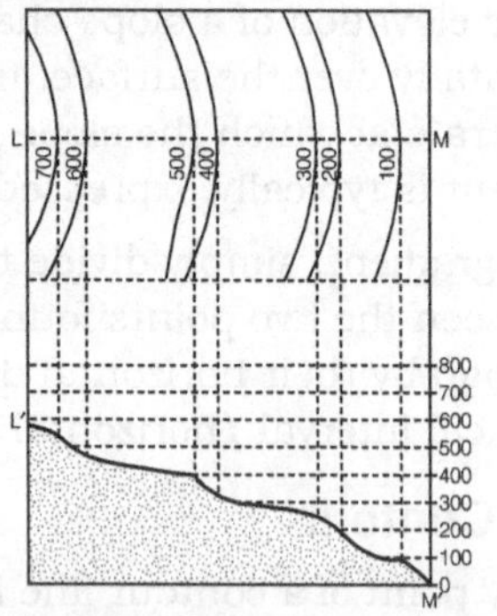

(iv) **Uniform Slope** When the rise or fall of the ground per unit horizontal distance is the same at every point, it is called a 'Uniform Slope'. Its contours are drawn at equal distance. *It has two sub-types*

(a) **Gentle Slope** In gentle slope, the change of elevation is gradual, e.g. 1:25 its gradient. Contours generally wide apart.

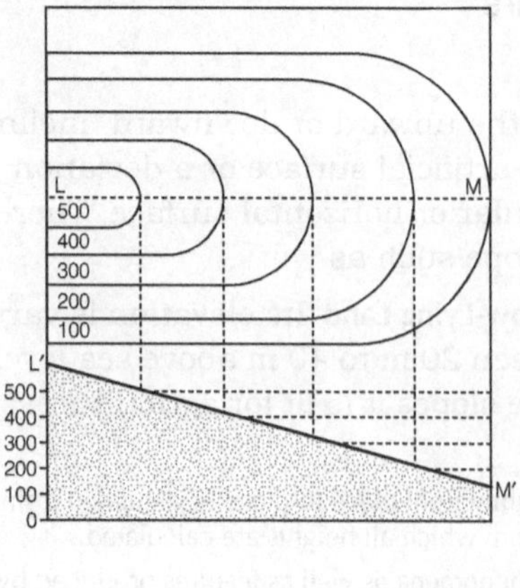

(b) **Steep Slope** In such a slope, the land suddenly slopes up or down. The contours of this slope are drawn close to one another.

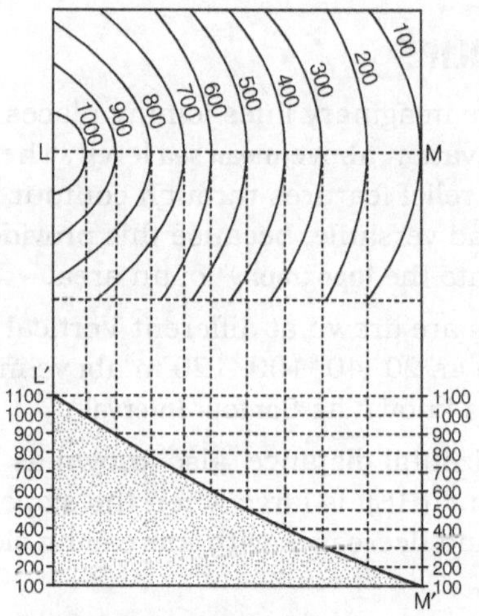

(v) **Concave Slope** When the contours are close together near the top of the hill and further apart downwards, this feature is called 'Concave Slope'. The top of a concave slope is visible from the foot. It is curved inwards.

(vi) **Convex Slope** Unlike concave slope in this type of slope the contours at the top are far apart and get closer at lower altitude, which give rise to a bulge in the middle instead of a depression.

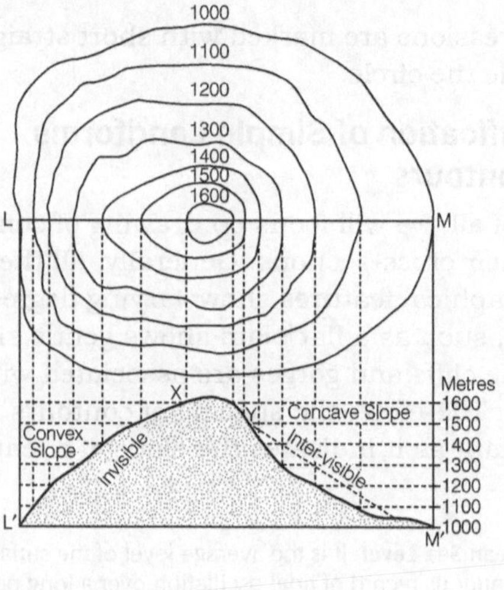

Conical Hill

A conical hill rises almost uniformly from the surrounding land. A conical hill with uniform slope and narrow top is represented by concentric contour spaced almost at regular intervals.

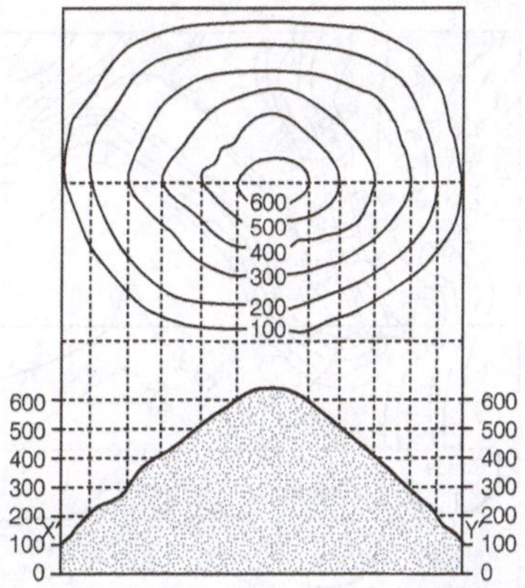

Plateau

A widely stretched flat-topped high land, with relatively steeper slopes, rising above the adjoining plain or sea is called a 'Plateau'. When a number of river valleys and streams cut the top of a plateau it is called 'Dissected Plateau' e.g. the Deccan plateau in India.

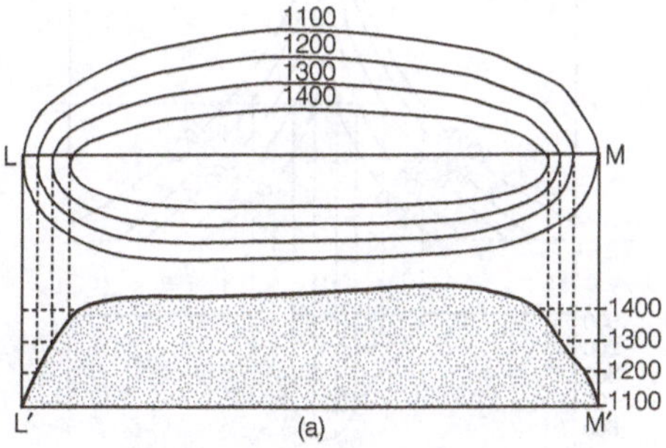

(a)

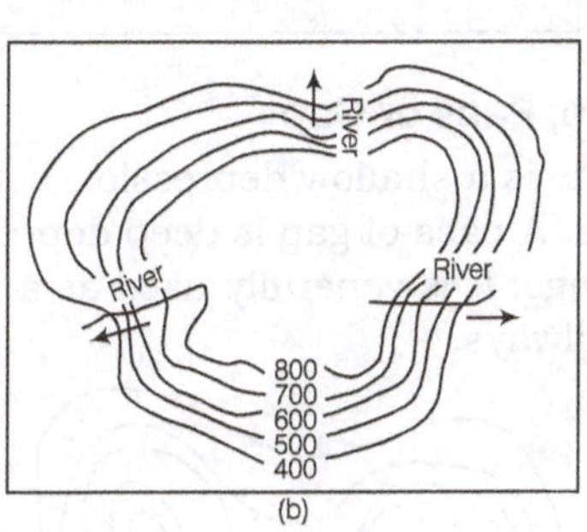

(b)

Escarpment

It is the abrupt, comparatively long and regular, steep face of any hill or a plateau. It has a narrow top with a steep slope on one side and a gentle slope on the other. It is a ridge with a steep scarp in the front and a dip slope on the back. This is formed by uneven erosional work of rocks on both the sides.

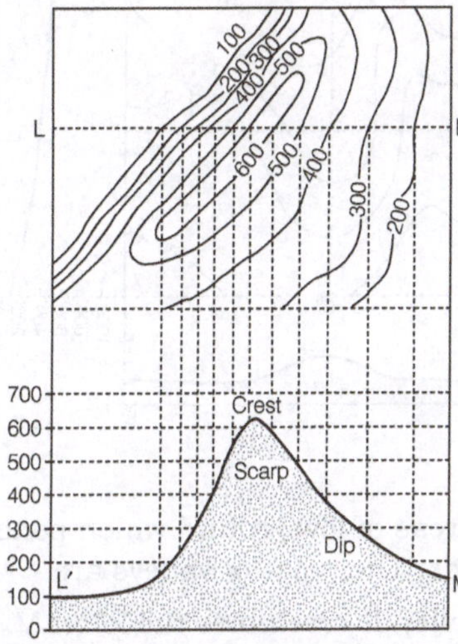

Waterfall

When there is a sudden fall of water over a steep rock into the river bed it is called 'Waterfall'. Due to steep slopes some contours are shown merging together.

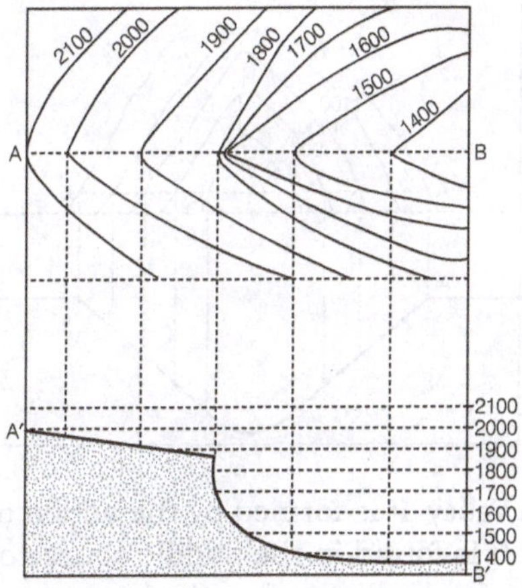

Spur

Spurs are projections of high land above a lower area. A spur is usually found projecting between two valleys. It is shown as V-shaped contour patterns.

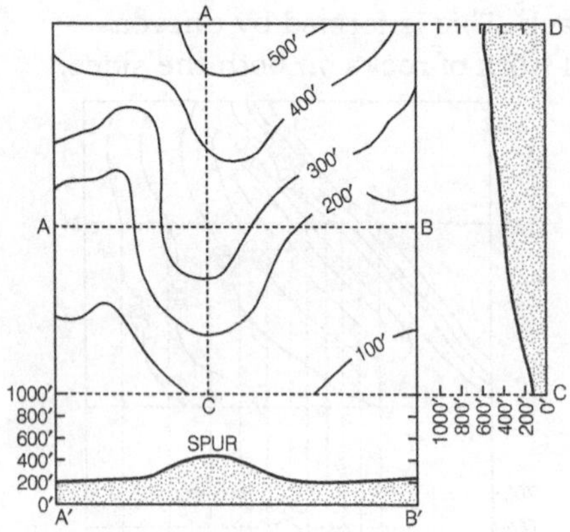

Valley

Valley are areas of low ground which penetrate into highlands. The types of valleys are

- **V-Shaped Valley** It resembles the letter V. It occurs in mountainous areas. The lowermost part of the V-shaped valley is shown by the innermost contour line. It has very small gap between its two sides and the lowest value of the contour is assigned to it.

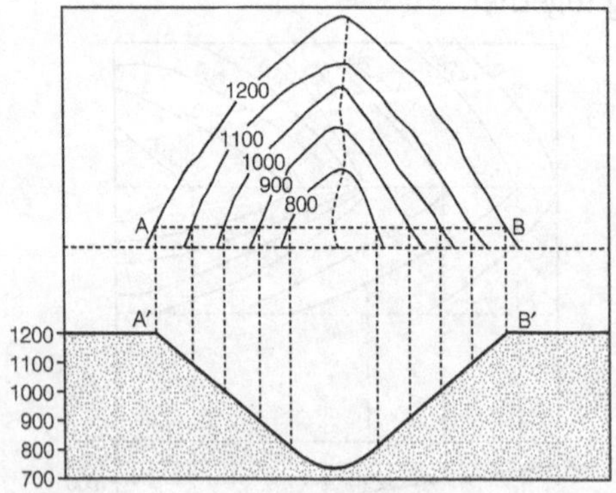

- **U-Shaped Valley** It is formed by the action of glaciers. It is found in the middle course of a river. These are generally flat from its base.
- **Hanging Valley** Glaciated tributary valleys break rapidly down a steep slope into the main valley below. The contours which cross the valley in close succession, are more or less V-shaped and they indicate waterfall.

- **Cirque** In glaciated mountainous regions the old catchment basins of glaciers have the appearance of steep-walled arm-chair hallows which are called 'cirques'.

C = Cirque,T = Tarn, H = Hanging valley

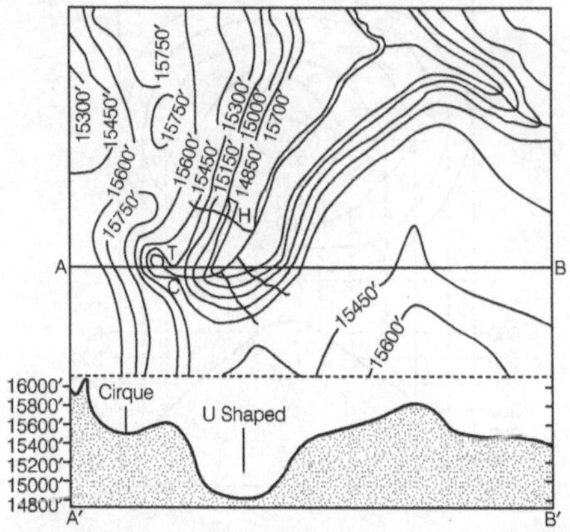

- **Gorge or Canyon** River which rise in mountains often flow through very narrow valley with steep banks on either side. Where the steep valley narrows, it becomes a gorge.

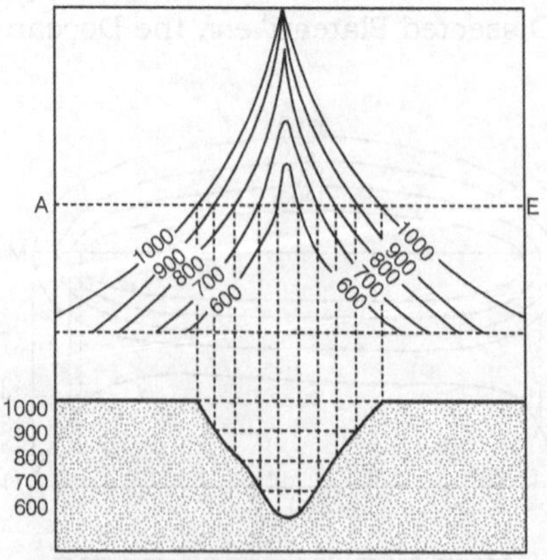

Col or Saddle, Pass or Gap

A col or saddle is a shallow depression between two hills or peaks. A pass of gap is deep depression in a mountain range. It is generally used as a route for roads and railways.

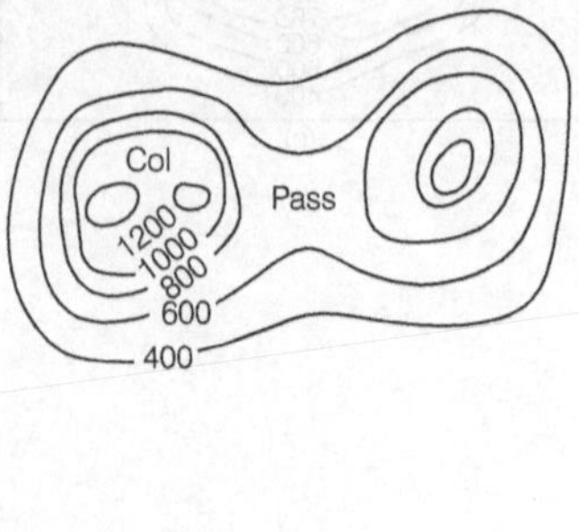

Identification of Drainage Pattern

The drainage pattern means the 'form' of the drainage systems and the spatial arrangement of streams in a particular locality or region.

The location, number and flow directions of different streams of a particular region depend on the nature of slope, structural control, lithological characteristics etc. Generally, the drainage patterns are divided into the following types

Trellis Drainage Pattern

It is like a rectangular drainage pattern where all the streams flow parallel to each other and join the main consequent stream at right angles.

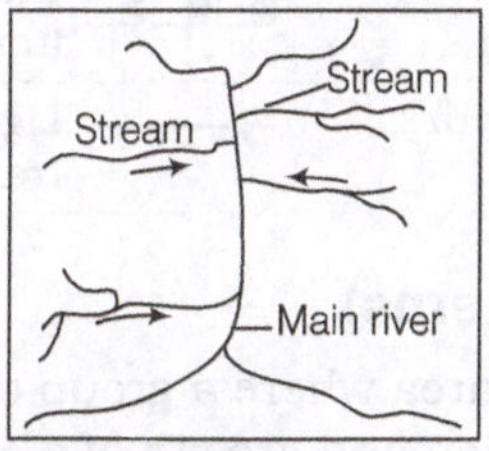

Dendritic Drainage Pattern

In this pattern, the tributaries come from all directions, to meet the main river.

The trunk or master stream resembles the branches and roots of a tree. It is generally founds over homogeneous and flat lands.

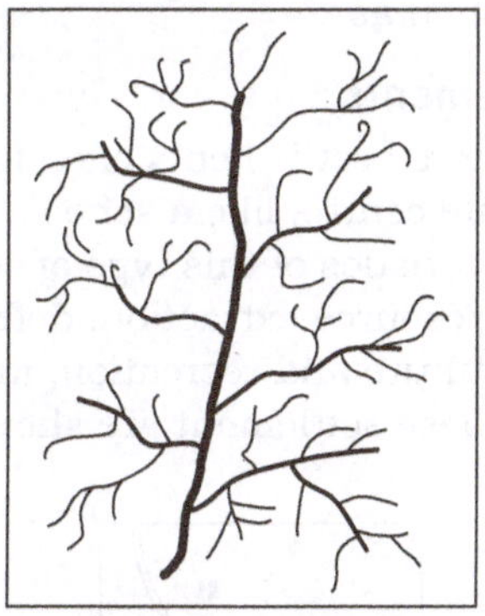

Radial Drainage Pattern

It is formed by the streams which diverge from a central higher point of a dome mountain in all directions.

These are basically the consequent streams as they follow the slope of the land. It is also known as 'Centrifugal Pattern'.

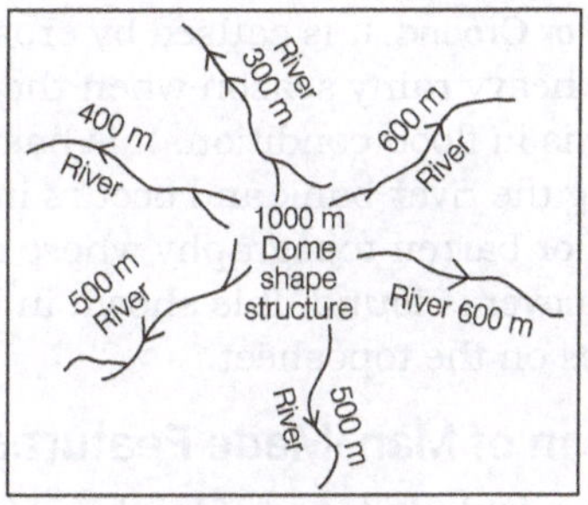

Centripetal Drainage Pattern

This pattern is formed by the covergence of streams in a depression or basin. It is just opposite to the radial drainage pattern as the streams emerge from the surrounding uplands.

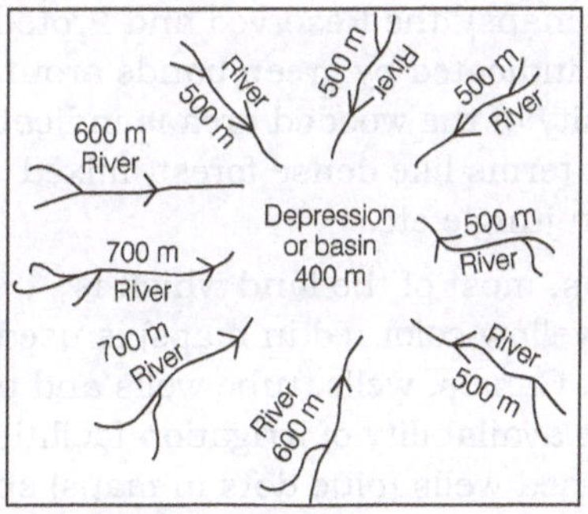

The Inland or Disappearing Drainage Pattern

Due to physical and climatic conditions, in some areas the streams are unable to reach the sea, lake or ocean and merge in the desert sands due to its porosity. Sometimes, due to scanty rainfall or excessive evaporation the streams disappear and may flow underground and reappear.

Feature of River and Valley on Toposheet

As given in the topographical map the drainage features are shown as

- **Perennial Rivers** These rivers carry water throughout the year and are shown in blue colour.
- **Seasonal Streams** The smaller streams that become dry during a part of the year. These are shown in black colour.

- **Irregular Streams** They disappear in the deserts or in limestone regions. These are shown as black dotted lines.
- **Broken Land or Ground** It is caused by erosion of soil during heavy rainy season when the river is overflow or is in flood condition. It is basically found along the river bank and occurs in the arid region or barren topography where no vegetation cover is found. It is shown in black curved lines on the toposheet.

Identification of Man-Made Features

These features include types of land use, means of communication, settlement pattern, rivers, means of irrigation etc.

Types of Land Use and Means of Irrigation

The type of vegetation is closely related to the relief of the land. In forested land (green coloured in maps), the Reserved and Protected Forests are indicated by green bands around them. Density of the wooded area is indicated by different terms like dense forest, mixed jungle, open jungle etc.

In the plains, most of the land which is cultivable (yellow coloured in maps) is used for agriculture. Canals, wells, tube wells and tanks indicate the availability of irrigation facilities. Perennial lined wells (blue dots in maps) show that the water table is high. In uncultivable land, we find features like open scrub, stony waste, rock outcrop, broken ground etc. Nothing is grown here.

Means of Transport and Communication

There are various means of transport and communication on the toposheet. This always depend on the type of relief and drainage e.g. in the plain areas there are better roads and rail connectivity available, where as in mountainous areas only roads are found, not railway tracks due to undulating topography.

These means of transport include national or state highways, cart tracks, pack tracks, causeways, metalled roads, unmetalled roads, footpaths with bridge, railway lines etc.

A part form these, there are also means of communication available like telephone lines, post offices, dak bungalow, telegraph line and other utilities/facilities like dispensary, police chauki etc.

Conventional Signs for Means of Transport and Communication

====	Metalled roads shown in red double lines.	—▭—	Railway : broad gauge
= = = =	Unmetalled roads shown in broken lines in red colours.	++++++	Metre gauge
---x---	Pack track (pagdandi)	+—+—+	Narrow gauge
———	Cart track	■□■□■□	Under construction (railways)
---)(---	Footpath with a bridge	+——+	Light railway or tramway

Settlement (Patterns)

A settlement is an area where a group of families live together. The location and growth of a settlement depend upon its site and situation. The site is the actual place where people decide to locate their settlement.

The growth of that settlement then depends upon its situation in relation to accessibility and availability of natural resources. Settlements generally follow some simple patterns such as

Nucleated Settlements

Nucleated or clustered settlements often form at crossroads or route centre, like a school, temple etc. The major characteristics of this type of settlement are trade, transport, resource extraction, defence, administration, culture and recreation, industrial production etc. These settlement are shown in red colour.

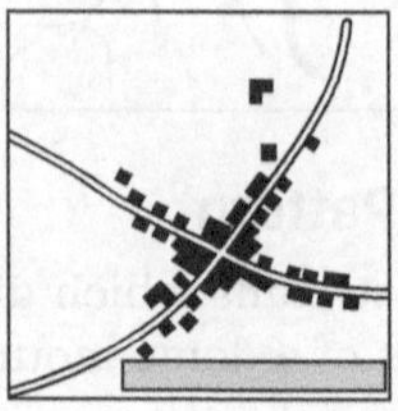

Dispersed or Scattered Settlements

These settlements have no obvious centre and are often hamlets spread over fertile farmland. These are so, due to high land topography, lack of availability of water, poor cultivated land etc. These settlement are shown in red squares on the toposheet map.

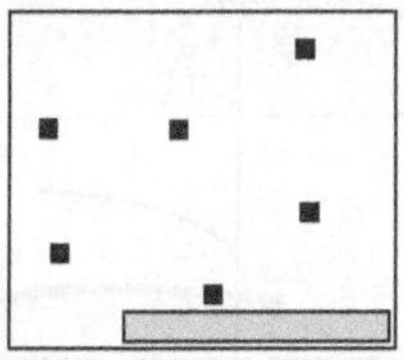

Linear Settlements

These settlements also known as 'Ribbon-Patterned' settlements. These settlements grow along a road i.e. in a narrow valley or along the coast.

Ribbon development is when housing grows out from a town along a main road. Presence of different attributes or facilities make the town or settlement important and bigger than the others.

These facilities include, post office, dak bungalow, police chauki, inspection bungalow, hotel, combined office, telegraph office, monuments like temple, church, chhatri, masjid, circuit house etc.

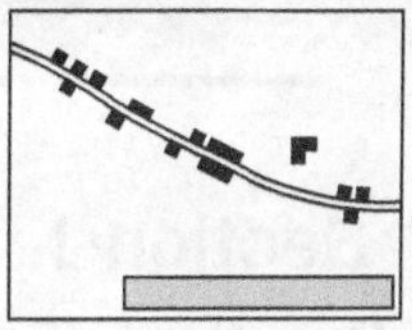

Occupations

The general occupations of the people of any area may be identified with the help of land use of the settlement or area e.g. presence of yellow patch or orchards shows that people of that area may indulge in cultivation, availability of meadows or scrubs infer cattle-grazing or animal husbandry, green patches on land area show forest cover area. Here, the occupation of the people may be forestry, lumbering or primitive agriculture.

Types of settlements show that in nucleated settlements people may engage in various activities due to presence of various factors like, industrial development, availability of public or government services etc.

On the other hand, in the dispersed settlement people may engage in animal rearing due to lack of availability of basic facilities.

Chapter Practice

Section-I

Multiple Choice Questions

1. Refer to the images and answer the question that follow

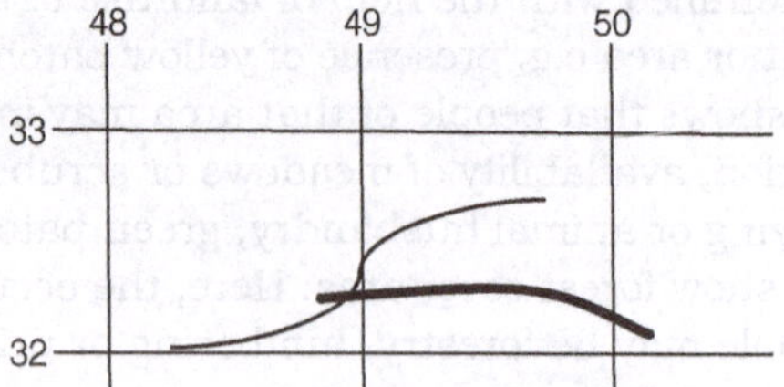

What does the black line in 4932 indicate?

(a) Open scrub (b) Dry land

(c) Broken land (d) Seasonal stream

Ans. (d) Seasonal stream

2. Refer to the images and answer the question that follow

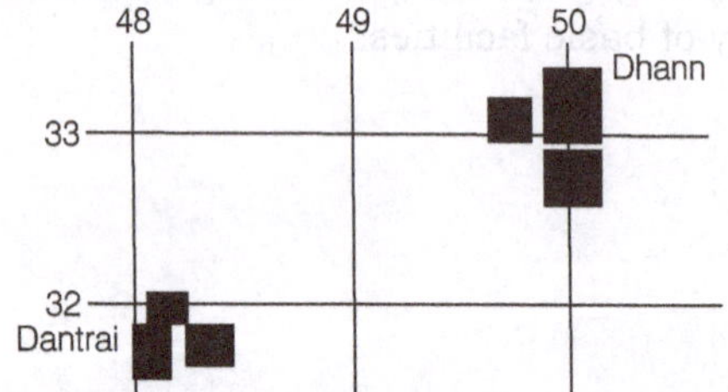

What is the direction of Dantrai from Dhann?

(a) North-East (b) North-West

(c) South-East (d) South-West

Ans. (d) South-West

3. Refer to the images and answer the question that follow.

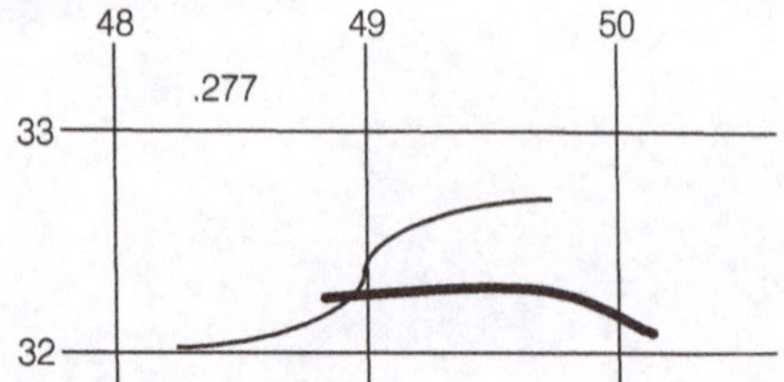

What is .277 in 4833?

(a) Spot height of 277 m (b) Spot height of 277 cm

(c) Spot height of 277 mm (d) Spot height of 277 km

Ans. (a) Spot height of 277 m

4. Refer to the images and answer the question that follow.

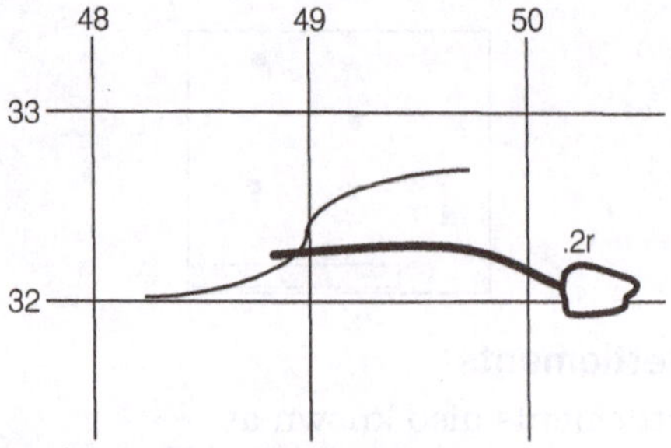

What does . 2r in 5032 indicate?

(a) The relative height of the tank is 2m.

(b) The relative height of the tank is 2 cm.

(c) The relative depth of the embankment is 2 m.

(d) The relative depth of the embankment is 2cm.

Ans. (a) The relative height of the tank is 2m

5. Refer to the images and answer the question that follow.

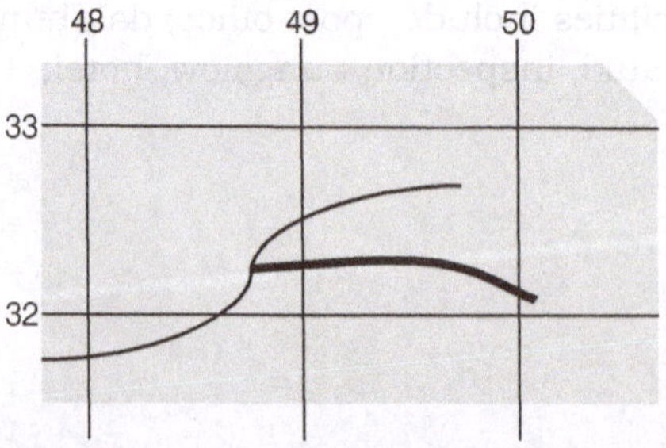

What is the main occupation of the people living in the area shown on the map extract?

(a) Mining (b) Agriculture

(c) Fishing (d) Sheep rearing

Ans. (b) Agriculture

6. Refer to the images and answer the question that follow.

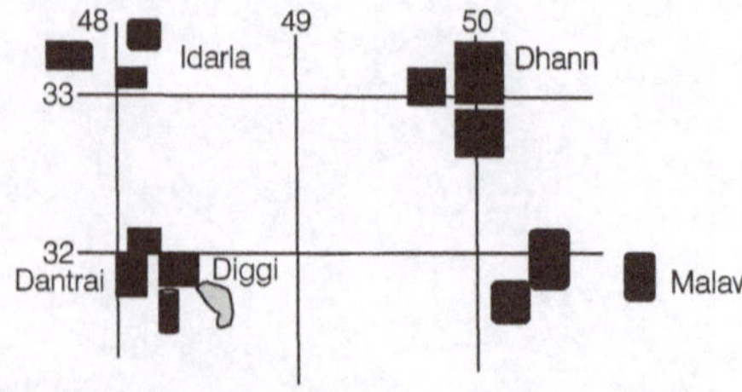

Which is the most important town in the above image?

(a) Idarla (b) Malawa

(c) Dantrai (d) Dhann

Ans. (a) Idarla

7. Refer to the images and answer the question that follow.

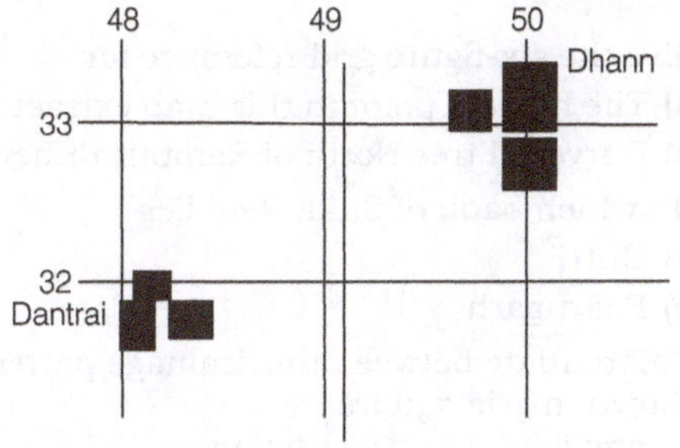

What is the black vertical line between 49 and 50 Easting?

(a) A line of latitude.
(b) A line of longitude.
(c) An Easting.
(d) A Northing.

Ans. (b) A line of longitude.

8. Refer to the images and answer the question that follow.

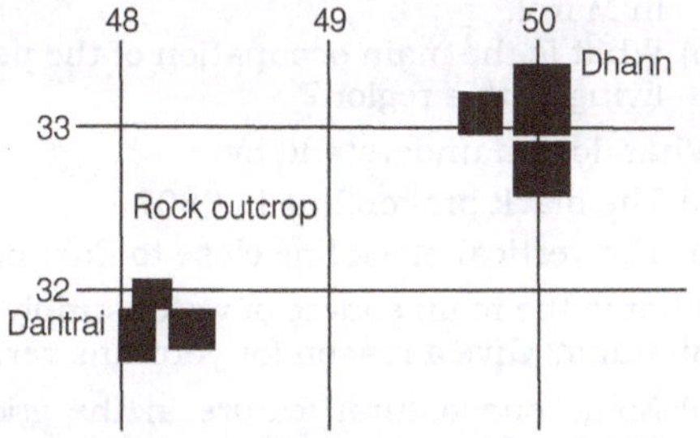

What is the four figure grid reference of rock outcrop?

(a) 4832 (b) 4933
(c) 3248 (d) 3349

Ans. (a) 4832

9. Refer to the images and answer the question that follow.

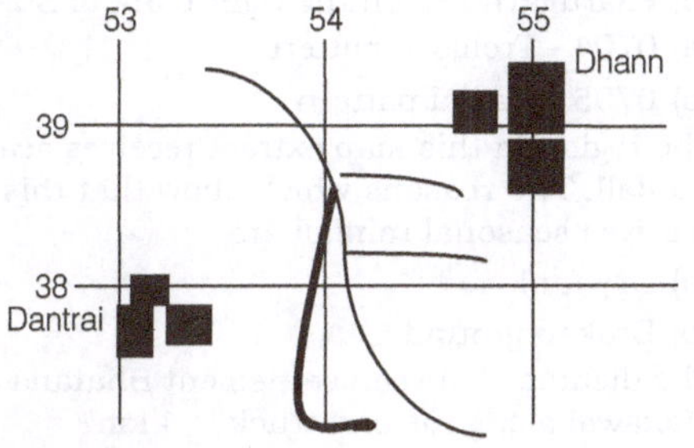

Which drainage pattern is seen in 5438?

(a) Radial
(b) Trellised
(c) Intermittent
(d) Dendritic

Ans. (b) Trellised

10. Refer to the images and answer the question that follow:

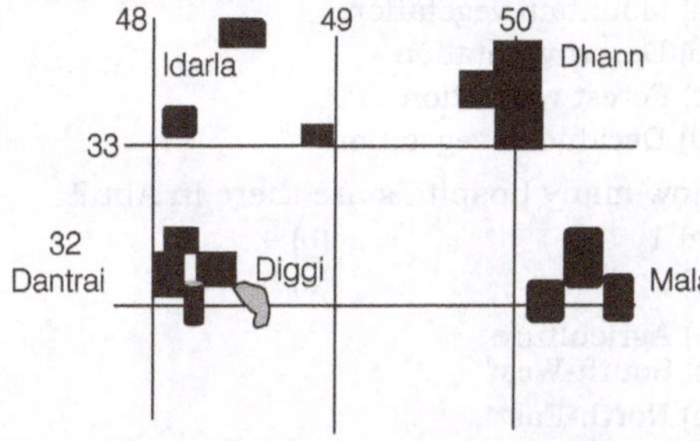

Name the settlement pattern in grid square 4833.

(a) Nucleated (b) Compact
(c) Scattered (d) Isolated

Ans. (d) Isolated

11. Study the Topographical Sheet Number 45D/10 and answer the following questions Eastings: 63 to 69, Northings: 32 to 41

(i) Name the occupation in which people of given the region are indulged.
(a) Agriculture (b) Government job
(c) Tourism (d) Trading

(ii) If a person has to walk from Mohabbatgarh to Anadra, which direction he needs to follow?
(a) South-East (b) North-East
(c) South-West (d) North-West

(iii) What is the general slope of the land shown the given toposheet .
(a) South-East (b) North-East
(c) South-West (d) North-West

(iv) If a person has to walk from Harmatiya to Mohabbatgarh, which direction he need to follow?
(a) South-East (b) North-East
(c) South-West (d) North-West

(v) What is the general climate of the given region?
(a) Summer
(b) Winter
(c) Heavy rainfall
(d) Tropical monsoon

(vi) Which is the most important settlement of the given region?
(a) Dak (b) Anadra
(c) Harmatiya (d) Hathal

(vii) What do you understand by 3r in the grid 6538?
(a) The relative height of the tank is 3 m.
(b) The relative depth of the embankment is 3 m.
(c) The relative depth of the embankment is 3 cm.
(d) The relative height of the tank is 3 cm.

(viii) Figure out the four figure grid reference of Spot height (437).
(a) 7040 (b) 7140
(c) 7041 (d) 7141

(ix) Which type of vegetation is found in the given region ?
(a) Mountain vegetation
(b) Desert vegetation
(c) Forest vegetation
(d) Deciduous vegetation

(x) How many hospitals are there in Abu?
(a) 1 (b) 4
(c) 2 (d) 5

Ans. (i) (a) Agriculture
(ii) (c) South-West
(iii) (b) North-East
(iv) (d) North-West
(v) (d) Tropical monsoon
(vi) (b) Anadra
(vii) (b) The relative depth of the embankment is 3 m.
(viii) (a) 7040
(ix) (c) Forest vegetation
(x) (d) 5

12. Study the extract of the Survey of India Map Sheet No. G43S7 and answer the following questions. (Eastings - 21 to 31, Northings - 86 to 96).

(i) (a) Give the four - figure grid reference of Δ317.
(b) What is the contour interval used in the given map extract ?

(ii) (a) What does the black line with dots in grid square 2486 indicate ?
(b) What does the brown square in grid square 2686 indicate ?

(iii) What do the following figures show ?
(a) 
(b) 

(iv) What do you understand by Representative Function (RF) ?

(v) (a) Vaghrol is which type of settlement ?
(b) What is the meaning of a black tree located in the grid square 2988 ?

Ans. (i) (a) 2487 (b) 20 metres
(ii) (a) This is main power line
(b) This is a temporary hut.
(iii) (a) It is a chhatri.
(b) It is a temple.
(iv) Representative Function (RF) is also known as Numerical Fraction. It is a type of scale on a map which indicates the relationship of distance measured on a map and the corresponding distance on the ground.
(v) (a) Vaghrol is a linear type of settlement.
(b) The black tree represents a surveyed tree.

13. Study the extract of the Survey of India Map Sheet No. 45D/10 and answer the following questions **[2017]**

(i) Give the six-figure grid reference for
(a) The highest point in this map extract.
(b) Surveyed tree North of Rampura Khera.

(ii) On which bank of Sukli Nadi lies
(a) Butri
(b) Paarugarh

(iii) Differentiate between the drainage pattern shown in grid square
(a) 0704 (b) 0705

(iv) The region in this map extract receives seasonal rainfall. Give two reasons for your answer.

(v) Calculate the distance in kilometre between settlement Bhatana and Makawal along the cart track.

(vi) State the compass direction of the following
(a) Dattani from Marol
(b) Dhavli from Makawal

(vii) (a) Mention of social activity of the people living in Marol.
(b) What is the main occupation of the people living in this region?

(viii) What do you understand by
(a) The black broken line in 0807
(b) The vertical black line close to Easting 10

(ix) What is the main source of water supply to Bhatana? Give a reason for your answer.

(x) (a) Name one natural feature in the grid square 0905.
(b) Identify one man made feature in the grid square 1003.

Ans. Survey of India Map Sheet No. 45D/10.
(i) (a) 087065
(b) 073074
(ii) (a) Butri lies on the left bank of Sukli river.
(b) Paarugarh lies on the right bank of Sukli river.
(iii) (a) 0704 - Trellised pattern
(b) 0705 - Radial pattern
(iv) The region in this map extract receives seasonal rainfall. Two reasons which show that this area receives seasonal rainfall are
(a) Dry tank
(b) Broken ground
(v) The distance between settlement Bhatana and Makawal along the cart truck is 4 km.
(2 cm = 1 km)
(vi) (a) Dattani from Marol = South-East direction.
(b) Dhavali from Makawal = North-East direction.

(vii) (a) People of Marol participate in fair activities every month.

(b) The main occupation of the people living in Marol is agriculture.

(viii) (a) The black broken line in grid square 0807 shows stream undefined.

(b) The vertical black line close to Easting 10 is longitude which shows 72° 35' East longitude of the area. Longitude is the angular distance represents in degrees, minutes and seconds of a point East or West of the Prime (Greenwich) Meridian.

(ix) The main source of water supply to Bhatana is perennial lined wells. The reason for this is the presence of blue dots on the map extract.

(x) (a) One natural feature in the grid square 0905 is broken ground along the bank of a stream. It is uncultivable land.

(b) One man made feature in the grid square 1003 is the dry tank with embarkment.

4. Study the extract of the Survey of India Map Sheet No. 45 D/10 and answer the following questions. **[2015]**

(i) Give the four-figure grid reference for a figure similar to the one given below. Identify the figure.

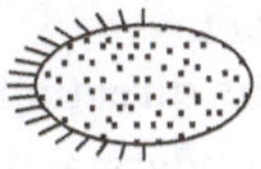

(ii) How is the drainage pattern in grid square 1606 different from that in grid square 1608?

(iii) Identify the correct six-figure grid reference for each of the following

(a) Gautam Maharishi Mandir — 200071; 071200; 201070

(b) 443 —172059; 052179; 179052

(iv) Name the most prominent settlement other than ABC. Give two reasons to support your answer.

(v) (a) What is the general slope of the land in the North-West corner of the map extract?

(b) What is the compass direction of Chandela (1803) from Hanumanji ka Mandir (2208)?

(vi) What do you understand by the following terms as used on the map extract?

(a) Causeway (1702)

(b) Falls 25 m (2307)

(vii) (a) If you were to cycle at 10 km an hour, how much time would it take to cover the North-South distance depicted on this map extract?

(b) Calculate the area enclosed by Eastings 19 to 22 and Northings 04 to 09.

(viii) (a) Identify one natural feature in grid square 1610.

(b) Identify one man-made feature in grid square 1903.

(ix) Give two probable reasons, other than dry water features, to indicate that the region depicted on the map extract receives seasonal rainfall.

(x) Calculate, in metres, the difference in height between the highest point on the map extract and the contour height given in grid square 2402.

Ans. (i) Four-figure grid reference is 1903. The figure is a dry man-made tank.

(ii) The drainage pattern in grid square 1606 is radial drainage while that in grid square 1608 is trellised drainage.

(iii) (a) Six-figure grid reference of Gautam Maharishi Mandir is 200071.

(b) Six-figure grid reference of point height 443 is 179052.

(iv) The most prominent settlement other than Abu is Anadra, as it is linked with a metalled road and has a post and Telegraph Office (PTO).

(v) (a) The land is sloping down gradually (contours far apart) from South-East to North-West in the North-West corner of the map extract i.e. (North-West of Abu).

(b) The compass direction of Chandela (1803) from Hanumanji ka Mandir (2208) is South-West.

(vi) (a) Causeway (1702) is a crossing of a usually dry river bed. Such a crossing may not be usable when water flows in the river, mostly during the rainy season.

(b) Falls 25 m (2307) represents a waterfall of height 25 m in the river.

(vii) (a) The scale of map is 2 cm = 1 km. Since, the North-South distance depicted on the map is 30 cm, the actual distance = 30/2 km = 15 km. Cycling at 10km /hour, it will take 15/10 or 1.5 hours to cover this distance.

(b) Area enclosed $= (22-19) \times (09-04)$

$= 3 \times 5 = 15$ sq km.

(viii) (a) The natural feature found in grid square 1610 is broken ground.

(b) The man-made feature found in grid square 1903 is an earthwork dam.

(ix) There are a number of causeway shown in the map, indicating that they are usable most of the year except during the rainy season. The other reason is presence of broken ground, indicating seasonal rainfall.

(x) The highest point in the map extract is triangulated height 1409 (in grid square 2212) and the contour height given in grid square 2402 is 268. The difference in height between these points = 1409 − 268 = 1141 metres.

15. Study the extract of the Survey of India Map sheet No. 45 D/10 and answer the following questions. **[2014]**

(i) (a) Give the four-figure grid reference of the settlement of Hamirpura.
(b) Give the six-figure grid reference of the temple in the settlement of Jolpur.

(ii) (a) What does the blue coloured circle in the grid square 0619 represent?
(b) What is the compass direction of Dantrai from Jolpur?

(iii) What is the difference between
(a) Pattern of settlements in 0725 and the settlement of Idarla
(b) Drainage pattern of the streams in 0624 and those in 0824

(iv) What is the value of the contour line in square 0226? What is the contour interval in the map?

(v) Mention any two factors which provide evidence that the region in the map extract is a rural region.

(vi) (a) How does the feature, indicated by the black curves in 0721, show that rainfall in this region is seasonal?
(b) Mention one man-made feature in the map which also provides evidence that the rainfall is seasonal.

(vii) (a) Name two natural features in 0527.
(b) Name two man-made features in 0325.

(viii) Name two features which make Dantrai a more important settlement than the other settlements in the map extract.

(ix) Calculate the area of the region which lies to the South of Northing 21 in sq km.

(x) What are the following?
(a) The black vertical line between Eastings 09 and 10.
(b) 302 in grid square 0425.

Ans. (i) (a) 0123 (b) 0781887

(ii) (a) Perennial lined well.
(b) It is North-West direction.

(iii) (a) Settlement in 0725 – Dispersed, scattered
Idarla — Nucleated/clustered
(b) Drainage of 0624 – Trellised, Drainage of 0824 – Dendritic

(iv) The value of the contour line in square 0226 is 300m. The contour interval in the map is 20 m.

(v) The two factors are
(a) No large settlement is there.
(b) No metalled road facility is available only cart-tracks are found.

(vi) (a) The black curved line in 0721 is Broken Ground. It is formed due to alternating dry and wet periods along the banks of seasonal river where the soil is soft.
(b) Large number of Perennial lined well.

(vii) (a) Two natural features in the grid square 0527 are seasonal stream and trees and barren land.
(b) Two man-made features in grid square 0325 are motorable road in dry season and settlement.

(viii) The settlement Dantrai has a police chauki and post office while other settlements do not have such utilities/facilities.

(ix) 30 km^2 as there are 30 grids South of the Northing 21.

(x) (a) It is longitude.
(b) 302 in grid square 0425 is a spot height.

16. Study the extract of the Survey of India Map Sheet No. G 43S7 and answer the following questions. (Eastings - 31 to 41, Northings - 01 to 10).

(i) (a) Give the four figure grid reference for ∆ 284.
(b) Give the four figure grid reference for ·269.

(ii) (a) What does the meaning of black line with dots shown in grid square 3409 ?
(b) What is the meaning of the blue square shown in grid square 3608 ?

(iii) (a) Name two important rivers of the given map extract.
(b) What is the direction of Varka river?

(iv) What do you understand by stony waste written on the map extract ?

(v) What is the meaning of the tiny black curved lines shown in the grid square 3709 ?

Ans. (i) (a) 3807 (b) 3606

(ii) (a) It is the power line with poles unsurveyed.
(b) It is the perennial covered tank.

(iii) (a) The two important rivers of the given map extract are Sipu river and Varka river.
(b) The direction of Varka river is from East to West.

(iv) Stony waste is a land which is mostly covered with rock boulders and stones. This area is unfit for agriculture. It is shown as a white patch on topographical maps.

(v) The tiny black curved lines shown in the grid square 3709 represent broken ground. It is the weathered part of the land caused due to erosion during heavy rain at the time of flooding. It is found mostly in dry regions around streams and rivers.

17. Study the extract of the Survey of India Map sheet No. 45 D/10 Eastings 11 to 21 and Northings 13 to 23 and answer the following questions.

(i) Name and give the four-figure grid reference of a settlement where the people of the region meet at least once a year.

(ii) What does the conventional symbol at grid reference 147132 mean?

(iii) If a man were to walk from Gulabganj (1820) to Harmatiya (1916)

(a) In which direction, would he be walking?

(b) Which are the two different kinds of roads that he would be using?

(iv) What is the following numbers in grid square 1718 and 1828 mean?

(a) 280 (b) 281

(v) What are the two differences between the settlement Bamba in 1914 and those in 1813?

(vi) Name four facilities that Anadra has which make it an important settlement.

(vii) What is the quickest means of communication for the people of Dab ani (1313)?

(viii) What is the following mean

(a) Brackish in 1915

(b) Causeway in 1715

(c) 6r in 1218

(ix) Mention two factors which support the following:

(a) The Sipu river is in its middle course.

(b) The rainfall in the region shown in the map extract is seasonal.

(x) What is the distance in kilo metres between the distance stone 20 in 1818 and the causeway in 1715 along the metalled road?

Ans. (i) Malgaon 1520.

(ii) It is a temple situated at a height of 270 m above mean sea level.

(iii) (a) South-East

(b) Cart track and metalled road.

(iv) (a) 280 is contour height of 280 m above sea level.

(b) 281 is the spot height of 281 m above sea level.

(v) 1914 is the temporary and nucleated settlement pattern. 1813 is the permanent and scattered or dispersed settlement pattern.

(vi) The four facilities in Anadra are Post and Telegraph Office, Dak Bungalow, Dispensary and Police Chauki.

(vii) Telephone line.

(viii) (a) Brackish means that the water has high salt content and unfit for drinking and irrigation.

(b) Causeway is a raised platform road across a stream or road.

(c) 6r is the relative height of the bank of the river i.e. 6 m.

(ix) (a) The Sipu river is in its middle course because it is flowing through a flat land or plain.

- Wider course with tributaries joining.
- It is meandering (any two).

(b) Streams are seasonal as there are dry tanks, broken ground cause ways etc.

(x) The distance is 3.25 km.

18. Study the extract of the Survey of India Map sheet No. 45 D/10 Eastings 03 to 13 and Northings 08 to 18 and answer the following questions. **[2011]**

(i) Give the six-figure grid reference of

(a) the brick kiln

(b) the temple near Asav

(ii) What is the difference in the pattern of drainage in grid square 0916 and in 0712?

(iii) Give the four-figure grid reference of each of the following

(a) Stony waste

(b) Open scrub

(iv) Calculate the distance in kilometres along the metalled road between the causeways in grid square 0512 and 0808.

(v) (a) What do the tiny curved black lines in grid square 0315 indicate?

(b) What is the main cause for this feature?

(vi) (a) What is the geographical name that you would give to the general pattern of settlements in the region shown on the map?

(b) Give a reason for your answer.

(vii) What is the general direction of flow of the Sipu nadi, given in the map extract? Give a reason to support your answer.

(viii) Name two probable occupations of the people in the settlement of Revdar in grid square 0313 and 0413.

(ix) What kind of roads connect

(a) Marol with Mitan and

(b) Revdar with Karaunti respectively?

(x) Give two reasons to show that the area depicted in the map experiences seasonal rainfall.

Ans. (i) (a) 088131

(b) 059128

(ii) 0916 – Radial, 0712 – Trellis

(iii) (a) 1014 (b) 0816

(iv) It is 5.7 km.

(v) (a) This indicates presence of broken ground.

(b) The main causes are flooding, hot and dry weather or spell.

(vi) (a) Nucleated settlement pattern.

(b) Settlements are close together and people built their houses in areas where there are wells and they can do some farming.

(vii) The direction of the river is North-East to South-West, because spot heights are receding from North-East to South-West and an arrow onto the bed of the main river indicates this.

(viii) Framing, cattle rearing and work in PTO, DB.

(ix) (a) Cart track

(b) Metalled road

(x) Two reasons that show that the area depicted in the map experiences seasonal rainfall are:
(a) Dry tanks
(b) Dry streams and broken grounds.

19. Study the extract of the Survey of India Map Sheet No. G 43S7 and answer the following questions. (Eastings - 28 to 38, Northings - 89 to 99).

(i) (a) Give the four-figure grid reference for Δ 216.
(b) Give a four-figure grid reference for. 196.

(ii) Which settlement is important in the given map extract and why ?

(iii) (a) What is the meaning of the line drawn on the grid square 3094 ?
(b) What is the meaning of the line drawn on the grid square 3092 ?

(iv) (a) What is the meaning of brown patches shown in the map extract ?
(b) These brown patches are found in which area?

(v) What do you understand by the following ?
(a) White patches
(b) Yellow wash

Ans. (i) (a) 3392
(b) 3090

(ii) Dantiwada is an important settlement in the given map extract. It is due to the fact that it has a post-office, a rest house or inspection bungalow, temples, a police station and several aqueducts.

(iii) (a) It is a masonary dam.
(b) It is an earthen dam.

(iv) (a) Brown patches shown in the map extract represent swampy area.
(b) Swampy is low land that is seasonally flooded. It is mostly found along the coastal areas.

(v) (a) White patches shown in the map extract represent uncultivated land, badlands or rocky area.
(b) Yellow wash shown in the map extract represents cultivated area.

20. Study the extract of the Survey of India Map Sheet No. G43S7 and answer the following questions. (Eastings - 28 to 38, Northings - 97 to 07).

(i) (a) Give the four figure grid reference for Jawar hill.
(b) Give the four figure grid reference for Annual fair (Feb).

(ii) What do you understand by the symbol Δ592 in grid square 3701 ?

(iii) Which type of drainage patterns shown in the following grids ?
(a) 3699
(b) 3499

(iv) The following settlements are located on which banks of Varka river ?
(a) Gangudra (b) Odha

(v) Name two important rivers of the map extract. Also state their direction of flow.

Ans. (i) (a) 3797
(b) 3601

(ii) Δ 592 in grid square 3701 represents triangulated height. When a point is accurately and shown with a triangle is called 'triangulated height'.
It is determined trignometrically, e.g. mountain peaks are indicated by triangulation points or heights on topographical maps.

(iii) (a) Radial drainage pattern
(b) Dendritic drainage pattern

(iv) (a) Gangudra settlement is located on the right bank of Varka river.
(b) Odha settlement is located on the left bank of Varka river.

(v) Two important rivers of the map extract are Sipu river and Varka river. The direction flow of Sipu river is from North to South and that of Varka river is from East to West.

21. Study the extract of the Survey of India Map Sheet No. G43S7 and answer the following questions. (Eastings 22 to 32, Northings - 01 to 11).

(i) (a) Give the four figure grid reference for. 200.
(b) Give the four figure grid reference for 20 r.

(ii) What do you understand by the tiny curved lines marked on the grid square 2607 ?

(iii) How would you say that the given map extract represents arid region ? State any two reasons.

(iv) (a) Name the important settlement of the map extract.
(b) Why is it an important settlement ?

(v) State any two features of Sipur river shown on the given map extract.

Ans. (i) (a) 2407 (b) 2707

(ii) The tiny curved lines marked on the grid square 2607 represent broken ground. It is found along the banks of a stream or river eroded due to flooding during rainy season. This is not fit for cultivation.

(iii) The reasons which explain that the given map extract represents grid region are as follows
(a) The area has many seasonal streams which dry up in summers.
(b) It has open scrub which shows arid or desert condition.

(iv) (a) Panthawada is an important settlement of the map extract.
(b) Panthawada has a police station, a post office, temples, perennial lined wells and it is connected by metalled roads.

(v) The two features of Sipur river are
(a) It is a dry river with water channel.
(b) It has islands and rocks.

22. Study the extract of the Survey of India Map sheet No. 45 D/10 Eastings 10 to 20 and Northings 01 to 10 and answer the following questions.

(i) Give a six-figure grid reference of
(a) Survey tree 277
(b) Δ 480

(ii) How does the drainage pattern in grid square 1304 differ from the drainage pattern in grid square 1506?

(iii) What are the two landforms represented by the pattern of contour in grid square 1608?

(iv) What is the ground distance in kilometres along the metalled road between the causeway in 1502 and the distance stone marked '14' in grid square 1203?

(v) What are the two main reasons for the absence of human habitation in the North-Eastern region of the map extract?

(vi) Name the type of rainfall experienced in the region shown in the map extract. Also give a reason to support your answer.

(vii) What is the difference between set patterns in grid square 1107 and in 1902?

(viii) State the difference in height between the highest spot height in the map extract and the contour height in grid square 1006.

(ix) (a) What is the compass direction of Patlawa ka Goliya (590) from Δ 480?
(b) Name the settlement that has a post office.

(x) What do you understand by the term causeway?

Ans. (i) (a) 177056
(b) 138045

(ii) 1304 - Radial drainage pattern.
1506 - Trellised drainage pattern.

(iii) These are pass and spur.

(iv) The distance is about 3.5 km.

(v) The reasons are
(a) The region is mountainous.
(b) The region does not have transport facility.

(vi) The rainfall type is seasonal as most of the streams are dry, not having water.

(vii) 1107-clustered or nucleated settlement.
1902-dispersed or scattered settlement.

(viii) The difference in highest spot height-1023 m
Contour height-260 m, 1023 - 260 = 763 m

(ix) (a) North-East direction
(b) Dattani

(x) Causeways are raised platforms across a dry stream. During the dry period, when the stream dries up people make a habit of crossing it. Thus, a footway is formed. Presence of many causeways show that the area gets seasonal or scanty rainfall.

23. Study the extract of the Survey of India Map Sheet no. 45 D/10 Eastings 02 to 12 and Northings 15 to 25 and answer the following questions.

(i) Give the six-figure grid reference of
(a) Temple near Jolpur
(b) The police chauki at Dantrai

(ii) Calculate the distance in km along the cart track between Dangrali and Dhann.

(iii) What is the difference in drainage pattern in grid square 0916 from that in 0221?

(iv) What is the probable occupation of the people living in the area of the map extract?

(v) How can we say that the area of the map extract experiences seasonal rainfall?

(vi) Name the most important settlement shown in the map extract. Also give a reason to support your answer.

(vii) What are the two different types of man-made features in grid square 0619?

(viii) (a) What is indicated by the tiny curved black lines in grid square 0720?
(b) How does it form?

(ix) (a) What is the direction of the main river given in the map extract?
(b) On which bank of Sukli Nadi is Bikanwas situated?

(x) Explain the meaning of the following features.
(a) 413 in grid square 0815.
(b) Stony waste in grid square 0918.

Ans. (i) (a) 078188
(b) 034238

(ii) The distance is about 3.5 km.

(iii) The drainage patterns are
0916-Radial type, 0221-Dendritic type.

(iv) The probable occupation of the people living in the area is agriculture as most of the map is coloured with a yellow wash.

(v) The area shown in the map extract experiences seasonal rainfall because of the presence of a number of dry tanks and seasonal streams.

(vi) The most important settlement is Dantrai as it has a Post Office (PO) and a Police Chauki.

(vii) One man-made feature is a perennial well (blue dot) and another is the permanent hut (shown by red square).

(viii) (a) his is broken ground.

(b) It is formed due to floods which occur during rainy season. Because of floods, the top soil is washed away developing into a badland which has loose soil and is unfit for cultivation.

(ix) (a) The direction is from North to South.

(b) Bikanwas is situated on the right bank of the river.

(x) (a) This is a triangulated height 413 m above mean sea level.

(b) Stony waste is the land which is mostly covered with rock boulders and stones and where cultivation is not possible.

24. Study the extract of the Survey of India Map Sheet no. 45 D/10 and answer the following questions. **[2019]**

(i) (a) Give the six-figure grid reference for the temple that is located to the South-West of Pithapura settlement.

(b) Give the four-figure grid reference for a settlement where people of the region meet socially and for trade at least once in a year.

(ii) (a) What is the pattern of drainage seen in the grid square 2118?

(b) What is the pattern of settlement seen in the grid square 1923?

(iii) What do each of the two numbers (281 printed in black colour and 20 printed in red colour) in the grid square 1818 indicate?

(iv) (a) Name any two man-made features in grid square 2419.

(b) Name any two natural features in grid square 2118.

(v) What is the significance of the following?

(a) Fire line in grid square 2417.

(b) Water body found in grid square 2221.

(vi) Calculate the area of the region between 16 and 19 Eastings and 18 and 22 Northings. Give your answer in kilometre square.

(vii) Give a reason for each of the following

(a) The water in some of the wells in the North-West quarter of the map is not fit for drinking.

(b) The region near Anadra and Gulabganj has many causeways.

(viii) (a) What is the main means of irrigation used by people living in the area shown on the map?

(b) What is the main occupation of the people of the region shown on the map?

(ix) According to you which is the most important settlement?

(x) Name any two means of transport used by the people living in the area shown on the map extract.

Ans. (i) (a) 201215

(b) 1622 settlement, 1520

(ii) (a) Radial

(b) Nucleated or compact settlement

(iii) 281 is the height of the land, whereas 20 is distance stone of the road.

(iv) (a) Houses / Huts, Cart track

(b) Rivers streams, Hills

(v) (a) It is wide path filled with water or sand to prevent forest fire.

(b) This is river with embankments to save the land from flooding.

(vi) Number of squares – 20

1: 50,000

Scale used 2 cm = 1 km

Area = 20 cm = 10 km

(vii) (a) Due to presence of brackish wells and water bodies marked in grid 1621.

(b) Causeway is a metalled raised road across a minor stream. A number of causeways are built in these regions is due to presence of numerous minor streams.

(viii) (a) Sipu nadi as many canal have been built from this along with number of distributing.

(b) Presence of cart track, park shows dependence infront. So they are involved in forest based occupations.

(ix) Pamgera 1622 presence of PS, PO compact settlement with annual fair.

(x) Cart track, Metalled road, footpath.

25. Study the extract of the Survey of India Map Sheet no. 45D/10 and answer the following questions **[2020]**

(i) (a) Give a six-figure grid reference for the spot height 324 in Northern part of the map extract.

(b) Give a four-figure grid reference for open scrub South of Dhad Talao.

(ii) (a) What is the meaning of the term "Contour interval"?

(b) What is the contour interval of the sheet provided to you?

(iii) What is the area in kilometre square of the region between 06 and 09 Eastings and 22 and 27 Northings?

(iv) What is the significance of the following colours used on the survey map?

(a) Yellow colour (b) Green colour.

(v) What is the compass direction of?
(a) Idarla (0825) from Bhamra (0420).
(b) Dhana (0623) from Amarapura (0124).

(vi) (a) Name the settlement pattern seen in the grid square 0819.
(b) Name the drainage pattern seen in the grid square 0827.

(vii) (a) Name two man-made features seen in the grid square 0723.
(b) Name two natural features seen in the grid square 0218.

(viii) (a) What is the black horizontal line drawn between 18 and 19 Northings?
(b) Name the most important settlement of the region shown on the map extract.

(ix) Draw the conventional symbol for each of the following
(i) Lined perennial well.
(ii) Seasonal tank.

(x) (a) Give one evidence to prove that the regions shown on the map extract receive scanty rainfall.
(b) What is .5r in the grid square 0321?

Ans. (i) (a) 076274
(b) 0721
(ii) (a) Contour lines are imaginery lines which join places of equal heights.
(b) 20 metre
(iii) 15 sq km.
(iv) (a) Yellow colour - agricultural land.
(b) Green colour- vegetation cover.
(v) (a) North-East
(b) North-West
(vi) (a) Dispersed Settlement Pattern
(b) Dendritic drainage Pattern
(vii) (a) Settlements and agricultural land.
(b) River and wasteland.
(viii) (a) Latitude.
(b) Dantrai
(ix) (a) 
(b) 
(x) (a) Seasonal nature of rivers and dry tanks represent that the regions shown on the map extract receive scanty rainfall.
(b) .5r represents relative height of the area.

26. Study the extract of the Survey of India Map Sheet No. G-13S7) and answer the following questions **[2023]**

(i) (a) Give the four-figure grid reference for A224.
(b) What is the contour interval used in the given map extract ?

(ii) (a) Mention two man made features seen in grid square 2706.
(b) Mention two natural features seen in grid square 2905.

(iii) (a) What do you understand by 1:50,000 printed below the map extract ?
(b) What is the pattern of drainage seen in the grid square 2505 ?

(iv) (a) What do you understand by 10r in 2709 ?
(b) What is th e compass direction of Mahudi Nani (2604) from Panswal (2909) ?

(v) Calculate the area in kilometre square of region enclosed between (Easting 26 to 29 and Northing 05 to 11).

Ans. (i) (a) 2706 (b) 20 metres
(ii) (a) Two man made features seen in gird square 2706 are covered tank and lime kilns.
(b) Two natural features seen in grid square 2905 are trees and seasonal streams.
(iii) (a) 1 : 50,000 is the scale of the given map.
(b) Dendritic drainage pattern
(iv) (a) 10r in grid square 2709 represents relative height of the area.
(b) The compass direction of Mahudi Nani (2604) from Panswal (2909) is South-West.
(v) The area in km sq. of the region enclosed between Eastings 26 to 29 and Northing 05 to 11 is 18 sq km.

CHAPTER

02

Map of India

SYLLABUS

On an outline map of India, candidates will be required to locate, mark and name the following:

- Mountains, Peaks and Plateaus: Himalayas, Karakoram, Aravali, Vindhyas, Satpura, Western and Eastern Ghats, Nilgiris, Garo, Khasi, Jaintia, Mount Godwin Austin (K2), Mount Kanchenjunga, Deccan Plateau, Chota Nagpur Plateau.
- Plains Gangetic Plains and Coastal plains –(Konkan, Kanara, Malabar, Coromandel, Northern Circars).
- Desert : Thar (The Great Indian Desert)
- Rivers: Indus, Ravi, Beas, Chenab, Jhelum, Satluj, Ganga, Yamuna, Ghaghra, Gomti, Gandak, Kosi, Chambal, Betwa, Son, Damodar, Brahmaputra, Narmada, Tapti, Mahanadi, Godavari, Krishna, Cauveri, Tungabhadra.
- Water Bodies: Gulf of Kutch, Gulf of Khambhat, Gulf of Mannar, Palk Strait, Andaman Sea, Chilka Lake, Wular Lake.
- Passes: Karakoram, Nathu-La Passes.
- Latitude and Longitudes: Tropic of Cancer, Standard Meridian (82° 30'E).
- Direction of Winds: South West Monsoons (Arabian Sea and Bay of Bengal Branches), North East Monsoons and Western Disturbances.
- Distribution of Minerals: Oil - Mumbai High (Offshore Oil Field) and Digboi. Iron – Singhbhum, Coal – Jharia.
- Soil Distribution – Alluvial, Laterite, Black and Red Soil.
- Cities - Delhi, Mumbai, Kolkata, Chennai, Hyderabad, Bengaluru, Kochi, Chandigarh, Srinagar, Vishakhapatnam, Allahabad.
- Population - Distribution of Population (Dense and sparse).

The main objective of giving map work in the examination is to test your knowledge about the location of different features on a map of India, e.g. mountains, plateaus, plains, rivers and water bodies, towns, coastal features, minerals, rainfalls, winds, latitudes and longitudes of India.

Assessment of Location and Labelling

- Marking the correct location of the feature. If a river is to be drawn on the map, it should have almost the correct shape of the channel, with the source and mouth marked at the correct place on the map.
- Appropriateness of symbol used, e.g. triangle or circle for a National Park, a square for the location of a mineral mine, the symbol | | for a dam on a river, etc.

Types of Maps Given

(i) **India Political Map** This is normally given to show political or administrative boundaries of states of India or any country. They can also indicate the location of major cities. These maps are used for most questions regarding identification or location and labelling of given features.

(ii) **India Outline Map** This is given rarely, but is used to mark the flow of a river, area of growth of a crop, major soil types, mining centres, monsoon winds direction and physiography of a specific area.

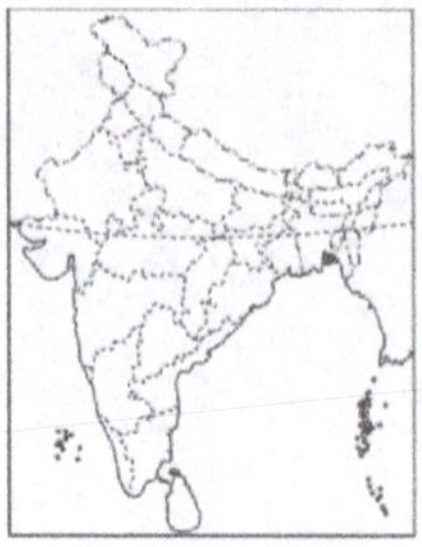
India Political

India Outline

Mountains, Peaks, Passes, Plains and Desert

Mountains and Peaks Himalayas, Karakoram, Aravali, Vindhyas, Satpura, Western and Eastern Ghats, Nilgiri Hills, Garo, Khasi, Jaintia, Mount Godwin Austin (K2), Mount Kanchenjunga

Passes Karakoram Pass, Nathu La Pass

Plains Gangetic Plains and Coastal Plains–Konkan Coast, Kanara Coast and Malabar Coast, Coromandel Coast and the Northern Circars.

Desert Thar (The Great Indian Desert)

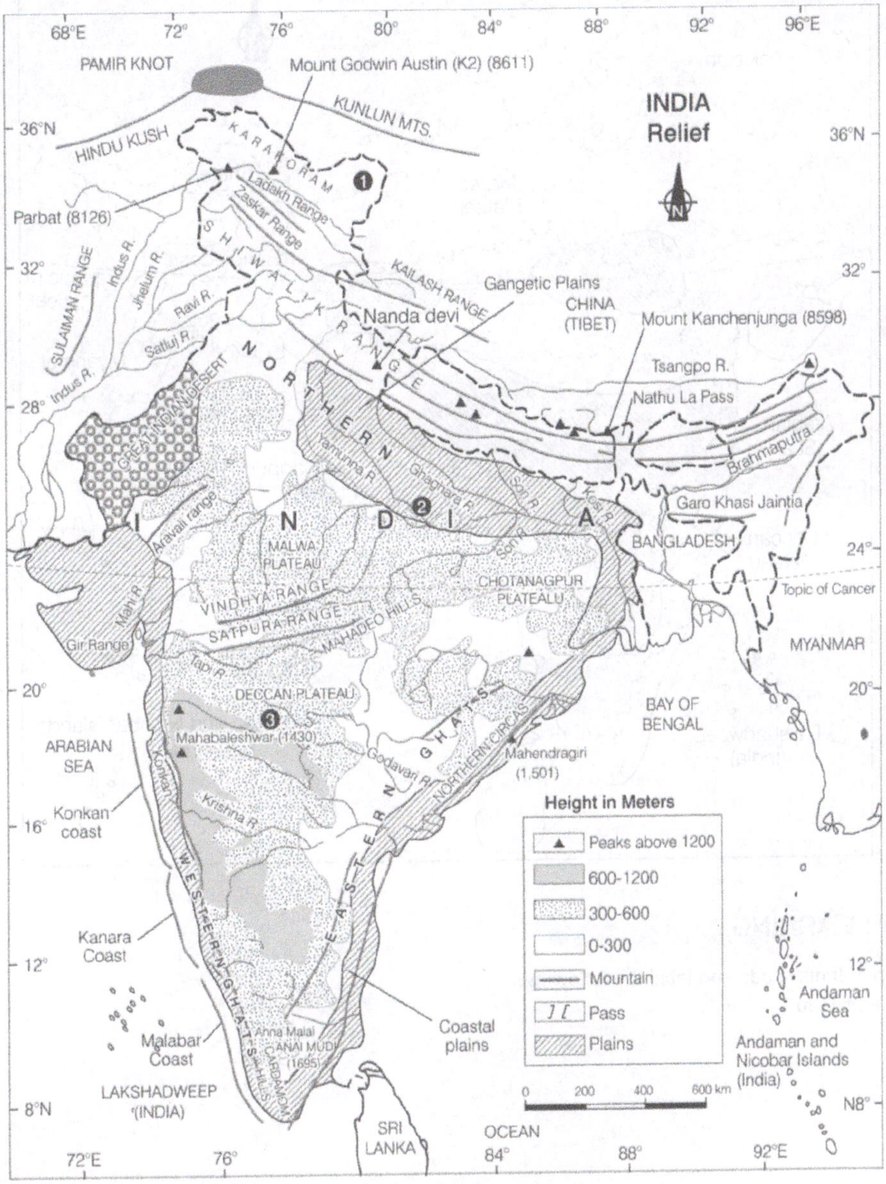

Check Your LEARNING...

1. On an outline map of India shade and label the following.
   (i) Himalayas
   (ii) Aravali Range
   (iii) Garo Hills
   (iv) Karakoram Pass
   (v) Konkan Coastal Plain

Plateaus

Deccan Plateau, Chota Nagpur Plateau, Malwa Plateau

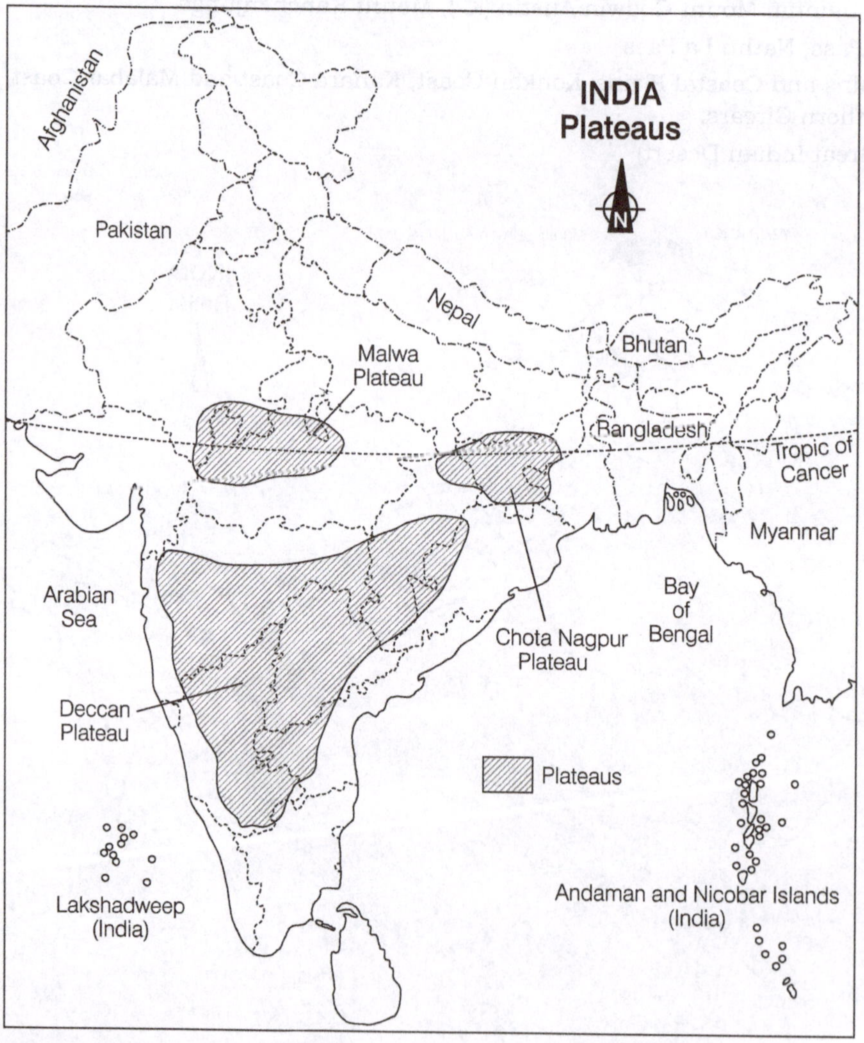

Check Your LEARNING...

2. On an outline map of India shade and label the following.
   (i) Chota Nagpur Plateau
   (ii) Malwa Plateau

Plains

Gangetic Plains, Coromandal Coast, Malabar Coast, Northern Circar

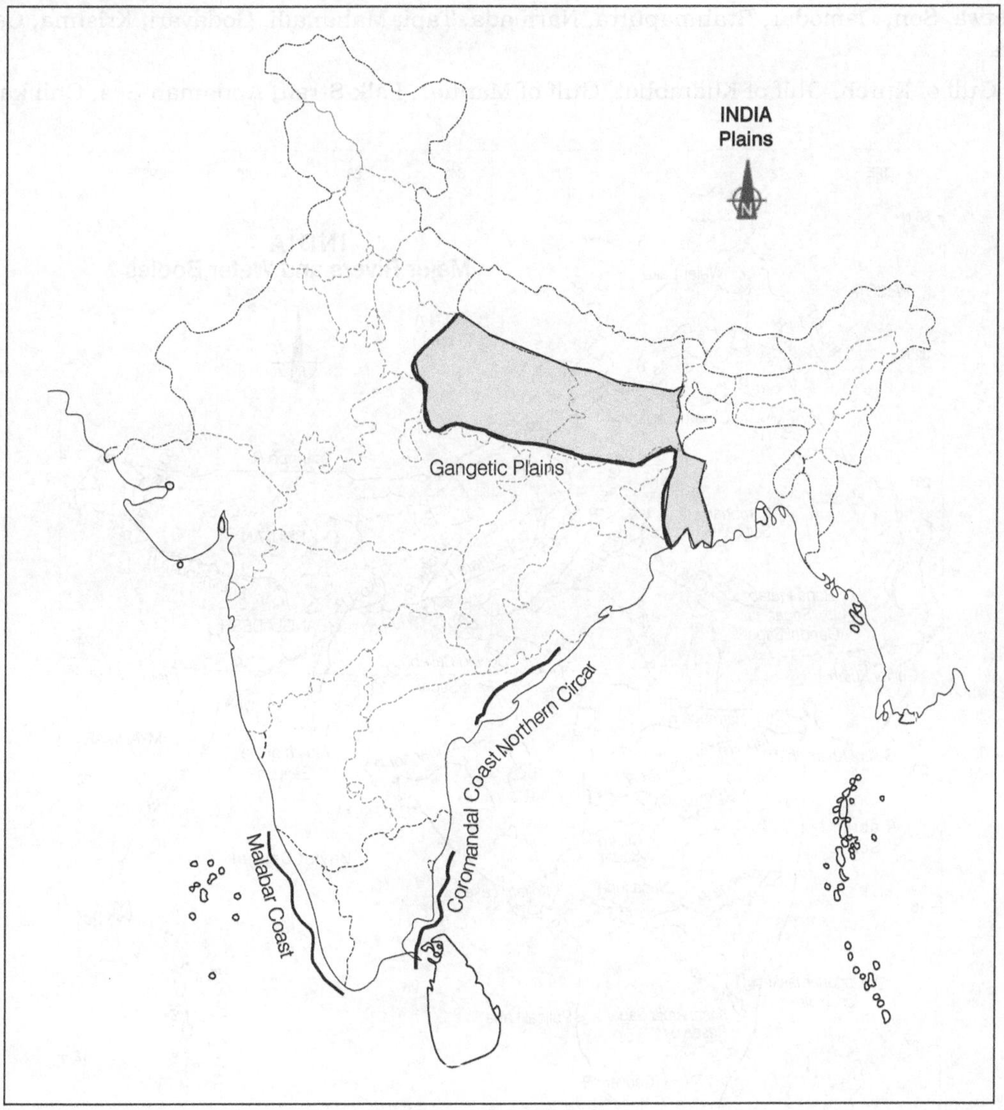

Check Your LEARNING...

3. On an outline map of India shade and label the following.
   (i) Gangetic Plains (ii) Northern Circar

Rivers and Water Bodies

Rivers Indus, Ravi, Beas, Chenab, Jhelum, Satluj, Ganga, Yamuna, Ghaghra, Gomti, Gandak, Kosi, Chambal, Betwa, Son, Damodar, Brahmaputra, Narmada, Tapi, Mahanadi, Godavari, Krishna, Cauvery, Tungabhadra

Water Bodies Gulf of Kutch, Gulf of Khambhat, Gulf of Mannar, Palk Strait, Andaman Sea, Chilika Lake, Wular Lake

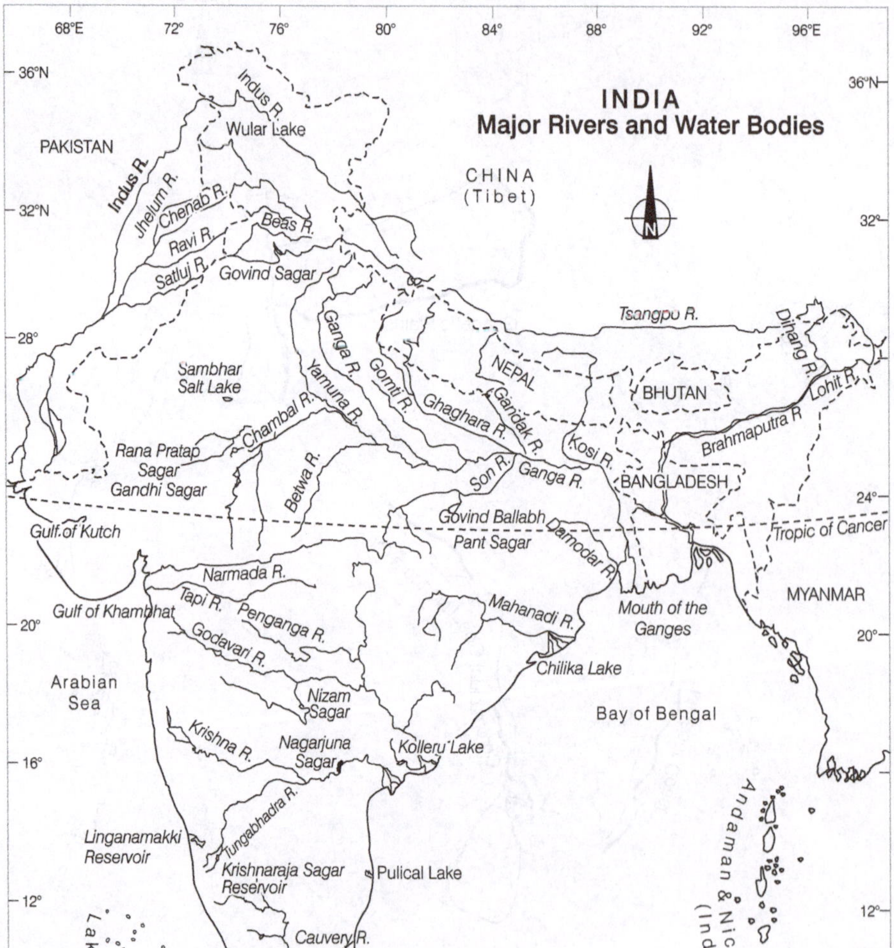

Check Your LEARNING...

4. On an outline map of India mark and label the following.
(i) Indus River
(ii) Godavari River
(iii) Chilika Lake
(iv) Gulf of Kutch
(v) Palk Strait

Latitudes and Longitudes

- **Tropic of Cancer** — (23°1/2° N) a parallel of latitude divides India into almost two equal halves.
- **Standard Meridian** — (82°30′ E) a meridian of longitude from where the Indian Standard Time (IST) has taken.

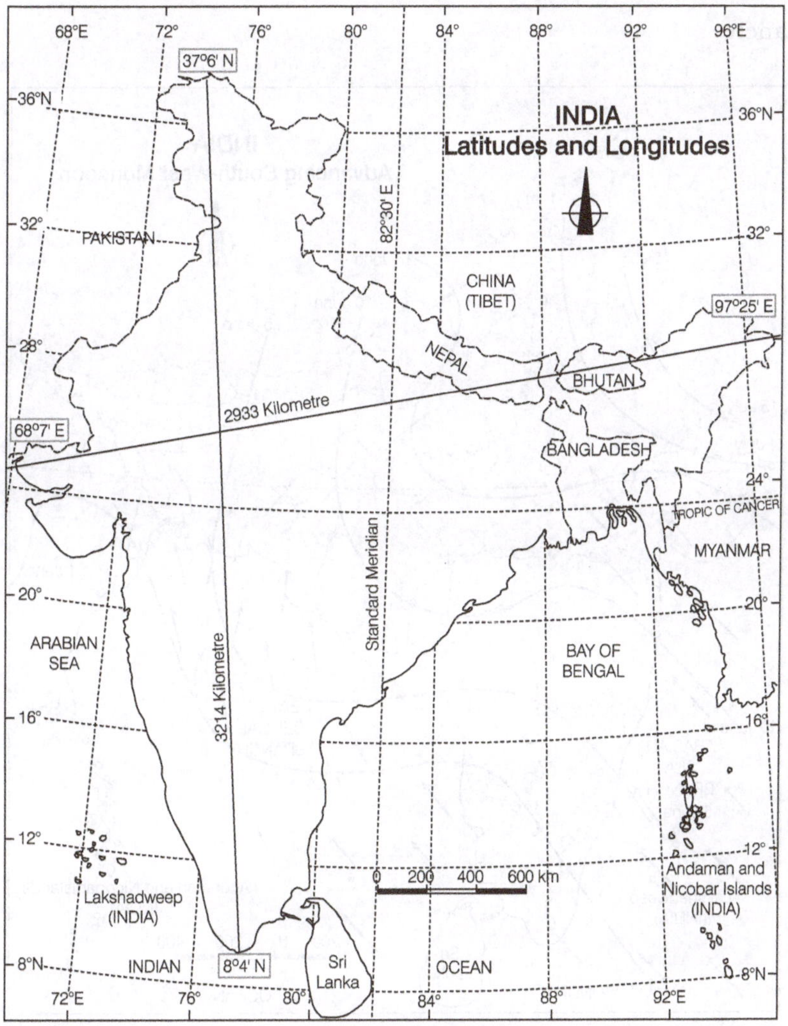

Check Your LEARNING...

5. On an outline map of India mark and label the following.
   (i) Tropic of cancer
   (ii) The meridian of longitude from where the Indian Standard Time (IST) has taken.

Direction of Monsoon

South-West Monsoon (June to September)

It has two branches

(i) Arabian Sea Branch

(ii) Bay of Bengal Branch

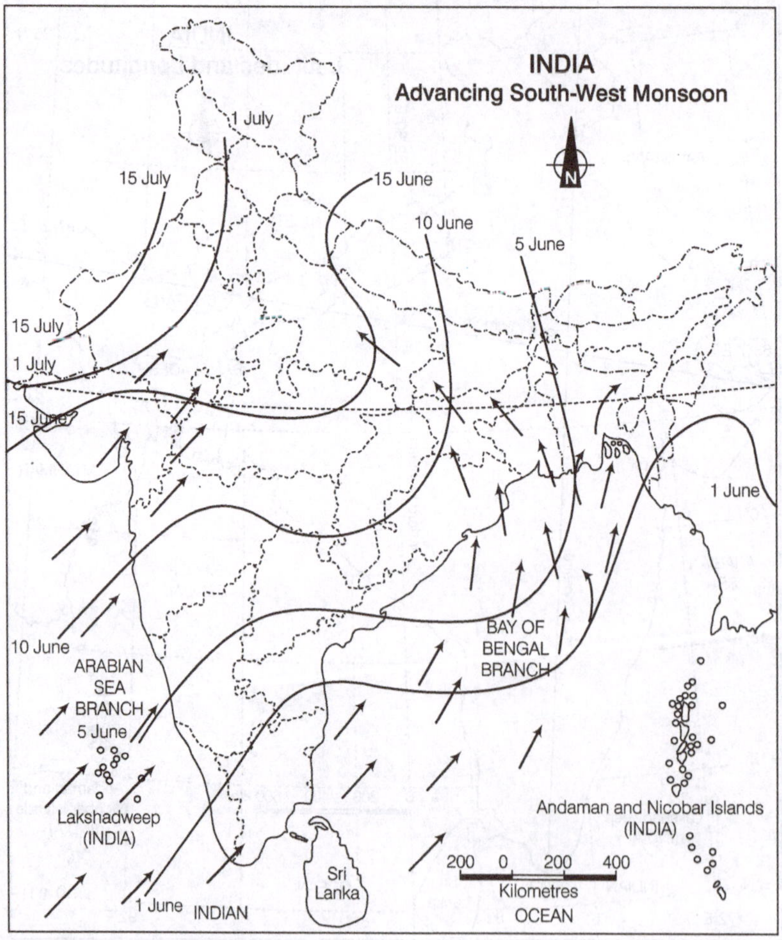

Check Your LEARNING...

6. On an outline map of India mark with arrows the location of winds of the following.
   (i) Arabian Sea Branch
   (ii) Bay of Bengal Branch

Withdrawal or Retreating of South-West Monsoon

The months of October and November are known as the Season of Retreating Monsoon.

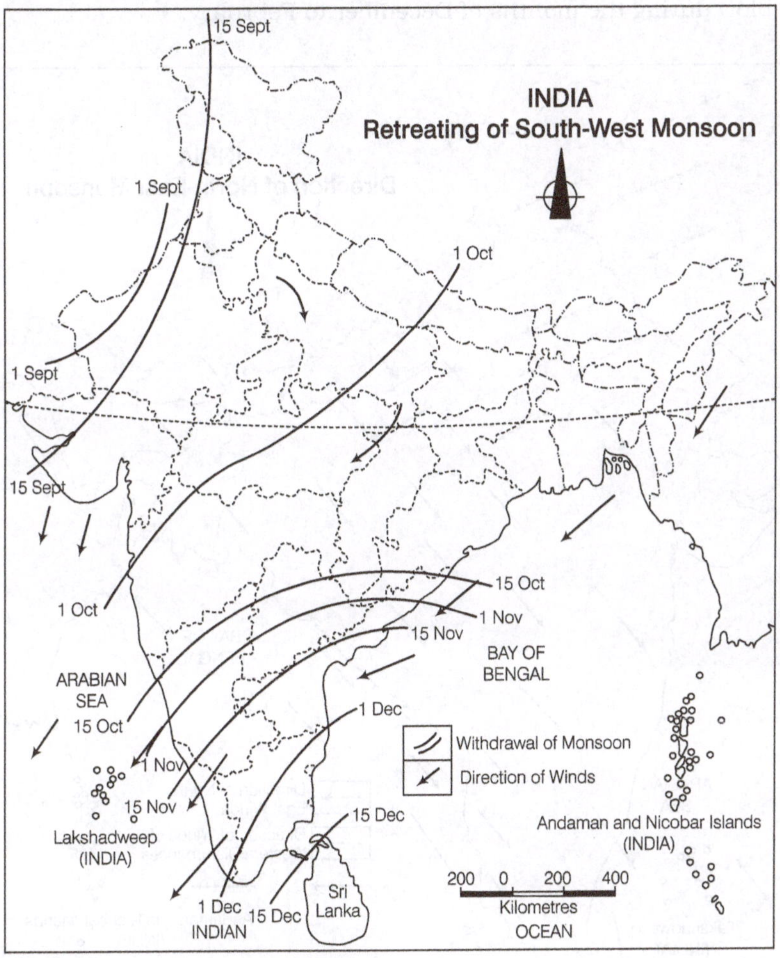

Check Your LEARNING...

7. On an outline map of India mark with single arrow the location of winds of the season of retreating monsoon.

Direction of North-East Monsoon (December to February) and Western Disturbances

These monsoon winds blow during the months of December to February.

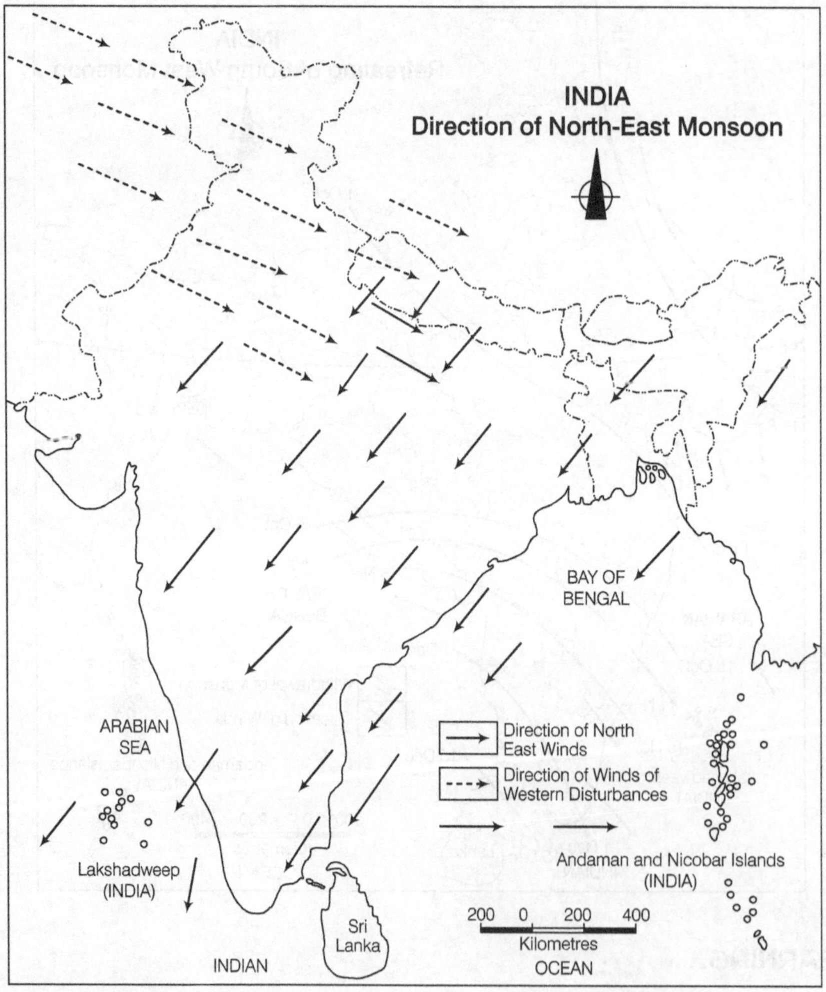

Check Your LEARNING...

8. On an outline map of India mark with a single arrow the location of winds of North-East monsoon.

Distribution Minerals*

(i) Oil Fields and Refineries

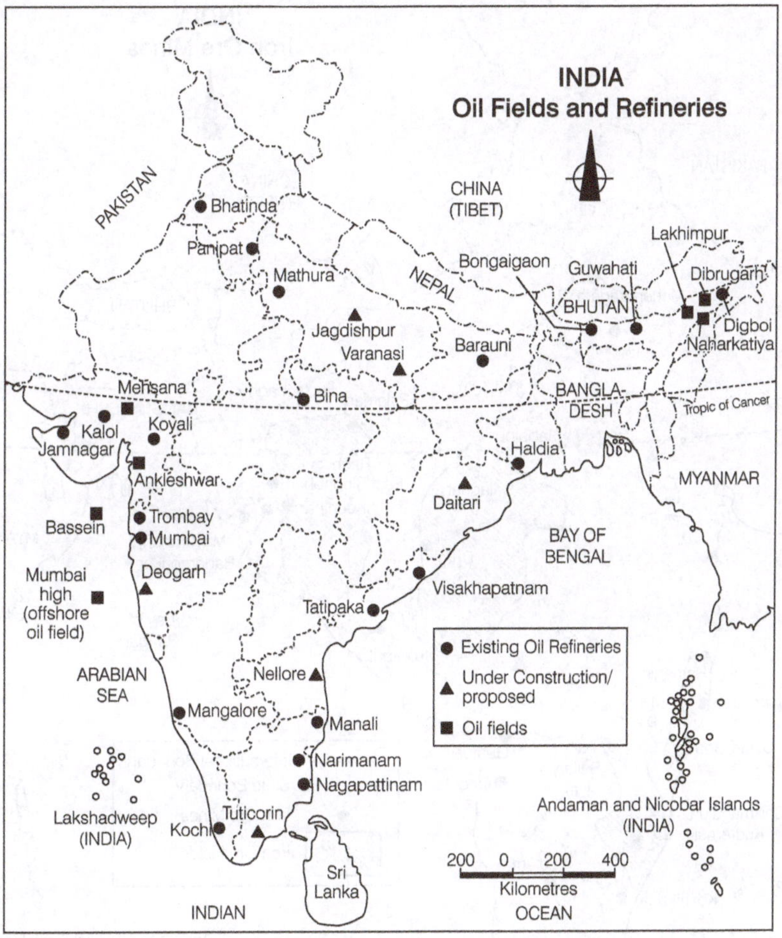

Check Your LEARNING...

9. On an outline map of India mark and label the following.
   (a) Mumbai High offshore oil field.
   (b) An oil field in North-Eastern region.

* In ICSE Geography X syllabus, only Mumbai High and Digboi as oil fields, Singhbhum as iron field and Jharia as coal field are given in Distribution of Minerals for locating and marking on map.

(ii) Iron ore Mines

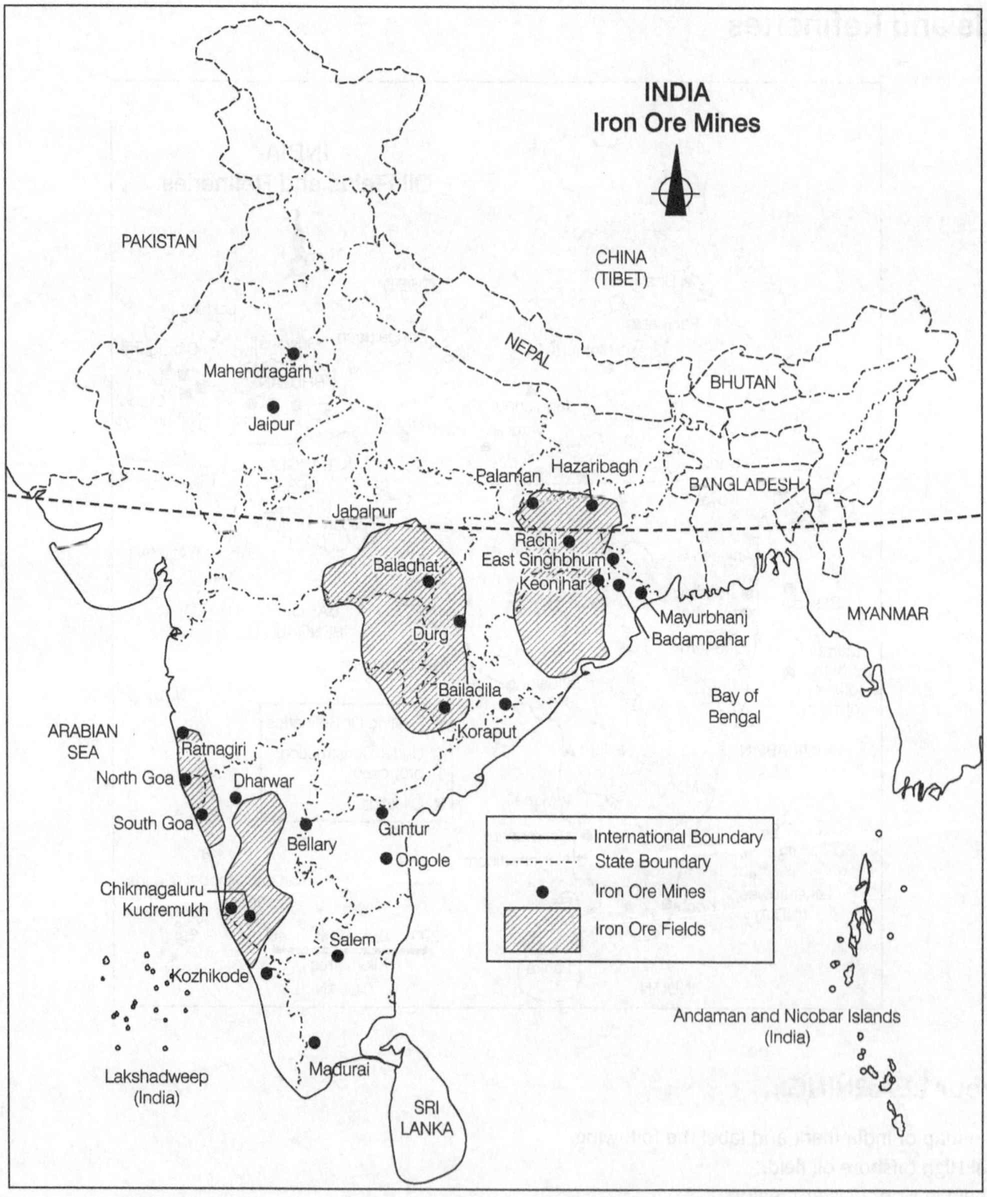

Check Your LEARNING...

10. On an outline map of India mark and label the following.
    (a) The Singhbhum iron ore mine
    (b) An iron ore mine located in Karnataka
    (c) Bellary iron ore mine

(iii) Coal Fields

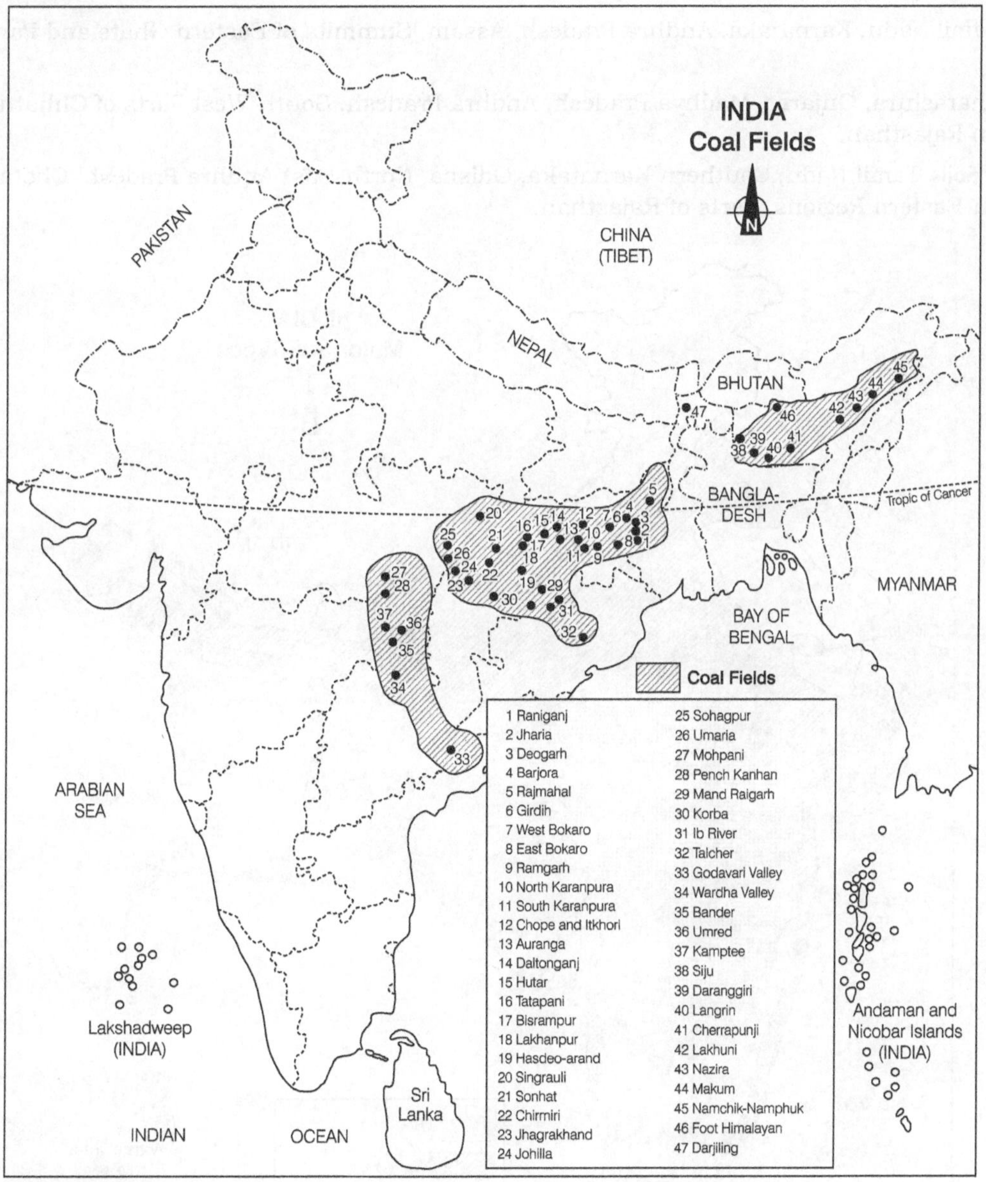

Check Your LEARNING...

11. On an outline map of India mark and label the following.
    (a) Jharia coal field.
    (b) Raniganj coal field.
    (c) Godavari Valley coal region/field.

Major Soil Distribution

Alluvial Soils Punjab, Haryana, Uttar Pradesh, Bihar, West Bengal, Assam, Coastal Plains (East-West).

Laterite Soils Tamil Nadu, Karnataka, Andhra Pradesh, Assam, Summits of Eastern Ghats and Parts of Odisha.

Black Soils Maharashtra, Gujarat, Madhya Pradesh, Andhra Pradesh, South-West Parts of Chhattisgarh, South-Eastern Rajasthan.

Red and Yellow Soils Tamil Nadu, Southern Karnataka, Odisha, North-East Andhra Pradesh, Chotanagpur Plateau, North-Eastern Regions, Parts of Rajasthan.

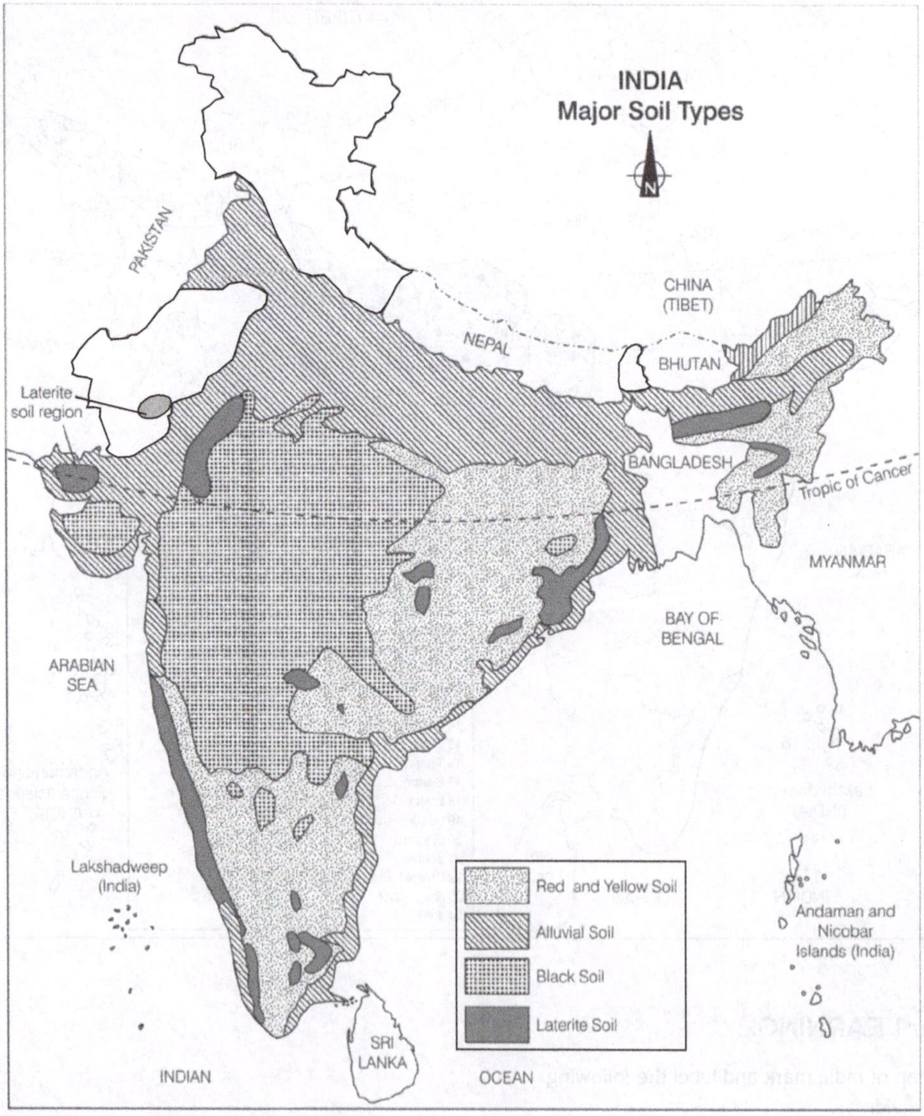

Check Your LEARNING...

12. On an outline map of India shade and label the following.
   (i) An area of laterite soil in the North India.
   (ii) An area of alluvial soil in the Peninsular India.
   (iii) A region with black soil.
   (iv) An area with red soil.
   (v) A region with laterite soil in the Eastern India.

Major Cities

Delhi (capital of India), Mumbai, Kolkata, Chennai, Hyderabad, Bengaluru, Kochi, Chandigarh, Srinagar, Visakhapatnam, Allahabad.

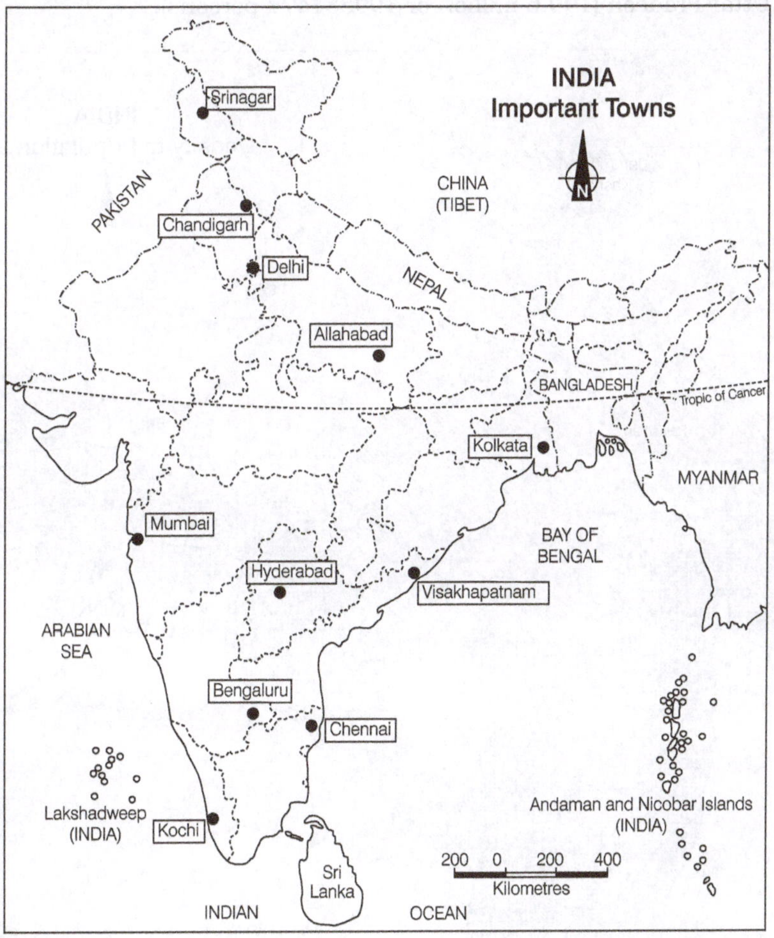

Check Your LEARNING...

13. On an outline map of India mark and label the following.
    - (i) Delhi
    - (ii) Kolkata
    - (iii) Hyderabad
    - (iv) Visakhapatnam
    - (v) Kochi

Population Distribution

As per 2011 Census

Sparsely Populated State Sikkim (0.6 million or 607688 persons).

Densely Populated State Uttar Pradesh (199.6 million or 199581477 persons).

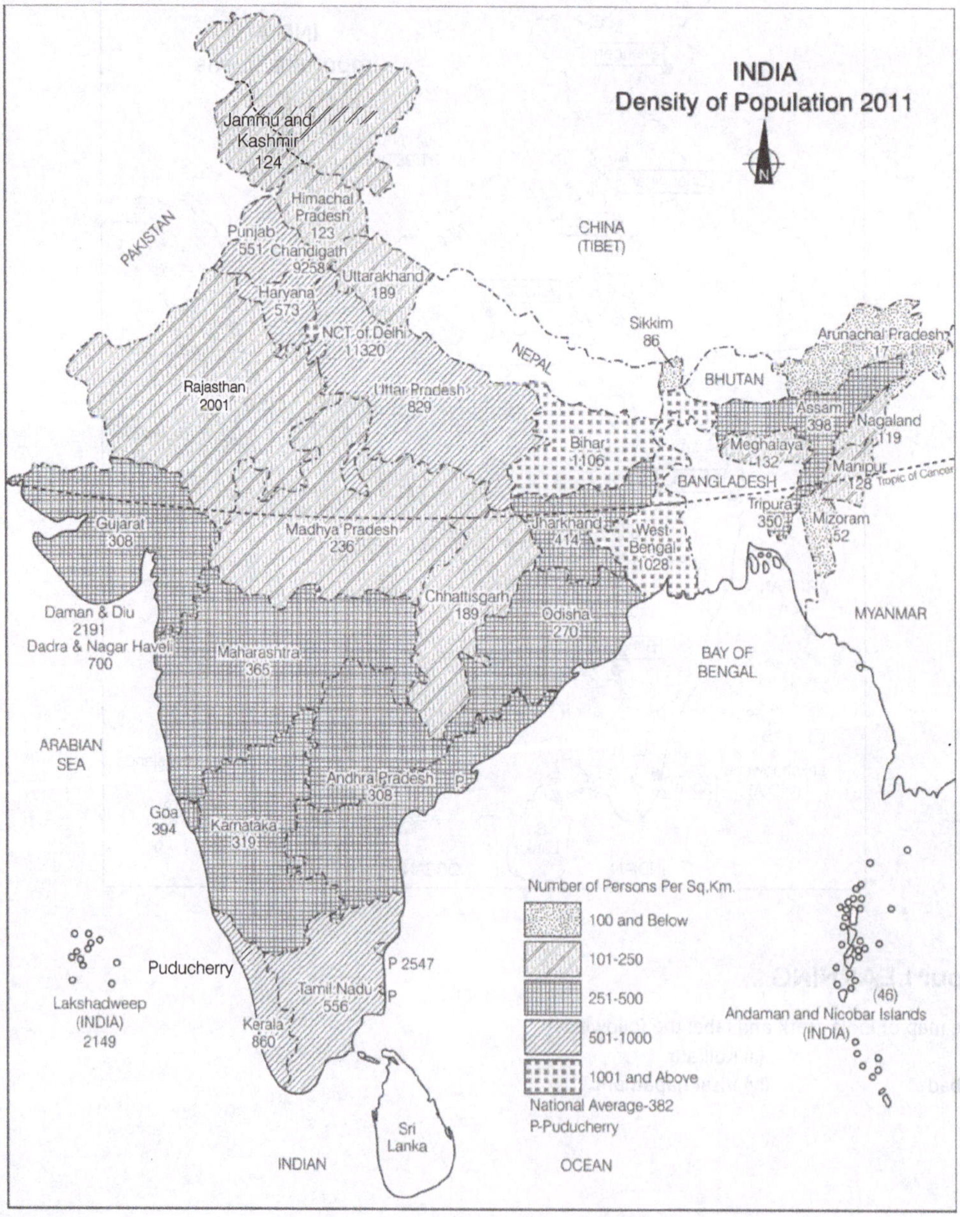

Check Your LEARNING...

14. On an outline map of India mark and label the following.
   (i) The densely populated state of India.
   (ii) The sparsely populated state of India.

Chapter Practice

Maps Based Questions

1.

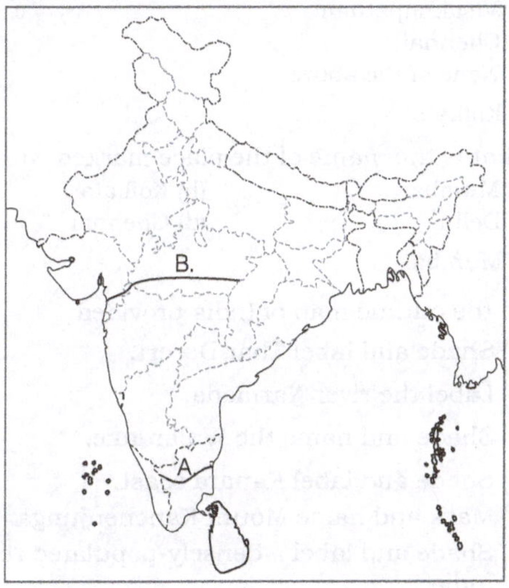

(i) What is the name of the river marked with A?

(a) Godavari (b) Krishna
(c) Kaveri (d) Mahanadi

Ans. (c) Kaveri

(ii) What is the name of the river marked with B?

(a) Narmada (b) Tapi
(c) Godavari (d) Krishna

Ans. (a) Narmada

2.

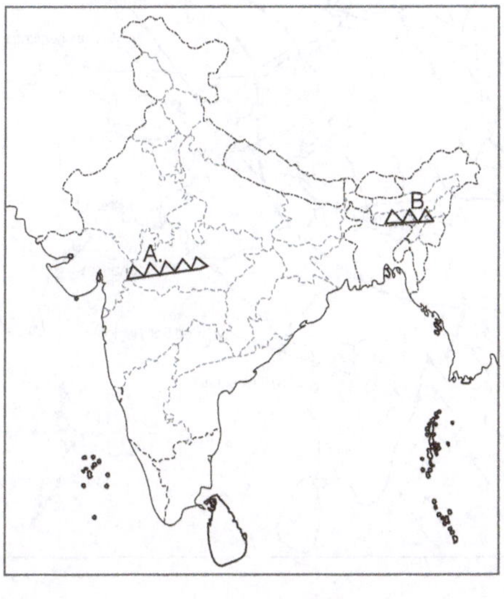

(i) What is the name of the hill marked with A?

(a) Aravali
(b) Nilgiri
(c) Satpura
(d) Western Ghat

Ans. (c) Satpura

(ii) What is the name of the hill marked with B?

(a) Garo Khasi Jaintia
(b) Nathu la
(c) Ladakh
(d) Nanda Devi

Ans. (a) Garo Khasi Jaintia

3.

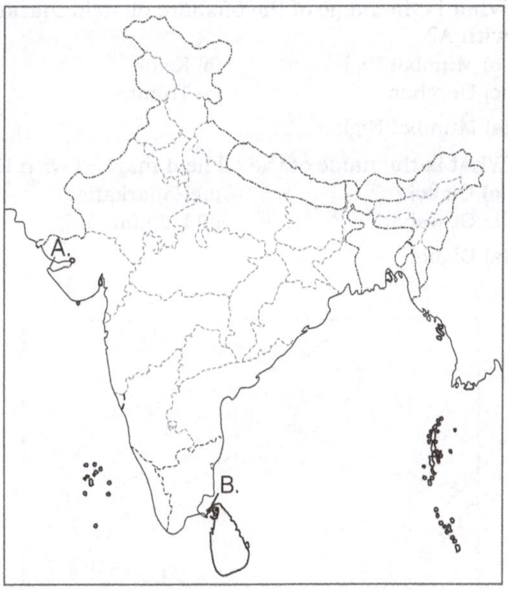

(i) What is the name of the point marked with A?

(a) Gulf of Khambhat
(b) Chilika Lake
(c) Palk strait
(d) Gulf of Kachchh

Ans. (d) Gulf of Kachchh

(ii) What is the name of the place marked with B ?

(a) Palk strait
(b) Gulf of Kutch
(c) Gulf of Khambhat
(d) None of the above

Ans. (a) Palk strait

4.

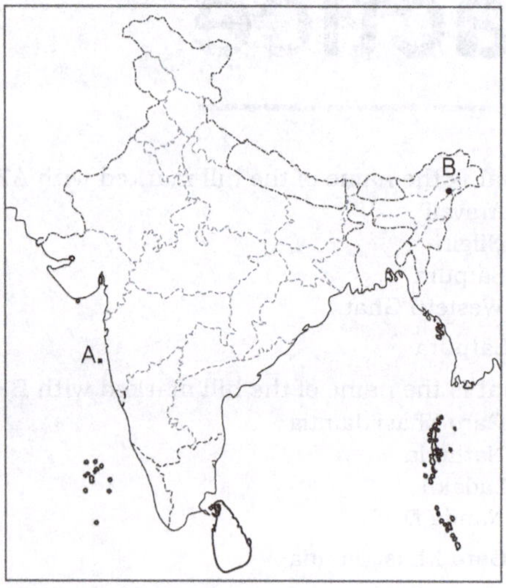

(i) What is the name of the offshore oil field marked with A?

(a) Mumbai High (b) Kalol
(c) Devghar (d) Trombay

Ans. (a) Mumbai High

(ii) What is the name of the oil field marked with B?

(a) Digboi (b) Naharkatiya
(c) Guwahati (d) Lakhimpur

Ans. (a) Digboi

5.

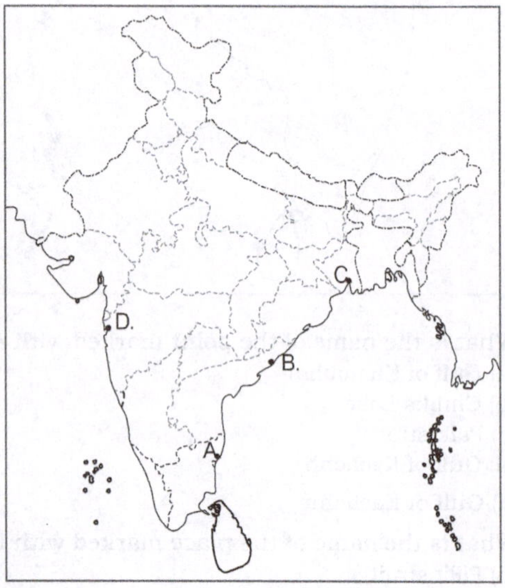

(i) What is the name of the place marked with A?

(a) Chennai (b) Kolkata
(c) Mumbai (d) Delhi

Ans. (a) Chennai

(ii) What is the name of the place marked with B?

(a) Visakhapatnam
(b) Chennai
(c) Kolkata
(d) Delhi

Ans. (a) Visakhapatnam

(iii) What is the name of the place marked with C?

(a) Kolkata
(b) Visakhapatnam
(c) Chennai
(d) None of the above

Ans. (a) Kolkata

(iv) What is the name of the place marked with D?

(a) Mumbai (b) Kolkata
(c) Delhi (d) Chennai

Ans. (a) Mumbai

6. On the outline map of India provided **[2018]**

(i) Shade and label Thar Desert.
(ii) Label the river Narmada.
(iii) Shade and name the Wular lake.
(iv) Shade and label Kanara coast.
(v) Mark and name Mount Kanchenjunga.
(vi) Shade and label a densely-populated region in India.
(vii) Shade and label a region with Red soil in India.
(viii) Mark with a dot and name Chennai.
(ix) Mark and label the Arabian Sea branch of S.W. Monsoon.
(x) Mark with a dot and name Singhbhum.

Ans.

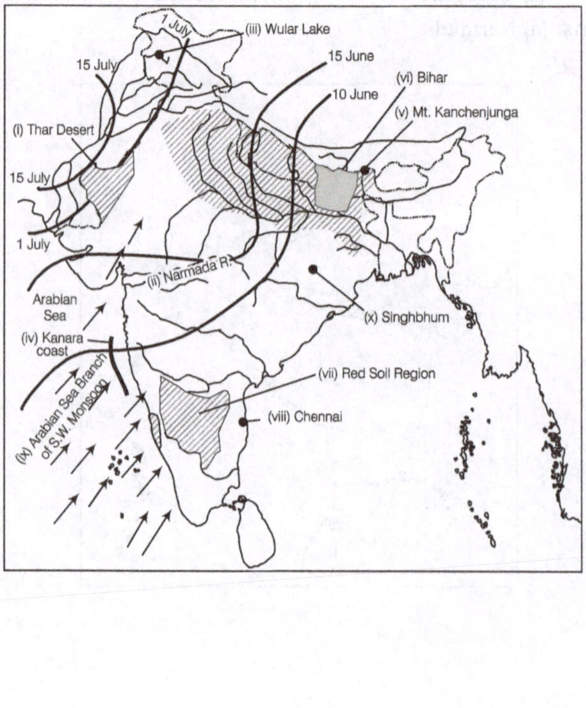

7. On the outline map of India provided [2017]

(i) Draw and name the Tropic of Cancer.
(ii) Label the river Godavari.
(iii) Mark and name the Garo Hills.
(iv) Mark C on the coal fields of Jharia.
(v) Mark with an arrow and name, the NE monsoon over the Bay of Bengal.
(vi) Shade and name the Gulf of Kachchh.
(vii) Shade and name the coastal plain that receives rainfall in October-November.
(viii) Mark with a dot and name Delhi.
(ix) Shade a region with black cotton soil.
(x) Use an arrow to point at a densely populated state in South India.

Ans.

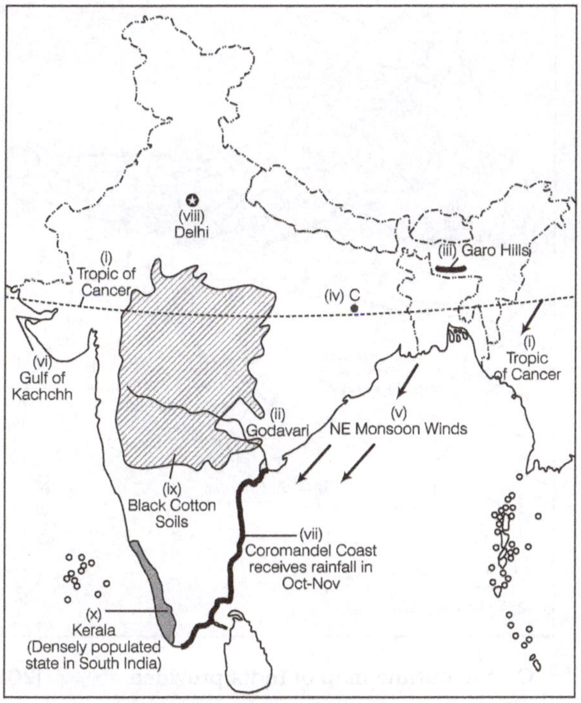

8. On the outline map of India provided [2016]

(i) Draw and number the Standard Meridian of India.
(ii) Label the river Mahanadi.
(iii) Mark and name lake Chilika.
(iv) Shade and name the Gulf of Mannar.
(v) Mark and name the Vindhya Mountains.
(vi) Shade and name a sparsely populated region in Western India.
(vii) Shade a region with alluvial soil in South India.
(viii) Mark and name Kolkata.
(ix) Mark with arrows and name South-West Monsoon winds over the Bay of Bengal.
(x) Mark and name Mumbai High.

Ans.

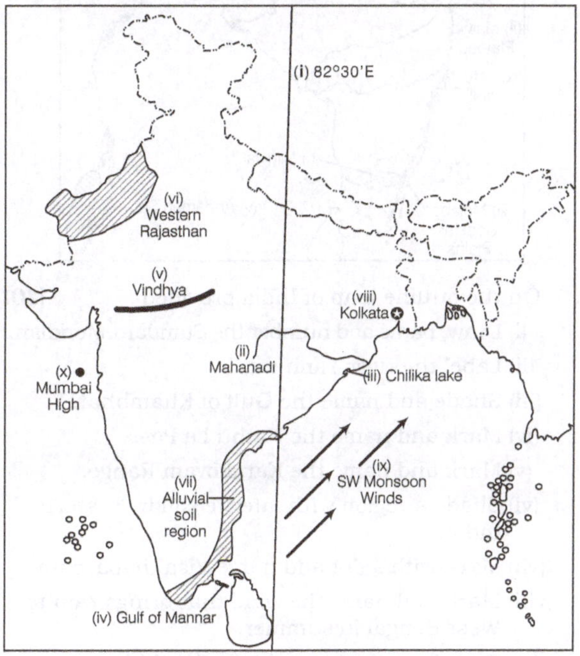

9. On the outline map of India provided [2015]

(i) Mark and name the Nilgiris.
(ii) Shade and label the Malwa Plateau.
(iii) Shade and label the Malabar Coastal Plains.
(iv) Mark and name the river Gomti.
(v) Shade and name the Andaman Sea.
(vi) Mark and name Allahabad.
(vii) Mark with a single arrow and name the winds that bring winter rain to North-West India.
(viii) Mark and name Digboi.
(ix) Mark an area with laterite soil below the Tropic of Cancer.
(x) Mark and name the Karakoram Pass.

Ans.

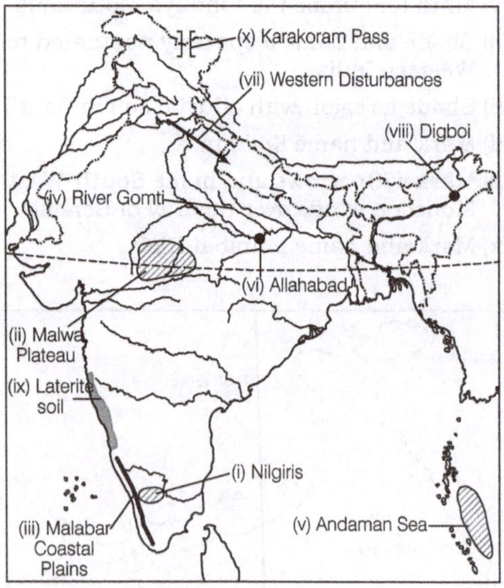

10. On the outline map of India provided **[2014]**

(i) Draw, name and number the Standard Meridian.

(ii) Label the river Yamuna.

(iii) Shade and name the Gulf of Khambhat.

(iv) Mark and name the Nathu La Pass.

(v) Mark and name the Karakoram Range.

(vi) Shade a region with laterite soil in Eastern India.

(vii) Mark with a dot and name Visakhapatnam.

(viii) Mark and name the wind that brings rain to West Bengal in summer.

(ix) Print S on the iron mine in Singhbhum.

(x) Shade and name a sparsely populated state in North-East India.

Ans.

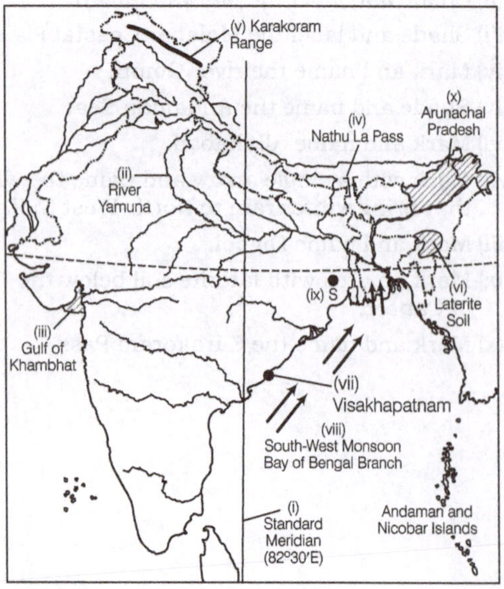

11. On the outline map of India provided **[2013]**

(i) Mark the name Chennai.

(ii) Label the river Godavari.

(iii) Shade and label the Chota Nagpur Plateau.

(iv) Shade and name the Gulf of Kachchh.

(v) Mark and name the Indo-Gangetic Plains.

(vi) Shade and label an area with red soil.

(vii) Mark and name the winds, which bring rain to Mumbai in July and August.

(viii) Mark and name the Satpura Range.

(ix) Mark and name the Jharia coal field.

(x) Shade and label the Northern Circars coastal region.

Ans.

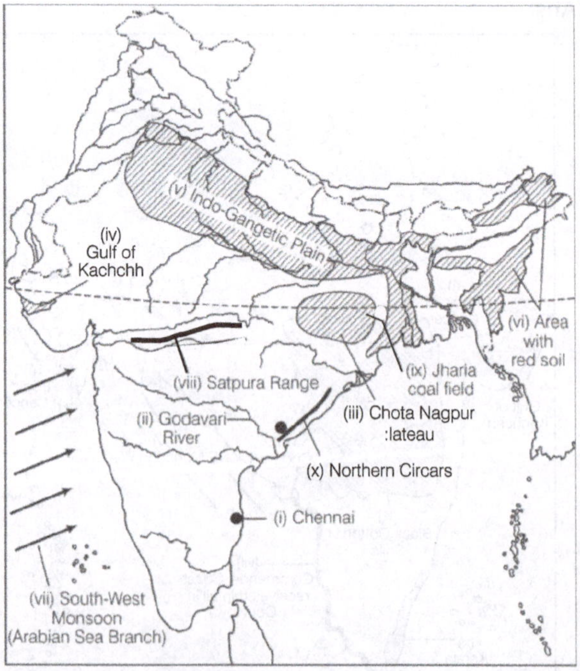

12. On the outline map of India provided **[2012]**

(i) Draw, name and number the Tropic of Cancer.

(ii) Label the river Narmada.

(iii) Shade and name Chilika lake.

(iv) Mark and name the Aravali mountains.

(v) Mark and name the Karakoram Pass.

(vi) Mark and name a densely populated state in South India.

(vii) Shade and name a region with black soil.

(viii) Mark with a dot and name Srinagar.

(ix) Mark and name the winds which bring rain in winter to the Coromandel coast.

(x) Name and print on an oilfield in North-East India.

Ans.

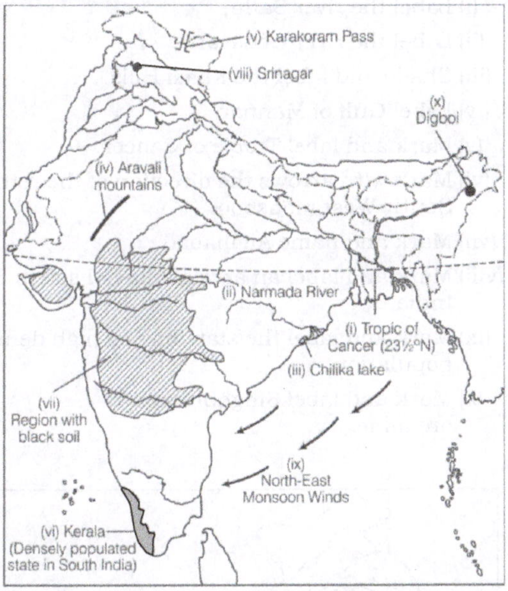

13. On the outline map of India provided **[2011]**

(i) Mark and name Kochi.
(ii) Label the river Krishna.
(iii) Shade and label the Malwa Plateau.
(iv) Mark and label the Konkan Coast.
(v) Shade and label the Gulf of Mannar.
(vi) Shade and label an alluvial soil area in the Peninsular India.
(vii) Mark with arrows the direction of the Arabian Sea branch of South-West monsoon winds.
(viii) Shade and label the Western Ghats.
(ix) Mark the Jharia coal field.
(x) Shade and name a densely populated area.

Ans.

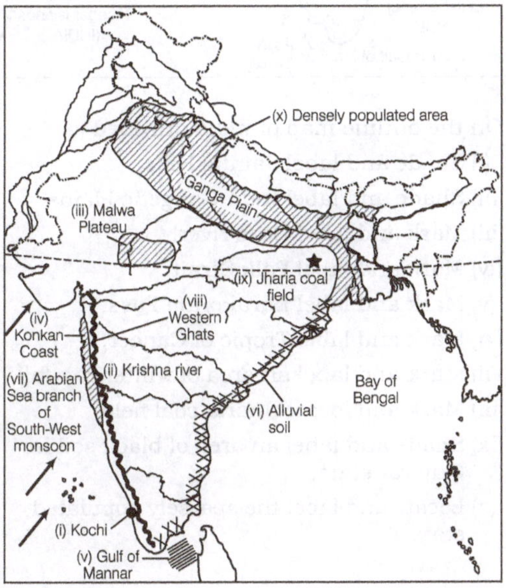

14. On the outline map of India provided **[2010]**

(i) Label the river Chenab.
(ii) Label the river Chambal.
(iii) Shade and label the Nilgiri Hills.
(iv) Mark and label the Eastern Ghats.
(v) Mark and name the port city of Pakistan.
(vi) Mark and label Hyderabad.
(vii) Shade and label the Sunderbans.
(viii) Mark and name the Palk Strait.
(ix) Mark and label a region North of the Tropic of Cancer where tea is grown extensively.
(x) Mark and name the winds which bring rain to Mumbai in July and August.

Ans.

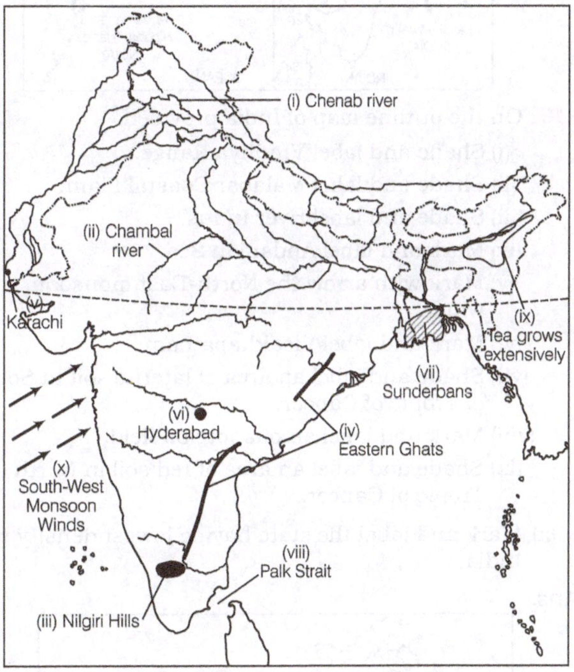

15. On the outline map of India provided

(i) Shade and label Coromandel Coastal Plains.
(ii) Shade and label the Himalayas.
(iii) Label the Betwa river.
(iv) Mark and label Palk Strait.
(v) Mark with arrows the direction of the winds which cause cyclones to occur in Andhra Pradesh and Odisha during October-November.
(vi) Mark and label Mumbai High.
(vii) Mark and label the Standard Meridian.
(viii) Shade an area of laterite soil in Western India.
(ix) Mark and label the city of Bengaluru.
(x) Mark and label the sparsely populated state of Western India.

Ans.

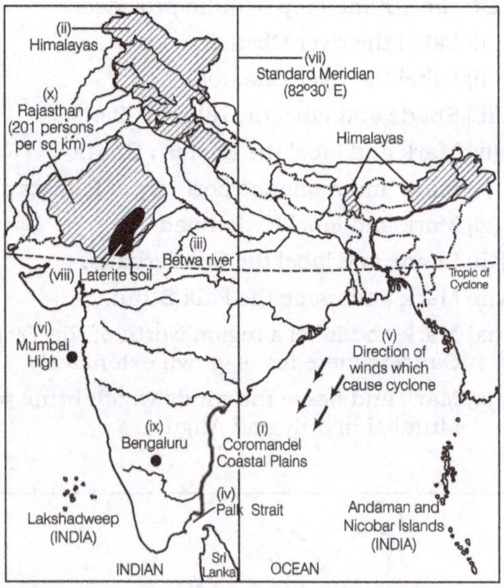

16. On the outline map of India provided

(i) Shade and label Vindhya Range.
(ii) Shade and label Malabar Coastal Plain.
(iii) Shade and label river Indus.
(iv) Mark and label Andaman Sea.
(v) Mark with arrow the North-East monsoon winds.
(vi) Mark and label Visakhapatnam.
(vii) Shade and label an area of laterite soil in South of Tropic of Cancer.
(viii) Mark and label an offshore oil field.
(ix) Shade and label an area of red soil in North of Tropic of Cancer.
(x) Mark and label the state having lowest density in India.

Ans.

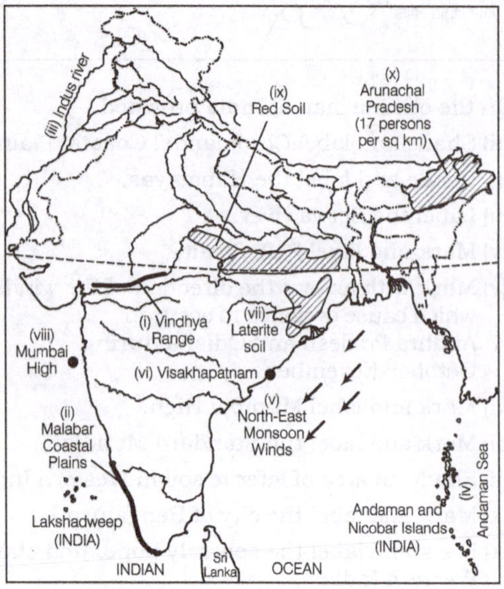

17. On the outline map of India provided

(i) Label the river Satluj.
(ii) Label the river Godavari.
(iii) Shade and label the Khasi Hills.
(iv) Label Gulf of Mannar.
(v) Mark and label Tropic of Cancer.
(vi) Mark with arrows the direction of the retreating South-West monsoon.
(vii) Mark and name Allahabad.
(viii) Mark and label an area of alluvial soil in South India.
(ix) Mark and label the state having high density of population.
(x) Mark and label Singhbhum iron ore mine.

Ans.

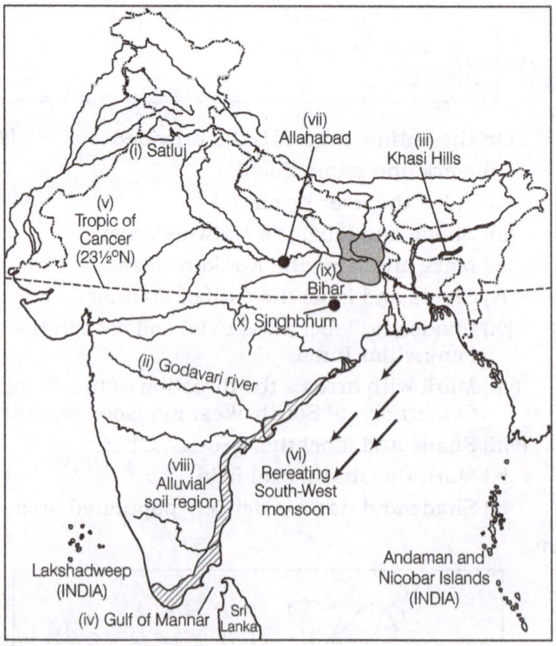

18. On the outline map of India provided

(i) Shade and label Jaintia Hills.
(ii) Shade and label Indo-Gangetic Plains.
(iii) Mark and label Beas river.
(iv) Mark and label Palk Strait.
(v) Mark and label Karakoram Pass.
(vi) Mark and label Tropic of Cancer.
(vii) Mark and label an area of winter rainfall.
(viii) Mark and locate Jharia coal field.
(ix) Shade and label an area of black soil in Gujarat state.
(x) Locate and label the sparsely populated state.

Ans.

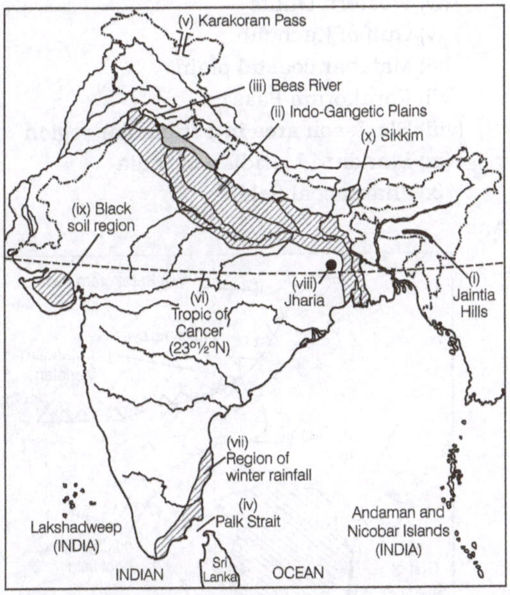

19. On the outline map of India provided **[2023]**

(i) Mark and label the Satpura.
(ii) Shade and label the Gulf of Kutch.
(iii) Mark and label the River Chambal
(iv) Mark and label Delhi.
(v) Mark and label 82° 30' E longitude.
(vi) Mark and label Jharia Coalfield.
(vii) Mark with arrows and name the South-West Monsoon winds.
(viii) Mark and label the Karakoram Pass.
(ix) Shade and label a sparsely populated region in Western India.
(x) Shade an area having alluvial soil.

Ans.

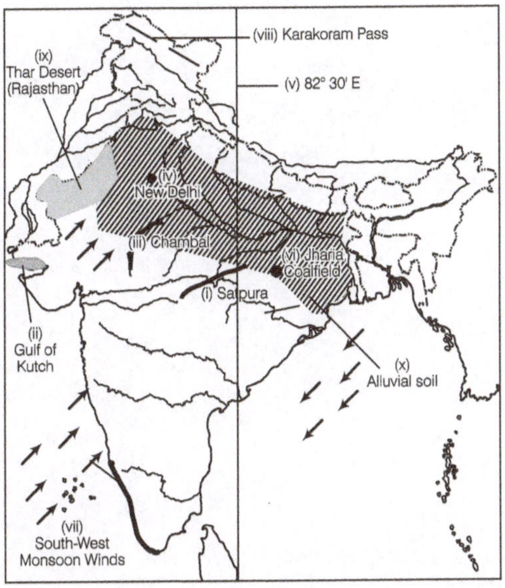

20. On the outline map of India provided **[2019]**

(i) Shade and label the Gangetic Plain.
(ii) Shade and label an area of laterite soil in North India.
(iii) Mark and label the Karakoram Mountains.
(iv) Mark and name the Palk Strait.
(v) Shade and label the river Kaveri.
(vi) Mark and name Mumbai.
(vii) Mark and name the Nathu La Pass.
(viii) Mark and name Digboi.
(ix) Shade and name the Deccan Plateau.
(x) Shade and label the river Jhelum.

Ans.

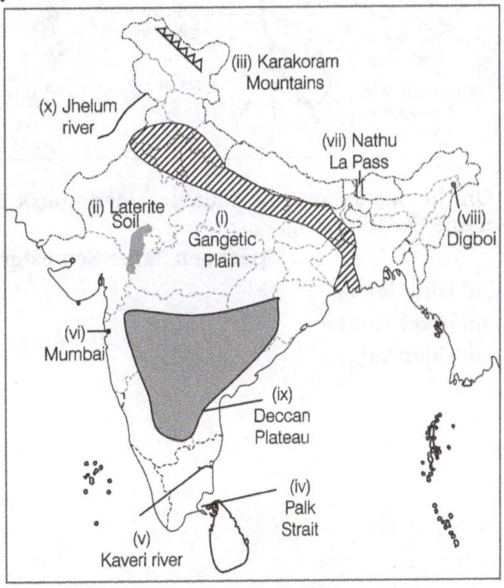

21. On the outline map of India provided **[2020]**

(i) Mark and name Nilgiris.
(ii) Mark and name Kochi.
(iii) Mark and name the Karakoram Pass.
(iv) Mark and name 82½°E Longitude,
(v) Shade and name the Coromandel Coastal Plain.
(vi) Mark and name the River Brahmaputra
(vii) Mark and name the Gulf of Kachchh.
(viii) Mark and name the Satpura.
(ix) Mark using arrows, the direction of the South West Monsoon wind during summer over the Arabian Sea and label it.
(x) Shade and label a sparsely populated region in India.

Ans.

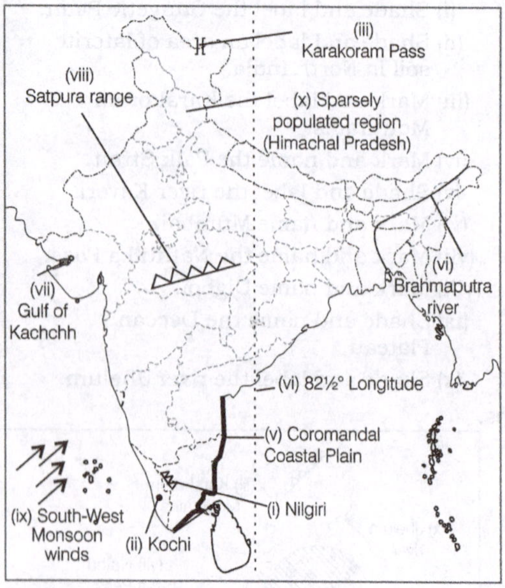

22. On the outline map of India provided, mark and name the following.
[Specimen Paper Semester-II 2022]

(i) Himalayas
(ii) River Ganga
(iii) Chennai
(iv) Western Ghats
(v) Gulf of Kachchh.
(vi) Malabar coastal plain
(vii) Karakoram Pass
(viii) Black soil area in peninsular region
(ix) Standard Meridian of India
(x) Jharia coal field

Ans.

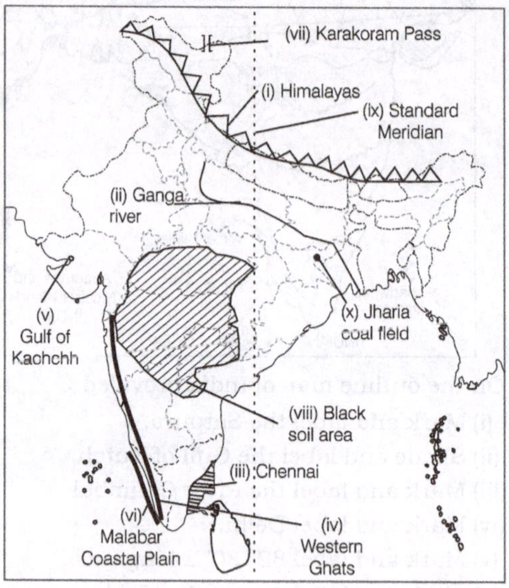

CHAPTER

03

Location, Extent and Physical Features

SYLLABUS

Location, Extent and Physical Features Position and Extent of India (through Map only).
- The Physical Features of India-mountain, plateaus, plains and river (through Map only).

India is the largest country in the Indian **sub-continent**[1] which consists of India, Pakistan, Nepal, Bhutan, Bangladesh, Sri Lanka and Maldives. It has derived its name from the river 'Indus' which flows through the North-Western part of the country.

Location

India is a vast country and located in the Northern hemisphere. It lies on the Western edge of Indian Ocean and in the middle of South-East and South-West Asia. Its mainland extends between latitudes 8°4'N and 37°6'N and longitudes 68°7'E and 97°25'E. It is divided into almost two equal parts by the **Tropic of Cancer**[2] (23°30'N) i.e. sub-tropical in the North and tropical zone in the South. It passes through 8 states i.e., Gujarat, Rajasthan, Madhya Pradesh, Chhattisgarh, Jharkhand, West Bengal, Tripura and Mizoram.

Two groups of islands belonging to India are the **Andaman and Nicobar Islands** in the Bay of Bengal (South-East of the main land) and the **Lakshadweep Islands** in the Arabian Sea (South-West of the mainland).

Size and Extent

India's landmass has an area of 3.287 million sq km. It occupies 2.4% of the total geographical area of the world. India is the 7th largest country of the world, after Russia, Canada, USA, China, Brazil and Australia. India has a land boundary that extends over 15,200 km and its coastline is about 7516.6 km.

The latitudinal as well as longitudinal extent of India is about 30° despite the fact that East-West extent appears to be smaller than the North-South extent. The latitudinal extent influences the duration of day and night as one moves from South to North.

1 **Sub-continent** A big landmass which stands out as a distinct geographical unit from the rest of the continent.
2 **Tropic of Cancer** It is an imaginary line at an angle of 23.5 degrees North from the Equator, that passes through the middle of India.

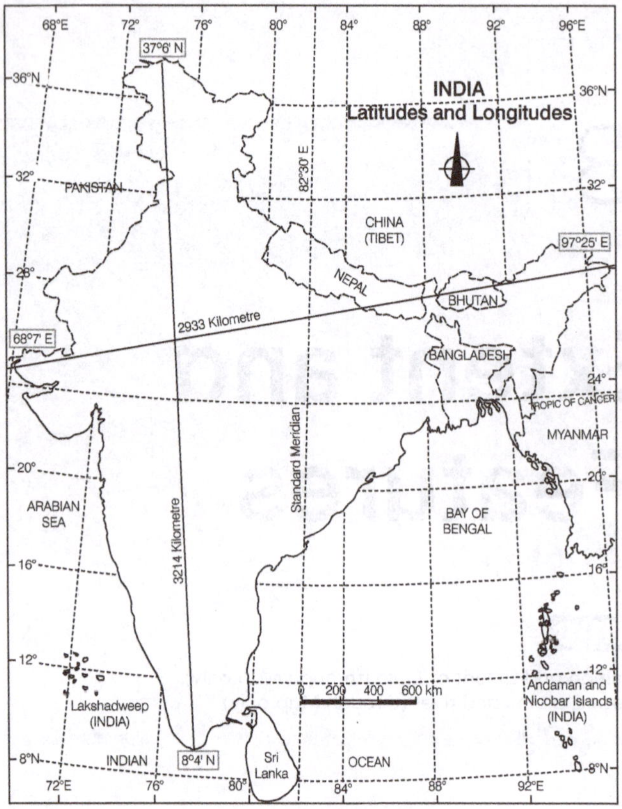

India : Size and Extent

Important Facts about India

Total Area	3.287 million km^2
Latitude	8°4 'N to 37°6'N
Longitude	68°7'E to 97°25'E
North to South Extent	3214 km
East to West Extent	2933 km
Main Land Coastline	6100 km
Total Coastline	7516.6 km
Land Boundary	15,200 km
Northern Most Point	Indira Col, Siachen Glacier J&K
Southern Most Point	Indira point (Great Nicobar) that got submerged under Indian Ocean in 2004 during the Tsunami.
Western Most Point	Guhar Moti (Gujarat)
Eastern Most Point	Kibithu (Arunachal Pradesh)
Highest Altitude	Kanchenjunga
Lowest Altitude	Kuttanad (Kerala)
Territorial Sea	12 nm (22.2 km)
State having Longest Coastline	Gujarat (1214.70 km)
State having Shortest Coastline	Goa (160.5 km)

India and Adjacent Countries

India has 28 States and 8 Union Territories. It shares its land boundaries with Pakistan and Afghanistan in the North-West, China, Nepal and Bhutan in the North-East and Myanmar and Bangladesh in the East. Two island countries i.e. Sri Lanka (separated by Palk Strait and Gulf of Mannar) and the Maldives, lie to the South of India across the Indian Ocean.

Indian Standard Time (IST)

There is a time difference of almost two hours between Gujarat in West to Arunachal Pradesh in North-East. Hence, time along the **Standard Meridian**[3] of India passing through Mirzapur (in Uttar Pradesh) is taken as the Indian Standard Time for the whole country. It is $5\frac{1}{2}$ hours ahead of **Greenwich Mean Time (GMT)**[4].

Physical Features of India

The physical features of India can be classified as

1. The Himalayan Mountains
2. The Northern Plains
3. The Peninsular Plateau
4. The Indian Desert
5. The Coastal Plains
6. The Islands

1. The Himalayan Mountains or Northern Mountains

The Himalayas run in a West-East direction from the Indus to the Brahmaputra rivers. They are the longest mountain range in India, covering an area of about 2400 km. Their width varies from 400 km in Kashmir to 150 km in Arunachal Pradesh.

Sub-Divisions of the Himalayan Mountains

- **Himadri or Inner Himalayas or Greater Himalaya**
  This is the Northern most and the highest mountain range with an average height of 6000 m. It is covered with snow throughout the year and thus, called Himadri. It contains all the prominent Himalayan peaks like **Mount Everest** (8,848 m), **Kanchenjunga** (8,598 m), Makalu (8,481 m), etc. It has many passes, namely Karakoram Pass, Shipki-La Pass, Mana Pass, Niti Pass, etc. Sharda, Ganga, Gandak and Kosi river originate from this mountain range.

3 **Standard Meridian** The longitude which passes through a country or region which is used to fix the standard time for that country or region.

4 **Greenwich Mean Time** (GMT) GMT is the time measured on the Earth's zero degree line of longitude or Meridian. This runs from North Pole to South Pole, passing through the old Royal Observatory in London suburb of Greenwich. From here all terrestrial longitudes are measured and the world's time zones are calculated.

- **Himachal or Lesser Himalayas or Western Himalayas** This range lies parallel to the Himadri in the South and forms the most rugged (uneven surface) mountain system. Its height vary from 3700 to 4500 m and its width is about 50 km. This range has a large vegetative cover. The peaks located in this range are Pir Panjal (longest), Dhaula Dhar and Mahabharat. It also include the valleys like Kashmir, Kangra, Kullu, etc.
- **Shiwaliks or Outer Himalayas** This is the outermost range of the Himalayas with height varying between 900 and 1100 m and width between 10 to 50 km. Shiwaliks are not a continuous mountain range, hence break can be seen in these ranges. **Doons**[5] like Dehradun, Kotlidun and Patlidun lie between the Himachal and Shiwaliks.
- **Purvanchal Range or the Eastern Himalayas** The Brahmaputra marks the Easternmost boundary of the Himalayas. Beyond Dihang gorge, this range turns South along the North-Eastern boundary of India. It includes the Patkai hills, the Naga hills, the Manipur hills and the Mizo hills.

Other Features of the Himalayas

- **Doons** 'Doon' or 'Dun' is a local word for valley, mainly an open valley in the Shiwalik or between the Shiwalik and Himachal ranges.
- **Bhabar** It is the gentle-sloping coarse alluvial zone below the Shiwalik Hills. The Himalayan river streams after descending from the mountains, deposit pebbles in a narrow belt of about 8 to 16 km in width which lies parallel to the slopes of the Shiwaliks and is known as Bhabar belt.
- **Terai** The 'Terai' or 'Tarai' is a lowland region in Northern India and Southern Nepal. In bhabar belt, the streams and rivers disappear into permeable sediments and suddenly appear and create a wet, swampy and marshy region known as terai. Terai area is mostly located in the Eastern region because Eastern Himalayas get heavier rainfall than the Western Himalayas.
- **Khadar and Bhangar** Khadar is the new alluvium which is brought down by the rivers in the low-lying areas and it is responsible for floods in these low-lying areas. Bhangar is the old alluvium which is found above the flood plains in the form of terraces in the river channels.

Significance of the Himalayas

- The Himalayas act as a natural barrier as it protects Northern India from severe cold in winters and stops the moisture-laden monsoon winds which bring heavy rain to the North Indian plains.
- The Himalayas are a source of many perennial rivers due to the presence of glaciers.
- The rivers that originate from Himalayas are major sources of hydal power as due to the topography of the Himalayas, the rivers form rapids and waterfalls. This provide conditions for the creation of reservoirs which can be utilised for the generation of hydroelectricity by constructing dams across the rivers.
- The Himalayas act as a physical barrier to the foreign invaders as it consists of all peaks which led to difficult route to travel.
- The Himalayas are rich in forest resources as it provides both hard wood and soft wood and is also a home to a wide variety of wild animals like yaks, bears, tigers, elephants, red pandas, snow leopard, etc.
- It is a store house of minerals like copper, lead, nickel, cobalt, tungsten, coal and also gold, silver and precious stones.

2. The Northern Plains

This plain is formed by three river systems, *viz* **the Indus, the Ganga** and **the Brahmaputra,** alongwith their tributaries. This plain is formed by alluvial soil. It spreads over an area of 7 lakh sq km. These plains are about 2400 km long and between 240 and 320 km broad. They are densely populated due to the fertile soil, adequate water supply, favourable climate and terrain.

Sub-Divisions of Northern Plains

- **Punjab Plain** It is the Western part of the Northern Plains. It has been formed by the Indus river and its tributaries. The Punjab Plains lie in India in Punjab, Haryana and Himachal Pradesh. **Doabs**[6] of five tributaries of Indus river is a significant feature of these plains. These tributaries are Jhelum, Chenab, Ravi, Sutlej and Beas.
- **Ganga Plain** It is the middle part of the Northern Plains. It extends from the Ghaggar river (in Haryana) to the Tista river (in West Bengal).

5 **Doons** These are longitudinal valleys lying between the lesser Himalayas and Shivaliks.
6 **Doab** It consists of two words like 'Do' means 'two' and 'ab' means 'water'.

It covers an area of about 1400 km through the states of Uttarakhand, Haryana, Delhi, Uttar Pradesh, Bihar, partly Jharkhand and West Bengal. It consist of a number of plains like Ganga, Yamuna doab, Mithila Plains and Awadh Plains.

- **Brahmaputra Plain** It is the Eastern part of the Northern Plains. It extends from Assam to Bangladesh. It is surrounded by the Eastern Himalayas of Arunachal Pradesh in the North, the Garo-Khasi-Jaintia and Mikir hills in the South, Patkai and Naga hills in the East and the lower Ganga plain in the West.
- Its length is about 640 km and it has been formed by deposits from the Brahmaputra river and its tributaries. It has a number of **riverine islands**[7] among which **Majuli** is the largest river island in the world.
- **Rajasthan Plain** This plain is an undulating (wave like) plain. Its average elevation is about 325 m above mean sea level. It extends from, the North-West India to Eastern Pakistan. The desert region in this plain is called **Marusthali** or the **Great Indian Desert** which forms a greater part of the Marwar plain. In this plain, the Eastern part of the Thar Desert up to the Aravali Range is a semi-arid plain known as **Rajasthan Bagar**. Luni is a significant rivers of this plain. This plain also includes some salt water lakes such as the Sambhar, Kuchaman and Didwana lakes.

Significance of Northern Plains

- Due to the presence of a good network of rivers and favourable climate, these plains support dense population.
- The fertile soil, perennial rivers and favourable climate have made the Northern Plains an excellent agricultural land.
- Large number of multi-purpose dams has been constructed across the rivers to provide water for irrigation and to generate electricity.
- Due to the flat level surface of the Northern Plains, construction of road network and railways is possible. The rivers are also navigable and allow comfortable transportation. It also facilitates easy access to good communication system.

3. The Peninsular Plateau

This is a **tableland** (a broad, high level region) composed of the old crystalline, igneous and metamorphic rocks. It was formed due to the breaking up and drifting of **Gondwana** land, thus it is a part of the oldest landmass.

The plateau has broad and shallow valleys and rounded hills.

Sub-divisions of Peninsular Plateau

- **Central Highlands** This part lies to the North of the Narmada river and Vindhyan range and Satpura ranges lie its South. Aravallis lies on the West and Kaimur and Maikal range lies to the East of Centre Highlands.
- It slopes from South-West to North-East as indicated by the flow of the Chambal, Sind, Betwa and Ken rivers. The Central Highlands are wider in the West, but narrower in the East. It comprises of Bundelkhand upland, Malwa Plateau and Mewar upland.
- **The Eastern Plateaus** This part lies to the North-East of the Malwa plateau which comprises of
  - (i) **The Baghelkhand Plateau** Rihand and Son rivers flow through it. It also has synclinal (up fold in layers of rocks) valleys and anticlinal (down folds in layer of rocks) hills.
  - (ii) **The Chota Nagpur Plateau** It lies to the East of Bundhelkhand in Jharkhand state. It is drained by two main rivers i.e. the Damodar and the Subarnarekha. It is a mineral- rich region and is known as the **Ruhr of India**.
  - (iii) **Bastar or Dandakaranya Upland** It lies to the South of the Bundelkhand. It has rugged and forested topography in its South.
- **The Northeastern Plateau** It is the North-East extension of the main Peninsular plateau. It has the Meghalaya plateau (lies beyond the Chota Nagpur Plateau) consisting of the Garo, Khasi and Jaintia hills. This region get heavy rainfall and it has many mineral resources like coal, iron ore, limestone and uranium.
- **Deccan Plateau** This triangular landmass lies to the South of the river Narmada. It includes the land between the Eastern Ghats and Western Ghats and the South part of the Maikal, Mahadeo and Satpura ranges. The Deccan plateau has higher slope in the Westward side and gentle scope in Eastward side. The Deccan plateau comprises of Maharashtra plateau, Telangana plateau and Karnataka plateau. The Western part of the Deccan plateau is known as the Deccan Trap. It contains black soil of volcanic origin.

---

7 **Riverine Islands** A riverine island is any exposed land surrounded by river water.

- **The Kathiawar and Kutch** These Peninsulas are made with Deccan lavas. They are joined to the Peninsular Plateaus by Gujarat Plains.

The Peninsular Mountains

The mountains of Peninsular Plateau are classified into Western Ghats, Eastern Ghats, Aravalli, Vindhya range and Satpura range.

Western Ghats

The Western Ghats also called **Sahyadri** lies parallel to the Western coast. The total length of the ghats is around 1600 km with an average elevation of about 900 to 1100 m. Western Ghats cause orographic rain by forcing the rain-bearing moist monsoon winds to rise along the Western slopes of the ghats. The height of the Western Ghats increases from North to South.

Anai Mudi (2695 m) and **Doda Betta** (2637 m) are the highest peak in these ghats. The Western Ghats are continuous and can be crossed through passes only. The famous hill stations of Western Ghats are Udagamandalam and Kodaikanal. Godavari, Cauvery and Krishna are the major rivers of Western Ghats.

Eastern Ghats

The Eastern Ghats stretch from the Mahanadi valley to the Nilgiris in the South with an average height of about 600 m. The Eastern Ghats are discontinuous and irregular and dissected by rivers draining into the Bay of Bengal. **Mahendragiri** (1501 m) is the highest peak in the Eastern Ghats. Shevroy hills and Javadi hills are located in the South-East of the Eastern Ghats. The Nilgiri hills in Tamil Nadu lie at the junction of the Eastern and Western Ghats.

Aravalli

Aravalli ranges are one of the oldest (very old) fold mountains range of the world and the oldest in India. They are stretched from North-East to South-West of India for about 800 km between Delhi and Palanpur in Gujarat. **Gurushikhar** (1722 m) located at Abu hill is the highest peak of Aravalli ranges. The Raisina hill of Delhi is the Northern most stretch of Aravalli ranges.

Vindhya Range

This range stretched from Bihar (sasaram) in the East to Gujarat (Jobat) in the West. It is a continuous block mountain range which separates Northern India from the Southern mainland. It is composed of sandstones, shales and quartzites. Narmada river flows in the South of the Vindhyan range which acts as a natural watershed between North and South India.

Satpura Range

It lies between Narmada valley in the North and Tapi valley in the South.

It stretched from Rajpipla hills in the West through Mahadeo hill to Maikal range in the East. The Northern and Southern borders of Satpura ranges are made up of sandstone. Eastern part of Satpura range is called Maikal plateau. The highest peak of this range is Dhupgarh (1,350 m) near Panchmarhi.

Significance of Peninsular Plateau

- The Peninsular Plateau is the home of India's most valuable metal reserves including iron, bauxite, mica, gold, copper, etc. Famous mines like Kolar, Bailadila, Singhbum, and Korba are located in the Peninsular plateau.
- The Peninsular Plateau include many premium coal mines of India. Famous mines like Ranighanj, Singareni and Jharia are located in the Peninsular Plateau.
- The black soil and the climatic conditions in the Peninsular Plateau make it a great location for the cultivation of cotton.
- The Western and Eastern Ghats which form the edges of the Peninsular Plateau are very rich in flora and fauna. They are also home to valuable timber woods like teak, sandalwood, rosewood, etc.

4. The Indian Desert

This lies on the Western margins of the Aravalli hills. It consists of wave like sandy plain with various types of sand dunes. It receives less than 150 mm rainfall annually. It has arid climate with low vegetation.

Here streams appear only during the monsoon season. Luni is the only large river in this region. Crescent shaped sand dunes called **Barchans**[8] cover most of this desert, but longitudinal dunes are also seen on the Western edge of this region near the Indo-Pakistan border. This desert is known as the Thar Desert.

8 **Barchans** These are crescent-shaped sand dunes produced by the action of wind predominately from one direction.

5. The Coastal Plains

The Deccan plateau is bounded by two coastal plains on either side of it i.e. the Western Coastal Plains and the Eastern Coastal Plains.

The Western Coastal Plains

The plains which lie along the Arabian sea are called Western Coastal plains. It consists of the following sub-divisions

- **Gujarat Plains** The plains are located to the South of Thar Desert.
- **The Kutch Peninsula** Rann of Kutch which lies in this region consist of Westernmost part of Western Coastal plains. During the dry season, marshes are formed in this region due to the composition of silt and salt.
- **Kathiawar Peninsula** It is also called **Saurashtra Peninsula**. It is bounded by the Little Rann (marsh) of Kachchh (Kutch) to the North, the Gulf of Khambhat to the East, the Arabian Sea to the South-West and the Gulf of Kachchh to the North-West. Rivers of Western Ghats bought alluvium to the Southern part of Kathiawar Peninsula and thus become rich in alluvium.
- **Konkan Coast** It extended from Daman to Goa (500 km). It is made up of basaltic trap rocks.
- **Kanara Coast** It runs from Goa to Cannanore. **Estuatries**[9] are formed in the stretch of Kanara coast.
- **Malabar Coast** It is the Southernmost stretch of Western Coastal Plains. It extends from Cannanore to the town of Cape Comorin in Tamil Nadu. It have lagoons or backwaters called **kayals**.

The Eastern Coastal Plains

The plains which lie along the Bay of Bengal are Eastern Coastal Plains. These are more wide and level. Eastern coastal plains have several depositional features like lagoons, **spits**[10] and many offshore **bars**[11].

In Northern part, the Eastern coastal Plain is known as **Northern Circar** (from mouth of Ganges to Nellore or between Mahanadi and Krishna rivers) and in Southern part, it is called as Coromandel Coast (from Nellore to Kanyakumari). Rivers like the Mahanadi, Godavari, Krishna and Kaveri have formed extensive deltas on this Coast. Lake **Chilika** is the largest salt water lake on the Eastern Coast (Odisha).

Significance of Coastal Plains

- They are the source of precious minerals.
- The Kerala coast has large quantities of monazite which is used for nuclear power.
- The sedimentary rocks of these coastal plains have large deposits of mineral oil.
- The ports of Eastern and Western Coastal Plains account for 98% of the international trade.
- Fisheries are an important activity in these coastal plains.

6. The Islands

India has two island groups. These are

(i) **The Lakshadweep Islands** These lies close to the Malabar Coast (Kerala). This group of 36 islands is composed of small coral islands. Earlier, they were known as Laccadive, Minicoy and Amindivis islands. In 1973, these were named as Lakshadweep. They cover a small area of 32 sq km. **Kavaratti** island is the administrative headquarters of Lakshadweep.

(ii) **The Andaman and Nicobar Islands** They are two chains of densely forested islands. The Andamans are bigger in size. They are more numerous and scattered. The entire group of islands is divided into two broad categories i.e. the Andamans in the North and the Nicobars in the South.

These islands are formed by elevated portion of submarine mountains or under sea mountains. These islands have an elevation of about 730 m. Andaman and Nicobar consist of more than 300 islands, most of which are very small.

India's only active volcano is found on Barren Island in the Andaman and Nicobar islands. There is great diversity of flora and fauna in

9 **Estuary** The wide part of a river (mouth) where it joins the sea.

10 **Spits** A spit is an extended stretch of sand emerging out into the sea from the land. Spits occur when there is a change in the shape of the landscape or there is a river mouth.

11 **Bars** Sometimes a spit can grow across a bay and joins two headlands together. This landform is known as a bar.

this group of islands. They lie close to equator and experience equatorial climate with thick forest cover.

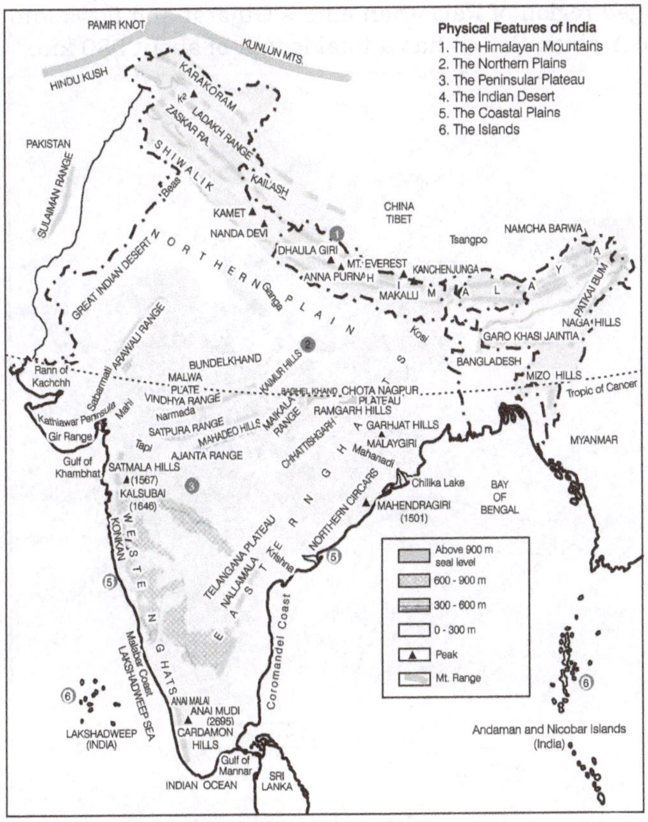

Physical Features of India

Major Rivers of India

Indus River

The Indus or Sindhu river originates from a glacier at the height of 4,164 m near Bokhar Chu (31° 15′N latitude and 81° 40′E longitude) in the Kailash mountain range in Tibetan region, where it is known as **Singi Khamban** or **Lion's mouth**.

It has a total length of 2,880 km and in India it has length of 1,114 km. It is one of the largest river basins of the world, covering an area of 11,65,000 sq km of which 321,289 sq km is in India. It is the Westernmost Himalayan river in India. It finally discharges into the Arabian Sea, East of Karachi.

Ganga River

It rises in the Gangotri glacier near Gaumukh (3900 m) in Uttarkashi district of Uttarakhand. Here it is known as the **Bhagirathi** and after joining the Alaknanda at Devprayag, it is known as the **Ganga**.

Its length is 2,525 km which is shared by Uttarakhand (110 km), Uttar Pradesh (1,450 km), Bihar (445 km) and West Bengal (520 km). The river finally discharges into the Bay of Bengal near the **Sagar Island**.

Brahmaputra River

It rises in the Chemayungdung glacier in the Kailash range near Mansarovar lake. It enters India in the West of Sadiya town in Arunachal Pradesh. It is known as Dihang in Arunachal Pradesh which flows South-West and joined by Dibang or Sikang and Lohit on its left bank, thereafter it is called the Brahmaputra. It finally falls in the Bay of Bengal.

Mahanadi River

It rises near Sihawa in Raipur district of Chhattisgarh. It flows for a distance of 851 km through the states of Chhattisgarh and Odisha and spreads over 1.42 lakh sq km of catchment area. About 53% of the drainage basin of this river lies in Madhya Pradesh and Chhattisgarh, while 47% lies in Odisha.

Godavari River

It rises in the Nasik district of Maharashtra and falls into the Bay of Bengal. It is also known as **Dakshin Ganga** as it is the **largest** and a sacred river of the Peninsular river system. It is 1,465 km long and covers the catchment area of 3.13 lakh sq km. About 49 per cent of its catchment area, lies in Maharashtra, 20 per cent in Madhya Pradesh and Chhattisgarh, and the rest in Andhra Pradesh.

Krishna River

It rises near Mahabaleshwar in Sahyadri and flows through Maharashtra, (about 27% catchment area) Karnataka (44% catchment area) and Andhra Pradesh and Telangana (29% catchment area). It is the **second largest river** of the Peninsular river system with the total length of 1401 km.

Kaveri River

It rises in Brahmagiri hills (1,341m) of Kogadu district in Karnataka. Its length is 800 km and drains an area of 81,155 sq km in the states of Kerala, (about 3% catchment area) Karnataka (41% catchment area) and Tamil Nadu (56% catchment area).

Narmada River

It originates on the Western flank of the Amarkantak plateau at a height of 1057 m. It flows through a rift valley between the Vindhyan in the North and the Satpura ranges in the South.

After flowing a distance of about 1,312 km, it meets the Arabian Sea South of Bharuch, forming a broad 27 km long estuary. Its catchment area is about 98,796 sq km and it forms a picturesque gorge in marble rocks and Dhuandhar waterfall near Jabalpur. Sardar Sarovar Dam project has been constructed on this river.

Tapi River

It rises in Multai of Betul district in Madhya Pradesh and flows Westwards. Its length is 724 km and flows through the states of Madhya Pradesh, (about 15% basin), Maharashtra (about 79% basin) and Gujarat (about 6% basin) covering a total area of 65,145 sq km.

Luni River

It rises in the Aravallis. It is the largest river of Rajasthan. It has a length of about 495 km.

Sabarmati River

It rises in the Aravalli Range of the Udaipur District of Rajasthan. It meets the Gulf of Khambhat of Arabian Sea after travelling 371 km in a south-westerly direction across Rajasthan and Gujarat.

Mahi River

It rises in Madhya Pradesh and after flowing through the Vagad region of Rajasthan enters Gujarat and flows into the Arabian Sea. It has a total length of about 580 km.

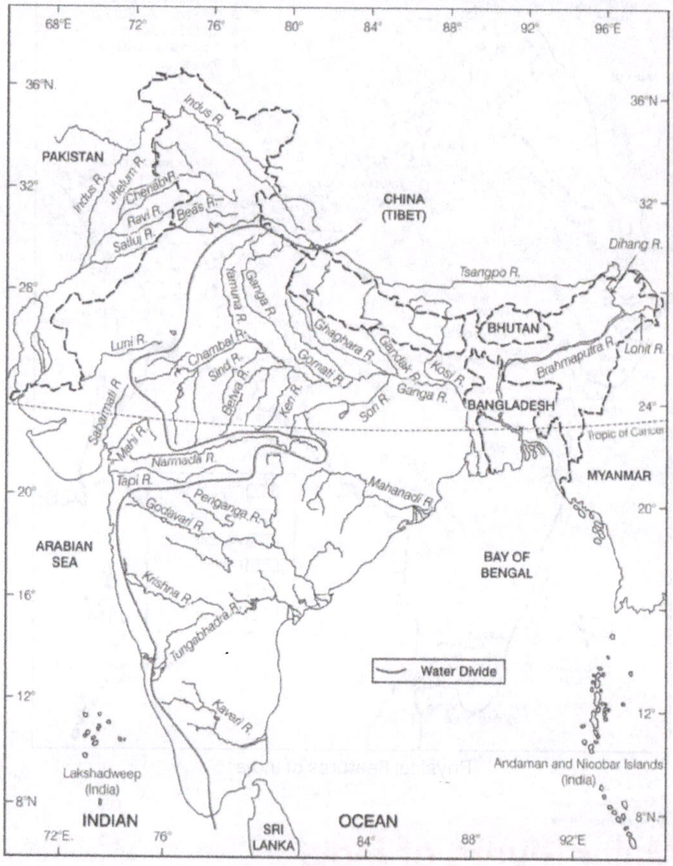

Major Rivers of India

CHAPTER

04

The Climate of India

SYLLABUS

Climate Distribution of temperature, rainfall, winds in summer and winter and factor affecting the climate of the area. • Monsoon and its mechanism.

Season March to May-Summer; June to September - Monsoon; October to November-Retreating Monsoon; December to February-Winter.

The term climate refers to the atmospheric conditions, which prevails in a large area over a long period of time. It is measured by assessing the patterns of variation in temperature, humidity, atmospheric pressure, wind, precipitation and other **meteorological**[1] variables in a given region over a long period of time.

India is called a tropical country because it lies in the tropical belt and the monsoon winds influence the climate of India which are largely confined to the tropics between 20°N and 20°S. The Tropic of Cancer, which passess through the centre of India divides it into two climatic zones, **sub-tropical zone** (Northern part) and **tropical zone** (Southern part). Due to tropical and sub-tropical regions, India experience high temperature and dry winters.

Regional Variations in Climate of India

India has a monsoon type of climate, however different regions of the country have variations in climate. For example, the climatic conditions in the Northern and Southern part of India differs largely but in spite of that both these parts have a similar monsoon climate.

The variations are realised due to different temperatures, rainfall, pattern of winds, rhythm of seasons and the degree of wetness or dryness. These regional variations are known as the **sub-types of monsoon climate.**

Distribution or Variations in Temperature

Regional variation in temperature is found in different parts of India. Even a single place has variations in day and night temperature. Some of the examples of these variations are

- Temperatures in the winter in North-West mountainous regions can go down to −45° C, while it is 22°C in Thiruvananthapuram in Kerala.
- Temperature can go upto 50°C in summer in some parts of Western Rajasthan and 20°C in Shillong.
- The regions to the South of the Tropic of Cancer $23\frac{1}{2}^\circ$N which are nearer to the equator (coastal areas) have a range of 25-27°C average temperature during the entire year due to the **moderating effect**[2] of the sea, e.g. Bengaluru, Mumbai, Chennai.

1 **Meteorological** Meteorology is a science that deals with the atmosphere and its phenomena and especially with weather and weather forecasting.

2 **Moderating effect** Climatic conditions that is neither too hot nor too cold.

- In June, Barmer in Rajasthan may record a temperature of 48°C or 50°C, while at the same time temperature hardly reaches 22°C at Pahalgam or Gulmarg in Kashmir. However, during winter, in Dras near Kargil, the temperatures may go down to -40°C.
- Tropical climate with warm and moist air is observed in the coastal state of Kerala, whereas in the landlocked state of Punjab, continental climate with severe heat alternating with severe cold is observed .
- In Kargil, in the month of December temperature goes down to as low as - 40°C, whereas Kerala records 20°C or 22°C in the same month.
- Along the Malabar Coast, the annual range of temperature is 3°C and more than 20°C in the interiors.
- The variation between day and night temperatures in the Andaman and Nicobar Islands and Kerala is 7 to 8°C, whereas the same goes upto 25 to 30 °C in the Thar desert.

Distribution of or Variations in Rainfall

The distribution of rainfall is uneven in India due to the pressure conditions, direction of relief features and winds bearing moisture and cyclonic depressions. Spatial variations in rainfall in India can be categorised under the following

- **Areas of Heavy Rainfall** These areas experience more than 200 cm of rainfall. It includes the region in the Western coast, slopes of Western Ghats, Assam, Arunachal Pradesh, West Bengal and Garo, Khasi and Jaintia hills of Meghalaya.
- **Areas of Moderate Rainfall** These areas receive 100-200 cm of rainfall. It includes the North Ganga Plain along the Sub-Himalayas and Cachar valley and Manipur, the East coast of Tamil Nadu, the Southern part of Gujarat and North-Eastern Peninsula covering Odisha, Jharkhand, Bihar and Eastern Madhya Pradesh.
- **Areas of Low Rainfall** These areas receive 50 to 100 cm of rainfall. These areas include Western Uttar Pradesh, Eastern Rajasthan and Gujarat, Delhi, Haryana, Punjab and Jammu and Kashmir and Deccan Plateau.
- **Areas of Inadequate Rainfall** These areas receive less than 50 cm of rainfall. This is the region of scanty or insufficient rainfall. These areas include part of Peninsula, especially in Andhra Pradesh, Karnataka and Maharashtra, Western Rajasthan and Ladakh.

Some examples of extreme difference in the rainfall amount are

- Cherrapunji and Mawsynram in Meghalaya get about 1100 cm rainfall in a year, whereas Jaisalmer in Rajasthan hardly receives 9 cm of rainfall in the same year.
- The amount of rainfall received by Tura in Meghalaya in a single day is equal to 10 years of rainfall at Jaisalmer in Rajasthan.
- The Ganga delta and the coastal plains of Odisha are hit by strong storms almost every third or fifth day during July and August, whereas the Coromandel coast remains dry during these months.
- The coastal areas of Tamil Nadu get rains in the beginning of the winter season, whereas most parts of India receive rainfall during June-September.
- The annual precipitation varies from over 400 cm in Meghalaya to less than 10 cm in Ladakh and Western Rajasthan.

Factors Affecting the Climate of India

- **Latitude** It is the measurement of distance of a point on the Earth's surface in North or South of the equator. It is measured from the equator which lies on 0°. Temperature changes with latitude.
- At the equator, the Sun's rays fall directly thus, temperatures are highest there. But when the distance of places increases from the equator, the Sun's rays become more slanting and cover large area thus, temperature reduces. It means the farther an area is from the equator, the lower is its temperature.
- **Altitude** Generally, with increase in height, temperature decreases, that is why Agra and Darjeeling are located in same latitude, but due to height difference, the weather conditions differ. For every 166 m rise in height, there is a decrease of 1°C in temperature. That is why hilly areas are cooler than the plains because of high altitude.
- **Himalayan Mountains** The Himalayas form a climatic barrier which separates Indian sub-continent from the rest of Asia. The Himalayas prevent the cold winds of Central Asia (Siberian winds) from entering into India. Thus, it protects the country from severely cold winters. It also traps the monsoon winds, forcing them to shed their moisture within the sub-continent.

- **Western Disturbances** Western disturbance is an extratropical storm or cyclones originating in Mediterranean Sea. These cyclones caused by weather condition during winter which are influenced by the distribution pattern of pressure in Central Asia and West Asia. This distribution of pressure led the **Westerlies**[3] to blow from 20°N to 50°N latitude due to which Northern India comes under the influence of the winds and cyclones. These cyclones give rains to Northern Plains and snowfall in Jammu and Kashmir.
- **The Monsoon Winds** The summer rains over India are caused due to the South-West monsoon winds and the winter rains are caused due to the North-East monsoon winds.
- **Jet Streams** The cold fast blowing winds that develop in the upper layers of the atmosphere are called jet streams. The easterly jet stream direct the **tropical depression**[4] over India while the westerly jet stream prevails over the North Indian plains during the winter months. The distribution pattern of the monsoon rainfall in the sub-continent are heavily influenced by these depressions as highest rainfall occurs along the course of these depressions. The speed of jet streams varies from about 110 km per hr in summer to about 184 km per hr in winter.
- **El-Nino Effect** El-Nino is warm ocean current which sometimes appears off the coast of Peru in South America during the month of December. Due to this the surface temperature of the sea is increased which affects the movement of monsoon winds in the Indian Ocean. This causes weak drought-like situation in the Indian sub-continent.
- **Influence of the Surrounding Seas** India is surrounded by three water bodies, namely, the Indian Ocean, the Bay of Bengal and the Arabian sea. These have a deep impact on the climate, especially in coastal areas. These water bodies act as the main source of moisture to the summer monsoons and bring heavy rainfall to the whole area. In fact, the coastal areas have moderate climate due to being close to the sea.
- **Distance from the Sea** The Southern half of India is surrounded by sea from the three sides, the Arabian sea, the Bay of Bengal and the Indian Ocean. Due to moderating influence of these seas, the Southern region is neither hot in summers nor very cold in winters. The North India far away from these seas has continental type (extreme type) of climate with very hot summers and very cold winters.
- **Tropical Cyclones** They influence Indian weather in summer season. They originate in the Bay of Bengal and Arabian sea and move towards the interior of the country. The amount of rainfall increases due to these cyclones.
- **Relief Features** The presence of mountains, plateaus, etc also affect the climate of India. For example, the Aravalli hills do not block the way of rain bearing winds, hence Western Rajasthan is dry. Likewise the windward side of Western Ghats gets heavy rainfall as these mountains prevent the moisture laden winds to cross them.

Check Your LEARNING...

1. Which type of climate India has?
2. Which regions of India experience - 45°C temperature?
3. Which regions of India faces low rainfall?
4. The Arabian sea lies in which direction?

Seasons

The large size of the country and its varied relief play a crucial role in determining the climatic variations in different parts of India.

On the basis of the monsoon variations, year may be divided into four seasons such as

(i) Summer Season (March to May)
(ii) Monsoon Season (June to September)
(iii) Retreating Monsoon Season (October to November)
(iv) Winter Season (December to February)

(i) Summer Season (March to May)

The months of March, April and May are the summer months in India. In these months, the Sun moves from over the equator towards the Tropic of Cancer (Northward movement) and **Inter Tropical Convergence Zone**[5] (ITCZ) shifts Northward. By 21st June, the Sun is directly overhead the Tropic of Cancer.

3 **Westerlies** The winds blowing from the West.

4 **Tropical Depression** It is an atmospheric low-pressure system originating in the tropics, especially a tropical cyclone in which the maximum sustained wind speed is 38 miles per hour or less.

5 **Inter Tropical Convergence Zone** (ITCZ) It is a belt of low pressure which circles the Earth generally near the equator, where trade winds of the Northern and Southern hemisphere come together.

Temperature Conditions

- During summer, the interior parts of North Indian plains covering Rajasthan, Punjab, Haryana and Western Uttar Pradesh are intensely hot. The daily maximum temperature in some of these parts is as high as 45-47°C.
- In the month of April, the **diurnal range**[6] of temperature ranges between 5° C and 6° C in coastal areas, but reaches 20° C in the interior parts of the country and in the North -West Sutlej Ganga plains. The average maximum temperature is above 33°C in the month of May at Delhi and Jodhpur. The mean minimum daily temperature in May also remains quite high being about 36°C at Delhi and Jaipur.

Pressure Conditions

In summer, high temperature in North India leads to low pressure condition and the ITCZ moves Northwards at 25° N in July. This elongates (make something longer) low pressure trough, extends from Thar desert in North-West to Patna and Chotanagpur plateau in East-South-East.

A high pressure area develops near Cape Comorin by the end of May which extends towards the Arabian Sea. By June, low pressure system become more intense and move Northwards over the Indus lowlands and Baluchistan.

Mechanism of Monsoon in Summer

The word 'monsoon' is derived from the Arabic word *'Mausim'* which means season. Monsoon refers to the seasonal reversal of the wind during a year which strongly influence climate of India.

During summer in May, June and July, the plains of the Indian sub-continent are heated by the vertical rays of the sun. Low pressure is developed due to this intense heat which is known as **monsoonal trough.** During these months, a high pressure area develops over the Indian Ocean. So, the South-East trade winds start to blow from the Indian Ocean towards North and North-West into Asia.

After crossing the equator, the, South-East trade winds deflect towards right (due to **Coriolis effect**[7] of the Earth) to the low pressure area of Indian Subcontinent and start blowing in the South-Western direction.

As they blow from the sea to the land, they get moisture and brings heavy rainfall in some parts of the Indian sub-continent, which is the summer monsoon in India. The summer monsoon winds blow from South-West, so the monsoon is known as the **South-West Summer Monsoon.**

Winds in Summer

- **Loo** The summer months experience rising temperature and falling air pressure in the Northern part of India because of the local wind named Loo. It is a gusty (wild), hot, dry wind blowing during the day over the North and North-Western India in the months of May and June. Temperature of these winds ranges between 45°C and 50°C.
- **South-West Summer Monsoon Winds** These winds blow from June to September. The direction of these winds is from South-West to North-East. These winds tend to carry moisture with them and cause rain in the entire country.
- **Mango-Showers** These are local winds which occur in South India during April-May. These carry little rain which help in blooming of coffee and cherries as well as ripening of mangoes. They are also known as **cherry blossoms** in Karnataka.
- **Kaal Baisakhi** It means 'the calamity of the months of Baisakhi'. These are the local winds in West Bengal. These winds are accompanied by thunder storms and bring rainfall in the months of April-May. This rain is good for the cultivation of tea in Assam and rice and jute in West Bengal. It is also known as **Norwester** due to its North-West direction and Bardoli Chheerha in Assam.

(ii) Monsoon Season (June to September)

This season remains from June to September and is also known as advancing monsoon or South-West monsoon. The low pressure areas over the Northern plains intensifies by mid-June and attracts the trade **winds**[8].

These trade winds originate over the warm tropical ocean in the Southern hemisphere. After crossing equator, these blow towards South-West entering peninsula as monsoon winds. They cover the entire sub-continent in just over one month and bring abundant rainfall.

6 **Diurnal Range** It is the difference between the maximum and minimum temperature of a day.

7 **Coriolis effect** As the earth rotates on its axis, circulating air is deflected towards the right in the Northern Hemisphere and towards the left in the Southern Hemisphere. This deflaction is called the Coriolis effect.

8 **Trade winds** Winds that blow steadily from East to West towards the equator over most of the equatorial zone.

Temperature Conditions

- The onset of South-West monsoons leads to significant fall in temperature i.e. 3°C to 6°C.
- The temperature remains less uniform throughout the rainy season. There is a rise in temperature whenever there is **break in the monsoon**.
- The diurnal range of temperature are experienced at places west of the Aravalli, e.g. 38°C to 40°C. This is due to lack of clouds and hot continental air masses. Other parts of North-West India also have temperatures above 30°C.
- Generally, in the afternoon of a scorching day (very hot), rains begin suddenly which is called **burst of the monsoon**[9].

Branches of South-West Monsoon

The South-West monsoon is divided into two branches which are

The Arabian Sea Branch

The monsoon winds over the Arabian sea advances Northwards by 1st June from the Kerala coast and reaches Mumbai by about 10th June. By mid-June, it spreads over Saurashtra, Kutch and Madhya Pradesh. This branch is divided into three sub-branches

(a) **First Branch** The moonsoon winds in this branch strikes the Western Ghats and cause heavy rainfall in the **windward side**[10]. After crossing the Ghats, these winds descend, get heated up and thereby, the humidity in the winds is reduced. Due to lack of moisture, these winds cause little rainfall in East of the Western Ghats and make it the rain shadow zone.

(b) **Second Branch** The moonsoon winds in this branch strikes the North coast of Mumbai. These winds move further along the Narmada and Tapi river valleys and bring a good amount of rainfall in Central India. After that, these winds enter the Ganga Plains and merges with the Bay of Bengal branch in the North-Western part (Punjab and Haryana) of the Ganga Plains.

(c) **Third Branch** The moonsoon winds in this branch strikes the Saurashtra Peninsula and the Kutch. After that, these winds passes over West Rajasthan and cause scanty rainfall along the Aravallis.

The Bay of Bengal Branch

The monsoon winds of Bay of Bengal branch first strikes Andaman and Nicobar Islands by about 25th of May and advances North-Eastward after collecting moisture from the Bay of Bengal. Then it rushes against the Myanmar coast and due to having the Arakan hills along the Myanmar coast, a large part of this branch deflects towards India and reaches Meghalaya, Mizoram and Tripura by about 1st June.

After that, the winds of this branch divides into two branches, one goes to Brahmaputra valley and second goes to the Ganga Plains.

The first branch rapidly spreads over most of Assam and causes the heaviest rainfall in the world at **Mawsynram** (in the Southern ranges of the Khasi hills in Meghalaya) about 1200 cm and **Cherrapunji** about 1100 cm annually. The second branch deflects Westward towards the Ganga Plains, where these winds reach Kolkata around 11th June.

In Delhi, Western Uttar Pradesh, Haryana and Punjab, the monsoon reaches around 1st July. It covers the other parts of India by 15th of July. The quantity of rainfall decreases as they move towards West over the Northern plains. For example, Kolkata receives 120 cm, Patna receives105 cm, Allahabad 91 cm, Delhi receives 56 cm, Bikaner recives 25 cm and Srinagar (Jammu and Kashmir) receives only 20 cm of rainfall in this season.

(iii) Retreating Monsoon Season (October to November)

This season remains from October to November and is also known as **Post-Monsoon season**. During this season, the Sun starts shifting towards the South. The South-West monsoon winds become weak and starts retreating or gradually withdrawing from North to South i.e. from land to sea.

While retreating, these winds pick up moisture from Bay of Bengal and cause rainfall in Coromandel Coast (Tamil Nadu). By the beginning of October, it retreats completely from Northern plains. This season is the period of transition from hot rainy season to cold winter season. This period is marked by clear sky, moist ground, high temperature and humidity which is known as **October heat**.

---

9 **Monsoon Burst** The sudden approach of the moisture laden winds which are associated violent thunder and lightning.

10 **Windward side** The side or slope of a mountain facing the moisture laden winds is known as windward side.

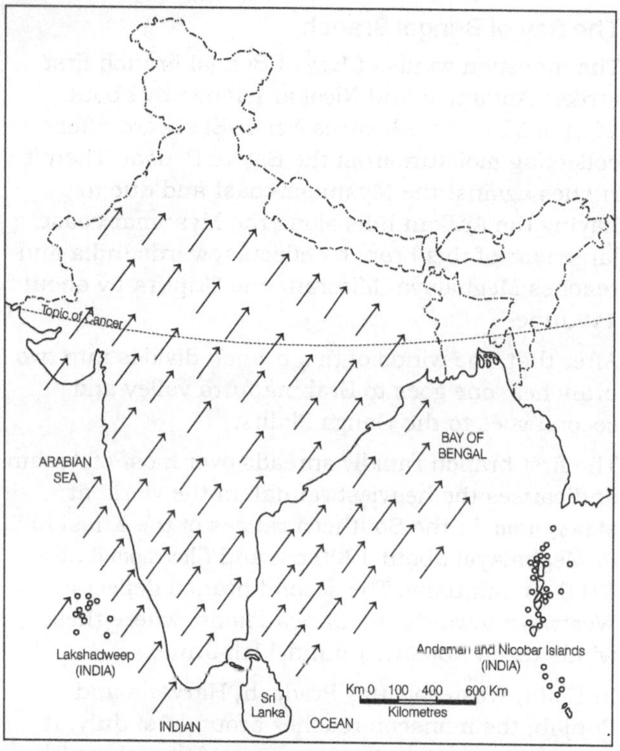

Retreating Monsoon Season

Temperature Conditions

- The temperature during this season is uniformally high being about 25°C in the beginning of October in Northern India and then it gradually decreases in November.
- The day temperature is fairly high, but nights become pleasant with the mean temperature going down to 20°C or even lower.

Pressure Conditions

In winter, the Sun's position is over the Tropic of Capricorn on 22nd December and low temperature conditions in Northern plains and the Central Asia prevailed. Due to these conditions, a feeble high pressure is formed over North and slightly low pressure in South. As a result, wind start blowing from North-Western high pressure zone to low pressure zone over the Indian Ocean in South.

Mechanism of Monsoon in Winter

During winter, a high pressure develops over a big landmass stretching from Central Asia upto North-West Indian Plains and a low pressure zone develops in the Indian Ocean. Thus, the North-East winds started to blow from the land to the sea and bring cold dry weather. But they are incapable of producing rain as they lack moisture.

They bring some rainfall when these winds blow over seas and pass over the adjoining land. The Southern Coromandel coast (Tamil Nadu and Southern tip of Andhra Pradesh) in India get rain from winter monsoons. The winter monsoon winds blow from North-East, so the monsoon is known as the **North-East Winter Monsoon.**

Cyclonic Depressions

During retreating monsoon, cyclonic depression originating over the Andaman Sea cause tropical cyclones on the coastline from Bangladesh to Tamil Nadu, as low pressure conditions get transferred to the Bay of Bengal.

These cyclones cause heavy and widespread rain and lots of destruction. These cyclones frequently struck the populated deltas of Godavari, Krishna and Kaveri. The Coromandel Coast gets monsoon rainfall due to these tropical cyclones.

(iv) Winter Season
(December to February)

This season remains from December to February in which January is the coldest month. Clear sky, low temperature, humidity and feeble (weak) variable winds are the characteristics of the weather during this season.

In February, the cold winds from the Caspian sea and Turkmenistan bring cold waves over the North-Western parts of India. Frost occurs in the Northern plains and snowfall occurs in the high mountainous regions of Himalayas.

Winds in Winter

- **Jet Streams** These are narrow belt of high altitude Westerly winds (above 12000 m) in the troposphere, which help in determining the arrival of monsoon.
- **North-East Monsoon Winds** These winds blow from the continent (Asia) to the ocean. During winter season, North-East trade winds prevail over India. These winds, being offshore do not give rain. They are dry except for the branch that blows over the Bay of Bengal and gives rainfall to the East coast of India.

Temperature Conditions

The temperature decrease from South to North. For example, the average temperature of Chennai on the Eastern coast is between 24-25°C while in Northern Plains, it ranges between 10-15°C. Here, days are warm and nights are cold. The average temperature lies between 20°C to 25°C in Peninsular India.

Cyclonic Depressions

During this season, there is an inflow of Western disturbances or temperate cyclones from the West and the North-West, which originate over the Mediterranean Sea and Western Asia. The frequency of these disturbance is 4 to 6 days per month between December and January.

Western disturbances cause small amount of winter rainfall which is highly beneficial to rabi crops. It is locally known as **Mahawat**. Besides, snowfall also occurs from the Western disturbances, which feed the glaciers of the Western Himalayas. The North-Eastern parts of India also get some rainfall during winter season due to these disturbances.

Check Your LEARNING...

1. What is the meaning of monsoonal trough?
2. Where did the Bay to Bengal Branch causes the heaviest rainfall in the world?
3. Which weather phenomenon gives rise to October heat?
4. Due to which weather phenomenon the North-Western region gets rainfall during winter season?

QUiCK Revision

- The term 'climate' refers to the atmospheric conditions, which prevails in a large area over a long period of time.
- Generally, the climate of India belongs to the tropical monsoon type. The Tropic of Cancer, which passes through the centre of the country, divides it into sub-tropical climate zone (Northern part) and tropical zone (Southern part).
- Different parts of the country can experience different types of climate. So the regional variation in the climate is one of the major characteristics of India.
- Climate of India is affected by various factors such as latitude, altitude, Himalayan mountains, pressure and surface winds, Western disturbances, distance from the sea, tropical cyclones, by relief features, Monsoon wind, jet stream and El-Nino.
- India generally has four seasons such as hot and dry summers, South-West monsoon, retreating monsoon and cool and dry winters or North-East monsoon.
- The hot and dry summer is experienced in India in the months of March, April and May and characterised by intensely hot weather and very little humidity.
- The mechanism of monsoon develops over Indian sub-continent by various factors such as the differential heating and cooling of land and water, ITCZ, presence of high pressure area East of Madagascar, heating of Tibetan plateau.
- After summer there is South-West Monsoon which occurs in June and last until September due to trade winds that originate over the warm tropical ocean in the Southern hemisphere and cover the entire sub-continent in just over one month.
- South-West monsoon has two branches namely the Arabian sea branch and the Bay of Bengal branch.
- Both the branches merge over the North-Western part of the Ganga plains and shed remaining moisture at the foothills of the Himalayas.
- During retreating monsoon, the Sun starts moving towards the South during October-November. This is the period of 'October heat'.
- During this season, tropical cyclones originate over the Andaman Sea and cause heavy and widespread rain over the Eastern coast of India and the Coromandel coast of India.
- At the advent of December the whole part of India experiences winter season that lasts from December to February.
- There is an inflow of cyclonic disturbances from West and the North-West, (low pressure depression) which originates in West Asia and in areas near the Mediterranean Sea which is called 'Western Disturbance'.

Chapter Practice

Section-I

Multiple Choice Questions

1. Name the type of climate experienced in India. **[Specimen Paper Semester-I 2022]**
(a) Tropical cyclonic type (b) Tropical monsoon type
(c) Temperate monsoon type (d) Sub-tropical monsoon

Ans. (b) Tropical monsoon type

2. Which of the following factor is responsible for the rise in the temperature of mainland of India in the month of March? **[Specimen Paper Semester-I 2022]**
(a) Southward migration of the Sun from the equator.
(b) Northward migration of the Sun from the equator.
(c) The pressure belts shift.
(d) The land breeze blows towards the sea.

Ans. (b) Northward migration of the Sun from the equator.

3. Why has Thar developed into a desert? **[Specimen Paper Semester-I 2022]**
(a) It has no cloud cover.
(b) It is near the sea.
(c) It is on the windward side of Western Ghats
(d) Aravalli is parallel to South-West Monsoon wind

Ans. (d) Aravalli is parallel to South-West Monsoon wind

4. The Western coast gets its heaviest rainfall during...............by South-West Monsoon winds.
(a) August (b) June (c) September (d) July

Ans. (b) June

5. Which of the following coasts of India is most affected by violent tropical cyclones?
(a) Malabar (b) Coromandel (c) Konkan (d) Kanara

Ans. (b) Coromandel

6. The places to the North of Tropic of Cancer experience............ type of climate.
(a) continental (b) moderate
(c) oceanic (d) equatorial

Ans. (a) continental

7. The places in Peninsular India even at higher altitude never experience any snowfall because of
(a) nearness to the Indian Ocean
(b) nearness to the Tropic of Cancer
(c) nearness to the Equator
(d) nearness to the Arabian Sea

Ans. (c) nearness to the Equator

8. The pre-monsoon mango showers occur predominantly in
(a) West Bengal and Assam (b) Deccan Plateau
(c) Gujarat and Maharashtra (d) Kerala and Karnataka

Ans. (a) West Bengal and Assam

9. In May-June each year, the monsoon winds approach the Southern tip of India from
(a) North direction
(b) North-Easterly direction
(c) North-Westerly direction
(d) South-Westerly direction

Ans. (d) South-Westerly direction

10. Which of the following area receives rain from the North-East monsoon ? **[2023]**
(a) Konkan coast
(b) Ganga basin
(c) Coromandel coast
(d) Malabar coast

Ans. (d) Malabar coast

11. The Eastern coast gets its maximum rainfall during.............
(a) summer season (b) rainy season
(c) autumn season (d) winter season

Ans. (d) winter season

12. Give reasons for the following. **[Specimen Paper Semester-I 2022]**
There is heavy rainfall in the Western coastal plains.
(a) Presence of Aravalli mountain range in Western India
(b) The Eastern coastal plains have no intercepting barrier
(c) Presence of Deccan Plateau
(d) Presence of Western Ghats

Ans. (d) Presence of Western Ghats

13. Give reasons for the following. **[Specimen Paper Semester-I 2022]**
In June, Bhopal is warmer than Kolkata
(a) due to its continental location.
(b) due to Kolkata's proximity to the sea.
(c) Bhopal is closer to the Tropic of Cancer.
(d) Himalayan hill station Darjeeling, is closer to Kolkata than it is to Bhopal.

Ans. (a) due to its continental location.

14. Give reasons for the following. **[Specimen Paper Semester-I 2022]**
The reason for Rajasthan being deficient in rainfall is
(a) The monsoon fail to reach this area.
(b) It is too hot.
(c) There is no water available and thus the winds remain dry.
(d) The winds do not come across any barrier to cause necessary uplift to be cooled.

Ans. (d) The winds do not come across any barrier to cause necessary uplift to be cooled.

15. Give the reason for the following.
The extreme of temperature between summer and winter is quite low in Southern part of peninsular India mainly because.
(a) the adjoining oceans moderate the temperature.
(b) the sky is generally cloudy.
(c) the Sun's rays are almost vertical throughout the year.
(d) strong winds flow throughout the year.

Ans. (a) the adjoining oceans moderate the temperature

16. Which one of the following statements is wrong regarding the "Norwesters" of Bengal?
(i) It is caused due to strong surface heating.
(ii) It originates in the Chota Nagpur Plateau region.
(iii) It is a kind of thunderstorm.

Codes
(a) Both (i) and (iii) (b) Both (i) and (ii)
(c) Both (ii) and (iii) (d) None of these

Ans. (d) None of these

17. Which one of the following statements is correct regarding the "Western disturbances affect the crops in North India".
(i) They cause heavy damage to the standing crops.
(ii) They bring in locusts which destroy the crops.
(iii) They are beneficial to the crops by causing winter rain.
(iv) They help in keeping the plants warm to some extent in winter.

Codes
(a) All of these (b) Only (i)
(c) Only (ii) (d) Only (iii)

Ans. (d) Only (iii)

18. Match the following.

Months	Characteristics
A. March to May	1. Cool and dry winters
B. June to September	2. Retreating monsoon
C. October to November	3. South-West monsoon
D. December to February	4. Hot and dry summer

Codes
(a) A-4, B-3, C-2, D-1 (b) A-1, B-2, C-3, D-4
(c) A-2, B-3, C-4, D-1 (d) A-4, B-1, C-2, D-3

Ans. (a)

19. Match the following.

States	Amount of rainfall
A. Meghalaya	1. Less than 50 cm
B. Jharkhand	2. More than 200 cm
C. Gujarat	3. 100-200 cm
D. Thar	4. 50- 100 cm

Codes
(a) A-4, B-3, C-2, D-1 (b) A-1, B-2, C-3, D-4
(c) A-2, B-3, C-4, D-1 (d) A-4, B-1, C-2, D-3

Ans. (c)

20. Match the following.

Branches of South-West Monsoon	Affected Regions
A. First branch of Arabian Sea	1. Western Ghats
B. Second branch of Arabian Sea	2. North coast of Mumbai
C. Third branch of Arabia Sea	3. Saurashtra Peninsula
D. First branch of Bay of Bengal	4. Most of Assam

Codes
(a) A-1, B-2, C-3, D-4 (b) A-4, B-3, C-1, D-2
(c) A-3, B-1, C-4, D-2 (d) A-4, B-3, C-2, D-1

Ans. (a)

Section-II

Short Questions

1. (i) What type of wind is 'Monsoon'? What is its direction during summer?
(ii) Mention two characteristics of the Indian monsoon. [2019]

Ans. (i) The word 'Monsoon' derived from the Arabic word 'Mausim' which means season. Monsoon is a seasonal wind system that reverses during a year which strongly influence climate of India. The direction of monsoon in summer is from South-West to North-East.
(ii) Two characteristics of monsoon in India are
(a) A large part of the country receives rainfall mainly in the summer from the South-West monsoon winds. Very little rain is caused in winter from the North-East winter monsoons.
(b) Erratic and unpredictable nature of monsoon causes heavy or very little rainfall in some years.

2. (i) Name the type of climate prevailing over India.
(ii) Mention any two factors responsible for it. [2012]

Or What is the name given to the climate of India? Mention any two factors responsible for such a type of climate. [2016]

Ans. (i) Tropical monsoon climate prevail over India.
(ii) The two factors responsible for climate of India are
(a) The Tropic of Cancer which passes through the middle of the country.
(b) The climate is influenced by the monsoon winds, altitude, distance from sea, relief etc.

3. What is the chief cause of the tropical monsoon type of climate?

Ans. The chief cause of the tropical monsoon climate is the differential heating and cooling of the land and the water and the resulting low pressure regions drawing in the winds.

4. Why are there great variations in the climate of the Indian subcontinent?

Ans. The Indian sub-continent extends from 8°4′ N to 37°6′ N latitude and a distance of 3214 km from North to South. Thus, there is a great variation in the climate (a great latitudinal extent, extending into two climatic zones i.e. Tropical and Sub-tropical zones).

5. Explain two factors that affect the climate of India giving a suitable example for each. [2015]

Ans. Two factors affecting the climate of India are

(i) **Latitude** It is the measurement of distance of a point on the Earth's surface in North or South of the equator. At the equator, the Sun's rays directly thus, temperatures are highest there. But when the distance of places increases from the equator, the Sun's rays become more slanting and cover large area thus, temperature reduces.

(ii) **Altitude** Generally, with increase in height, temperature decreases. For every 166 m rise in height, there is a decrease of 1°C in temperature. That is why hilly areas are cooler than the plains because of high altitude.

6. Define jet streams. Also explain how do they affect the climate of India?

Ans. Jet stream are Westerly winds which blow in the upper layers of the atmosphere. These winds blow at a speed of 110 kmph in summers and 184 kmph in winters.

These winds are air currents and greatly help in determining the arrival of monsoons in India.

7. Answer the following questions.

(i) Name a state that is the first to experience the onset of the monsoon.

(ii) How does the 'Mango Shower' influence the state of Karnataka? [2018]

Ans. (i) Kerala is the first state in India to experience the onset of the monsoon from Arabian branch of monsoon.

(ii) Mango shower influences the state of Karnataka because it helps in early ripening of mangoes in Karnataka and parts of Tamil Nadu.

8. How do the water bodies influence the climate of India?

Ans. The water bodies influence the climate of India in the following ways

(i) The water bodies surrounding India on three sides have a moderating influence due to which the coastal areas enjoy equable climate.

(ii) Monsoon winds carry moisture from the water bodies that surround India.

9. Name the places that experience continentality.

Ans. The places of India which experience continentality are Agra, Delhi, Jaipur, Udaipur, Jaisalmer, Jodhpur, Pokaran, Bhopal, Meerut, Bareilly, Amritsar, Lucknow, Ludhiana, Indore, Patna, Kanpur, Chandigarh, Nagpur, Hyderabad, Bikaner, Ajmer, Jabalpur, Mathura, Ambala and Varanasi.

10. Name the places that experience oceanic or coastal or maritime climate in India.

Ans. The places of India which experience maritime climate are Kandla, Dwarka, Porbandar, Diu, Mumbai, Ratnagiri, Panaji, Murmagao, Karwar, Mangalore, Kannur, Kozhikode, Kochi, Thiruvananthapuram, Kanyakumari, Tuticorin, Nagapatnam, Puducherry, Chennai, Kakinada, Visakhapatnam, Haldia, Kolkata, Machilipatnam, etc.

11. Why Agra's temperature in January is higher than Darjeeling in spite of having same latitudinal locations?

Ans. The difference in temperatures of Agra and Darjeeling is due to the elevation levels at which these places are located. With rise in elevation, the temperature and pressure falls. Darjeeling is situated in the mountains where the temperature is less than plain areas where Agra is located.

12. Why are the South facing slopes of the Garo, Khasi, Jaintia hills or Himalayas or Shivaliks warmer than the North facing slopes of these hills or mountains?

Ans. The Garo, Khasi, Jaintia hills or Himalayas or Shivaliks are in the Northern hemisphere and have an East-West alignment. The South facing slopes are warmer as they get more direct sun rays as the Sun rays strike at a steeper angle than the North facing slopes and hence, they are less intense.

13. Define loo.

Ans. Loo is a gusty (wild), hot, dry wind blowing during the day over the North and North-Western India in the months of May and June.

14. State two differences between the rainfalls that occur from June to September and that from December to February in North India. [2015]

Ans. Differences between South-West monsoon and North-East monsoon are

South-West Monsoon	North-East Monsoon
These winds start blowing during the months of June to September.	These winds start blowing during December to February.
These winds bring rain to almost whole part of India.	These winds bring rain only to Tamil Nadu coast and a little to some parts of North-East regions.

15. Mangalore and Chennai lie approximately on the same latitude, yet Mangalore receives its rainfall from June to September, while Chennai receives its main rain in November to February. What are the reason for this difference?

Ans. Mangalore lies on the West coast of India and experience the South-West monsoon of the Arabian Sea branch which blooms from June to September. This place is on the windward side of the Western

Ghats hence, receives rain during this period. While Chennai lies on the East coast of India and this place experiences the North-East monsoons during the months of November to February. These monsoons bring rain to Chennai in winter that lies on the windward side of the Eastern Ghats.

16. Name the four seasons into which the climatic conditions of India is divided.

Or Mention the four seasons that prevails in India stating the months for each. [2017]

Or Name the seasons of India and mention the duration of each season. [2023]

Ans. The four seasons are

(i) Summer season (March to May)

(ii) Advancing or South-West monsoon season (June to September)

(iii) Retreating monsoon season (October to November)

(iv) Winter season (December to February)

17. With reference to the summer season in India, answer the following questions. [2019]

(i) Mention the duration of the summer season in India.

(ii) What is the atmospheric pressure condition during summer season over the central part of India?

Ans. (i) The months of March, April and May are the summer months in India when the Sun moves from the equator towards the Tropic of Cancer (Northward movement) and the global heat belt shifts Northward. By 21st June, it is directly overhead the Tropic of Cancer.

(ii) The atmospheric pressure conditions in Central India is low in summer as the region experiences high temperature and heat waves during summer.

18. "Rainfall in India is orographic in nature." Give an example with reference to the distribution of rainfall and the effect of relief on its distribution. [2011]

Ans. Relief plays a very important role in the distribution of rainfall in India. The windward slopes of the Western Ghats obstruct the moist winds from the sea and cause heavy rainfall, while the leeward slopes remain dry. Thus, Western Ghats receive more than 200 cm rainfall.

19. (i) Name one state in the North-Western part of India that receives rainfall during winter. [2020]

(ii) What is the source of this rainfall?

Ans. (i) Punjab in North-Western part of India receives rainfall in winter.

(ii) The North-Western plains of India experience winter rainfall due to the invasion of the Western disturbances rising from the Mediterranean sea, led by the westerly jetstream. As the Western disturbances are associated with the cyclonic winds, they bring rainfall.

20. State the benefits that are derived from the local winds that blow in summer in the following states. [2014]

(i) Kerala (ii) West Bengal

Ans. (i) **Kerala** The local wind is called 'Mango Shower'. These winds bring little rain in April and May, which is helpful in the early ripening of mangoes, tea and coffee plants.

(ii) **West Bengal** The local wind is called 'Norwesters or Kaal Baisakhi'. This rain is useful for the cultivation of rice and jute in West Bengal.

21. Name the following [2016]

(i) The winds bring heavy rain in Cherrapunji.

(ii) The local winds that bring a light rainfall to South India and is good for tea and coffee crops.

Ans. (i) The Bay of Bengal branch of South-West monsoon.

(ii) Mango showers or cherry blossoms.

22. Give two important characteristics of the hot and dry summer in India.

Ans. Two characteristics of the hot and dry summer in India are

(i) It is a dry season with high temperature and low humidity.

(ii) The tornado like duststorms, hot wind (loo) and the Norwesters are the characteristics of summer season.

23. Which Indian state is the first to receive the South-West monsoons? Give a reason to justify your answer.

Ans. The first state that receives South-West monsoon is Kerala. Kerala lies on the South-West of India from where the Arabian Sea branch of the South-West monsoon enters India.

24. Name the state which experiences the longest monsoon season and another state or UT which experiences the shortest monsoon season.

Ans. Kerala experiences the longest monsoon season. The Union Territory of Jammu and Kashmir experiences the shortest monsoon season.

25. Give two important characteristics of the Indian monsoon season in India.

Ans. Two important characteristics of the Indian monsoon season in India are

(i) **Uneven Distribution of Rainfall** Monsoon winds cause uneven rainfall over India. Some areas like Western slopes of Western Ghats and North-East India receive heavy rainfall, whereas some areas receive less rainfall.

(ii) **Heavy Rainfall in Short Duration** Heavy rainfall occurs only during monsoon season which is of a short duration period i.e. from June to September.

26. Which winds are responsible for the rainfall experienced over the greater part of India? **[2006]**

Ans. South-West monsoon winds are responsible for the rainfall experienced over the greater part of India. These winds blow from June to September. These winds tend to carry moisture with them and cause rain in the entire country.

27. Mention two features of the Arabian Sea branch of the South-West monsoons.

Ans. Following are the features of the Arabian Sea branch of the South-West monsoon

(i) This branch originates from the Arabian Sea and advances Northwards.

(ii) This branch gives voluminous rainfall throughout the country except the parts of Western Rajasthan and Gujarat as they lie on the leeward side of the Aravalli range.

28. Mention two features of the Bay of Bengal branch of the South-West monsoon.

Ans. The two features of the Bay of Bengal branch are

(i) This branch originates from the Bay of Bengal and gives heavy rainfall in the Eastern and North-Eastern parts of India.

(ii) The winds of this branch divides into two branches, one goes to Brahmaputra valley and second goes to the Ganga Plains.

29. Why has Mawsynram become the place that receive highest rainfall in the world?

Ans. Mawsynram receive highest rainfall in the world as it lies in the Southern ranges of the Khasi hills in Meghalaya. Here, the Bay of Bengal branch of the South-West monsoon offer collecting moisture dashes against the hills and cause 1200 cm of rainfall.

30. Mention two differences in the climatic conditions which prevail over Kerala and Uttar Pradesh in the month of June. **[2010]**

Ans. The differences in the climatic conditions which prevail over Kerala and Uttar Pradesh in the months of June are

Climatic conditions in Kerala in the month of June	Climatic conditions in Uttar Pradesh in the month of June
High pressure prevails in Kerala.	Low pressure prevails in Uttar Pradesh.
Lower temperature as compared to Uttar Pradesh prevails in the region due to moderating effect of the sea.	High temperature prevails in the region.

31. Why do much of the Central Maharashtra and Central Deccan plateau have only light rainfall?

Ans. Central Maharashtra and Deccan plateau region get light rainfall as they lie in the rain shadow area of the Western Ghats. These mountains block the way of the rain bearing winds coming from the Arabian sea.

32. Mumbai receives rainfall in the summer season while Chennai receives rainfall from October to December. Why? **[2009]**

Ans. Mumbai is situated in the West coast of India thus it gets rainfall from the South-West monsoons that bring rainfall in summer from June to September. Chennai is situated in the East coast thus it receives rainfall from North-East monsoons during winters from December to February.

33. Western coastal plains receive more rainfall than Eastern coastal plains. Give a reason.

Ans. Western coastal plains receive more rainfall because they lie in the windward side of the Western Ghats that block the way of rain bearing winds coming from the Arabian Sea. While the Eastern coastal plains lie on the leeward side of the Western Ghats and receives less rainfall.

34. Name two types of cyclonic systems that affect India and two areas that receive rainfall from these systems. **[2013]**

Ans. Two cyclonic systems that affect India are

(i) **Temperate Cyclones** Two areas that receive rainfall from these cyclones are Punjab and Haryana.

(ii) **Tropical Cyclones** Areas which receive rainfall from these cyclones are Andhra Pradesh, Tamil Nadu, Odisha and West Bengal.

35. Give two important facts about retreating of South-West monsoon.

Ans. The two important facts of the retreating monsoon in India are

(i) October and November are the months of retreating monsoon. During this season, low monsoon trough becomes weak and is replaced by high pressure. Thus, monsoon begins to retreat. By the beginning of October, it retreats completely from Northern plains.

(ii) This is the period of transition from hot rainy season to cold winter season. It is marked by clear sky, moist ground and high temperature giving birth to October heat.

36. Define 'October Heat'.

Ans. The period of transition from hot rainy season to cold winter season which is marked by clear sky, moist ground and high temperature is known as October heat.

37. Mention the different sources of rain in Punjab and Tamil Nadu during the winter season. **[2014]**

Ans. The different sources of rain in Punjab and Tamil Nadu during the winter season are

(i) Punjab receives rainfall due to the cyclonic disturbances (Westerly disturbances), that originate over the Eastern Mediterranean Sea during the winter season.

(ii) Tamil Nadu receives rainfall from North-East monsoon wind during the winter season.

38. Give a reason for each of the following [2020]

(a) Rainy season in India comes after the summer season.

(b) Tamil Nadu has more rainy months than Kerala, yet, Kerala receives more rainfall than Tamil Nadu.

Ans. (a) Rainy season always comes after summer season because during summer, there is a lot of water loss due to sweating by humans and transpiration by plants due to excessive heat. This increases the amount of moisture and humidity in the atmosphere which ultimately results in rainfall.

(b) Tamil Nadu has more rainy months than Kerala because it receives rainfall from both-South- West monsoon winds and North-West monsoon winds (during winters), but Kerala receives rainfall only from South-West monsoon winds. The South-West monsoon winds first strike Kerala and give abundant rainfall there. Thus, Kerala gets more rainfall than Tamil Nadu.

Long Questions

1. How is the winter rainfall of the North-West part of India different from the winter rainfall of the South-East of India? [2018]

Ans. The North-West India receives winter rainfall from low pressure systems, called the Western disturbances. These disturbance travel Eastward across Iran and Pakistan from Mediterranean Sea and Gulf of Persia and reach India during the winter season. They cause much rainfall over plain areas of North-West regions of India.

On the other hand, the South-East of India receives rainfall in winter due to North-East monsoons. During winter season, several cyclonic storms develop in Bay of Bengal which moves from the North-East to South-West causing substantial rainfall on the coast of Tamil Nadu.

2. "Location and relief are important factors in determining the climate of India." Explain the statement.

Ans. Location and relief are important factors as they affect the climate of India in

(i) **Location** The amount of solar energy varies according to latitude. Air temperature generally decreases on moving from equator to poles. That is why, Antarctic is the coldest region. When we move from the surface of the Earth to higher altitudes, the atmosphere becomes less denser and temperature decreases. The hills, therefore, are cooler during summers.

(ii) **Relief** Relief features like high mountains act as barriers for cold and hot winds. They may also cause precipitation, if they are high enough and lie in the path of rain bearing winds. For example, the windward side of mountains gets more rainfall.

3. What is the most important feature of the tropical monsoon type of climate?

Ans. The most important feature of the tropical monsoon type of climate is the 'alteration of season'. During winter, the interior of the large land mass in Asia becomes very cold and develops a high pressure centre.

The cold surface winds move out towards the surrounding sea as the North-East monsoon. In summer, the interior of the land masses become extremely hot, which causes the development of low pressure areas. Winds then begin to blow from the high pressure areas in Australia to low pressure regions. These winds on crossing the equator deflect to the right and become the South-West monsoon winds.

4. The Thar Desert has sandy and rocky soils while the Indo-Gangetic plain has alluvial soil. Which place would have greater diurnal range in temperature and why?

Ans. The Thar Desert would have a greater diurnal range in temperature because of the nature of its soil which is rocky and sandy and hence, it has an extreme climate. This is because sandy and rocky soils do not retain water and is heated rapidly and cools rapidly. On the other hand, the Indo-Gangetic plain have Alluvial soil. This soil has the ability to retain water hence, this soil is heated slowly and cools slowly, thus the Indo-Gangetic plain will have a small range in temperature resulting in an equable climate.

5. Name the region of India which experiences the highest diurnal range of temperature. Also give its reason.

Ans. The North-Western part of India comprising the Indian desert experiences the highest diurnal range of temperature. This is because of the fact that sand (found in ample quantity in this region) gains and loses heat very quickly. As a result of this phenomenon, there is a wide difference between day and night temperatures in this region. The day temperature may rise to 50°C and drop down to near 15°C the same night.

6. How do the Himalayas play an important role in influencing the climate of Indian sub-continent?

Ans. The role of Himalayas in influencing the climate of the Indian sub-continent is

(i) The Himalayan mountains act as a natural barrier against the cold winds of Central Asia and Siberia to enter India thus, preventing a severe cold climate.

(ii) The Himalayas trap the rain bearing winds of South-West monsoon causing them to shed their moisture in the Indian sub-continent thus, making agriculture possible on a large scale.

7. "Chennai gets more rainfall in winter than in summer." Give two reasons.

Ans. Chennai gets more rainfall in winter than in summer due to following reasons

- Tropical cyclones originate in winter over the Bay of Bengal and the Indian Ocean. These cyclones cause heavy rainfall in Tamil Nadu, Andhra Pradesh and Odisha coast.
- During October and November, North East monsoon while crossing over the Bay of Bengal, picks up moisture and causes rainfall.
- The region gets lesser rainfall from the summer monsoon as it lies in the rain shadow area of the Bay of Bengal branch.

8. Why does Jodhpur do not get much rainfall?

Ans. Jodhpur does not get much rainfall due to the following reasons

- Jodhpur is situated on the outskirts of Thar Desert or in the Western part of Rajasthan. When the monsoon winds pass over Western part of Rajasthan, i.e. Thar Desert, they become warmer and increase their capacity to hold moisture instead of shedding moisture.
- Aravalli hills lie in Rajasthan which fall parallel to the Arabian Sea branch of the South-West monsoon. These hills do not act as barriers to these winds. Hence, they do not cause any rainfall in Jodhpur.

9. What is extreme type of climate? Name three places of extreme climate in India.

Ans. The climate which has high annual range of temperature and great variation in the amount of rainfall over the year is known as extreme climate. It is also known as continental or interior type of climate, as it is found in the interior parts of the continents.

Examples of extreme type of climate are Jodhpur, Delhi, Kanpur.

10. Distinguish between Arabian sea branch and Bay of Bengal branch of South-West monsoon.

Ans. The differences between Arabian sea branch and Bay of Bengal branch of South-West monsoon are

Arabian Sea Branch	Bay of Bengal Branch
This branch is more powerful.	This branch is less powerful.
This branch covers large part of Indian sub-continent consisting of Western Ghats, Deccan Plateau and then moves on to Northern plains.	This covers North-East India, Ganga-Brahmaputra delta and Northern plains.
This branch picks up moisture from the Arabian Sea.	This branch picks up moisture from the Bay of Bengal.

11. How does the change in pressure conditions over the Southern oceans affect the monsoons?

Ans. Southern oceans affect the monsoons over the change in conditions due to the following reasons

- When the tropical Eastern-South Pacific Ocean experiences high pressure, the tropical Eastern Indian Ocean experiences low pressure. In this condition, the monsoon rainfall will be average.
- In some years, this condition gets reverse when pressure differences are negative. It leads below average and late monsoon.

12. Why are the delta regions of Eastern India struck by cyclones?

Ans. The delta-regions of Eastern India struck by cyclones when transfer of low pressure conditions occurs over Bay of Bengal. This shift or transfer generate cyclonic depressions over Andaman Sea. The cyclone coming under influence of retreating monsoon winds generally cross the Eastern coast and struck the thickly populated delta region of Godavari, Krishna and Kaveri rivers. These are often destructive and cause great damage to life and property.

13. (i) What do you understand by the term 'Burst of Monsoon'? Name the state that experiences the 'Burst of Monsoon'. **[2020]**

(ii) Even though India gets abundant rainfall during the rainy season, yet some places experience drought. Explain giving suitable examples.

(iii) Why is Shimla colder than Delhi during summer?

Ans. (i) Around the time of the arrival of the monsoons, the normal rainfall increases suddenly and continues constantly for several days. This is known as the 'burst of the monsoon'. This branch is responsible for giving Meghalaya the highest rainfall in the world.

(ii) Even though India gets abundant rainfall during the rainy season, yet some places experience drought because rainfall is uncertain and unreliable. Distribution of rainfall in the country is uneven. While some states receive abundant rainfall during monsoon, whereas some states face drought like condition due to scanty rainfall e.g. Rajasthan and Haryana.

(iii) Shimla is colder than Delhi in summer because Shimla is situated at a higher altitude where the atmosphere is cooler. Delhi is in the plains where atmosphere gets heated up fast.

14. Give a geographic reason for each of the following. **[2015]**

(i) Kerala has the longest rainy season.

(ii) The Konkan coast experiences orographic rainfall.

(iii) The city of Kanpur in Uttar Pradesh has a higher range of temperature than that of Chennai in Tamil Nadu.

Ans. (i) Kerala has the longest rainy season because Kerala is surrounded by water bodies i.e. Arabian Sea on West. When monsoon arrives it brings rainfall from the Arabian Sea and strikes on the Western Ghats. This results in frequent and long rain in Kerala.

(ii) Orographic rainfall is mainly caused by the presence of a relief barrier. The Konkan coast lies on the windward side of the Western Ghats which obstructs the onshore Arabian Sea branch of the South-West monsoon winds. Thus, this causes heavy rainfall on the Western slopes of the Western Ghats and hence, Konkan coast experiences orographic rainfall.

(iii) Kanpur has an interior location while Chennai has a coastal location. The areas in the interior of the country have an extreme type of climate resulting in high annual range of temperature while the coastal areas have a moderate climate. This is mainly due to the influence of land and sea breeze caused by differential heating and cooling of land and sea.

15. Mention a geographical reason for each of the following. **[2014]**

(i) Patna receives heavier rain than Delhi.

(ii) Western Rajasthan receives no rain from the Arabian Sea branch of the South-West monsoon winds.

(iii) Mangalore is not cold even in the month of December.

Ans. (i) Patna receives heavier rain than Delhi because it lies to the East of Delhi and receives rainfall from the Bay of Bengal branch of South-West monsoon. The moisture of the branch decreases from East to West.

(ii) Western Rajasthan receives no rain from the Arabian Sea branch because these winds run parallel to the Aravalli ranges and do not cross it to give rainfall in Western Rajasthan. Also the temperature is so high that monsoon winds become dry and do not shed any moisture there.

(iii) Mangalore is not cold even in the month of December because it lies on the Western coast of India and therefore have the moderating influence of the sea.

16. Give reasons for the following. **[2013]**

(i) When the Malabar coast is receiving heavy rainfall in July, the Tamil Nadu coast is comparatively dry.

(ii) The Northern plains of India have a continental type of climate.

(iii) Central Maharashtra receives little rainfall.

Ans. (i) When the Malabar coast is receiving heavy rainfall in July, the Tamil Nadu coast is dry because it lies in the rain shadow region of Arabian Sea branch and Bay of Bengal is parallel to the coast.

(ii) The Northern plains of India are far away from the sea and there is no moderating influence of the sea so, it experiences a continental type of climate.

(iii) Central Maharashtra receives little rainfall because it lies in the rain shadow region of the Western Ghats.

17. Give geographical reasons for the following. **[2012]**

(i) Even in summer Shimla is cooler than Delhi.

(ii) The Northern Plains of India do not freeze in winter.

(iii) Kochi has a lesser annual range of temperature than Agra.

Ans. (i) Refer to answer of Long Questions Q. 13 (iii).

(ii) Northern Plains do not freeze in winters because the Himalayan mountains act as a natural barrier against the cold winds coming from North.

(iii) Kochi is located on the Western coast due to which it enjoys marine climate. The moderating influence of the sea keeps the temperature average throughout the year. On the other hand, Agra lies in the interiors as it is far away from the sea so it experiences continental type of climate and has more range of temperature.

18. Give a reason for each of the following.

(i) Patna gets a heavier rainfall than Varanasi.

(ii) The Arabian Sea branch of the South-West monsoon does not shed any moisture in Western Rajasthan.

(iii) India has varied climatic conditions.

Ans. (i) The quantity of rainfall decreases as the monsoon winds moves westwards from sea towards the land. Patna is situated more towards the East than Varanasi, so it gets heavier rainfall.

(ii) Western Rajasthan receives no rain from the Arabian Sea branch because these winds run parallel to the Aravalli ranges and do not cross it to give rainfall in Western Rajasthan. Also, the temperature is so high that monsoon winds become dry and do not shed any moisture there.

(iii) India has varied climatic conditions due to different factors that affect the climate of India like pressure and winds, distance from the sea, relief, cyclonic disturbances etc.

19. Give a reason for each of the following. **[2019]**

(i) Goa receives heavier rainfall than Puducherry.

(ii) Mawsynram receives the highest average annual rainfall.

(iii) Mangaluru is cooler than Delhi in summer season.

Ans. (i) Goa is situated in the West coast of India where it gets rainfall from the South-West monsoon which brings heavy rainfall in summer (from June to September). While Puducherry is situated in the Eastern Ghats where South-West monsoon does not give much rain, therefore Goa gets heavier rainfall than Puducherry.

(ii) Mawsynram lies on the windward side of Khasi hills. The place is enclosed by hills on all the three sides due to which it gives a funnel shaped location to Mawsynram. The monsoon winds get trapped in this region causing heavy rainfall again and again thereby making it the highest average annual rainfall place.

(iii) Mangaluru is cooler than Delhi because it lies on the Western cost of India and therefore has moderating influence of sea in summer, whereas Delhi is located in interior of India and has continental type of climate (extremely hot in summer and extremely cold in winter).

20. Give a geographical reason for each of the following. **[2023]**

(i) The Malabar coast receives heavy rainfall in the month of July but the Coromandel coast during this time remains comparatively dry.

(ii) Punjab receives rainfall in winter season.

(iii) Mumbai is warmer than Delhi in the month of December.

Ans. (i) Malabar coast receives heavy rainfall from the Arabian Sea branch of South West Monsoon during June to October as it lies in the windward side of Western Ghats. On the other hand, Coromandel Coast gets very low rainfall from South-West monsoon as it lies in the leeward side of Western Ghats.

(ii) The cyclones originating in the Mediterranean sea during the winter gradually shifts towards the East and reaches India. This causes winter rainfall in Northern plains, especially in the Punjab region.

(iii) Mumbai is warmer than Delhi in the month of December because it has an equable climate due to coastal location, while Delhi is an inland town. The presence of land and sea breezes keep the nights warm at Mumbai.

21. Write three differences between summer monsoon and retreating monsoon season. **[2018]**

Ans. The differences between summer monsoon and retreating monsoon are

Summer Monsoon	Retreating Monsoon
These winds or monsoon winds blow from June to September.	These winds blow from October to November.
This monsoon covers the whole India and gives heavy rainfall.	This monsoon covers little regions of India but the coastal areas of Tamil Nadu receives maximum rainfall.
The temperature is humid and pressure is low on the land.	The temperature goes up and the humidity becomes high.

22. How does India get rainfall in winters and what is the importance of this rainfall for India?

Ans. India gets rainfall in the winter months between December and January by the cyclonic or Western disturbances. The Western disturbances originate over the Mediterranean Sea and Western Asia. It causes rainfall in the North and North-West of India. The importance of these Western disturbances is that in the Himalayan mountain region, these cause snowfall which feed the glaciers of Western Himalayas. The North-Eastern parts of India also get some rainfall during the winters from Western disturbances.

23. Give a reason to explain the following. **[2011]**

(i) The coastal areas of India do not experience a significant variation in temperature between summer and winter months.

(ii) The annual rainfall in Rajasthan is less than 25 cm.

(iii) The Coromandel Coast gets most of its rain during the winter season.

Ans. (i) The coastal areas of India do not experience a significant variation in temperature between summer and winter months due to the effect of land and sea breeze caused by differential rate of heating and cooling of the land and sea which results in an equable and moderate climatic conditions.

(ii) Rajasthan gets less than 25 cm of rainfall or very little rainfall as it lies in the rain shadow of the Aravalli ranges. The Bay of Bengal branch of South-West monsoon is almost exhausted by the time it reaches Rajasthan while the Arabian Sea branch blows parallel to the Aravalli ranges.

(iii) Coromandel coast gets most of its rainfall from the North-East monsoon winds that travel from land to sea. On the way, these winds pick moisture from Bay of Bengal and cause rainfall in Coromandel Coast that includes parts of Andhra Pradesh and Chennai.

24. Give reasons for the following. **[2010]**

(i) The North-East monsoons bring almost no rain to most of India.

(ii) The Mango showers are beneficial local winds.

(iii) The latitudinal extent of India is responsible for the variation in the climatic conditions which prevail in the country.

Ans. (i) The North-East monsoons bring almost no rain to most of India as these winds travel from land towards sea.

(ii) Mango showers are beneficial local winds as they bring rain to Kerala in the month of May which is good for the growth of mangoes.

(iii) The latitudinal extent is responsible for the variation in climatic conditions of India as the place (latitudinal extent) which is farther from the equator experience low temperature as compared to the place nearer to the equator which experience high temperature.

25. Name the following.

(i) The winds that provide relief rainfall to Andhra Pradesh coast.

(ii) A region receiving orographic rain.

(iii) A region receiving cyclonic rain.

Ans. (i) South-West monsoon winds
(ii) Windward side of the Western Ghats
(iii) Punjab

26. Distinguish between South-West monsoon and North-East monsoon.

Ans. The differences between South-West monsoon and North-East monsoon are

South-West Monsoon	North-East Monsoon
These winds blow from sea to land.	These winds blow from land to sea.
In this season oppressive heat and humidity is felt, which is known as 'October Heat'.	In this season pleasant weather with low temperature, low humidity and clear skies are experienced.
These winds have two branches i.e. the Arabian Sea and Bay of Bengal branch.	These winds have only one branch.

27. Distinguish between cool dry winters and hot dry summers.

Ans. The differences between cool dry winters and hot dry summers are

Cool Dry Winters	Hot Dry Summer
The months of December, January and February are cool dry winters.	The months of March, April and May have hot dry summers.
This season has low temperature, low humidity and clear skies.	This season has high temperature and low humidity.
A little precipitation takes place that causes rainfall in North-West India and snowfall in Himalayas.	Duststorms, hot winds (Loo) and Norwesters blow in hot dry summers.

28. Differentiate between tropical cyclones and temperate cyclones.

Ans. The differences between tropical cyclones and temperate cyclones are

Tropical Cyclones	Temperate Cyclones
Tropical cyclones originate in the tropical zone that is why called as 'Tropical Cyclones'.	These cyclones originate in the temperate zone that is why they are known as 'Temperate Cyclones'.
They are circular in shape and generally small in size as compared to temperate cyclones.	These cyclones are of oval shape and larger than that of tropical cyclones.
They develop over the oceans or seas.	They develop over continents.

29. Give a reason for each of the following. [2017]
(i) Kolkata receives heavier rain than Lucknow.
(ii) The summer monsoon winds blows over the Arabian Sea from the South-West.
(iii) Thar is a desert.

Ans. (i) Kolkata receives heavier rain than Lucknow because Kolkata lies in the lower Ganga plain so it receives more rainfall but by the time the Bay of Bengal branch of South-West monsoons reach Lucknow their moisture holding capacity decreases, therefore it sheds less rainfall.
(ii) The summer monsoon winds blow over the Arabian Sea from the South-West because during the summer season in the Northern hemisphere, the Indian subcontinent landmass gets heated up and develops low pressure. As a result of this, the South-East Trade winds are attracted towards the Indian sub-continent and become the South-West Monsoon winds in the Indian sub-continent due to Coriolis force.
(iii) Thar is a desert because the soil of the Thar Desert remains dry for most of the year due to having a scanty rainfall. There are very few local tree species and the sand in the desert is highly mobile due to strong winds.

30. Give a geographical reason for each of the following. [2016]
(i) Kanpur has extreme temperature conditions.
(ii) Kochi is warmer than Mumbai even though both lie on the Western Coast of India.
(iii) The Ganga Plain gets the monsoon rain much later than the West Coast of India.

Ans. (i) Kanpur has extreme temperature condition as it is located in the interiors and has no moderating influence of the sea. Therefore, it is very hot in summers and very cold in winters.
(ii) Although Kochi and Mumbai lie on the West Coast of India, yet Kochi is warmer because it is situated closer to the equator and get adequate sunshine throughout the year.
(iii) The West Coast of India gets monsoon rains first as the Arabian Sea branch of the South-West monsoon enters India from there. Then it moves upwards from Deccan Plateau in Central India towards Ganga plains in North. So, the Ganga Plain gets monsoon rain later than West coast.

31. State the agricultural benefits derived from
(i) The Westerly depressions in Punjab. [2017]
(ii) The Kaal Baisakhi in Assam.

Ans. (i) **The Westerly Depression in Punjab** The Westerly depression in Punjab causes rain during winter. This is good for rabi crop. Rabi crops are sown at the start of winter and harvested in spring or at the start of summer. Rabi crops mainly wheat and barley in Punjab get sufficient precipitation during winter months due to the Western temperature cyclone or Westerly depression.
(ii) **The Kaal Baisakhi in Assam** The 'Kaal Baisakhi' wind usually blows in North-West direction. These winds are accompanied by thunderstorms and brings heavy rainfall. This rain in the month of April to May is good for tea crop in Assam.

32. What is the direction of the summer monsoon? Why? [2012]

Ans. The direction of the summer monsoon is from South-West to North-East.

In summer, due to high temperature, low pressure areas develops over the North-Western India and high pressure over the sea. Air from high pressure areas blow from Southern hemisphere towards the region as this region attracts moisture bearing winds from South. After crossing the equator these winds deflected to the right and blow over India and give windespread rainfall over the mainland. These are known as 'the South-West monsoon' winds.

33. Give a reason for each of the following. [2018]

(i) Kanyakumari experiences equable climate.

(ii) Central Maharashtra gets less rainfall than coastal area of Maharashtra.

(iii) Jaipur has a higher annual range of temperature than Mumbai.

Ans. (i) Kanyakumari experiences equable climate because it is located near the coast and there is not much difference between the temperatures during the summer and winter due to the sea effect.

(ii) Central Maharashtra gets less rainfall than coastal area of Maharashtra because Central Maharashtra lies in the rain shadow zone of the Western Ghats. On the other side, coastal area of Maharashtra is humid, means water vapours are present and moist wind comes from sea which strikes to Western Ghats, therefore it gets heavy rainfall.

(iii) Jaipur lies in the interiors far away from the sea, so it experiences higher temperature, whereas Mumbai lies on the Western coast, so it experiences moderate type of temperature.

Data Based Questions

1. Study the climatic data given below and answer the questions that follow [2017]

Month	Temp. °C	Rainfall cm	Month	Temp. °C	Rainfall cm
Jan	12.0	1.5	Jul	36.0	25.3
Feb	25.5	0.1	Aug	35.9	27.2
Mar	26.3	0.0	Sep	30.3	24.0
Apr	27.1	1.4	Oct	28.4	9.4
May	30.0	1.1	Nov	21.0	1.5
Jun	36.2	21.0	Dec	16.6	0.4

(i) What is the annual range of temperature of the station?

(ii) What is the total annual rainfall experienced by the station?

(iii) Why would it be correct to presume that the station lies in the interior and not on the coast?

Ans. (i) The annual range of temperature of the station is 36.2°C-12°C = 24.2 °C

(ii) The total annual rainfall is 1.5 + 0.1 +0.0 + 1.4 + 1.1 + 21.0 + 25.3 + 27.2 + 24.0 + 9.4 + 1.5 + 0.4 = 112.9 cm.

(iii) The Western coast gets its heaviest rainfall during June by South-West monsoon, while Eastern coast gets its maximum rainfall in winter. But in the given table there is no heavy rainfall either in summer or in winter. Besides, the annual range of temperature is also very high. Thus, it is correct to presume that the station lies in the interior and not on the coast.

2. Study the climatic data of station X given below and answer the questions that follow [2016]

Month	Temp. °C	Rainfall cm	Month	Temp. °C	Rainfall cm
Jan	24.5	4.3	Jul	31.0	8.6
Feb	25.7	1.6	Aug	30.2	11.4
Mar	27.7	1.7	Sep	29.8	11.8
Apr	28.4	2.4	Oct	28.0	30.6
May	30.0	2.8	Nov	25.9	35.0
Jun	32.5	4.6	Dec	24.7	13.9

(i) Calculate the total annual rainfall experienced by the station.

(ii) What is the annual range of temperature?

(iii) On which coast of India does the station lie? Give a reason for your answer.

Ans. (i) The annual rainfall is 4.3 + 1.6 + 1.7 + 2.4 + 2.8 + 4.6 + 8.6 + 11.4 + 11.8 + 30.6 + 35.0 + 13.9 = 128.7 cm.

(ii) The annual range of temperature is
32.5° C – 24.5° C = 8° C

(iii) The station lies on the East coast as maximum rainfall is in the months of October-November i.e. in retreating monsoon season.

3. Study the climatic data given below and answer the questions that follow. [2015]

Month	Temp. °C	Rainfall cm	Month	Temp. °C	Rainfall cm
Jan	21.0	5.1	Jul	26.1	8.4
Feb	21.9	2.8	Aug	25.4	11.4
Mar	24.3	1.2	Sep	25.0	11.9
Apr	27.2	1.7	Oct	26.0	31.6
May	28.0	3.9	Nov	23.8	34.5
Jun	26.4	4.6	Dec	21.2	14.8

(i) Identify the hottest month.

(ii) Calculate the annual rainfall.

(iii) Name the winds that bring the maximum rainfall to this city.

Ans. (i) Hottest month is May.

(ii) Total annual rainfall is 5.1 + 2.8 + 1.2 + 1.7 + 3. 9 + 4.6 + 8.4 + 11.4 + 11.9 + 31. 6 + 34.5 + 14.8 = 131.9 cm.

(iii) As the maximum amount of rainfall is received during the months of October and November. We can deduce that they are caused by the winds of retreating monsoon.

4. Study the climatic data given below and answer the questions that follow [2014]

Month	Temp. °C	Rainfall cm	Month	Temp. °C	Rainfall cm
Jan	25.0	24.5	Jul	36.0	9.3
Feb	25.5	23.1	Aug	35.9	7.2
Mar	26.3	15.0	Sep	30.3	4.0
Apr	27.1	2.4	Oct	28.4	9.4
May	30.0	0.1	Nov	27.0	14.5
Jun	36.2	11.0	Dec	24.6	20.4

(i) Calculate the annual range of temperature.

(ii) What is the total annual rainfall?

(iii) Presuming that the station is located in India, give a reason for its location being on the East Coast or the West Coast of India.

Ans. (i) Annual range of temperature is

$36.2°C - 24.6°C = 11.6°C$

(ii) Total annual rainfall is

$24.5 + 23.1 + 15.0 + 2.4 + 0.1 + 11.0$
$+ 9.3 + 7.2 + 4.0 + 9.4 + 14.5 + 20.4 = 140.9$ cm

(iii) The station is located on the Eastern coast of India, because heavy rainfall is observed in winter season.

5. Study the climatic data given below and answer the questions that follow [2013]

Month	Temp. °C	Rainfall cm	Month	Temp. °C	Rainfall cm
Jan	23.1	15.3	Jul	33.1	6.1
Feb	24.8	10.1	Aug	32.1	10.2
Mar	26.5	0.3	Sep	30.5	10.5
Apr	29.3	0.1	Oct	29.3	20.1
May	32.0	1.3	Nov	28.7	16.8
Jun	32.8	4.5	Dec	26.1	19.0

(i) Calculate the annual rainfall experienced by the station.

(ii) Suggest a name of this station, giving a reason for your answer.

(iii) Name the season during which the rainfall is highest.

Ans. (i) Annual rainfall = 15.3 + 10.1 + 0.3 + 0.1 + 1.3 + 4.5 + 6.1 + 10.2 + 10.5 + 20.1 + 16.0 + 19.0 = 114.3 cm

(ii) Suggested name is Chennai, because the station is receiving most of its rain in October and November.

(iii) Rainfall is high in winter season.

6. Study the climatic data given below and answer the questions that follow [2012]

Month	Temp. °C	Rainfall cm	Month	Temp. °C	Rainfall cm
Jan	23.8	0	Jul	30.4	46.5
Feb	25.0	0	Aug	33.3	45.4
Mar	27.7	1.1	Sep	30.0	43.3
Apr	28.3	1.5	Oct	30.3	20.1
May	30.2	2.1	Nov	25.5	3.0
Jun	30.3	45.3	Dec	24.2	0.1

(i) Calculate the mean annual temperature.

(ii) What is the total rainfall during the monsoon season?

(iii) Does the station have a maritime or a continental climate? Give a reason for your answer.

Ans. (i) The mean annual temperature

$$= \frac{\text{Sum of all observations}}{\text{No. of observations}} = \frac{339}{12}$$

= is 28.25° C

(ii) The total rainfall during the monsoon season (June to October) is 200.6 cm.

(iii) The station has a maritime type of climate because it has less temperature variation (from 30.4°C to 23.8°C).

7. Study the climatic data given below and answer the questions that follow [2011]

Month	Temp. °C	Rainfall cm	Month	Temp. °C	Rainfall cm
Jan	24.5	4.6	Jul	31.0	8.7
Feb	25.7	1.8	Aug	30.2	11.3
Mar	27.7	1.3	Sep	29.8	11.9
Apr	20.4	1.8	Oct	28.0	30.6
May	30.0	3.8	Nov	25.9	35.0
Jun	32.5	4.5	Dec	24.7	13.9

(i) Name the driest month.

(ii) Calculate the annual rainfall experienced by the station.

(iii) What is the annual range of temperature?

Ans. (i) The driest month is March (1.3 cm).

(ii) The annual rainfall experienced by the station is 4.6 + 1.8 + 1.3 + 1.8 + 3.8 + 4.5 + 8.7 + 11.3 + 11.9 + 30.6 + 35.0 + 13.9 = 129.2 cm.

(iii) The annual range of temperature is 20.4 to 32.5°C-20.4°C = 12.1°C.

8. Study the following climatic data and answer the questions that follow

Month	Temp. °C	Rainfall cm	Month	Temp. °C	Rainfall cm
Jan	14.4	2.5	Jul	30.3	19.3
Feb	16.7	1.5	Aug	29.4	17.8
Mar	23.3	1.3	Sep	28.9	11.9
Apr	30.0	1.0	Oct	25.6	1.3
May	33.2	1.8	Nov	19.4	0.2
Jun	33.3	7.4	Dec	15.6	1.0

(i) Name the rainiest month of the year. How much is the rainfall in this month?
(ii) What is the annual range of temperature here?
(iii) Name the hottest month and write the temperature.

Ans. (i) The rainiest month of the year is July. The rainfall in this month is 19.3 cm.
(ii) The annual range of temperature is
33.3° C – 14.4° C
= 18.9° C
(iii) The hottest month of the year is June and the temperature is 33.3° C.

9. Given below is the climatic data of a station. Study the table and answer the questions that follow

Month	Temp. °C	Rainfall cm	Month	Temp. °C	Rainfall cm
Jan	24.5	4.6	Jul	31.0	8.7
Feb	25.7	1.3	Aug	30.2	11.3
Mar	27.7	1.3	Sep	29.8	11.9
Apr	20.4	1.8	Oct	28.0	30.6
May	30.0	3.8	Nov	25.9	30.5
Jun	32.5	4.5	Dec	24.7	13.9

(i) Calculate the annual rainfall experienced by the station.
(ii) What is the annual range of temperature?
(iii) Name the wettest month.

Ans. (i) Annual rainfall experienced by the station
= 4.6 + 1.3 + 1.3 + 1.8 + 3.8 + 4.5 + 8.7 + 11.3 + 11.9 + 30.6 + 30.5 + 13.9 = 124.2 cm.
(ii) The annual range of temperature is
= 32.5 °C –20.4 °C
= 12.1° C
(iii) The wettest month is October with the highest rainfall 30.6 cm.

10. Study the climate data of Station X and answer the questions that follow

Month	Temp. in °C	Rainfall (cms)
Jan	21.0	5.1
Feb	21.9	2.8
Mar	24.2	1.2
Apr	27.2	1.7
May	28.0	3.8
Jun	26.4	4.6
Jul	26.1	8.4
Aug	25.4	11.4
Sep	26.0	11.9
Oct	26.0	31.5
Nov	23.8	34.5
Dec	21.2	14.8

(i) Calculate the annual range of temperature of Station X.
(ii) Name the wind that brings most of the rainfall to this station.
(iii) On which coast of India is Station X located ?

Ans. (i) The annual range of temperature is
28.0 – 21.0 = 7 °C.
(ii) North-East monsoon (iii) Tamil Nadu

11. Study the climatic data given below and answer the questions that follow [2020]

Month	Temp. in °C	Rainfall cm
Jan	8.4	1.5
Feb	11.5	0.9
Mar	21.6	0.5
Apr	28.3	–
May	35.1	–
Jun	38.5	12.5
Jul	41.0	17.8
Aug	38.0	18.5
Sep	30.8	12.5
Oct	29.2	12.5
Nov	15.6	6.2
Dec	10.2	2.1

(i) Calculate the annual range of temperature.
(ii) State whether the station is located in the coastal area or in the continental interior.
(iii) Name the wind that brings most of the rainfall to this area.

Ans. (i) The annual range of temperature is 41.0- 8.4 = 32.6°C.
(ii) The station is located in the continental interior due to having long range of temperature.
(iii) The wind that brings most of the rainfall to this area is South-west monsoon winds as most of the rainfall occur from June to September which is a period of South-west monsoon season.

Chapter Assessment

Section-I

Multiple Choice Questions

1. Which of the following wind blows from the Mediterranean Sea to the North-Western parts of India?
   (a) Western disturbances (b) Norwesters
   (c) Loo (d) Mango showers
2. The average annual temperature of a meteorological station is 26°C. Its average annual rainfall is 63 cm and the annual range of temperature is 9°C. The station in the question is.............. .
   (a) Allahabad (b) Chennai
   (c) Cherrapunji (d) Kolkata
3. The retreating monsoon withdraws itself from
   (a) the West coast to the East coast
   (b) North-east India to the West coast
   (c) the North to the South
   (d) North-west India to Bengal and then to Kerala.
4. Which of the following factors does not have influence on the Indian climate?
   (a) Presence of Indian Ocean (b) Nearness to Equator
   (c) Ocean currents (d) Monsoons
5. Which of the following is recognised as a season by the meteorological department of India?
   (a) Cold weather (b) Hot weather
   (c) Retreating monsoon (d) North-East monsoon

Section-II

Short Questions

1. Why is Chennai warmer in December than Delhi?
2. The Northern Plains experience what kind of climate?
3. What are the pressure conditions and wind directions during the hot weather season in India?
4. State two characteristic of the retreating monsoon.
5. Which state receive the maximum rainfall in winter season and why?
6. What is the duration of the monsoon season in Western Rajasthan?
7. In which season does the heat belt shift Northwards.
8. October heat is the main phenomenon of which season?

Long Questions

1. What is windward side? Define.
2. How do Himalayas act as 'climate divide'?
3. Briefly explain how does relief affect the climate of India?
4. What is retreating monsoon and name any two months associated with them? Normally by what date does the monsoon advance into Kerala?

CHAPTER

05

Soil Resources

SYLLABUS

Soil Resources Types of Soil (alluvial, black, red and laterite) distribution, composition and characteristics such as colour, texture, minerals and crops associated.
Soil Erosion Causes, Prevention and Conservation.

Soil can be simply defined as a mixture of small rock particles and organic materials like humus. It develops the topmost layer on the Earth's surface and support growth of plants. Agricultural production depends on the fertility of soil because if soils are fertile, production is more and such areas support a high density of population.

Types of Soil in India

The Indian Council of Agricultural Research (ICAR) has divided the soils found in India into major groups which are

Alluvial Soil

This soil is formed by deposition of very fine particles of soil called alluvium by three important Himalayan river systems i.e. the Indus, the Ganga and the Brahmaputra. Alluvial soil is also known as **riverine soil** because it is mainly found in the river basins. This soil is highly fertile. It is ex-situ or transported soil, as the soil has been transported by the rivers to its current location.

Characteristics of Alluvial Soil

- **Colour** The colour of this soil varies from light grey to ash grey, depending on the depth of deposition, texture of material and time taken for attaining maturity.
- **Texture** The alluvial soils found in the Upper Ganga Valley are dry, porous, sandy, faint yellow which contain clay and organic matter. On the other hand, the alluvial soils of lower Ganga Valley, West Bengal and Bangladesh are more compact, less coarse and more moist.
- **Minerals** This soil is fertile due to having minerals like potash, lime, but is deficient in nitrogen and humus. The alluvial soils of the Ganga deltaic region are rich in humus contents.
- **Composition** Alluvial soil is made up of a mixture of silt, sand and clay which are collectively known as loams. It is more loamy and clayey in lower and middle Ganga valley and Brahmaputra valley. The sand content decreases in this soil from West to East.
- **Crops Associated** Alluvial soil is good for most of the crops (Kharif and Rabi) like rice, wheat, sugarcane, cotton, jute, oilseeds, pulses, etc.

Types of Alluvial Soils

Alluvial soils are classified into two types on the basis of their age which are

(i) **Bhangar** The older alluvial soil, found above the flood level of rivers is known as bhangar. It contains higher concentration of kankar nodules. It presents a terrace-like structure and covers large parts of the North Indian plains. It is clayey and non-porous.

(ii) **Khadar** The newer alluvial soil near the river is known as khadar. It is finer in texture. It is found in the lower levels in the plains near the rivers. It is loamy (smooth) and porous soil. It is more fertile than bhangar as new layers of this soil are deposited year after year during monsoonal floods.

Difference between Khadar and Bhangar

Bhangar	Khadar
This is old alluvial soil.	This is newer alluvial soil.
This soil is found far from the river basins.	This soil is found close to the river basins.
This soil is less fertile and therefore, not suitable for agriculture.	This soil is very fertile and therefore, very suitable for agriculture.

Distribution of Alluvial Soil

- **Inland Alluvium** This type of alluvial soil is found on the plains of the Ganga, the Brahmaputra and the Indus river, extending from Punjab and Sindh (Pakistan) to Bangladesh and Assam (India). It is also found in Uttarakhand, Uttar Pradesh, Bihar, West Bengal, Punjab, Haryana and in some parts of Gujarat and Rajasthan.
- **Deltaic Alluvium** This type of alluvial soil is found in the deltas of the Mahanadi, Godavari, Ganga-Brahmaputra, Krishna and Kaveri rivers.
- **Coastal Alluvium** This type of alluvial soil is tidal in origin and is found in the coastal strips of Peninsular India. It is also found in the plains region of Gujarat.

Black Soil

This soil is also known as **regur soil or black cotton soil.** It is formed after solidification of molten lava during volcanic activity, thus it is also known as lava soil. It is **in situ**[1] or residual soil.

Characteristics of Black Soil

- **Colour** This soil is deep black, medium black or dark brown in colour because it is volcanic in origin.
- **Texture** This soil is fine textured and clayey in nature. It develops deep cracks during hot summer, which helps in **aeration**[2] of the soil, but it becomes sticky (due to high moisture retention) when it is in wet condition. It has self ploughing quality and holds moisture when becomes wet.
- **Minerals and Composition** This soil is rich and composed of minerals like lime, potash, iron, magnesia and alumina but it lack in phosphorus, nitrogen and organic matter.
- **Crops Associated** Cotton, sugarcane, groundnut, millets, rice, wheat, oilseeds, cereals, citrus fruits, vegetables and tobacco are the important crops that grow well in this soil.

Distribution of Black Soil

It is found in the Deccan trap (Basalt lava region) and covers the plateau areas of Gujarat, Maharashtra, Malwa of Madhya Pradesh, parts of Andhra Pradesh, Northern Karnataka, Rajasthan and some parts of Tamil Nadu. It is also found along the valleys of the Godavari and Krishna rivers.

Red Soil

This soil is formed due to weathering of old crystalline rocks like igneous and metamorphic rocks in the areas of low rainfall. Red soils differ from place to place on the basis of the parental rocks and climatic conditions. It is not fertile and thus, need fertilisers and irrigation support.

Characteristics of Red Soil

- **Colour** This soil is red, yellow, brown and reddish in colour. The red colour of this soil is due to the diffusion of iron particles into crystalline and metamorphic rocks. It looks yellow when it is in the hydrated form.
- **Texture** This soil is more sandy and less clayey. It is porous and has friable (dry) structure. It is slightly acidic. Its pH value generally ranges from 6.6 to 8.0. It does not retain moisture. Soil aggregates (kankars) are absent in the soils.
- **Minerals and Composition** This soil is rich and composed of minerals like iron, magnesium and potash but it lacks in nitrogen, phosphorus and humus.
- **Crops Associated** Wheat, rice, millet, gram, sugarcane, groundnut, coconut, ragi, oilseeds, pulses and cotton are the important crops grown in this soil. Red soil is ideal for dry farming as it does not require much moisture.

1 **In-situ** It refers to the original place.

2 **Aeration** It involves entering the soil with small holes to allow air, water and nutrients to penetrate the grass roots.

Types of Red Soil

Red soil is classified into three types which are

(i) **Red Loamy Soil** These are dark red in colour and loamy in texture.

(ii) **Red Gravelly Soil** These are dark red and gravelly (consisting of gravels) in texture.

(iii) **Mixed Red and Black Soil** These soils are found in areas that integrate into black soil regions.

Distribution of Red Soil

It is found in low rainfall areas of the Deccan plateau (Eastern and Southern parts). It is thus found in parts of Tamil Nadu, Odisha, Madhya Pradesh, Karnataka, Maharashtra, Andhra Pradesh, the Chota Nagpur plateau areas of Chhattisgarh and Jharkhand, Bundelkhand, Meghalaya, Mizoram, Manipur, Telangana and Nagaland. It is also found in some districts of West Bengal, Uttar Pradesh and Rajasthan.

Laterite or Lateritic Soil

The word 'Laterite' has been derived from the Latin word 'Later' which means 'brick'. Laterite soil is a residual soil, formed as a result of intense leaching due to tropical rainfall. It develops in areas of high temperature and heavy rainfall. It can be made cultivable with adequate amounts of manure and chemical fertilizers.

Characteristics of Laterite Soil

- **Colour** The soil is compact, reddish or yellowish-red in colour and turns black on exposure to the Sun.
- **Texture** This soil is of coarse texture, soft and fragile. It becomes hard when exposed to air and suitable for construction purpose. It is not capable of retaining moisture due to its acidic nature.
- **Minerals and Composition** This soil is rich and composed of minerals like iron-oxide, aluminium and potash but it lacks in phosphate, calcium, nitrogen and organic matter.
- **Crops Associated** Tea, coffee, cashewnuts, rubber, coconut, rice, ragi sugarcane are the important crops grown in this soil.

Types of Laterite Soil

Laterite soil is of two types

(i) **Upland Laterites** These soils are formed over the hilly areas or uplands.

(ii) **Lowland Laterites** These soils are transported by streams from hilly areas (uplands) to lower areas (lowlands).

Distribution of Laterite Soil

This soil is found in the areas of Peninsular plateaus i.e. Eastern and Western Ghats, Rajmala hill and many other hilly areas of Eastern part of Peninsula. It is also found in Odisha, Karnataka, Kerala, Tamil Nadu, Madhya Pradesh, Andhra Pradesh, Maharashtra, West Bengal, Telangana, etc.

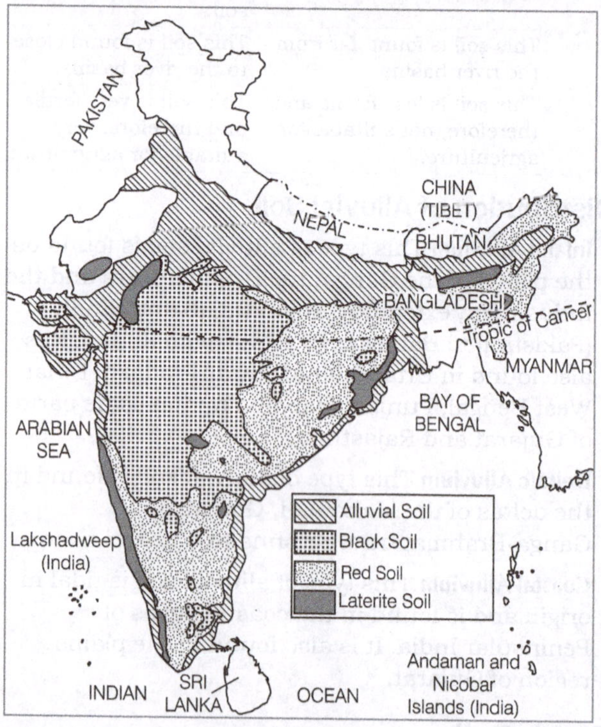

Soils in India

Check Your LEARNING...

1. What is the composition of alluvial soil?
2. Mention the other name of black soil.
3. Which soil is formed due to weathering of crystalline rocks?
4. Name the soil formed due to high temperature and heavy rainfall.

Soil Erosion

Soil erosion is the removal of top layer of soil by the forces of nature, particularly wind and water and human activities. e.g. deforestation, over-grazing, faulty agricultural practices, construction, mining, dumping of chemicals and waste materials on land, etc.

The top layer of soil is very rich in nutrients and it is fertile. When this top layer is removed by soil erosion, it becomes unfit for the growth of crops, plants, trees and vegetation.

Problems caused by soil erosion are

- Loss of valuable top soil
- Damage to fields
- Fall in plant productivity
- Desertification
- Land infertility
- Leads to devastating floods
- Land degradation
- Reduce in level of groundwater

Natural Causes of Soil Erosion

Water Erosion

Water erosion takes place in different forms such as

- **Sheet Erosion** Sometimes water flows as a sheet over large areas down a slope. In such cases, the top soil is washed away. This is known as sheet erosion.
- **Rill Erosion** It is the removal of soil by concentrated water running through small channels and making finger-shaped **rills**[3] and **grooves**[4] on the land surface. Rills are created when sheet erosion continues for long time.
- **Gully Erosion** When heavy rainfall takes place, deep gullies (deep channels) are formed on bare soils due to surface water run-off. Gullies are formed on extensive areas which turn the whole areas into **bad land**[5] topography. This type of erosion removes nutrients from the soils and make them improductive. Sandy soils are more prone to formation of gullies, e.g. **ravines**[6] of Yamuna and Chambal basin have been formed in this manner.
- **Bank Erosion** In this type of erosion, the continuously flowing water erodes the banks of streams and rivers, e.g. the flood plains of Ganga, Yamuna and other rivers. This type of erosion can be seen in Uttar Pradesh, Madhya Pradesh, Rajasthan, etc.
- **Seashore Erosion or Littoral Erosion** In this type of erosion, tidal water of sea cause considerable damage to the soil along the sea coast. The powerful waves strikes against sea-coast and break hanging **cliff**[7] rocks which is then removed by the retreating sea waves. This type of erosion is seen throughout the Eastern and Western Coasts of India.
- **Leaching** It is the loss of soluble substances from the top layer of the soil by precipitation. Farmers leave the soils bare for some time, after harvesting the crop. During rainfall, the nutrients in the top soil are leached or washed out into lower sub-soil.

Wind Erosion

It refers to the movement and deposition of soil particles by wind from one location to another. Wind erosion is active in arid and semi-arid areas which have less or no vegetation cover. It is common in Rajasthan and the adjoining areas of Haryana, Punjab and Gujarat.

There are three types of wind erosion

(i) **Surface Creep** It involves rolling and moving of large soil particles (0.5 mm to 2 mm in diameter) across the surface.

(ii) **Saltation** It involves rolling and moving of middle-sized soil particles (0.05 mm to 0.5 mm in diameter) off the surface.

(iii) **Suspension** It involves rolling and moving of tiny soil particles (less than 0.1 mm in diameter) which include fine grains of sand, clay particles and organic matter.

Human Causes of Soil Erosion

Human interferences lead to soil erosion in a variety of ways which are

Faulty Practices of Farming

Most of the soil erosion in India is caused by faulty practices of farming which are

- **Faulty Ploughing** If the fields are ploughed along the slope, there is no obstruction to the flow of water and the water washes away the top soil easily. In some parts of the country, the same crop is grown in a repeated manner which spoils the chemical balance of the soil. Thus, soil is exhausted and is easily eroded by wind or water.

---

3 **Rill** It is a small stream.

4 **Groove** It is a long deep line that is cut in the surface of something.

5 **Badland** A land which is unfit for cultivation.

6 **Ravine** Cutting of a gully bed into the soil with a drop of 3 to 4 metres and becomes flattened is known as ravine.

7 **Cliff** It is a high area of rock with a very steep side, often on a coast.

- **Lack of Mulching** Mulching is the process of covering the top soil with plant material such as leaves, grass, etc. It provides protection against splash erosion, restrict the velocity of run off and helps to keep the soil particles bound together and retain moisture.

  However this process is not practiced in most parts of India due to the use of **agricultural residue**[8] as fuel and high incidence of multiple cropping. Therefore, the soils are more exposed to erosion by running water as well as wind.

Overgrazing

The continous grazing by animals on the same piece of land without sufficient recovery periods is known as overgrazing. It leads to the removal of plant cover on a large-scale and becomes open to erosion by wind and water. The grazing animals also demolish the soil by the hoofs and teeth. Thus, the soil loosened and easily washed away when heavy showers take place.

Erosion due to overgrazing is very common over the hilly areas of Madhya Pradesh, Himachal Pradesh, Jammu and Kashmir and in arid and semi-arid areas of Rajasthan, Maharashtra, Karnataka and Andhra Pradesh.

Deforestation

The cutting down of forests on a large scale which leaves an open and exposed landscape also lead to soil erosion. It cause leaching or flash floods. Deforestation is caused by constructional activities by men, e.g. construction of roads, railway lines, buildings and agricultural practices which cause sheet, rill or gully erosion.

Soil Conservation

Soil Conservation is a method to maintain soil fertility, prevent soil erosion and exhaustion and improve the degraded condition of the soil. There is a need to conserve soil due to the following reasons

- Loss of top layer of soil led to loss of mineral nutrient that are necessary for agricultural productivity and soil fertility.
- Soil conservation is needed to lower the underground water table and decreasing soil moisture.
- Soil erosion increase the frequency of droughts and floods and recurrence of landslides, thus soil conservation is needed.

Methods for Prevention of Soil Erosion

Farming Methods that Reduce Soil Erosion

- **Strip Cropping** It is a method of farming in which large fields can be divided into strips and strips of grass are left to grow between the crops. This breaks up the force of the wind and the strips soak up the rainwater and keep the water run off slow.
- **Contour Tillage or Cropping** It is the practice of ploughing the field in which crops are planted in curving rows to follow the contour of hills. It leads to formation of ridges and **furrow**[9] against the direction of flow of water. The furrows stop the flow of water and encourage **percolation**[10] in the soil.
- **Shelter Belts** In this method, rows of trees are planted between the fields which slow down the wind and reduce wind erosion.
- **Terrace Farming** In this farming method, step-like terraces are built on slopes. They prevent the soil from being washed away by running water.
- **Stone Walls or Bunds** In this method, low stone walls are built along the contour of a hill. These walls hold water and allow it to reach into the soil rather than flowing downhill.
- **Crop Rotation** It is a farming method in which a systematic succession of different crops is grown on the same piece of land. This retains soil fertility and provides soil cover.
- **Plugging Gullies** During heavy rains, the gullies made in the soil are plugged (obstructed) with deposition of silt which prevents the soil erosion.

Controlled Overgrazing and Afforestation

There should be controlled grazing on the same land and there are separate lands where pastures should be grown extensively. Afforestation should be adopted as planting trees will reduce the intensity of water run off which is responsible for soil erosion.

8 **Agricultural Residue** Remains of plants when the grains have been removed from them.
9 **Furrow** A long, narrow ditch made in the ground by a plough, especially for irrigation.
10 **Percolation** The movement of water through the soil or underlying porous rock.

It increases the seepage of water to the underground water-table. Forests can be grown along the banks of rivers, canals, lakes, roads and railway tracks to overcome the problem of soil erosion.

Reclamation of Saline and Alkaline Soils

Some of the steps which can be taken to overcome the problem of **salinity**[11] and **alkalinity**[12] of soil, are levelling of land, drainage improvement, optimum irrigation, flushing (remove or clean) the salts by flooding the fields and plantation of salt tolerant vegetation and crops such as cotton, barley, date, palm, rapeseed and fodder crops.

Flood Control and Construction of Dams

Flood is a major factor which cause soil erosion on a large-scale in India. Therefore, efforts should be made for the storage of flood water and diversion of additional rainwater. Soil erosion is caused by the flow of rivers. Thus, to control this phenomenon, dams should be built in the upper course of rivers.

Soil Conservation Schemes

In India, the government has taken special conservation measures for soil. Some of these are

- Scheme of Integrated Watershed Management
- Scheme for Reclamation and development of ravine areas (Madhya Pradesh, Uttar Pradesh and Rajasthan)
- Scheme for control of shifting cultivation.
- National Project on Development and Use of Bio-Fertilizers
- Rainwater Harvesting.

Check Your LEARNING...

1. What is the meaning of sheet erosion?
2. Which process helps in reducing soil erosion by using plant residue?
3. Mention any one reason for the need to conserve soil.
4. What is crop rotation?

QUiCK Revision

- Soil is a non-renewable natural resource that supports all life forms on the Earth.
- Soil formation is a very long process, begins with the weathering of rocks into small fragments, with the help of various erosional agents like river, wind, sea and glacier.
- Factors that help to form soil are parent material, climate, living organisms and topography.
- According to Indian Council of Agricultural Research (ICAR) the soils of India are grouped as alluvial soils, black soils, red soils, laterite soils, forest or mountain soils and arid soils.
- Alluvial soils are the most widespread soil in India. This soil has been deposited by Himalayan rivers. This soil is very fertile for growing paddy, wheat, sugarcane, cotton, jute, oilseeds and other crops.
- Black soil is also known as black cotton soil or regur soil. It is formed after solidification of molten lava during volcanic activity. It is good for cotton, sugarcane groundnut, millets and so on.
- Red and yellow soils are formed due to old crystalline rocks like igneous and metamorphic rocks in the areas of low rainfall. It is good for wheat, rice, millets, gram, etc.
- Laterite soils mainly known as brick soil due to its colour which is red because of high iron content. It is good for tea, coffee, cashewnuts, rubber, etc.
- Soil erosion takes place after the action of various natural agents such as water, wind (natural processes) and overgrazing, faulty practices of farming and deforestation (human factors).
- Soil erosion removes top layer of soil which makes it unfit for cultivation and pasture land.
- There is a need for soil conservation which can be possible by various soil conservation methods such as adopting appropriate farming method, Plugging Gullies, controlled overgrazing, afforestation, reclamation of saline and alkaline soils, flood control and construction of dams. Government has also introduced some soil conservation schemes.

11 **Salinity** It refers to the amount of dissolved salts that are present in water or soil.

12 **Alkalinity** It is a measurement of dissolved alkaline substances in water or soil.

Chapter Practice

Section-I

Multiple Choice Questions

1. The soil is a mixture of sand, clay and silt which is collectively known as ....
   (a) desert (b) clayey
   (c) sandy (d) loamy

Ans. (d) loamy

2. Khadar is more fertile than Bhangar
   (a) presence of micro-organisms.
   (b) presence of vegetation cover.
   (c) new layers are deposited year after year during monsoonal floods.
   (d) due to huge erosion.

Ans. (c) new layers are deposited year after year during monsoonal floods.

3. Which of the following crops is/are suitable for growing on black soil?
   (a) Cotton (b) Wheat
   (c) Gram (d) All of these

Ans. (d) All of these

4. Which of the following types of soil have a marked capacity to retain water?
   (a) Desert soil (b)Red soil
   (c) Laterite soil (d) Regur soil

Ans. (d) Regur soil

5. Which of the following soil is most suitable for the cultivation of cotton and sugarcane? **[Specimen Paper Semester-I 2022]**
   (a) Laterite soil (b) Black soil
   (c) Red soil (d) Alluvial Soil

Ans. (b) Black soil

6. What is the main reason for the red colour of red soil? **[Specimen Paper Semester-I 2022]**
   (a) Abundance of magnesium
   (b) Accumulated humus
   (c) Presence of ferric oxides
   (d) Abundance of phosphates

Ans. (c) Presence of ferric oxides

7. Which of the following factor is responsible for acidic nature of laterite soil? **[Specimen Paper Semester-I 2022]**
   (a) As it is friable in nature.
   (b) As it can retain moisture.
   (c) As the bases leached down from the top soil.
   (d) All the above

Ans. (c) As the bases leached down from the top soil.

8. Under which climatic conditions does the laterite soil develop?
   (a) Wet tropical climate
   (b) Hot and dry climate
   (c) Cold temperature climate
   (d) Mediterranean type of climate

Ans. (a) Wet tropical climate

9. Favourable conditions for the formation of laterite soil are
   (a) high temperature and heavy rainfall.
   (b) low temperature and heavy rainfall.
   (c) low temperature and low rainfall.
   (d) high temperature and low rainfall.

Ans. (a) high temperature and heavy rainfall.

10. Which is the most widespread soil of India ? **[2023]**
   (a) Red soil (b) Alluvial soil
   (c) Laterite soil (d) Black soil

Ans. (b) Alluvial soil

11. The causes of desertification are
   (a) overgrazing (b) deforestation
   (c) over cultivation (d) All of these

Ans. (d) All of these

12. Name the process of removal of soluble mineral salts, especially the bases and silica from horizon A or the top soil by percolating rain water. **[Specimen Paper Semester-I 2022]**
   (a) Pedogenesis (b) Leaching
   (c) Lithification (d) Conglomeration

Ans. (b) Leaching

13. Advantages of organic manure are
   (a) it binds the soil.
   (b) it improves the water-holding capacity of soil.
   (c) Both (a) and (b)
   (d) it binds the soil, but decreases its water retention capacity.

Ans. (c) Both (a) and (b)

14. Which of the following is not a cause of soil erosion?
   (a) Drainage (b) Deforestation
   (c) Weathering (d) Grazing

Ans. (c) Weathering

15. Afforestation prevents soil erosion because **[Specimen Paper Semester-I 2022]**
   (a) it reduces pollution.
   (b) it protects the soil from being exposed.
   (c) the roots of the trees bind the soil particles.
   (d) trees produce fruits.

Ans. (c) the roots of the trees bind the soil particles

16. Choose the correct statement regarding the characteristics of alluvial soil.
(a) The soil is immature and has weak profile due to its recent origin.
(b) The soil is porous.
(c) This soil is constantly replenished by the recurrent floods.
(d) All of the above

Ans. (d) All of the above

17. Give reason for the following.
Wind erosion is active in arid and semi arid area.
(a) The area is full of vegetation
(b) The area is devoid of vegetation cover.
(c) The wind speed increase here with increasing slope
(d) Due to the earth rotation.

Ans. (b) The area is devoid of vegetation cover.

18. Give reason for the following.
Mulching is the important for soil.
(a) It provides protection against splash erosion.
(b) It provides fertility to the soil.
(c) It doesn't restrict the velocity of run-off.
(d) It helps to keep the roosts bound together.

Ans. (a) It provides protection against splash erosion.

19. Give reason for the following.
Soil degradation takes place in irrigated cultivated land in India
(a) because of silting of land
(b) because of gully erosion
(c) because of alkalisation and salinity of soil
(d) because of wind erosion

Ans. (c) because of alkalisation and salinity of soil

20. Which of the following is/are not the characteristics of red soil?
(i) It is derived from weathering of old crystalline and metamorphic rocks.
(ii) It contain iron oxides.
(iii) It has high water retention capacity.
(iv) It has high nitrogen content.

Codes
(a) (i) and (ii) (b) Only (ii)
(c) Only (iv) (d) (iii) and (iv)

Ans. (d) (iii) and (iv)

21. Match the following.

	Term		Definition
A.	Ravine	1.	A land unfit for cultivation
B.	Abrasion	2.	Cutting of gully beds
C.	Badland	3.	The wearing down of rocks
D.	In-situ	4.	Natural Place

Codes

	A	B	C	D		A	B	C	D
(a)	4	3	2	1	(b)	1	2	3	4
(c)	2	3	1	4	(d)	4	1	2	3

Ans. (c)

22. Match the following.

	Soil		Major Crops
A.	Alluvial	1.	Cotton, sugarcane
B.	Black Soil	2.	Rice and wheat
C.	Red and yellow soil	3.	Millet, gram
D.	Laterite	4.	Tea, coffee

Codes

	A	B	C	D		A	B	C	D
(a)	4	3	2	1	(b)	1	2	3	4
(c)	2	3	1	4	(d)	4	1	2	3

Ans. (d)

23. Match the following.

	Soil		Major Crops
A.	Alluvial	1.	Deccan Trap
B.	Black Soil	2.	Southern India
C.	Red Soil	3.	Low rainfall areas of Deccan Trap
D.	Laterite	4.	Northern Plains

Codes

	A	B	C	D		A	B	C	D
(a)	4	1	3	2	(b)	1	2	4	3
(c)	2	3	1	4	(d)	2	1	3	4

Ans. (a)

24. Study the map and answer the following questions **[Specimen Paper Semester-II 2022]**

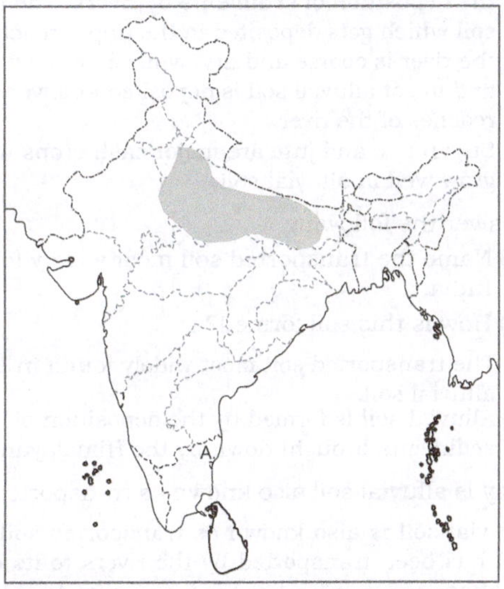

(i) Which soil is found in the shaded region?
(a) Black soil (b) Alluvial soil
(c) Red soil (d) Laterite soil

Ans. (b) Alluvial soil

(ii) How is this type of soil formed?
(a) Formed by the deposition of silt brought down by rivers.
(b) Formed by weathering of alluvium.

Ans. (a) Formed by the deposition of silt brought down by rivers.

Section-II

Short Questions

1. Define soil.

Ans. Soil can be simply defined as a mixture of small rock particles and organic materials/humus which develops on the Earth's surface and support growth of plants.

2. How is soil important for us?

Ans. Soil is important for us in the following ways

- Soil is the most important renewable natural resource and a living system which supports many types of living organisms.
- Only a productive soil base can ensure prosperous agriculture which in turn forms the basis of economic advancement and a higher standard of living in a society.

3. State an important feature of soil formation.

Ans. An important feature of soil formation is that it is a time taking process which takes millions of years to be formed or replenished.

4. Answer the following.
   (i) Why does alluvial soil differ in texture? [2018]
   (ii) State two cash crops that grow well in alluvial soil.

Ans. (i) Alluvial soil differs in texture, as it is formed by the deposition of sediments by rivers. The alluvial soil which gets deposited in the upper reaches of the river is coarse and dry, while extremely fine and moist alluvial soil is deposited at lower reaches of the river.
(ii) Sugarcane and jute are major cash crops which grow well in alluvial soil.

5. Answer the following.
   (i) Name the transported soil most widely found in India.
   (ii) How is this soil formed?

Ans. (i) The transported soil most widely found in India is alluvial soil.
(ii) Alluvial soil is formed by the deposition of sediments brought down by the Himalayan rivers.

6. Why is alluvial soil also known as transported soil?

Ans. Alluvial soil is also known as transported soil as the soil has been transported by the rivers to its current location.

7. State two differences between Bhangar and Khadar. [2013]

Ans. The differences between Bhangar and Khadar are

Bhangar	Khadar
This is old Alluvial soil	This is new Alluvial soil.
This soil is found far from the river basins.	This soil is found close to the river basins.

8. Name the following. [2020]
   (i) A soil that occurs in-situ and is good for cotton crop due to high temperature and heavy rainfall.
   (ii) Soil that is formed with reference to alluvial Soil.

Ans. (i) Black soil is the soil that occurs in-situ and is good for cotton crop. It is due to high temperature and heavy rainfall.
(ii) Khadar soil is formed with reference to Alluvial Soil.

9. Mention two differences between alluvial soil and black cotton soil. [2017]

Ans. Two differences between alluvial soil and black cotton soil are

Alluvial Soil	Black Soil
Alluvial soil is coarse in nature and contain kankar, pebbles and gravels.	Black cotton soil is fine grained in texture with more than 60% clay. They do not contain gravel or sand.
Alluvial soil is very fertile.	Black soil is less fertile in uplands.

10. Answer the following.
    (i) How is black soil formed?
    (ii) Name one cash crop for which black soil is most suited.

Ans. (i) Black soil is formed by the weathering of igneous rocks which are made by volcanic lava.
(ii) Black soil is most suited for cotton cultivation.

11. Mention any two characteristics of black soil. [2023]

Ans. The two characteristics of black soil are
(i) It has been formed by weathering of the parent rock material found in Deccan Plateau i.e. igneous rocks and is called Regur soil.
(ii) It is made up of extremely fine particles i.e. clayey material.

12. Answer the following.
    (i) Name the soil which is formed due to the weathering of basic igneous rocks.
    (ii) Name two states of India where this type of soil is found. [2019]

Ans. (i) Black soil has been formed by weathering of basic igneous rocks.
(ii) Black soil is found in the Deccan trap (Basalt lava region) and covers the plateau areas of Saurastrian Gujarat, Maharashtra, Malwa of Madhya Pradesh, parts of Andhra Pradesh, Northern Karnataka, parts of Tamil Nadu, Chhattisgarh and also along the valleys of the Godavari and Krishna rivers.

13. Name two states in India where regur soil is found. In what way does regur soil help agriculture? [2011]

Ans. Black soil is also called regur soil and it is found in the states of Gujarat and Maharashtra.

Regur soil help in agriculture as it is rich in minerals. It supports the growth of cotton cultivation and also suitable for sugarcane cultivation.

14. State the characteristic of each of the soils named below that makes them most suitable for crop cultivation. [2015]
(i) Black soil (ii) Red soil

Ans. (i) **Black Soil** It is suitable for the cultivation of cotton as it is rich in calcium carbonate, magnesium carbonate, potash and lime.
(ii) **Red Soil** It is suitable for the cultivation of wheat, rice, cotton and sugarcane as it is rich in iron and potash.

15. Answer the following.
(i) Name the parent rock that contributes to the formation of red soil. [2020]
(ii) How does this soil get its 'red' colour?

Ans. (i) Metamorphic rocks and old crystalline rocks are the most common parent materials that contribute to the formation of red soil.
(ii) The colour of the soil is red due to iron oxide content in it.

16. With reference to black soil answer the following. [2018]
(i) Name one imortant crop which grows in this soil.
(ii) Give one chemical property of this soil.

Ans. (i) The important crop which grows in black soil is cotton.
(ii) The chemical property of the black soil is that it is rich in calcium, potassium and magnesium.

17. Mention two main characteristics of laterite soil.

Ans. The characteristics of laterite soil are [2011]
(i) The soil is compact, reddish or yellowish-red in colour and turns black on exposure to the sun.
(ii) It is not capable of retaining moisture due to its acidic nature.

18. Mention any two differences between alluvial soil and red soil. [2014]

Ans. The differences between alluvial soil and red soil are

Alluvial Soil	Red Soil
This soil is very fertile due to the presence of minerals like lime, potash and humus.	This soil is less fertile as it lacks humus, lime and phosphorus.
This soil is transported soil.	This soil is in situ-soil.

19. Mention two similarities between red soil and laterite soil. [2016]

Ans. The similarities between red and laterite soils are
(i) Red soil and laterite soil have similar colour i.e. red, reddish yellow and brown.
(ii) Both red soil and laterite soil are not very fertile due to lack of humus.

20. State the geographic term for each of the following processes. [2015]
(i) The process by which soluble minerals dissolve in rainwater and percolate to the bottom, leaving the top soil infertile.
(ii) The process by which rainwater, flowing in definite paths, removes the top soil, thus, causing deep cuts to the surface of the land.

Ans. (i) Leaching (ii) Gully erosion

21. Name the following.
(i) An important transported soil of India.
(ii) Soil that is rich in iron oxide. [2019]

Ans. (i) Alluvial soil is an important transported soil of India.
(ii) Red soil is rich in iron oxide.

22. What is soil erosion? Mention two steps that could be taken to prevent soil erosion. [2016]

Ans. Soil erosion is the removal of top soil by different agents of weathering such as wind, water etc.
The contour bunding and afforestation are the two important measures to prevent soil erosion.

23. Name the process by which laterite soil is formed. What climatic conditions are responsible for its formation?

Ans. Laterite soil is formed due to the intensive leaching brought by heavy rains.
It is formed in regions having high temperature and heavy rainfall.

24. Name an area in India in which each of the following processes takes place. [2017]
(i) Sheet erosion (ii) Gully erosion

Ans. (i) **Sheet Erosion** Flood plains of Brahmaputra, Ganga, Kosi and Nilgiris.
(ii) **Gully Erosion** Chambal valley

25. State two methods of controlling the erosion of soil caused by running water. [2012]

Ans. Two methods of controlling the erosion of soil caused by running water are
(i) Soil erosion can be prevented by growing more trees and grass to bind the soil.
(ii) Plugging of gullies and ravines.

26. Explain two points to show that it is the human action that has caused massive soil erosion.

Ans. The two points which shows the human actions causing massive soil erosion are
(i) Faulty farming practices leads to removal of top soil.
(ii) Cutting of trees for shifting cultivation leads to soil erosion.

27. How does the lack of vegetation cover increase soil erosion?

Ans. Lack of vegetation cover exposes the landscape to running water and wind. Heavy rains and moving wind then wash away the top soil causing massive soil erosion.

28. What is soil conservation? How does re-afforestation help in soil conservation? **[2010]**

Ans. Soil Conservation is a method to maintain soil fertility, prevent soil erosion and exhaustion and improve the degraded condition of the soil.

Re-afforestation means replanting trees which have been cut down. For every tree that is cut, two trees are to be planted. Thus, in this way forest cover is increased and help in soil conservation.

29. State any two methods of controlling soil erosion. **[2014]**

Ans. Two methods of controlling soil erosion are

(i) **Strip Cropping** It is a method of farming in which large fields can be divided into strips and strips of grass are left to grow between the crops. This breaks up the force of the wind and the strips soak up the rainwater and keep the water run off slow.

(ii) **Afforestation** It refers to growing trees on open grounds to reduce the intensity of runoff and preventing soil erosion.

Long Questions

1. Differentiate between transported soil and in situ soil, quoting a suitable example for each. **[2013]**

Ans. Differences between transported soil and in situ soil are

Transported Soil	In situ Soil
This soil is found at places where they got transported by agents of erosion i.e. wind and rivers.	This soil is found at places where they are formed by disintegration and weathering of rocks.
It is found in river valleys.	It is found in Deccan trap.
It is very fertile as it is rich in humus and minerals	It is less fertile as it is poor in humus.

2. How is alluvial soil formed? Why is this soil agriculturally important?

Ans. Alluvial soil is formed by the sediments brought down by the rivers. The river deposit very fine silt called alluvium in their plains, during the course of their journey which starts from their source in the mountains and ending till its mouth.

Alluvial soil is agriculturally very important because it is a mixture of sand, clay and silt (loam) which makes it very fertile. It is rich in potash and lime. It is light and porous therefore, easily tillable. It is suitable for growing large variety of rabi and kharif crops.

3. State the difference between alluvial soils found in the lower coarses and the upper coarses of the rivers. **[2011]**

Ans. The differences between alluvial soils in the lower and upper caorses of the river are

Upper Coarse	Lower Coarse
It is finer in the lowest section. It is known as Khadar soil.	It is coarser i.e. particles bigger in size. It is known as Bhangar soil.
It is more moist and more compact.	It is dry, less compact.
It is more fertile than the upper coarse soil as new layers are deposited year after year during monsoonal floods.	It is less fertile than the soils of lower coarses.

4. Describe alluvial soil under the following heads.
(i) Formation (ii) Distribution (iii) Nutrients

Ans. (i) **Formation** Alluvial soil is made up of silt, sand and clay. It is deposited by three important Himalayan river systems i.e. the Indus, the Ganga and the Brahmaputra. It is bigger and coarser in the upper reaches of the river and becomes finer as the river flows down.

(ii) **Distribution** Alluvial soil is distributed along the river valleys of the Northern plains, strips in Gujarat, Rajasthan, Eastern Coastal Plains in the Delta region of Mahanadi, Godavari, Krishna, Kaveri and in the foothills of piedmant plains.

(iii) **Nutrients** Alluvial soil is rich in nutrients like potash, phosphoric acid and lime.

5. State three main characteristics of the alluvial soil found in the river deltas of the Indian Coasts.

Ans. Refer to chapter theory page no. 80.

6. Mention three differences in the alluvial soil of the Northern Plains and the alluvial soil of the Coastal Plains of India.

Ans. The differences between alluvial soil of the Northern plains and the alluvial soil of the Coastal plains are

Alluvial Soil of the Northern Plains	Alluvial Soil of the Coastal Plains
The Alluvial soil of the Northern Plains is formed due to the deposition of alluvium which is brought from the Himalayan region.	The Alluvial soil of the Coastal Plains is formed due to the deposition of alluvium brought mainly from the Deccan Trap region which is volcanic in origin.
The main rivers which deposit alluvium in this region are the Himalayan rivers i.e. Indus, Ganga and Brahmaputra rivers.	The main rivers which deposit alluvium in this region are the Peninsular rivers i.e. Godavari, Krishna, Narmada and Tapi rivers.
This soil is light in colour.	This soil is dark in colour.

7. Answer the following.
(i) What are the two types of Alluvial Soil?
(ii) Name an area where alluvial soil is found.
(iii) Name two crops that grow well in this soil. **[2020]**

Ans. (i) Alluvial soil can be classified into two groups on the basis of its age which are

- **Khadar** It is light in colour and is made up of newer deposits.
- **Bhangar** It is the older alluvium and is composed of lime nodules or kankar and its composition is clayey.

(ii) The entire Northern Plains including parts of Arunachal Pradesh, Assam, Bihar (almost entirely), Chandigarh, Delhi (almost entirely), Haryana, Himachal Pradesh, Madhya Pradesh, Punjab, Rajasthan, Uttarakhand, Uttar Pradesh and West Bengal are made of alluvial soil.

(iii) Two cash crops which grow well in alluvial soil are sugarcane and cotton.

8. Mention any three characteristics of black soil which makes the soil fertile. **[2012]**

Ans. The characteristics of black soil that make it fertile are

(i) Black soil is rich in lime, iron, potash, magnesium carbonate and calcium carbonate that is good for cotton crops.

(ii) It is made up of extremely fine clayey material that gives it a fine texture.

(iii) It has the capacity to hold or retain moisture that is useful for the crops.

9. Which geographical factors are responsible for the evolution of black soil? Why it is considered the most suitable for growing cotton?

Ans. Geographical factors which are responsible for the evolution/formation of black soil are temperature, rainfall and weathering of parent rock material i.e. volcanic rocks.

Black soil is considered the most suitable for growing crop because

- It has high capacity to hold moisture.
- It is rich in line, potash, iron, magnesium etc.
- It develops deep cracks during hot weather, which helps in the proper aeration of the soil.

10. Define the term 'leaching'. Why it is also an environmental concern?

Ans. In agriculture, leaching may refer to the loss of water soluble plant nutrients from the soil, due to rain and over irrigation. Leaching is an environmental concern also when it contributes to groundwater contamination. As water from rain, flooding or other sources seeps into the ground, it can dissolve chemicals and carry them into the underground water supply. As it removes vital nutrients and micronutrients from the soil, it causes potential deficiencies in crops.

11. Answer the following.

(i) State mineral composition of laterite soil.

(ii) How is red soil formed? State two reasons for low productivity of red soil.

(iii) State any three problems caused by soil erosion.

Ans. (i) Laterite soil is rich in iron, phosphate and aluminium compounds. Laterite soil is poor in silica, potash, nitrogen, magnesium, lime, organic matter and phosphoric acid.

(ii) Red soil is formed by the weathering of old crystalline and metamorphic rocks in the areas of low rainfall.

Reasons for low productivity of red soil are

(a) It is poor in phosphorus, lime, manganese, nitrogen and humus.

(b) It is more sandy so does not retain moisture.

(iii) Three problems caused by soil erosion are

(a) Loss of valuable top soil.

(b) Plant productivity declines.

(c) Land degradation occurs.

12. With reference to red soils in India, answer the following questions. **[2013]**

(i) Name two states where it is found.

(ii) State two advantages of this type of soil.

(iii) Mention two important crops grown in this soil.

Ans. (i) Red soil is found in Tamil Nadu and Karnataka.

(ii) Advantages of red soil are

(a) It has high iron oxide content and potash.

(b) It becomes productive with fertilisers.

(iii) Important crops grown in red soil are rice and sugarcane.

13. Give one geographical reason for each of the following. **[2018]**

(i) Red soil requires irrigation.

(ii) Afforestation prevents soil from getting eroded.

(iii) Laterite soil is red in colour.

Ans. (i) Red soil is a type of soil that develops in a warm, temperate, moist-climate and generally derived from crystalline rock. That is why red soil requires irrigation.

(ii) Trees reduce the rate of erosion by protecting the soil from the impact of rain. It also bind the soil to sloping land with their roots. Thus, afforestation prevents soil from getting eroded.

(iii) Laterite soil is made up of high level of iron oxides in the form of minerals like goethite and hematite. Thus, it appears red in colour.

14. Give a geographical reason for each of the following. **[2019]**

(i) Terrace farming is an ideal soil conservation method for hilly regions.

(ii) Dry farming is preferred in areas with red soil.

(iii) Wind is a common agent of soil erosion in arid regions.

Ans. (i) Terrace farming is an ideal soil conservation method for hilly regions because in this farming technique, step-like terraces are built on slopes which prevent water run off from rushing downhill and carrying away the soil.

(ii) Red soil is found in the low rainfall areas of India. Thus, dry farming is done in this soil because this farming does not need much water.

(iii) Wind erosion is active in arid and semi-arid areas which are devoid of vegetative cover. Soil erosion by wind is performed through wind picking up soil particles and carrying them away, and through abrasion. Soil erosion by wind is common in Rajasthan and the adjoining areas of Haryana, Punjab and Gujarat.

15. Name the soil [2023]
   (i) That is found on the summits of Eastern and Western Ghats.
   (ii) That is suitable for dry farming
   (iii) That varies in texture.

Ans. (i) Laterite soil (ii) Black soil (iii) Alluvial soil

16. Give a geographical reason for each of the following. [2023]
   (i) Terrace farming is an ideal soil conservation method for hilly areas.
   (ii) Khadar soils are preferred over Bhangar soils.
   (iii) Foothills of Himalayas have been affected by soil erosion.

Ans. (i) Terrace farming is an ideal soil conservation method for hilly areas as it prevents rain from washing away soil, hence preventing soil erosion. In terrace farming, a terrace is a piece of the sloped plane that is cut into a series of successively receding platforms, that resemble steps.
   (ii) Khadar soil is preferred over Bhangar because it is more fertile as it is replenished every year by floods.
   (iii) The foothills of Himalayas are prone to severe soil erosion because of the topography as well as inherent soil properties such as coarse texture, poor water holding capacity, surface stoniness, etc.

17. (i) Define the term 'Residual' soil. [2020]
   (ii) Name two crops that are grown on laterite soil.
   (iii) Name two important agents of soil erosion.

Ans. (i) Residual soil can be defined as a soil material whic h is the result of weathering and deco mposition of rocks that has not been transported from its original place.
   (ii) The two crops that are grown on laterite soil are tea and rubber.
   (iii) The agents of soil erosion are the same as of other types of erosion i.e. water, ice, wind and gravity.

18. Give a geographical reason for each of the following.
   (i) Alluvial soil differs in texture. [2016]
   (ii) Black soil does not get leached.
   (iii) Khadar is more fertile than Bhangar.

Ans. (i) Alluvial soil is coarse in the upper valley of the rivers because the eroded matter is carried away by the fast flowing river, while in the lower coarse, the river reduces its speed and the soil particles become finer due to attrition or because the sediments itself get eroded.
   (ii) Black soil does not get leached because it is clayey and sticky and moisture retentive and therefore the rain cannot wash out the silicates.
   (iii) Khadar is more fertile than Bhangar as new layers are deposited year after year in Khadar soil during monsoon floods.

19. Name the soil which [2017]
   (i) is good for cultivation of sugarcane.
   (ii) is acidic in nature.
   (iii) occurs in-situ.

Ans. (i) Black soil is considered good for sugarcane cultivation because it is made up of extremely fine clayey material and has self-ploughing quality and holds moisture when becomes wet.
   (ii) Laterite soil is acidic in nature as it has low humus content, because the micro-organisms get destroyed due to high temperature.
   (iii) Black soil is considered in-situ or residual soil that means it is found where it is formed.

20. Define the following: [2015]
   (i) Pedogenesis (ii) Humus (iii) Bhangar

Ans. (i) **Pedogenesis** It is the study of the process of soil formation.
   (ii) **Humus** It is the decayed organic matter present in top soil that increases the fertility of the soil.
   (iii) **Bhangar** It is old alluvium soil and consists of kankars. It is coarse in texture and less fertile.

21. Name the soil which [2014]
   (i) is good for the cultivation of cashewnuts.
   (ii) covers almost all of West Bengal.
   (iii) is a result of leaching.

Ans. (i) Laterite soil (ii) Alluvial soil (iii) Laterite soil

22. Name the soil which [2010]
   (i) covers the summits of the Eastern Ghats.
   (ii) makes up the Delta of the river Ganga.
   (iii) is the most suitable for the cultivation of cotton.
   (iv) is sticky when wet and cracks when dry.

Ans. (i) Laterite Soil (ii) Alluvial Soil
   (iii) Black Soil (iv) Black Soil

23. What is soil conservation? State a method of soil conservation in the [2017]
   (i) arid and semi-arid region.
   (ii) river valleys prone to flood.

Ans. Soil Conservation is a method to maintain soil fertility, prevent soil erosion and exhaustion and improve the degraded condition of the soil.
   (i) **Arid and Semi-arid Region** In these regions, overgrazing of forests and grassland by animals should be checked, separate grazing grounds should be provided. Belts of trees and shrubs should be planted to check the velocity of wind and thus, prevent wind erosion.
   (ii) **River Valleys Prone to Flood** Soil erosion by floods can be checked by constructing dams or barrages over such rivers which are responsible for flood.

24. Name two important agents of erosion. For each, state one method of controlling the erosion caused. [2011]

Ans. The two important agents of erosion are water and wind. Methods of controlling erosion are
   (i) **Erosion by Water** During heavy downpours, deep 'gullies' are made on account of water run off. Gully erosion can be stopped by plugging it with stones and pebbles or quick growing grasses can be grown in gullies to stop its expansion.

(ii) **Erosion by Wind** Wind erosion reduces the productive capacity of the soil by removing the loose particles of soil with the high velocity wind. Therefore, more and more trees should be planted along the edges of the fields, the waste land and also on the steep slopes. If it is difficult to grow trees, so grass should be grown but no land should be left devoid of plants.

25. (i) What is soil erosion? [2018]
(ii) Mention two causes of soil erosion in India.

Ans. (i) Soil erosion is a displacement of the upper layer of soil by the dynamic activity of erosion agents like water, ice, snow, wind, plants, animals and humans.
(ii) The two causes of soil erosion in India are
(a) **Running Water** It is the prime factor of soil erosion as it disturbs the agricultural pattern.
(b) **Deforestation** Removal of forest cover which functions as a binder of the top layer of the soil with increasing land demand, have resulted in enhancing extent of soil erosion.

26. Give a geographic reason for each of the following.
(i) Alluvial soil is extremely fertile. [2015]
(ii) Need for soil conservation.
(iii) Re-afforestation should be practiced extensively.

Ans. (i) Alluvial soil is extremely fertile because it is rich in various minerals such as potash, iron and lime, Moreover, it is clayey in nature and has high water holding capacity. This makes it suitable for the cultivation of various types of crops.
(ii) Soil consevation is necessary as the removal of the top soil layer results in loss of fertility, decreasing soil moisture, drying of vegetation and increase in the frequency of floods and droughts.
(iii) Re-afforestation should be practiced extensively in order to compensate for the large-scale deforestation occurring because of industrialisation and other factors, which would certainly result in soil erosion and land degradation.

27. Briefly answer the following. [2019]
(i) Mention one way in which man is responsible for soil erosion.
(ii) How can deepening of the river bed help in preventing soil erosion?
(iii) Mention a physical characteristic of laterite soil.

Ans. (i) Faulty practice of farming like faulty ways of ploughing, shifting cultivation, etc done by man is responsible for soil erosion.
(ii) Deepening of the river bed help in preventing soil erosion as by deepening a river can hold more water during heavy rainy season and water would get more space to flow easily without breaching the river beds. Thus, the river bed could hold embankment and nearby areas.
(iii) The laterite soil is compact, reddish or yellowish-red in colour and turns black on exposure to the Sun.

28. Give a geographical reason for the following. [2014]
(i) Different regions in India having different kinds of soil.
(ii) Black soil being suitable for growth of cotton.
(iii) The conservation of soil as a natural resource.

Ans. (i) Factors affecting soil formation are climate, vegetation, parent rock, relief and slope of the land. India has varied relief features, land forms, climatic realms and vegetation types. These have led to the development of a variety of soils in the country.
(ii) Black soil contains lime, alumina, iron, potash, magnesium and calcium and also retains moisture which helps in the growth of cotton plants.
(iii) The soil helps us to get most of our food and clothing directly or indirectly and also ensures agricultural prosperity of a country, thus, soil conservation as a natural resource is important and essential.

29. Define the following. [2016]
(i) Sheet erosion (ii) Soil conservation
(iii) In-situ soils

Ans. (i) **Sheet erosion** Sometimes water flows as a sheet over large areas down a slope. In such cases, the top soil is washed away. This is known as sheet erosion.
(ii) **Soil conservation** It is an effort made by man to prevent soil erosion to retain fertility of soil.
(iii) **In-situ soils** These soils are formed in their original position by breaking up of parent rocks. They include black soil, red soil, etc.

Picture Based Question

1. Study the diagram given below and answer the questions that follow.

(i) What type of farming is shown in the picture given above?
(ii) Name another method used which is similar to the one shown above.
(iii) Write a benefit of this farming.

Ans. (i) Terrace farming (ii) Contour ploughing
(iii) Terrace farming prevents erosion of the top soil from running water or wind rushing downhill and carrying away the soil.

Chapter Assessment

Section-I

Multiple Choice Questions

1. Black cotton soil of the Deccan region of India is associated with ....
(a) Volcanic rocks (b) Plutonic rocks
(c) Sedimentary rocks (d) Igneous rocks

2. Soil erosion in desert area can be prevented by
(a) Strip ploughing
(b) Using manure
(c) Afforestation
(d) Shifting cultivation

3. .... soil has higher iron content and found in Manipur and Mizoram.
(a) Laterite (b) Red
(c) Black (d) Alluvial

4. Which of the following is/are not the characteristics of red soil?
I. It is derived from weathering of old crystalline and metamorphic rocks
II. It contain iron oxides
III. It has high water retention capacity
IV. It has high nitrogen content

Codes
(a) I and II (b) Only II
(c) Only IV (d) III and IV

Section-II

Short Questions

1. How would you define 'soil'?
2. Which organic matter is responsible for soil fertility?
3. The soil forming material is obtained by which rock?
4. State two examples of 'In Situ' soil.
5. Alluvial soil is deficient in which minerals?
6. State two difference between red soil and black soil.

Long Questions

1. Distinguish between old alluvium and new alluvium.
2. Compare and contrast between alluvial soil and laterite soil.
3. What is soil erosion? Name the causes of soil erosion with a suitable diagram.
4. State the problems which are caused by soil erosion.
5. Compare and contrast between sheet erosion and gully erosion.
6. By which process badland and ravines are developed? Explain in brief.
7. Define the need for soil conservation and the useful farming practices which can help to reduce soil erosion.

CHAPTER 06

Natural Vegetation of India

SYLLABUS

Natural Vegetation Importance of Forests.
• Types of Vegetation (Tropical Evergreen, Tropical Deciduous, Tropical Desert, Littoral and Mountain).
• Distribution and Correlation with the Environment • Forest Conservation.

The term forest implies 'natural vegetation' of the area, existing from thousands of years and supporting a variety of biodiversity, forming a complex ecosystem. Natural vegetation includes all plant life such as trees, bushes, herbs, etc that grow naturally in an area which have been left undisturbed by humans for a long time.

Importance of Forests

- Forests are an important part of the Earth's climate because the presence of a variety of plants produce massive amount of oxygen and enable organisms to breathe.
- Forests provide home to diverse animals and plant species which not only provide biodiversity on the Earth, but each species has an important role in the ecosystem.
- About one-fourth of all the natural medicines that is produced, originates from tropical rainforest. Thus, they are known as **world's largest pharmacy**.
- Forests are major producers of timber, cellulose pulp, matchwood, firewood, charcoal wood, sal, teak, gurjan, deodar, etc.
- Forests provides habitat to wildlife and recreation to humans through various Wildlife Sanctuaries, National Parks, etc.
- Forests provide many minor products like grasses, bamboo, canes, oils, fibres, gums, resins, drugs, tanning products and dye-stuffs, spices, leaves, edible products and animal products like lac, honey and wax, etc.
- Forests play an important role in the prevention and control of soil erosion, desertification and floods.
- Forests regulate the water cycle. The trees absorb water from ground and release it into the atmosphere which helps to form clouds and precipitation.

Types of Vegetation

On the basis of climate, soil, relief and structure, Indian forests can be divided into the following categories

1. Tropical Evergreen Forests
2. Tropical Deciduous Forests
3. Tropical Desert Forests
4. Littoral Forests
5. Mountain Forests

1. Tropical Evergreen or Rainforest

These forests are very dense with tall trees and also have a number of lianas (climbing plants) and **epiphytes**[1]. Due to continuous rainfall throughout the year, the trees do not shed their leaves and hence, such forests are called evergreen forests. Due to having hard and durable timber, these forests have high economic value.

The characteristic features of Tropical Evergreen forests are

- They are dense and have a variety of trees and shrubs.
- The trees of these forests reach at a height of 60 m or above.
- Due to thick canopy of trees, herbs and grasses cannot grow in these forests.
- These forests do not have any fixed period of time for shedding of leave.

Some of the important species of Tropical Evergreen forests are rosewood, gurjan, ebony, toon, mahogany and sheesham.

Tropical Evergreen Forests

Climatic Conditions

These are also called 'tropical rainforests' as they are found in the areas where the annual rainfall is over 200 cm with a short dry season. The average temperature is about 25°C to 27°C which is hot and extremely humid (more than 70% humidity) with almost no seasonal variation.

Distribution

These forests are found on Western slopes of the Western Ghats, both groups of islands (Lakshadweep, Andaman and Nicobar Islands), coast of Tamil Nadu, Odisha, Bhabar and Terai regions, in North-Eastern India (in parts of Assam, Meghalaya, Tripura, Manipur and Nagaland).

Correlation with the Environment

The Tropical Evergreen forests are quite dense with heavy undergrowth of ferns and shrubs due to warm, moist and humid climate. The trees have multi-storeyed structures with good **canopies**[2], e.g. the lower layer consists of mosses, ferns, herbs, the middle layer has a dense growth of shrubs and short trees and the topmost layer consists of the tall emergent trees.

2. Tropical Deciduous Forests

These are the most widespread forests in India and are also called the **monsoon forests**. The trees of these forests have a height of 30-35 m with dense bushes and an undergrowth of grasses. Some of the important species of tropical deciduous forests are sal, teak, sheesham, jamun, bamboo and sandalwood.

Types of Tropical Deciduous Forests

On the basis of the availability of water, Tropical Deciduous forests are of two types

(i) **Tropical Moist Deciduous Forests** The trees of these forests shed their leaves from six to eight weeks during spring and early summer. These forests are the most commercially exploited forests in India. These forests have trees found in pure stands (having trees of single species and not mixed with other vegetation). These forests provide valuable timber and they are great source of various other products. The sandalwood found in these forests are in great demand in India and abroad.

(ii) **Tropical Dry Deciduous Forests** These forests survive in accordance with the climatic condition of that particular region. The trees of these forests completely shed their leaves and look like a vast tract of grasslands. These trees provide timber, fruits and other useful products. Large tracts of these forests have been cleared for agricultural activities.

1 **Epiphyte** A plant which grows on the outside of another plant, using that plant just for support, e.g. lichens, mosses, orchids.

2 **Canopies** The uppermost branches of the trees in a forest.

Climatic Conditions

Tropical Moist Deciduous forests are found in areas receiving low or moderate annual rainfall of 100 to 200 cm and temperature of 24°C to 27°C. They are found in areas of humidity between 50 to 80%.

Tropical Dry Deciduous forests are found in the areas having annual rainfall between 70 and 100 cm with humidity of 51 to 58% and annual temperature between 23°C and 27°C.

Distribution

Tropical Moist Deciduous forests exist mostly in the Eastern part of the country such as North-Eastern states, along the foothills of the Himalayas, Jharkhand, West Odisha, Chhattisgarh, Madhya Pradesh, Chota Nagpur Plateau, Shiwalik including the Bhabar and Terai regions and the Eastern slopes of the Western Ghats.

Tropical Dry Deciduous forests are found in the rainier parts of the Peninsular Plateau and the plains of Bihar and Uttar Pradesh.

Correlation with the Environment

Tropical Deciduous forests occur in those regions which have a distinct dry season. The trees shed their leaves for about 1-2 months during spring and summer due to lack of adequate moisture in the environment.

3. Tropical Desert Forests

These forests are limited in nature and have long roots which penetrate deep into the soil in order to get moisture. Leaves of the trees of these forests are mostly thick and small to minimise evaporation. The stems are succulent (juicy) to conserve water.

Ber fruit of these forests is eaten raw or processed and made into pickle or beverages. The timber of these forests is hard, durable and tough. It is used to make legs for bedsteads, boat ribs, agricultural implements, charcoal, etc. Some of the trees of these forests such as neem, babool tree's bark and gum have medicinal value. The main characteristic features of Tropical Desert forests are

- Due to scanty rainfall, the forests have **xerophytic**[3] vegetation.
- The trees of these forests are stunted and have large patches of coarse grasses.
- The trees of these forests remain leafless.
- The forest looks like scrub vegetation.
- Some of the important species of tropical desert forests are babool, date, palms, kikar, catechu and palash.

Types of Tropical Desert Forests

Tropical Desert forests can be divided into two broad groups

(i) **Semi-Arid Vegetation** This vegetation is also known as dry thorn vegetation and occurs where rainfall is between 25 and 50 cm per year.

(ii) **Arid Vegetation** This type of vegetation is found in extreme dry condition where rainfall is less than 25 cm annually. Due to less rainfall, the land is mostly covered by **sand dunes**[4].

Climatic Conditions

Tropical Desert forests are found in the regions having annual rainfall between 25 and 50 cm and the average temperature between 25°C to 27°C with humidity below 47%.

Distribution

These forests are found in Southern parts of Punjab, Haryana, Eastern and Central Rajasthan, Gujarat, Madhya Pradesh, parts of Maharashtra, Andhra Pradesh Karnataka and Chhattirgarh.

Correlation with the Environment

Tropical Desert forests can easily tolerate extreme dry conditions, low or scanty rainfall, low humidity and high temperatures.

They have adaptation characteristics which make them to survive in the hot deserts. The trees found in Tropical deserts are babool or acaciaber, date palm, khair, etc.

4. Littoral or Mangrove Forests

This type of vegetation flourishes in wet marshy areas in river deltas, saline or other swampy areas, river mouths and sea coasts. These forests helps in the formation of delta by blocking the sediments and prevent seashore from erosion by blocking tidal waves. These regions act as nursery for the marine micro-organisms.

---

3 **Xerophytic** They are species of plant that has adaptations to survive in an environment with little water.

4 **Sand dunes** A hill of sand near an ocean or in a desert that is formed by the wind.

The tidal trees of these forests yields hardwood which is strong and durable and is used for making boats and boxes. These forests have Sundari trees that is why they are called **Sunderbans** in the Ganga Delta. Sundari trees of these forests provide hard durable timber whereas mangrove trees are utilised for fuel.

Littoral or Mangrove Forests

The main characteristic features of Littoral forests are

- These forests are dense, evergreen and of varying heights.
- The trees of these forests have long roots submerged under water and have pores which help them to breathe during high tide.
- Some of the important species of these forests are sundari, mangrove, kora, amur, canes, palms, etc.
- These forests have breathing roots called pneumatophores.

Climatic Conditions

Littoral forests grows in coastal areas where the saline sea water encroaches at the time of high tides and fresh water of rivers continuously mixes with the saline water. So, these can survive in salty as well as in fresh water. These forests occur in areas receiving rainfall of 100 to 150 cm and have temperatures ranging between 25°C and 27°C.

Distribution

The deltaic tracts of Ganga, Godavari, Krishna, Kaveri and Mahanadi are ideally suited for this type of forests. In India, these forest are mainly found in coast of Odisha, Andhra Pradesh, West Bengal (Sunderbans), Tamil Nadu and along the coastal areas of Kutch, Kathiawar, Gulf of Khambhat and Andaman and Nicobar Islands.

Correlation with the Environment

These forests are quite sensitive, thus the proper ratio of both the fresh and saline water is necessary for them and if there is a deficit or excess in any of the two, it may cause damage to the vegetation.

5. Mountain or Montane Forests

These forests are found in mountainous areas in high altitude and usually vary to a great extent along the slopes of mountain. These forests provide different variety of timber which has great economic value and the trees of these forests are used as fuel wood in rural areas. These trees bring benefits to the agriculture, forestry and fishing sectors.

These forests also provide useful medicinal plants like Himalayan Yew. Himalayan Yew species has a variety of uses in traditional medicine. But now classified as endangered species by the IUCN due to its high exploitation.

The main characteristics of Mountain forests are

- These forests consists of mixed species of broad leafed evergreen trees and conifers.
- The forests are mainly found at an altitude between 1000 to 4000 m.
- Some of the important trees of Mountain forests are chir, deodar, silver-fir, blue-pine and spruce.

Mountain or Montane Forests

Types of Mountain Forests

- **Wet Temperature Forests** These forests are found at lower altitudes between 1000 and 2000 m with evergreen broad leaf trees such as oak and chestnut. The height of these trees are 15 to 20 m with dense canopy.

- **Temperate Forests** These forest are found at altitude between 1500 and 3350 m. These trees have a height of up to 45 m. Coniferous trees like pine, deodar, silver-fir, spruce and cedar are found in these forests. These forests cover mostly the Southern slopes of the Himalayas, places having high altitude in Southern and North-East India.
- **Temperate Grasslands** These are found at an altitude above 3600 m. Silver-firs, pines, junipers, birches, etc are common trees in these forests. These trees progressively hinder the growth as they approach **snow line or tree line**[5].
- **Alpine Vegetation** This vegetation is found in the higher reaches of the Himalayas (above 3500 to 4000 m). Alpine vegetation through shrubs and scrubs combined with alpine grasslands are used by nomadic tribes like Gujjars and Bakarwals for grazing.

  This type of vegetation has **rhododendrons**[6], barberries, birch and stunted trees of junipers. Above this vegetation mosses and lichens are found which are part of tundra vegetation.

Climatic Conditions

Mountain forests are mainly based on relief and change with corresponding change in temperature. These forests are found in areas receiving annual rainfall between 100 and 300 cm and annual temperature of 12°C to 13°C with humidity between 56 and 65%.

Distribution

These forests are found in mountainous areas of Jammu and Kashmir, Himachal Pradesh, Uttarakhand, Sikkim and Arunachal Pradesh. They are also found in Vindhyas, Nilgiris and Western Ghats.

Correlation with the Environment

There is difference in nature of vegetation of these forests found in lower slopes and upper slopes (above 1500 m). At higher altitudes, temperature falls and precipitation increases. Therefore, in these forests vegetation tends to become evergreen.

The altitudinal zone between 1500 to 3350 m above the sea level where the temperature is lower and annual rainfall ranges between 100 to 250 cm, wet temperate forests are found.

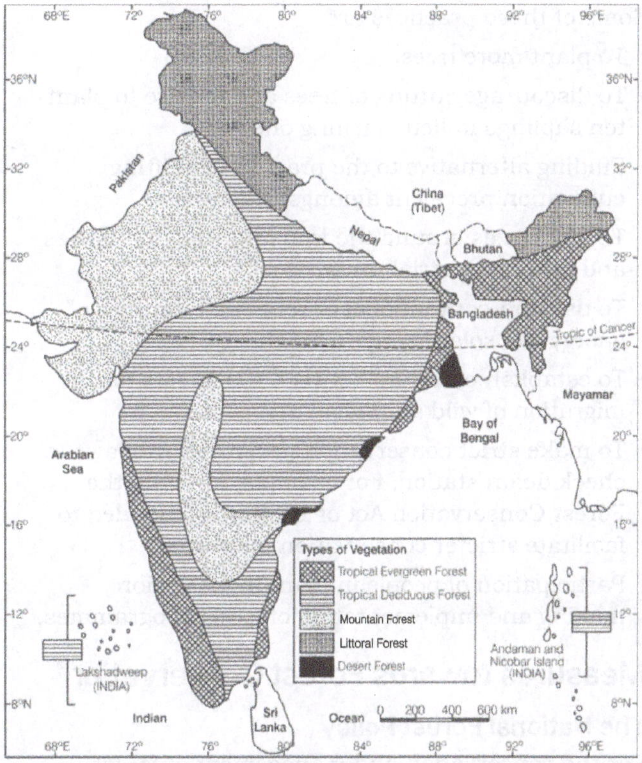

Types of Vegetation

Check Your LEARNING...

1. Natural vegetation includes which type of plants?
2. Which forests are considered as a degraded version of the moist deciduous forests?
3. Xerophytes are the characteristic feature of which type of forest cover in India?
4. Which climatic conditions are best suited for littoral type of forests?

Forest Conservation

It is the practice of planting and maintaining forested areas for the benefit and sustainability of future generations. It is necessary as forests are declining at a rapid rate. Some reasons that led to the decline in the forest are

- Increasing population
- Converting forests into pasture lands
- Overgrazing of animals
- Increasing demand of timber
- Construction of multi-purpose river valley projects

In order to conserve forests, many practices have to be undertaken.

5 **Tree line/Snow line** The altitude above which no trees and plants can grow because of the intense cold and presence of ice cover.
6 **Rhododendron** It is large class of widely cultivated shrubs and trees with alternate leaves and showy flowers.

Some of these practices are

- To plant more trees.
- To discourage cutting of trees and ensure to plant ten saplings in lieu of felling one tree.
- Finding alternative to the practice of shifting cultivation prevalent amongst the tribals.
- To grow trees around the iron and steel industries and other industrial units.
- To use non-conventional or renewable sources of energy like solar energy, tidal energy, etc.
- To establish corridors between the forests for the migration of wild animals.
- To make strict conservation measures and laws to check deforestation. For example, in 1988, the Forest Conservation Act of 1980 was amended to facilitate stricter conservation measures.
- Participation of people in planning, decision making and implementation of forest programmes.

Measures towards Forest Conservation

The National Forest Policy

For the conservation and management of forest cover, India has a forest policy in operation since 1894, which was revised in 1952 and 1988. The main aim of the revised National Forest Policy of 1988 is protection, conservation and development of forests. It led to a programme named Joint Forest Management. This policy proposed that specific villages in association with the forest department will manage specific forest blocks.

Some other objectives of this policy are

- Restoration of ecological balance.
- Maintenance of environmental stability.
- Preserving natural forests through wide variety of flora and fauna.
- Checking soil erosion and the extension of sand-dunes in the desert areas.
- To increase forest cover area through extensive afforestation and social forestry programmes.
- Encouraging the use of forest produce.

People's Participation

Many tribal communities still live in the forests of India and depend on forest products for their livelihood and also worship them. Thus, these communities are working with the government to conserve forests.

Some important examples are

- In Sariska Tiger Reserve (Rajasthan), villagers fought against mining activities.
- Chipko Movement started in 1970's in district Chamoli (Uttarakhand) was a non-violent movement based on Gandhian philosophy. It aimed at protection and conservation of trees and forests from being destroyed.

Van Mahotsav

It was launched in the year 1950 by **Shri Kanhaiyalal M Munshi**, the then Union Minister for Agriculture and Food. This initiative was taken to create an enthusiasm in the mind for the preservation of forest and planting of trees. It is a week long festival of tree planting, which organises every year in the month of July all across India and lakhs of trees are planted.

Social Forestry

It refers to managing and protecting forests and planting trees on barren lands with an objective to help in the environmental, social and rural development. The main objective of social forestry is to reduce pressure on traditional forests by plantation of fuelwood, fodder, timber and grasses. Agro-forestry, community forestry, commercial farm forestry, non-commercial farm forestry and urban forestry are the main components of social forestry.

Agro-Forestry

It is a part of social forestry and it represents the intermediate stage between forestry and agriculture. It refers the sustainable system in which trees or shrubs are grown around or among crops or pasture land. The main aim of agro-forestry is to provide conservation of the land and to achieve a combined produce of forest and agricultural crops through the improvement of land.

Joint Forest Management (JFM) Programmes

These programmes have been launched by various state governments. Under such programmes, village communities are entrusted with the protection and management of nearby forests. The areas concerned are usually degraded or even deforested areas.

Check Your LEARNING...

1. Van Mahotsav is based on which concept?
2. In which year Van Mahotsav is launched?
3. Agro-forestry is a part of which type of forestry?
4. What are JFM programmes?

QUiCK Revision

- Natural vegetation includes all plant life such as trees, bushes, herbs, etc that grow naturally in an area and have been left undisturbed by humans for a long time.
- Forest implies natural vegetation of the area that provides various natural resources to human beings and shelter/habitat to fauna.
- Forests provide firewood, timber and raw material for many industrial purposes in the form of oils, paints, resins etc.
- India is one of the twelve mega-biodiversity countries of the world and has varied types of forests and tree cover, ranging from the rainforest of Kerala in the South to the alpine pastures of Ladakh in the North, from the desert of Rajasthan in the West to the evergreen forests in the North-East.
- Forest cover of India is affected by a variety of factors such as relief (land, soil), climate (temperature, rainfall, sunlight) etc.
- The forests of India are classified into five major types. First is tropical evergreen/rain forests, which are found in the Western Ghats, Indian island groups (Lakshadweep and Andaman and Nicobar), Tamil Nadu and Himalayan region.
- Second is tropical deciduous forests which are mostly found in the Central and Eastern Indian states.
- Third is tropical desert forests which are mainly occurred in the North-Western part of India and Deccan Plateau region.
- Fourth is littoral/swampy/mangrove forests which are mainly found in the deltaic regions and on the sea coasts.
- Fifth type of forests are the mountain/montane forests which are widely found in the Himalayan regions.
- These forests also give a wide variety of flora and fauna which is very useful for commercial and domestic purposes like, medicinal plants, timber wood, fuelwood, etc.
- The conservation of forest resources is very important for the sustainable development of our environment and for survival of all the living beings.
- The government has took various steps in this regard and now encouraging people to conserve forest by providing sufficient incentives and technical assistance in this direction.
- Van Mahotsav was launched in 1950 for the preservation of forests and planting of trees.
- Social forestry is a measure initiative which aims to reduce pressure on traditional forests by plantation of fuelwood, fodder, timber and grasses.

Chapter Practice

Section-I

Multiple Choice Questions

1. In which vegetation belt multiple layers of trees are found? **[Specimen Paper Semester-I 2022]**
(a) Tropical Deciduous (b) Tropical Evergreen
(c) Thorn and scrub forest (d) Tidal forest

Ans. (b) Tropical Evergreen

2. A Tropical Deciduous tree special to the Deccan Plateau is............
(a) Teak (b) Shisham (c) Sandalwood (d) Sal

Ans. (c) Sandalwood

3. The most important commercial forests of India are
(a) Tropical evergreen (b) Mangrove
(c) Tropical deciduous (d) Coniferous

Ans. (c) Tropical deciduous

4. Which type of forest is found mostly in the coastal areas of India ? **[2023]**
(a) Tropical Evergreen Forest
(b) Tropical Desert Forest
(c) Littoral Forest
(d) Tropical Deciduous Forest

Ans. (a) Tropical Evergreen Forest

5. Which of the following is not a species of tropical moist deciduous forests?
(a) Mahogany (b) Sal (c) Shisham (d) Teak

Ans. (a) Mahogany

6. Open stunted forests with bushes and having long roots and sharp thorns or spines are found in
(a) Eastern Odisha
(b) North-Eastern Tamil Nadu
(c) Shiwaliks and Terai regions
(d) Western Andhra Pradesh

Ans. (d) Western Andhra Pradesh

7. Choose the correct statement.
What are the chief characteristics of monsoon forests? **[Specimen Paper Semester-I 2022]**
(a) These regions receive a moderate rainfall.
(b) The trees shed their leaves in the dry season.
(c) The trees are found in pure stand.
(d) All of the above

Ans. (d) All of the above

8. In Tropical Desert forests, the trees are stunted with large patches of coarse grasses. This Vegitation is known as
(a) Alpine (b) Littoral
(c) Xerophytic (d) None of these

Ans. (c) Xerophytic

9. Which of the following features is not associated with thorn and scrub forest? **[Specimen Paper Semester-I 2022]**
(a) Xerophyte or drought resistant
(b) Evergreen and multilayered
(c) Long roots going deep in the ground
(d) Leaves turned into spines

Ans. (b) Evergreen and multilayered

10. The Mangrove forests of Ganga delta are known as
(a) Monsoon forest (b) Sunderbans
(c) Tropical forest (d) Swamp forest

Ans. (b) Sunderbans

11. .... trees are used for extracting oil and its flowers for making wine and are largely found in Madhya Pradesh.
(a) Semul (b) Palash
(c) Mahua (d) Teak

Ans. (c) Mahua

12. .... trees provide hard durable timber for construction purposes and boat making.
(a) Sundari (b) Deodar
(c) Sal (d) Ebony

Ans. (a) Sundari

13. What is the other name of Littoral forests? **[Specimen Paper Semester-I 2022]**
(a) Rain forests (b) Monsoon forests
(c) Tidal forests (d) Scrub lands

Ans. (c) Tidal forests

14. Give a reason for the following.
Sundarbans name is given because **[Specimen Paper Semester-I 2022]**
(a) the abundance of breathing roots.
(b) a beautiful forest.
(c) the abundance of Sundari trees.
(d) ban on cutting of trees.

Ans. (c) the abundance of Sundari trees.

15. Choose the correct statement.
What is Social Forestry? **[Specimen Paper Semester-I 2022]**
(i) The management and protection of forests and afforestation on barren lands with the purpose of helping in the social development.
(ii) The practice of growing trees on Farm lands.
(iii) Growing trees by social workers.
(iv) Forest used for social gathering.

Codes
(a) Only (i) (b) (i), (ii) and (iii)
(c) All of these (d) None of these

Ans. (a) Only (i)

16. Which of the following statements is/are valid for saying forests are important for human beings?
(i) They support industries and provide livelihood
(ii) They control wind force and temperature and cause rainfall.

Codes
(a) Only (i) (b) Only (ii)
(c) Both (i) and (ii) (d) None of these

Ans. (c) Both (i) and (ii).

17. Match the following

Term	Definition
A. Epiphyte	1. The altitude above which no trees and plants can grow.
B. Canopies	2. A hill of sand
C. Sand dunes	3. A plant which grows on the outside of another plant.
D. Snow line	4. The upper most branches of trees in the forest.

Codes

	A	B	C	D		A	B	C	D
(a)	1	2	3	4	(b)	2	1	3	4
(c)	3	4	2	1	(d)	4	3	2	1

Ans. (c)

18. Match the following

Forest	Distribution
A. Tropical Evergreen	1. North Eastern States
B. Tropical Deciduous	2. Thar Desert
C. Tropical Desert	3. Delta regions
D. Littoral	4. Western slopes of Western Ghat

Codes

	A	B	C	D		A	B	C	D
(a)	1	2	3	4	(b)	4	2	3	1
(c)	1	3	2	4	(d)	4	1	2	3

Ans. (d)

Section-II

Short Questions

1. A great variety of flora is found in India. Give three geographical factors responsible for this diversification of flora.

Ans. Three geographical factors responsible for a great variety of flora found in India are
(i) Varied relief features
(ii) Varied landforms
(iii) Range of daily and annual temperature

2. Briefly explain two reasons for forests being an important natural resource. [2013]

Ans. Forests are important natural resource because
(i) they provide timber, medicinal plants etc.
(ii) they help in purifying air and giving rain.

3. How do forests [2014]
(i) have a favourable effect on the climate of the region?
(ii) act as a flood control measure?

Ans. (i) Forests transmit moisture into the air by means of transpiration and induce precipitation. Forests turn carbon dioxide into oxygen and thus help the organisms to survive.
(ii) The roots of plants and trees hold the soil and thus, forests check or prevent soil erosion, especially in hilly areas. Hence, they also help in controlling floods.

4. State two ways by which forests help in protecting the environment. [2020]

Ans. Two ways by which forests help in protecting the environment are
(i) After oceans, forests are the world's largest storehouses of carbon. These absorb harmful greenhouse gases that produce climate change.
(ii) It provide habitats to a number of wild animals and birds.

5. Mention two main characteristics of Tropical Rainforests. [2013]

Ans. Two main characteristics of Tropical Rainforests are
(i) Due to continuous rainfall throughout the year, the trees of these forests do not shed their leaves at the same time and hence, such forests are called 'evergreen forests'.
(ii) They are dense and have a variety of trees and shrubs.

6. (i) Name the forests which grow on the windward slope of the Western Ghats. [2016]
(ii) Why do such forests grow in this region?

Ans. (i) Tropical Evergreen forests grow on the windward slope of the Western Ghats.
(ii) Tropical Evergreen forests grow on the windward slope of the Western Ghats because of the favourable climatic conditions such as rainfall is more than 200 cm, average annual temperature is between 25° to 27°C and humidity is more than 70%.

7. (i) Name an area in India where Tropical Monsoon forest is found. [2018]
(ii) How is this forest of great commercial value to India?

Ans. (i) The Tropical Monsoon forest is found in the Andaman and Nicobar Islands, the Western Ghats and the Coastline of Peninsular India and also in Assam region of North-East India.
(ii) The Tropical Monsoon forests contain several tree species of great commercial value. For example, teak, Indian rosewood, etc.

8. With reference to Tropical Deciduous forests, answer the following questions: [2020]
(i) Name two states where it is found.
(ii) Name two important trees found in these forests.

Ans. (i) Tropical Deciduous forests are found in Madhya Pradesh and Uttar Pradesh.

(ii) Teak and Sal are important trees found in these forests.

9. State two characteristics of the Tropical Deciduous forests. **[2015]**

Ans. Two characteristics of Tropical Deciduous forests are

(i) The trees in these forests shed their leaves for 6 to 8 weeks during spring and early summer.

(ii) These forests provides valuable timber and other forest products.

10. Write two reasons why Monsoon Deciduous forests are commercially more valuable than other types of forests. **[2014]**

Ans. Monsoon Deciduous forests are commercially more valuable than other forests because

(i) Tree in these forest are more appropriate for commercial exploitation.

(ii) These forest are not so dense as the tropical evergreen forests. The tree species like Sal, Sheesham, Teak, Jamun, etc are very durable woods and are in great demand. These are mainly used for furniture making, railway slippers, agricultural equipments, house constructional work, etc.

11. (i) Name the forest which is commercially most important in India. **[2016]**

(ii) Name two trees which grow in these forests.

Ans. (i) Tropical Deciduous forests is commercially most important in India

(ii) Sal and Teak grows in these forests.

12. How do trees in the Tropical Desert forests adapt themselves to the dry climate? **[2017]**

Ans. The trees in Tropical Desert forests adapt themselves to the dry climate as in the lack of moisture, the trees growing here have very small leaves and long plant roots penetrate deep into the soil and spread in a radial pattern in search of water.

13. What are 'tidal forests'? Name two typical trees found there. **[2011]**

Ans. Tidal forests are found in wet marshy areas, in river deltas, saline or swampy areas along the sea coast. These forests consist of evergreen species with stilt roots which are submerged under water. Two typical trees found in these forests are Sundari and Casuarina.

14. Give two characteristics of tidal forests. **[2012]**

Ans. Two characteristics of Tidal forest are

(i) These forests help in formation of delta by blocking the sea.

(ii) These forests also act as a major carbon sink.

15. Define Sunderbans.

Ans. The forests found on the Ganga-Brahmaputra delta covering the coasts of West Bengal and Bangladesh are called Sunderbans because of the abundance of Sundari trees.

16. Name the tree as per its characteristics given below. **[2017]**

(i) The wood is hard and suitable for shipbuilding.

(ii) The stilt roots are underwater during high tide.

Ans. (i) Teak (ii) Sundari

17. With reference to littoral forest, answer the following questions. **[2018]**

(i) Why do the trees in this forest grow aerial roots?

(ii) Name one area in India where this forest is found.

Ans. (i) Littoral forests refer to trees that grow at shore region. In such regions, soil is accumulated with salt and cannot be aerated as normal soils, so trees grow upwards. Such roots are called as aerial roots and they are adventitious (unplanned) in nature.

(ii) Littoral forests or tidal forests are found in delta regions and along the marshy coasts. Sunderbans in West Bengal is one of the areas in India where littoral forests are found.

18. Give two reasons to explain as to why we need to conserve our forest resources. **[2019]**

Ans. We need to conserve forest resources because

- Forests are an important part of the Earth's climate. It is primarily because of the presence of a variety of plants which due to their high density produce massive amount of oxygen and enables other organisms to breathe.
- Forests provide home to diverse animals and plant species which not only provide biodiversity on the Earth, but each species has an important role in the ecosystem.

19. State two ways in which forests help in protecting the environment. **[2023]**

Ans. Forests help in protecting the environment in the following ways

(i) Forests contribute in preserving soil and supporting wildlife that leads to protection of environment.

(ii) Forests play an important role in the global water cycle, moving water across the Earth by releasing water vapour and capturing rainfall.

20. What is JFM?

Ans. Joint Forest Management programmes have been launched by various state governments. Under such programmes, village communities are entrusted with the protection and management of nearby forests. The concerned areas are usually degraded or even deforested areas.

Long Questions

1. What is meant by vegetation? How much natural is the natural vegetation of India today?

Ans. Vegetation includes all plant life such as trees, bushes, herbs, etc that grow naturally in an area and have been left undisturbed by humans for a long time.

Today, natural vegetation has not been left natural anymore because of the following reasons

- Various new species of plants are raised in laboratories and they are planted to have better results.
- Human interference is continuously increasing day by day which is deteriorating the quality of nature and is harmful for humans too.

2. Briefly explain the following.

(i) Why are Tropical Evergreen forests called 'Evergreen'? [2020]

(ii) Why is afforestation essential in the cities that have iron and steel industries?

(iii) How do forests act as a source of income for the people?

Ans. (i) The regions of Tropical Evergreen forests receive heavy rainfall throughout the year. As there is no particular dry season, the trees do not shed their leaves at the same time. Thus, the forests always appear green. This is the reason due to which they are called Evergreen forests.

(ii) Afforestation is essential in and around iron and steel industries because it provides a clean environment as trees take up carbon dioxide and give out oxygen.

(iii) Forests provide important sources of income to many rural people. Forest products such as bushes and fuel wood are gathered and traded at local and regional markets. Forests also provide the raw materials for artisan and processing activities.

3. What are the favourable climatic conditions for Tropical Evergreen forests? Also mention the regions where these are found.

Ans. Tropical Evergreen or Rainforest requires following climatic conditions

(i) These are found in areas where the annual rainfall is over 200 cm with a short dry season.

(ii) The average temperature is about 25°C to 27°C which is hot and extremely humid (more than 70% humidity) with almost no seasonal variation.

These forests are found on Western slopes of the Western Ghats, both groups of islands (Lakshadweep, Andaman and Nicobar Islands), coast of Tamil Nadu, Odisha, Bhabar and Terai regions, in North-Eastern India (in parts of Assam, Meghalaya, Tripura, Manipur and Nagaland).

4. Name the type of forests found in the Western part of the Western Ghats. Give two reasons why these forests are so named? [2011]

Ans. The Tropical Evergreen forests are found in the Western part of the Western Ghats.

These forests are named as Tropical Evergreen Forests because

(i) The trees in these forests do not have a fixed time to shed their leaves. Thus, they appear evergreen throughout the year.

(ii) This region receives an annual rainfall over 200 cm with short dry season. Thus, they remain green all the time.

5. Write any three difference between tropical evergreen and tropical desert forest.

Ans. The three difference between Tropical Evergreen and Tropical Desert forest are

Tropical Evergreen Forests	Tropical Desert Forests
These are found on Westward slope of the Westward Ghats and North-Eastern parts of Assam, Meghalaya.	These are found in the Panjab, Haryana and in the Southern peninsula.
These are found where rainfall is over 200 cm.	These are found where rainfall is less than 50 cm.
The main species are ebony, rosewood, sheesham etc.	The main species are neem, babool, kikar etc.

6. State the correlation of Tropical Evergreen forests with their surrounding environment.

Ans. The Tropical Evergreen forests are quite dense with heavy undergrowth of ferns and shrubs due to warm, moist and humid climate. The trees have multi-storeyed structures with good canopies, e.g. the lower layer consists of mosses, ferns, herbs, the middle layer has a dense growth of shrubs and short trees and the topmost layer consists of the tall emergent trees.

7. (i) Give two reasons to explain as to why the Tropical Evergreen forests are difficult to exploit for commercial purpose. [2019]

(ii) Name any two trees found in Tropical Evergreen Forests.

Ans. (i) Two reasons for difficulty in exploiting Tropical Evergreen Forests for commercial purpose are

- Tropical Evergreen Forests do not occur in pure stands i.e. main canopy do not consist of single species.
- These forests are dark and dense, so it is difficult for commercial exploitation.

(ii) Gurjan, ebony, rosewood, etc are found in Tropical Evergreen forests.

8. State the correlation of Tropical Deciduous forests with their surrounding environment.

Ans. Tropical deciduous forests occur in those regions which have a distinct dry season. The trees shed their leaves for about 1-2 months during spring and summer due to lack of adequate moisture in the environment.

9. Name any three trees found in Monsoon Deciduos forests and state one use of each of these trees. [2012]

Ans. Three trees of Monsoon Deciduous forests and their uses are

(i) **Sal** It is used for furniture making, railway sleepers, etc.

(ii) **Teak** It is used for house construction and furniture making.

(iii) **Sandalwood** It is used in cosmetic and making handicrafts, perfumes, etc.

10. Explain three main features of Tropical Moist Deciduous forests.

Ans. The main features of Tropical Moist Deciduous forests are

(i) These forests are found in the areas receiving rainfall of 100 to 200 cm.

(ii) The height and density of the trees in these forests are much lower than the Tropical Evergreen forests.

(iii) Due to seasonality of moisture, the trees in these forests shed their leaves for about 6 to 8 weeks in dry summer.

11. Briefly explain each of the following.

(i) The trees in the Tropical Desert forests have stunted growth. [2019]

(ii) There is a gradual increase in the forest cover in India in recent times.

(iii) The trees in Monsoon Deciduous forests shed their leaves for about 6-8 weeks during March and April.

Ans. (i) The trees of Tropical Desert forests have stunted growth because they receive low or scanty rainfall, due to low humidity and high temperature.

(ii) There is a gradual increase in the forest cover in India in recent times due to the work of central government in the direction to increase the forest cover areas in the country by formulating different policies and programmes.

(iii) Monsoon Deciduous forests shed their leaves for about 6-8 weeks during March and April to conserve water or to better survive winter weather conditions. Further, they must regrow new foliage during the next suitable growing seasons.

12. Explain three characteristics of Tropical Dry Deciduous forests.

Ans. The characteristics of Tropical Dry Deciduous forests are

(i) These are found in areas of slightly lower rainfall between 70 and 100 cm with a more pronounced seasonality.

(ii) Most of the trees shed their leaves during the long dry season.

(iii) These forests are economically very important.

13. Differentiate between Moist Deciduous forests and Dry Deciduous forests.

Ans. The differences between Moist Deciduous and Dry Deciduous forests are

Moist Deciduous Forests	Dry Deciduous Forests
These forests are found in areas with annual rainfall between 100 to 200 cm.	These forests are found in areas with annual rainfall between 70 to 100 cm.
Teak, bamboo, sal, sheesham, sandalwood, khair, kusum, arjun and mulberry trees are found in these forests.	Teak, sal, neem and peepal trees are found in these forests.
Not many areas of these forests have been cleared for commercial activities.	Large areas of these forests have been cleared for cultivation and grazing.

14. In which geographical or climatic condition do Tropical Desert forests thrive?

Ans. The geographical conditions in which Tropical Desert forests thrive are

(i) Regions having annual rainfall of 50 cm.

(ii) Regions having average temperature between 25°C to 27°C.

(iii) Evaporation rate is higher than precipitation due to high temperature.

15. Explain any three features of the Tropical Desert forests or thorn and scrubs.

Ans. The features of Tropical Desert forests or thorn and scrubs are

(i) Trees of these forests are scattered and have long roots penetrating deep into the soil in order to get moisture.

(ii) The stems of the trees in these forests are succulent to conserve water.

(iii) Leaves of the trees in these forests are mostly thick and small to minimise evaporation.

16. (i) Mention two conditions required for the growth of Littoral forest. [2019]

(ii) State one characteristic feature of the forest found in the Nilgiri Hills.

Ans. (i) The conditions required for the growth of Littoral forests are

(a) Littoral forests are specialised tropical type of vegetation that grows in coastal areas where the saline sea water encroaches at the time of high tides and fresh water of rivers continuously mixes with the saline water. So, these can survive in salty as well as in fresh water.

(b) These forests occur in areas receiving 100 to 150 cm rainfall and have temperatures ranging between 25°C to 27°C.

(ii) Forests found in the Nilgiri Hills are also known as monsoon forests. A feature of these forests is that they spread over the region receiving rainfall between 70 and 200 cm.

17. Name the regions where Mangrove forests are found.

Ans. The deltaic tracts of Ganga, Godavari, Krishna, Kaveri and Mahanadi are ideally suited for Mangrove type of forests. In India, these forest are mainly found in coast of Odisha, Andhra Pradesh, West Bengal (Sunderbans), Tamil Nadu and along the coastal areas of Kutch, Kathiawar, Gulf of Khambhat and Andaman and Nicobar Islands.

18. Name the natural vegetation extensively found at the following altitudes.
(i) At lower altitudes between 1000-2000 m.
(ii) At altitudes between 1500-3000 m.
(iii) At higher reaches of the Himalayas above 3500-4000 m.

Ans. (i) Wet temperate forests are found at lower altitudes between 1000 and 2000m with evergreen broad leaf trees such as oak and chestnut.
(ii) Temperate forests are found at altitude between 1500 and 3000 m. Coniferous trees like pine, deodar, silver-fir, spruce and cedar are found in these forests.
(iii) Alpine vegetation is found at altitude between 3500 and 4000m.

19. (i) Name one region in India where Tropical Evergreen Forest is found. **[2023]**
(ii) Mention the temperature and rainfall conditions found suitable for its growth.

Ans. (i) Western Ghats
(ii) The Tropical Evergreen Forest requires a condition of 200 cm of rainfall and a temperature of 15-30 degrees Celsius for its growth.

20. (i) Name a state in India where thorn and scrub forest is found. **[2018]**
(ii) Give two ways by which the trees that are found here have adapted to the climate.

Ans. (i) Rajasthan, Punjab, Haryana and Deccan are the major states where thorn and scrub forests are found.
(ii) The trees of thorn and scrub forests adapted to the dry climate in the following ways
(a) The thorn and scrub forest trees have long tapering roots which go deep to tap water. The trees are stunted as there is no enough rain for tree growth.
(b) The thorny branches reduce loss of water by transpiration and the fleshy leaves prevent loss of water by evaporation.

21. Identify the tree as per its characteristics mentioned below. **[2015]**
(i) It yields wood that is hard and scented and is usually found in high altitudes.
(ii) It is generally found in deltaic regions and is used to make boats.
(iii) The furniture made from the wood of this tree is generally the most expensive.

Ans. (i) Deodar
(ii) Sundari
(iii) Mahogany

22. Name the natural vegetation largely found in the following regions. **[2014]**
(i) The delta of the Ganga river.
(ii) The windward side of the Western Ghats.
(iii) The Deccan Plateau.

Ans. (i) Mangrove or Littoral forests
(ii) Tropical Evergreen forests
(iii) Tropical Deciduous forests

23. Name the tree, the timber of which could be used for the following. **[2013]**
(i) A soft and white timber used for making toys and match boxes.
(ii) A hard durable timber used for ship building and furniture making.
(iii) A sweet smelling timber which yields an oil, used for making handicrafts.

Ans. (i) Semal (ii) Teak
(iii) Sandalwood

24. (i) Name one region of India for each of the following. **[2013]**
(a) Tidal forests
(b) Thorn and scrub
(ii) Explain why thorn and scrub forests are found in the above mentioned regions.

Ans. (i) **Tidal Forests** Deltas of Ganga, Mahanadi, Godavari, Krishna and Kaveri.
Thorn and Scrub Forests Rajasthan and Gujarat.
(ii) Thorn and scrub forests are found in the above mentioned regions because these areas get less than 25 cm of rainfall and average temperature of 25° to 27°C.

25. Answer the following. **[2020]**
(i) The Tropical Deciduous forest is commercially the most important forest belt in India.
(ii) Tropical Evergreen forests occur on the windward side of Western Ghats.
(iii) It is very difficult to move through Tidal forests.

Ans. (i) Tropical Decidious forests are the most commercially important tropical forest type found in India. They contain important timber providing trees such as teak and Sal. The trees are located in forests which are readily accessible by various transport methods.
(ii) The Tropical Evergreen forests grow on the windward side of the Western Ghats because this region receives heavy rainfall above 250 cm annual.
(iii) It is very difficult to move through Tidal forests because they are muddy due to soil erosion and the silt carried by the rivers and their tributaries downstream.

26. To which type of forest do the following trees belong? [2016]
(i) Hintal and Sundari (ii) Rosewood and Ebony
(iii) Deodar and Chir Pine

Ans. (i) Littoral or Tidal forest
(ii) Tropical Evergreen or Rainforest
(iii) Montane forest

27. Name the natural vegetation found in the following regions. [2017]
(i) The Western slopes of the Western Ghats
(ii) The Nilgiris
(iii) Western Rajasthan

Ans. (i) Tropical Evergreen forest
(ii) Tropical Evergreen
(iii) Desert and semi-desert vegetation and scrub and thorn forests.

28. State one important use of each of the following types of trees. [2014]
(i) Sundari (ii) Sandalwood (iii) Rosewood

Ans. (i) **Sundari** It is used mainly for making boats.
(ii) **Sandalwood** It is used for making incense sticks, furniture goods etc.
(iii) **Rosewood** It is used in manufacture of furniture plyboards, etc.

29. Explain why the forest cover in India is shrinking. [2017]

Or Give three reasons for rapid depletion of forest resources in India in the past. [2016]

Ans. The forest cover in India is shrinking as a consequences of indiscriminate cutting down of the trees. This deforestation has brought complete deficiency of flora and fauna in our country.

The main reasons depletion of forests resources in the past are

- It is a consequence of indiscriminate cutting down of the trees due to Jhooming (or slash and burn) practices to clear the forests for cultivation and construction purposes.
- There is uncontrolled and unauthorised cutting down of trees by dishonest timber merchants for the purpose of trade.
- Trees have been cut due to agricultural expansion, development of railways, mining and commercial reasons.

30. Mention three reasons why forests must be conserved. [2012]

Ans. Reasons for conservation of forests are
(i) Forest conservation is needed to prevent soil erosion.
(ii) It helps to save the habitat of the wild animals.
(iii) It also prevents desertification and floods.

31. Answer the following [2018]
(i) Give two ways in which forests are important.
(ii) Mention one forest conservation method followed in India.

Ans. (i) The two ways in which forests are important are
(a) **Forests help us Breathe** They give us oxygen and absorb the carbon dioxide.
(b) **People Live in Forests** Many people live in forests worldwide and their survival depends almost on the forests.
(ii) To conserve the forest in India, government is regulating and planning the cutting of trees and checking over forest clearance for agricultural habitation purpose.

32. Differentiate between afforestation and deforestation. State a disadvantage of deforestation. [2015]

Ans. Afforestation is the planting of trees in abandoned areas or any other suitable place, in order to improve our environment. On the other hand, deforestation is the process of cutting down of trees for various purposes like industrialisation, urbanisation, etc. A disadvantage of deforestation is loosening of soil particles, which eventually results in soil erosion and land degradation.

Picture Based Questions

1. Study the diagram below and answer the questions that follow

(i) Identify the type of vegetation.
(ii) Name the two regions where this vegetation is found.

Ans. (i) Tropical Evergreen forests
(ii) These forests are found in Western slopes of Western Ghats, Coast of Tamil Nadu and Odisha.

2. Study the diagram below and answer the questions that follows.

(i) Identify the type of vegetation.
(ii) Name the two regions where the vegetation is found.

Ans. (i) Mangrove forests/vegetation.
(ii) These forests are found in the deltaic tracts of Ganga, Godavari, Krishna, Kaveri and Mahanadi.

Chapter Assessment

Section-I

Multiple Choice Questions

1. Which of the following areas of India is covered by Tropical Evergreen forests?
   (a) Semi-arid areas of Gujarat
   (b) Eastern Ghats
   (c) Western Ghats
   (d) Madhya Pradesh

2. What is the altitude of temperate grasslands?
   (a) 1000-2000 m (b) Above 4000 m
   (c) 2000 to 3500 m (d) Above 3500 m

3. With reference to Indian forests, consider the following pairs:
   (i) Tropical Moist Deciduous Forests-Sandalwood
   (ii) Tropical Dry Deciduous Forests-Sal
   (iii) Tropical Thorn Forests-Shisham

   Which of the pairs given above is/are correctly matched?
   (a) Only (i)
   (b) (i) and (ii)
   (c) (ii) and (iii)
   (d) (i), (ii) and (iii)

Section-II

Short Questions

1. Define the term 'Forest'.
2. What do you understand by the term 'xerophytes'?
3. Why are tidal forests important for us?
4. Who launched the Van Mahotsav and what is its importance?
5. What is the difference between Xerophytic vegetation and Tundra vegetation?

Long Quesions

1. Which factors are responsible for variation in natural vegetation?
2. Explain why are forests important for human beings.
3. Differentiate between Thorn and Scrubs forests and Mangrove forests.
4. Discuss the various measures and schemes that the government had adopted in order to conserve forests resources.
5. Briefly explain about social forestry.
6. State the important features of Joint Forest Management (JFM) programme.

CHAPTER

07

Water Resources

SYLLABUS

Water Resources Source (Surface water and Groundwater) Need for conservation and conservation practices (Rain water harvesting and its importance). ***Irrigation*** Importance and Methods

Water is essential for humans, living organisms and natural habitat. Water resources are used for drinking, cleaning, agriculture, transportation, animal husbandry, hydroelectricity, industrial and commercial use.

Sources of Water

97% of water available on the Earth is saline water and the remaining 3% is fresh water. Over 2.3% of this fresh water is frozen in glacier and polar ice caps. Out of the remaining 0.7% freshwater, 0.66% is groundwater and 0.03% is freshwater found in rivers, lakes and streams. The sources of water are

- **Surface Water** Water present on the surface of the Earth such as in a river, lake, wetland or ocean is called surface water. India's 60% of surface water is provided by the rivers like Indus, Ganga and Brahmaputra, etc.
- **Groundwater** Water present under the surface of the Earth is called groundwater. Groundwater makes up 98% of the fresh water on the planet. About 3/4th of the total groundwater is used for irrigation.

Conservation of Water

Conservation of water is the practice of using water efficiently and to prevent and control the unnecessary wastage of water.

Need for Conservation of Water

Conservation of water is necessary due to following reasons

- Rapid industrialisation and urbanisation are continuously declining availability of water and exerting a lot of pressure on the available water resources in the country.
- Greater demand for water due to growing population, leads to falling ground water level.
- Hydro-electric power also requires water for its production.
- Rainfall is unevenly distributed over time and space as different area receive different amount of rainfall.
- Irrigation consume more than 90% of total fresh water.
- In inland saline areas, the fresh water is becoming saline due to excessive withdrawal of ground water.

Practices for Conservation of Water

There are majorly two practices for the conservation of water i.e. watershed management and rainwater harvesting.

Watershed Management

It refers to the efficient management and conservation of both the surface and groundwater resources.

It include

- Prevention of surface runoff.
- Storage and recharge of groundwater by different methods such as percolation tanks, recharge wells, etc.
- The conservation, regeneration and judicious use of all natural resources (land, water, plants and animals) and human resources within a watershed.

A watershed development project has been started by the Central Government of India called **Haryali.** It aims at enabling the rural people to conserve water for irrigation, drinking, fisheries and afforestation.

Rainwater Harvesting

In this method, rain water is collected, stored and used for land irrigation. There are two ways of rainwater harvesting which are

(i) Surface Runoff Harvesting or Recharge of Groundwater

Surface runoff water harvesting is the collection, accumulation and storing of rain water for its eventual reuse.

It has various structures which are used to recharge or refill groundwater such as

- **Recharge Pits** These pits are constructed for recharging the **shallow acquifers**[1], where permeable rocks are exposed on the land surface or near the ground.
- **Trenches** These are built when the permeable rock layers are present at shallow depths.
- **Dug Wells** The dug well is recharged by drainpipes which carry the water via filtration tank. Rain water that is collected on rooftop of buildings is also diverted to the dug wells.
- **Trench with Recharge Well** It is developed in areas where the surface soil is impervious (not allowing water to pass through) and large quantities of roof water or surface run-off is available within a very short period of heavy rainfall. The use of trench/pits is made to store water in a filter medium. It subsequently recharges the groundwater through especially constructed recharge wells.

(ii) Rooftop Rainwater Harvesting

It is a system of collecting rainwater. In this technique, the roof becomes the catchments and the rainwater is collected from the roof of the building. This method is less expensive and very effective. It helps in improving the groundwater level of the surface, if it is implemented properly. This systems mainly constitutes the following sub-components

- **Catchment** The surface that receives rainfall directly is the catchment, e.g. sloping roof or flat roof.
- **Water Pipes** Rainwater from rooftop is carried down through water pipes or drains to the storage/harvesting system. Water pipes should be UV resistant of required capacity.
- **First Flush** It is a device used to flush off the water received in first shower. First rain contains contaminants of the atmosphere and catchment roof, thus first rain separator should be made at outlet of each drain pipe.
- **Filteration** Filters are used for treatment of water to effectively remove **turbidity**[2]. There are different types of filters which are used like Sand Gravel Filter, Charcoal Filter and PVC-Pipe Filter.

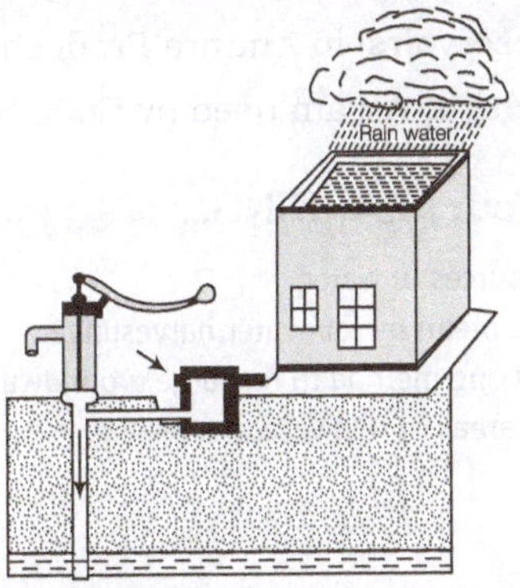

Rooftop Rainwater Harvesting

Advantages or Needs of Rainwater Harvesting

- It reduces flood like situation from water runoff, erosion and contamination of surface water with pesticides, sediments, metals and fertilisers.
- It promotes both water and energy conservation.
- Rainwater is excellent source of water for landscape irrigation, with no chemicals, dissolved salts and minerals from the soil.

1 **Shallow Acquifers** They are underground layer of water bearing permeable rocks.
2 **Turbidity** It is the colourless or haziness of a fluid caused by large number of individual particles and suspended matter.

Disadvantages of Rainwater Harvesting

- Rainwater harvesting is not possible in areas with limited and uncertain rainfall.
- The payback period varies depending on the size of storage and complexity of the system.
- Rainwater harvesting system requires some technical skills to install and regular maintenance.

Areas of Rainwater Harvesting

Rain water harvesting is very popular in Rajasthan, Gujarat, Andhra Pradesh, Assam and Karnataka. Some of the regional names of rainwater harvesting systems in India are

- Johads (Eastern dam) and Kunds (covered underground tanks) in Rajasthan.
- Tankas (underground small tanks) and Khadin (a long Eastern embankment to store runoff water) in Gujarat.
- Bhandaras or Kere (tanks) in the Deccan Plateau.
- Surangam (tunnel well) in Western Ghats and Korambu (temporary dam) in Eastern Ghats.
- Kuhe in Western Himalayas and Zing in Ladakh.
- Cheruvu (reservoirs) in Andhra Pradesh.
- Dongs (ponds) in Assam used by Bodo tribes.

Check Your LEARNING...

1. Name two sources of water.
2. What do you mean by rainwater harvesting?
3. Mention any one method to recharge groundwater.
4. Name some areas of rainwater harvesting.

Irrigation

The artificial means of supplying water to the agricultural fields from wells, tanks, canals, etc is known as irrigation. There are various types of irrigation practices in different parts of India.

Importance of Irrigation

The following points visualise the importance of irrigation in India

- **Unpredictable Rainfall** Insufficient and irregular rain causes uncertainty in agriculture. So, irrigation is necessary to provide sufficient moisture to the agricultural fields in order to stop crop failure.
- **Multiple Cropping Possible** Irrigation facilities help in the growing of two or three crops in a year which enhance agriculture production and productivity.
- **Bringing more Land under Cultivation** Irrigation helps in maximisation of land under cultivation as India's agricultural land requires substantial capital investment to make land fit for cultivation.
- **Increases in Employment** Irrigation increases employment potential by developing allied activities like means of transport, etc.
- **Crop Requirements** Different quantities of water are required by different crops. For example,
  - The requirements of water for rabi, kharif and zaid crops are different.
  - Some crops require water before maturing and some require water during maturing period.
  - High yielding varieties require more water.
  - Commercial crops like sugarcane need high quantity of water.

Thus, irrigation is important for different crops according to their need.

- **Nature of the Soil** The irrigation requirements of a crop depend on the nature of soil in which the crop is grown. There are two types of soil i.e. sandy soil and clayey soil. Sandy soil is highly porous having high permeability. Thus, crop cultivated in sandy soil needs more frequent irrigation. On the other hand, the clayey soil is less permeable than sandy soil due to which the crop grown in a clayey soil needs less irrigation.
- **Utilisation of River Water Effectively** There is a wide disparity in the water flow from year to year. Many rivers in India are not perennial and carry insignificant flows during the rabi season. The rivers of Central and Southern India remain largely dry during the eight months of the year. Therefore, to effectively utilise the water of these rivers, means of irrigation have to be used.
- **Increase or Maximise Production** Irrigation maximise or increase the production as according to agricultural scientists, the irrigated crops give more productivity than the unirrigated crops.

Methods of Irrigation

The methods of irrigation depend upon various factor like topography, soils, rainfall, availability of groundwater, nature of rivers and requirements of crops. The methods of irrigation can be categorised into traditional and modern methods.

Traditional Methods of Irrigation

(i) Canal Irrigation

This method of irrigation is very popular in Northern part of the country due to **perennial**[3] flow of water on flat **terrain**[4]. There are two main requirements for digging canal which are

(i) Fertile soil with low level relief.

(ii) Sources of water should be perennial which means snow-fed rivers.

The canals for irrigition are of the two types

(i) **Inundation Canals** These canals are taken out directly from the rivers. They do not have any kind of **weirs**[5] and barrages to regulate the flow of water from the rivers. These types of canal are found on the Sutlej-Ganga Plains and Brahmaputra valley.

(ii) **Perennial Canals** These canals maintain its water flow throughout the year either from the river or from reservoir of the river projects. A weir is built below the intake of the canal and the intake itself is being regulated by **sluice**[6] gates.

Important Canal Systems in India

- **Northern India** In Northern India, upper Ganga canal, lower Ganga canal, East Yamuna canal, Sharda canal and Agra canal are the important canal systems of Uttar Pradesh.

  Sirhind canal, Upper Bari Doab canal and Nangal dam canal are important in Haryana and Indira Gandhi canal and Chambal Project canal are important in Rajasthan.
- **Southern India** In Sourthern India, Godavari canal system, Krishna delta canal and Tungabhadra project canal are the important canal systems of Andhra Pradesh. The Koyana project is important in Maharashtra, the Hirakud project is important in Odisha and the Kakrapar project is important in Gujarat.

Advantages of Canal Irrigation

- Canals carry a lot of sediment brought down by the rivers which gets deposited in the agricultural fields and add to the fertility of the soil.
- The perennial canals provide constant supply of water and save the crops from drought situations.
- Canal irrigation has benefitted the sandy areas of Rajasthan which are yielding good agricultural crops.
- Canal irrigation has converted Punjab and Haryana into a Granary of the country.
- Although the initial investment for constructing a canal is high but it is quite cheap in the long run.

Disadvantages of Canal Irrigation

- During rainy season, many canals overflow and flooded the already cultivated areas.
- In areas where the water is excessively flowing in fields, canals raises the ground water level and results in bringing the alkaline salts to the surface. This makes the field unfit for agriculture or unproductive.
- Canal irrigation led to water logging due to which the capacity of soil to absorb water reduces and this destroys the standing crops, stored grains, etc.
- Canal irrigation is suitable mainly in plain areas.

(ii) Tank Irrigation

Tanks are constructed by building Earthen walls built across a depression or valley behind which rainwater collects. Tank is a reservoir of any specific size. It is popular in the peninsular plateau area i.e. Andhra Pradesh, Tamil Nadu and Maharashtra because these areas have uneven and seasonal rainfall. This method of irrigation is also important in Deccan region as the rivers of Deccan mainly depends on rainwater which become dry up when there is not rain.

Advantages of Tank Irrigation

- It is inexpensive as tanks are mostly natural.
- It is highly significant because it stores the abundant rainwater and reduces the waste of the excessive flowing water.
- Since wells and tubewells cannot be dug in the rocky surface, tanks irrigation is possible.

Disadvantages of Tank Irrigation

- In the absence of rainwater during dry season, the tanks become dry and fail to provide water for irrigation.

---

3 **Perennial** It means something which last or exist for a long or infinite time.

4 **Terrain** A piece of ground having specific characteristics.

5 **Weirs** A low dam built across a stream to raise its level or divert its flow.

6 **Sluice** A sliding gate for controlling the flow of water.

- Due to deposition of sediments, the tanks get blocked up soon and deblocking is necessary for making irrigation suitable which is expensive.
- Tanks occupy large fertile areas which could be used for agricultural purposes.
- Since tanks are very extensive and shallow, there is possibility of loss of stored water through evaporation.

(iii) Well Irrigation

Wells are the traditional method for supplying water for domestic purpose, agriculture and drinking. India's irrigated area through wells is about 40%. Wells are two types i.e. lined wells and unlined wells

(i) **Lined Wells** These wells are man-made. They are constructed artificially by digging into the ground and making a supporting wall of bricks in a circular pattern.

(ii) **Unlined Wells** These wells are formed naturally and are not protected by wall of bricks around it.

Well irrigation is practised in the states of Uttar Pradesh, Punjab, Haryana, Bihar, Goa, Gujarat, Rajasthan, Maharashtra, Madhya Pradesh, Andhra Pradesh, Karnataka and Tamil Nadu.

Methods of Lifting Water From Well

- **Persian Wheel Method** Persian wheel is a mechanical water lifting device operated usually by bullocks, buffaloes, camels or elephants, to lift water from open shallow wells. The method is mainly used in Punjab, Haryana and Western Rajasthan.
- **Lever Method** It is a very economical and efficient method of lifting water from shallow wells to a height of 3.5 to 4.5m. In this method, a large wheel is used to pull water which is attached to a pulley that is used to move the wheel. It is widely practised in Bihar and Andhra Pradesh.
- **Inclined Plane Method** This method is also known as **mhote.** In this method, a pair of bullocks is used to lift water from wells.
- **Table Wells** In this method, power-driven pumps are used to lift water from tube wells from depths below 15 m. They can be dug at very low costs and hence can be used even by poor farmers.

Advantages of Well Irrigation

- It is less expensive.
- Wells can be dug anywhere where the soil is soft.
- By using pumps and tubewells, water can be lifted from great depths.

Disadvantages of Well Irrigation

- It is difficult to dig wells in the hilly regions and in the rocky areas of Southern Peninsula.
- Due to uneven distribution of underground water resources in different areas, wells do not function effectively.
- Due to excessive withdrawal of underground water and lowering of water table, the traditional wells dry up.

(iv) Tube Well Irrigation

In this methods, a deep borewell is digged at a depth of about 30 m and water is taken out with the help of an electric or diesel motor. It is also called **lift method.** Tube wells are important means of irrigation in Northern India especially in Punjab, Haryana, Uttar Pradesh, Bihar, West Bengal, etc.

Advantages of Tube well Irrigation

- Tube well is able to irrigate a larger agricultural land.
- Large amount of underground water is easily available through this method.
- This method is reliable during dry season when the surface water dries up as the tube well is drilled up to the permanent water table.
- A good amount of water can be pulled out in a short period of time through this method.

Disadvantages of Tube well Irrigation

- Tube well irrigation is not possible if the groundwater is salty.
- It is costly as it requires regular supply of electricity.
- It is not possible if the underground water level is low.
- Excessive use of tube well leads to lowering of groundwater level.

Modern Methods of Irrigation

- **Sprinkler Irrigation** It is a method of distributing water through a system of pipes in which water is supplied to plants uniformly. This is the best method of conserving water because it does not involve any loss of water by seepage or evaporation. It is suitable for arid and semi-arid region.

- **Drip Irrigation** It is also known as **trickle irrigation.** In this method, plastic pipes are used to place between the rows of crops or buried along the roots of plants and water is given or dripped directly to the crops.
- **Furrow Irrigation** It is a type of surface irrigation in which furrows are dug between the rows of the crops and water is evenly distributed to the entire field.
- **Spray Irrigation** In this method, a long **hose**[7] is set to water source on one side and water is released from the other side by spray guns to the cultivated land. It is an expensive, but water efficient method. However, evaporation takes place in this method and plant diseases occur due to excess moisture by over watering.

Check Your LEARNING...

1. State any one importance of irrigation.
2. What is the role of irrigation in providing employment?
3. How is tank irrigation different from well irrigation?
4. Which method of irrigation is used in semi-arid regions?

QUiCK Revision

- Water is essential for human civilisation, living organisms and natural habitat.
- About 97% of water available on earth is saline water and only 3% is freshwater.
- Surface water and groundwater are the sources of water.
- Major river basin in India are Indus system, Ganga-Brahmaputra system and East and West flowing peninsular rivers.
- Indian agriculture is totally dependent on monsoon system, but the distribution of water is highly uneven. Thus, irrigation system is required.
- Conservation of water means prevention and controlling of fresh water which encompasses through policies, strategies and activities to meet the current and future human demands.
- Irrigation is important due to unpredictable rainfall, multiple cropping to bring more land into cultivation and to fullfil crop requirements.
- Water harvesting is incorporated with all the different methods of conserving and collecting rainwater.
- Rainwater harvesting is the method of collecting, storing and using water for landscape irrigation.
- Johads, Tankas, Cheruvu, Dongs and Kere are some of the names of rainwater harvesting techniques in India.
- There two major methods of irrigation i.e. traditional methods and modern methods.
- Traditional methods of irrigation include wells, tanks, canals and tube wells.
- Modern methods means of irrigation include sprinkler irrigation, drip irrigation, furrow irrigation, spray irrigation, etc.
- In tube well irrigation, a deep borewell is digged at a depth of about 30 m and water is taken out by diesel or electric motor.

7 **Hose** A flexible tube for conveying a liquid or gas.

Chapter Practice

Section-I

Multiple Choice Questions

1. Watershed management does not refer to
   (a) prevention of runoff.
   (b) prevention of use of water.
   (c) efficient management and conservation of both surface and groundwater.
   (d) storage and recharge of groundwater by methods like percolation pits, recharge wells, etc.

Ans. (b) prevention of use of water.

2. The most important measure that Government should adopt to handle water crisis.
   (a) Watershed development project called Haryali.
   (b) Dig more tube wells and bore wells.
   (c) Start development and infrastructure projects in catchment areas.
   (d) Supply water to every house.

Ans. (a) Watershed development project called Haryali.

3. Name the rain water harvesting system practiced in Deccan plateau.
   (a) Khatri (b) Korambu
   (c) Surangam (d) Bhandaras and Kere

Ans. (d) Bhandaras and Kere

4. Which of the following is a ground water source ? [2023]
   (a) Pond (b) Lake
   (c) Spring (d) River

Ans. (c) Spring

5. What is the meaning of irrigation? **[Specimen Paper Semester-I 2022]**
   (a) The water received by rainfall.
   (b) The man-made arrangements of supplying water to the fields.
   (c) The storage of rain water.
   (d) The growing of crops.

Ans. (b) The man-made arrangements of supplying water to the fields.

6. Why do the inundation canals have limited use? **[Specimen Paper Semester-I 2022]**
   (a) They get water only when the rivers are in flood
   (b) They are taken out from a perennial river
   (c) They are constructed to store rain water
   (d) It occupies lot of space.

Ans. (a) They get water only when the rivers are in flood

7. Which of the following is a type of canal found in India? **[Specimen Paper Semester-I 2022]**
   (a) Perennial canal (b) River canal
   (c) Artificial canal (d) Ground canal

Ans. (a) Perennial canal

8. .... and .... states are the nucleus of Green Revolution.
   (a) Uttar Pradesh, Haryana
   (b) Punjab, Haryana
   (c) Madhya Pradesh, Bihar
   (d) Tamil Nadu, Karnataka

Ans. (b) Punjab, Haryana

9. The oldest and the cheapest means of irrigation is
   (a) tube wells
   (b) sprinkers
   (c) unlined and lined wells
   (d) drip irrigation

Ans. (c) unlined and lined wells

10. Tank irrigation is an important method of irrigation in Karnataka because
    (a) most of Karnataka is fed by perennial rivers.
    (b) Karnataka is a plain land and the rivers are fed by glaciers.
    (c) Karnataka being in the Deccan region, has natural depressions and hard sub-surface.
    (d) Karnataka has large tracts of land covered in sand.

Ans. (c) Karnataka being in the Deccan region, has natural depressions and hard sub surface.

11. Which of the following is the main drawback of conventional method of irrigation ?
    (a) Optimum utilisation of water by irrigation.
    (b) Reduces seepage and evaporation.
    (c) Subject to cyclic changes of flooding and water stress situations resulting in poor yield.
    (d) Very good water management.

Ans. (c) Subject to cyclic changes of flooding and water stress situations resulting in poor yield.

12. 'Without irrigation, development of agriculture is difficult in India'. Why?
    (a) There is an increase in demand of food and cash crops.
    (b) use of high yielding seeds.
    (c) crops like rice and sugarcane need more water.
    (d) India receives rainfall throughout the year.

Ans. (a) There is an increase in demand of food and cash crops.

13. Sprinkler irrigation is efficient, but is still not a very commonly used method of irrigation by the Indian farmers. Why? **[Specimen Paper Semester-I 2022]**
    (a) There is no loss of water by seepage
    (b) It is an expensive method of irrigation
    (c) There is no loss of water by evaporation
    (d) Farmers are scared of getting wet

Ans. (b) It is an expensive method of irrigation

14. Which is the most advanced and efficient method of irrigation? [Specimen Paper Semester-I 2022]
(a) Canal irrigation (b) Well irrigation
(c) Drip irrigation (d) Tank irrigation

Ans. (c) Drip irrigation

15. Give reason for the following.
Sprinkler irrigation is practiced in arid and semi-arid regions.
(a) It is cheap and easy to install.
(b) It reduces loss of water due to evaporation and seepage.
(c) It can be used for all types of crops.
(d) It requires simple machinery.

Ans. (b) It reduces loss of water due to evaporation and seepage.

16. Give reason for the following.
The tube wells are popular in India because
(a) they can be dug anywhere.
(b) large area can be irrigated by cheap electricity made available.
(c) they need a network of channels to irrigate the fields.
(d) they saturate the soil and make it swampy.

Ans. (b) large area can be irrigated by cheap electricity made available.

17. Choose the correct statement.
(i) About 3/4th of the total groundwater is used for irrigation.
(ii) About 1/4th of the total groundwater is used for irrigation.
(iii) About 1/2nd of the total groundwater is used for irrigation.
(iv) None of the above

Codes
(a) Only (i) (b) Only (ii)
(c) Only (iii) (d) None of these

Ans. (a) Only (i)

18. We do not need to conserve water because
(i) 71% of Earth is covered by water.
(ii) there is an increase in demand due to increase in population, irrigation and industrialisation.
(iii) loss of vegetation causes reduction in rainfall resulting in drought.
(iv) the water resources are polluted.

Codes
(a) Only (i) (b) Only (ii)
(c) Only (iii) (d) None of these

Ans. (a) Only (i)

19. Choose the correct statement regarding to the rainwater harvesting.
(i) Limited and uncertain local rainfall is the disadvantage of rainwater harvesting.
(ii) Technical skill is not required.
(iii) It promotes both water and energy conservation.
(iv) It does not reduce the flood.

Codes
(a) Only (i) and (ii) (b) Only (i) and (iii)
(c) Only (i) and (iv) (d) None of these

Ans. (b) Only (i) and (iii)

20. Choose the correct statement regarding to bamboo irrigation system.
(i) It is 200 years old system.
(ii) Mostly practised on North-East India.
(iii) It is one modern method of irrigation.
(iv) About 20 liters of water enters the bamboo pipe system.

Codes
(a) Only (i) and (ii) (b) Only (ii) and (iii)
(c) Only (iii) and (iv) (d) All of these

Ans. (d) All of these

21. Match the following.

Term	Definition
A. Crevices	1. A narrow opening in rock or wall.
B. Sluice	2. A piece of ground having specific characteristic.
C. Weir	3. A low dam built across a stream to rise its level or divert its flow.
D. Terrain	4. A sliding gate for controlling the flow of water

Codes

	A	B	C	D
(a)	1	4	3	2
(b)	1	2	3	4
(c)	2	1	4	3
(d)	4	1	3	2

Ans. (a)

22. Match the following. [Specimen Paper Semester-I 2022]

List I	List II
A. Khatri	1. Western Ghats
B. Johad	2. Ladakh
C. Zing	3. Western Himalayas
D. Surangam	4. Central India

Codes

	A	B	C	D
(a)	3	4	2	1
(b)	1	2	3	4
(c)	2	3	1	4
(d)	4	2	3	1

Ans. (a)

Section-II

Short Questions

1. Answer the following questions.
(i) What is the percentage of water on Earth?
(ii) Name the sources of surface water.

Ans. (i) 71 per cent of the Earth's surface is covered with water and the oceans holds 97 per cent of Earth's total water which is saline.
(ii) The sources of surface water are rivers, lakes, ponds, lagoons and backwater (a part of river).

2. Why is per capita availability of water getting decline?

Ans. The per capita availability of water is getting decline because of rapid industrialisation and urbanisation which is putting a lot of pressure on the available water resources. Hence, it is necessary to conserve water.

3. Give two main reasons why water scarcity occurs in India. **[2013]**

Ans. The two main reasons due to which water scarcity occurs in India are

(i) There is water scarcity due to industrialisation, rapid growth of modernisation of agriculture and urbanisation as they pollute the river water.

(ii) Rainfall is erratic and unreliable in India.

4. What are check dams?

Ans. Check dams are small barriers built across the direction of water flow on shallow rivers and streams for the purpose of water harvesting.

5. Answer the following questions.

(i) What is rainwater harvesting? **[2016]**

(ii) Mention two objectives of rainwater harvesting.

Ans. (i) Rainwater harvesting is the system of collecting rainwater directly or recharging it into the ground to improve groundwater storage in aquifer.

(ii) Two objectives of rainwater harvesting are

(a) Recharging the groundwater and raising its level.

(b) Preventing the rainwater from being wasted as there is water scarcity.

6. Mention any two methods of recharging ground water aquifers. **[2020]**

Ans. Two methods of recharging ground water aquifers are

(i) Constructing recharging wells.

(ii) Constructing recharge pits and shafts.

7. Mention two techniques of rooftop rainwater harvesting.

Ans. The two techniques of rooftop rainwater harvesting are

(i) Catchment

(ii) First Flush

8. Mention two advantages of rainwater harvesting.

Ans. Two advantages of rainwater harvesting are

(i) It makes use of water and reduces flood like situation from water runoff, erosion and contamination of surface water with pesticides, sediments, metals and fertilisers.

(ii) It is an excellent source of water for landscape irrigation, with no chemicals such as fluoride and chlorine and no dissolved salts and minerals from the soil.

9. Answer the following questions

(i) Name any two traditional rainwater harvesting methods.

(ii) What do you mean by tanka and kul?

Ans. (i) Kuls of Himachal Pradesh and Khadins of Gujarat are two traditional rainwater harvesting method.

(ii) Tankas are underground tank for storing drinking water. Kul is a circular village tank from which water is released as and when required.

10. Answer the following questions

(i) What do you understand by irrigation?

(ii) Mention any two factors on which the source of irrigation depend.

Ans. (i) Irrigation refers to the process of supplying water to agricultural plants through wells, tanks, tube wells and canals.

(ii) Topography and rainfall are two main factors on which the source of irrigation depends.

11. "Without irrigation, development of agriculture is difficult in India." Clarify the statement by giving two reasons. **[2016]**

Ans. "Without irrigation, development of agriculture is difficult in India" because of

(i) the erratic and unpredictable monsoon of India which makes irrigation difficult.

(ii) uneven distribution of rainfall in different parts of the country.

12. Why do we need different modes of irrigation?

Ans. We need different modes of irrigation because of topographical features, availability of surface water, groundwater, soils and climatic condition.

13. Answer the following questions

(i) Name three traditional means of irrigation. **[2018]**

(ii) Give a reason why traditional means of irrigation are still important in most parts of India.

Ans. (i) The three traditional means of irrigation are

(a) Tank irrigation (b) Canal irrigation

(c) Well irrigation

(ii) Traditional means of irrigation are still important in most parts of India because these are less efficient, but more sustainable due to which farmers use water judiciously.

14. Answer the following questions

(i) Name the most common means of irrigation used in India.

(ii) Give one reason for the popularity of this means of irrigation in our country. **[2020]**

Ans. (i) Canals are the most common source of irrigation used in India. In Punjab, Haryana, Delhi, Uttar Pradesh, Bihar and Northern Rajasthan, canals are used to irrigate the soil.

(ii) Reasons for the popularity of canal irrigation is

- As Compared to conventional watering, higher productivity per hectare land is obtained due to canals.
- The canals constructed are permanent means of irrigation which can be used when there is fluctuation in rainfall.

15. What are inundation canals?

Ans. Inundation canals are taken out directly from the rivers and they do not have any kind of weirs and barrages to regulate the flow of water from the rivers. These types of canal are found on the Sutlej-Ganga Plains and Brahmaputra valley.

16. Why are inundation canals being converted to perennial canals? Give two reasons. [2012]

Ans. Inundation canals are converted to perennial canals because

(i) Inundation canals depend on flood water and dry up during the summer.

(ii) Perennial canals can provide water throughout the year.

17. There is plenty of rain in India during the rainy season, yet we need irrigation. Give two reasons to support this statement. [2018]

Ans. There is plenty of rain in India, but yet we need irrigation because

(i) the spatio-temporal variation in monsoon i.e. rainfall by monsoon is not same at every place.

(ii) rainfall fluctuates every year i.e. there may be good rainfall in one year and may be drought to another year.

18. How people of West Bengal harvest water in the flood plains?

Ans. People of Bengal harvest water by building inundation canals.

19. Answer the following questions

(i) What are perennial canals? (ii) What is a tank?

Ans. (i) Perennial canals maintain their water flow throughout the year either from the river or from reservoir of the river projects.

(ii) Tank is a man-made/natural structure which is used for preserving rainwater.

20. State two reasons why tank irrigation is popular in South India. [2014]

Ans. Tank irrigation is popular in South India due to following reasons

(i) South India consists of hard rock surface which makes it difficult to dig canals and wells.

(ii) Tank irrigation is the simplest and cheapest source of irrigation.

21. In which states of India, well irrigation is used?

Ans. Uttar Pradesh, Goa, Punjab, Haryana, Bihar, Rajasthan, Gujarat, Maharashtra, Madhya Pradesh, Andhra Pradesh, Karnataka and Tamil Nadu are the states where well irrigation is used.

22. Give a reason for the significance of irrigation in

(i) Punjab (ii) Rajasthan [2017]

Ans. (i) **Punjab** The demand for irrigation is greater in Punjab as it is predominantly an agricultural region. With supply of water, i.e. proper irrigation, crops like rice and sugarcane is grown which consume a lot of water.

(ii) **Rajasthan** Rajasthan receives less rainfall over the year. Thus, irrigation through canal system is adopted here. In Rajasthan, Indira Gandhi canal, Rajasthan canal and Chambal project canal are important projects for irrigation which are adopted by the government.

23. Answer the following questions

(i) Why is sprinkler irrigation method suitable for arid and semi-arid region?

(ii) Which area of India is famous for bamboo irrigation system?

Ans. (i) Sprinkler irrigation method is suitable for arid and semi-arid region because these do not involve any loss of water by seepage or evaporation.

(ii) The bamboo irrigation system is very popular in North-East part of India. This is 200 years old system used by the tribal farmers of Khasi and Jaintia hills.

24. Name two modern methods of irrigation. State one important reason for their growing popularity. [2015]

Ans. Two modern methods of irrigation are as follows

(i) Drip irrigation method

(ii) Sprinkler irrigation method

In the conventional methods of irrigation a large quantity of water is wasted due to water logging and often results in gradual salinity of the soil. This has made the modern methods of irrigation more popular.

25. "The modern means of irrigation are gaining popularity." Give two reasons to justify this statement. [2019]

Ans. The modern methods of irrigation are gaining popularity because

- In the conventional methods of irrigation a large quantity of water is wasted.
- These create water logging issue and often results in gradual salinity of the soil.

26. Name two states in which tube wells are extensively used. Give a reason to explain its importance as a source of irrigation. [2013]

Ans. Uttar Pradesh and Punjab states have extensive use of tube wells.

The importance of tube wells as a source of irrigation are

(i) Tube wells are very useful during drought conditions when surface wells dry up.

(ii) Tube wells can irrigate a large number of area as compared to surface wells.

27. Mention two factors that favour the development of tubewell irrigation in Punjab.

Ans. The factors for the development of tubewells as a source of irrigation in Punjab are

(i) The level of water table is high in Punjab due to which tubewell irrigation is favourable.

(ii) The soil in Punjab is soft which makes it easier to dug holes required for tubewell irrigation.

28. Mention two factors which are essential for the development of tubewell irrigation. [2016]

Ans. The factors essential for the development of tube wells irrigation are

(i) Water level should be high with perennial water supply.

(ii) The ground should be soft, preferably alluvial soil, so as to facilitate deep digging.

Long Questions

1. Answer the following questions.

(i) Differentiate between surface water and groundwater. [2018]

(ii) Mention two reasons to explain as to why we are facing water scarcity in recent times.

Ans. (i) Surface water is found in a river or a lake. It is exposed to many different contaminants such as animal wastes, pesticides, algae, etc and not useful for drinking directly.

On the other hand, groundwater is contained by a sub-surface layer of soil or rock and contaminants found in it are dissolved minerals, therefore it is used as drinking water directly.

(ii) Refer to answer of Short Question Q. 3.

2. Give three reasons for conservation of water resources. [2014, 2011]

Ans. Conservation of water resources is essential in India due to following reasons

(i) To safeguard ourselves from health hazards as the quality of water is badly affected by discharge of urban wastes, industrial effluents, pesticides and fertilisers.

(ii) The underground water has been exploited and the water table has been lowered.

(iii) Many regions of India face shortage issue or drought like condition, e.g. North-Western parts of India.

3. What are the factors of water scarcity?

Ans. The factors of water scarcity are

- Industrialisation and urbanisation
- Lack of water management
- Disposition of waste substance
- Low water table
- Unequal access of water among different social groups.

4. Answer the following questions.

(i) How is freshwater obtained?

(ii) How is freshwater being renewed?

Ans. (i) The freshwater is obtained from surface run off and groundwater that is continually being renewed.

(ii) The freshwater is being renewed through the hydrological cycle.

5. Answer the following questions.

(i) What type of regions are expected to face water shortage?

(ii) In which areas, rainwater harvesting is used?

(iii) Name regions where these rainwater harvesting techniques are used.

(a) Dongs (b) Cheruva

Ans. (i) Regions with low rainfall, low water table, desert and drought prone areas are expected to face water shortage.

(ii) Rainwater harvesting is used in the states of Rajasthan, Gujarat, Andhra Pradesh, Assam and Karnataka.

(iii) (a) Dongs technique is used in Assam by Bodo tribes.

(b) Cheruva technique is used in Andhra Pradesh.

6. Mention any three water harvesting systems practiced in India. [2011]

Ans. The three water harvesting systems practiced in India are

(i) **Rooftop Rainwater Harvesting** It is a system of catching rainwater where it falls. In this technique, the roof becomes the catchment and the rainwater is collected from the roof of the building.

(ii) **Kuls** In hills and mountainous regions, people built diversion channels like the 'guls' or 'kuls'. It is common in Western Himalayas and largely used for irrigation.

(iii) **Johads and Khadins** In arid and semi-arid regions, agricultural fields were converted into rain fed storage structures that allowed the water to retain and moisten the soil. This is known as 'Khadins in Jaisalmer and Johads in other parts of Rajasthan.

7. (i) Name two methods of water harvesting in India.

(ii) Mention any two objectives of rainwater harvesting. [2018, 2013]

Ans. (i) The two methods of water harvesting in India are

(a) Rooftop rainwater harvesting.

(b) Recharge of groundwater.

(ii) The two objectives of rainwater harvesting are

(a) It check the rainwater from flowing far away so, as to prevent soil erosion or flooding of the surrounding area.

(b) It meet the demands of water requirement in dry season.

8. State any three components of rooftop rainwater harvesting system.

Ans. The components of rooftop rainwater harvesting are

(i) **Catchment** The surface that receives rainfall directly is the catchment, e.g. sloping roof or flat roof.

(ii) **Water Pipes** Rainwater from rooftop is carried down through water pipes or drains to the storage/ harvesting system.

(iii) **First Flush** It is a device used to flush off the water received in first shower. First rain contains contaminants of the atmosphere and catchment roof thus, first rain separator should be made at outlet of each drain pipe.

9. Write down the different regional names of rainwater harvesting in India.

Ans. The different regional names of rainwater harvesting in India are

- Johads (Eastern dam), Kunds (covered underground tanks) in Rajasthan.
- Tankas (underground small tanks) and Khadin (a long Eastern embankment to store runoff water) in Gujarat.
- Bhandaras or Kere (tanks) in the Deccan Plateau.
- Surangam in Western Ghats and Korambu in Eastern Ghats.
- Khatri or Kuhe in Western Himalayas and Zing in Ladakh.
- Cheruvu (reservoirs) in Andhra Pradesh.
- Dongs (ponds) in Assam used by Bodo tribes.

10. Briefly explain the following terms. **[2019]**

(i) Inundation canal
(ii) Rooftop rainwater harvesting
(iii) Surface water

Ans. (i) Inundation canals are taken out from the rivers and do not have any kind of weirs and barrages to regulate the flow of water from the rivers.

(ii) Rooftop rainwater harvesting is a system of collecting rainwater. In this technique, the roof becomes the catchments and the rainwater is collected at the roof of the building. This method is less expensive and very effective and if implemented properly, it helps in augmenting the groundwater level of the area.

(iii) Surface water is the water present in the water bodies which are found on the surface of the ground, e.g. rivers, lakes, ponds, lagoons, backwater, etc.

11. State any three reasons why irrigation is important to a country like India.

Ans. Irrigation is important to a country like India as

- **Unpredictable Rainfall** Insufficient and irregular rain causes uncertainty in agriculture. So, irrigation is necessary to provide sufficient moisture to the agricultural fields in order to stop crop failure.
- **Multiple Cropping Possible** Irrigation facilities help in the growing of two or three crops in a year which enhance agriculture production and productivity.
- **Bringing more Land under Cultivation** Irrigation helps in maximisation of land under cultivation as India's agricultural land requires substantial capital investment to make land fit for cultivation.

12. Answer the following questions. **[2020]**

(i) What geographical conditions make irrigation necessary in the country?
(ii) How has irrigation changed the cropping pattern in India?
(iii) Why is there a scarcity of surface water in our country?

Ans. (i) The physical and climatic diversity of India has made it necessary to have irrigation facility to provide water for both agricultural purpose.

(ii) Availability of adequate water for irrigation has changed the cropping pattern of various regions. Many farmers because of the increased availability of water have switched over to the cultivation of water intensive commercial crops such as jute, cotton and tea, rather than food grains such as bajra, wheat and ragi.

(iii) Water scarcity may be caused by climate change, such as altered weather patterns including droughts or floods, increased pollution, and increased human demand and overuse of water. Water scarcity is being driven by two converging phenomena, growing freshwater use and depletion of usable freshwater resources.

13. Give one geographical reason of each of the following. **[2014]**

(i) Irrigation is necessary despite the monsoon.
(ii) The drip method of irrigation is the best method among all modern methods of irrigation.
(iii) Canal irrigation leads to the ground around it becoming unproductive.

Ans. (i) Irrigation is necessary is because Indian monsoon is erratic and unpredictable.

(ii) Drip method of irrigation is the best among all modern methods of irrigation because it adheres highest water application efficiency and directly reaches the roots of plant, thus conserving water.

(iii) Canal irrigation leads to the ground around it unproductive because it lead to water logging.

14. Answer the following questions.

(i) Name two states where perennial canals are widely used. **[2013]**
(ii) Briefly explain two reasons for perennial canals being a popular form of irrigation in the named states.

Ans. (i) The two states where perennial canals are widely used are Punjab and Haryana.

(ii) The two reasons for perennial canals being a popular form of irrigation in the named states are

(a) As these canals serve throughout the year, the agricultural production in the areas of less or uncertain rainfall has increased considerably.

(b) During hot season, the large traits of land of these states can also be cultivated through these perennial canals.

15. Give a reason for each of the following. **[2019]**

(i) Most of the South Indian states are not suitable for development of canal irrigation.
(ii) There is an urgent need for water conservation in India.
(iii) Development of irrigation is essential for the growth of the agriculture sector of India.

Ans. (i) Most of the South Indian states are located over a hard rocky surface. The digging of canals in rocky and uneven areas is difficult and uneconomic. Thus, these states are not suitable for canal irrigation.

(ii) Conservation of water resources is essential in India due to following reasons

(a) To safeguard ourselves from health hazards as the quality of water is badly affected by discharge of urban wastes, industrial effluents, pesticides and fertilisers.

(b) The underground water has been exploited and the water table has been lowered.

(iii) Development of irrigation is essential for the growth of the agriculture sector of India because the Indian agriculture mostly depends on monsoon rainfall which is inadequate and fluctuates every year. Thus to minimise this dependence, different methods of irrigation should be developed in the country.

16. Give one reason for each of the following. **[2016]**

(i) The Northern Plain of India is found suitable for canal irrigation.

(ii) Tank irrigation is an important method of irrigation in Karnataka.

(iii) Although expensive, yet sprinkler irrigation is gaining popularity in recent times.

Ans. (i) The Northern Plain of India is suitable for canal irrigation because it has low level relief, deep fertile soils and perennial source of water.

(ii) Tank irrigation is an important method of irrigation in Karnataka because most of the area here is uneven with many natural depression where the tanks can be built.

(iii) Although considered as an expensive source, sprinkler irrigation is gaining popularity in recent times because there is no loss of water by seepage and evaporation.

17. Answer the following questions.

(i) Name two states of India where canal irrigation is extensively used.

(ii) Name the types of canals used in India.

(iii) Mention one point of difference between the types of canals mentioned by you. **[2020]**

Ans. (i) Canal irrigation is mostly followed in Uttar Pradesh, Andhra Pradesh, Punjab, Haryana, West Bengal and Bihar. In canal irrigation, Uttar Pradesh stands first followed by Punjab and Haryana.

(ii) Inundation canals and perennial canals are used in India.

(iii) Inundation canals are taken out from the rivers without constructing dams, barrage, and embankments. On the other hand, prennial canals are taken out from the rivers or reservoirs by constructing dams or barrages.

18. Where are tanks most widely used in India? Why?

Ans. Tanks are mostly used in peninsular India i.e. Andhra Pradesh, Tamil Nadu and Maharashtra. This is because

- The undulating relief and hard rocks make it difficult to dig canals and wells.
- There is little percolation of rainwater due to hard rock structure and groundwater is not available in large quantity.
- There are several streams which become torrential during rainy season. The only way to make best use of this water is to impound it by constructing bunds and building tanks. Otherwise this water would go waste to the sea.

19. (i) Why is well irrigation still a popular means of irrigation? Give two reasons to support your answer **[2013]**

(ii) State the significance of rainwater harvesting.

Ans. (i) Well irrigation is a popular method of irrigation due to the following reasons

(a) Wells can be dug very easily in areas of soft soil.

(b) By the use of pumps and tubewells, water can be lifted even from great depths.

(ii) The significance of rainwater harvesting is

- This method helps to raise the groundwater table by recharging of groundwater reserves.
- It helps to reduce surface runoff and avoid flooding.

20. Give one geographical reason for each of the following. **[2017]**

(i) Sprinkler irrigation is practiced in arid and semi-arid regions.

(ii) A tube well should be installed in a fertile and productive regions.

(iii) Canal irrigation is more suitable in the Northern Plains.

Ans. (i) Refer to answer of Short Question Q. 23 (i).

(ii) A tube well should be installed in a fertile and productive regions because water table should be high with perennial water supply for tube well.

(iii) Canal irrigation is more suitable in the Northern Plains because here the rivers are perennial and flow through flat terrain.

21. Why is drip irrigation called 'trickle irrigation'? Give its two advantages.

Ans. Drip irrigation is called 'trickle irrigation' because in this method irrigation is done through dripping steadily rather than fast flow of water.

Its two advantages are

(i) Water keeps on dripping steadily which avoid wastage.

(ii) It takes water directly to the roots of the plants or trees.

22. Give two advantages and one disadvantage that tubewells have over surface wells.

Ans. Advantages of tube wells are

(i) Tube well do not result in evaporation of water like suface wells.

(ii) It irrigates large area (400 hectares) as compared to surface wells.

A disadvantage of tube well is that it is only possible in areas where the groundwater level is not too low and power is needed to drain water. On the other hand, water can be stored in surface well even if their is no ground water.

23. Answer the following questions.

(i) Give two advantages of tube wells as a method of irrigation.

(ii) What are the conditions necessary for tube wells ?

Ans. (i) Two advantages of tube wells as method of irrigation are

(a) Tube wells can irrigate a larger area about 400 hectares.

(b) This method of irrigation is quicker and more convenient.

(ii) The conditions necessary for tube wells are

(a) sufficient ground water.

(b) cheap electric power must be made available.

24. Distinguish between Inundation canal and Perennial canal. [2023]

Ans. The differences between Inundation canal and Perennial canal are

Inundation Canal	Perennial Canal
The supply of water is uncertain.	The water supply is certain.
It irrigates only low-lying areas of land.	It irrigates all types of areas of land.

Picture Based Questions

1. Study the diagram below and answer the questions that follow. [2017]

(i) Name the activity shown in the diagram.

(ii) Give two objectives of the activity.

Ans. (i) The activity shown in the diagram is of rooftop rainwater harvesting method.

(ii) Two objectives of rainwater harvesting method are

(a) It is simple scheme to replenish the groundwater and increase its level.

(b) The purpose of rainwater harvesting is to utilise the rainwater to its maximum and not to let it runoff or go waste.

2. Study the diagram below and answer the questions that follow.

(i) What does the picture shows?

(ii) What can be done in this regard?

Ans. (i) The picture shows to save the precious water on the Earth.

(ii) We can do various things to save water such as

(a) Recycle and reuse water.

(b) Use rainwater harvesting system to avoid rainwater runoff.

Chapter Assessment

Section-I

Multiple Choice Questions

1. The most advanced and efficient method of irrigation is
   (a) Canal Irrigation (b) Well Irrigation
   (c) Drip Irrigation (d) Tank irrigation
2. The man-made arrangements of supplying water to the fields is known as
   (a) water logging (b) irrigation
   (c) harvesting (d) None of these
3. .... type of canal is found in India.
   (a) Perennial canal (b) River canal
   (c) Artificial canal (d) Ground canal
4. Why sprinkler is not a very commonly used method of irrigation by the Indian farmers ?
   (a) There is no loss of water by seepage. (b) It is an expensive method of irrigation.
   (c) There is no loss of water by evaporation. (d) Farmers are scared of getting wet.

Section-II

Short Questions

1. Give the name of the various sources of surface water.
2. Name the states of India where well irrigation is in practice.
3. In Rajasthan and Meghalaya which type of water harvesting is popular?
4. What is Persian well method?

Long Questions

1. Why irrigation is important in India? Give any three reasons.
2. Explain three modern methods of irrigation.
3. Why there is a need to conserve water resource? Explain.
4. What are the advantages and disadvantages of tube well irrigation?

CHAPTER 08

Minerals and Energy Resources

SYLLABUS

Minerals and Energy Resources Iron ore, Manganese, copper, bauxite - uses and their distribution.

- Conventional sources : Coal, petroleum, natural gas (distribution, advantages and disadvantages)
- Hydel power (Bhakra Nangal Dam and Hirakud)
- Non-conventional sources : Solar, wind, tidal, geo-thermal, nuclear and bio-gas (generation and advantages)

Minerals

A mineral is a combination of two or more than two elements with definite chemical composition which is formed by inorganic processes. It is generally found in the Earth's crust in the form of ore which is used for various purposes by processing. All minerals get potential value after extraction and processing. Some unique characteristics of minerals are

- Distribution of minerals over the Earth's surface is uneven.
- There is inverse relationship between the quantity and quality of minerals i.e. good quality minerals are less in quantity and low quality minerals are found in large quantities.
- Minerals are exhaustible, once used they cannot be replenished immediately at the time of need. So, minerals have to be conserved and used judiciously.

Types of Minerals

Minerals are found in three forms i.e. metallic, non-metallic and energy minerals

(i) **Metallic Minerals** These are found in igneous rocks and contain metals. These minerals play an important role in the industrialisation and economic growth of the country. Some of these minerals are iron ore, manganese, bauxite, nickel, copper and gold.

(ii) **Non-Metallic Minerals** These minerals are found in sedimentary rocks and contain no metal. Some of these minerals are mica, limestone and gypsum.

(iii) **Energy Minerals** These minerals are also known as **fossil fuels**. They are major sources of energy. Some of these minerals are coal, petroleum and natural gas.

Metallic Minerals

Iron Ore

Iron ore is abundantly found on the Earth's crust. It provides the backbone to the **basic industry**[1]. India is the largest iron producing country in Asia. The deposits of iron ore are found near the areas producing coal, limestone, dolomite and manganese. These minerals are well utilised in several iron and steel plants. There are four types of iron ore found in India. They are

(i) **Magnetite (Black Ore)** Magnetite constitutes best quality of iron ore (70% iron content). It has strong magnetic property, hence, it is called magnetite. It is black in colour. It is obtained from Tamil Nadu and Karnataka.

1 **Basic Industry** These industries are backbone of industrial system as these industries make machines for other industries.

(ii) **Haematite** It is the second best quality of iron ore with 50% to 60% iron content. It contains pure iron and is known as 'oxide of iron'.

It is reddish in colour and also known as red iron. It is obtained from Jharkhand, Odisha, Chhattisgarh, Karnataka and Maharashtra.

(iii) **Limonite** It is inferior quality of iron ore which contains 40% to 60% pure iron. It is also known as 'hydrated iron-oxide'. It is found in yellow or light brown colour and is obtained from Raniganj (West Bengal), Uttar Pradesh, Uttarakhand and Himachal Pradesh.

(iv) **Siderite** It is low quality iron ore with 10% to 40% of pure iron and many impurities. It is also known as 'iron carbonate'.

Uses of Iron

- 90% of iron ore is used to make steel. Raw iron combined with other elements is used for construction, automobiles, railways machineries, etc.
- Black iron oxide is used as **pigments**[2] in polishing compounds, medicine and magnetic inks.
- Low grade iron ore is used in manufacturing sponge iron.
- Iron blue is used in blueprints, inks, paints, enamels, crayons, linoleum, etc.

Distribution of Iron Ore

Around 20% of world's total reserves of iron ore are found in India. It is obtained from peninsular India. Important iron ore producing states of India are

- **Odisha** Iron ore found in Odisha contain 55 to 68% iron content and belongs to haematite variety. Important mines are located at Gorumahisani, Sulaipet and Badampahar in Mayurbhanj district, Kiruburuaburu in Kendujhar district and Bonai in Sundergarh district.
- **Karnataka** It has large reserves of haematite and magnetite. Important mines are located at Donai Malai in Bellary-Hospet region, Baba Budan hills in Chikmagalur district and Kudremukh in Chitradurg district.
- **Chhattisgarh** Important mines are located at Dalli Rajhara in Durg district and Bailadilla in Bastar district.
- **Jharkhand** Important mines are located at Noamundi, Singhbhum and Palamu districts.
- **Goa** It supplies iron for household purposes and for export. The iron ore of Goa is of inferior limonite and siderite variety. In Goa, the richer and larger deposits are confined to North Goa.
- **Andhra Pradesh** In Andhra Pradesh, the iron ore producing areas are located in Anantpur, Krishna, Kurnool, Cuddapah and Nellore districts. The iron content in these deposits vary from 55 to 62 per cent.
- **Tamil Nadu** In Tamil Nadu, iron ore is found in Salem, North Arcot, Tiruchirapalli, Coimbatore and Madurai.
- **Maharashtra** In Maharashtra, iron ore deposits are found in the Ratnagiri and Chandrapur districts.
- **Rajasthan** In Rajasthan, iron ore deposits are found in Moriza in Bhilwara and Udaipur districts.

Manganese

It is an iron like metal occurs as natural oxide. It is a hard and black metal which is used in industries like in steel industry, dry battery industry and dye manufacturing industry.

Uses of Manganese

- It is used to improve the quality of many **alloys**[3], e.g. iron and steel. For manufacturing one tonne of steel, 10 kg of manganese is used.
- It is used in industries for manufacturing bleaching powder and insecticides.
- It is used to prepare alloys or mixture of different metals to accquire special properties for the minerals, e.g. ferro-manganese alloys.
- It is used to manufacture coloured glass.
- It is used to regulate blood sugar levels, supports immune system, involved in bone development and reproduction.
- It is also useful in plant growth as it reduces nitrates in green plants and algae.

Distribution of Manganese

India's manganese ore is produced by following states

- **Odisha** It is the leading manganese producer of India. Important mines are located in the districts of Bonai, Kendujhar, Sundergarh, Gangpur, Kalahandi and Balangir.

2 **Pigment** Dry colouring material, especially a powder to be mixed with a liquid to produce paint and hard coating.

3 **Alloy** A mixture containing two or more metallic elements or non-metallic elements usually dissolving into each other when molten.

- **Karnataka** In Karnataka, the mines are located in Dharwar, Ballari, Belgaum (Belagavi), North Canara, Chikkmagaluru, Shivamogga, Chitradurg and Tumakuru.
- **Maharashtra** Manganese is mainly mined in Nagpur, Bhandara and Ratnagiri districts. The main disadvantage of these mines is that they are located far from steel plants.
- **Madhya Pradesh** In Madhya Pradesh, manganese is found in a belt that extends through Balaghat-Chhindwara-Nimar-Mandla and Jhabua districts.
- **Others** Other minor producers of manganese are Telangana, Goa and Jharkhand.

Iron ore and Manganese Distribution in India

Copper

Copper is 'the red metal'. It is a non-ferrous base metal. It is one of the few metals that occur in the nature in directly usable metallic form with three principal elements i.e. sulphides, oxides and carbonate. Copper is malleable (flexible), easy to shape and ductile.

Uses of Copper

- It is used in electrical industry in the form of copper wires and other numerous kinds of electrical equipments because it is a good conductor of electricity.
- It is used in meterological sector as rain gauges.
- Copper is good conductor of heat, so it is extremely useful in refrigeration, utensils and in wires.
- It is used in space programmes and telecommunication.
- It is used in automobiles and in defence industries.
- It is alloyed (combined) with nickel and iron to make stainless steel.
- It is alloyed with aluminium to make duralumin.
- When it is alloyed with zinc, it is called brass and when it is alloyed with tin, it is called bronze.
- Copper is also used in construction, plumbing and ship building.

Distribution of Copper

Copper production in India is only about 3.4 per cent of the world production which makes India to depend on import for copper need.

The leading producers of copper are

- **Jharkhand** In Jharkhand, Singhbhum and Hazaribagh districts have good reserves of copper.
- **Madhya Pradesh** Malanjkhand copper belt and the Balaghat district have rich reserves of copper in Madhya Pradesh.
- **Rajasthan** Khetri copper belt, Jhunjhunu and Dariba in Alwar district have important reserves of copper in Rajasthan.
- **Maharashtra** Bhandara, Chandrapur, Gadchiroli and Nagpur districts are copper producing regions in Maharashtra.
- **Andra Pradesh** Guntur, Prakasam and Kurnool are the copper producing regions of Andhra Pradesh.

Bauxite

It is the ore of aluminium. It is mainly found in tertiary deposits and related to laterite rocks found on the plateau region or hilly area of peninsular India and also from coastal areas.

Uses of Bauxite

- It is used for making aluminium that is obtained in the form of hydrated aluminium oxides from bauxite.
- Aluminium from bauxite is used for making aircrafts, ships and utensils, as it is light in weight and resists rust.

- It is good conductor of electricity hence, it is used in electrical industry.
- It is also used in making mirrors, headlight reflectors and in telescopes.

Distribution of Bauxite

The major bauxite producing states in India are

- **Odisha** It is the largest producer of bauxite and the important producing areas in the Odisha are Kalahandi, Sambalpur, Balangir and Koraput.
- **Jharkhand** The patlands of Lohardaga in Jharkhand have rich deposits of bauxite.
- **Gujarat** Bhavanagar and Jamnagar in Gujarat have major deposits of bauxite.
- **Chhattisgarh** Amarkantak plateau region in Chhattisgarh has large deposits of bauxite.
- **Madhya Pradesh** Katni-Jabalpur area of Balaghat have important deposits of bauxite.
- **Maharashtra** Kolaba, Thane, Ratnagiri, Satara, Pune and Kolhapur are important producers of bauxite in Maharashtra.
- **Others** Tamil Nadu, Karnataka and Goa are the minor producers of bauxite in Maharashtra.

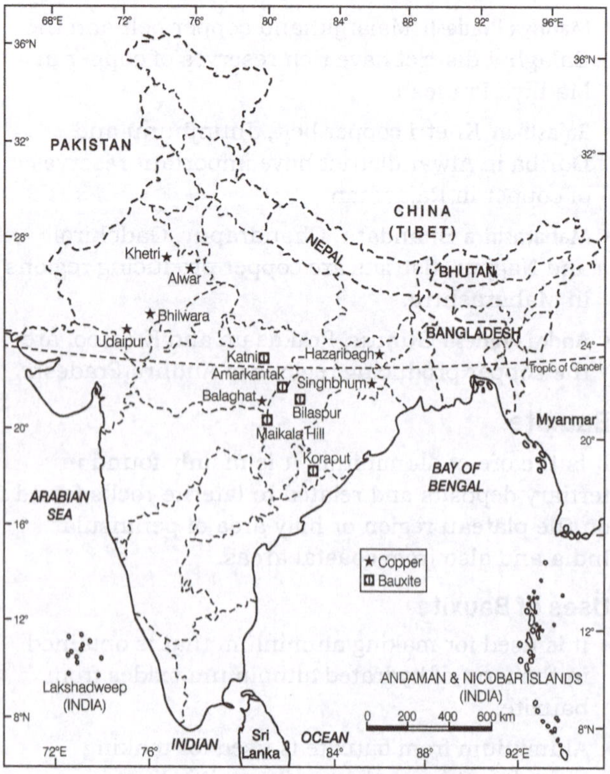

Copper and Bauxite Distribution in India

4 **Calorific Value** It is the amount of heat energy present in fuel.

Check Your LEARNING...

1. Name two metallic minerals.
2. Which variety of iron-ore contains maximum amount of pure iron?
3. Name the metal which is hard and black in nature.
4. Name two leading states producing bauxite.

Energy Resources

These include resources which are used for generating power or energy. These resources are categorised into conventional and non-conventional energy sources.

Conventional Sources of Energy

These sources of energy are being used since a long time. These resources cannot be renewed or replenished. They are exhaustible in nature.

For example, all fossil fuels like coal, petroleum, natural gas and hydel power. Except hydel power, these sources are costly and present in limited quantity.

Coal

It is formed by the accumulation of dead vegetation in swampy areas, coastal plains and basin lowlands. It is a kind of fossil fuel found in sedimentary rocks and also an inflammable organic substance. Coal is composed of carbon, hydrogen, oxygen, nitrogen and small amount of sulphur and phosphorus.

Types of Coal

On the basis of amount of moisture, carbon and voltaic matter, there are four types of coal as peat, lignite, bituminous and anthracite

Anthracite Coal

- It is a hard and compressed variety of coal with highest carbon content of 90%.
- It is associated with strongly deformed sedimentary rocks which were subjected to higher pressure and temperature.
- It burn slowly and leaves behind little ash after burning.
- It is lustrous, shiny and jet black in colour.
- It has high **calorific value**[4] and is good for domestic use since it is smokeless.
- It is found only in Jammu and Kashmir.

Bituminous Coal

- It is a black, hard, brittle and compact coal with 50% to 80% of carbon content in it.
- Due to high carbon content, its calorific value is very high and it has low moisture content.
- It is used as steam coal, household coal, coking coal, gas coal, etc. Steam coal is the best bituminous coal since it contains 80% carbon in it.
- Bituminous coal is black and lustrous and is widely used for domestic purposes.
- It is relatively a soft coal and contains tar like substance called bitumen.
- The highest grade bituminous coal is the coking coal which is an important ingredient in iron and steel smelting in blast furnaces
- Bituminous coal is found in Odisha, Jharkhand, Chhattisgarh, West Bengal and Madhya Pradesh.

Lignite Coal

- It is also referred to as brown coal.
- It is a soft brown combustible sedimentary rock.
- It has a carbon content of only 40%.
- It is a low grade coal due to its relative low heat content.
- It has high moisture content and is less combustible.
- It is found in Tamil Nadu, Rajasthan, Kerala, West Bengal and Puducherry.

Peat Coal

- Peat is an accumulation of partially decayed vegetative or organic matter which has undergone varying degree of decomposition and carbonisation.
- It has less carbon content and is of inferior grade as compared to the varieties of coal.
- The formation of Peat is the first step in the geological formation of other fossil fuels.
- Peat contains high moisture and small percentage of volatile matter.
- It is found in the regions of Nilgiri Mountain, in the Kashmir Valley and in the swampy areas of coastal plains.

Distribution of Coal

In India, coal is found in two rock sequences i.e **Gondwana deposits** and **Tertiary coal deposits.**

Gondwana Coal Fields

Most important Gondwana coal fields are located in the Damodar valley. It lies in West Bengal-Jharkhand region. Jharia (largest coal field), Raniganj (second largest field), Bokaro, Giridih, Karanpura are important Gondwana coal fields. Other river valleys associated with coal are Godavari, Mahanadi and Sone. The important coal mining centres are

- **Jharkhand** The important coal fields are Jharia, Giridih, North and South Karanpura, Ramgarh, Bokaro and Daltonganj. The **Jharia** coalfield is the **largest in India** which produces the best variety of coking coal.
- **Odisha** The important coalfields are Talcher, Rampur. They are situated in the Mahanadi basin.
- **Chhattisgarh** The important coal fields are **Korba** coal mine, Jhilimili and Bishrampur.
- **West Bengal** The important coalfields are found in Raniganj and Mejia. **Raniganj** coal field is the second largest coalfield in India while Mejia in Bankura district of West Bengal is a recently discovered large coal field.
- **Telangana** The major coalfields are Singareni, Tandur, Kothagudem and Yellandu.
- **Maharashtra** The major coalfields are found in Nagpur-Wardha region. The important mining areas are Wardha, Ballarpur, Chanda and Kamptee.
- **Madhya Pradesh** The major coal mines are Umaria, Sohagpur, Singrauli and Pench valley.

Tertiary Coal Fields

These are found in Assam, Arunachal Pradesh, Meghalaya, Nagaland and Kashmir. The important coal mining areas are

- Darangiri, Cherrapunji, Mewlong and Langrin in Meghalaya.
- Makum, Joypur and Nazira in Assam.
- Namchik- Namphuk in Arunachal Pradesh.
- Kalakot in Jammu and Kashmir.

Advantages of Coal

- It is easy to burn.
- It produces high energy upon its combustion.
- It is used for running **dynamos**[5], machines, trains and ships.
- It is also used for making iron and steel.
- It is safer as compared to nuclear energy.
- It is also used for domestic purposes, building materials and in potteries.
- It is used in Thermal Power Plant as raw material.

Disadvantages of Coal

- Its mining activity is dangerous for mining workers.
- Due to its mining, deforestation and land degradation take place and also habitats of wildlife get affected.
- Carbon emissions due to burning of coal have a negative impact on environment and cause climate change and global warming, acid rain, etc.
- Production and transportation cost of coal is very high.
- It is non-renewable source of energy.

Petroleum

The word 'petroleum' has been derived from two Latin words '*Petra*' which means 'rock' and '*Oleum*' which means 'oil'. Thus, it signifies 'rock oil'. Petroleum is formed from the remains of dead plants and animals decomposed millions of years ago. It is the main source of kerosene, diesel oil, paraffin wax, vaseline and benzene.

Petroleum has an organic origin and it is found in sedimentary basins, shallow depressions and in the seas. Petroleum is known as **liquid gold** due to its scarcity and different uses. The liquid form of petroleum is called crude petroleum, the gas form is called natural gas and the solid form is called asphalt, tar, bitumen, etc.

Crude petroleum consists of hydrocarbons of liquid and gaseous states varying in chemical composition, colour and specific gravity.

Oil refineries are industrial units where crude petroleum is refined and processed to produce useful products like gasoline, petroleum naphtha, LPG and diesel oil, asphalt base, etc.

Some of the oil refineries of India are Mathura Refinery, Mumbai Refinery, Haldia Refinery, Barauni Refinery and Panipat Refinery.

Distribution of Petroleum

The main oil deposits in India, in accordance to their importance are

- **Mumbai High** It is an offshore oil producing region located 160 km off Mumbai in the Arabian sea.

  It produces superior quality of crude oil as compared to Middle East countries. It was discovered in 1973 and started production in 1976. The oil in Mumbai High is drilled with the drillship Sagar Samrat which has a maximum drill depth of 20,000 feet.
- **Oilfields of Eastern Region** The oldest and the biggest oilfield in India is Digboi oilfield situated in Lakshmipur district of upper Assam. The other oilfields in this region are Moran, Bappapung, Hausanpung and Hugirijang.
- **Oilfields of Western Region** Cambay Basin in Gujarat is the main oilfield in the Western Region of India. The other important oilfields in Gujarat are Kalol, Koyali, Kosamba, Sanad, Kathana, Ankleshwar and Navgaon.

Distribution of Major Oil Refineries in India

State	Oil Refineries
Assam	Assam Oil Company, Digboi, Bongaigaon Refinery and Petroleum Limited
Bihar	Indian Oil Corporation, Barauni
West Bengal	Indian Oil Corporation, Haldia
Gujarat	Indian Oil Corporation, Koyali, Jamnagar Refineries
Maharashtra	Bharat Petroleum Corporation, Mumbai Hindustan Petroleum Corporation, Mumbai
Andhra Pradesh	Hindustan Petroleum Corporation, Visakhapatnam
Tamil Nadu	Madras Refineries, Chennai
Kerala	Kochi Refineries
Uttar Pradesh	Mathura Oil Refinery

Advantages of Petroleum

- Petroleum is a major energy source in India after coal.
- Transportation of petroleum is easy and can be done through pipelines or tankers to areas which uses it.
- Petroleum has high density i.e. 1 kg oil generate 10,000 kcal of energy.

5 **Dynamos** They are the machines used for converting mechanical energy into electricity.

- It supports many industries, mainly the petrochemical, fertilisers and chemical industries.
- Petroleum contain many hydrocarbons and it is used both as fuel and raw material.

Disadvantages of Petroleum

- The burning of petroleum emits large amounts of Carbon dioxide (CO_2) or greenhouse gas, which leads to global warming.
- It is a non-renewable source of energy.
- It is toxic to humans, animals and other forms of wildlife like plants and animals.
- Everything surrounding the use and processing of petroleum is expensive. The equipments to harness the oil is also very expensive.
- If petroleum spills in water bodies such as oceans and seas, it cause adverse effects to marine life. This spill can cause massive ocean pollution, causing the death of animals and fishes.
- Petroleum is inflammable and can cause fire.

Natural Gas

It is a naturally occurring hydrocarbon gas consisting primarily methane and small amount of propane and ethane. It is toxic, colourless and odourless gas. Natural gas is a fossil fuel used as a source of energy for heating, cooking and electricity generation.

Natural gas in compressed form is used as fuel for vehicles which is known as CNG (Compressed Natural Gas). It is a fuel which is used in place of petrol, diesel and LPG. In CNG, methane is stored at high pressure. The gas which is supplied to household for cooking purposes is known as LPG (Liquefied Petroleum Gas).

It is an odourless gas. However, the LPG gas cylinder in households gives out the foul smell because ethyl mercaptan is added to it so that if there is any leakage it can be easily detected. LPG is also being replaced in some places with PNG (Piped Natural Gas) which is supplied through pipeline instead of storing in the cylinder.

Distribution of Natural Gas

Natural gas is found mainly in the following regions

- **Mumbai** The largest gas reserves have been found in this region (about 70% of India's natural gas reserves).
- **Andhra Pradesh** The Reliance Group of Industries have discovered gas near Krishna-Godavari basin in Andhra Pradesh.
- **Rajasthan** Natural gas reserves are found in Khambhat Basin, Jaisalmer. It is also found in Tamil Nadu, Gujarat, Assam, Tripura.

Advantages of Natural Gas

- It can be directly used for burning.
- It is cheaper and eco-friendly.
- It has multiple uses, e.g. generating electric power, powering vehicles, fertilisers, etc.
- It is used in dyes and inks.

Disadvantages of Natural Gas

- Its reserves are limited.
- Leakage of natural gas cannot be detect and can proved extremely dangerous, e.g. causes fire or explosions.
- It is non-renewable source of energy.
- When it is used as a fuel in cars, the mileage is lower than gasoline.

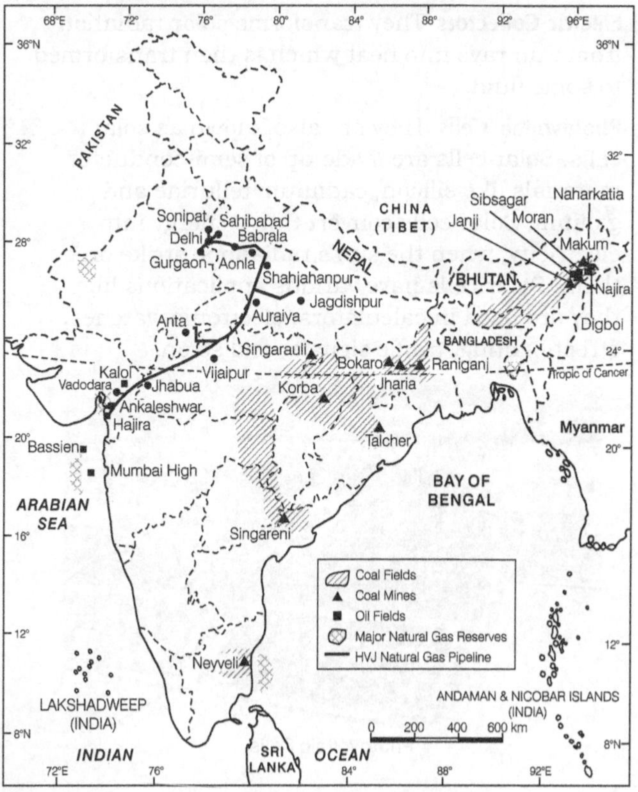

Conventional Energy Resources

Check Your LEARNING...

1. Good quality of coal is found in which two states of India?
2. Mention any one advantage of petroleum.
3. Name the region with largest gas reserves in India.
4. Natural gas is which type of energy source?

Non-Conventional Sources of Energy

Non-conventional or renewable sources of energy are automatically replenished by nature, i.e. suns rays, water, tides, wind, air, etc. These sources include solar energy, wind energy, tidal energy, geothermal energy, nuclear energy and Biogas.

Solar Energy

Energy produced through the sunlight is called solar energy. India receives about 5000 trillion KWh solar energy per year. Indian solar grid had a cumulative capacity of 15.60 GW with about 300 clear and sunny days in a year in most parts of the country.

Generation

Solar energy can be generated through the following

- **Electric Collectors** They transforms solar radiation from Sun rays into heat which is then transformed to some fluid.
- **Photovoltaic Cells** They are also known as solar cells. Solar cells are made up of semi-conductor materials like silicon, cadmium telluride and gallium. Solar cells convert Sun's energy into electricity, when the sun's radiations strike on them. Solar cells have various applications like they are used in calculators, electronic watches, street lighting, traffic signals, and so on.

Photovoltaic Cells

- **Solar Cooker and Heater** It consist of a glass topped box into which the light enters and gets trapped. It is painted back from insides for efficient absorption of light. It is generally used for cooking. Solar heater is a device that capture sunlight to heat water.

Advantages of Solar Energy

- Solar energy is renewable and inexhaustible source of energy.
- Large amount of free energy can be produced due to high availability of sunlight.
- It can be used in heating, drying and cooking.
- It saves fossil fuels and used to produce electricity.

Wind Energy

Energy produce through wind is called wind energy. It is produced by the motion of wind turbines. It involves the use of windmills to produce power for heating and lighting purposes. Wind speed may vary within minutes and affect the power generation.

In India, largest wind farms are situated in Tamil Nadu, Andhra Pradesh, Gujarat, Karnataka, Kerala, Maharashtra and Lakshadweep.

Generation

Wind power is generated by using wind mills. The windmills are installed in open areas, in costal regions or in hilly areas. The blades of wind mills rotate because of the wind and generate electricity. The blades consists of a number of machines like water pumps, flour mills and electric generators.

Advantages of Wind Energy

- Wind power is cost-effective and a clean fuel source.
- Wind is a domestic source of energy. It is abundant and inexhaustible.
- It is sustainable source of energy.
- It has low operational cost.

Tidal Energy

The gravitational forces of the Sun and Moon which cause rise and fall of the sea water or tides, creates tidal energy.

In India, the Gulf of Cambay and the Gulf of Kutch in Gujarat on the West coast have the maximum tidal range which is ideal for harnessing tidal energy.

Generation

Tidal energy is generated by movement of oceanic tides, which can be used to generate electricity. For this, **floodgate dams**[6] are built across inlets. During high tide, water flows into the inlet and gets trapped when the gate is closed. After the tide falls outside the floodgate, the water inside it flows back to the sea via a pipe that carries it through power generating turbine. In this way, electricity is generated.

Advantages of Tidal Energy

- It is cleaner and safer form of energy generation.
- It involves simple and less complex procedures.
- It has high energy capacity.
- It is more efficient compared to solar or wind energy.
- The maintenance of tidal plants are quite low.

Geothermal Energy

It refers to energy generated by the tremendous heat of magma that comes over the Earth's surface from the interior of the Earth. Geothermal energy is enormous and clean power resource.

Geothermal Energy

Generation

Geothermal energy is generated when water seeps into the Earth's crust through cracks and gets heated due to high temperature inside. The heated water becomes steam.

This steam is channelised to rotate turbines that activates a generator which produces electricity.

The geothermal energy is important in both electricity production and direct use.

Advantages of Geothermal Energy

- It is renewable and eco-friendly energy resource as it has low emissions of sulphur, carbon dioxide and greenhouse gases.
- It is inexpensive and widely available resource.
- It is highly efficient and its maintenance is low.

Nuclear Power

It is the energy generated by the nuclei of atoms of naturally occurring radioactive elements.

India developed its nuclear power in August 1956. There are seven nuclear power plants in India namely, Kaiga, Kakrapara, Kudankulam, Chennai, Narora, Rajasthan and Tarapur.

Generation

Nuclear power is generated by the process of nuclear fission through nuclear reactors. Nuclear fission is the process in which the atoms of radioactive substances react and split apart Nuclear fission produces heat which is used to heat water and make steams.

The steams are channelised to rotate the turbines to produce electricity. Both uranium and thorium are used for generating nuclear power. The nuclear reactors used to generate electricity are Pressurised Water Reactors (PWR) and Boiling Water Reactors (BWR).

Advantages of Nuclear Power

- The nuclear power plant is more economical as compared to thermal power plant.
- There is no problem of fuel transportation, storage and handling.
- Less man power is required for the operation of nuclear power plant.
- Nuclear power plant occupies less space than thermal power plant.
- Nuclear power is a clean source of energy.

Biogas

It typically refers to a mixture of different gas produced by decomposition of organic matter in the absence of oxygen. It is composed of carbon dioxide, methane, hydrogen and hydrogen sulphide.

6 **Floodgate Dams** They are a type of dams in which its gates are used to control the flow of water.

Generation

Biogas is generated in a digester tank which is filled with bacteria. The bacteria absorbs the organic waste and give flammable gas i.e. biogas. Biogas can be generated from raw material such as agriculture waste, manure, municipal waste, plant material, sewage, green waste or food waste.

Advantages of Biogas

- Biogas is a clean and non-polluting energy.
- It reduces soil and water pollution.
- It produces organic fertiliser.
- It is available all the time and is cost effective.
- It is a renewable energy that can be used for heating, electricity and many other operations.

Hydel Power

Hydro power or hydel power is derived from the energy of falling water or fast running water. It is a source used for generating electricity. It is cheap, clean, environmental friendly and renewable source of energy. It plays an important role in reducing greenhouse gas emissions. The major dams used to generate hydel power are

Bhakra Nangal Dam

The Bhakra Nangal multi-purpose dam was among the earliest river valley development schemes undertaken by India after independence. The Bhakra Nangal project is a joint venture of the Governments of Punjab, Rajasthan and Himachal Pradesh. The Bhakra Dam is the second highest (226 metres) dam which is 518 metres long and 362 metres wide.

The main aim of this dam was to prevent floods in the Satluj Beas River Valley, to provide irrigation to nearby states and to generate electricity.

The Bhakra Nangal project comprises of two dams which are

(i) **The Bhakra Dam** It is one of the highest dams in the world. Gobind Sagar is the name of the reservoir of Bhakra Dam. It is the third largest water reservoir in India. It has the storage capacity of 9.3 billion cubic meters.

(ii) **The Nangal Dam** It has been constructed on river Sutlej about 13 kms downstream of the Bhakra Dam. It is an auxiliary dam (a supporting dam) which serves as a balancing reservoir. It is one of the longest cemented canals of the world. It supplies water to Bhakra irrigation canals.

Bhakra Nangal Dam also comprises of four power houses and Bhakra Canal System. The four power houses are Ganguwal, Kotla, Right Bank power house and Left Bank power house.

All these power houses have an installed capacity of 1204 MW. The Bhakra Canal system is 174 km long and it provides irrigation in the states of Haryana, Punjab and Rajasthan.

Hirakud Dam

Hirakud Dam is built across the Mahanadi river about 15 km from Sambalpur in Odisha. It is one of the first major multi-purpose river valley projects started after India's independence.

The Hirakud Dam is the longest major Earthen dam in the world. The dam support two different hydroelectric power houses i.e. Power House-I and Power House-II.

The dam helps to control floods in the Mahanadi Delta, irrigate 75000 sq. km of land and generate electricity. Hirakud Dam has three canals i.e. Bargarh main canal, **Sason canal** and **Sambalpur canal.** This project provides irrigation in district of Subarnapur, Bargarh, Sambalpur and Bolangir. Water from the Hirakud Dam is also used in various industries, e.g. in minerals processing and thermal power plants.

Advantages of Hydel Power

- There is less pollution due to absence of burning fuel.
- It is cheaper that electricity produced from fossil fuel and nuclear power.
- It plays an important role in reducing Greenhouse Gas emissions.
- It is reliable, renewable and sustainable.
- The reservoirs and dams built to produce hydroelectricity helps in saving and restoring water.

Disadvantages of Hydel Power

- It is expensive due to its high investment costs to build dams.
- Construction of dams can cause water access problems as it can change the water-table level.
- The building of large dams can cause serious geological damage like it can cause earthquakes.
- Displacement of people living in the villages and towns in the regions to be flooded loses their farms and business and is physically and psychologically disturbed.

Check Your LEARNING...

1. Name two main hydel power plants in India.
2. Name few non-conventional energy sources.
3. Mention any one advantage of wind energy.
4. Name any two nuclear power plants in India.

QUiCK Revision

- A mineral is a combination of two or more than two elements through definite chemical composition which is formed by inorganic processes.
- Minerals are found in the three forms i.e. metallic minerals, non-metallic minerals and energy minerals.
- Iron ore is used in the production of iron and steel and is used in the making of all machinery.
- Manganese is mainly used in the manufacturing of steel and ferro-manganese.
- Major producers of most of the minerals in India are Jharkhand, Odisha, Chhattisgarh and Madhya Pradesh.
- Copper production of India is 3.4 per cent of world's production.
- Copper is a non-ferrous base metal and used in railways, space programmes, telecommunication and cables.
- Bauxite is the ore of aluminium. It is mainly found in tertiary deposits.
- Conventional sources of energy cannot be renewed and they are exhaustible.
- Coal, petroleum and natural gas are important sources of energy in India that are conventional and non-renewable.
- Bhakra Nangal Dam project is a joint venture of Punjab, Rajasthan and Himachal Pradesh.
- Bhakra Dam is one of the highest dams in the world.
- Nangal Dam is constructed on Sutlej river.
- Nuclear power is another important source of energy in India.
- Biogas helps in reducing soil and water pollution and also produce organic fertiliser.

Chapter Practice

Section-I

Multiple Choice Questions

1. Minerals are deposited and accumulated in the stratified form of .... rocks.
   (a) sedimentary (b) igneous
   (c) metamorphic (d) Sandstone

Ans. (a) Sedimentary

2. Iron ore from the Kudremukh mines is transported as slurry through pipelines to a port near
   (a) Mangalore (b) Visakhapatnam
   (c) Kolkata (d) Marmagao

Ans. (a) Mangalore

3. Balaghat mines are the largest producer of
   (a) Coal (b) Mica (c) Gold (d) Copper

Ans. (d) Copper

4. Koderma in Jharkhand is the leading producer of
   (a) Bauxite (b) Iron ore
   (c) Copper (d) Mica

Ans. (d) Mica

5. Hirakud dam is based on which of the following rivers ? [2023]
   (a) River Godavari (b) River Mahanadi
   (c) River Krishna (d) River Narmada

Ans. (b) River Mahanadi

6. Which among the following is a Conventional source of energy?
   (a) Natural gas (b) Wind energy
   (c) Tidal energy (d) Hydel energy

Ans. (a) Natural gas

7. In which state of India is the largest wind farm cluster located?
   (a) Rajasthan (b) Gujarat
   (c) Tamil Nadu (d) Kerala

Ans. (c) Tamil Nadu

8. The most ideal place in India for producing tidal energy is
   (a) Arabian sea (b) Sunderbans Delta
   (c) Gulf of Kutch (d) Bay of Bengal

Ans. (c) Gulf of Kutch

9. Give reason for the following.
   Minerals need to be conserved because
   (a) they are expensive (b) they are hard to find
   (c) they are exhaustible (d) None of the above

Ans. (c) they are exhaustible

10. Give reason for the following.
    Anthracite is used for domestic purposes.
    (a) It is cheap in price
    (b) It is abundant in nature
    (c) High carbon content and less smoke
    (d) None of the above

Ans. (c) High carbon content and less smoke

11. Choose the correct statement related to hydel power
    (i) The cost of building dams for producing hydroelectricity is quite high.
    (ii) Building a large dam alters the natural water-table level.
    (iii) Building a large dam can cause serious geological damage like triggering earthquakes in the area.
    (iv) Building of dams to produce electricity, displaces many people from the area and disturbs their life physically, mentally and psychologically.

Codes
(a) Only (i) (ii) and (iii) (b) Only (ii) and (iii)
(c) Only (iii) and (iv) (d) All of these

Ans. (d) All of these

12. Choose the correct statement related to wind energy
    (i) Wind energy is a renewable source of energy which can be produced again and again.
    (ii) It is the cleanest form of renewable energy which produces no pollution.
    (iii) It reduces our dependence on the fossil fuels.
    (iv) Land owners can look for additional income by installing wind turbines on land that can even be used for agricultural purposes.

Codes
(a) Only (i), (ii) and (iii) (b) Only (ii) and (iii)
(c) Only (iii) and (iv) (d) All of these

Ans. (d) All of these

13. Match the following.

	Minerals		Distribution
A.	Iron ore	1.	Balaghat
B.	Manganese	2.	Ratnagiri
C.	Copper	3.	Gorumohishani
D.	Bauxite	4	Korapur

Codes

	A	B	C	D
(a)	1	2	3	4
(b)	3	1	2	4
(c)	3	4	2	1
(d)	4	3	2	1

Ans. (b)

14. Match the following.

	List I		List II
A.	Coal	1.	Assam
B.	Petroleum	2.	Jharkhand
C.	Natural Gas	3.	South-West India
D.	Wind Energy	4	Mumbai

Codes

	A	B	C	D		A	B	C	D
(a)	1	2	3	4	(b)	4	3	2	1
(c)	3	1	4	2	(d)	2	1	4	3

Ans. (d)

Section-II

Short Questions

1. What do you understand by minerals?

Ans. Minerals are the combination of two or more than two elements through definite chemical composition which are formed by inorganic processes.

2. What are ferrous minerals? Give examples.

Ans. The minerals which contain iron are known as 'ferrous minerals'. For example, nickel, manganese, cobalt, etc.

3. What is an ore? Name any two iron ores.

Ans. A naturally occurring solid materials from which a valuable metallic mineral can be extracted profitably is called as 'ore'.

Two iron ores are haematite and magnetite.

4. Which iron ore is called 'Black ore'? State any one characteristics of this.

Ans. Magnetite is called 'Black ore'.

It is a black, magnetic mineral that leaves a black streak when rubbed across a hard rough surface.

5. (i) Why is iron ore called the back bone of our modern industry? [2020]

(ii) Mention two uses of iron ore.

Ans. (i) Iron ore is called as the backbone of the modern civilisation because it provides raw materials ,all types of machinery to run other industries. This sector has helped in the generation of several small scale industries supporting power, transport and communication industries in India.

(ii) The uses of iron ore are

(a) The primary use of iron ore (98%) is to make steel.

(b) The remaining 2% is used in various other applications such as for certain types of steels, magnets, auto parts and catalysts.

6. Give the names of four important types of iron ore found in India. [2017]

Ans. Magnetite, haematite, limonite and siderite are four important iron ores found in India.

7. Answer the following.

(i) Name two varieties of iron ore used in industry.

(ii) How is the low grade iron ore utilised?

Ans. (i) Haematite and magnetite are used in industry.

(ii) The low grade iron ore variety is often used in manufacturing sponge iron and converted into pellets and then exported.

8. State the most important use of the following. [2015]

(i) Iron ore

(ii) Bauxite

Ans. (i) **Iron Ore** It is mainly used to make steel. Raw iron is alloyed with other elements to make good quality steel which is used for construction, automobiles and other forms of transportation, etc.

(ii) **Bauxite** It is the main source of aluminium which is light weight, strong and rust resistant. Aluminium is mainly used for making automobiles, aircrafts, wagons, coaches and used in shipping industry, etc.

9. Where do the following iron and steel plants get their supply of iron ore from? [2019]

(i) Bhilai Iron and Steel Plant.

(ii) Vishakhapatnam Steel Plant.

Ans. (i) Iron ore is available from Dalli-Rajhara range which is just 80 km South of Bhilai.

(ii) Iron ore is available from Bailadila mines of Chhattisgarh.

10. (i) Name two manganese producing States in India.

(ii) Name one use of the mineral.

Ans. (i) Odisha and Karnataka are manganese producing States in India.

(ii) Mineral is used to improve the quality of many alloys, e.g. iron and steel.

11. Mention any two uses of manganese. [2014]

Ans. The uses of manganese are

(i) Manganese is used to increase the strength of steel.

(ii) It is also used as raw material for manufacturing paints, glass wares, insecticides, bleaching powder and dry cell batteries.

12. Why is copper used in electrical appliances?

Ans. Copper is used in electrical appliances because it is a good conductor of heat.

13. Name any two industrial products for which limestone is used as a source of raw material. [2013]

Ans. Two industrial products for which limestone is used as source of raw material are Iron and steel and cement

14. What are conventional source of energy?

Ans. These are the non-renewable source of energy which cannot be used again. For example, petroleum and coal.

15. Which of the different varieties of coal is used for domestic purposes and why? **[2014]**

Ans. Bituminous is used for domestic purposes as it has very high carbon content and emits very less smoke.

16. (i) Name the state of India that leads in the production of manganese. **[2023]**

(ii) What is the importance of manganese for the iron and Steel industry ?

Ans. (i) Madhya Pradesh

(ii) The presence of manganese contributes to its increasing hardness. That is why it is used as an alloy to manufacture steel.

17. (i) Name any three types of coal found in India. **[2016]**

(ii) Which type of coal is mostly used in iron and steel industries?

Ans. (i) There are four variety of coal found in India i.e. lignite, peat, bituminous and anthracite.

(ii) Anthracite is mostly used in iron and steel industries.

18. What is lignite? Name thc two areas where lignite is found in India. **[2011]**

Ans. Lignite refers to inferior variety of coal which contains about 60% of carbon and a good amount of moisture and less of combustible matter. Two states where lignite is found are Tamil Nadu and Kerala.

19. Name the following. **[2016]**

(i) An offshore oil field of India.

(ii) An iron ore mine of Karnataka.

Ans. (i) Mumbai High is offshore oil field of India.

(ii) Kemmangundi is iron ore mine of Karnataka.

20. Name the following. **[2017]**

(i) An off-shore oil field in the Gulf of Cambay.

(ii) An oil refinery in Bihar.

Ans. (i) Aliabet island close to Bhavangarh is an off-shore oil field in the Gulf of Cambay.

(ii) An oil refinery in Bihar is Barauni refinery.

21. Give two advantages that non-conventional energy sources have over conventional energy sources. **[2018]**

Ans. Two advantages that non-conventional energy sources have over conventional energy sources are

(i) Most of the non-conventional energy sources are cheaper and renewable.

(ii) They are environment friendly and create very less greenhouse gases.

22. Write two advantages of hydro electric power?

Ans. Two advantages of hydro electric power are

(i) Hydel power is inexhaustible and pollution free source of energy.

(ii) It produces many benefits like flood control, irrigation and water supply.

23. Give two advantages of using natural gas over coal. **[Specimen Paper Semester-II 2022]**

Ans. Two advantages of using natural gas over coal are

(i) Natural gas is eco-friendly fuel than coal.

(ii) It has multiple uses like generating electric power, powering vehicles, fertilisers, etc.

24. Mention one agricultural and one industrial problem solved by the Bhakra Nangal Dam. **[2020]**

Ans. Bhakra Nangal Dam solved the agricultural problem of soil erosion. It also solved the energy crists of industries by providing regular electricity supply.

25. Mention two purposes of solar energy.

Ans. Two purposes of solar energy are

(i) Solar energy is used for solar heating and solar electricity production.

(ii) It conserve non-renewable sources of energy and is cost effective.

Long Questions

1. State four economic uses of mineral resources.

Ans. Four economic uses of mineral are

(i) They form the basis for industries.

(ii) They are the important sources of energy, for example, coal and petroleum.

(iii) Energy minerals are used to produce electricity fuel for transportation, etc.

(iv) They are used to earn foreign exchange by their exports.

2. Explain about the four types of iron ore found in India.

Ans. The four types of iron ore are

(i) **Magnetite (Black Ore)** Magnetite constitutes best quality of iron ore (70% iron content). It has strong magnetic property, hence, it is called 'magnetite'. It is black in colour.

(ii) **Haematite** It is the second best quality of iron ore with 50% to 60% iron content. It contains pure iron and is known as 'oxide of iron'. It is reddish in colour and also known as red iron.

(iii) **Limonite** It is inferior quality of iron-ore which contains 40% to 60% pure iron. It is also known as 'hydrated iron-oxide'. It is found in yellow or light brown colour.

(iv) **Siderite** It is low quality iron ore with 10% to 40% of pure iron and many impurities. It is also known as 'iron carbonate'.

3. Mention the important iron ore producing regions found in India. Explain any two of them.

Ans. The important iron ore producing regions are

- **Odisha** Iron-ore faund in Odisha contain 55 to 68% iron content and belongs to haemetite variety. Important mines are located at Gorumahisani, Sulaipet and Badampahar in Mayurbhanj district, Kiruburuaburu in Kendujhar district and Bonai in Sundergarh district.

- **Karnataka** It has large reserves of haematite and magnetite. Important mines are located at Donai Malai in Bellary-Hospet region, Baba Budan hills in Chikmagalur district and Kudremukh in Chitradurg district.

4. Explain the distribution of copper in India.

Ans. The distribution of copper in India are

- **Jharkhand** In Jharkhand, Singhbhum and Hazaribagh districts have good reserves of copper.
- **Madhya Pradesh** Malanjkhand copper belt and the Balaghat district have rich reserves of copper in Madhya Pradesh.
- **Rajasthan** Khetri copper belt, Jhunjhunu and Dariba in Alwar district have important reserves of copper in Rajasthan.
- **Maharashtra** Bhandara, Chandrapur, Gadchiroli and Nagpur districts are copper producing regions in Maharashtra.
- **Andra Pradesh** Guntur, Prakasam and Kurnool are the copper producing regions of Andhra Pradesh.

5. (i) Name the metal extracted from bauxite.
(ii) Mention two uses of this metal. [2016]

Ans. (i) Aluminium is the metal extracted from bauxite.
(ii) (a) Aluminium is a good conductor of electricity, hence, it is used in electrical industry.
(b) Aluminium is used for making aircrafts and utensils.

6. Answer the following. [2018]
(i) State one industrial use of copper.
(ii) Mention one advantage of generating power from biogas.
(iii) Name the mineral that toughens steel and makes it rust-proof.

Ans. (i) Copper is used in electrical industry in the form of copper wires and other numerous kinds of electrical equipments.
(ii) Biogas is a renewable as well as a clean source of energy and it reduces greenhouse emissions.
(iii) Chromium is hard and tough in nature, therefore it is used in steel industries to make steel tough and rust-proof.

7. Answer the following questions. [2018]
(i) Name the metal obtained from bauxite. Give any one use of the metal mentioned by you.
(ii) Which multipurpose project provides power to both Punjab and Himachal Pradesh?

Ans. (i) Aluminium metal is obtained from bauxite. Aluminium is used in a huge variety of products including cans, foils, kitchen utensils, aeroplane parts, etc.
(ii) The Bhakra Nangal multipurpose dam provides power to both Punjab and Himachal Pradesh. It is built on river Sutlej.

8. Give a geographical reason for each of the following. [2015]
(i) Many port cities have their own oil refineries.
(ii) Petroleum is called a 'fossil fuel'.
(iii) Coal is called a 'versatile mineral'.

Ans. (i) Many port cities have their own oil refineries as the location of the oil refineries near the coast minimises the cost of transport and also reduces the risk of transporting the oil inside the country due to its inflammable nature.
(ii) Petroleum is made of fossil remains of vegetations, that is why they are called fossil fuel. It is formed by the accumulation of vegetative matter. This vegetative matter when subjected to heat and pressure results in physical and chemical changes due to the increasing weight of the overlying layers of sediments and Earth movements.
(iii) Coal is known as a 'versatile mineral' due to its varied uses such as
- It is used as a source of power for running machines, trains, ships, etc.
- It is used in manufacturing of steel.

9. (i) Name the state that is the leading producer of manganese. [2020]
(ii) Name the mineral oil field of India which is the largest producer of petroleum.
(iii) Mention two advantages of using geothermal energy over coal.

Ans. (i) Madhya Pradesh is the leading producer of manganese.
(ii) Rajasthan have the mineral oil fields which are the largest producers of petroleum in India. These oil fields are Mangala oil field, Saraswati and Rajeshwari.
(iii) The advantages of using geothermal energy over coal are
(a) **Environmentally Friendly** Geothermal energy is more environmentally friendly than conventional fuel sources such as coal and other fossil fuels. In addition, the carbon footprint of a geothermal power plant is low.
(b) **Renewable** Geothermal energy is a source of renewable energy. The hot reservoirs within the Earth are naturally replenished, making it both renewable and sustainable.

10. Name the two states where limestone is found. Mention two important uses of limestone. [2017, 2011]

Ans. Limestone is found in Rajasthan and Madhya Pradesh.
Two important uses of limestone are
(i) Limestone is used as flux in the iron and steel industry.
(ii) It is used in production of chemicals such as bleaching powder, caustic soda, glass, fertilisers etc.

11. Name the mineral used in the manufacture of
(i) Cement (ii) Aluminium
(iii) Synthetics **[2014]**

Ans. (i) **Cement** Limestone is used in the manufacturing of cement.
(ii) **Aluminium** Bauxite is used in the manufacturing of Aluminium.
(iii) **Synthetics** Petroleum is used to manufacture synthetics.

12. State an important industrial use of **[2017]**
(i) Manganese (ii) Coal (iii) Aluminium

Ans. (i) **Manganese** It is used to improve the quality of many alloys, e.g. iron and steel.
(ii) **Coal** It is used in generating power and thermal electricity.
(iii) **Aluminium** It is used for making aircrafts, ships and utensils, as it is light in weight and resists rust.

13. Which state is the leading producer of the following minerals? **[2014]**
(i) Coal (ii) Oil
(iii) Manganese

Ans. (i) **Coal** Jharkhand leads in coal production and coal reserves in the country.
(ii) **Oil** Maharashtra is the largest producer of oil in India.
(iii) **Manganese** Odisha is the leading producer of manganese in India.

14. Name the following. **[2015]**
(i) Largest oil refinery in the public sector.
(ii) State that is the largest producer of coal.
(iii) Best variety of iron ore.

Ans. (i) Panipat refinery is the largest oil refinery in the public sector in India.
(ii) Jharkhand is the largest producer of coal in India.
(iii) The best variety of iron ore is magnetite which constitutes best quality of iron ore.

15. Name the following. **[2016]**
(i) Largest coal field of India
(ii) Oldest oil-field of India
(iii) Best variety of iron ore

Ans. (i) Jharia in Jharkhand is the largest coal field in India.
(ii) The oldest and one of the largest oil fields in India is at Digboi in Assam.
(iii) Magnetite is best quality of iron ore.

16. (i) Which state is the largest producer of mineral oil?
(ii) Name two coastal and two inland oil refineries in India. **[2013]**

Ans. (i) Maharashtra is the largest producer of mineral oil in India.
(ii) **Coastal Refineries** The coastal refineries are Mumbai High and Kochi oil refinery. Mumbai High is an offshore oil field which is about 176 km off the coast of Mumbai. Kochi oil refinery is a public crude oil refinery in the city of Kochi, Kerala.
Inland Refineries The inland refineries are Barauni refinery and Bongaigaon refinery. Barauni refinery in the Bihar state was built in collaboration with the Soviet Union, in 1964. It is situated 125 km from Patna. Bongaigaon is located in Assam. It was incorporated in 1974 by the Government of India.

17. Give geographical reasons, why?
(i) Anthracite is used for domestic purposes.
(ii) Oil refineries are located close to oil fields or near ports.
(iii) The location of coal fields is an important factor in industrial development.

Ans. (i) Anthracite is used for domestic purposes as it has very high carbon content and emits very less smoke.
(ii) Oil refineries are located near the oil fields which help to transport crude oil through pipelines and hence, reduce the transport cost. Moreover, if located near the port it helps to import the crude oil and export of its products.
(iii) The location of coal fields is an important factor in industrial development as coal is a bulky and heavy raw material and if the industries are located away from coalfields, they will incur huge transport cost and it affects the cost of production on a large scale.

18. (i) Mention one advantage of use of natural gas over coal or petroleum. **[2018]**
(ii) Name one offshore oil field in India.

Ans. (i) Natural gas is the cleanest burning fossil fuel because the combustion process for natural gas is almost very perfect as very few by-products are emitted into the atmosphere as pollutants.
(ii) Mumbai High is one of the offshore oil field in India.

19. With reference to Bhakra Nangal dam answer the following. **[Specimen Paper Semester-II 2022]**
(i) On which river is it situated?
(ii) Name any two states benefitted by Bhakra Nangal.

Ans. (i) Bhakra Nangal dam is situated on Sutlej river.
(ii) States like Himachal Pradesh and Punjab are benefitted by Bhakra Nangal dam.

20. Answer the following questions.

(i) Mention one disadvantage of using natural gas as a source of power. [2020]

(ii) How is the residue from a bio-gas plant put to use?

(iii) Why is the use of alternative sources of energy becoming essential in modern time?

Ans. (i) Natural gas is explosive and can cause a fire hazard if the pipeline bursts.

(ii) The residue left out in the biogas plant is slurry which is essentially used in the manure.

(iii) As the consumption of energy grows, the population depends more and more on fossil fuels such as coal, oil and gas day by day. Thus, there is a need to use alternative sources of energy.

21. What is geothermal energy? Name any two project which are set-up to harness this energy.

Ans. Geothermal energy refers to the heat produced in the interior of the Earth. This heat when turn into steam is used to drive turbines and generates electricity.

Two experimental projects have been set-up in India to harness the geothermal energy are Parvati valley in Himachal Pradesh and Puga valley in Ladakh.

22. Answer the following questions.

(i) Mention two advantages of using biogas.

(ii) How has the nuclear power contributed in reducing the pressure on conventional sources of energy? [Specimen Paper Semester-II 2022]

Ans. (i) Two advantages of using biogas are

(a) Biogas is eco-friendly.

(b) It reduces soil and water pollution.

(ii) The nuclear power has contributed in reducing the pressure on conventional sources of energy in the following ways

- It keeps the air clean by removing thousands of tones of harmful air pollutants each year that contribute to acid rain, smog, lung cancer and cardiovascular disease.
- Nuclear energy produces more electricity on less land than other conventional sources of energy, thus it has contributed in reducing the pressure on conventional sources of energy.

Picture Based Questions

1. Study the picture given below and answer the following questions.

(i) Identify the dam given in the picture.

(ii) What is the main aim of this dam?

Ans. (i) The dam given in the picture is Bhakra Nangal Dam.

(ii) The main aim of this dam is to prevent floods in the Sutlej-Beas river valley, to provide irrigation to nearby states and to generate electricity.

2. Study the picture given below and answer the following questions.

(i) Which energy is generated by the activity given in the picture?

(ii) Mention any four advantages of this energy.

Ans. (i) Wind energy is generated by this activity.

(ii) The advantages of wind energy are

(a) Wind power is cost-effective.

(b) It is a clean fuel source.

(c) Wind is a domestic source of energy. It is abundant and inexhaustible.

(d) It is sustainable source of energy.

Chapter Assessment

Section-I

Multiple Choice Questions

1. Which is the oldest oil producing state in India?
   (a) Maharashtra (b) Assam
   (c) Goa (d) Gujarat
2. Coal is formed in .... rocks.
   (a) sedimentary (b) igneous
   (c) metamorphic (d) igneous and metamorphic
3. What mineral occurs in the beds or layers of sedimentary rocks?
   (a) Coal (b) Bauxite
   (c) Magnesium (d) Bromine
4. Which of these minerals is used in electric wires?
   (a) Silica (b) Iron
   (c) Copper (d) Rutile
5. The State of Jharkhand is known for production of
   (a) Natural gas (b) Coal
   (c) Copper (d) Petroleum

Section-II

Short Questions

1. Define minerals.
2. Which minerals are considered as the 'backbone' of the development of metallurgical industry?
3. Metallic minerals are found in which type of rocks.
4. Name the plateau region where more than 90% of the mineral deposits of India are located.
5. Which metal is considered as 'iron like metal'?

Long Questions

1. State any three difference between metallic minerals and non-metallic minerals.
2. Mention the important properties of anthracite coal.
3. Name alignite coalfield in the following states.
   (i) Tamil Nadu (ii) Rajasthan
   (iii) Kashmir
4. Name any three recently discovered oil fields of India.
5. Name the oil refineries found in the following locations.
   (i) Visakhapatnam
   (ii) Bongaigaon
   (iii) Koyali
6. What are non-conventional sources of energy? Explain any two sources.

CHAPTER 09

Agriculture in India

SYLLABUS

Indian Agriculture • Importance, problems and reforms.
• Types of farming in India: subsistence and commercial : shifting, intensive, extensive, plantation and mixed. • Agricultural seasons (rabi, kharif, zaid)

The term agriculture has been formed from two Latin words, '*Ager*' which means 'Land' and '*Culture*' which means 'Cultivation'. India is primarily an agricultural country as its two-third part of population depends on agriculture. The development of agriculture in India is the result of necessary conditions like vast expanse of level land, rich soil, wide climatic variations, sufficient sunshine and a long growing season.

Importance of Agriculture

- Agriculture sector provides employment to a large section of the population in India.
- It provides food and food products to human population and fodder for **livestock**[1].
- It is the source of raw material for many agro-based as well as non-agro based industries.
- It brings foreign exchange through export of many crops like tea, jute, cotton etc.
- Agricultural practices have provided impetus to the automobiles and machine producing industries like tractors, threshers, harvesters and fertilisers, pesticides and *vice-versa*.

Problems of Indian Agriculture

There are many problems in agriculture which lead to low yield. These are caused by several factors such as

Environmental Factors

- **Erratic Rainfall** The agricultural sector in India is still dependent on rainfall which is very unreliable and irregular. Around 55 per cent of the net sown area is dependent on rainfall rather than irrigation. Monsoon in India is often affected by many factors and its failure or late arrival causes serious problems for the farmers of India.
- **Problem of Soil Erosion** It is also an increasing problem causing loss of soil fertility and productivity. The indiscriminate clearing of forests, overgrazing by cattles and faulty agricultural practices have led to the degradation of soil quality. Soil erosion is responsible for low crop yields.

1 **Livestock** These are domesticated animals raised by farmers to produce food (meat) and other products for commercial and domestic purposes.

- **Frequent Floods and Drought** Flood is the most **detrimental**[2] element which leads to damage of crops as well as decrease the fertility of soil. Flood is more common in Northern part of India while drought is common in Deccan Peninsular part mainly in Eastern Maharashtra which leads to drying up of crops.

Institutional Factors

- **Limitations in Irrigational Facilities** India is a vast country with large irrigated area but still a large portion of area lacks good irrigation facilities and still dependent on rainfall.
- **Fragmented and Small Landholdings** Fragmented landholdings refers to a small or incomplete part or piece of land, separated from the whole land to which it originally belongs. Majority of farmers in India are not rich and they possess very small landholding. It limits the usage of latest machineries and modern irrigation equipments. Even fertile land and productive labour cannot give good returns on small landholdings.

Technological Factors

- **Old Methods of Cultivation** Majority of Indian farmers are illiterate and lack in technical knowledge. They adopt old and inefficient methods of farming, e.g. wooden plough, bullocks, which lead to low production per hectare.
- **Poverty and Lack of Knowledge** Due to poverty or lack of knowledge farmers are not able to buy or use good quality manure, fertilisers or pesticides. This reduces agricultural production greatly. They are not able to understand the various crop diseases or find their remedies due to lack of education. Government provides **subsidy**[3] on various pesticides and herbicides in order to make it easy and cheaper for farmer to use it. Farmers should be educated properly for effective usage of these fertilisers.

Economic Factors

- **Poor Quality of Seeds** The poor farmers of India are often out of reach of good high yielding varieties of seeds. This limitation causes low productivity.
- **Demand for Food Crops** There are two main food crops which are grown extensively with repetition in the country, i.e. rice and wheat. Due to repetition these crops deplete the soil fertility.
- **Decrease in Net Sown Area** In recent decades, India is experiencing a gradual shift from food crops to commercial crops in order to gain more profit through exports, e.g. fruits, vegetables, oil-seeds and industrial crops. It has declined the net sown area under cereals and pulses. Besides this, land is being used for different non-agricultural purposes e.g. housing, etc has resulted in decline the net sown area in India.
- **Exploitation of Farmers** Small farmers and landless labourers are highly exploited by the land tenure system. This system was an important reason for low productivity in the country.
- Many landowners have become absentee landlords and get their cultivation done through tenants, sharecroppers, landless labourers who get very low wages and work as bonded labourers. Thus, they are exploited by these landowners.
- **Practice of Subsistence Agriculture** Subsistence agriculture is still practised in India. In this type of agriculture, farmers grow food crops on small landholdings only to meet the needs of themselves and their families and not for selling the crops in the market.
- **Globalisation** Indian farmers are facing many challenges due to globalisation which are
  - As the Indian government has reduced its subsidy on fertilisers, it raised the cost of production of crops.
  - There is reduction of import duty on agricultural products in India that increase international competition and further posed great problem for the Indian farmers.
  - The cost of agricultural crops is increasing in Indian market while it is decreasing in the international markets due to use of modern techniques and biotechnology in agriculture and providing heavy subsidies to the farmers in developed countries.
- **Low Productivity** The yield of crops is low in India as compared to the international levels. Per hectare output of crops like rice, wheat, cotton and oilseeds in India is very low as compared to USA, Russia, Japan etc. Yields are also low in rainfed drylands which mostly grow coarse cereals, pulses and oilseeds. Labour productivity is also

2 **Detrimental** The things which cause harm or damage.

3 **Subsidy** It is the sum of money granted by government to keep the price of a commodity very low.

low in India in comparison to international level because of very high pressure on land resources.

- **Financial Constraints and Indebtedness** Crop failures and low returns from agriculture force the small and marginal farmers to fall in the trap of indebtedness. As the modern inputs of agriculture are very expensive, it becomes difficult for these farmers to invest in agriculture. They have to take credit from various institutions and moneylenders to buy expensive input resources.

Reforms in Agriculture

Institutional Reforms

Major insitutional reforms include **collectivisation**[4], consolidation of landholdings (Chakbandi), development of cooperative societies, abolition of zamindari, **Right of inheritance**[5], fragmentation of landholding, etc.

Reforms for Farmers

These reforms improve the condition of the farmers. This is done by providing crop insurance to farmers against drought, flood, cyclone, fire, crop disease, etc. Government also provides loans at lower rate of interest to the farmers. For this, it established grameen banks, cooperative societies, etc.

Technological Reforms

These reforms improve the way of crop production by use of modern technology. In 1960s, Indian Government introduced **Green Revolution** where modern technology like HYV seeds, modern machinery, fertilisers were introduced in the production of rice and wheat.

Some important elements of Green Revolution are

- Adoption of modern scientific methods of farming.
- Use of High Yielding Varieties (HYV) of seeds, chemical fertilisers, insecticides and pesticides.
- Use of large capital and technological inputs.
- Extension of irrigation facilities, particularly ground water resources.
- Improvement in marketing and storage facilities.

The impacts of Green Revolution were

- It changed the scenario of Indian agriculture from subsistence to commercial and market-oriented.
- It improved the agricultural production and made the India self-sufficient in respect of food grains.
- It created more employment opportunities in agriculture sector.
- It increased the income of many farmers by utilising the modern agricultural inputs.

However, it had some bad impacts like land degradation due to overuse of fertilisers and pesticides, drying up of aquifers and vanishing biodiversity.

Other Reforms

- **Indian Council of Agricultural Research (ICAR),** agricultural universities, veterinary services, animal breeding centres, horticulture development, etc. were set up for promoting agricultural research.
- **Kisan Call Centres** were set up by the Government of India in 2004. Besides, this soil testing laboratories have been set up in India to check health and fertility of soil resources.
- **Kisan Credit Cards** were issued to farmers so that they could get cheap and early loans. Government also provides Personal Accident Insurance Scheme (PAIS) to KCC holders.
- **Subsidy** is provided to farmers by reducing the cost of agricultural inputs like seeds, electricity, irrigation facility at subsidised rates.
- **Minimum Support Price (MSP)** for essential agricultural products is announced by the Government to ensure that farmers are able to sell their products at proper rates.
- To improve irrigation system, an **Accelerated Irrigation Benefit Programme** has been started to ensure completion of irrigation projects.
- The Government has made many efforts to provide irrigation facilities to more areas, e.g. promotion of better management practices, installation of sprinklers and drip irrigation systems in water scarce and drought prone areas, appropriate use of surface and ground water resources and farmer's participation to improve irrigation system.

4 **Collectivisation** This is meant that small farms would be gathered together to form one large massive one.
5 **Right of Inheritance** It is the passing of property, rights and obligations from father to son after his death.

National Agricultural Policy (NAP)

The National Agricultural Policy is the Government initiative which came in the year 2000, to increase the potential of Indian agriculture. Some objectives of this policy are

- To strengthen rural infrastructure
- To support faster agricultural development
- Accelerate the growth of agro-business
- Create employment in rural areas
- Secure a fair standard of living of farmers and agricultural workers
- Face the challenge arising out of economic liberalisation and globalisation.
- Annual growth rate of over 4 per cent.
- Private sector participation to be promoted through contract farming and land leasing.
- Wider coverage of future markets to minimise fluctuations in price and other risks.
- Plant varieties to be protected through legislation.
- Animal husbandry, poultry, dairy and aquaculture to receive high priority to diversify agriculture.
- New location-specific and economically viable improved varieties of agriculture and horticulture crops to be developed.
- Restrictions on movement of agricultural commodities will be removed.
- Institutionalisation of farm credit.
- Priority to rural electrification.
- National Agriculture Insurance Scheme to cover every aspect of agriculture.

Check Your LEARNING...

1. Which crops bring foreign exchange in India? Name them.
2. Mention any one problem faced by Indian farmers in agriculture.
3. Name one technological change introduced by government.
4. What does PAIS stand for?

Types of Farming in India

India is an agricultural country with undulating **topography**[6] and varied climate. On the basis of these characteristics of India, different types of farming are practiced in different parts of the country. The types of farming are

Shifting Farming

It is also known as **slash and burn** agriculture. This type of agriculture is mainly practiced in North-East India and hilly areas. In this type, a patch of forest is cleared by cutting trees and burning the remaining vegetation. The ash after fire is used as manure. The cleared ground is then cultivated for 2-3 years until the fertility of the soil is exhausted. After couple of years, the farmer abandons the land and moves to a fresh piece of land to repeat the same process for few years.

The feature of shifting farming are

- This type of cultivation is known by different local names in different areas like Jhum in Assam, Podu in Andhra Pradesh/Telangana, Ponam in Kerala, Koman or Bringer in Odisha, Kuruwa in Jharkhand, Khil in Himalayan region, and Bewar, Masha, Penda and Hera in Madhya Pradesh.
- This type of agriculture was discouraged by the government due to its detrimental effects on the environment. For example, soil erosion, floods and silting in the lower reaches of the riverine flood plains.
- Intercropping is being used as an alternative to shifting farming. It is a practice of sowing two or more crops next to each other which do not harm the fertility, nutrients, and soil moisture.

Subsistence Farming

This method of farming is practiced by majority of the farmers in India who produce exclusively for their own consumption. The features of subsistence farming are

- In this type of farming, the farmers have very scattered and small landholding and primitive tools like hoe or dao and digging sticks are used by their families and community labour.
- This type of farming is dominated by food crops and it is highly dependent on monsoon since there is no irrigation facilities.
- This farming practice also depends on the natural fertility of the soil.

Intensive Farming

This is the type of farming in which small piece of land is cultivated intensively. The main focus is on increasing the yield per hectare by using biochemical inputs, fertilisers, high quality seeds and best irrigation facilities.

The features of intensive farming are

- It is practiced in densely populated areas and employs huge manual labour.
- In this farming, usually more than one crop is cultivated on the same field and the land is under one crop or the other throughout the year. Thus, there is enormous pressure on agricultural land.

6 **Topography** It is the distribution of natural physical features on the surface of an area.

- The crops grown in this type of farming are rice and wheat.
- It is popular mainly in Northern plains of India and the coastal areas of South India which has proper irrigation facilities.

Extensive Farming

This type of farming is practiced on lands of comparatively large size in which considerable amount of capital and labour are used in which the input of labour per unit area is low and machines are used. The features of extensive farming are

- It is characterised by crop specialisation i.e. the farmer specialises in a couple of major commercial crops which mainly includes rice, wheat, sugarcane, etc.
- Farmers mainly focus on to increase their production.
- In this farming, the productivity is based on natural fertility of soil, climate and terrain of the area thus, it is practised on large farms to achieve higher yields.
- The total crop production is high due to large landholding, but low in terms of per unit production.
- It is an environment- friendly method of farming as less amount of chemical fertilisers and pesticides are used.
- This type of agriculture is practiced in North-Western parts of India (Punjab, Haryana and Uttar Pradesh) and Terai region.

Plantation Farming

This type of farming is practiced on a large (continuous) piece of land where cultivation of a single crop (mainly cash crops) like tea, coffee, rubber, spices, etc is done on a large scale. This farming was introduced by the Britishers in the 19th century.

The features of planation farming are

- This farming practice involves large capital, vast agricultural land, managerial ability, fertilisers, modern and sophisticated machineries as well as scientific techniques.
- Plantation crops are used for export purposes and earn foreign exchange.
- Technical knowledge and fluent transport facilities are main demands for this type of farming.
- Plantation farming is mainly practiced in Assam hills, Northern Bengal, hills of South India like Nilgiri, Anaimalai and Cardamom hills.

Mixed Farming

The practice of cultivation of crops as well as raising of animals/livestock simultaneously is popularly known as mixed farming. Sometimes, fruits and vegetables are also grown along with poultry farming.

The features of mixed farming are

- Modern technology and machineries, high quality seeds, chemical fertilisers are used in this farming to grow two or more crops together, having different maturing periods.
- **Crop rotation**[7] is an important feature of this farming.
- Mixed farming is very helpful for the farmers because even if the crops fail they can rely on cattle rearing for income.
- This type of agriculture is most commonly practised in developed countries as they are possessed with large land holdings and latest technology.

Commercial Farming

In this type of farming, crops are cultivated mainly for commercial purpose i.e. for selling in the market, e.g. sugarcane, tobacco, oilseeds, etc. These crops are called cash crops that include cotton, jute, sugarcane etc.

The features of commercial farming are

- This type of farming incorporates High Quality Seeds, (HYVs) expensive fertiliser, pesticides, etc.
- It is generally practiced in those areas where farms are large and population is sparse.
- The degree of commercialisation of this farming varies in different parts of India e.g. rice is a commercial crop in Punjab and Haryana, whereas in Odisha, it is a subsistence crop.
- This type of farming cannot be practised on small landholdings.

7 **Crop Rotation** It is a practice of growing different crops in same area across a sequence of growing seasons.

- Commercial farming have been successful mainly in Punjab, Haryana, Gujarat, Western Uttar Pradesh and Andhra Pradesh.

Agricultural Seasons

There are three main crop seasons in India

(i) **Kharif** These crops are grown during the month of June and July and harvested in September and October during autumn months. This season is associated with South-West monsoon season. Major kharif crops are rice, bajra, ragi, maize, sugarcane, cotton and jute.

(ii) **Rabi** These crops are grown in October and November during winter season and harvested in March and April. Due to low temperature conditions during this season, sub-tropical or temperate type of crops like wheat, barley, peas, linseed, rapeseed, gram, mustard, etc are grown.

(ii) **Zaid Crops** These crops are grown for a short time period between kharif and rabi crops, mainly from March to June. Some of the crops of this season are cucumber, muskmelon, vegetables and fodder crops.

Zaid Kharif and Zaid Rabi Crops

Zaid kharif crops are grown in August and September and harvested in December and January. Most of the oilseeds like mustard are zaid kharif crops.

Zaid rabi crops are sown at the beginning of the summers in February and March and harvested in the months of April and May. For example, summer vegetables, jowar, maize, watermelons, cucumbers, etc.

Cropping Seasons in India

Cropping Season	Major Crops Cultivated	
	Northern States	Southern States
Kharif (June-September)	Rice, Cotton, Bajra, Maize, Jowar, Tur	Rice, Maize, Ragi, Jowar, Groundnut
Rabi (October-March)	Wheat, Gram, Rapeseeds and Mustard, Barley	Rice, Maize, Ragi, Groundnut, Jowar
Zaid (April-June)	Vegetables, Fruits, Fodder	Rice, Vegetables, Fodder

Check Your LEARNING...

1. In which type of farming a land is cultivated for only 2-3 years?
2. Name the farming practice which is done only for the farmer's own consumption.
3. Name two commercial crops in India.
4. Mention the name of the crops grown in rabi season.

QUiCK Revision

- India is primarily an agricultural country as its two-third part of population depends on agriculture.
- Agriculture sector provides employment to a large section of the population in India.
- Indian agriculture is facing a number of problems like erratic rainfall, small and fragmented landholdings, old methods of cultivation, soil erosion, lack of technical know-how and so on.
- Government of India made some strong efforts to modernise agriculture through establishment of Indian Council of Agriculture Research (ICAR), agricultural universities, veterinary services and animal breeding centres, horticulture research and development in the field of meteorology and weather forecast, etc along with improving the rural infrastructure.
- Apart from these, many other reforms, development programmes and schemes for farmers have taken place in order to improve the scenario of the Indian farming and boost up the Indian economy.
- Many types of agricultural practices have developed in India. Shifting agriculture, subsistence farming, intensive farming are done in small piece of land.
- Extensive farming, plantation farming, commercial farming are done on large land areas with use of machinery.
- In India, there are three agricultural seasons i.e. Kharif, Rabi and Zaid.
- Kharif crops are grown during the month of June and July and harvested in September and October, e.g. rice, jowar, bajra, ragi, etc.
- Rabi crops are grown in October and November, e.g. wheat, barley, peas, gram, etc.
- Zaid crops are grown in August and September, while harvested in December and January, e.g. watermelon, maize, cucumber, etc.

Chapter Practice

Section-I

Multiple Choice Questions

1. After independence, what was given priority to bring about institutional reforms of agriculture in the country?
   (a) Abolition of the zamindari system
   (b) Consolidation of landholdings
   (c) Collectivisation of landholdings
   (d) All of the above

Ans. (d) All of the above

2. In which of the following states has the Green Revolution helped the growth of Rabi crops especially wheat?
   (a) New Delhi
   (b) Western Uttar Pradesh
   (c) Madhya Pradesh
   (d) Eastern Himachal Pradesh

Ans. (b) Western Uttar Pradesh

3. Modernisation of agriculture in India was made possible due to the establishment of which of the following organisations?
   (a) Food Corporation of India (FCI)
   (b) Indian Council of Agricultural Research (ICAR)
   (c) International Crop Research Institute (ICRI)
   (d) Indian Agricultural University (IAU)

Ans. (b) Indian Council of Agricultural Research (ICAR)

4. Which type of farming is practiced in areas which have high population pressure on land?
   (a) Intensive farming (b) Commercial farming
   (c) Jhumming farming (d) Extensive farming

Ans. (a) Intensive Farming

5. HYV seeds, chemical fertilisers, insecticides and pesticides are usually used in which type of farming?
   (a) Subsistence farming (b) Commercial farming
   (c) Sedentary farming (d) Shifting agriculture

Ans. (b) Commercial farming

6. What crop is a commercial crop in Haryana, but a subsistence crop in Odisha?
   (a) Wheat (b) Rice
   (c) Jowar (d) Bajra

Ans. (b) Rice

7. Which agricultural season is associated with South-West monsoon season?
   (a) Rabi (b) Kharif
   (c) Zaid (d) Zaid- Kharif

Ans. (b) Kharif

8. Which of the following is not a problem of Indian agriculture ? **[2023]**
   (a) Dependence on monsoon (b) Small land holdings
   (c) Two main cropping seasons
   (d) Use of traditional methods of farming

Ans. (c) Two main cropping seasons

9. In Meghalaya, Assam, Mizoram and Nagaland, shifting agriculture is called ....
   (a) Pamlou (b) Jhumming
   (c) Deepa (d) Khil

Ans. (b) Jhumming

10. A powerful tool that helps to develop new hybrid varieties of seeds is ....
   (a) Genetic engineering (b) Bio-fuelling
   (c) Genetic disorder (d) Genetic drift

Ans. (a) Genetic engineering

11. Given reason for the following
   Agriculture is an important economic sector for a country like India.
   (a) India has a large population size.
   (b) Agriculture provides its maximum share to GDP.
   (c) Many industries get their raw material from agriculture.
   (d) All of the above

Ans. (d) All of the above

12. Given reason for the following
   The Green Revolution was considered a 'New Agricultural Strategy'.
   (a) Due to adoption of modern scientific methods of farming.
   (b) Due to application of High Yielding Varieties (HYV) of seeds.
   (c) Because of the use of large capital and technological inputs.
   (d) All of the above

Ans. (d) All of the above

13. Given reason for the following.
   The Green revolution was successful in Punjab, Haryana, Western Uttar Pradesh and parts of Rajasthan.
   (a) These states have small landholdings for cultivation of crops.
   (b) There is proper development of transport network in these states.
   (c) Farmers are well-educated to use advanced technology in farming practice.
   (d) Green revolution was started by a group of farmers of these states.

Ans. (c) Farmers are well-educated to use advanced technology in farming practice.

14. Given reason for the following.
Indian farmers are facing many challenges in the international markets
(a) Indian government has reduced its subsidy on fertilisers, it raised the cost of production of crops.
(b) There is reduction of import duty on agricultural products in India.
(c) The cost of agricultural crops is increasing in Indian market while decreasing in the international markets.
(d) All of the above

Ans. (d) All of the above

15. Give reason for the following.
In India Jhumming is a primitive form of cultivation.
(a) No use of HYV seeds.
(b) It is done by family members of farmers.
(c) Farmers use primitive tools like hoe, dao, digging sticks.
(d) All of the above

Ans. (d) All of the above

16. Which of the following statements is correct about the major drawback of agriculture in India?
(i) Use of HYV seeds is not appropriate for Indian farming practices.
(ii) Use of organic manure is not appropriate for agriculture.
(iii) Mechanisation of agriculture degrades the soil fertility.
(iv) Dependence on monsoon is the major problem of Indian agriculture.

Codes
(a) Only (i) (b) Only (ii)
(c) (ii) and (iii) (d) Only (iv)

Ans. (d) Only (iv)

17. Which one of the following statements is incorrect as regards to commercial farming?
(i) Use of heavy doses of modern inputs.
(ii) Crops are grown for sale.
(iii) Family members are involved in growing crops.
(iv) Practised on large landholdings.

Codes
(a) Only (i) (b) (i) and (iii)
(c) Only (iii) (d) (ii) and (iv)

Ans. (c) Only (iii)

18. Match the following.

List-I	List-II
A. Kharif	1. October – March
B. Rabi	2. April–June
C. Zaid	3. February-March
D. Zaid- Rabi	4. June-September

Codes

	A	B	C	D		A	B	C	D
(a)	1	2	3	4	(b)	2	1	4	3
(c)	3	4	1	2	(d)	4	1	2	3

Ans. (d)

19. Match the following.

List-I	List-II
A. Intensive Farming	1. Terai region
B. Extensive Farming	2. Northern India
C. Plantation Farming	3. Andhra Pradesh
D. Commercial Farming	4. Assam

Codes

	A	B	C	D		A	B	C	D
(a)	1	2	3	4	(b)	2	1	4	3
(c)	3	4	1	2	(d)	4	3	2	1

Ans. (b)

20. Match the following.

List-I	List-II
A. Intensive Farming	1. Practice of cultivation and raising of animals
B. Extensive Farming	2. A type of monoculture
C. Plantation Farming	3. Uses heavy machinery
D. Mixed Farming	4. Aims to gain high productivity from a small land

Codes

	A	B	C	D		A	B	C	D
(a)	1	2	3	4	(b)	2	3	4	1
(c)	3	4	1	2	(d)	4	3	2	1

Ans. (d)

Section-I

Short Questions

1. What do you understand by the term 'agriculture'?

Ans. The term agriculture is formed from two Latin words, *'Ager'* which means 'Land' and *'Culture'* which means 'Cultivation'. The basic purpose of agriculture is to produce food and fodder.

2. What is the importance of agriculture in India? Mention two factors. **[2012]**

Or Mention any two reasons for the importance of agriculture in India.

[Specimen paper Semester-II 2022]

Ans. The importance of agriculture in India is
(i) Agriculture sector provides employment to vast section of the population in our country.
(ii) It provides food and food products like rice, wheat milk, etc. to human population and fodder for livestock.

3. Name the major factors which significantly influence the method of cultivation in India.

Ans. Physical environment, technological knowledge and socio-cultural practices are some major factors that influence the method of cultivation in India.

4. How have poverty and fragmentation of land become problems of agricultural India? [2014]

Ans. Majority of farmers in India are not very rich and they possess very small landholding which limits the usage of latest machinery, fertilisers and modern irrigational equipments on their pieces of land.

These small and fragmented pieces of lands lead to wastage of time, labour and a lot of fertile land is wasted in raising boundaries. These limitations do not allow high yield and proper income.

5. Mention any two problems of agriculture in India. [2011]

Ans. There are many problems in agriculture which lead to low yield, these are

(i) **Erratic Rainfall** The agriculture sector in India is still dependent on rainfall which is very unreliable and irregular. Its failure or late arrival causes serious problem for the farmers.

(ii) **Limitations in Irrigational Facilities** India is a vast country with large irrigated area, but still a large portion of area lacks good irrigation facilities and is still dependent on rainfall.

6. How is proper use of manure important in agriculture?

Ans. Proper use of manure and fertilisers are very essential for keeping the quality of the soil intact and to raise the productivity from agriculture.

7. Mention two steps taken by the government to boost agricultural production in India. [2019]

Ans. Two steps taken by government to boost agricultural production in India are

(i) Introduction of Green Revolution in India and use of High yielding varieties of seeds (HYVs).

(ii) Providing subsidy to farmers by reducing the cost of agricultural inputs like seeds, electricity, irrigation facility at subsidised rates.

8. What do you mean by jhumming?

Or Explain shifting cultivation. [2016]

Ans. Shifting agriculture is also known as 'slash and burn agriculture' or 'jhumming'. Shifting cultivation involves a patch of forest which is cleared, trees are cut down and the stumps are set on fire. The patch is then cultivated for a few years and when the soil becomes infertile, the cultivator moves to a fresh piece of land and repeats the same procedure.

9. Mention two disadvantages of shifting cultivation in India.

Ans. The disadvantages of shifting cultivation are

(i) When the land is abandoned, it leads to soil erosion.

(ii) It amounts to low production of crops.

10. Mention two differences between shifting agriculture and plantation agriculture.

Ans. The two differences between shifting and plantation agriculture are

Shifting Agriculture	Plantation Agriculture
It is practised on a small piece of land for a few years.	It is practised on a large piece of land continuously.
It is primitive type of agriculture.	It uses modern technology.

11. Mention any two features of extensive agriculture.

Ans. The features of extensive agriculture are

(i) This type of farming is practised on lands of comparatively large size in which small amount of capital and labour are used.

(ii) This farming is mainly carried out with the help of big machines. The farmer focusses on a few important commercial crops.

12. Explain two important characteristics of plantation farming. Name two important plantation crop.

Or Mention any two features of plantation farming stating two examples. [2014]

Ans. The characteristics of plantation farming are

(i) This type of agricultural practice involves large capital and vast agriculture land for cultivation of single crop.

(ii) These farms employ labour on large scale. Tea, coffee, rubber, spices (mainly cash crops) are its examples.

13. What do you mean by mixed farming? Give its one advantage.

Or What is mixed farming? Mention any one benefit of mixed farming. [2017]

Or Give a reason why practicing mixed farming gives security to farmers. [2019]

Ans. The practise of cultivation of crops as well as raising of animals/livestock simultaneously is popularly known as mixed farming.

The benefit or advantage of mixed farming is that it gives security to the farmers because even if the crops fail they can rely on their cattle rearing for income.

14. What do you understand by commercial farming?

Ans. In commercial farming, crops are cultivated mainly for commercial purpose i.e. to sale it in the market. Sugarcane, oilseeds, fibre crops like cotton and jute are the main cash crops.

15. Name some crops of commercial farming. State any one characteristics of this farming.

Ans. Tea, coffee, rubber, sugarcane etc. are the crops of commercial farming. A characteristic of this farming is the use of high doses of modern inputs, like high yielding varieties of seeds, chemical, fertilisers, insecticides and pesticides in order to obtain higher productivity.

16. Distinguish between intensive commercial farming and extensive commercial farming. [2013]

Or Differentiate between intensive farming and extensive farming. [2023]

Ans. Differences between intensive and extensive farming are

Intensive	Extensive
This type of farming is practised on a small piece of land.	This is practised on comparatively large piece of land.
It employs huge manual labour.	It is carried out with the help of big machines.

17. Mention two points of difference between subsistence agriculture and commerical agriculture. [2020]

Ans. The differences between subsistence agriculture and commercial agriculture are

Subsistence Agriculture	Commercial Agriculture
In this type of agriculture farmer produces exclusively for his own consumption.	In this type of agriculture crops are cultivated for commercial purpose.
It is devoid of facilities like fertilisers, high quality seeds etc.	It incorporates high quality seeds, expensive fertilisers etc.

18. Answer the following questions.
   (i) When are kharif crops sown and harvested?
   (ii) Name the cash crop which is also a kharif crop.

Ans. (i) Kharif crops are sown in June and July with the arrival of the monsoon rains. They are harvested in October and November.
(ii) Cotton is a cash crop and also a kharif crop in peninsular India.

19. (i) Name two agriculture seasons of India. [Specimen Paper Semester-II 2022]
   (ii) Name one crop that grows in each of the season

Ans. (i) Two agriculture seasons of India are rabi and kharif.
(ii) Wheat is a rabi crop and rice is a kharif crop.

Long Questions

1. Explain how lack of quality seeds and modern technology have affected the agriculture?

Ans. Lack of quality seeds and modern technology have severely affected the agriculture by the following ways

(i) **Poor Quality Seeds** The poor farmers of India are often out of reach of good high yielding varieties of seeds. This limitation causes low production.

(ii) **Lack of Reach of Modern Technology** Farmers are out of reach of latest technology and methods. Due to this, they do not get proper yield per hectare. Efforts should be made to provide education for modern means of farming to the farmers through radio, television, schools etc.

2. Explain the different features of subsistence farming.

Ans. The features of subsistence farming are

- In this type of farming, the farmers have very scattered and small landholding and primitive tools like hoe or dao and digging sticks are used by their families and community labour.
- As the farmers are poor, they are devoid of the facilities like fertilisers, high quality seeds, electricity and irrigation. This results in very low production and hence, they use it for their own consumption and snarely sell in the market. It is dominated by food crops.
- This type of farming is dominated by food crops and it is highly dependent on monsoon since there is no irrigation facilities.

3. State any three important features of plantation farming in India. [2011]

Ans. Important features of plantation farming are

(i) It is mainly used for commercial purposes and helpful in earning foreign exports by export of plantation crops.

(ii) This farming also facilitates their workers by providing schools, houses, market places, hospitals and other facilities. In India, it is practised in Assam, Darjeeling, Nilgiri and Anaimalai hills, etc.

(iii) The important crops grown on plantations are tea, coffee, coconut, oil palm, spices, banana, cinchona and rubber. Many of these crops are developed as single cash crops on a vast scale and are exported.

4. Differentiate between a rabi crop and a kharif crop. [2015]

Ans. Differences between rabi crop and kharif crop are

Rabi Crop	Kharif Crop
Rabi crops are sown in October-November and harvested in March-April.	Kharif crops are sown in June-July and harvested in September-October.
It is sown mainly in winter season.	It is sown mainly in summer season.
Examples of rabi crops are wheat, peas, gram, oilseeds, barley, etc.	Examples of kharif crops are rice, maize, cotton, groundnut, jowar, bajra, etc.

5. Answer the following questions.
   (i) Why is agriculture important in India? [2018]
   (ii) Name the two main agricultural seasons in India.
   (iii) What is mixed farming?

Ans. (i) Agriculture is important in India because it provides employment to the vast population of our country.
(ii) The two main agricultural seasons in India are rabi season and kharif season.
(iii) The practice of cultivation of crops as well as raising of animals/livestock simultaneously is popularly known as mixed farming.

6. What is commercial farming? What are its features?

Ans. Commercial farming is the cultivation of crops mainly for the purpose of selling in the market or exporting it. The example of commercial crops are sugarcane, tobacco, oilseeds, cotton, jute, etc. Features of commercial farming are

- It require good quality seeds, proper irrigation, fertilisers in adequate amount and pesticides.
- Large land area and big farms are used.
- Commercial farming of different crops varied place to place. For example, rice is a commercial crop in Punjab.
- It is successful in filling the gap of food security in India.

7. How can mixed farming help farmers towards a sustainable income?

Ans. Mixed farming is raising of animals/livestock and growing of crops simultaneously. It provides a sustainable income to the farmers, as even if the crop of farmer fails, he will be able to get income from rearing his cattles, by selling milk, eggs, etc. This type of agriculture can help the small farmers who mainly depend on their crops for survival.

Picture Based Question

1. With reference to the given picture answer the following questions.

(i) Which type of farming is shown in above picture?
(ii) Name two places where this farming takes place.
(iii) Mention the another name of this farming.

Ans. (i) The farming shown in the picture is known as shifting cultivation.
(ii) The two places where shifting farming takes place are Andhra Pradesh and Kerala.
(iii) Another name of shifting cultivation is 'slash and burn' method.

Chapter Assessment

Section-I

Multiple Choice Questions

1. Grouping of small landholdings into a bigger one is called ....
(a) ceiling on landholdings
(b) collectivisation
(c) co-operative farming
(d) consolidation of landholdings

2. Farmers clear a patch of land, produce food, and abandon it when soil fertility decreases. What is it called?
(a) Viable agriculture
(b) Slash and burn agriculture
(c) Productive agriculture
(d) Burnt dead seed agriculture

3. Intensive farming is practised in area of ....
(a) low population (b) high population
(c) deserts (d) thick forests

4. Which of the following crops are grown with the onset of monsoons and are harvested in the months of September-October?
(a) Rabi (b) Kharif
(c) Zaid (d) None of these

Section-II

Short Questions

1. How does the monsoon affect cultivation in India?
2. How is soil erosion becoming a problem for Indian agriculture?
3. Where is Jhumming practised in India and what are its disadvantages?
4. State two characteristics of plantation agriculture.
5. What is the importance of agriculture?
6. Mention any two problems of Indian agriculture.
7. State any two reforms of agriculture.
8. Give any two features of shifting farming.
9. Differentiate between mixed farming and commercial farming.

Long Questions

1. Why is agriculture known as 'backbone of India's economic system'?
2. What are the types of agriculture practised in India? Which is the most common farming in India and why?
3. Explain Green Revolution.

CHAPTER

10

Food and Fibre Crops of India

SYLLABUS

Food and Fibre Crops of India • Climatic conditions, soil requirements, method of cultivation, processing and distribution of the following crop:
• Rice, wheat, millets, pulses, cotton and jute.

Food Crops of India

Food crops have important place in Indian agricultural economy as these occupy about two-third of total cropped area in the country. Food crops are part of cereals. Cereals are also called grains. They are any grass yielding starchy seeds which are suitable for food. Important cereals are rice, wheat, maize, millets, etc.

Rice

It is the most important staple food crop of India. It supports half of the Indian population. Rice accounts for one-third production of food-grains in India. It is grown all over the country mainly in North-East and Southern parts (in highest concentration) of the country.

Rice is a kharif crop in North India while it can be grown throughout the year in South if proper irrigation is available. Rice grows in well watered lowland plain that can be flooded. Rice crop in India divided into two categories

(i) **Upland Rice** The rice grown in hilly areas is called 'dry' or 'upland rice' because the supply of water to hilly regions is not as much as on the plains. The rice in upland areas is grown without flooding the fields. This type of rice is sown in March-April and harvested in September-October. Upland rice cultivation depends on the distribution of rainfall only. The entire crop is consumed by the local people.

(ii) **Lowland Rice** The rice grown in lowland fields (plains) are called lowland rice. These fields are rainfed or irrigated. This type of rice is sown in June and harvested in October. Lowland rice needs plenty of water and its production is used for local consumption as well as for commercial purpose.

Climatic Conditions and Soil Requirement

- **Temperature** Rice requires an average temperature of about 24°C. The mean temperature for flowering and fertilisation ranges from 16°C to 20°C whereas during ripening, it needs temperature from 18°C to 32°C. Temperature beyond 35°C is not suitable and it needs sufficient amount of sunshine as well as water.
- **Rainfall** Rice cultivation requires sufficient amount of water and the average rainfall required is about 150 cm to 300 cm. Flooded fields with **stagnant**[1] water (around 5 cm to 10 cm) during the early

1 **Stagnant** The standing or immobile fluid which shows no activity.

period of growing season is required. Thus, the monsoon lands, flood plains, river valleys, coastal plains, deltas, estuaries, etc. are best suited for rice cultivation.

- **Soil** Rice cultivation require deep fertile clayey or loamy soils. It is cultivated in the alluvial soils around the river banks. The soil should be capable to retain water in the field. This condition protects the plant from pests, which can't survive under water. Soil needs manure and fertilisers to get a higher yield.

Methods of Cultivation

Rice can be cultivated by two methods which are

(i) **The Dry Method** This method of cultivation is mainly practiced in areas which depends on rain and do not have adequate irrigation facilities. In this method, farmers use drills to sow the seeds in rows in heavy rainfall areas and in moderate rainfall areas, they scatter seeds by hands.

(ii) **The Puddled or Wet Method** It is practised in areas which have adequate supply of water. Farmers plough the land and fill it with 3-5cm of standing water. This water is maintained in the fields up to a depth of 2-3 cm till the seedlings are well established.

Sowing

Rice is sown in the following ways

- **Broadcasting Method** It involves sprinkling seeds all over the field by hand, after ploughing it. The yield is low in this method of cultivation. This method is commonly used in those regions where labour is scarce and soil is infertile. It is done before the onset of monsoon.
- **Drilling Method** This method is prevalent in peninsular India (South India). In this method, seeds are dropped in the **furrow**[2] through a bamboo shaft attached to the plough. The seeds fall in the furrows thereby saving the wastage of seeds, but it is time consuming. The germination rate of the seeds in this method is high.
- **Dibbling Method** A dibble is a planting bar, which is used to make holes in the ground for seeds or plants. In this method, seeds are sown at regular intervals in the furrows made by the farmers with the help of plough.
- **Transplantation Method** This method is dominant in the areas of fertile, deltaic soil with abundant rainfall and plenty of sunshine. In this method, the seeds are first sown in nurseries after soaking them in water for 24 hours.

  After about 4 to 5 weeks when the seedlings attain about 20 to 25 cm of height, they are removed with their roots and transplanted in the flooded fields, so that they can grow again. After sowing the seeds in the field, farmers fill the field with 2-3 cm deep water. Gradually, they increase the depth of water level to 4-6 cm till the crop matures. This method of rice cultivation is popular because it gives a higher yield. As compared to broadcasting method, there is less wastage of seeds in transplantation method.
- **Japanese Method** This method was introduced in 1953. In this method, good quality seeds are used, but in less quantity. The seeds are sown on a raised nursery bed at a regular distance of 20 cm to 25 cm, so that the **weeding**[3] and fertilising process are made easy for the farmers. In this method, heavy use of fertilisers and hybrid seeds called 'Japonica' are included which results in high yield of rice.

Harvesting

Harvesting of rice is done by hand with a sickle, but in commercial farming it is done by machines. The crop which is cut is kept in the field to let it dry for about 3 to 4 days. Each stem of rice is cut about 60 cm below the grain which helps to facilitate proper threshing.

Processing

The processing of rice include the following methods

- **Threshing** Rice is threshed and crushed by bullocks to separate the **kernel**[4] from the seed. It is done in the rice fields in order to minimise the cost of transporation.
- **Winnowing** The process removing unwanted husk from the grain is called winnowing. It involve pouring the grain.
- **Milling** It is the process of removing the yellowish outer cover of the grain. The rice is then polished which makes it attractive, but lesser in nutrients.

---

2 **Furrow** It is a long, narrow trench made in the ground by a plough, especially for planting seeds or irrigation.
3 **Weeding** Removal of unwanted plants from the field.
4 **Kernel** A soft, edible part of a nut, seed or fruit contain within its hard shell.

Distribution

- **West Bengal** Rice is the leading crop of West Bengal. Farmers grow three varities of rice in West Bengal called 'aus', 'boro' and 'aman'.
- **Uttar Pradesh** In the Easter region of Uttar Pradesh, rice is an important crop. Basti, Deoria, Gorakhpur, Maharajganj, Siddharth Nagar and Azamgarh are the major rice producing districts of Uttar Pradesh.
- **Punjab** The major rice producing areas of Punjab are Amritsar, Jalandhar, Faridkot and Patiala. A major part of rice growth in these areas are exported.
- **Tamil Nadu** The major rice producing area of Tamil Nadu are Thanjavur, South Arcot, Chingleput, North Arcot and Madurai.
- **Other States** Haryana, Karnataka, Odisha, Madhya Pradesh, Bihar, Assam, Gujarat, etc are the other rice producing States of India.

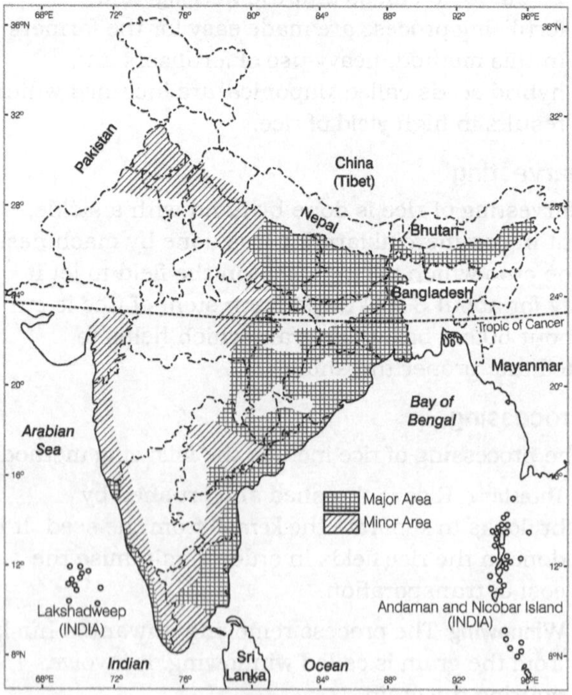

Rice Producing Areas

Wheat

It is the second most important staple food in India after rice. It is high in protein, vitamins and carbohydrates. Wheat is a rabi crop grown in winter and harvested in March or April. About 14 per cent of the total cropped area in the country is under wheat cultivation. It is a staple food crop for the Northern and North-Western India.Wheat is a winter crop in state like Punjab, Haryana, Rajasthan, UP and Bihar.

Climatic Conditions and Soil Requirement

- **Temperature** Wheat is a temperate crop and needs a cool climate with moderate amount of rainfall. It requires an average temperature of about 10°C to 15°C at the time of sowing. But higher temperature (20° C to 25° C) at the time of ripening and harvesting is needed.

  Gradual increase in temperature is more suitable than fast increase. Winter temperature of the North India is more favourable for wheat production. Wheat is generally not grown in South due to very high temperature even in winters.
- **Rainfall** Wheat requires rainfall of about 50 cm to 100 cm during growing period. Too much rainfall is harmful for wheat while the shortage of rain may dry the crop. Irrigation becomes important when there is shortage of rainfall.

  Winter rainfall is good for this crop in the North-Western India. Due to excessive rainfall it is not grown in North-East and Southern states of India.
- **Soil** Wheat cultivation is practised best in well drained, fertile, loamy and alluvial soils of clayey type. In India, it is mainly grown in flat alluvial plains of North India.

  The deep soil provides the required moisture to wheat crop. Wheat can also be grown in black cotton soil. Different types of seeds have different soil requirements. For example, the common bread wheat is grown on the alluvial soils of the Great Plains, whereas macaroni wheat is grown on the black soils of Central and Southern parts of India and emmer wheat Triticumdicoccum grows on the red soils of the Nilgiri Hills.

Methods of Cultivation

- **Sowing** Wheat seeds are sown by various methods like broadcasting, dibbling and drilling. As wheat is a rabi crop, the condition of fairly low temperature in the month of October-November and the rainfall in winters are very helpful for sowing wheat.

  For good germination, the seed-bed is prepared many times before the seed is sown. The seeds germinate in about 3 or 4 days when the plant is about 15 cm to 20 cm tall, it needs good irrigation.

The temperature should be generally low in the growing season. Wheat crop need 3 or 4 times irrigation during the growing period.

- **Harvesting** The crop starts to ripen in March when temperature is around 21°C and is harvested in the month of April when temperature reaches up to 27°C.
- Harvesting is carried out by sickle, but it is being replaced by machines now, especially in Punjab, Haryana and Western Uttar Pradesh. Warm and sunny weather condition is helpful in the ripening of the crop. Hailstorms, frost or rain are very harmful at the time of harvesting.
- **Processing** Wheat is processed into various grades of flour by cleaning, tempering, grinding, sifting (refining) and purifying. Then flour is sold in the markets.

Distribution

Uttar Pradesh, Punjab, Haryana, Madhya Pradesh and Rajashthan are leading producers of wheat in India. Punjab is called **Granary of India**. The other major wheat producing states are Bihar, Maharashtra, Gujarat, Karnataka, West Bengal and Uttarakhand. The yield level of wheat is very high (above 4,000 k.g. per ha) in Punjab and Haryana whereas, Uttar Pradesh, Rajasthan and Bihar have moderate yields.

In the states like Madhya Pradesh, Himachal Pradesh and Jammu and Kashmir wheat is grown under rain-fed conditions which results in low yield.

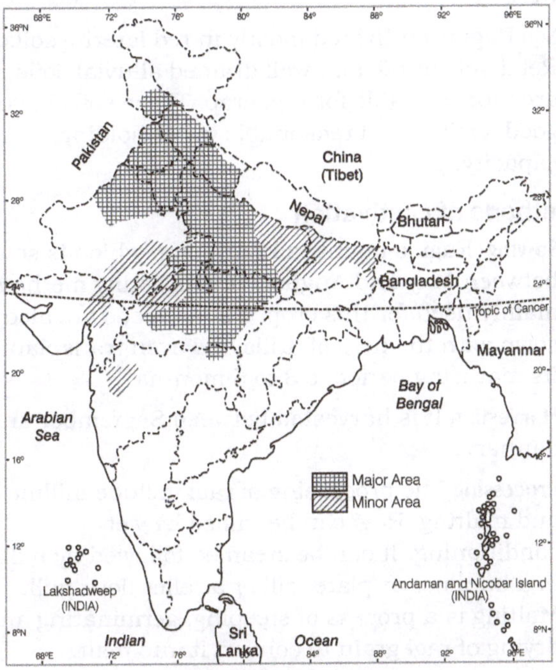

Wheat Producing Areas

Millets (Jowar, Bajra and Ragi)

Millets are kharif crops grown in comparatively less fertile areas where rice and wheat cannot be cultivated. Millets are food of the poor people and provide an important fodder for cattle. These are drought resistant crops and do not require specific soil, but loamy, sandy and clayey soils are better for production.

Millets are very nutritious and digestible food grains. They are good source of iron, calcium, zinc and magnesium. These are short duration crops which take 3-4 months.

Jowar

Jowar or sorghum is among the important food crops of India which accounts for 5.3 per cent of total cropped area. It is an important food crop in the dry parts of the Peninsular Plateau where rice or wheat cannot be grown. Jowar can be both kharif and rabi crop.

It needs little water for growth and can grow well even in the dry farming areas. It is mostly grown in plains, but can also be grown on gentle slopes up to 1200 m height.

Climatic Conditions and Soil Requirement

- **Temperature** Jowar requires 27°C to 32°C of temperature for its optimum cultivation.
- **Rainfall** It requires rainfall ranging from 40 cm to 100 cm. Rainfall above 100 cm causes damage to the crop. It is grown in arid and semi-arid areas.
- **Soil** Jowar can be grown in regur, heavy and light alluvium soils, red soils, grey and yellow loams and clayey black soils. Kharif jowar is grown in sandy soil while rabi jowar is grown in black regur soils. The black clayey loams of Peninsular Plateau is most suitable for the cultivation of jowar.

Methods of Cultivation

- **Sowing** This crop does not need a thorough and continuous preparation of the fields. But the soil management before sowing is important for the crops of dry farming areas. Dibbling and broadcasting methods are used for sowing jowar seeds. It takes 4 to 5 months to mature the crop.
- **Harvesting** Jowar should be harvested when the grain is ripe and dried in the layer. It should not be heaped to avoid the loss of seed viability.

- **Processing** In the processing of jowar, threshing may be done with mechanical threshers or stone roller threshing or cattle threshing may be done. The grain should be stored in airtight containers like seed bins. Grain should be dried thoroughly before storing. Periodical drying of grain once a month will control the store grain from pests.

Distribution

Maharashtra is the largest producer of jowar. It is also grown in Karnataka, Madhya Pradesh, Andhra Pradesh, Telangana, Tamil Nadu, Rajasthan, Gujarat and Uttar Pradesh.

Bajra

Bajra or bulrush millet is a short season kharif crop which is used both as food as well as fodder in India. In some parts of the country, it is used as **thatching**[5] material for the roof and staple food crop in North-Western Rajasthan and Gujarat. It is also grown as a mixed crop with cotton, jowar or ragi. Due to its rainfed nature, it needs less irrigation.

Climatic Conditions and Soil Requirement

- **Temperature** Bajra requires a temperature ranging from 25°C to 30°C.
- **Rainfall** It requires a rainfall between 40 cm to 50 cm. It grows very well in bright sunshine just after light monsoon showers. It is lessly grown in areas where rainfall exceeds 100 cm.
- **Soil** It can be grown in poor, light sandy soils as well as black and red or gravelly soils.

Methods of Cultivation

- **Sowing** Bajra is sown in the middle or last week of July through drilling or dibbling method. Generally the crop requires low quantity of nutrients. Fertilisers are applied in split doses, half of nitrogen, full phosphorus and potash should be placed at the time of sowing .

  The organic manures must be applied 20 days before the sowing of the seeds for full decomposition. One-fourth dose of nitrogen should be applied about 30 days and 60 days after sowing.
- **Harvesting** It is harvested when grains become hard enough and contain moisture. Two methods are adopted for harvesting the crop
  (i) Cutting earhead from standing crop followed by cutting of remaining plants later
  (ii) Cutting of entire plants by sticks and stalking the plants for 5 days in sun for obtaining grains.
- **Processing** Bajra grains are separated either by beating the earheads with sticks or by trampling the earheads under bullock feet. The separated grains must be cleaned and dried in sun to bring about 12-14% moisture after which the grains may be bagged and stored in a moisture proof store.

Distribution

India is the largest producer of Bajra. It is grown mainly in Rajasthan, Maharashtra, Gujarat, Uttar Pradesh, Tamil Nadu and Haryana.

Ragi

Ragi or buckwheat is not a season bound crop and hence can be cultivated throughout the year, if moisture is available. It is grown in dry region of South India and some parts of North India. The main season of Ragi is from June to September.

Climatic Conditions and Soil Requirement

- **Temperature** Ragi require an average temperature of about 20°C to 30°C.
- **Rainfall** It is suited for cultivation in areas with annual rainfall of 50 cm to 100 cm. It can be grown under severe drought conditions and very low rainfall.
- **Soil** Ragi is cultivated mostly in red laterite soils. Relatively fertile and well drained alluvial soils are most suitable for ragi crop. These soils have good fertility and reasonable water holding capacity.

Methods of Cultivation

- **Sowing** Ragi is mainly a kharif crop which is sown between May and August. Broadcasting method is mainly used for this crop, but its seeds are also sown with the help of drills and even transplanted. Its maturing period is 3 to 5 months.
- **Harvesting** It is harvested between September and January.
- **Processing** The processing of ragi include milling and malting. Ragi can be milled by wet conditioning. It can be steamed followed by milling in a hammer or plate mill or a roller flour mill. Malting is a process of steeping, germinating and drying of ragi grain to convert it into malt.

5 **Thatching** It is a craft of building a roof with dry vegetation such as straw or similar material.

Distribution

Around 1.3 per cent of the total cropped area is occupied by ragi crop. It occupies around 5 per cent of the total cereals. Karnataka and Tamil Nadu are the leading producers of ragi in the India. Other important producers are Uttarakhand, Maharashtra, Andhra Pradesh, Odisha, Jharkhand and Gujarat.

Pulses

Pulses are main source of protein in a vegetarian diet. They occupy about 11 per cent of the total cropped area in India. Pulses are rabi crop which provides essential vegetable proteins. They are leguminous plants with root nodules which have the capacity to fix and use atmospheric nitrogen in the soil.

These are often rotated with other crops to keep the fertility of the soil intact. They are often used as food for cattle.

Gram and tur (*arhar*) are the main pulses of India. Other pulses are *urad* (black gram), *moong* (green gram), *masoor* (lentil), *matar* (peas), *kulthi*, *khesari* and moth. Among other pulses Gram is the leading pulse crop.

It occupies about two-fifths of the total area under all pulses. Gram is raised as a rabi crop in those areas which receive about 10 cm of rainfall during winter. It is a mixed crop which is sown with wheat. It is the crop of North and Central India.

Tur, *urad* and *moong* are raised as kharif crops almost throughout India. *Khesari* and *masur* are raised as rabi crops in North India.

Climatic Conditions and Soil Requirement

- **Temperature** Pulses can be cultivated in a wide range of climatic conditions, but it grows best in mild, cool and comparatively dry climate with temperature ranging from 20°C to 25°C.
- **Rainfall** Pulses needs rainfall of about 50 cm to 75 cm.
- **Soil** Pulses are produced in loamy, alluvial and dry type of soil. Heavier soils with more water retention capacity are considered ideal for cultivation of pulses. Pulses cannot be grown on saline and acidic soils.

Methods of Cultivation

- **Sowing** Being a rabi crop, pulses are sown between September and November after maturing in about 5-6 months.
- **Harvesting** Pulses are harvested in February and April. It is pulled out and is kept in the open area to dry.
- **Processing** The processing of pulses is done in the following ways
  - **Cleaning and Grading** Pulses are cleaned from dust, chaff, grits, etc and graded according to size by a reel type cleaner.
  - **Pitting** In this process, the clean pulses are passed through an emery roller machine. Husk is cracked and scratched in this operation. Some of the pulses are de-husked and split during this operation which are then separated by sieving.
  - **Pretreatments with Oil** The scratched or pitted pulses are passed through a screw conveyor and mixed with some edible oil like linseed oil (1.5 to 2.5 kg/tone of pulses). Then they are kept for about 12 hours for diffusion of the oil.
  - **Conditioning** Conditioning of pulses is done by alternate wetting and drying. After sun drying for a certain period, 3-5 % moisture is added to the pulse and tempered for about eight flours and again dried in the Sun.

    The whole process of alternate wetting and drying is continued for two to four days until all pulses are sufficiently conditioned. Pulses are finally dried to about 10 to 12 % moisture content.
  - **De-husking** Emery rollers, known as Gota machine are used for the de-husking and splitting of conditioned pulses.
  - **Polishing** Polish is given to the de-husked and split pulses by treating them with a small quantity of oil and/or water.

Distribution

The cultivation of pulses in the country is largely concentrated in the dry lands of Deccan and Central plateaus and North-Western parts of the country. Pulses are mainly grown in Madhya Pradesh, Maharashtra, Uttar Pradesh, Himachal Pradesh, Rajasthan, Haryana, Andhra Pradesh, West Bengal, Karnataka, etc.

Check Your LEARNING...

1. What kind of soil is required for the cultivation of rice?
2. In which season wheat is harvested?
3. Name a crop, which can be grown in both kharif and rabi season.
4. State any one reason which made pulses an important crop in India.

Fibre Crops of India

Cotton and Jute are the main fibre crops that are produced on a large scale in India.

Cotton

It is very important fibre crop that supplies raw material to textile industry. Cotton seed is an important source of edible oil. Cotton is a tropical crop and it is grown in India as a kharif crop. On the basis of length, strength and structure, cotton is of following types

- **Short Staple Cotton** Its length is less than 20 mm. This is an inferior quality of cotton and is produced in the upper Ganges valley. It is produced in Punjab.
- **Medium Staple Cotton** It has a length of about 20 to 24 mm. In India, majority of cotton output is of this type. It is produced in North-Western Deccan region.
- **Superior Medium Cotton** It contributes 37% of India's output and is grown in Punjab, Tamil Nadu, Madhya Pradesh, Uttar Pradesh, Karnataka and Maharashtra.
- **Long Staple Cotton** It has the longest fibre whose length ranges from 24 to 30 mm. The fibre is of superior quality and shiny. It is used to make fine quality of cotton clothes. It is produced in Central and Southern Deccan region.
- **Superior Long Staple Cotton** It is longer than 27 mm. It consist of 33% of India's total production of cotton.

Climatic Conditions and Soil Requirement

- **Temperature** Cotton needs mild, cool and comparatively dry climate having temperature 21°C to 30°C and abundant sunshine is necessary during its growth period.

  A long period of 200 (frost free) days are essential for the plant to mature. It needs the day temperature above 26°C during October, which helps the ripening and bursting of cotton balls under the sunny skies. The minimum temperature should not fall below 20°C as it stops plant growth.
- **Rainfall** Cotton plant need a moderate rainfall of 50 cm to 80 cm which should be well distributed throughout the year. Stagnant water and excessive rainfall are injurious for the growth of cotton.
- **Soil** Cotton is grown on variety of soils, but it is grown mainly in the black (regur) soil of the Deccan Plateau and Malwa Plateau, as this soil has the ability to retain moisture. It also grows well in the alluvial soil of Satluj-Ganga plains and in red and laterite soils of the peninsular regions.

Methods of Cultivation

- **Sowing** Cotton is sown in April-May (before onset of monsoon) and mainly as kharif crop in case of long staple varieties and in September in case of short and medium staple varieties.

  It takes 6 to 8 months to mature. Bright and sunny days helps in ripening at bursting of cotton balls. In Punjab and Haryana, it is sown as a rabi crop while in peninsular India, it is grown as kharif crop because of the fear of frost. The seeds are sown by the broadcasting method. Irrigation helps the crops to grow better.
- **Harvesting** In peninsular India, it is harvested between January and March, whereas in Northern India, it is harvested in December and January before the winter frost which is very harmful for the crop.
- **Processing** Picking and ginning are the main activities under processing of cotton which is mostly done by hand. The picking season normally continues for 3 months as the cotton balls continue to mature. A lot of labour is required for picking process because it cannot be mechanised.

  Ginning is the process of separation of seeds and fibre from the raw material known as **lint**. It is known as **roller gins** in India. After separating, the lint is tied in bales and sent to the cotton mills for cleaning and spinning into threads.

  After cleaning by washing, these bales are combed and made into an untwisted rope called a **sliver**. Then a spinning frame turns these slivers directly into cotton yarns.

  Finally, the yarn is dyed and looms are used to weave it into garments and fabrics. Cotton seeds that are obtained from cotton after ginning are used to obtain oil. The oil cake is used as a fodder for the cattle and also as a manure.

Distribution

India has the largest area under cotton cultivation, such as 4.7% of total cropped areas. It is grown mainly in three regions

(i) **North-West Region** It includes Punjab, Haryana, Rajasthan and Western Uttar Pradesh.

(ii) **Southern Region** It includes Tamil Nadu, Andhra Pradesh and Karnataka.

(iii) **Central Region** It includes Madhya Pradesh, Gujarat (largest producer), Maharashtra (second largest producer) and Telangana.

Jute

It is also an important fibre crop. It is known as **golden fibre** of India because it earns valuable foreign exchange by exporting good quality of jute. It is also known as **brown paper bag** as its sacks are used for packing wheat, rice, sugar, cement, etc. It is also used for making gunny bags, ropes, strings, carpets, etc. However, it is getting stiff competition from plastic and synthetic fibres.

Jute is a cash crop in West Bengal and adjoining Eastern parts of the country. Being concentrated only in a few states, this crop accounts for only about 0.5 per cent of total cropped area in India.

The height of jute plant is of 2 to 4 metres. Its fibre in the inner bark is soft and strong and can be drawn out into yarn of good lengths. Mesta is used as an inferior substitute for jute. It can tolerate drought conditions. Therefore, it is grown where jute cannot be grown. Bags for rough use are made from Mesta. Its cultivation is undertaken in Assam, Bihar, Odisha and Kerala.

There are two types of jute produced in India

(i) **White Jute** This is grown in deltas of lowlands and highland. It is hard and highly adaptable.

(ii) **Tossa Jute** It is grown only on uplands because it cannot grow in flooded area.

Climatic Conditions and Soil Requirement

- **Temperature** Jute requires a temperature ranging from 24°C to 37°C. Hot and humid climate is very useful for jute production.
- **Rainfall** It requires high relative humidity of about 80% to 90%. It requires huge rainfall of 150 cm to 200 cm. However, continuous and untimely rainfall and continuous droughts are harmful for the plants.
- **Soil** Jute grows best in the soil rich with alluvium i.e. flood plains, hence light sandy or clayey loams are considered to be best for jute cultivation. The clayey soil gives the heaviest yield of jute fibre, but the fibre becomes sticky while sandy soil produce coarse fibre.

Methods of Cultivation

- **Sowing** Jute is generally sown in February on lowlands and in March-June on upland. Sowing is mostly done by drilling or broadcasting method. Weeding is very important in the early stages of growth. Relatively higher yields are obtained from the crop sown during the winter season.
- **Harvesting** Jute plant is harvested from July to September. A delay in harvest also adds to yields, but usually produces coarse fibre. The plant are generally uprooted, if the area is flooded, otherwise it is cut to ground length. Some part of the crops is left behind in the fields to develop the seed.
- **Processing** Retting is used for processing jute. After harvesting the plant, it is tied into bundles. It is dried and stripped of unwanted leaves and is kept submerged in water for 2 to 3 weeks.

  This process is known as **retting**. Retting is a micro-biological process. It softens the outer bark and facilitates the easy removability of the fibres from the stalk.

  As soon as it is easy to separate the fibre from the stalk, the bark is peeled and fibres are removed. After it is dried, the fibres are loosely spun, woven and pressed into large bundles called bales.

Distribution

- **West Bengal** It accounts for about three-fourth (about 60%) of the jute production in India. The major producers of jute in West Bengal are Hooghly, Murshidabad, 24 Pargoanas, Jalpaiguri, Dinajpur, Malda and Burdwan districts. West Bengal is the leading jute producer in India due to the following reasons
  - West Bengal has hot and humid climate which is favourable for jute production.
  - It is rich in alluvial and loamy soil.
  - It has plenty of cheap labour availability.
- **Assam** In Assam, jute is cultivated in the districts of Tezpur, Darrang, Nowgong, Goalpare, Sibsagar and Kamrup.
- **Uttar Pradesh** The major producers of jute in Uttar Pradesh are Khetri, Sitapur and Bahraich districts.
- **Odisha** In Odisha, major producers of jute are Cuttack, Puri and Bolangir districts.
- **Bihar** The major producers of jute in Bihar are Darbhanga, Purnea and Saharsa districts.

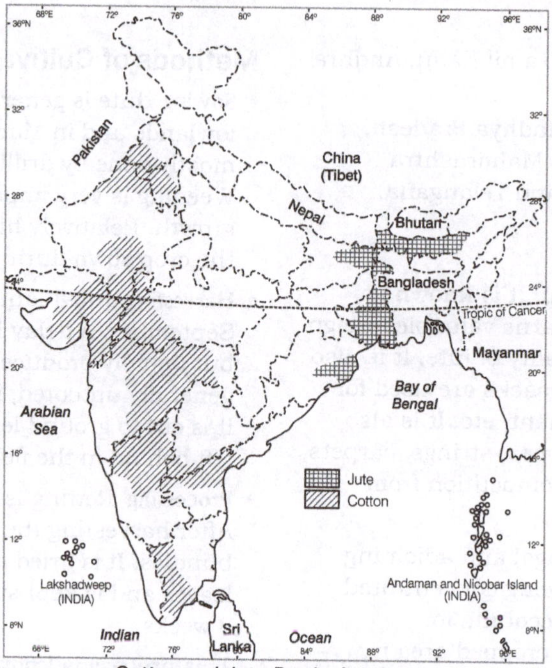

Cotton and Jute Producing Areas

Check Your LEARNING...

1. Which part of cotton is an important source of edible oil?
2. In which region long staple cotton is produced?
3. What is the other name for jute?
4. West Bengal is rich in which type of soil?

QUiCK Revision

- Rice is the most important staple food crop of India. It is a kharif crop and requires 18°C to 32°C temperature with 150 to 300 cm rainfall. West Bengal is the leading producer of rice.
- Rice can be cultivate by two methods i.e. dry method and puddled or wet method.
- Major rice producing states are West Bengal, Uttar Pradesh, Punjab, Tamil Nadu, etc.
- Wheat is second important staple food in India after rice. About 14% of the total cropped areas in India is under wheat cultivation. Wheat cultivation is practised in well drained, fertile, loamy and alluvial soils of clayey type.
- Wheat is processed into various grades of flour by cleaning, tempering, grinding, sifting and purifying.
- Major wheat producing states are Uttar Pradesh, Punjab, Haryana, Madhya Pradesh and Rajasthan.
- Millets are foodgrains that grow well even in dry areas. They are major food of the poor people.
- Millets include jowar, bajra and ragi. Jowar requires 27°C to 32°C of temperature and rainfall from 40 cm to 100 cm. Bajra requires 25°C to 30°C of temperature and rainfall from 40 cm to 50 cm. Ragi requires 20°C to 30°C of temperature and rainfall from 50 cm to 100 cm.
- Pulses are rabi crops which have the capacity to fix and use atmospheric nitrogen in the soil. They are major source of protein.
- Pulses occupies about 11% of the total cropped area in India.
- Pulses requires 20°C to 25°C of tempreature and rainfall of about 50 cm to 75 cm. They are produced in loamy, alluvial and dry soil.
- Major pulses producing states are Uttar Pradesh, Maharashtra, Himachal Pradesh, Rajasthan, Haryana, West Bengal, etc.
- Cotton and jute are important non-food crops of India and form the base of agro-based industries.
- Cotton is important fibre crop. India has the largest area under cotton cultivation (4.7% of total cropped area).
- On the basis of length, strength and structure, the types of cotton are short staple cotton, medium staple cotton, superior medium cotton, long staple cotton and superior long staple cotton.
- Major cotton producing states are Haryana, Rajasthan, Uttar Pradesh, Karnataka, Tamil Nadu, Gujarat, Maharashtra, etc.
- Jute is a very important fibre crop in India after cotton. It is also known as 'golden fibre' of India.
- Jute requires 24°C to 37°C of temperature and rainfall from 150 cm to 200 cm. It grows well in the soil rich with alluvium such as sandy or clayey loam soil.
- Major jute producing states are West Bengal, Assam, Uttar Pradesh, Odisha and Bihar.

Chapter Practice

Section-I

Multiple Choice Questions

1. Which of the following soils is suitable for rice cultivation?
   (a) Deep fertile clayey soil (b) Loamy soil
   (c) Alluvial soil (d) All of these

Ans. (d) All of these

2. Which of the following is the method of cultivation of rice?
   (a) Broadcasting method (b) Drilling method
   (c) Dibbling method (d) All of the above

Ans. (d) All of the above

3. Which state of the Peninsular India tops in the production of paddy?
   (a) Kerala (b) Tamil Nadu
   (c) Karnataka (d) Andhra Pradesh

Ans. (d) Andhra Pradesh

4. Which of the following is a staple food grain of India? **[2023]**
   (a) Rice (b) Gram
   (c) Arhar (d) Wheat

Ans. (a) Rice

5. .... method of rice cultivation is popular because it gives a higher yield.
   (a) Drilling (b) Transplantation
   (c) Japanese (d) Dibbling

Ans. (b) Transplantation

6. .... is the second most important staple food in India.
   (a) Rice (b) Wheat
   (c) Jowar (d) Bajra

Ans. (b) Wheat

7. The foremost crop of the Peninsular India is
   (a) jute (b) cotton
   (c) sugarcane (d) pulse

Ans. (b) cotton

8. Which of the following is one of the fibre crops in India?
   (a) Jute (b) Paddy
   (c) Sugarcane (d) Coffee

Ans. (a) Jute

9. Give reason for the following
   Cultivation of pulses is lagging behind.
   (a) Most of the farmers are given preference to other cash crops.
   (b) Lack of HYV seeds for pulses.
   (c) Farmers do not have much knowledge about its cultivation.
   (d) Both (a) and (b)

Ans. (d) Both (a) and (b)

10. Give reason for the following.
    Cotton grows well in Deccan plateau.
    (a) Cotton needs warm climate.
    (b) Abundant sunshine necessary during the growth of cotton plants.
    (c) The Southern part of India has maritime climate.
    (d) All of the above

Ans. (d) All of the above

11. Give reason for the following.
    Cotton is a labour-intensive crop.
    (a) Cotton has a variety of short staple cotton.
    (b) India is the largest producer of cotton.
    (c) The population size of India is large.
    (d) Cotton balls are to be plucked manually.

Ans. (d) Cotton balls are to be plucked manually.

12. Give reason for the following.
    Jute has to be retted.
    (a) Jute is a fibre crop.
    (b) Jute needs warm climate.
    (c) Fibre can be removed through retting process.
    (d) Both (a) and (c)

Ans. (d) Both (a) and (c)

13. Give reason for the following
    Rice is successfully grown in India.
    (a) Rice is a tropical plant.
    (b) Rice needs hot and humid climate.
    (c) Punjab and Haryana have assured irrigation facilities.
    (d) All of the above

Ans. (d) All of the above

14. Which one of the following statement is incorrect?
    (i) Rice is a type of millet.
    (ii) Ragi is not a season bound crop.
    (iii) Pulses are the main source of protein.

    Codes
    (a) Only (i) (b) (ii) and (iii)
    (c) Only (iii) (d) All of these

Ans. (b) (ii) and (iii)

15. Which of the following statements is correct about millets?
    (i) Millets are kharif crops.
    (ii) These are grown in comparatively inferior areas where rice and wheat cannot be cultivated.
    (iii) These are called food of poor.

Codes
(a) Only (i) (b) Only (ii)
(c) Only (iii) (d) All of these

Ans. (d) All of these

16. Match the following.

List-I	List-II
A. Rank of India in rice production	1. Sixth
B. Rank of India in wheat production	2. First
C. Rank of India in pulses production	3. Second
D. Rank of India in jowar production	4. Second after China

Codes

	A	B	C	D		A	B	C	D
(a)	1	2	3	4	(b)	2	1	4	3
(c)	3	4	1	2	(d)	4	3	2	1

Ans. (d)

17. Match the following.

List-I	List-II
A. Kharif crop	1. Jowar
B. Rabi crop	2. Vegetables
C. Zaid crop	3. Wheat
D. Zaid- Rabi crop	4. Rice

Codes

	A	B	C	D		A	B	C	D
(a)	1	2	3	4	(b)	2	1	4	3
(c)	3	4	1	2	(d)	4	3	2	1

Ans. (d)

18. Match the following.

List-I	List-II
A. Wheat	1. Maharashtra
B. Rice	2. Madhya Pradesh
C. Jowar	3. Uttar Pradesh
D. Pulses	4. West Bengal

Codes

	A	B	C	D		A	B	C	D
(a)	1	2	3	4	(b)	2	1	4	3
(c)	3	4	1	2	(d)	4	3	2	1

Ans. (c)

Section-II

Short Questions

1. What do you understand by cereals?

Ans. Cereals are all kinds of grass like plants, which have starchy, edible seeds. The most common cereals are rice, wheat, maize, barley, oats, millets etc. They have formed a basic diet for humans due to its high nutritional value.

2. Name all the types of soils in which rice can be grown.

Ans. The major soil groups where rice is grown well are montane, terai, laterite, coastal alluvium, red sandy, mixed red and black and medium and shallow black soils.

3. What are the different methods for sowing rice?

Ans. Rice can be cultivated by different types of methods. For example, broadcasting, dibbling, drilling, transplantation and Japanese method.

4. Which is the most preferred method of sowing of rice? In which areas it is dominated?

Ans. Transplantation method is the most important method for sowing of rice. This method is dominant in the areas of fertile, deltaic soil with abundant rainfall and plenty of sunshine.

5. With reference to rice cultivation, answer the following. **[2016]**

(i) Why does rice grow well in a soil with clay like subsoil?

(ii) What is the advantage of growing rice in nurseries before it is transplanted?

Ans. (i) Rice grow well in a clay like subsoil because the rice fields need standing water and clay like subsoil do not let the water percolate. (filter gradually through a porous surface).

(ii) By planting the rice seeds in nurseries before transplantation, fertilisers and pesticides can be properly added. This also quickens the germination process and reduces wastage as unhealthy seeds and weeds are eliminated.

6. State two climatic requirements for the growth of wheat in India. **[2011]**

Ans. Two climatic requirements for growth of wheat in India are

(i) **Temperature** Wheat requires an average temperature of about 10°C to 15°C at the time of sowing, but higher temperature at the time of ripening and harvesting.

(ii) **Rainfall** It requires rainfall of about 50 cm to 100 cm during growing period.

7. In which season is wheat grown in Northern India? What are the rainfall and soil requirements of this crop?

Ans. In rabi season i.e. winter wheat is grown in Northern India.

Its cultivation is practised best in well drained, fertile, loamy, alluvial soils of clayey type. In India, it is mainly grown in flat alluvial plains of North India.

8. Why is cultivation of wheat is confined to the Northern part of India? **[2019]**

Ans. Wheat is a temperate crop and needs a cool climate with moderate amount of rainfall. It requires an average temperature of about 10°C to 15°C at the time of sowing, but higher temperature at the time of ripening and harvesting (20° C to 25° C), though sudden rise of temperature is harmful. The winter temperature and rainfall of North India is more favourable for wheat production so, it is confined to Northern part of India.

9. With reference to the wheat crop answer the following questions [2020]
   (i) Name the state which is the leading producer of this crop in India.
   (ii) Mention the climatic condition found suitable for the cultivation of this crop.

Ans. (i) Uttar Pradesh is the leading producer of wheat crop in India.
(ii) The climatic conditions for the cultivation of wheat are
- **Temperature** Wheat requires an average temperature of about 10°C to 15°C at the time of sowing. But higher temperature (20° C to 25° C) at the time of ripening and harvesting, though sudden rise of temperature is harmful.
- **Rainfall** Wheat requires rainfall of about 50 cm to 100 cm during growing period. Too much rainfall is harmful for wheat while the shortage of rain may dry the crop.

10. State the three grains (millets) grown in India. Name three major producing states of these crops.

Ans. The three types of millets grown in India are Jowar, Bajra and Ragi. The major producing states are Maharashtra, Rajasthan and Karnataka.

11. Why are millets called 'dry crops'? Name any two millet crops grown widely in India.
Or Millets are known as dry crops. Give a geographical reason. [2017]

Ans. Millets are hard and tough crops and these can be grown in regions of low rainfall and poor soils, thus these are called 'dry crops'.
Two millet crops are Jowar and Bajra.

12. (i) Name two varieties of millet grown in India.
(ii) What is the soil requirement for growing millet? [2019]

Ans. (i) Jowar and ragi are grown in India.
(ii) Millets are drought resistant crops and do not require specific soil, but loamy, sandy and clayey soils are better for production.

13. Explain why?
   (i) Pulses are grown as rotation crops.
   (ii) Millets are referred to as dry crops.

Ans. (i) Pulses are grown as a rotation crop because these have the capacity to fix atmospheric nitrogen in the soil into nitrogenous compound, which is needed for crop growth.
(ii) Refer to answer of Short Question Q. 11.

14. Give two reasons for pulses being grown extensively in India. Name any two pulses.

Ans. Pulses are grown extensively in India because
(i) It forms a major part of the diet of vegetarian people. It is a good source of proteins.
(ii) It is a leguminous crop which increases the nitrogen content of the soil. Two pulses are gram (chana) and tur (arhar).

15. Name a pulse crop cultivated in India.
   (i) During the rabi season.
   (ii) During the kharif season.

Ans. (i) Pulses grown during rabi season are gram and *masoor.*
(ii) Pulses grown during kharif season are tur and *urad.*

16. Name a state which produces short staple cotton. Which climatic and soil conditions favour the cultivation of cotton in the state mentioned? [2012]

Ans. Punjab produces short staple cotton.
The climatic conditions favouring the cultivation of cotton are mild, cool and dry climate with no frost. The soil here is alluvial and light, which suits this crop.

17. Name the state in India which leads cotton cultivation. Mention two climatic factors which affect the cotton cultivation adversely. [2010]

Ans. Maharashtra leads in cotton cultivation.
Frost and excess cold at the time of ripening of cotton balls affect cotton cultivation adversely.

18. Give a geographical reason for each of the following [2018]
   (i) Cotton is a labour intensive crop.
   (ii) Retting is a processing method of jute.
   (iii) Growing of pulses is important in India.

Ans. (i) Cotton is a labour intensive crop because a lot of labour is required for picking process.
(ii) Retting is a processing method of jute under which bundles of jute are immersed in soft running water for 2 to 3 weeks to remove fibre from the stalk.
(iii) Refer to answer of Short Question Q. 14.

Long Questions

1. What do you understand by the following.
   (i) Drilling Method (ii) Dibbling Method

Ans. (i) **Drilling Method** This method is prevalent in peninsular India (South India). In this method, seeds are dropped in the furrow through a bamboo shaft attached to the plough. The seeds fall in the furrows thereby saving the wastage of seeds, but it is time consuming. The germination rate of the seeds in this method is high.

(ii) **Dibbling Method** A dibble is a planting bar, which is used to make holes in the ground for seeds or plants. In this type of method, seeds are sown at regular intervals in the furrows made by the farmers with the help of plough.

2. Mention three differences in the geographical and climatic conditions and cultivation of rice and wheat. **[2014]**

Ans. The differences between geographical and climatic conditions of rice and wheat are

Rice	Wheat
It is a kharif crop that requires 18°C to 32°C of temperature.	It is a rabi crop that requires 10°C to 15°C of temperature.
It needs rainfall of 150 to 300 cm and fertile alluvial soil that allows water to stand.	It needs rainfall of 50 to 100 cm and loamy black soils.
The methods of farming are broadcasting, dibbling, drilling and transplanting. Japanese method is also there.	The farming method is drilling.

3. Explain the transplantation method of rice cultivation.

Ans. The transplantation method of rice cultivation is dominant in regions of deltaic soil that get abundant rainfall and plenty of sunshine. In this method, seeds are sown in rows in nurseries after soaking them for 24 hours. When the seeds germinate into seedlings and are 20 to 25 cm tall, then the seeds are uprooted and planted in fields. Therefore, the seeds are transplanted from nurseries to the field hence, it is named as transplantation method.

4. State three important aspects of the Japanese method of rice cultivation.

Ans. Important aspects of the Japanese method of rice cultivation are

(i) Use of good quality seeds which are of the high yielding variety.

(ii) Sowing the seeds in raised nursery beds.

(iii) Transplanting the seedlings in rows to make weeding and fertilising easier.

5. Name any three rice producing areas in India.

Ans. Three rice producing areas in India are

(i) **Lower and Middle Gangetic Plains** Rice is the staple food crop of this region. Here soil is very fertile, which is favourable for rice cultivation.

(ii) **Brahmaputra Valley** In the Brahmaputra valley three crops of rice in an agricultural year are grown. Here the rice seasons include

- **Sali** During winter paddy season
- **Bao** During March and April months
- **Ahu** During Autumn season
- **Boro** During Rabi season (December and January).

(iii) **East and West Coastal Regions** West Coastal region includes Kerala and Konkan Coasts. East Coast includes the non-delta regions of Tamil Nadu.

6. Answer the following question

(i) With reference to rice cultivation, name two leading states in the production of rice. **[2013]**

(ii) Give two advantages of growing rice in nurseries.

Ans. (i) West Bengal and Uttar Pradesh.

(ii) The advantages of growing rice in nurseries are

(a) The process of transplantation allows better penetration (deeper penetration) of the roots in the soil.

(b) The process of transplantation greatly increases the yield of the crop.

7. With reference to wheat cultivation answer the following.

(i) Name the soil found suitable for its growth.

(ii) Name the state that is the largest producer of this crop in India.

(iii) Why is this crop not grown in Southern parts of India? **[Specimen Paper Semester-II 2022]**

Ans. (i) Well drained, fertile, loamy, alluvial soils of clayey type is best suitable for wheat crop.

(ii) Uttar Pradesh is the largest producer of wheat crop.

(iii) Wheat is not grown in Southern parts of India because these regions have very high temperature even in winters.

8. Give a geographical reason for each of the following **[2020]**

(i) Cultivation of rice requires flat level land.

(ii) Pulses are important rotation crops.

(iii) Bajra and jowar are grown as dry crops.

Ans. (i) Cultivation of rice requires flat level land because rice need more water. Flooded fields with stagnant water (around 5 to 10 cm) during the early part of growing season is very helpful. Therefore, flat land is best suited for rice cultivation.

(ii) Refer to answer of Short Question Q. 13(i).

(iii) Bajra and jowar are a variety of millets which are drought resistant crops. These do not require much water for their growth. Thus, are grown as dry crops.

9. Why pulses are important food crops? **[2015]**

Ans. Pulses are important for the following reasons

- Pulses are rich in proteins and found to be main source of protein to vegetarian people.
- It is second important constituent of Indian diet after cereals.
- They provide raw material to various industries. For example, dal industry, roasted grain industry, papad industry etc.

10. What are three important places where cotton is grown extensively?

Ans. The places where cotton is grown extensively are

(i) **North-West Region** It includes Punjab, Haryana, Rajasthan and Western Uttar Pradesh.

(ii) **Southern Region** It includes Tamil Nadu, Andhra Pradesh and Karnataka.

(iii) **Central Region** It includes Madhya Pradesh, Gujarat (largest producer) and Maharashtra (second largest producer). Leading producers of this crop are Gujarat, Maharashtra and Telangana.

11. Cotton grows widely in Maharashtra, give a geographical reason for it. **[2014]**

Ans. Cotton is grown widely in Maharashtra because this crop grows well in well drained clayey soil i.e. black soil which is widely found there. Also while growing cotton, the minimum temperature should not drop below 21°C and rainfall should be moderate. All these climatic conditions exist in Maharashtra and thus, it is widely grown here.

12. State an important difference between the climatic requirements for growing cotton and jute. **[2015]**

Ans. Differences between climatic requirements for growing cotton and jute are as follows

Cotton	Jute
Cotton is the crop of tropical and sub-tropical areas.	Jute is the crop of hot and humid climate.
It requires a temperature 21°C to 27°C.	It requires temperature 24°C to 37°C.
It requires rainfall between 50 cm to 80 cm.	It requires rainfall between 150 cm to 200 cm.

13. State main characteristics of each type of cotton.

Ans. The types of cotton with their characteristics are

- **Short Staple Cotton** Its length is less than 20 mm. This is an inferior quality of cotton and is produced in the upper Ganges valley. It is produced in Punjab.
- **Medium Staple Cotton** It has a length of about 20 to 24 mm. In India, majority of cotton output is of this type. It is produced in North-Western Deccan region.
- **Superior Medium Cotton** It contributes 37% of India's output and is grown in Punjab, Tamil Nadu, Madhya Pradesh, Uttar Pradesh, Karnataka and Maharashtra.
- **Long Staple Cotton** It has the longest fibre whose length ranges from 24 to 30 mm. The fibre is of superior quality and shiny. It is used to make fine quality of cotton clothes. It is produced in Central and Southern Deccan region.
- **Superior Long Staple** It is longer than 27 mm. It consist of 33% of India's total production of cotton.

14. Answer the following questions.

(i) Name the most important fibre crop in West Bengal.

(ii) Describe two climatic conditions which favour the growth of this crop.

Ans. (i) Jute is the most important fibre crop in West Bengal.

(ii) The climatic conditions which favour the growth of jute are

(a) **Temperature** Jute requires a temperature ranging from 24°C to 37°C. Hot and humid climate is very useful for jute production.

(b) **Rainfall** It requires high relative humidity of about 80% to 90%. It requires huge rainfall of 150 cm to 200 cm. However, continuous and untimely rainfall and continuous droughts are harmful for the plants.

15. Explain in brief the following. **[2013]**

(i) Retting (ii) Ginning (iii) Broadcasting

Ans. (i) **Retting** It is a processing technique of jute, under which the bundles of jute are immersed in soft running water for 2 to 3 weeks to remove fibre from the stalk.

(ii) **Ginning** It is associated with cotton. Ginning is a process by which fibre is seperated from the raw material.

(iii) **Broadcasting** It is a method of sowing rice seeds under which seeds are scattered in the field by hand.

Picture Based Questions

1. Study the picture given below and answer the following questions. **[2010]**

(i) Name the crop which is being planted. Give one benefit of this method of planting this crop.

(ii) Mention the climatic conditions which favour the cultivation of the crop being planted.

Ans. (i) Rice is being planted using the transplantation method.
One benefit is that weeds (wild/unwanted plants) are removed at the time of transplantation.
(ii) Rice require 16°C to 32°C temperature and rainfall ranging from 150 to 300 cm.

2. Study the picture given below and answer the questions that follow.

(i) Mention the climatic condition that is suitable for the cultivation of this crop.
(ii) Name the state that produces the largest amount of this crop.
(iii) In which cropping season is the crop grown in India?

Ans. (i) This crop is cotton. Cotton needs mild, cool and comparatively dry climate having temperature 21°C to 27°C and abundant sunshine is necessary during its growth period. A long period of 200 (frost free) days are essential for the plant to mature. Cotton plant need a moderate rainfall of 50 cm to 80 cm which should be well distributed throughout the year.
(ii) Gujarat is the largest producer of cotton.
(iii) Cotton is grown in India as a kharif crop.

Chapter Assessment

Section-I

Multiple Choice Questions

1. Which of the following is the important region of rice production?
(a) Lower Gangetic plain (b) Middle Gangetic plain
(c) Brahmaputra valley (d) All of these
2. Jowar comes next in ranking to rice and .... in terms of both area and production.
(a) bajra (b) ragi (c) pulses (d) wheat
3. Picking and ginning are associated with which of the following crops?
(a) Cotton (b) Jute (c) Wheat (d) Bajra
4. Among other pulses .... is the leading pulse crop.
(a) masoor (b) moong
(c) gram (d) All of these

Section-II

Short Questions

1. Agricultural crops in India can be divided into how many categories?
2. Name any two food crops.
3. Name the most important staple food crop of India.
4. Which crop is high in protein, vitamins and carbohydrates?
5. Millets are grown in which crop season of India?
6. What are the soil requirements for cultivation of rice?
7. Mention the climatic conditions required for the cultivation of wheat.
8. Name some regions of cotton cultivation.
9. Sowing in jute cultivation is done by which method?

Long Questions

1. Name the improved method of transplantation. State any three features of this method.
2. Give geographical reasons for each of the following
(i) West Bengal is the largest producer of both rice and jute.
(ii) Pulses increases soil fertility.
(iii) Karnataka is the leading producer of ragi.
3. What are the two types of jute produced in India? What are their region of growth?

CHAPTER 11

Cash Crops of India

SYLLABUS

Climatic conditions, soil requirements, method of cultivation, processing and distribution of the following crops • Sugarcane, oilseeds (groundnut, mustard and soybean) • Tea and coffee

The cash crops are grown for commercial purposes i.e. to provide raw materials to agro-based industries. Some crops like oilseeds, sugarcane, beverage (tea and coffee) are cash crops. Fibre crops like cotton and jute are also called cash crops.

Oilseeds

In India all the primary oilseeds like groundnut, linseed, sesame, mustard, rapeseed, castor, soybean, sunflower, etc are grown. They are used as raw material for the manufacture of paints, varnishes, hydrogenated oils, soaps and many lubricants. The oil extracted from oilseeds is used as a cooking medium. Castor and linseed are two non-edible oilseeds. Some of the oilseeds are discussed below

Groundnut

It is the most important edible oilseed of India. It is both a kharif and rabi crop, but is mostly grown as a kharif crop. Groundnut is also known as **peanut** or **monkey nut**. It was introduced in India from Brazil during the 16th century.

About 42% oil is extracted from the nuts which is found in the roots of the groundnut plant. Its oil is used as a cooking medium and its **oil cake**[1] is used as fodder for cattle. Its oil is also used in medical emulsions and soaps.

Groundnut plants are of two types

(i) **The Bunch Type** They grow upto a height of 40 cm.

(ii) **The Runner Type** They grow horizontally unlike bunch type and spread over a large area. They are shorter in height.

Climatic Conditions and Soil Requirement

- **Temperature** It requires a temperature ranging from 20°C to 25°C. It is a tropical crop. Warm and dry weather is suitable for the ripening of the crop. Higher altitudes with cooler climates are not suitable for groundnut production. It is generally a rainfed kharif crop, but in Odisha and Southern states, it is a rabi crop.
- **Rainfall** It requires about 50 to 100 cm of rainfall. Continuous drought and rain or stagnant water and frost, interrupt the growth of this crop.
- **Soil** Groundnut grows well in sandy loams, red and black soils which allow enough **aeration**[2]. Red, yellow and black cotton soils of Peninsular India are good for this crop.

1 **Oil Cake** It is the residue left after the extraction of oil from the oilseeds and is used as a fodder for animals and also serves a good manure in the fields.

2 **Aeration** The introduction of air into a material.

Methods of Cultivation

- **Sowing** The seeds of the plant are sown in the month of June or July generally by the process of broadcasting or drilling. Its pods (seed vessels) grow underground and hence, they are called groundnuts. The plant bears flower on maturing. The flower stalk increases after self-pollination and move downwards.

  The whole crop takes a time of about 4-5 months to be ready for harvesting. It is used as a rotation crop for millets and other crops as well.
- **Harvesting and Processing** It is harvested in the months from October to December. The whole plant is removed from the soil, including its roots. After that they are collected and dried in the Sun. They are shelled and seeds are collected and then sent to mills after packaging (in sacks).

Distribution

The major producers of groundnut are Rajasthan, Uttar Pradesh, Haryana and Madhya Pradesh. Other producers of groundnut are Bihar, Odisha, West Bengal, Gujarat, Assam and Jammu and Kashmir.

Mustard (Sarson)

It is a tropical crop which is grown in rabi season (winter season). The seeds are pressed to obtain mustard oil. It is an edible oil and one of the most important seeds produced in India. Oil cake of mustard is used as an important cattle feed and its leaves are eaten as vegetable in Uttar Pradesh, Punjab and Haryana. Oil content of Mustard is about 25-43%. It is grown mostly as a rabi crop or mixed with wheat, gram and barley.

Climatic Conditions and Soil Requirement

- **Temperature** Mustard is a tropical crop which need a moderate, cool climate with temperature range of 10°C to 20°C.
- **Rainfall** It require a rainfall of about 25 to 40 cm.
- **Soil** It grows best in alluvial soils of Northern Plains of Ganga and Sutlej. These plains are rich in alluvial deposits. It is also grown on loamy and heavier soils.

Methods of Cultivation

- **Sowing** Mustard is sown by broadcasting and drilling method. Mustard and rapeseed take around 4 to 5 months to mature.
- **Harvesting** Mustard is harvested about 1 or 2 week before the main crop. After harvesting, it is collected in heaps in the granary. The seeds are separated by crushing them under the bullock's feet.
- **Processing** Processing of mustard involves the following steps
  - Seed pre-cleaning for removal of extraneous material like stones, mud, etc.
  - Seed grading to obtain uniform size seeds.
  - Conditioning the cleaned seeds for de-husking.
  - Separation of de-husked granules and husk part.
  - Proper conditioning of de-husked granules for obtaining oil.

Distribution

As mustard needs only cool climate that is why, it is widely grown in the Sutlej-Ganga plain. A very less proportion of mustard is grown in the Peninsular States.

It is grown extensively in Rajasthan, Uttar Pradesh, Madhya Pradesh, Punjab and Haryana. Other producers of mustard are West Bengal, Odisha, Gujarat, Chhattisgarh, Bihar, Assam and Jammu and Kashmir.

Soybean

It is a rainfed kharif crop of India. It is a rich source of protein and vitamins. It is in great demand due to its varied use like soybean oil, soya milk, soya sauce, cheese etc and industrial products like paints, varnish, linoleum, etc. Soybean is considered as a substitute for animal proteins. It is a leguminous crop, thus it increases the nitrogen content in soil.

Climatic Conditions and Soil Requirement

- **Temperature** Soybean requires the temperature between 13°C and 24°C . During the time of flowering, the temperature should be within 20°C to 25°C.
- **Rainfall** The plant grows well in dry areas so it requires rainfall from 40cm to 60cm.
- **Soil** The soil needed for the cultivation of soybean is the one that can retain moisture i.e. well drained fertile loamy acidic soil.

Method of Cultivation

- **Sowing** Soybean is sown in the summer month (June). It is sown by drill method in rows, 40 to 50 cm apart from each other. The depth of sowing is 5 to 10 cm. It is irrigated 3 to 4 times during its growing period.
- **Harvesting** It is harvested in October before the arrival of winters. Thus, the crop gets ready within 3-4 months.
- **Processing** Processing of soybean include the following steps
  - The first step in processing is to properly prepare the soybean for dehulling which involves using magnets to remove metal and screening to remove impurities. Mechanical rollers are used to make thin flakes containing the soybean oil.
  - After this extraction process is used in which the soybean oil is washed from the prepared soybean flakes by using hexane or other solvents.
  - After this desolventising process is used in which solvent is removed from both the flakes and soybean oil. The desoventised flakes are now a product and ready for sale. The soybean oil can be further refined from a crude product to an edible product.

Distribution

In India, soybean is generally grown in the states of Madhya Pradesh, Maharashtra, Andhra Pradesh, Rajasthan, Chhattisgarh, Gujarat, parts of Punjab and Uttar Pradesh.

Sugarcane

It is one of the important cash/commercial crops of India. It is a tropical crop which belongs to the bamboo family and it is **indigenous**[3] to India. It has hard thick stem which grows to height of 3.5 m or more. Sugarcane is the main source of sugar, gur and khandsari. It is also used as fodder for the cattle in rural areas. It is also eaten raw and its juice is widely popular in India, especially in summer season.

India accounts for about 19 per cent of the world production of sugarcane. But it occupies only 2.4 per cent of total cropped area in the country.

Its yield is high in Southern India and low in Northern India. Gur and Khandsari industries consume about two-third of the sugarcane produced in the country and only about a third of it is used to make sugar.

Climatic Conditions and Soil Requirement

- **Temperature** Sugarcane requires hot and humid climate with temperature ranging from 20°C to 24°C. Both high and low temperature are very detrimental for the growth of sugarcane plant. Frost is also very harmful for the crop. Cool and moderate temperature favours the ripening process of sugarcane.
- **Rainfall** It requires a rainfall of about 100 cm to 150 cm. It cannot resist water stagnation. Sugarcane needs moderately dry sunny weather. If heavy rain occurs for long time its sucrose content decreases, whereas in the rainfall deficiency areas, it grows as a fibrous crop.
- **Soil** There are variety of soils which are good for sugarcane cultivation, but it grows best in alluvial clayey loams of the Indo-Gangetic Plains and the black soil of Southern India. It is also grown on brown or reddish loams and laterite soils. The soil should be high in nitrogen, calcium and phosphorus contents. As sugarcane exhaust the fertility of soils, thus proper manuring is needed.

Methods of Cultivation

- **Sowing** Sugarcane is generally sown from January to April, in most part of the country. The field is prepared by ploughing and clearing all vegetation and also by **harrowing**[4]. Heavy amount of manure is applied before planting as the crops exhaust the fertility of the soil. Sugarcane can be planted through the following methods
  - (i) **Sett Method** In this method, planting is done by cutting the old healthy cane into two to three new canes and planted horizontially in well prepared furrows at regular intervals. Sugarcane takes about 8 to 12 months to mature.

3 **Indigenous** A crop, animal, plant, etc which is naturally belong to a particular place.

4 **Harrowing** It is a type of method to till and break the soil to make it suitable for cultivation.

(ii) **Ratooning** It is the method in which the sugarcane is cut leaving the root very much intact in the soil. The stalk which has been left behind grows out into new shoots or ratoons. The second or any other successive crop obtained from the roots of the first sugarcane plant is called ratoon.

(iii) **By Seeds** It is an obsolete method in which sugarcane is planted by seeds. It is now practised in some parts of India. In this method sugarcane is planted in furrows and covered with soil. Farmers maintain enough gap between furrows (30-45 cm) to facilitate hoeing, **weeding**[5], irrigation and harvesting.

- **Harvesting** Harvesting is done with the use of a long curved knife before the cane begins to flower. Its harvesting and crushing period is from October- November till April. Sugarcane must be cut near the ground because the stem contains most of the sucrose content. Farmers in the Northern India cut sugarcane before the winter season due to frost which is bad for it.
- **Processing** The sugarcane must be processed within 48 hours of cutting to preserve its sugar content. This is the reason why most of the sugar factories are located near the sugarcane fields in order to save the transportation time. In the mills, the sugarcane is trampled/crushed between rollers. It is boiled soon after the juice is extracted. Lime is added to it to remove the impurities. The sugarcane juice crystallises and forms raw brown sugar.

Distribution

Sugarcane is cultivated in the Sutlej-Ganga Plains of Uttar Pradesh, Punjab and Bihar in North India. The soil in these regions are fertile alluvium that gets replenished every year by rivers and streams flowing here.

It is also cultivated in the black soils region of Maharashtra and Tamil Nadu along the Eastern slopes of the Western Ghats and the coastal Andhra Pradesh and Krishna valley.

In South India, the yield per hectare of sugarcane is higher but there is competition from other cash crops like cotton and groundnut.

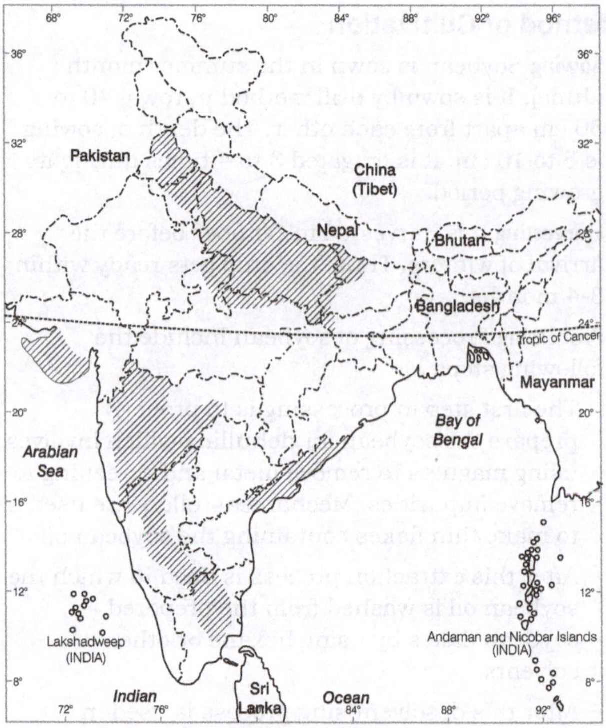

Distribution of Sugarcane

Check Your LEARNING...

1. State two uses of oilseeds.
2. In which crop season, soybean is grown?
3. Name a crop that belongs to bamboo family.
4. Raw brown sugar is made by which process?

Beverages

Tea

It is an important beverage crop in India. In 1823, Major Robert Bruce discovered indigenous tea bushes on the hill sides of upper Assam. Commercial planting of tea was started in India in 1840's in Brahmaputra valley of Assam. Tea is grown best on hill slopes to avoid waterlogging. It can also be grown in the valleys. Tea is grown on various elevations, ranging from 600 m to 1500 m above sea level. Tea cultivation is a fine example of plantation agriculture in India. There are mainly four varieties of tea

(i) Black tea (ii) Green tea
(iii) Oolong tea (iv) Brick Tea

5 **Weeding** It refers to remove unwanted plants from an area.

Black tea is preferred in India and Europe, while Green and Oolong tea are more popular in China, Japan and Taiwan. Brick tea is normally consumed in Russia and Tibet.

Climatic Conditions and Soil Requirement

- **Temperature** Tea plant requires a temperature ranging from 20°C to 30°C, but ideal temperature would be 25°C. Alternate cool and warm breeze are very helpful for tea plants. Tea grows best in the shade and hence, shady trees are required in tea plantations along with tea plants.
- **Rainfall** It requires heavy rainfall of about 150 cm to 250 cm distributed well throughout the year. Due to heavy rainfall tea grows well in Assam (annual rainfall between 125 cm and 375 cm), Duar and Darjeeling districts (annual rainfall between 250 cm to 500 cm). High amount of humidity, heavy dew and morning fog help the leaves to grow rapidly, but prolonged dry spell is very detrimental for tea plants.
- **Soil** It requires well drained, deep, friable (easily crumbled) light loamy soils. The soil should be rich in humus and iron content. It must be deep and have a moderate open texture. Tea is very soil exhausting crop and hence, regular use of fertilisers and manures is essential. Phosphorus and potash add special flavour to tea. Regular tilling of the soil to remove the weed is preferable.

Methods of Cultivation

- **Sowing** The sowing of tea plants include following methods
  - (i) **Transplantation Method** In this method, first the seeds are sown in small germination beds or nursery and are allowed to grow for 9 to 12 months into proper seedlings. Good amount of fertilisers are applied in the meantime. The well developed seedlings are then transplanted within a year to the tea gardens.
  - (ii) **Clonal Planting** Under this method, tea plants can be grown from cuttings of a good high yielding mother plant instead of seeds. This method is called clone planting because the new plant has the qualities of the mother plant. These small cuttings (or Sapling when grown to 20 cm high) are then planted in the regular germination bed and again transplanted to the tea gardens.
- **Harvesting** Tea planters start the **pruning**[6] of the bush after two years. It is done in order to maintain the height and diameter of the tea plant limited to one metre. In India tea is picked every ten days during the growing season at lower elevations and every fifteen days, at higher altitudes. But during the South-West monsoon season from early April to mid-November, picking goes on all the time. Frequent pruning is essential for the rapid production of fresh leaves and shoots.

  Tea-picking is mainly done by women because it is a skilful job which requires patience and women can be employed at relatively cheaper wages. Two tender leaves and a bud or shoot (known as fine plucking) are usually plucked from each stem.
- **Processing** Processing of tea includes the following steps
  - (i) **Withering** This is performed to reduce the moisture from the gathered tea leaves and to make them soft and flexible. This is done by spreading the leaves over shelves (racks) and hot air is blown over the leaves.
  - (ii) **Rolling** This is done to provide tea its special flavour. Under this process, the leaves are twisted which breaks the leaf cells and crushed between rollers to squeeze out the juice.
  - (iii) **Fermentation** Under this process, the tea leaves are spread out on trays and the tannin acid in tea is partly oxidised changing the colour of the leaves to copper red. This whole process is done under controlled temperature and humidity.
  - (iv) **Drying** (*or Fixing*) In this process, the tea leaves are put on a conveyor belt and are slowly passed through tiered dryers. After this, the leaves become dry and turns to rich black colour.
  - (v) **Sorting** After drying the leaves, it is sorted out according to their size.
  - (vi) **Blending** In this method, tea planter prepares his own brand on the basis of its flavour, colour and texture.

6 **Pruning** To cut branches or part of branches of a tree.

(vii) Packing A lot of care is taken to pack the prepared tea to protect its flavour. They are packed in plywood cases with lining of aluminium foil paper to keep the tea fresh.

Distribution

- In India, tea is mainly produced in North-East India and South India.
- Assam accounts for about 53.2 per cent of the total cropped area under tea plants and contributes more than half of total production of tea in the country.
- In West Bengal, tea is majorly grown in Darjeeling hills and Duars region.
- Tamil Nadu produces 15.9 per cent of tea in India. It is grown in Nilgiri hills in the region of Coimbatore, Kanyakumari and Madurai.
- In Kerala, tea is produced in Kottayam, Kollam, Thiruvananthapuram, Thrissur, Palakkad, Kozhikode and Kannur.
- Minor amount of tea are also produced in Kangra valley of Himachal Pradesh, Garhwal region of Uttarakhand, Ratnagiri of Maharashtra, Mysore, Coorg of Karnataka.

Coffee

It is extracted from the coffee fruit that grows in clusters. It is the second most important beverage of India after tea. Coffee is the oldest plantation crop of India. Coffee is very popular in urban areas especially among the young generation and in South India. It is a native plant of Ethiopia (Abyssinia plateau) from where it was brought to Arabia. The first plantation of coffee in India was set up by the Britishers near Chikmagalur in **Karnataka** in 1840. There are three varieties of coffee which are grown in India

(i) **Arabica** Arabica is known for its superior quality and it is most expensive. It is known for its fine flavour. In India, it is produced more than 70% of total cultivation. It's main varieties are chicks, coorgs, kents, etc.

(ii) **Robusta** It is cheaper variety of coffee because the cost of production is less and the yield per acre is higher. It yields poorer quality coffees. It is grown in lower elevation (300-610 m) districts of South India. It is disease resistant and can survive even in arid conditions.

(iii) **Liberica** It is used in making instant coffee. It gives heavy yields of moderate quality coffee. It is also hardy and disease resistant coffee.

Climatic Conditions and Soil Requirement

- **Temperature** Coffee is a tropical plant which requires high temperature, ranging from 15°C to 28°C throughout the year. Bright sunlight and warm weather are neccessary for harvesting and growth of the berries. Frost, snow and strong sunlight are harmful for coffee plants. Therefore, coffee plant should be grown under shady trees like bananas, jackfruit, etc. The coffee plant cannot tolerate high temperature above 30°C.
- **Rainfall** Coffee plant requires a rainfall of about 150 to 200 cm which should be well distributed throughout the year. Stagnant water is very detrimental for the coffee plant. Continuous drought is also harmful for the coffee plant. It is always grown on hill slopes at an elevation ranging from 600 to 1600 m above sea level.
- **Soil** Coffee plant grows well in deep, porous soil having high humus content and minerals like iron and calcium. The soil must be properly manured to retain and replenish the fertility. Lava soils, red soils and laterite soils of Deccan plateau are very well suited for coffee plantation. Cattle manure, oil cakes, bone meal and fertilisers are used as manures.

Methods of Cultivation

- **Sowing** The coffee seeds are grown in nursery for 9 to 12 months, till it grows into a proper seedling. Good amount of fertilisers are also applied. The well developed seedlings are then picked out and transferred to the coffee gardens. In the early stage, it is grown under shady tree like silver oak, jackfruit. The height of the trees is kept to 1.5 to 2.5 m. It is grown on slopes so that water does not stagnate.
- **Harvesting** Usually, harvesting of coffee is done in the 4th or 5th year after planting. Coffee picking is done by hand by removing the ripe berries from the stalk. Indiscriminate picking of both a ripe and unripe berries results in coffee beans of inferior quality which gives low surplus amount.

- **Processing** There are two methods of processing the coffee berries which are
  (i) **Wet Method** The coffee which is processed by the wet method is called plantation coffee. Under this method, crushing, **fermenting**[7], washing and drying is done. Machines are also used in this method.
  (ii) **Dry Process** The coffee which is processed by dry process is called cherry or native method. Under this method, cherries are put under the Sun to dry. After drying, the covering is removed and the seeds are obtained.

  They are then sorted according to their size and quality. Then they are roasted which gives it a brown colour and pleasing smell and taste. Freshly roasted beans are better and preferred more. After roasting, coffee beans are crushed and then coffee powder is used to make the beverage.

Distribution

The coffee in India is majorly produced in three states i.e. Karnataka, Kerala and Tamil Nadu. The states are referred as traditional coffee producing areas.

In Karnataka, coffee is majorly produced in Coorg, Chikmagalpur, Hassan, Mysore and Shimoga. In Kerala, coffee is majorly produced in Kozhikode, Palakkad, Idukki, Wayanad, etc. In Tamil Nadu, coffee is majorly produced in Nilgiris, Madurai, Coimbatore, Salem, Tirunelveli, etc.

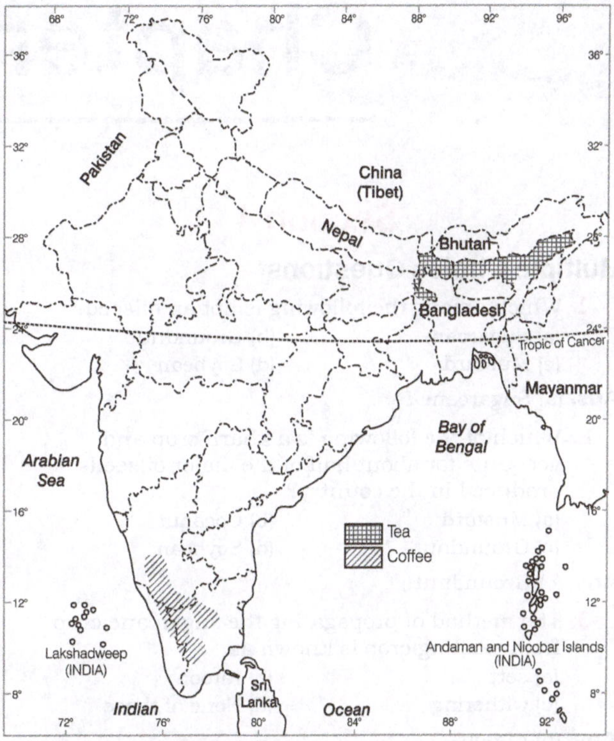

Distribution of Tea and Coffee

Check Your LEARNING...

1. Name the country other than India where black tea is preferred the most.
2. Under which method farmers use cutting from a good high yielding mother plant instead of seeds?
3. After which process sorting of coffee is done?
4. Coffee is which type of crop?

QUiCK Revision

- India has the largest area under production of oilseeds.
- Important oilseeds are groundnut, linseed, sesame, mustard, rapeseed, castor, soybean, sunflower, etc.
- Groundnut is the most important edible oilseed of India. It is both a kharif and rabi crop, but is mostly grown as a kharif crop.
- Mustard is a tropical crop which is grown in rabi season (winter season).
- Soybean is a kharif crop of India. It is a rich source of proteins and vitamins.
- Sugarcane is an important commercial crop of India. It is a tropical crop. It belongs to the bamboo family of plants and is indigenous to India. It is used to make sugar, gur and khandsari.
- The sugarcane must be processed within 48 hours of cutting to preserve its sugar content.
- Tea is the most important beverage crop of India which is popular in both rural and urban areas. There are three varieties of tea i.e. Black Tea, Green Tea, Oolong Tea.
- Coffee is the second most important beverage crop of India after tea. It is more popular in urban areas than in rural and grown mainly in South India.

7 **Fermentation** It is a metabolic process in which an organism converts carbohydrates into alchol or acid.

Chapter Practice

Section-I

Multiple Choice Questions

1. Which among the following is not an oilseed?
(a) Sugarcane (b) Groundnut
(c) Mustard (d) Soybean

Ans. (a) Sugarcane

2. Which of the following is a kharif crop and accounts for about half of the major oilseeds produced in the country?
(a) Mustard (b) Coconut
(c) Groundnut (d) Soybean

Ans. (c) Groundnut

3. The method of propagating the sugarcane crop from existing crop is known as
(a) sett (b) ratoon
(c) withering (d) None of these

Ans. (b) ratoon

4. Short stalks from which sugarcane is propagated is known as ....
(a) setts (b) ratoon
(c) fermenting (d) None of these

Ans. (a) setts

5. How long does sugarcane take to grow?
(a) Six months (b) Three months
(c) Two years (d) Almost a year

Ans. (d) Almost a year

6. .... is the main source of jaggary, khandsari and molasses.
(a) Arhar (b) Coconut
(c) Linseed (d) Sugarcane

Ans. (d) Sugarcane

7. Which one of the following is the example of plantation agriculture?
(a) Jute (b) Wheat (c) Tea (d) Oilseeds

Ans. (c) Tea

8. Cultivation of coffee is confined to which of the following hills?
(a) Nilgiri (b) Aravalli
(c) Shivalik (d) None of these

Ans. (a) Nilgiri

9. Of which one of the following beverage crops, India is the leading producer as well as exporter in the world?
(a) Coffee (b) Pulses (c) Tea (d) Rice

Ans. (c) Tea

10. .... crops are known as beverage crops.
(a) Castor seed and sunflower (b) Peas and gram
(c) Cotton and jute (d) Tea and coffee

Ans. (d) Tea and coffee

11. Give reason for the following
Mustard is widely grown in the Sutlej- Ganga plain.
(a) It needs only cool climate.
(b) It needs loo type of winds to grow.
(c) It needs dry conditions.
(d) None of the above

Ans. (a) It needs only cool climate.

12. Give reason for the following
Cultivation of oilseeds is lagging behind in recent times in India.
(a) Climatic fluctuation hampers the growth of oilseeds.
(b) Low market value.
(c) Lack of High Yielding varieties of seeds
(d) All of the above

Ans. (d) All of the above

13. Give reason for the following
A lot of labour is required for cultivation of sugarcane.
(a) Sugarcane stalks need careful cutting.
(b) Sugarcane is a heavy crop which needs more labour.
(c) Sugarcane sucrose content is large in quantity which collected by only labour force.
(d) All of the above

Ans. (a) Sugarcane stalks need careful cutting.

14. Give reason for the following
In Northern India, the yield per hectare of sugarcane is low.
(a) The unfavorable climatic conditions prevailing in the region.
(b) The crushing season is very short there.
(c) The factories in this region are very old and use obsolete machinery and techniques.
(d) All of the above

Ans. (d) All of the above

15. Give reason for the following
Soybean is in great demand in India.
(a) It is a rich source of protein.
(b) It has varied uses like soyabean oil, soya milk, cheese etc.
(c) It is a kharif crop.
(d) Both (a) and (b)

Ans. (d) Both (a) and (b)

16. Which of the following statements is correct about groundnut?
(i) Groundnut is a kharif crop.
(ii) It is called monkey nut.
(iii) Its oil is used for cooking purpose.

Codes
(a) Only (i) (b) Only (ii) (c) Only (iii) (d) (ii) and (iii)

Ans. (d) (ii) and (iii)

17. Which of the following statements is incorrect?
(i) Mustard is a sub-tropical crop.
(ii) Broadcasting and drilling methods are used to sown mustard seeds.
(iii) Mustard is grown with other crops like wheat, gram etc.

Codes
(a) Only (i) (b) Only (ii)
(c) Only (iii) (d) (ii) and (iii)

Ans. (d) (ii) and (iii)

18. Match the following.

List I	List II
A. Rank of India in oilseeds production	1. Second
B. Rank of India in groundnut production	2. First
C. Rank of India in sugarcane production	3. Second after China
D. Rank of India in tea production	4. Second after Brazil

Codes

	A	B	C	D		A	B	C	D
(a)	1	2	3	4	(b)	2	1	4	3
(c)	3	4	1	2	(d)	4	3	2	1

Ans. (b)

19. Match the following.

List I	List II
A. Sett method	1. Coffee
B. Broadcasting	2. Tea
C. Clonal Planting	3. Oilseeds
D. Transplantation	4. Sugarcane

Codes

	A	B	C	D		A	B	C	D
(a)	1	2	3	4	(b)	2	1	4	3
(c)	3	4	1	2	(d)	4	3	2	1

Ans. (d)

20. Match the following.

List I	List II
A. Sugarcane	1. Karnataka
B. Tea	2. Madhya Pradesh
C. Coffee	3. Uttar Pradesh
D. Soybean	4. Assam

Codes

	A	B	C	D		A	B	C	D
(a)	1	2	3	4	(b)	2	1	4	3
(c)	3	4	1	2	(d)	4	3	2	1

Ans. (c)

Section-II

Short Questions

1. What are cash crops?

Ans. Cash crops are grown for commercial purpose i.e. to provide raw material to agro-based industries, e.g. oilseed, sugarcane and beverages.

2. (i) Name two non-edible oilseed .
(ii) After oil extraction, what other uses can the oilseed be put to?

Ans. (i) Two non-edible oilseeds are linseed and castor.
(ii) After oil extraction, the oilseed can be used as fodder for animals or as manure in fields.

3. State important characteristics of groundnut.

Ans. Important characteristics of groundnut are
(i) Groundnut is the most important edible oilseed of India.
(ii) It is both a kharif as well as rabi crop.

4. Define the method of cultivation of groundnuts.

Ans. The seeds of the groundnut are sown in the month of June or July and generally by the process of broadcasting or drilling. It is harvested from October to December.

5. Explain the following in terms of mustard crop.
(i) Its soil type
(ii) Its temperature condition

Ans. (i) **Soil** Mustard grows best in alluvial soils of Northern plains of Ganga and Sutlej. These plains are rich in alluvial deposits.
(ii) **Temperature** Mustard is a tropical crop which need moderate, cool climate with temperature range of 10°C to 20°C.

6. Explain the term oil cake.

Ans. Oil cake is the solid residue that is left after oil from oilseeds has been extracted. It is used as cattle fodder or fertiliser.

7. Discuss the following conditions for soybean
(i) Soil (ii) Temperature

Ans. (i) **Soil** The soil needed for the cultivation of soybean is the one that can retain moisture i.e. well drained fertile loamy soil.
(ii) **Temperature** The temperature should range between 13°C to 24°C. During the time of flowering, the temperature should be within 20°C to 25°C.

8. What is the method used for the cultivation of soybean? Give any two regions suitable for its cultivation.

Ans. Soyabean is sown in the summer months (June). It is sown by drill method in rows, 40 to 50 cm apart from each other. The depth of sowing is 5 to 10 cm. It is harvested in October before the arrival of winters. Thus, the crop gets ready within 3-4 months.

Two regions suitable for its cultivation are Madhya Pradesh and Maharashtra.

9. State two reasons to explain why the cultivation of oilseeds is lagging behind in recent times.

Ans. Two major reasons due to which oilseeds cultivation is lagging behind are

(i) The low productivity is recorded in oilseeds due to lack of high yielding varieties, irrigation facilities etc.

(ii) Low market value discourage farmers more towards commercial crops.

10. Give the climatic requirements for the cultivation of sugarcane. **[2017]**

Ans. Sugarcane requires around 100-150 cm of rainfall throughout the year. It grows best in well drained rich alluvial soil with 20°C to 24°C temperature.

11. Define the following terms

(i) Molasses (ii) Bagasse

Ans. (i) **Molasses** It is one of the important by-product which is dark brown syrup like liquid formed after recrystalisation of sugar. It is used as organic fertilisers, fodder for the cattle, as fuel in mills and as a raw material in the manufacturing of paper industry.

(ii) **Bagasse** It is the crushed form of sugarcane after the juice has been extracted. It is used as a biofuel and in the manufacture of pulp and building materials.

12. What is press-mud? State any one use of it.

Ans. Press-mud is generally the residue of the filtration of sugarcane juice. The clarification process separates the juice into a clear juice that rises to the top and a mud that collects at the bottom is press-mud.

It is generally used as organic fertiliser, as a fodder and fuel for mills.

13. Why is ratoon cropping gaining popularity among sugarcane cultivators? **[2019]**

Ans. Ratoon cropping is gaining popularity among sugarcane cultivators because in ratoon cropping the crops are not required to be planted again. The ratoons have comparatively low maturation period. It is cheaper as planting of crops is not needed. As the successive crop goes on, its productivity decreases, therefore only one or two ratoon crops are generally harvested.

14. What is ratooning? **[2020]**

Ans. Ratooning is a method of cultivation of sugarcane. In this method, during the first harvest, the sugarcane is cut leaving a little bit of the stalk in the soil with the roots. The stalk soon puts out new shoots or ratoons. The second or any other successive crop obtained from the roots of the leftover crop is called ratoon.

15. Name the regions where these varieties of tea are popular.

(i) Black tea (ii) Green tea.

Ans. (i) **Black tea** It is more popular in India and Europe.

(ii) **Green tea** It is more popular in China, Japan and Taiwan.

16. Which temperature conditions are suitable for tea plantation?

Ans. Tea plant requires a temperature ranging from 20°C to 30°C, but ideal temperature would be 25°C. Alternate cool and warm breeze are very helpful for tea plants. Tea grows best in the shade and hence, shady trees are grown along with tea plants.

17. Define the terms.

(i) Drying (ii) Blending

Ans. (i) **Drying** In this process, the tea leaves are put on a conveyor belt and are slowly passed through tiered dryers. Too much high temperature and too low temperature are harmful for tea. After this, the leaves are dry and turns to rich black colour.

(ii) **Blending** In this method, tea planter prepares his own brand on the basis of its flavour, colour and texture.

18. Name the suitable soils for the following crops.

(i) Sugarcane (ii) Mustard
(iii) Coffee (iv) Tea

Ans. (i) **Sugarcane** Alluvial clayey loams, black soil, brown or reddish loams and laterite soils.

(ii) **Mustard** Alluvial soils.

(iii) **Coffee** Deep, porous soil, lava soils, red soils and laterite soils.

(iv) **Tea** Mountain soils.

Long Questions

1. Why are oilseed crops important for Indian farming? State any three reasons.

Ans. Three reasons due to which oilseed crops important for Indian farming are

(i) They can be grown in all kinds of soils.

(ii) These are valuable crops and a source of foreign exchange.

(iii) They provide raw material for many industries e.g. paints, varnishes, soaps, lubricating oils etc.

2. Answer the following questions.

(i) What are the climatic conditions necessary for the cultivation of groundnuts?

(ii) What climatic conditions adversely affect the groundnut crops?

(iii) Name two non-edible oilseeds grown.

Ans. (i) Groundnuts require tropical or sub-tropical climate with a temperature range of 20°C to 25°C and rainfall between 50 to 70 cm annually.
(ii) Continuous rain, stagnant water, frost or drought adversely affect the groundnut crops.
(iii) Castor and linseed are two non-edible oilseeds grown.

3. Answer the following question.
(i) Why the yield of sugarcane is higher in the Deccan? Give two reasons for this.
(ii) Give one advantage and disadvantage of ratoon cropping.

Ans. (i) Two reasons for higher yield of sugarcane in the Deccan are
(a) Black lava soil with high fertility and water retention is favourable for this crop which is found in abundance there.
(b) Absence of loo during summer and frost during winter in the Deccan helps in better growth.
(ii) The advantage and disadvantage of ratoon cropping are
- **Advantage** It requires less labour and is time saving.
- **Disadvantage** It yields thinner canes with lower sucrose content.

4. Answer the following questions with reference to sugarcane. **[2010]**
(i) Mention two different ways in which it is propagated.
(ii) Why lot of labour required for its cultivation?
(iii) Why most of the sugar mills be near the sugar fields?

Ans. (i) The sett method and ratooning are two different ways used to propagate sugarcane.
(ii) At the time of cultivation, furrows and cuttings are made and manuring is done two or three times. Thus, a lot of labour is required for sugarcane cultivation.
(iii) The sugar mills must be near the fields because, sugarcane contains sucrose and if it is not processed within 24 hours, the content of sucrose will start reducing, thus, reducing the sugar output.

5. What is withering? Why is it important? **[2011]**

Ans. Withering is a process which is used to remove excess water from the tea leaves and allows a very slight amount of oxidation. The tea leaves can be either put under the Sun or left in a cool breezy room to pull moisture out from the leaves.

The leaves sometimes loose more than a quarter of their weight in water during withering.

The process of withering is important in promoting the breakdown of leaf proteins into free amino acids and increases the availability of freed caffeine, both of which change the taste of the tea.

6. Give geographical reasons for the following. **[2017]**
(i) Regular pruning is essential for tea bushes.
(ii) Coffee beans are roasted.

Ans. (i) Pruning is the method in which the branches of tea bush are cut off. This method encourages the growth of new shoots with softer leaves and to keep the plant about 1.2 m, high so that the leaves can be picked up easily. So, regular pruning is essential for tea bushes.
(ii) Coffee beans are roasted before grinding. This is done to add the specific brown colour to the coffee beans, and for adding aroma and taste.

7. With reference to the cultivation of tea, answer the following. **[2018]**
(i) Why is tea grown on hill slopes?
(ii) Why tea bushes have to be pruned at regular intervals?

Ans. (i) Tea grows on hill slopes because tea plantation demands evenly distributed rainfall with no water-logging issues. The hill slopes provide an easy drainage of the rainwater. Moreover, the tea plants grow well in the loamy soil which is found mostly over the hill slopes.
(ii) Refer to answer of Long Question Q. 6 (i).

8. Give a geographical reason for each of the following.
(i) Tea is cultivated on hill slopes. **[2015]**
(ii) The yield per hectare of sugarcane is higher in Southern states.

Ans. (i) Refer to answer to Long Question Q. 7(i).
(ii) Due to favourable climatic condition the sucrose content is higher so, yield per hectare is high in Southern India as compared to Northern India.

9. Give geographical reasons for the followings. **[2010]**
(i) Tea bushes are pruned at regular intervals.
(ii) Tapping of rubber trees is usually done in the morning hours.
(iii) Oil cake is a useful residue.

Ans. (i) Refer to answer of Long Question Q. 6 (i).
(ii) Tapping of rubber trees is done in the morning, as latex (a milky fluid found is plants) flows freely at this time.
(iii) Oil cake is a useful residue as it is used as manure and can be used as fodder for cattle.

10. Answer the following question. **[Specimen Paper Semester -II 2022]**

(i) Name the largest producer of tea in India.

(ii) What is ginning?

(iii) Why is pruning essential for tea crop?

Ans. (i) The largest producer of tea in India is Assam state.

(ii) Ginning is associated with cotton. Ginning is a process by which fibre is separated from the raw material. Earlier it was done by hands, but now machines are also used for ginning.

(iii) Refer to answer of Long Question Q. 6 (i).

11. With reference to the cultivation of coffee in Southern India. **[2011]**

(i) Name the two varieties of coffee plants grown on commercial scale.

(ii) Why are coffee estates inter-planted with orange trees, cardamom and pepper vines?

(iii) Name one state where coffee is grown extensively.

Ans. (i) Arabica and Robusta are two main varieties of coffee grown on commercial scale.

(ii) Coffee estates are inter-planted with orange trees, cardamom and pepper vines as they supplement the farmer's income and provide shade to the young coffee plants.

(iii) Coffee is grown extensively in Karnataka.

12. Answer the following questions.

(i) Give a brief description about following.

(a) Arabica (b) Robusta

(ii) Why are the following trees commonly grown in a coffee estate?

(a) Dalap and silver oak

(b) Orange and Plum

Ans. (i) (a) **Arabica** Arabica coffees have a delicate flavour and balanced aroma coupled with a sharp and sweet taste. These are harvested between November to January.

(b) **Robusta** It has a very strong taste and a grainy essence. These coffee plants are harvested from December to February.

(ii) (a) Dalap and silver oak are grown to provide shade to the young coffee plants.

(b) Orange and plum are grown to provide extra income to the farmers.

13. (i) Name two states where coffee plantations are found. **[2013]**

(ii) What condition of soil and climate are favourable for the cultivation of coffee?

Ans. Two states where coffee plantations are found are

(i) (a) **Karnataka** It contributes about more than 70% of the total production.

(b) **Tamil Nadu** It contributes about more than 5% of the total production. Arabica coffee forms the major part of the total coffee produced in the state.

(ii) Soil and climate conditions that are favourable for the cultivation of coffee are

- **Temperature** Coffee is a tropical plant which requires high temperature, ranging from 15°C to 28°C throughout the year.
- **Rainfall** Coffee plant requires a rainfall of about 150 to 200 cm which should be well distributed throughout the year.
- **Soil** Coffee plant grows well in deep, porous soil having high humus content and minerals like iron and calcium. The soil must be properly manured to retain and replenish the fertility. Lava soils, red soils and laterite soils of Deccan plateau are very well suited for coffee plantation.

14. State the two important methods of processing the coffee.

Ans. The two important methods of processing the coffee are

(i) **Wet Method** The coffee which is processed by the wet method is called plantation coffee. Under this method, pulping, fermenting, washing and drying is done. Machines are also used in this method.

(ii) **Dry Process** The coffee which is processed by dry process is called cherry or native method. Under this method, cherries are put under the Sun to dry. After drying, the covering is removed and the seeds are obtained.

They are then sorted according to their size and quality. Then they are roasted which gives it a brown colour and pleasing smell and taste. Freshly roasted beans are better and preferred more. After roasting, coffee beans are crushed and then coffee powder is used to make the beverage.

15. Give a geographical reason for each of the following. **[2014]**

(i) Clonal planting is the best method for tea propagation.

(ii) Oilseeds are an important commercial crop grown in India.

Ans. (i) Clonal planting is best as it helps to produce superior quality, better yield and also contains special flavour of the mother plants.

(ii) Oilseeds are important as they provide raw material to various industries which extract the oil for different uses.

16. Give the geographic term for each of the following. **[2015]**

(i) Cultivation of sugarcane from the root stock of the cane which has been cut.

(ii) The residue left behind after the crushing of oilseeds.

(iii) The process by which latex is converted into a thick spongy mass by adding acetic acid or formic acid.

Ans. (i) Ratooning (ii) Oil cake

(iii) Coagulation

Picture Based Question

1. Study the picture given below and answer the questions that follow. [2016]

(i) Name one state where this crop grows well.
(ii) Why are mostly women employed to harvest it?
(iii) Mention two geographical conditions suitable for the cultivation of this crop.

Ans. (i) The crop is tea and it grows well in Assam, West Bengal, parts of Tamil Nadu and Kerala.
(ii) Women labour is mostly employed to pluck it as women have nimble-fingers and take better care of the fragile and precious leaves as it requires fine plucking i.e. two leaves and a bud.
(iii) Two geographical conditions suitable for the cultivation of this crop are

Temperature Tea plant requires a temperature ranging from 20°C to 30°C, but ideal temperature would be 25°C. Alternate cool and warm breeze are very helpful for tea plants. Tea grows best in the shade and hence, shady trees are required in tea plantations along with tea plants.

Rainfall It requires heavy rainfall of about 150 cm to 250 cm distributed well throughout the year. Due to heavy rainfall tea grows well in Assam (annual rainfall between 125 cm and 375 cm), Duar and Darjeeling districts (annual rainfall between 250 cm to 500 cm). High amount of humidity, heavy dew and morning fog help the leaves to grow rapidly, but prolonged dry spell is very detrimental for tea plants.

Chapter Assessment

Section-I

Multiple Choice Questions

1. Which type of groundnut is grown in India?
(a) Brunch type (b) Bunch type
(c) Runner type (d) Both (b) and (c)

2. The largest producer of mustard is ....
(a) Rajasthan (b) Madhya Pradesh
(c) Assam (d) Chhattisgarh

3. Which of the following is a variety of tea?
(a) Robusta (b) Green tea
(c) Oolong tea (d) Both (b) and (c)

4. In the coffee production, the rank of India is ....
(a) first (b) second
(c) fifth (d) eighth

Section-II

Short Questions

1. Groundnut, linseed, mustard come under which type of crop?
2. Name two types of groundnut.
3. What is done in fermentation of tea crop?
4. Why coffee is grown on hill slopes?
5. Mention the climatic and geographical conditions suitable for the growth of groundnut.
6. Name some regions where cultivation of mustard takes place in India.
7. State the methods used for cultivation of sugarcane.
8. What is transplantation method?

Long Questions

1. Explain the advantages of ratooning.
2. Explain how the cultivation of sugarcane of North India is different from South India?
3. Differentiate between wet method and dry method of coffee cultivation.
4. What is the difference between climate conditions and soil requirement of mustard and soybean ?
5. Explain sugarcane's method of cultivation.

CHAPTER 12

Manufacturing Industries

SYLLABUS

Importance and Classification • Agro based Industry-Sugar, Textile (Cotton and Silk)
• Mineral based Industry-Iron and Steel (TISCO, Bhilai, Rourkela, Visakhapatnam)
Petro Chemical and Electronics.

India is one of the important industrialised countries in the world. India has diversified natural resources, large population which provide cheap labour and huge market to sell the manufactured goods. The process of using the raw material from natural resources into a finished, ready to use product is called 'manufacturing'.

Importance of Industries in India

- Industries are backbone of an economy. It provides finished goods for consumption and intermediate goods for other sectors.
- Industries helps to strengthen our agricultural system as industry provides tools and implements to be used in agriculture.
- Industries are very important source to provide employment on a large-scale.
- Industries help to produce goods and equipments for the defence of the country.
- Industries help to reduce dependency on foreign countries and make India self-reliant and become self-sufficient.
- Expansion of industries is required to fill the gap between developed and under-developed regions in India.
- Industries help to maintain a favourable balance of trade by producing goods of better quality that can be exported.

Classification of Industries

On the basis of type of raw material, its size, location, type of the product manufactured, industries can be classified into the following groups

On the Basis of Raw Material

- **Agro-Based Industries** These industries use the produce of agricultural sector as their raw material. Some examples of these industries are sugar, jute, cotton, vegetable oil, coffee, tea and other food processing industries.
- **Mineral Based Industries** These industries use minerals as their raw material like ferrous metallic minerals, non-ferrous metallic minerals and non-metallic minerals. Some examples of these industries are iron and steel, aluminium, heavy engineering and machine tools, cement, fertilisers, chemicals and ship building industries.

- **Animal Based Industries** These industries depend on animals for their supply of raw material. Some examples of these industries are woollens, silk, dairy products, hides, skin and poultry, etc.
- **Forest Based Industries** These industries receive their raw material from the forest and forest products, e.g. paper, cardboard, tanning of leather and timber industries. Some pharmaceutical industries also depend on forest produces and medicinal plants.

On the Basis of Nature of Products

- **Heavy Industries** These industries produce capital goods and **consumer durables**[1]. These industries need huge capital, sophisticated machinery, skilled and unskilled labour, large quantity of raw material and scientific knowledge, e.g. iron and steel industry, locomotives and automobile industry.
- **Light Industries** These industries produce goods of light weight like electronic goods, cycles, sewing machines, etc. They don't require huge capital like heavy industries and work with less number of workers. Some examples of these industries are electronic goods, sewing machines, TV, fridge, fan, etc.

On the Basis of Size and Investment

- **Large-Scale Industries** These industries need large amount of investment and large number of labour. The investment is above 10 crore. They produce machinery and goods on a large-scale like iron and steel industry, shipbuilding, automobile, etc. They use more capital so they are capital intensive.
- **Medium-Scale Industries** These industries are neither very large nor very small. They require everything on a medium-scale. The investment is upto 10 crore. Some examples of these industries are paper mills, radio and cycle manufacturing industries.
- **Small-Scale Industries** These industries are very small and are managed by private individuals. They do not require large capital and only employ few workers. They use more labour instead of capital and also called 'labour intensive industries'. The investment is less than 1 crore. Some examples of these industries are weaving industry, silk industry, etc.

On the Basis of Ownership and Management

- **Public Sector Industries** These industries are owned and managed either by the Central Government or by the State Government. These industries comprise of railways, post and telegraph, oil refineries, irrigation projects, defence management, etc. The most important industries in this group are Bharat Heavy Electrical Limited (BHEL), Gas Authority of India Limited (GAIL), Indian Oil Corporation (IOC), etc.
- **Private Sector Industries** These industries are owned and managed by an individual or some group of people. They can be large or small-scale industries. For example, Reliance India Limited (RIL), Wipro, Infosys, etc.
- **Joint Sector Industries** These industries are owned, managed and controlled jointly by the private individuals or groups and the government. For example, Automobile Corporation of Goa Ltd. and Ipitata Sponge Iron Ltd. have been established with TELCO and TISCO of the Tata House as private group, respectively.
- **Co-operative**[2] **Sector Industries** These industries are owned and managed on cooperative basis by those who are producers of the raw materials required for the industry. Some examples of these industries are sugar mills (run by the cultivators of sugarcane), dairy industry (Amul), etc.

On the Basis of Location and Market

- **Rural Industries** These industries get their basic requirements like raw material, skilled labour, etc from the rural area in which they are set up. Some examples of these industries are handloom, pottery making, food processing, pickles, khadi, etc.
- **Cottage Industries** In these industries, the business activity is performed at home and hence, they are also known as **household industries**. These are organised by individuals who can invest their private resources and carry out their activity with households assistance. They employ local resources and labours. Some examples of these industries are carpet weaving, handloom, handicraft industry, etc.

---

1 **Consumer Durables** Large goods that people buy for their own use like cars.

2 **Cooperative** It is a group of people where these people with limited resources share their physical and material resources with each other.

On the Basis of the Finished Product or Functions

- **Basic Industries** These are the group of core industries on which other industries are dependent for their manufacturing. For example, iron and steel industry, petroleum industry.
- **Secondary or Consumer Industry** These industries process the basic raw materials and convert them into primary goods for direct utilisation by the consumers. For example, bakeries, textiles, paper, sugar, etc.
- **Tertiary Industries** These industries provide public utility based services like railways, roads, banking, post and telegraph, etc.
- **Ancillary Industries** These industries prepare spare parts and components for big industries engaged in the manufacturing of buses, aircraft, heavy electrical industry, engines and locomotives.

Check Your LEARNING...

1. Name the industry which is owned and managed by individuals.
2. State two components of heavy industries.
3. State two examples of tertiary activities.
4. Iron ore is which type of industry?

Agro-Based Industries

The main agro-based industries in India are sugar and textile industries.

Sugar Industry

India is known for producing sugar since decades. It is the second largest organised industry in India after cotton textiles. India contributes around 8% of the total sugar production in the world. The sugar industry relies heavily on the supply of fresh cane hence, most of the industries are located near the sugarcane producing fields generally in a radius of around 25 km.

Byproducts of Sugarcane

Molasses It is a thick, dark brown syrup. It is obtained in the process of sugar manufacture which involves the process of crystallisation and **centrifugation**[3]. It is used for the manufacture of fertiliser, DDT powder, alcohol, synthetic rubber, plastic, rum and cattle feed.

Bagasse It is the leftover cane after crushing. It is used as raw material for paper industry and making cardboard. It is also used as a energy source to produce power (steam) for sugar industry.

Pressmud It is used for making wax, carbon paper, shoe polish, etc.

Distribution of Sugar Industry in India

- **Maharashtra** It is the leading producer of sugar in India which contributes more than one-third of the total production of sugar in the country. It has ideal conditions for the cultivation of sugarcane. Manmad in the North to Kolhapur in the South is the narrow belt in Maharashtra which is famous for sugar production. The crushing period in the mills in this state is more than 140 days which is a very favourable factor.
- **North India** Uttar Pradesh is the second largest producer of sugar in India. Sugar factories are located in the Ganga-Yamuna doab and the Terai belt in Uttar Pradesh. Saharanpur, Meerut, Baghpat, Muzaffarnagar, Bulandshahr and Ghaziabad are the main sugar producing centres in the Ganga-Yamuna doab while Basti, Bahraich, Gonda, Gorakhpur and Lakhimpur Kheri are the main centres in the Terai area. The other sugar producing states in North India are Bihar, Punjab, Haryana, Madhya Pradesh and Gujarat.
- **Peninsular India** Many favourable conditions along with new machinery has led to higher output of sugar in peninsular or South India. In South India, major sugar factories in Tamil Nadu are located in Coimbatore, Vellore, Tiruvanamalai and Tiruchirappalli. In Andhra Pradesh, major sugar factories are located in Vijayawada, East and West Godavari, Kakinada, Chittoor and Srikakulam.

Shifting of Sugar Mills from North India to South India

In recent years, there is a tendency for the mills to shift and concentrate in the Southern and Western states, especially in Maharashtra. This is because of the following reasons

- The cane produced in South India has higher sucrose content which is of superior quality and gives higher yield especially in Tamil Nadu state.
- The cooler climate (maritime climate due to sea effect) and absence of Loo in South India ensure a longer sugarcane crushing season.
- The region has black soil which is favourable for sugarcane cultivation.
- Sugarcane farms are larger in South India as compared to North India.

3 Centrifugation It is a process which is used to separate two homogeneous substances.

- Many states in South India have favourable transportation facilities. These states also have export markets.
- Moreover, the cooperatives are more successful in South India who take care of large sugarcane farms and have good access to many facilities like good quality seeds, fertilisers, irrigation methods and so on.
- The sugar mills/factories in South India are located near the sugarcane farms which reduces the loss of sucrose content and provide quick access of raw material to the factories.
- Introduction of new machineries and longer crushing season in South India are also a favourable factors for the location of sugar mills.

Sugar Industrial Centres

Uttar Pradesh	The Western belt includes Meerut, Bijnor, Saharanpur, Muzaffarnagar and Moradabad and the Eastern belt includes Gorakhpur, Deoria, Basti and Gonda.
Maharashtra	Nasik, Pune, Satara, Sangli, Kolhapur, Solapur are the centres well integrated in the cooperative sector in terms of cultivation and sugar factories.
Tamil Nadu	Nalikupuram, Pandyarajpuram, Coimbatore and Pugulur. Villupuram, Vellore, Tiruvanamalai, Thiruvallur, Thanjavur, Perambalur, Cuddalore and Dharmapuri districts.
Andhra Pradesh	Vijayawada, West and East Godavari, Kakinada, Vishakhapatnam, Srikakulam and Chittoor.
Karnataka	Munirabad, Shimoga and Mandya.
Bihar	Extension of the Eastern Uttar Pradesh belt, which includes Darbhanga, Saran, Champaran and Muzaffarpur.
Odisha	Bargarh and Rayagada
Madhya Pradesh	Sehore
Punjab	The centres are mainly located in the Eastern side in Phagwara, Dhuri.

Problems of the Sugar Industry

- The quality of sugarcane produced in India is poor having low yield and sucrose content is also very low.
- Due to inefficient nature of production, the cost of production is high. Crushing season is short and the location of sugarcane cultivating fields are farther from the mills.
- Generally, entire stock of sugarcane is harvested at the same time, which creates pressure on factories to process the sugarcane hence, some amount of cane goes waste. This increases in the cost of production.
- The sugar mills do not run throughout the year thus, creating problem of regular income for the workers.
- The by-products produced by the sugar industry are not utilised properly. Hence, they can't be converted into different useful products to further reduce the cost of production.
- The machines in the factories especially in Northern India are old and obsolete. This hampers the production of sugar.
- The sugarcane is grown by small farmers who sell their crops to sugar factories at fixed prices by the government. When farmers do not get attractive prices they switch the other profit-making crops.

Textile Industries

When we refer the word textile it includes all the five fibres i.e. cotton, jute, wool, silk and synthetic fibre. In India, textile industry occupies an important place as it generates huge employment opportunity. The major textile industries in India include cotton and silk industries.

Cotton Textile Industry

Cotton textile manufacturing is the largest organised modern industry in the country. Cotton textiles employs huge number of people thereby supporting the economy of the country. It is more concentrated in the cotton growing region.

In India the cotton textile industry is divided into two sectors namely, **power loom** and **handloom.** Maharashtra, Gujarat and Tamil Nadu have the most important cotton mills in power loom. These states account for three-fourths of the total output of yarn and cotton cloth.

The remaining one-fourth is produced by West Bengal, Uttar Pradesh, Rajasthan, Madhya Pradesh, Andhra Pradesh, and Karnataka.

Handloom industry is located all over India. Its important centres are Mumbai, Ahmedabad, Coimbatore, Kanpur, Delhi and Howrah. Other important states are Rajasthan, Kerala, Karnataka, Punjab, Bihar, and Assam.

Distribution of Cotton Textile Industry in India

- **Maharashtra** Mumbai is the most important centre of cotton textile in India. It is often called as **cottonopolis**[4] **of India.** The state produces about 40% of the mill cloth in India. Mumbai is also known as Lancashire (in England) of India.
- **Gujarat** It is renowned as the second largest producer of cotton textile in India. It contributes about 23% of the total mill cloth production in India. Ahmedabad is the second largest cotton manufacturing city of India and is popularly known as **Manchester (city of England) of India.**
- **Tamil Nadu** It produces about 6% of the total mill cloth of India and it leads in yarn production. Coimbatore is an important cotton textile producer which is also called **The Manchester of South India.** Coimbatore, Madurai, Salem, Tuticorin, Tiruchirappalli, Tirunelveli and Ramanathapuram are the chief centres.
- **West Bengal** Kolkata is the most popular textile centre of West Bengal, which has various advantages as it is a port city. It has huge supply of cheap labour and has high demand of cotton clothes due to humid climate. It receives water for the production of cotton from Hooghly river. It is also facilitated with good network of roads and railways.
- **Uttar Pradesh** In Uttar Pradesh, majority of Cotton Textile Industry has emerged along its Western part. The largest centre in Uttar Pradesh is Kanpur. Lucknow, Moradabad, Modinagar, Etawah, Agra and Saharanpur are other important centres.

Cotton Textile Industry in India

Maharashtra	Mumbai, Pune, Aurangabad, Kolhapur and Solapur.
Gujarat	Ahmedabad, Surat, Jamnagar and Bhavnagar
West Bengal	Kolkata
Tamil Nadu	Chennai, Salem, Coimbatore, Tuticorin and Madurai.
Madhya Pradesh	Gwalior, Indore and Bhopal
Rajasthan	Kota, Bhilwara and Jaipur
Uttar Pradesh	Modinagar, Kanpur, Varanasi, Moradabad and Lucknow
Andhra Pradesh	Anantpur and Vijayawada
Kerala	Kollam and Thiruvananthapuram

Problems of Cotton Textile Industry

- **Lack of Raw Material** After the partition, India had to bear a huge loss of long-staple cotton as most of the centres went to Pakistan. Thus in order to fulfil its requirement, India imports cotton from Pakistan, Kenya, Uganda, Sudan, Egypt, USA and Peru.
- **Old and Obsolete Machinery** Many mills in India are very old and are very inefficient. They have **obsolete**[5] machineries as compared to some other developed countries. This proves to be an obstruction in higher production.
- **Shortage of Power Supply** There is serious problem of power shortage for cotton textile mills. The industries suffer a lot due to load shedding and frequent power cut. This causes loss in production to huge extent.
- **Low Labour Productivity** As compared to other developed countries, the labour productivity of India is low and it is a drawback for the cotton industry.
- **Stiff Competition** Indian cotton textiles have to face stiff competition from synthetic fibres which are cheaper and need less maintenance.
- **Foreign Market** Indian cotton textile industry is facing a tough competition in foreign markets of Taiwan, Japan, South Korea and China whose proudcts are both cheaper and better in quality.
- **Sick Units/Mills** Due to various reasons as mentioned above, many mills in India are going in loss and are declared as sick mills. These sick units are in the need of huge financial investments to replace it with modern technology and machineries. The government has setup **National Textile Corporation** to solve the problems of the sick mills and many of the sick and unproductive mills have been taken over by the government.

Silk Textile Industry

India is one of the leading producers of silk in the world. It produces all the four varieties of silk *viz* mulberry, eri, tassar and muga. Silk Industry is considered as a small-scale industry in India. Very little investment is required in it but it requires more labour. India holds a monopoly in golden-yellow muga silk which is produced in Assam.

The rearing of silkworms for the production of silk is called **sericulture**. Sericulture engages women in rearing of silkworms while men work in the plantations.

4 **Cottonopolis** A major cotton trading centre.
5 **Obsolete** Outdated when new technology is invented.

The raw material is obtained by silkworm reared on mulberry bushes. The East India Company established the first modern silk textile factory of India in 1832.

In India, mulberry silk accounts for about 90% of total natural silk produced. Mulberry silk is produced in Karnataka, Andhra Pradesh, Tamil Nadu, West Bengal, Kashmir and Himachal Pradesh. Important mulberry producing centres are Bengaluru, Mysore, Belgaun and Srinagar.

Distribution of Silk Textile Industry in India

- Karnataka is the leading silk producing state in India (about 70%).
- Andhra Pradesh accounts for almost 17.83% of India's total silk production.
- West Bengal accounts for almost 8.3% of India's total production.
- Assam, Jharkhand, Bihar, Odisha and Meghalaya produces muga and tussar varieties of silk.

Silk Industry in India

Karnataka	Bengaluru, Hubli, Dharwar, Mysore and Belgaum, Kollegal, Melkote, Kolar, Mandya, Tumkur, Belgavi, Chikkabollapura, Ramanagaram, Chamarajanagar and Coorg.
West Bengal	Murshidabad, Bankura and Bishnpur, Birbhum, Malda, Baswa, Raghunathpur, Rishra, Chak and Islampur.
Uttar Pradesh	Varanasi, Mirzapur and Shahjahanpur.
Tamil Nadu	Salem, Tirunelveli, Nilgiris, Kanchipuram and Thanjavur
J & K	Srinagar
Bihar and Jharkhand	Bhagalpur, Palamau, Hozavibag, Ranchi (Largest tasar producing states in India).
Assam	Goalpara in Kamrup and Nagaon, Sualkuchi (Assam is only muga-producing region in India.)
Punjab	Amritsar, Jalandhar and Ludhiana
Gujarat	Ahmedabad, Surat and Cambay
Telangana	Warangal, Mahbubnagar, Karimnagar, Adilabad
Andhra Pradesh	Anantpur, Chittoor, Visakhapatnam and Kurnool, Pochampally

Problems of Silk Industry

- It is facing tough competition from artificial silk which is cheaper and needs less maintenance.
- The import of cheaper and better quality silk from China is proving to be very harmful for the Indian silk industry.
- The fluctuation in the prices of raw silk has an adverse effect on the silk industry.
- As compared to advanced countries like Japan and China, India does not have systematic testing and grading of silk.
- Latest and modern technology is required for increasing the production.

Artificial Silk (Synthetic Fibre)

It is man-made or synthetic fibre which is in huge demand due to its variety, durability, cheaper price and strength.This sillk is also called **art silk**. **Cellulose**[6] (rayon and acetate[7]) and non-cellulose (nylon and polyester) are two types of man-made fibres.

Caustic soda, sodium sulphate and sulphuric acid are chief raw material required to produce these fibres. Alcohol and cotton are the chief or primary raw material needed for acetate yarn and staple fibre. The popular areas of production of these yarns are Kerala, Andhra Pradesh, Gujarat, Kota, Mumbai and Modinagar.

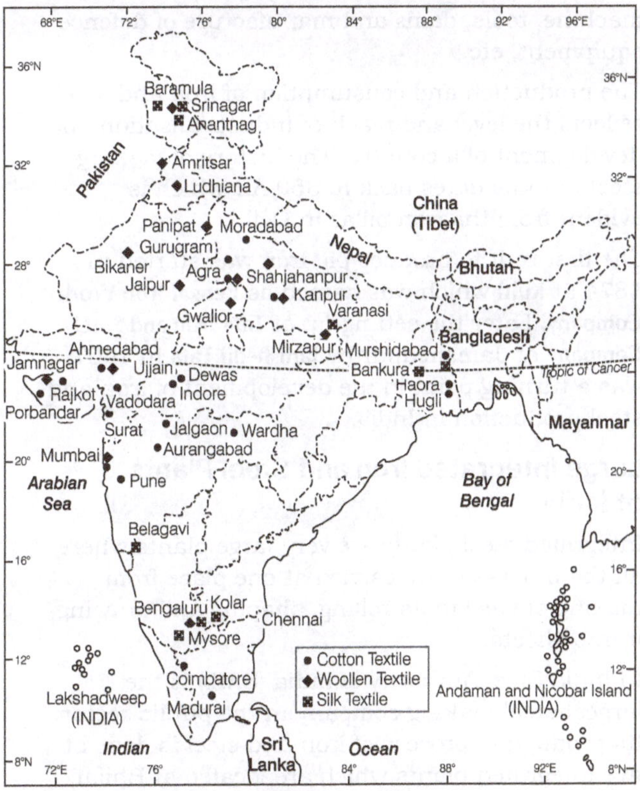

Textile Industries in India

6 **Cellulose** Plant material used in making of natural fibres.
7 **Acetate** Smooth artificial cloth made from chemicals and acetic acid.

Check Your LEARNING...

1. Name any one by product of sugarcane.
2. Name any two sugar producing centres of Uttar Pradesh.
3. Mention any one problem of cotton textile industry.
4. Name a silk producing region of Karnataka.

Mineral Based Industry

The industries that require minerals as their raw material are called mineral based industry. For example, iron and steel industry is a mineral based industry as it is based on iron ore and other minerals.

Iron and Steel Industry

Iron and steel is a central element in the heavy industrial structure and forms the backbone of industrial development. This industry converts iron ore into iron and then to steel which becomes the major input for other industries like automobile, locomotives, railways, shipbuilding, machine, tools, dams and manufacture of defence equipment, etc.

The production and consumption of iron and steel reflects the level and reach of industrialisation and development of a country. The history of making steel in India dates back to 350 AD which is evident from the iron pillar in Delhi.

The first unit to produce pig iron was started in 1874 at **Kulti** which was named as **Bengal Iron Work Company.** Later the setting up of **Tata Iron and Steel Company** at Jamshedpur by **Jamshedji Tata** in 1907 was a turning point in the development of iron and steel production in India.

Large Integrated Iron and Steel Plants of India

Integrated steel plants are very large plants where all the processes are carried at one place from making of steel to its rolling, shaping and drawing it into sheets.

In India Steel Authority of India (SAIL) is the largest steel making company in the public sector. Its production process of iron and steel is done at five integrated plants which are located at Bhilai, Durgapur, Rourkela, Bokaro and Burnpur and three special steel plants at Salem, Durgapur and Bhadravati.

Chandrapur in Maharashtra is also has a Ferro Alloy plant. Private sector also has many integrated steel plants, the largest being Tata Iron and Steel plant which is located at Jamshedpur.

Some important iron and steel plants in India are

Tata Iron and Steel Company (TISCO)

This is the oldest manufacturing plant in India and one of the largest manufacturing plant in Asia. It is a private sector iron and steel plant established in 1907 by **Jamshedji Tata** at Sakchi in Jamshedpur in Jharkhand.

The production of this plant started in 1911. This plant is responsible for producing many variety of goods like iron sheets, rail sleepers for railway wheels, etc. TISCO produces high grade carbon steel, acid steel and special alloy steel.

Carbon steel is used in structural fittings and tin plates, acid steel is used in making railway wheels, axles, bars, rods sheets, and special alloy steel is used for making bulletproof armour plates.

Tata Iron and Steel Plants

The given factors were responsible for the establishment of TISCO in Jamshedpur

- High quality of iron-ore available from Noamundi of Singhbhum region (Jharkhand) and Mayurbhanj (Odisha).
- Availability of coal from Jharia and Bokaro coal mines of Jharkhand.
- Availability of manganese from Joda in Keonjher district of Odisha.
- Dolomite, limestone and fire clay are available from Sundargarh district of Odisha.
- Water for cooling purpose is provided from the river Subarnarekha and also from the Kharkai dam.

- Raw materials as well as finished goods can be transported from Jamshedpur to Kolkata, Mumbai, Chennai as it is well connected by roads and railways.
- Availability of cheap labour from Jharkhand and nearby Odisha region.
- Nearness to Kolkata (about 240 km) as it provides important market for the consumption of iron and steel goods and also has facilities for export of finished goods.

Bhilai Iron and Steel Plant

This plant was set up in collaboration with the erstwhile USSR in Durg district of Chhattisgarh and started its production in 1959.

This was the **first plant** under the public sector and was established to bring prosperity and development in Durg region. This plant produces rails, railway sleepers, beems, billets, angles, etc. Bhilai iron and steel plant produces heavy rails, structurals, billets, rolled wire, beams. It provides plates to shipbuilding industry. Besides these, this plant also produces many by-products like ammonium sulphate, benzol, coal tar and sulphate acid.

Bhilai Iron and Steel Plant

The important factors which were favourable for this plant are

- Availability of iron ore from Dalli-Rajhara range which is just 80 km South of Bhilai.
- Coal is available from Korba (Chhattisgarh) and Kargali fields. High quality coal is further brought from Jharia and Bokaro.
- Limestone is obtained from quarries of Nandini which is few kilometres away.
- Manganese is available from Balaghat of Madhya Pradesh.
- Dolomite is available from Bilaspur and energy supply is available from Korba thermal power plant in Chhattisgarh.
- Important water supply is available from Tendula canal.
- Cheap labour is easily available from Bihar, Jharkhand and Madhya Pradesh.
- The region is well connected with Kolkata-Nagpur railway line. There was a construction of another railway line to transport iron ore from Dalli to Bhilai steel works.

Rourkela Steel Plant

This plant was set up in the Sundergarh district of Odisha with the technical help of German firm, Krupps and Demag in 1959 during the Second Five Year Plan. This plant is located at the confluence of two rivers the sankha and Koel which flow as a single river called Brahmani.

This plant has produced specialised steel for the vehicles related to Indian Space Satellite Programme. It also supports various fertiliser plants which utilises the by-products released by it.

It provides many products like hot-rolled sheets and strips, cold- rolled sheets, galvanized sheets, electrical steel plates and so on. Besides these, it also produces large quantity of nitrogen as a by-product which is utilised for making fertilisers and other chemicals.

Some of the favourable factors for this plant are

- Availability of iron ore from Sundergarh and Keonjhar district which is very close to its location.
- Coal is available from Jharia, Talcher and Korba coal fields.
- Power is supplied from Hirakud Dam.
- Manganese is obtained from Barajamda. Dolomite is obtained from Baradwar and Hirni mines of Madhya Pradesh while limestone from Birmitrapur.
- Water supply is available from the nearby Brahmani river and Mahanadi river.
- Abundance of cheap labour from the nearby areas.

- There is good connectivity from the plant to Kolkata through roads and railways. Kolkata provides good port facilities for both the raw materials and finished goods.

Visakhapatnam Steel Plant

This plant is the most modern steel plant and is the latest integrated iron and steel plant. It is also the **first seashore based steel plant** which started its production in 1992. It is managed by Rashtriya Ispat Nigam. This plant contributes heavily to the shipbuilding industry and uses the advantage of being a large sea port of India. It produces liquid steel and saleable steel which is exported to China and South-East Asia.

Some of the favourable factors contributing to this plant are

- Iron ore is available from Bailadila mines of Chhattisgarh.
- Cooking coal is obtained from Pookie and Bhalore coal mines of Jharkhand.
- Limestone is obtained from Jaggayyapeta of Andhra Pradesh and dolomite is brought from Birmitrapur in Odisha and Khammam in Andhra Pradesh.

Mini Steel Plants

Mini steel plants are small unit plants. These plants generally use ferrous scrap, pig iron or sponge iron as their raw material. They are located away from integrated large steel plants. They work through electric furnaces and have a capacity from 10,000 tonnes to about 5 lakh tonnes per year. Their period of construction and gestation is also short. Some of the mini steel plants are located at Kanpur, Jaipur, Hyderabad, Delhi, Pune and Ranchi. The Government of India is planning to set up more mini steel plants due to following advantages

- They use scrap iron which is easily available and is comparatively cheap.
- They are environment-friendly as they depend on electric power and do not cause pollution.
- They do not require heavy investment.
- These plants need not be located near the source of raw material as they use scrap iron of integrated steel plants.
- These plants can meet the demands of local market and reduce pressure on large plants.

Problems of Iron and Steel Industry

- **Huge Investment** This is a large-scale industry that requires huge capital for its set up. It is difficult for a developing country like India to invest huge capital required in this type of industry.
- **Outdated and Low Technical Development** Outdated machinery has increased the cost of production of iron and steel. This has also reduced the profit margin of the iron and steel plants.
- **Inefficiency in Production** The production units do not utilise the full potential of employees. Labour productivity is low as compared to other countries which increases the cost of production.
- **Rise in Import** India has to import iron and steel from foreign countries as it is not able to fulfil its demand for steel. The rise in import leads to greater spending of foreign exchange.
- **Lack of Availability of Resources** There should be proper availability of all the natural resources at one place such as iron-ore mines, energy sources and water resources. If even one of the natural resources is not available, then the development of the industry becomes very difficult.
- **Limited Availability of Coking Coal** Despite of having huge deposits of high grade iron-ore, India has limited coking coal reserves which is mainly used for smelting iron-ore. Thus, many steel plants are forced to import coking coal e.g. Visakhapatnam steel plant imports coal from Australia.
- **Sick Industrial Units** Many small iron and steel plants are either experiencing sickness or have been closed due to the inadequate supply of power and sharp increase in the cost of raw materials.
- **Control on Prices** The manufacturers of steel do not get much profit as the government has fixed price for iron and steel.
- **Inefficiently Managed Public Sector** Iron and steel plants in the public sector are facing many problems like strikes, lockouts, energy crisis, etc. These problems result into heavy investment on social overheads, poor labour relations, inefficient management and under-utilisation of capacity.

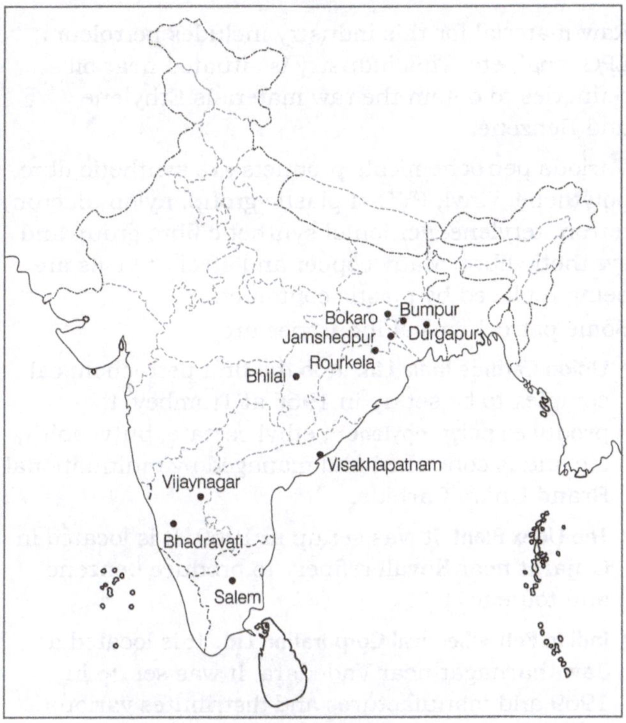

Iron and Steel Plants in India

Check Your LEARNING...

1. Name any two large integrated iron and steel plants of India.
2. Mention any one favourable factor for the set up of Rourkela steel plant in Sundergarh.
3. Give any one problem of iron and steel industry.
4. Vishakhapatnam steel plant imports coal from which country?

Electronics

The electronics sector in India covers a wide range of products which includes television, transistors, telephone exchange, cellular telecom, pagers, computers and various equipments for post and telegraph, defence, railway and **meteorological**[8] phenomena.

It developed from 1950s and has improved the lifestyle of the people. There is a great demand of Indian hardware and softwere worldwide. The electronic industry is a fast growing tertiary occupation which is mostly concentrated in the South India.

Important electronic industries are

Electronic Goods Industries

- **The India Telephone Industries** (ITI) It was the first public sector undertaking to be set up after independence, near Bengaluru in 1950.

Bengaluru is known as **Electronic city** or **Electronic capital of India** as it is the largest centre of electronics goods production.

ITI produces equipments for fulfilling the requirement of post and telegraph departments, railways, defence, overseas communication services and electricity boards.

It also manufactures automatic telephone switching systems, long distance transmission systems and teleprinter exchanges. ITI has seven manufacturing units in India. Two units are in Bengaluru, and other five are at Naini, Rae Bareli, Mankapur, Palakkad and Srinagar.

- **The Bharat Electronics Ltd.** (BEL) It was set up in 1956 in Bengaluru as a public sector undertaking. It fulfils the requirement of defence services, All India Radio and the Meteorological Department. It manufactures equipments for communication purpose, radar, fire control system for tanks and other optical system.
- **Electronics Corporation of India Ltd.** (ECIL) It was set up in 1970 in Hyderabad. It is an indigenous unit which manufactures modular systems for nuclear application and for the use in medical, agricultural and industrial fields. Various other products like metal oxide resistors, analog computers and online digital process control computers are also manufactured.

Software Industry

Software has developed as a major industry. India has vast reservoir of technically sound manpower which is the main reason for the rapid development of software industry. From the 90's (between 1991 and 1996), software sector of India made a major progress.

India has well developed software industry which provides cost effective, high quality, high reliability, speedy deliveries and the use of state of the art technologies in the software industry. India has attained a capacity of designing and building super computers. The leading centres for software industries in India are Bengaluru and Hyderabad.

Space Technology

The space technology in India is supported by the electronics industry. India has successfully launched many indigenously built satellites like the **Aryabhatta** and the **INSAT** series.

8 **Meteorological** It is a phenomena dealing with atmosphere and weather.

The Indian Space Research Organisation (ISRO) at **Bengaluru**, the Satellite Launching Station at **Sriharikota** and the National Remote Sensing Agency at **Hyderabad** are the major centres of developments in the field of space technology.

India has the capability to launch satellites into **Geosynchronous**[9] Transfer Orbit (GTO) and is among the six countries to do so. ISRO has developed two types of rockets, **Polar Satellite Launch Vehicle** (PSLV) to put the satellite into polar orbits and the **Geosynchronous Satellite Launch Vehicle** (GSLV) to put the satellite into **geostationary**[10] orbits.

Space industry is the top most marketing agency for subsystem and components for satellites. It also provides launch facilities and trekking and training services. In 2008, **Chandrayaan-I** was launched as India's first Scientific Mission to moon and Chandrayaan-II was launched in 2019. India has become the first country in the world to reach Mars planet on its first attempt in September, 2014.

The Mars Orbiter Mission (MOM), also called **Mangalyaan** was a space probe orbiting Mars which was India's first interplanetary mission. It made ISRO the fourth space agency to reach Mars, after Roscosmos, NASA, and the European Space Agency.

Television and Audio

The television and audio industries came into existence in the 1990s due to progress of the electronics industry. The audio industry produces many products like mono players, stereo players, mini systems, CD based systems and audio systems. Mumbai, Kolkata, Chennai and Pune are important centres of production.

Petrochemical Industry

It is an important organic chemical industry which derive its chemicals from petroleum resources and products like LPG and Coal. Petrochemicals are used for manufacturing various goods like synthetic rubber, synthetic fibre, ferrous, non-ferrous metals, plastics, dyestuffs, drugs, insecticides and many pharmaceuticals. This industry also produces resins, adhesives, plastic sheets, paints and furniture covering for household items.

Raw material for this industry includes petroleum, LPG, coal, etc. This industry is situated near oil refineries to obtain the raw materials Ethylene and Benzene.

Various petrochemicals products are synthetic fibre, polythene, vinyl, PVC of plastic group, nylon, dacron, tetron, terylene, acrilon of synthetic fibre group and synthetic fibre. Many copper and steel utensils are being replaced by plastic containers.

Some petrochemical industries are

- **Union Carbide India Ltd.** It is the first petrochemical complex to be set up in 1966 at Trombey. It produces **polypropylene**[11], ethyl ecetate, butyl spirit, etc and is controlled and managed by multinational Brand Union Carbide.
- **The Udex Plant** It was set up in 1969. It is located in Gujarat near Koyali refinery to produce benzene and toluene.
- **Indian Petrochemical Corporation Ltd.** It is located at Jawaharnagar near Vadodara. It was set up in 1969 and manufactures and distributes various petrochemicals like polymers, synthetic organic chemicals and fibres.
- **Petrofils Cooperative Limited** (PCL) It was set up as a joint venture of the Government of India and Weaver's Cooperative Societies. It is set up at Vadodara and Naldheri in Gujarat. It produces yarn which is used for making swim suits, undergarments, polyester filament yarn and nylon chips.
- **The Bongaigaon Petrochemicals Ltd.** It is located at Bongaigaon in the State of Assam and it gets its raw material from the Bongaigaon and Noonmati refineries and produces polyester fibre and orthorycline.
- **National Organic Chemical Industries Ltd.** It is the biggest unit in India which is managed by Mafatlals at Thane (near Mumbai). It is based on the latest technology and enjoys the title of being the first integrated plant in India. It produces ethylene, benzene, PVC, etc.
- **Haldia Petrochemicals Ltd.** It is located at Haldia in West Bengal which is based on Naphtha. It produces polyolefins and chemicals like benzene, butadiene, cyclo-pentane, etc.

9 **Geosynchronous** Being or having an orbit around the Earth with a period equal to one sidereal day i.e. the time a planet takes to turn once on its axis, with respect to a fixed point in the sky.

10 **Geostationary** Artificial satellite of the Earth moving in a circular geosynchromous orbit in the plane of the equator.

11 **Polypropylene** It is a thermoplastic polymer used in a wide variety of application.

- **The India Oil Corporation** It has built three world class mega petrochemical complex. These are
  (i) Linear Alkyl Benzene (LAB) Plant in Gujarat.
  (ii) Paraxylene purified Terephthalic Acid (Px/PTA) at Panipat.
  (iii) Naphtha Cracker Plant at Panipat.
- **Herdillia Chemicals Ltd** It was established in Chennai in collaboration with the Distillers Co. Ltd. of UK and Hercules Power Co. of the USA. Its important products are heavy organic chemicals like acetone, diacetone alcohol, phenol and their derivatives, by-products, co- products and compounds.
- **Reliance Industries** It is located at Hazira in Gujarat. It is the largest producer of petrochemicals in India. It produces many petrochemical products like polyester, aromatics, fibre-intermediates, etc.

Advantages of Petrochemical Products

- They are cheaper as compared to other products as they are generally manufactured on a large-scale.
- They are cost effective and economically stable as they have a definite market.
- The raw material is easily available for these products.
- They do not depend on agricultural raw material as with the case of jute, cotton, etc.

Check Your LEARNING...

1. Which city is called the 'Electronic capital of India'?
2. Mention some products of petrochemical industry.
3. Mention any one advantage of petrochemical products.
4. Name the largest producer of petrochemicals in India.

QUiCK Revision

- India has made a huge transformation toward industrial development.
- The process of using the raw material from natural resources into a finished good is called 'manufacturing'.
- Industries can be classified into various types based on the raw material, size, location, type of the product manufactured by it and its location is also dependent on both geographical and commercial factors.
- Agro-based industry are the one which are dependent on agricultural product for their raw material.
- Cotton textiles employ huge number of people. Maximum number of mills are located in Maharashtra, Gujarat and Tamil Nadu.
- India produces all the four varieties of silk *viz* mulberry, eri, tassar and muga.
- Iron and steel is a pivotal element in the heavy industry structure and forms the backbone of industrial development. It gives input for other industries as well.
- Visakhapatnam steel plant is the first sea shore based steel plant which started production in 1992.
- Integrated steel plant is the one where all the three important processes are carried out, i.e. from melting of iron, to steel making followed by shaping of the metal by rolling.
- Mini steel plants are the secondary units. These have electric furnaces and do not posses all the facilities at one place and require separate units for manufacturing steel.
- Electronic sector in India covers a wide range of products which includes television, transistors, telephone exchange, cellular telecom, pagers, computer and various other equipment for post and telegraph. Hyderabad and Bengaluru are two important centres.
- India has a well developed software industry which provides cost effective, high quality, high reliability, speed deliveries and the use of the state of art technology in software industry.
- Petrochemical industry produces products derived from petroleum resources, LPG, coal, etc. These type of chemicals are used for manufacturing various goods like synthetic rubber, synthetic fibre, plastic, etc.

Chapter Practice

Section-I

Multiple Choice Questions

1. Which sector is known as the backbone of development in general and economic development in particular?
   (a) Agriculture (b) Mining
   (c) Manufacturing (d) Service

Ans. (c) Manufacturing

2. An example of the joint sector company is ....
   (a) Hindustan Lever Limited (b) Bajaj Auto Limited
   (c) Tata Consultancy Services
   (d) Ipitata Sponge Iron Ltd

Ans. (d) Ipitata Sponge Iron Ltd

3. The first successful textile mill in India was set up at Mumbai in which year?
   (a) 1792 (b) 1825 (c) 1854 (d) 1919

Ans. (c) 1854

4. India exports yarn to which of the following countries?
   (a) Japan (b) US
   (c) UAE (d) Canada

Ans. (a) Japan

5. Varanasi is famous for ....
   (a) Cotton (b) Wool
   (c) Silk (d) Synthetic fiber

Ans. (c) Silk

6. Which of the following is a basic/key industry? [2023]
   (a) Iron and steel industry (b) Silk industry
   (c) Electronic industry (d) Cotton textile industry

Ans. (d) Cotton textile industry

7. Which of these agencies markets steel from public sector plants in India?
   (a) HAIL (b) SAIL
   (c) BAIL (d) GAIL

Ans. (b) SAIL

8. Where is the headquarters of TISCO?
   (a) Mumbai (b) West Bengal
   (c) Chhattisgarh (d) Odisha

Ans. (a) Mumbai

9. Which of the following industries manufactures telephones, computers?
   (a) Steel (b) Aluminium
   (c) Electronics (d) Information technology

Ans. (c) Electronics

10. Railway diesel engines are manufactured in Uttar Pradesh at ....
    (a) Lucknow (b) Naraura
    (c) Allahabad (d) Varanasi

Ans. (d) Varanasi

11. Give reason for the following.
    Large scale industries are capital intensive.
    (a) They need vast land to set up industry.
    (b) They need more labour.
    (c) They need heavy machinery to run its business.
    (d) All of the above

Ans. (d) All of the above

12. Give reason for the following.
    Small scale industry is called labour intensive industry.
    (a) It needs skilled white collar workers.
    (b) It uses more labour instead of capital.
    (c) Its capital need is also more.
    (d) In this industry workers are needed in weaving industry only.

Ans. (b) It uses more labour instead of capital.

13. Give reason for the following.
    Petroleum industry is a basic industry.
    (a) It is a large industry.
    (b) It provides its products to other industries.
    (c) It gets raw materials from other industries.
    (d) All of the above

Ans. (b) It provides its products to other industries.

14. Give reason for the following.
    Sugar industries are located in the vicinity of sugarcane producing fields.
    (a) Sugarcane is the second important raw material for sugar industry.
    (b) Sugarcane must be crushed within 24 hours after harvesting.
    (c) Sugar industries are small scale industries which need small area.
    (d) None of the above

Ans. (b) Sugarcane must be crushed within 24 hours after harvesting.

15. Give reason for the following.
    The cost of sugar production is high in India.
    (a) Sugarcane crushing season is short in India.
    (b) Old and obsolete machinery restricts the growth of sugar industries.
    (c) Labor output is very low in sugar industry.
    (d) All of the above

Ans. (d) All of the above

16. Which of the following statements is correct about manufacturing?
(i) It helps to strengthen agriculture.
(ii) It provides employment to a large population of India.
(iii) It produces goods for defense purposes.

Codes
(a) Only (i) (b) Only (ii) (c) Only (iii) (d) All of these

Ans. (d) All of these

17. Which of the following statements is incorrect?
(i) Agro-based industry is classified on the basis of raw material.
(ii) Sugar, jute, cotton industries etc. are examples of cottage industry.
(iii) TISCO is an example of public sector industry.

Codes
(a) Only (i) (b) Only (ii)
(c) Only (iii) (d) Both (ii) and (iii)

Ans. (d) Both (ii) and (iii)

18. Match the following.

List-I	List-II
A. Mineral based industry	1. Basis of ownership and management
B. Heavy industry	2. Basis of size and investment
C. Large scale industry	3. Basis of nature of products
D. Joint sector	4. Basis of raw material

Codes

	A	B	C	D		A	B	C	D
(a)	1	2	3	4	(b)	2	1	4	3
(c)	3	4	1	2	(d)	4	3	2	1

Ans. (d)

19. Match the following.

List-I (Industries)	List-II (Examples)
A. Mineral based industry	1. Iron and steel Industry
B. Heavy industry	2. Shipbuilding industry
C. Medium scale industry	3. Amul
D. Cooperative sector	4. Cycle manufacturing

Codes

	A	B	C	D		A	B	C	D
(a)	1	2	3	4	(b)	2	1	4	3
(c)	3	4	1	2	(d)	4	3	2	1

Ans. (b)

20. Match the following.

List-I	List-II
A. Maharashtra	1. Solapur cotton textile centre
B. Gujarat	2. Surat cotton textile centre
C. West Bengal	3. Kolkata cotton textile centre
D. Madhya Pradesh	4. Gwalior cotton textile centre

Codes

	A	B	C	D		A	B	C	D
(a)	1	2	3	4	(b)	2	1	4	3
(c)	3	4	1	2	(d)	4	3	2	1

Ans. (a)

Section-II

Short Questions

1. (i) How has industrialisation helped India?
(ii) What is the need of rapid industrialisation in India?

Ans. (i) Industrialisation has helped India by transforming it towards industrial development.
(ii) Rapid industrilisation strengthens the economy by providing employment to a large number of population.

2. Mention two reasons, why industrial development is important for India?
Or How are the industries important for India? **[2023]**

Ans. Two reasons why industrial development is important for India are
(i) It provides employment to a large number of people.
(ii) It supports agriculture by providing farm machinery, fertilisers etc.

3. (i) How would you classify industries?
(ii) How would you classify the industries on the basis of ownership in India?

Ans. (i) The industries are classified on the basis of raw materials, size, location, type of product manufactured etc.
(ii) The industries are classified on the basis of ownership in India as public sector, private sector, joint sector, co-operative sector.

4. Differentiate between agro-based and mineral based industry giving one example for each. **[2017]**

Ans. Differences between agro-based and mineral-based industry are

Agro-based	Mineral-based
The industries that depend on agricultural products for raw materials are agro-based industry.	The industries that depend on minerals for raw materials are mineral based industry.
For example, cotton and textile industry.	For example, iron and steel industry.

5. What is the difference between a public sector industry and one which is in the private sector? Give an example of industry in each of the two sectors. **[Specimen Paper Semester-2 [2022]**

Ans. Differences between public sector and private sector industries are

Public Sector	Private Sector
Owned and controlled by the Government (State or Central)	Owned and controlled by private group of people or individual
For example, Oil India, Railways, GAIL, BHEL.	For example, TISCO, Reliance, Wipro, Birla Mills.

6. What do you understand by ancillary industries?

Ans. Ancillary industries are the type which prepare spare parts and components for big industries engaged in the manufacturing of buses, aircraft, heavy electrical industry, engines and locomotives.

7. Distinguish between the industries that require huge capital and the industries that use more labour.

Ans. Differences between industries which require huge capital and industries which require more labour are

Industries which require huge capital	Industries which require more labour
The industries that require huge capital are large scale industries.	The industries that require more labour are small scale industries.
These are also called capital intensive industries.	These are also called labour intensive industries.

8. (i) Mention two reasons why the sugar industry has developed in Maharashtra.

(ii) Give two reasons for the importance of the silk industry in India.

Ans. (i) Sugar industry has developed in Maharashtra due to following reasons

(a) Due to large production of sugarcane.

(b) Crushing period is more.

(ii) Two reasons for the importance of the silk industry in India are

(a) India earns foreign exchange by exporting it.

(b) It provides employment to a large number of people.

9. Mention two problems faced by the sugar industry in India.

Ans. The two problems faced by the sugar industry are

(i) The quality of sugarcane produced in India is poor having low yield and sucrose content is also very low.

(ii) The sugar mills do not run throughout the year thus, creating problem of regular income for the workers.

10. "Though Uttar Pradesh has the largest number of sugar mills yet Maharashtra is the largest producer of sugar." Give any two reasons to justify the statement. **[2017]**

Ans. The two reasons for Maharashtra being the largest producer of sugar are

(i) Maharashtra has maritime climate therefore, it does not face extreme weather conditions like frost and loo as in Uttar Pradesh.

(ii) The black soil available in Maharashtra is more suitable for cultivation of sugarcane than Alluvial soil. Also the state has better transport facilities.

11. Mention two problems of the cotton textile industry in India. **[2018, 2016]**

Ans. The problems faced by the cotton textile industries are

(i) Textile industry depends on cotton and its cultivation depends on seasons which creates a problem of availability.

(ii) Indian textile industry is facing the problem of outdated machinery.

12. Give two reasons for the importance of the jute industry in the Ganga-Brahmaputra delta region. **[2016]**

Ans. The reasons for the importance of the jute industry in the Ganga-Brahmaputra delta region are

(i) The Ganga-Brahmaputra basin supplies the raw material, it constitutes about 90% of the jute production.

(ii) The region is well-connected with network of transport and also water transport is easily available.

13. (i) Why is the silk industry considered as a small scale industry? Name the two types of silk produced in India.

(ii) Name two important silk-weaving centres in Karnataka.

Ans. (i) Silk industry is considered as a small scale industry as it requires little investment and more labour. So it is a labour intensive industry.

Two types of silk produced in India is tassar silk and muga silk.

(ii) Two important silk weaving centres in Karnataka are Mysore and Bengaluru.

14. What is sericulture? Name any two types of silk. **[2010]**

Ans. The rearing of silkworms for the production of silk is called 'sericulture'.

The two types of silk are Tussar and Muga silk.

15. 'Karnataka has developed as an important state for the growth of the silk industry.' State any two factors. **[2019]**

Or State two factors which favour the silk industry in Karnataka. **[2012]**

Ans. Factors favouring the silk industry in Karnataka are

(i) Karnataka has ideal climate conditions for the rearing of silkworms.

(ii) Mulberry trees which are suited for raring silkworms grow well in Karnataka.

16. (i) State two problems faced by the silk industry of India.

(ii) Mention the most important factor for location of sugar industries. **[2020]**

Ans. (i) The two problems faced by the silk industry of India are

(a) It is facing tough competition from artificial silk which is cheaper and needs less maintenance.

(b) The import of cheaper and better quality silk from China is proving to be very harmful for the Indian silk industry.

(ii) Favourable factors for location of sugar industries are

- Availability of raw inaterial i.e. sugarcane.
- Availability of capital.
- Availability of cheap labour.

17. Identify the type of indsutry for the following products.

(i) Carpet weaving (ii) Post and telegraph

(iii) Silk industry

Ans. (i) Cottage industry (ii) Electronic industry

(iii) Small scale/Animal based industry

18. State two problems of steel industry.

Ans. Problems of steel industry are as follows

(i) **Huge Investment** It needs huge capital for its set-up.

(ii) **Inefficiency in Production** This increases cost of production as labour is not utilised properly.

19. Answer the following questions

(i) What are basic industries?

(ii) Give one example of a basic industry in India. [2020]

Ans. (i) Basic industries are those industries which supply their products or raw materials to manufacture other goods.

(ii) Iron and steel, copper smelting and aluminium smelting are the examples of basic industries.

20. Name one integrated iron and steel plant in the private sector. Where does it obtain its iron and coal from? [2018, 2014]

Ans. Tata iron and steel plant is the integrated steel plant in the private sector. It obtain its iron and coal from

- **Iron** Singhbhum in Jharkhand.
- **Coal** Jharia in Jharkhand.

21. "The Iron and steel industry constitutes the backbone of modern industrial economy." Give two reasons to justify the statement. [2017]

Ans. Iron and steel industry constitutes the backbone of modern industrial economy as it lays the foundation of other industries due to the following reasons

(i) Most of the other industries such as automobiles, locomotives, rail tracks, shipbuilding, machine building, bridges, dams and many other industries and commercial activities depend upon iron and steel industry for raw material.

(ii) It also provides employment to a large number of people.

22. Answer the following questions.

(i) Define a mini steel plant.

(ii) With which large scale industry would you identify the following manufacturing centres?

(a) Kanpur (b) Rourkela

(c) Pune (d) Mangalore

Ans. (i) A mini steel plant produce alloy steel, mild steel and stainless steel. Mini steel plants utilise scrap or sponge iron from large steel plants as raw materials. So, they help in recycling of iron.

(ii) (a) Cotton textile

(b) Iron and Steel Industry

(c) Automobile

(d) Chemical and fertiliser

23. Mention two advantages that a mini-steel plant has over an integrated iron and steel plant. [2016]

Ans. The two advantages of mini steel plant over an integrated iron and steel plant are

(i) It uses an electric arc furnace which conserves coal.

(ii) It requires small capital investment as compared to large steel plants.

24. (i) Name an iron and steel plant which was established with British collaboration. [2018, 2016]

(ii) From where does it get its supply of

(a) Iron ore (b) Manganese

(c) Coal

Ans. (i) Durgapur steel plant was established with British collaboration.

(ii) Durgapur steel plant gets its supply of

(a) iron-ore from Singhbhum and Keonjhar

(b) manganese from Sundergarh

(c) coal from Jhansi, Raniganj.

25. (i) Name an iron and steel industry setup in Odisha with the help of a famous German firm.

(ii) From where does the industry get its iron ore and manganese? [2017]

Ans. (i) The Rourkela steel plant was set up in Odisha with collaboration of the West German firm Krupps and Demag during the Second Five Year Plan. It started its production in 1959.

(ii) Rourkela steel plant gets its iron ore from Sundergarh and Keonjhar districts of Odisha and manganese from Barajmda of Jharkhand.

26. Where do the following iron and steel plants get their supply of iron ore from? [2019]

(i) Bhilai iron and steel plant.

(ii) Visakhapatnam steel plant.

Ans. (i) Bhilai iron and steel plant get its supply of iron ore from Dalli-Rajhara range which is just 80 km South of Bhilai.

(ii) Visakhapatnam steel plant get its supply of iron ore from Bailadila mines of Chhattisgarh.

27. Give two geographical reasons for the growth of IT industries in Bengaluru. [2011]

Ans. The two geographical reasons for growth of IT industries in Bengaluru are

(i) Presence of already existing electronic industry made it easier.

(ii) Availabitity of highly skilled labour.

28. Answer the following questions.
(i) State the importance of electronics in defence.
(ii) Mention one important requirement of the electronics industry.

Ans. (i) Electronics provides the modern means of communication used in defence.
(ii) It requires huge investment and research facilities.

29. Mention two reasons for the development of the petrochemical industry in India. [2010]

Ans. Two reasons for the development of petrochemical industry in India are
(i) Petrochemical industries do not depend on agriculture hence, they are not seasonal.
(ii) The raw material used in the petrochemical industry is easily available.

30. What are petrochemicals? Name any two products made from petrochemicals. [2012]

Ans. The petrochemicals are mainly chemicals derived from petroleum resources like coal, gas and petroleum.

Plastics and acrylic fibres are two products made from petrochemicals.

31. Name two raw materials used in the petrochemical industry and state two advantages of petrochemical products. [2014]

Ans. Two raw materials used in petrochemical industry are ethylene and benzene.

Two advantages of petrochemical industries are
(i) The raw material are easily available since they are not agro-based.
(ii) The products produced under this industry are durable.

32. (i) Mention two reasons for the importance of the electronic industry in India's development.
(ii) What is a petrochemical industry? Mention two reasons why petrochemical products are replacing traditional raw materials.

Ans. (i) Two reasons for the importance of electronic industry are
(a) Electronic industry provides telecommunication equipments.
(b) Electronic industry provides tools and implements needed in other industries.
(ii) Petrochemical industry is an industry where organic chemicals are derived from petroleum and then they are processed into various synthetic products.
Petrochemical products are replacing traditional raw materials because they are cheaper, easily available and needs less maintenance.

Long Questions

1. Differentiate between the following.
(i) Public sector and private sector.
(ii) Large scale and small scale industries.
(iii) Agro-based and mineral-based industry.

Ans. (i) Public sector industries are owned and managed either by the Central Government or by the State Government. On the other hand, private sector industries are owned and managed by an individual or some group of people.
(ii) Large-scale industries need large amount of investment and large number of labour. They use more capital so they are capital intensive. On the other hand, small-scale industries are very small and are managed by private individuals. They do not require large capital and only employ few workers.
(iii) Agro-based industries use the produce of agricultural sector. Some examples of these industries are sugar, jute, cotton, vegetable oil, coffee, tea and other food processing industries. On the other hand, mineral based industries use minerals as their raw material like ferrous metallic minerals, non-ferrous metallic minerals and non-metallic minerals.

2. Differentiate the industries on the basis of the finished goods or end product they provide.

Ans. On the basis of finished goods or end product the industries are classified as heavy and light industry. Differences between these two are

Heavy Industries	Light Industries
Heavy industries produce capital goods and consumer durables that are bulky.	Light industries produce goods of light weight
E.g. cars, engineering goods, machines.	E.g. electronics, cycles, computers.
Heavy industries require huge capital, scientific knowledge, large labour force and huge amount of raw materials.	Light industries require less capital and labour in comparison to heavy industries.

3. Answer the following questions
(i) State two reasons for the concentration of the sugar industry in Uttar Pradesh.
(ii) Mention any two ways in which the agro-based industries have affected the economy of India.

Ans. (i) The two reasons for the concentration of sugar industry in Uttar Pradesh are
(a) Sugarcane grows well in the fertile plains of Uttar Pradesh.
(b) There is cheap and easy availability of labour to work in the sugar mills.

(ii) The two ways in which agro-based industries have affected the economy are
  (a) Agro-based industries increase the demand and efficiency of the agricultural products.
  (b) They provide employment to a large section of the society.

4. Answer the following questions
  (i) Explain why sugarcane must be crushed within 24 hours of harvesting.
  (ii) Name four sugar mill centres in the Northern plains.

Ans. (i) Sugarcane must be crushed within 24 hours of harvesting as the sucrose content present in it, that is used to make sugar, keeps on decreasing in the sugarcane.
  (ii) Four sugar mill centres in Northern Plains are Saharanpur, Meerut, Gonda and Gorakhpur.

5. Mention three factors that have helped the sugar industry flourish in the peninsular region rather than in the Northern regions of India.

Ans. Three factors favouring sugar industry in peninsular region than Northern India are
  (i) The peninsular India has tropical climate throughout the year that favours the growth of sugarcane.
  (ii) The sucrose content in sugarcane is higher and crushing season is longer in peninsular India.
  (iii) States like Maharashtra, Tamil Nadu in peninsular India have better transportation facilities and modern sugar mills.

6. With reference to sugar industries answer the following questions. [2019]
  (i) Why should these industries be located close to the sugarcane growing areas?
  (ii) Name two by-products of the sugar industry.
  (iii) Mention one leading sugar producing state in North India and one in South India.

Ans. (i) Sugarcane must be crushed within 24 hours of harvesting as the sucrose content present in it, that is used ot make sugar, keeps on decrasing in the sugarcane. Thus, sugar industries should be located close to the sugrcane growing areas.
  (ii) Molasses and bagasse are by-products of the sugar industry.
  (iii) Leading sugar producing state in North India is Uttar Pradesh and leading sugar producing state in South India is Maharashtra.

7. Mention three factors, that favour the concentration of the cotton textile mills in Mumbai.

Ans. The factors that favour the concentration of cotton textile mills in Mumbai are
  (i) Mumbai has proper network of roads and railways that facilitates easy transportation from mills.
  (ii) It has proper network of banks that provides credit for setting up of cotton mills.
  (iii) It is a very important port that provides opportunity for import and export of cotton goods.

8. Give three factors that favour the cotton industry in Kolkata.

Ans. Three factors that favour the cotton textile industry in Kolkata are
  (i) It has proper supply of coal from Raniganj to run the industries.
  (ii) It has huge supply of cheap labour and also has high demand of cotton due to humid climate.
  (iii) It is facilitated with good network of roads and railways.

9. (i) Mention two reasons for the importance of the cotton textile industry. **[Specimen Paper Semester-II 2022]**
  (ii) Mention two reasons responsible for its poor performance.

Ans. (i) The two reasons for importance of the cotton textile industry are
  (a) It provides employment to huge section of population.
  (b) It brings lot of foreign exchange.
  (ii) Two reasons responsible for the poor performance of cotton textile industry are
  (a) **Lack of Raw Material** After the partition, India had to bear a huge loss of long-staple cotton as most of the centres went to Pakistan. Thus in order to fulfil its requirement, India imports cotton from Pakistan, Kenya, Uganda, Sudan, Egypt, USA and Peru.
  (b) **Old and Obsolete Machinery** Many mills in India are very old and are very inefficient. They have obsolete machineries as compared to some other developed countries. This proves to be an obstruction in higher production.

10. How is cotton facing stiff competition from other goods?

Ans. Cotton is facing stiff competition from synthetic fibres or artificial fibres that are made from petrochemicals like nylon, terylene etc in the following ways
- These are cheaper and needs less maintenance.
- These synthetic fibres are more durable than natural fibre like cotton and readily pick-up different dyes.
- As compared to natural fibres, many synthetic fibres are more water resistant and stain resistant.
- Natural fibres like cotton are much more sensitive than synthetic fibres.

11. With reference to cotton textile industry, answer the following question. [2020, 2017]
  (i) Give two reasons why Mumbai is an important cotton textile industry.
  (ii) Mention two more important centres of cotton textile industry in India.

Ans. (i) Refer to answer of Long Question Q. 7.
  (ii) Two important centres of cotton textile industry in India are Ahmedabad and Madurai.

12. State the contribution of Maharashtra in sugar and cotton industries.

Ans. The contribution of Maharashtra in sugar and cotton industries are

- Maharashtra is the largest producer of sugar in India. It contributes to more than 1/3rd of the total production of sugar in the country.
- Maharashtra is also the largest producer of cotton in India. It produces about 46 per cent of the total production and is also called 'Lancashire' of India.

13. Give a geographical reason for each of the following. [2018]

(i) Silk industry is doing particularly well in Karnataka.

(ii) Petrochemical products are gaining popularity in modern times.

(iii) The electronics industry is proving to be an asset for our country in the field of education.

Ans. (i) Silk industry is doing particularly well in Karnataka because of the temperature as it ranges from 16°C to 31°C and other favourable climatic conditions prevailing in Karnataka.

(ii) Petrochemical products are gaining popularity in modern times because they have greater variety and are cheaper. These products are more durable and require less maintenance.

(iii) The electronics industry is proved to be an asset for India in the field of education because it makes revolution to encourage the education related electronic items like personal computers, calculators, GPS automotive, digital cameras, etc.

14. Give geographical reasons for the following.

(i) Kolkata has many cotton mills though cotton is not grown in West Bengal.

(ii) Karnataka is an important centre for silk.

(iii) India produces very little sugar though it is one of the largest producers of sugarcane in the world.

Ans. (i) Kolkata has many cotton mills though cotton is not grown in West Bengal because Kolkata is well connected, has a port, banking facilities, cheap labour and power supply, so lots of cotton manufacturing units are set up there. Due to humid weather conditions, there is high demand for cotton.

(ii) Refer to answer of Short Questions Q. 15 (i).

(iii) Though India is the largest producer of sugarcane yet it produces very little sugar because the sugar mills have old and obsolete machinery which hampers sugar production. Also the location of sugar mills are far from sugarcane fields.

15. With reference to the silk industry, answer the following.

(i) Why is Karnataka the largest producer of mulberry silk?

(ii) Mention two varieties of non-mulberry silk produced in India.

(iii) Name one silk weaving centre each in UP and in Tamil Nadu. [2016]

Ans. (i) The most important factors responsible for making Karnataka the largest producer in mulberry silk are

- Availability of favourable climate for rearing silkworm
- Availability of Bombyx mori silkworm
- Recent introduction of new technology of handling Bombyx mori silkworm.

(ii) Non-mulberry silk produced in India are Tussar and Muga.

(iii) Silk weaving centre in UP is Varanasi and in Tamil Nadu is Kanchipuram.

16. Give the geographic term for each of the following.

(i) Non-mulberry silk produced in Madhya Pradesh.

(ii) Rejected cane after crushing.

(iii) The rearing of silkworms to obtain silk. [2017]

Ans. (i) Tussar silk (ii) Bagasse (iii) Sericulture

17. Give a reason for each of the following. [2019]

(i) Ahmedabad is an important cotton textile producing centre in India.

(ii) Cottage industries are significant for our economy.

(iii) Petrochemical industries are usually located close to the oil refineries.

Ans. (i) Ahmedabad is an important cotton textile producing centre as it is situated in the heart of cotton growing area, hence the major raw material is easily available. The humid climate is ideal for spinning and weaving. The flat terrain and easy availability of land and cheap labour from densely populated states of Gujarat and Maharashtra are suitable for the establishment of the cotton mills here.

(ii) Cottage industries are significant for our economy as it help in increasing employment and economic development of India. These improve the growth of the country by increasing urban and rural growth. These also create self empolyment and reduce unemployment. Thus, these industries are significant for economy.

(iii) Raw material for petrochemical industry includes petroleum, LPG, coal, etc. Thus, this industry is situated near oil refineries to obtain the raw materials Ethylene and Benzene.

18. State any three advantages of mini steel plants.

Ans. Three advantages of mini steel plants are

(i) Mini steel plants do not require huge capital investment like integrated steel plant.

(ii) Mini steel plants use scrap or sponge iron as raw materials, that is easily available and also helps in recycling of iron.

(iii) These plants are set up at local areas so they suit local needs and cater to local demands.

19. (i) Mention two problems faced by the sugar industry of India. **[2023]**
(ii) Where is Tata Steel located ?
(iii) Why is the Silk industry losing the market in recent time ?

Ans. (i) Two problems faced by sugar industry are
- Old and inefficient methods of production
- Lack of efficient transportation

(ii) Tata Steel is located in the city of Jamshedpur.
(iii) Silk industry is losing the market in recent times because domestic silk manufacturers are facing intense competition from China and India's share in the global market is declining gradually.

20. With reference to the steel plants in India answer the following questions. **[2010]**
(i) What are integrated steel plants?
(ii) Name one integrated steel plant in the public sector. From where does this plant get its requirement of iron ore and coal?

Ans. (i) Integrated steel plants are the plants where all the processes of making steel such as melting of iron ore, processing of steel and shaping of metals are carried out at one place.
(ii) One integrated steel plant in the public sector is Rourkela steel plant.
This plant gets iron ore from Sundargarh and Keonjhar district and coal from Jharia, Talcher and Korba fields.

21. Write three favourable factors that led to the development of Bhilai steel plant.

Ans. The factors that led to the development of Bhilai steel plant are
(i) Availability of iron ore, coal, limestone, manganese from the nearby mines lying within a range of 30-80 kms.
(ii) Availability of cheap labour and regular water supply from the nearby areas.
(iii) The steel plant located in the Kolkata-Nagpur railway line for easy transportation of goods.

22. With reference to Rourkela steel plant answer the following. **[Specimen Paper Semester-II 2022]**
(i) Name the state in which it is located.
(ii) Which country helped India to establish this steel plant?
(iii) From where it gets
(a) Iron ore (b) Coal
(c) Limestone

Ans. (i) Rourkela steel plant is situated in the Sundergarh district of Odisha.
(ii) Germany helped India to establish Rourkela Steel plant in the country in 1959 during the Second Five Year Plan.
(iii) (a) Iron ore Iron ore comes from Bonaigarh, Mayurbanj and Keonjhar districts.
(b) Coal It gets coal from Raniganj, Jharia and Talcher.
(c) Limestone Birmitrapur.

23. Briefly answer the following. **[2020]**
(i) From where does the Rourkela Steel Plant obtain its supply of coal?
(ii) From where does the Tata Iron and Steel Plant obtain its supply of iron ore?
(iii) Name two cities that are important for the production of Electronics.

Ans. (i) Rourkela Steel Plant obtain its supply of coal from Jharia, Talcher and Korba coal fields.
(ii) Tata iron and steel plants obtains its supply of iron ore from Noamundi of Singhbhum region and Mayurbhauj.
(iii) Bengaluru and Hyderabad are important for the production of electronics.

24. Name the following.
(i) First seashore based city on the East Coast of India which has a iron and steel industry.
(ii) The iron and steel plant set-up with German collaboration.
(iii) A city which has a plant manufacturing Maruti cars.

Ans. (i) Visakhapatnam is the first seashore based steel plant which was started in 1992.
(ii) Rourkela plant was set up in the Sundergarh district of Odisha with the technical help of German firm Krupps and Demag in 1959 during the Second Five Year Plan.
(iii) Gurugram in Haryana has a plant manufacturing Maruti cars.

25. Give one important centre of production of each of the following.
(i) Integral Coach Factory (ICF)
(ii) Bharat Heavy Electrical Limited (BHEL)
(iii) Hindustan Machine Tools (HMT)

Ans. (i) Integral Coach Factory (ICF) is a manufacturer of rail coaches located in Chennai, Tamil Nadu. It was established in 1952, is owned and operated by the Indian Railways.
(ii) Bharat Heavy Electricals Limited (BHEL) owned and founded by the Government of India, is an engineering and manufacturing company based in New Delhi. It was established in 1964. It is India's largest power generation equipment manufacturer.
(iii) Hindustan Machine Tools Limited (HMT) is a state-owned manufacturing company. Its 6 manufacturing units are situated at Bengaluru (Mother unit), Kochi, Hyderabad (2 units), Pinjore and Ajmer.

26. Give a reason for each of the following.

(i) The largest mineral based industry in India.

(ii) Mini steel plants cause less pollution than integrated steel plants.

(iii) The electronic industries has made an impact on both entertainment and education.

Ans. (i) Iron and steel industry is the largest mineral based industry in India as iron and steel is a pivotal element in the heavy industrial-structure and forms the backbone of industrial development. It gives the raw material for other industries such as automobile, locomotives, railways, shipbuilding, machine and tools, dams, manufacture of defence equipment etc.

(ii) Mini steel plants causes less pollution because they uses electric and induction furnace for processing.

(iii) Electronic industry give us various products like television, computers, laptops, tabs, radio, DTH etc. All these electronic products have become the major source of entertainments as well as education. For example, electronic gadgets with help of internet provides us the information we require for educating ourself and our childrens.

27. Name a manufacturing centre for each of the following industries. **[2014]**

(i) Engines for MIG aircraft. (ii) Diesel locomotives

(iii) Software

Ans. (i) Koraput has the engine division of Hindustan Aeronautics Limited (HAL), which is a defence enterprise of the Government of India. This factory manufactures aircraft engines for MIG and Sukhoi fighter aircraft.

(ii) The diesel locomotives are manufactured by the diesel locomotive works in Varanasi.

(iii) The manufacturing centres of software industries are Bengaluru and Pune.

28. Answer the following questions.

(i) What is the significance of the electronics industry in recent times?

(ii) Name two cities that have leading software companies.

Ans. (i) The significance of the electronics industry is that it has revolutionised the lifestyle of the people today. It covers a wide range of products including transistor sets, televisions, telephone exchanges, telecommunication, computers and various equipments for posts and telegraph, defence, railway and meteorological departments.

(ii) The cities that have leading software companies are

(a) **Bengaluru** It is the IT capital of India and a global information technology hub in the country. The city is known as the 'Silicon Valley' of India with large number of software companies in India and many top Indian firms like Infosys, Wipro, Mindtree are headquartered in Bengaluru.

(b) **Hyderabad** It is also known as 'Cyberabad' and 'HITEC City'. It is the second largest IT exporter in India and the first destination in India for the microsoft development centre.

29. Name the following. **[2018]**

(i) A city most famous for electronics and hence called 'The Electronics Capital of India'.

(ii) The location of an iron and steel industry set up with German collaboration.

(iii) A by-product of sugar industry which is used in the manufacture of wax and shoe polish.

Ans. (i) Bangalore also known as Bengaluru is the electronic capital of India because the presence of software industries, aerospace, telecommunications and heavy industries.

(ii) Rourkela steel plant in Odisha was set up by German collaboration in 1960s. It is operated by Steel Authority of India Limited (SAIL).

(iii) Pressmud is a by-product of sugar industry which is used in the manufacture of wax and shoe polish. This by-product is also known as sugarcane filter cake mud.

30. Name two products for each of the following industries. **[2017]**

(i) Petrochemical industry

(ii) Heavy engineering industry

(iii) Electronic industry

Ans. (i) Two products of petrochemical industry are polythene and PVC.

(ii) Two product of heavy engineering industry are ships and aircrafts.

(iii) Two products of electronic industries are computers and television.

31. Give a reason for each of the following. **[2016]**

(i) Products made from petrochemicals are growing in popularity.

(ii) A heavy engineering industry requires huge capital investment.

(iii) The electronics industry contributes to the development of the country.

Ans. (i) Refer to answer of Long Questions Q. 13. (ii)

(ii) A heavy engineering industry requires huge capital investment because it requires heavy machinery, large scale labours, heavy infrastructure etc.

(iii) The electronics industry contributes to the development of the country because it covers diverse areas such as space exploration, defence equipments.

32. (i) What are the benefits of using petrochemical products? **[Specimen Paper Semester-II 2022]**
(ii) Who has the electronic industry revolutionised the entertainment sector?

Ans. (i) Following are the benefits of using petrochemical products
- These products are made from petrochemicals thus, have greater variety and are cheaper.
- These products are moe durable and require less maintenance.

(ii) The electronic industry has revolutionised the entertainment sector by proving a side range of products including transistor sets, televisions, telephone exchanges, telecommunication, and computers and so on.

33. Answer the following questions.
(i) Name any two textile industries using any animal fibres. Name an important state where these industries are located.
(ii) Give two reasons for each of the following.
(a) Kolkata is an important cotton manufacturing centre even though West Bengal is not a leading producer of cotton.
(b) The wool industry is not as well developed as compared to the cotton industry in India.

Ans. (i) Wool industry in Punjab and Silk industry in Karnataka use animal fibres.
(ii) (a) The soil and climatic conditions in West Bengal are not suited for cotton cultivation. However, Kolkata is well connected, has a port, banking facilities, cheap labour and power supply, so lots of cotton manufacturing units are set up there. Due to humid weather conditions, there is high demand for cotton.
(b) Wool industry is restricted to Northern India as winters are very cold over there. Rest of the country have tropical type of climate and does not need woollens. So, the demand for cotton is throughout the country while demand for wool in restricted to North India only.

34. Answer the following questions.
(i) Name and define two important by-products of the sugar industry.
(ii) Give two reasons why the state of Punjab is the largest producer of woollen textiles. **[2011]**

Ans. (i) The two important by-products of sugar industry are
(a) **Molasses** It is thick, dark brown syrup. It is obtained in the process of sugar manufacture which involves the process of crystallisation and centrifugation.
(b) **Bagasse** It is the left over cane after crushing. It is used as raw material for paper industry.

(ii) The state of Punjab is a leading producer of woollens because
(a) Raw material i.e. wool is available from Jammu and Kashmir.
(b) Due to cold winters, demand of woollens is high there.

Picture Based Question

1. Study the picture given below and answer the following questions.

TISCO

(i) What is the full form of the plant shown in the picture?
(ii) To which sector does this plant belong?
(iii) Where it is located?

Ans. (i) The full form of TISCO is Tata Iron and Steel Company.
(ii) The plant belongs to private sector.
(iii) It is located in Jamshedpur in Jharkhand.

2. Study the picture given below and answer the following questions.

(i) Name the industry shown in the picture.
(ii) Give a brief description of this industry.

Ans. (i) Petrochemical industry.
(ii) It is an important organic chemical industry which derives its chemicals from petroleum resources and product likes LPG and Coal. Petrochemicals are used for manufacturing various goods like synthetic rubber, synthetic fibre, ferrous, non-ferrous metals, plastics, dyestuffs, drugs, insecticides and many pharmaceuticals. This industry also produces resins, adhesives, plastic sheets, paints and furniture covering for household items.

Chapter Assessment

Section-I

Multiple Choice Questions

1. Which one of the following favour the location of Industry?
   (a) Accessible to forest
   (b) Availability of entertainment facility
   (c) Availability of raw material
   (d) Availability of food
2. In the present day world of globalisation, India needs to be ....
   (a) less competitive and close the doors to globalisation.
   (b) produce goods in quantity disregarding quality.
   (c) more efficient in industry.
   (d) more dependent on agriculture.
3. Tata steel is a company in the .... sector.
   (a) public
   (b) private
   (c) joint
   (d) co-operative
4. Most of the integrated steel plants in India are located in which region?
   (a) Malwa Plateau
   (b) Bundelkhand Plateau
   (c) Meghalaya Plateau
   (d) Chotanagpur Plateau

Section-II

Short Questions

1. What is the importance of iron and steel plant in India?
2. What is the importance of heavy industries in India?
3. State three examples of heavy engineering industries.
4. Explain the development of aircraft industry.
5. What do you understand by medium-scale industry?
6. (i) Why is the iron and steel industry called a 'basic industry'?
   (ii) Define a mini steel plant.
7. With which industry would you identify the following manufacturing centres?
   (i) Kanpur (ii) Rourkela
   (iii) Pune (iv) Mangalore
8. Why is the cotton textile industry called an 'agro-based industry'?
9. Name the state that produces the most cotton and silk products respectively.

Long Questions

1. Write in details about the advantage of petrochemical products.
2. Write in details about the different production units of petrochemical industries.
3. Explain in details about the distribution of sugar industry in India.
4. Explain few problems faced by the cotton industries as well as jute industries.
5. Write about the features of mulberry silk.
6. (i) State two reasons for the growing importance in the status of petrochemical industries.
   (ii) Name two products of the petroleum industry.
7. State two conditions necessary for the setting up of a heavy engineering industry.
8. (i) State two major problems faced by the sugar industry.
   (ii) Name two by-products of the sugar industry. Also mention their uses.
9. (i) State one of the main problems of the silk industry.
   (ii) Why are synthetic fibres popular?

CHAPTER 13

Transport

SYLLABUS

Transport • Importance and Modes • Roadways, Railways, Airways and Waterways • Advantages and disadvantages.

The system through which people and goods move from one place to another is called transport system. Good transport network helps in the development of industrialisation and urbanisation. A developing country like India needs an efficient and wide transport system.

Importance of Transport

- Transport links the backward areas to the urban cities and reduces regional industrial disparity.
- It helps in proper utilisation of natural resources lying in hills and forest.
- It protects the people during war, natural calamities and crisis.
- It helps in transportation of raw material to industries.
- It helps in the movement of goods during any calamities.

Modes of Transport

The modes of transport include roadways, railways, airways and waterways.

Roadways

It is very important means of transportation for the development of a country as, it is capable of connecting each and every area of a region with another. India has the second largest road network in the world after USA with about 56 lakh kilometre (approx) of roads. Road networks are classified into various types, which are

National Highways

These are the roads constructed and maintained by Central Government. These are well constructed long metalled roads which are stretched through length and breadth of the country.

These roads are meant for inter-state transport and movement of defence men and material in strategic areas. These also connect the state capitals, major cities, important ports, railway junctions, etc. The longest highway in India is NH-7, which is from Varanasi to Kanyakumari. The National Highways constitute only about 2 per cent of the total road length, but carry 40 per cent of the road traffic.

The **National Highway Authority of India** (NHAI) is responsible for the development, maintenance and management of National Highways in India. The National Highways Authority of India (NHAI) was operationalised in 1995.

Major projects undertaken by NHAI are

- **Golden Quadrilateral (GQ)** It is the largest express highway project (super highway) in India which is 5,846 km long, 4/6 lane, high density traffic corridor. It connects India's four largest metropolitan cities namely, Delhi, Mumbai, Kolkata and Chennai and thus, forms a quadrilateral. Bengaluru, Pune, Ahmedabad and Surat are also connected by this network.

- **North-South and East-West Corridors** These are part of Golden Quadrilateral project. It consists of 4/6 lane expressways. North-South corridor aims at connecting Srinagar in Jammu and Kashmir with Kanniyakumari in Tamil Nadu (including Kochchi-Salem Spur). The East-West corridor has been planned to connect Silchar in Assam with the port town of Porbandar in Gujarat.

Freeways

Freeways are characterised as the highest class of controlled access highways. These are designed for high speed vehicular traffic. There are only two freeways in India Eastern Freeway and Western Freeway (or Coastal Freeway), to reduce traffic congestion in Mumbai (Island City).

Bandra Worli Sea Link (5,600 m), a part of Western Freeway, is India's first eight-lane freeway which was opened in 2009. It is officially known as the Rajiv Gandhi Sea-Link.

Expressways

Expressways are the most important features of land transport. These are highways which are planned for high-speed traffic, having few intersections, limited points of entry or exit.

The major expressways of India are

- **Agra-Lucknow Expressway** It is a 6 lane expressway which has reduced the travelling period between Agra and Lucknow. It has automatic traffic management systems which help to reduce road accidents and help even fog condition.
- **Yamuna Expressway** It is a controlled-access expressway which connects Greater Noida with Agra. It has 6 lanes and was formally inaugurated in 2012.
- **Ahmedabad-Vadodara Expressway** It is the first expressway of India which was opened in 2001. It is also India's **first 4 lane** and dual carriageway expressway project.
- **Delhi-Gurgaon Expressway** It is a part of Golden Quadrilateral Highway project which was opened for the public in 2008.
- **Mumbai-Pune Expressway** It is India's first 6 lane, concrete, high-speed, tolled expressway.
- **Noida-Greater Noida Expressway** This expressway is a 6 lane highway. It connects Noida (an industrial **suburb**[1] area) with Greater Noida (a new **suburb**) in Uttar Pradesh.
- **Delhi-Noida Direct Flyway** It is an 8 lane expressway. It connects Delhi to Noida, an industrial suburb.
- **Panipat Expressway** It is an elevated highway at Panipat in Haryana with a length of 10 km. It is a 6 lane expressway. It was built to decongest traffic on the Delhi-Amritsar route.
- **Bengaluru-Mysore Infrastructure Corridor** It is a 4 to 6 lane expressway in Karnataka with a length of 111 km. It connects Bengaluru with Mysore.

Some Other Expressways in India

Expressway Name	Distance	State
Jaipur-Kishangarh Expressway	90 km	Rajasthan
Allahabad Bypass	86 km	Uttar Pradesh
Durgapur Expressway	65 km	West Bengal
Chennai Bypass	32 km	Tamil Nadu
PV Narasimha Rao Elevated Expressway	11.6 km	Telangana
Hosur Road Elevated Expressway	9.9 km	Karnataka
Kona Expressway	08 km	West Bengal
Nehru Outer Ring Road [Hyderabad]	158 km	Telangana
Raipur-Bhilai-Durg Expressway	26 km	Chhattisgarh

State Highways

The roads linking to the state capital with its district headquarters are called State Highways. These are constructed and maintained by State Public Works Department. These roads are connected to the National Highways and State Highways of nearby states. These constitute 4 per cent of total road length in the country.

District Roads

The roads that connect district headquarters with tehsil headquarters and other rural areas of district are called district roads. They account for 14 per cent of the total road length of the country. These are maintained by Zila Parishad of the district.

Rural Roads

The roads that connect different villages to district are called rural roads. These roads cover about 80 per cent of the total road length in the country. There is regional variation in the density of rural roads because these are influenced by the nature of the terrain.

Border Roads

These are strategically important roads along the Northern and North-Eastern boundary of India. Border Roads Organisation (BRO) constructs and maintains roads in the border areas of the country. It was established in May 1960.

1 **Suburb** An area where people live, that is outside the central part of a town of city.

Advantages of Roadways

- Roadways helps to connect the remotest villages and hilly areas to towns, cities and plain areas.
- The cost of construction of roads is less than railway lines.
- Roads can be constructed even in irregular land and hilly regions where other transport system is difficult to develop.
- Roads provide the facility of door to door service which is very favourable and minimise the cost of loading and unloading of products and goods.
- The movement of products is safer in road transport as it has less chance of theft.
- Road transport is complimentary to the other means of transport as it offers a connection between railway stations and ports.

Disadvantages of Roadways

- Most of the roads are irregular, hence they are not suitable for regular vehicular traffic.
- Roads in India are not properly maintained.
- Roads in India are not strongly built. Most of it have weak pavement, unbridged level crossings and lack of wayside amenities and safety measures.
- Most of the Indian roads are heavily infested with traffic especially in cities. Same road is utilised by all type of vehicles with varied speeds.
- Road accidents frequently takes place and thus, it is not considered safe mode of transport.

Railways

Railways constitutes a principle means of transportation for freight and passengers. It provides the basic facilities to the people. The railways in India started in 1853 from Mumbai to Thane which covered a distance of about 34 km. After this, another railway line was opened from Kolkata and Raniganj in 1859. After Independence, huge development was made in railways.

India has one of the largest and busiest rail networks in the world. **Suburban rail**[2] networks constructed in many big cities to cater a large number of commuters. Mumbai, Chennai, Delhi, Kolkata, Hyderabad, Pune and Lucknow are the cities which currently have their own suburban networks. Metro networks are constructed in New Delhi, Kolkata, Chennai and Mumbai.

The overall railway system is managed by the Railway Board. Indian Railway transport a wide variety of goods ranging from mineral ores, fertilisers, iron and steel, etc. There are total **17 railway zones** in which the railway network has been divided. These zones are further divided into divisions.

Indian Railway Zones and Headquarters

Railway Zones	Headquarters
Central	Mumbai CST
Eastern	Kolkata
East Central	Hajipur
East Coast	Bhubaneswar
Northern	New Delhi
North Central	Allahabad
North Eastern	Gorakhpur
North East Frontier	Maligaon (Guwahati)
North Western	Jaipur
Southern	Chennai
South Central	Secunderabad
South Eastern	Kolkata
South East Central	Bilaspur
South Western	Hubli
Southern Coast	Visakhapatnam
Western	Mumbai (Church Gate)
West Central	Jabalpur

Railway Gauges

There are three types of railway gauges, which are based on width of track. These are

(i) **Broad Gauge** It has the width of about 1.676 metres and is installed in most part of the country. Broad gauge is also called 'India gauge' as it links major parts of India with the towns and Industrial centres.

(ii) **Metre Gauge** It is one metre in width and is mostly used in Northern Uttar Pradesh, Bihar, Assam, Western Rajasthan, Gujarat, Maharashtra, Karnataka and Tamil Nadu.

(iii) **Narrow Gauge** It is about 0.762 m in width. It is used mainly in mountainous regions such as Kalka, Shimla, Siliguri, Darjeeling and Otacamund.

Konkan Railway

One of the important achievements of the Indian Railways has been the construction of Konkan Railway in 1998. It is a broad gauge railway line. It is 760-km long rail route connecting Roha in Maharashtra to Mangalore in Karnataka. Asia's largest tunnel which is nearly 6.5 km long, also lies on this route. This is an undertaking of the governments of Maharashtra, Goa and Karnataka.

2 **Suburban Rail** It is passenger rail transport service that primarily operates within a metropolitan area, connecting commuters to a central city from adjacent suburbs or commuter town.

Advantages of Railways

- Railways are the chief means of transportation which help in smooth movement of heavy goods as well as perishable commodities to distant areas.
- It helps to move the raw material to the production point and manufactured goods to the markets.
- It helps in minimising the sufferings during natural disasters and helps to send the required food products and aid to the affected area.
- It has played a major role to bring the rural areas very close to the urban centres and reduced the travel time effectively.
- With its huge network stretched throughout the country, railways has helped to integrate and connect the whole country into a whole.
- It provides smooth movement of police forces, armed forces and defence equipments during the time of crisis.
- It is very comfortable form of journey as it allows the passenger to stretch and walk along the corridors.
- Modern berths are installed to allow the passengers to sleep comfortably during long distance travelling.

Disadvantages of Railways

- Rail tracks are very difficult to lay on irregular land such as hilly and forested areas as compared to Northern place which have dense network of railways.
- Train journey sometimes are very long and tiring, especially if we compare it with air journey.
- Trains cannot cross seas and oceans. It cannot be laid on the landscape which has loose soil base.
- Due to the electrification of trains there is an increase in the consumption of electricity and train fares.
- Lack of cleanliness and other basic facilities adds to the disadvantage of the railways.
- Rail transportation cannot provide door to door service.
- High cost is involved in construction of railway tracks.

Check Your LEARNING...

1. Which mode of transport provides door to door service?
2. What is suburb?
3. Name the first railway route of India.
4. Name the different gauges present in Indian Railways.
5. Name the headquarters of North Central railway zone.

Airways

Air transport is the fastest and most comfortable mode of transport. Air transport in India was started in 1911 when airmail operation commenced over a little distance of 10 km between Allahabad and Naini. Its real development took place in post-Independent period. The air transport was nationalised in 1953.

The **Airports Authority of India** (AAI) setup on 1st April, 1995 is responsible to enhance the expansion and modernisation of the operational, terminal and cargo facilities at the airports in the country. It is the nodal agency which provides safe and efficient air traffic services and **aeronautical**[3] communication services in the country.

Earlier, the air transport in India was managed by Air India and Indian Airlines, but these two corporations were merged into a single entity in 2007 and is combinely called 'Air India'. Air India has emerged as the 16th largest airline in Asia. It provides both domestic and International air services.

There are a number of private airlines dealing with air transport other than Air India such as Jet Airways (India) Ltd, Jet Lite Airlines, Spicejet Ltd., Vistara, Go Airlines (India) Pvt. Ltd. and Inter Globe Aviation Ltd. which is popularly known as 'Indigo'. These private airlines provide extensive range of flights and transportation to the different parts of India as well as outside the country.

Four important airports of India are

(i) Indira Gandhi International Airport, Delhi
(ii) Chhatrapati Shivaji International Airport, Mumbai
(iii) Netaji Subhash Chandra Bose International Airport, Kolkata
(iv) Chennai International Airport, Chennai

Pawan Hans

Pawan Hans Helicopters Ltd. (PHHL) was formed in 1985. It was set up to provide helicopter support services to the petroleum sector and Oil India Ltd. in offshore exploration in the mountainous regions that are inaccessible. It also provides services to some State Government and also to North-Eastern states. It also makes flights for promotion of tourism in India.

Advantages of Airways

- In a vast country, like India, air transport plays a significant role in transportation, covering long distances between major cities.

3 **Aeronautical** A science that deals with airplanes and flying.

- It connects major international cities with each other.
- It is comfortable and fastest means of transportation which acts as a link between major cities located far away from each other.
- It helps us to move swiftly and allow us to cross any mountain barriers, deserts, seas and oceans and all other inaccessible areas unlike rail and road networks.
- Air transport provides unparallel service during the time of natural calamities. It provides air-lift facilities to the people in affected areas and also could drop food, medicines, etc in the affected areas.

Disadvantages of Airways

- Air transport provides comfortable, but costly services. Its maintenance cost is also high.
- It depends mainly on prevalent weather conditions and when the weather is not favourable, it is often delayed.
- It runs on fuel based on petroleum which is a non-renewable source of energy.
- The rate of freight charges are very high in air transport.

Waterways

It is considered as the cheapest mode of transport. India has a huge cover of waterways such as rivers, lakes, canals, **backwaters**[4] and has a long coastline of about 7517 km. It is a very favourable transport system for carrying heavy and bulky goods from one place to another. Water transport can be broadly categorised into two groups which are

(i) Inland Waterways

The water bodies like rivers, canals, lakes, backwaters and creeks which are deep enough to provide the safe navigation of boats and ships are included in inland waterways.

Inland Waterways Authority of India (IWAI) is the statutory authority which look after the development and regulation of inland waterways for shipping and navigation. It was constituted on 27th October, 1986.

The following waterways have been declared as the National Waterways by the Inland Waterways Authority of India (IWAI)

- **National Waterway No.1** It consists of the Ganga-Bhagirathi-Hooghly system which connects Haldia- Kolkata- Farakka-Munger-Patna-Varanasi-Allahabad. It is a navigable waterway which stretches to more than 1620 km. This waterway is navigable by mechanical boats up to Patna and by ordinary boats up to Haridwar. It is divided into three parts for developmental purposes. These are Haldia-Farakka (560 km), Farakka-Patna (460 km) and Patna- Allahabad (600 km).
- **National Waterway No.2** It consists of the Brahmaputra river between Sadiya and Dhubri stretch (891 km). It connects Dhubri-Pandu-(Guwahati)-Tezpur- Neamati- Dibrugarh-Sadiya. It was declared as National Waterway no. 2 in 1988. This waterway connects the North-East region with Kolkata and Haldia ports through Bangladesh and Sunderbans waterways.
- **National Waterway No.3** It consists of Kottapuram-Kollam stretch (205 km) which includes 168 km of west coast canal along with Champakkara (14 km) and Udyogamandal canals (23 km). It was declared as National Waterway no. 3 in 1993. It is significant in terms of tourism.
- **National Waterway No.4** It consists of stretches of Godavari and Krishna rivers along with Kakinada Puducherry stretch of canals (1028 km). It connects Andhra Pradesh, Tamil Nadu and the Union Territory of Puducherry. It was declared as National Waterway no. 4 in 2008.
- **National Waterway No.5** It consists of stretches of river Brahmani (Talchar-Dhamra stretch) along with Matai river (Charbatia- Dhamra stretch), delta channels of Mahanadi river and East coast canal (Geonkhali- Charbatia stretch). It is 588 km in length. It was declared as National Waterway no. 5 in 2008.

(ii) Oceanic Waterways

Oceanic waterways play an important role in the transport sector of India's economy. The ocean routes in India supports about 95 per cent of foreign trade by volume and about 70 per cent by value. They are also utilised for transportation between the islands and the other parts of the country. There are major and minor ports which provide infrastructure support to oceanic routes.

4 **Backwaters** It is a part of a river where the water moves slowly because it is away from the main part of the river.

Ports

A port is a maritime facility comprising one or more loading areas, where ships load and discharge cargo and passengers. The ports are grouped as major, minor and intermediate ports which have their own administrative significance.

Major ports in India is administered by the Central Shipping Ministry and the minor and intermediate ports are administered by the ministries in the nine coastal states such as Odisha, West Bengal, Andhra Pradesh, Tamil Nadu, Kerala, Karnataka, Goa, Maharashtra and Gujarat. The major ports of India are

- **Kandla Port** It is located in Kuchchh of Gujarat, a free trade zone on the West Coast of India. It was the first port developed soon after Independence to ease the volume of trade on the Mumbai port. Kandla is a tidal port which is also known as the **Deendayal port**. It carry crude oil, petroleum products, edible oil, food grains, etc.
- **Mumbai Port** It is located in Maharashtra on the West Coast of India. It is the biggest port and natural harbour. It handles maximum traffic of cargoes like mineral oil and dry cargo.
- **The Jawaharlal Nehru Port** It is located in Maharashtra on the West Coast of India. It is the biggest ultra-modern port of Mumbai. It was planned with a view to decongest the Mumbai port and serve as a hub port for this region. It is also known as **Nhava Sheva**. It is the largest artificial port and the largest container port of India which is equipped with modern facilities.
- **Marmagao Port** It is located in Goa on the West Coast of India. It is a natural harbour which is situated on the **estuary**[5] of the river Zuari. It is the premier iron ore exporting port of the country. It accounts for about 50 per cent of India's iron ore export.
- **New Mangalore Port** It is located in Karnataka on the West Coast of India. It caters to the export of iron ore concentrates from Kudremukh mines and imports of fertiliser, petroleum, etc.
- **Kochchi Port** It is located in Kerala on the West Coast of India. It is the extreme South-Western port, located at the entrance of a lagoon with a natural harbour. It handles exports of spices, tea, coffee, salts and imports of petroleum and fertilisers.
- **Tuticorin Port** It is located in Tamil Nadu on the East Coast of India. This port has a natural harbour and rich **hinterland**[6]. Thus, it handles of a large variety of cargoes like coal, salt, edible oil, dry cargo, fertilisers and petroleum products, etc. Even neighbouring countries like Sri Lanka, Maldives, etc get their cargo handled from this port.
- **Chennai Port** It is located in Tamil Nadu on the East Coast of India. It is one of the oldest artificial ports of the country. It handles petroleum products, crude oil, fertilisers, iron ore and dry cargo etc.
- **Ennor Port** It is located in Tamil Nadu on the East Coast of India. It is India's first **corporatised**[7] port which is located 24 km from Chennai port. It is the first port in India which is a public company. This satellite port was developed to decongest the busy Chennai port and also to improve the environmental quality of the later port.
- **Visakhapatnam Port** It is located in Andhra Pradesh on East Coast of India. It is the deepest landlocked and well-protected port. It handles crude oil and petroleum products.
- **Paradwip Port** It is located in Odisha on East Coast of India. It handles the export of iron ore and coal.
- **Kolkata Port** It is located on the bank of Hooghly river in West Bengal on the East Coast of India. It is an **inland riverine port**[8]. It handles diversified goods coming from South-East Asian countries, Australia and New Zealand.
- **Haldia Port** It is located on the bank of Hooghly river in West Bengal on the East Coast of India. It was developed as a subsidiary port, in order to relieve growing pressure on the Kolkata port.

Advantages of Waterways

- It provides favourable means to carry heavy and bulky material.
- It consumes less fuel and is very safe in terms of conservation of environment.

5 **Estuary** An estuary is an area where a freshwater river or stream meets the ocean.
6 **Hinterland** It is the remote areas of a country away from the coast or the banks of rivers.
7 **Corporatise** To convert a state organisation into an independent commercial company.
8 **Inland Riverine Port** They are the ports located on the river front.

- Ships and cruise provides very comfortable form of travelling as it offers a lot of space and other facilities such as catering, entertainment, sports, medical facilities, communication, etc.
- The traffic in waterways are very less as compared to other modes of transport like roadways and railways.
- It provides employment to thousands of people and promotes tourism.
- It requires less capital investment as there is no cost of construction like roadways and railways.

Disadvantages of Waterways

- Many ports are not well linked with their hinterland which obstructs the smooth movement of goods.
- Waterways is dependent on the weather conditions which obstructs its potential.
- It demands long travelling hours which tends to make people ill.
- It is limited to the areas having navigable rivers and oceanic modes. At many places, diversion of river water for irrigation purposes make waterways non-navigable in large parts of their courses.
- Many ports in India are not well planned and lack basic facilities.
- The shipping companies incur huge losses due to slow handling of the cargo at port and undue delays as well.

Major Ports and Some International Airports

Check Your LEARNING...

1. State any one advantage of air transport.
2. Pawan Hans provides which type of service?
3. Who administer the major, intermediate and minor ports in India ?
4. Mention any one disadvantage of waterways.
5. Haldia port is located in which coast of India?

QUiCK Revision

- Transport helps in the better utilisation of the resources of the backward areas by connecting them with other developed areas. It helps in the movement of raw material, fuel, machinery, etc, from one point of production to the other point.
- Roadways are capable of connecting each and every area of a region with another. India has one of the largest road networks in the world.
- National Highways are the roads constructed by the Central Government. It passes through various states and cities.
- The National Highway Authority of India is an autonomous body of the Government of India which was constituted in 1988. It is responsible for the development, maintenance and management of National Highways in India.
- Railways constitute a principle means of transportation for freight and passengers.
- The railway system in India started in 1853 from Mumbai to Thane, which covered a distance of about 34 km. After this, another railway line was opened from Kolkata and Raniganj in 1859.
- Airways was started in India with a 10 km air mail operation from Allahabad to Naini in 1911. The air transport was nationalised in the year 1953.
- The Airports Authority of India (AAI) was set up on 1st April, 1995 by merging the International Airports Authority of India and the National Airports Authority.
- Pawan Hans Helicopters Ltd. (PHHL) was formed in 1985, which was set up to provide helicopter support services to the petroleum sector, offshore exploration and mountainous regions.
- Waterway is considered the cheapest mode of transport. India has huge cover of waterways such as rivers, lakes, canals, backwaters and has a long coastline of about 7517 km.
- The water bodies like rivers, canals, lakes, backwaters and creeks which are deep enough to provide the safe navigation of boats and ships are included in Inland waterways.
- Ports are divided into major, minor and intermediate ports.
- Major ports of India are Kolkata, Haldia, Paradwip, Visakhapatnam, Chennai, Tuticorin, Kandla, Mumbai, etc. They handle over 95% of all cargo traffic.

Chapter Practice

Section-I

Multiple Choice Questions

1. Sher Shah Suri Marg is known by which National Highway?
   (a) No. 1 (b) No. 2
   (c) No. 7 (d) No.15

Ans. (b) No. 2

2. How many lanes are there in super highways?
   (a) Two (b) Four
   (c) Six (d) Eight

Ans. (c) Six

3. The Northern terminal of the North-South corridor is which of the following?
   (a) Srinagar (b) Nangal
   (c) Kashmir (d) Gulmarg

Ans. (a) Srinagar

4. Roads that link a state capital with its district headquarters are called
   (a) National Highways
   (b) State Highways
   (c) District roads
   (d) Rural roads

Ans. (b) State Highways

5. District roads are maintained by the
   (a) State Public Works Department
   (b) Zila Parishad
   (c) Block Development Office
   (d) Panchayat

Ans. (b) Zila Parishad

6. .... provides door-to-door service.
   (a) Roadways (b) Railways
   (c) Pipelines (d) Airways

Ans. (a) Roadways

7. Which one of the following is the most important mode of transport in India?
   (a) Pipeline (b) Railways
   (c) Roadways (d) Airways

Ans. (b) Railways

8. There is a dense network of railways in India in the
   (a) Northern plains
   (b) Deccan plateau
   (c) Thar Desert
   (d) Swamps of Gujarat and forested areas of Central India

Ans. (a) Northern plains

9. The length of the longest National Waterway in India is .... km.
   (a) 205 (b) 891 (c) 1620 (d) 1890

Ans. (c) 1620

10. Give reason for the following.
    Good roads are the precursor of economic development of a country.
    (a) It helps to connect remote areas and hilly regions to towns, and cities.
    (b) Only goods can be transported through road network.
    (c) These provide door to door services and deliver commodities direct to the manufacturer.
    (d) Both (a) and (c)

Ans. (d) Both (a) and (c)

11. Give reason for the following.
    Expressways are the most important features of land transport.
    (a) These are highways which are planned for high-speed traffic.
    (b) These have few intersections and limited points of entry or exit.
    (c) Expressways provide many facilities like access ramps, lane dividers, telephone booths, CCTV cameras and mobile radars and so on.
    (d) All of the above

Ans. (d) All of the above

12. Give reason for the following.
    Golden Quadrilateral is important from economic point of view.
    (a) It interconnects many major cities and ports of India.
    (b) It enables the industrial growth of all small towns through which it passes.
    (c) It helps in the movement of agricultural produce from the hinterland to major cities and ports for export.
    (d) All of the above

Ans. (d) All of the above

13. Give reason for the following.
    Konkan Railway is considered an engineering marvel.
    (a) It is a narrow gauge railway line.
    (b) It crosses 146 rivers, streams, nearly 2000 bridges and 91 tunnels.
    (c) Asia's largest river lies on this route.
    (d) The states of Maharashtra, Delhi and Karnataka are partners in this undertaking.

Ans. (b) It crosses 146 rivers, streams, nearly 2000 bridges and 91 tunnels.

14. Give reason for the following.
Indian Railway is facing many challenges in recent times.
(a) Ticketless travelling incurs huge losses.
(b) Railways need replacement of tracks, equipments and machineries as these have become obsolete.
(c) Trains do not provide comfortable journey to passengers.
(d) Both (a) and (b)

Ans. (d) Both (a) and (b)

15. Which of the following statements is correct about transportation?
(i) It links backward regions to urban cities.
(ii) It helps to utilise natural resources found in the hilly areas.
(iii) It provides food, clothes etc during natural calamities.
(iv) It helps in the economic growth of a region.

Codes
(a) Only (i) (b) Only (ii)
(c) Only (iii) (d) All of these

Ans. (d) All of these

16. Which of the following statements is incorrect?
(i) Rural roads are all- weather roads.
(ii) Rural roads are maintained by NHAI.
(iii) These roads cover about 80 per cent of the total road length in India.

Codes
(a) Only (i) (b) (i) and (ii) (c) Only (ii) (d) All of these

Ans. (b) (i) and (ii)

17. Match the following.

List-I	List-II
A. National Highways	1. Account for 2 per cent of total road length in the country.
B. District Roads	2. Account for 14 per cent of the total road length of the country.
C. State Highways	3. Account for 80 per cent of the total road length of the country.
D. Rural Roads	4. Account for 4 per cent of the total road length of the country.

Codes

	A	B	C	D		A	B	C	D
(a)	1	2	4	3	(b)	2	1	4	3
(c)	3	4	1	2	(d)	4	3	2	1

Ans. (a)

18. Match the following.

List-I	List-II
A. Central Railway Zone	1. Allahabad headquarters
B. Eastern Railway Zone	2. Bhubaneswar headquarters
C. East Coast Railway Zone	3. Kolkata headquarters
D. North Central Railway Zone	4. Mumbai headquarters

Codes

	A	B	C	D		A	B	C	D
(a)	1	2	3	4	(b)	2	1	4	3
(c)	3	4	1	2	(d)	4	3	2	1

Ans. (d)

19. Match the following.

List-I	List-II
A. NW 1	1. Kottapuram-Kollam stretch
B. NW 2	2. Stretches of Godavari and Krishna rivers along with Kakinada Puducherry stretch of canals
C. NW 3	3. Allahabad-Haldia stretch
D. NW 4	4. Sadiya-Dhubri stretch

Codes

	A	B	C	D		A	B	C	D
(a)	1	2	3	4	(b)	2	1	4	3
(c)	3	4	1	2	(d)	4	3	2	1

Ans. (c)

Section-II

Short Questions

1. What do you understand by transport system?

Ans. The system through which people and goods move from one place to another is called transport system. Better transport helps in the better ultilisation of the resources of the backward areas by connecting them with other developed areas.

2. Give two reasons for the 'means of transport' being called the lifelines of a nation's economy. [2018]

Ans. The two reasons for the means of transport being called the lifelines of a nation's economy are
(i) It helps in the production and movement of goods and services.
(ii) It helps us in interacting with others in all parts of the world which has brought the world closer.

3. Why is road transport preferred in Northern Plains of India?

Ans. The road transport preferred in the Northern Plains of India due to flat surface and high density of population. The necessary material for constructing roads is also available from the nearby hilly areas.

4. What do you understand by National Highway?

Ans. National Highways are the roads constructed and maintained by Central Government. These are well constructed long metalled roads which stretches through length and breadth of the country.

5. What do you understand by 'Expressway'?

Ans. Expressways are 6 to 8 lane type highways with controlled access. These are well cemented and designed to offer smooth and highspeed movement of vehicles with hindrance-free facility.

6. Name two government agencies that work for the construction and maintenance of roads in India.

Ans. The government agencies that work for the construction and maintenance of roads in India are

(i) **The National Highway Authority (NHAI)** It is an autonomous body of the Government of India which was constituted in 1988. It is responsible for maintenance and management of National Highways in India.

(ii) **State Public Works Department (PWDs)** It is responsible for the development, construction, maintenance and management of State Highways.

7. Distinguish between national highway and expressway.

Ans. Differences between national highways and expressways are

National Highways	Expressways
These are maintained by the Central Government.	These may or may not be constructed by the Central Government.
These connect two remote places.	These are built to reduce congestion and travel time.

8. Distinguish between National Highway and State Highway.

Ans. Differences between National Highways and State Highways are

National Highways	State Highways
These are maintained by the Central Government.	These are maintained by the State Government.
These highways run over two or more states.	These highways run within the same state.

9. Roadways are always considered more important than any other means of transportation. Give two reasons in support of the statement. **[2016]**

Or Roadways are an important means of transport in India. Give two reasons to justify the statement. **[2019]**

Or Even through all means of transport are well developed in India, yet, road transport remains the most popular means of transport. Justify this statement. **[2020]**

Ans. Roadways are always considered as more important than any other means of transport because

(i) It is more suitable for short distance travel and it connects small villages and places where other means of transport cannot reach.

(ii) It saves cost of transportation from one station to another station and it saves the time.

10. Give two ways in which rail transport is useful for the people of India. **[2018]**

Ans. The two ways in which rail transport is useful for the people of India are

(i) It is money saving as it is cheaper than roadways and airways.

(ii) It helps people to connect their family from far away and transport the goods over long distance.

11. (i) Why are roadways considered more important than any other means of transport?

(ii) Mention two advantages of using railways as means of transport. **[2023]**

Ans. (i) Road transport is the most economical for short distances as compared to other means of transport as it offers door to door services and provide long distance links through highways, motorways, etc.

(ii) Two advantages of using railways as means of transport are

(a) It facilitates long distance travel and transport of bulky goods which are not easily transported through motor vehicles.

(b) It is a quick and more regular form of transport because it helps in the transportation of goods with speed and certainty.

12. (i) Why is the railways an important means of transport as compared to airways? **[2015]**

Or Mention two reasons why more people use railways rather than airways. **[2017]**

(ii) State one economic benefit of the Golden Quadrilateral Project.

Ans. (i) Railways is an important means of transport as compared to railways because

(a) Railways is a cheap mode of transport as compared to air transport which are easily reachable for the poor people.

(b) Railway can carry loads at cheaper rate to every corner of the country as compared to air transport,

(ii) The economic benefit of the Golden Quadrilateral is that it transports the goods at cheaper rate to the market where the demand is more.

13. Distinguish between broad gauge and metre gauge.

Ans. Differences between broad gauge and metre gauge are

Broad Gauge	Metre Gauge
In broad gauge, the distance between the railway track lines is 1.676 m.	In metre gauge, the distance between the railway track lines is 1 m.
Total route length of broad gauge line is 63,949 km.	It covers, 2402 km of route length.

14. Distinguish between metre gauge and narrow gauge.

Ans. Differences between metre gauge and narrow gauge are

Metre Gauge	Narrow Gauge
In metre gauge, the distance between railway track lines is 1m.	In narrow gauge, the distance between railway tracks is 0.762 m and 0.610 m.
It covers 2402 km of route length.	It covers 1809 km of route length.

15. What is AAI and when was it formed?

Ans. The Airports Authority of India (AAI) was set up on 1st April, 1995 by merging the International Airports Authority of India and the National Airports Authority.

16. What is 'Pawan Hans'? Why was it set up?

Ans. Pawan Hans Helicopters Ltd. (PHHL) was formed in 1985. It was set up to provide helicopter support services to the petroleum sector and Oil India Ltd. in offshore exploration. It operate in the mountainous region which is inaccessible.

17. Why is it important to have a well developed means of transport in India ? **[2023]**

Ans. A well-developed transport system is essential to achieve economic development and an efficient use of natural resources. It is also needed to transport people from one place to another.

18. Name two areas where helicopter services may be used. **[2012]**

Ans. Helicopter services can be used mainly in following areas

(i) Areas of mountains.

(ii) Areas affected with natural calamities like flood, earthquake, etc.

19. Mention one advantage and one disadvantage of air transport. **[2011]**

Ans. An advantage of air transport is that it provide unparallel service during the time of natural calamities. It provides air-lift facilities to the people in affected areas and also could drop food, medicines etc. in the affected areas.

A disadvantage of air transport is that it provides comfortable, but costly services.

20. Give one advantage of air transport. Why is it still a popular means of transportation in India? **[2013]**

Ans. An advantage of air transport is that it is the fastest mode of transport. It is indispensable for the business people, for defence and for making communication in hilly regions and border areas. So, it is a popular means of transportation in India.

21. Mention one advantage and one disadvantage of the inland waterways. **[2014]**

Ans. An advantage of inland waterway is that it is the most suitable for carrying heavy and bulky goods. A disadvantage of inland waterway is that it depends on the weather conditions which obstructs its potential.

22. (i) What do you mean by inland waterways?

(ii) Name the authority which handle the waterways in India.

Ans. (i) The water bodies like rivers, canals, lakes, backwaters and creeks which are deep enough to provide the safe navigation of boats and ships are called waterways.

(ii) Inland Waterways Authority of India (IWAI) is the statutory authority which handle the waterways in India. It was constituted on 27th October, 1986.

23. Why is inland waterways declining in its importance? Give two reasons for your answer. **[2017]**

Or Why has the importance of inland waterways declined? Give any two reasons. **[2012]**

Ans. Inland waterway is declining in its importance due to following reasons

(i) Areas of water transport is restricted. It provides access to limited areas.

(ii) It demands long travelling hours which tends to make people ill.

24. With reference to waterways answer the following questions. **[2020]**

(i) Mention two advantages of inland water transport.

(ii) Why is inland water transport not well developed in India?

Ans. (i) Two advantages of inland water transport are as

(a) It is suitable for heavy and bulky goods to transport from one region to another.

(b) Rivers are the only means of transport in thick forested areas of heavy rainfall.

(ii) Refer to answer of Short Question Q. 23.

25. (i) Why are South Indian rivers not ideal for the inland water transport?

(ii) Mention one advantage of coastal shipping. **[2019]**

Ans. (i) The rivers in South India are non-perennial and during dry season these have less water which is not suitable for navigation. These river also form steep waterfalls due to which navigation is not possible, thus, importance of inland waterways is declining here.

(ii) Coastal shipping is a cost effective way to transport domestic cargo along the coastal states.

26. Name the following.

(i) Cheapest mode of transport.

(ii) Fastest mode of transport.

Ans. (i) Waterways are the cheapest mode of transport which provides favourable means to carry heavy and bulky goods.

(ii) Airways are the fastest mode of transport. It saves our travelling time.

Long Questions

1. Mention three benefits of Golden Quadrilateral. **[Specimen Paper Semester-II 2022]**

Ans. Three benefits of Golden Quadrilateral are

(i) The Golden Quadrilateral Highway enhance the Indian economy as it provides links to port cities, industrial centres and enables truck transport throughout the country.

(ii) Its construction helps in reducing the time, distance and cost of movements among mega cities. It connects India's four big metro cities of Delhi-Mumbai-Chennai-Kokata.

(iii) It has also connected Bengaluru, Pune, Ahmedabad and Surat.

2. State any three features of the Border Roads?

Ans. Three features of the border roads are

(i) Border Roads are the lifeline of Border areas of Northern and North-Eastern part of India.

(ii) These roads have increased the accessibility in the difficult terrain areas of India.

(iii) These roads are constructed and maintained by Border Roads Organisation.

3. (i) "The railway is an important means of transport as compared to airways." State two reasons to support the statement.

(ii) Mention one disadvantage of rail transport. **[2019]**

Ans. (i) Refer to answer of Short Question Q.12 (i).

(ii) A disadvantage of rail transport is that train journey sometimes very long and tiring, especially if we compare it with airways.

4. Write any three problems faced by the roadways in India.

Ans. The problems faced by the roadways in India are

(i) Most of the roads are irregular, hence they are not suitable for regular vehicular traffic.

(ii) Roads in India are not properly maintained.

(iii) Roads in India are not strongly built. Most of it have weak pavement, unbridged level crossings and lack of wayside amenities and safety measures.

5. In accordance to the railway transport, answer the following questions.

(i) Why railways is suitable for long distance travel?

(ii) Why it requires high cost construction and maintenance?

(iii) First railway line in India connected which two places.

Ans. (i) Railways is suitable for long distance travel as it reduce the cost of long distance travelling as compared to other modes of transport. As compared to airways, travelling through railways is easy and comfortable as one can move during his/her travelling time and does not stuck in his/her seat for endless amount of hours.

(ii) Rail tracks are very difficult to lay on irregular terrain thus, high cost is involved in construction and maintenance of railway tracks.

(iii) The first railway line was started in 1853 from Mumbai to Thane.

6. (i) State one advantage of inland waterways. **[2018]**

(ii) State one advantage of roadways.

(iii) State one disadvantage of water transport.

Ans. (i) An advantage of inland waterway is that it is the cheapest means of transport and is most suitable for carrying heavy and bulky material.

(ii) An advantage of roadway is that it can go through dissected and undulating land areas and through steep mountains. It also provide door-to-door services.

(iii) A disadvantage of water transport is that it is a slow means of transport and unsuitable for small business.

7. (i) Give reasons to explain the lack of rail transport in North-East India.

(ii) Why is road transport favoured in the Northern Plains of India?

Ans. (i) There is lack of rail transport in North-East India because it has a hilly region and it is difficult to lay the railway tracks in this hilly terrain with uneven areas.

(ii) Road transport is favoured in the Northern Plains of India because

(a) Northern Plains are the fertile and levelled region which has a high density of population.

(b) Roadways in Northern Plains help in easy transportation of crops, perishable food items and raw materials within short distances quickly.

8. Mention any three problems being faced by the Indian Railways. **[2012]**

Ans. The problems faced by the Indian Railways are

(i) Rail tracks are very difficult to lay on irregular land such as hilly and forested areas as compared to Northern place which have dense network of railways.

(ii) Train journey sometimes are very long and tiring, especially if we compare it with air journey.

(iii) Majority of the train in India still runs on coal and thus, produces lot of air and noise pollution.

9. What are the three disadvantages of using air transport? **[Specimen Paper Semester-II 2022]**

Ans. Three disadvantages of using air transport are

(i) It provides costly services.

(ii) It depends greatly on weather conditions.

(iii) Its maintenance cost is too high.

10. (i) Give two disadvantages of airways.

(ii) Why is there an increase of airway traffic in recent years? **[2020]**

Ans. (i) Refer to answer of Long Question. Q. 9.

(ii) There is an increase of airway traffic in recent years due to economic and demographic growth and the emergence of low-cost airlines that offer holiday packages at cheaper rates.

11. (i) State one important difference between an expressway and a highway. **[2015]**

(ii) Name the first expressway constructed in the country.

(iii) State a reason why the Northern rivers are more suitable for navigation than the Deccan rivers.

Ans. (i) Expressways has controlled access, where a vehicle can enter it only through a limited place and no other road merges/crosses the expressway anywhere, thereby avoiding possible accidents. On the other hand, in the case of highways, there are multiple roads which merge with/across the highways at many places.

(ii) Ahmedabad-Vadodara expressway was the first expressway to be constructed in the country.

(iii) The Northern rivers are more suitable for navigation than the Deccan rivers because

(a) Deccan rivers are not perennial as compared to Northern rivers.

(b) Deccan rivers are seasonal in nature and only fed by rainfall.

(c) Decean rivers have lots of waterfalls and rapids as compared to Northern rivers.

12. Give three reasons as to why airways are becoming a popular means of transport in modern India.

Ans. The three reasons due to which airways are becoming a popular means of transport in modern India are

(i) It is the fastest means of movement from one place to the other for a vast country like India.

(ii) It has reduced the distance by minimising the travel time.

(iii) It helps to reach the large and difficult terrain places which are inaccessible through other modes of transport.

13. Mention two advantages and one disadvantage of waterways. **[2016]**

Or Mention two advantages of using waterways. **[Specimen Paper Semester-II 2022]**

Ans. For advantages of waterways, refer to chapter theory on page 204.

A disadvantage of waterway is that many ports are not well linked with their hinterland which obstructs the smooth movement of goods.

14. Give a reason for each of the following **[2019]**

(i) Nearly seventy per cent of Indians do not use air transport.

(ii) A well-developed transport is important for industrial growth.

(iii) Water transport is not as popular as land transport in India.

Ans. (i) Air transport provides comfortable, but costly services. The rate of freight charges are very high in air transport. Thus, Indians mostly do not use air transport.

(ii) Good transport network helps in the development of industrialisation and urbanisation as it links the backward areas to the urban cities and reduces regional industrial disparity. It helps in transportation of raw material to industries. Thus, well developed transport is important for industrial growth.

(iii) Water transport depends on the weather conditions which obstructs its potential, whereas land transport can be used in any season. Water transport is restricted to the areas having navigable rivers and oceanic modes while land transport helps to connect the remotest villages and hilly areas to towns, cities and plain areas. Thus, water transport is less popular than land transport in India.

15. Give a reason for each of the following **[2020]**

(i) Roadways is not well-developed in North-East India.

(ii) Railways are under the public sector.

(iii) A good network of transport is of great help for the development of the economy.

Ans. (i) Roadways is not well-developed in North-East India because this region is a hilly area which has undulating topography.

(ii) Railways are managed by the public sectors of the government, as the government has a majority of share in the railway sector. The public sector companies are involved with development and expansion of the railways.

(iii) A good network of transport is of great help for the development of the economy because it can broaden the market for goods. It can also make easy movement of raw materials, fuels, equipment, etc to the places of production, easy.

Picture Based Question

1. Study the diagram below and answer the questions that follow.

(i) In which part of India is this means of transport is most popular?

(ii) Name the first commercial train journey in India.

Ans. (i) This means of transport is most popular in the Northern Plains.

(ii) The first commercial train journey was started in 1853 from Mumbai to Thane.

Chapter Assessment

Section-I

Multiple Choice Questions

1. Border Roads Organisation was established in .... for the development of the roads of strategic importance in the Northern and North-Eastern borders.
   (a) 1960 (b) 1948
   (c) 1950 (d) 1937
2. Which of the following is the headquarters of South-Central Railway?
   (a) Hyderabad
   (b) Secunderabad
   (c) Bengaluru
   (d) Mumbai Churchgate
3. The length of inland waterways in India is .... km.
   (a) 2,369 (b) 7,425
   (c) 14,500 (d) 23,700
4. The seaport which is located in Navi Mumbai is ....
   (a) Chennai
   (b) Jawaharlal Nehru port
   (c) Marmagao
   (d) Tuticorin

Section-II

Short Questions

1. How does transport plays an important role in human life?
2. How have National Highways helped the country's economy?
3. Explain in detail about the National Highway Authority of India.
4. How are rural roads important?
5. Mention any two advantages of roadways.
6. Give any two disadvantages of railways.
7. Name some important airports of India.
8. Give a brief description about Inland waterways.
9. Mention any one advantage and disadvantage of waterways.

Long Questions

1. Explain in brief about Airport Authority of India.
2. Explain in details about the National Waterway.
3. Explain in details about the major ports of India.

CHAPTER 14

Waste Management

SYLLABUS

Waste Management • Impacts of waste accumulation-spoilage of landscape, pollution, health hazards, effects on terrestrial, aquatic (fresh water and marine) life. • Need for waste management. • Methods of safe disposal-segregation, dumping and composting. • Need and methods for reducing, reusing and recycling waste.

Waste Material

The products that has been used in any activity and now is rejected for further usage is known as waste. The Environment Protection Act, 1990, has defined waste material as

- Waste materials are the substance, which constitute a discarded material or an effluent or any other unwanted residue, which has come out from any activity.
- Waste material is any substance or article, which requires to be disposed of as being broken, worn out, contaminate or otherwise spoiled.

Classification of Waste

Wastes are classified into biodegradable , non-biodegradable, toxic and non-toxic wastes

- **Biodegradable Waste** These can be decomposed by bacteria, e.g. vegetable peels, wood, paper, dead animals, plants, etc.
- **Non-biodegradable Waste** These cannot be broken down or degraded by bacteria. They are harmful for the environment, e.g. glass, plastics, polythene bags, etc.
- **Toxic Waste** These are poisonous wastes and also known as 'hazardous waste' or 'radioactive wastes'. They can cause a serious threat to human health, e.g. industrial wastes and effluents, pesticides, fluoride wastes, medical wastes like blood samples, unused drugs, etc.
- **Non-Toxic Waste** The waste produced by offices, shops, schools etc that do not pose a serious threat to environment are called non-toxic waste.

Sources of Waste

The sources of waste or the ways by which waste are generated are

- **Industrial Waste** Waste generated by various industries are called industrial wastes. In recent years, industrial effluents as waste have become a major source of land and water pollution in many parts of the country. Industrial wastes include paints, sand, chemicals, metals, paper, etc.
- **Agriculture Waste** Wastes generated by agricultural activities are called agricultural wastes. Agricultural wastes can cause many environmental problems if they are not disposed of properly. For example, it can create a breeding ground for harmful insects and rodents on the ground. It includes crop residue, wood waste, saw dust, husks, rubber waste, manure, etc.
- **Domestic Waste** Wastes generated by domestic households are called domestic wastes. It include vegetable peels, plastics, paper, food wastes, etc.

- **Biomedical Waste** Wastes generated by hospitals, medical stores and dispensaries are called biomedical wastes. It includes bandages, expired medicines, plasters and syringes.
- **Nuclear Waste** It includes toxic wastes from nuclear plants, e.g. radioactive elements.
- **Mining Waste** Wastes generated through mining activities are known as mining wastes. These include debris, huge amount of dust, etc. Mining sites are abandoned after excavation work is complete leaving deep scars and traces of over-burdening on land. In states like Jharkhand, Chhattisgarh, Madhya Pradesh and Odisha, deforestation due to mining have caused severe land degradation.
- **Construction Waste** Wastes generated by construction activities like demolition and construction remains are known as construction wastes. It includes bricks, roofing, plastics, insulating materials, etc.
- **Electronic Waste** Wastes generated through electronic items are called electronic wastes. These include discarded refrigerators, televisions, washing machines, microwaves, mobile phones, etc. The use and throw concept is the main reason of the e-waste generation. These wastes are difficult to recycle as they mostly contain halogens with plastic resin which make recycling difficult. It includes TVs, computer monitors, printers, etc.

Impacts of Waste Accumulation

Waste accumulation is the gradual gathering of due to improper waste management. Dumping of wastes indiscriminately not only gives an undesirable, ugly look and foul smell, but also cause serious health hazards. Many **pathogenic**[1] bacteria, virus and fungi grow in these wastes. This causes air and water pollution.

Some of the impacts of waste accumulation are

Spoilage of Landscape

It refers to the accumulation of garbage, rubbish and trash in an open area which is left untreated. Dumping of garbage in an open area ruin the natural beauty of the place and serves as a potential disease breeding ground. All type of insects, flies, mosquitoes, rodents, etc breed on this garbage. The poisonous substance may seep into the groundwater or rivers and contaminate it. The soil may be contaminated and thus, these pollutants may even enter the food chain through water and soil pollution.

Pollution

The undesirable and unfavourable addition of certain things in the environment, entirely or partly due to direct or indirect actions of human being is called pollution. Pollution is caused by human activity, by addition of waste and toxic chemicals in the atmosphere. The substances that causes pollution are called pollutants.

Sources of Pollution

Air Pollution

When any chemical particulate matter, toxic waste material or biological material are added into the atmosphere by direct or indirect actions of human beings and causes the degradation or damage to the quality of the ecosystem, it is known as air pollution.

The pollutants that causes air pollution are of many forms such as solid particles, liquid matter or gases. These are of two types, which are

(i) **Primary Pollutants** The pollutants which are emitted directly in the air are referred as primary pollutants, e.g. ash from household, volcanic eruption, carbon monoxide from motor vehicles exhausts, sulphur dioxide from power plants, nitrogen oxide and **Suspended Particulate Matter**[2] (SPM).

(ii) **Secondary Pollutants** The pollutants which generates from the reaction taking place among various primary pollutants are known as secondary pollutants.

Water Pollution

Any addition of chemicals and waste material in the water bodies, which reduces the quality of the water by changing its colour, odour and composition and also reduces the natural cleansing process of water bodies, is known as water pollution.

1 **Pathogenic** Something that causes disease such as bacteria or a virus.

2 **Suspended Particulate Matter** They are finely divided solids or liquids that are dispersed through the air from compustion process, industrial activity or natural sources.

Harmful waste from the surrounding area reaches the water bodies like ponds, lakes, rivers and groundwater and contaminates it. The sewage waste coming from factories and industries reaches the water bodies and causes many water related diseases like diarrhoea and typhoid. These sewage must be properly treated before releasing them into the environment.

Soil Pollution

The degradation and **deterioration**[3] of soil quality due to addition of certain solid and semi solid wastes from agricultural practices, industrial processes, household, etc. is termed as soil pollution.

There are many different ways by which soil can become polluted, such as sewage from a landfill, discharge of industrial waste into the soil, flowing of contaminated water into the soil, breakage of underground storage tanks, excess application of pesticides, herbicides or fertilisers and solid waste sewage.

The most common chemicals involved in causing soil pollution are petroleum hydrocarbons, heavy metals, pesticides, solvents, etc.

Health Hazards

- Indiscriminate dumping of toxic and non-toxic matter causes serious health problems. The accumulations of these harmful waste can cause the outbreak of serious epidemics.
- Carbon monoxide present in air lowers the amount of oxygen that enters our blood, slows our reflexes and makes us confused and sleepy.
- Lead is present in petrol, diesel, lead batteries, paints, hair dye products, etc. and affects mainly children. It can cause nervous system damage and digestive problems and in some cases, cause cancer.
- The dumping grounds are open pits and thus, become the breeding ground for mosquitoes, flies, insects which cause malaria and dengue.
- Sulphur dioxide (SO_2) produced from burning coal, mainly in thermal power plants is a major contributor to smog and acid rain and can lead to lung disease.
- The unhygienic disposal of plastic may generate toxic substances that is harmful for human health.
- Recycling of toxic matter may also cause great risks for workers as they may experience toxic exposure. Some chemicals like cyanides, polychlorinated biphenyls and mercury are highly toxic and exposure to them lead to disease or death.
- Radioactive waste is responsible for serious environmental and health problems, which is produced by nuclear reactors and weapon factories. Even the small quantity of radioactive waste is extremely harmful to human health.

Effects on Terrestrial Life

Terrestrial life consists of all the living beings that live on Earth such as humans, plants and animals. Hazardous wastes may pollute soil, air, surface water and underground water. The soil pollutants may affect human being, plants and animals.

These toxic substances are transferred to different organisms through the food chain and cause a number of complications in living organisms. Some of these impacts are

Effect on Plants and Animals

- Many toxic chemicals, pesticides, other agricultural wastes released into the environment are taken up by the plants from air, water and soil. These toxins cause different types of leaf injuries premature leaf fall, decrease in transpiration, reduction in the rate of photosynthesis, reduction in biological nitrogen fixation.
- Exposure to high concentration of pollutants may cause acute injuries like chlorosis and discoloration. Sulphur dioxide is the most toxic pollutant which damages the crops.
- When leaves are covered by dust, it blocks stomata of plants which decreases rate of transpiration, and also reduces the absorption of nutritients from soil.
- Smoke also causes reduction in root and short lengths, number of leaves and grains, e.g. Wheat crop.

Effect on Animal Life and Birds

- When birds eat waste materials like agricultural wastes. These cause defective egg shells and increase mortality rate.
- Several domestic animals like cow, buffalo, goat, etc. often eat polythene and plastic bags along with food material which ultimately reach to their alimentary canal causing many disorders and even death.

3 **Deteriorate** To become worse as time passes.

Effect on Aquatic Life

Freshwater Life

- Large amount of wastes of human society are disposed of in the freshwater bodies like rivers, lakes, ponds and other aquatic bodies. These make the water polluted which is not fit for drinking and other domestic purposes.
- Oxygen concentration is reduced considerably due to heavy accumulation of toxic wastes and sewage drained from cities into the water bodies like canals, lakes and rivers. This process is known as **eutrophication**. In eutrophication process, nutrients become abundant due to waste accumulation and the growth of phytoplanton and algae increases which reduce the penetration of oxygen, light and heat into water body. Thus, affecting the life of fishes and other aquatic population.
- Sewage from municipalities and **tanneries**[4] that is discharged into the rivers, canals and lakes, etc carry many species of bacterias and other microbes which cause diseases in aquatic organism.
- Some pollutants, for example heavy metals, chemical waste and several other organic and inorganic compounds are harmful to aquatic organisms. Many of them especially non-biodegradable ones, accumulate in the body of organisms and cause long-term effects.

Marine Water Life

- Marine water includes sea water or ocean water. The growth of marine algae is affected through waste accumulation.
- Massive oil spills not only spoil innumerable beaches and estuaries, but also cause widespread damage to marine life.
- Herbicides and pesticides (especially the organ chlorides) reach the oceans *via* the wind and rivers and contaminate marine water.
- Thermal and radioactive pollution have disturbed the life of fishes in estuaries and coastal ecosystems. Their breeding is also affected adversely.
- Due to plastic debris in the oceans many marine animals including mammals, turtles, fish, sharks, etc are killed each year. This plastic waste breaks down into smaller pieces, which are easily ingested by marine animals causing blockages in their digestive tracts and eventually death.
- The aquatic organisms are also affected by biomagnification process which means increasing the concentration of various toxic substances along the food chain. Toxic substances which are found at the level of primary producers move to other trophic level of food chain. The phenomenon deposition of concentrated toxic at the higher trophic level is known as bio-accumulation.
- Mercury is also harmful for marine animals. Sources of mercury are wastes of industries like paper and pulp industry, chlorine industry, pesticide industry. For example, due to consuming mercury contaminated fishes many fishermen got ill who caught these fishes from the Minamata Bay in Japan. It also killed different sea bird species feeding on fishes. This epidemic in Minamata is known as **Minamata disease**.

Global Problems due to Waste Accumulation

Global Warming

Global warming is the production of carbon dioxide and methane gases as a result of decomposition of organic waste. These are called green house gases.

The effects of global warming are

- Due to Global Warming, global temperature is likely to rise by 2°C to 5°C during the next century.
- Rise in global temperature is very dangerous which will lead to melting of ice caps on the Earth's poles. It will result into the rise of the sea level and many low lying areas will submerge.
- The rise in temperature will lead serious climatic changes.
- Due to Global Warming insects and pests will increase in the warmer climatic conditions. Thus, pathogenic diseases will increase.

Ozone Layer Depletion

Ozone is an important layer which lies in the Stratosphere. It absorbs ultraviolet rays and infrared rays of the Sun and stops these from reaching the Earth directly. However, there are many causes which destroy ozone layer. For example, Chemical reaction of Oxides of Nitrogen (NO and NO_2) with ozone, nitrogen gas emitted by supersonic aeroplanes and Chlorofluorocarbons (CFCs), etc. A hole has been observed in the ozone layer in the Stratosphere near Antarctica.

4 **Tanneries** It is a place where animal skin is converted into leather.

This hole allows the ultraviolet rays of the Sun to reach the Earth directly without any obstacle. The ultraviolet rays can cause many diseases like skin cancer and cataract, genetic disorders and so on. It also disturbs ecological balance in marine ecosystem.

Acid Rain

When acids exceed in rain water it is known as acid rain. Burning of coal and petroleum produces sulphur and nitrogen which react with oxygen and are converted into sulphur dioxide and nitrogen dioxide, respectively. These are soluble in water and. thus, when these acids mix with rain, they form acid rain.

The effects of acid rain are

- Acid rain destroys forests and crops when acidity increases in the soil.
- It badly affects buildings, monuments, statues, bridges, fences and railings, e.g. turning of white marble surface of the Taj Mahal into yellow.
- It causes neurological diseases.
- It affects aquatic life.
- Plant growth is affected as plant leaves get burnt and dry due to acid rain.

Measures to Control Waste Accumulation

- To control the growth of population.
- Suitable and necessary infrastructure should be prepared.
- Waste material should be disposed properly in closed vans.
- Strict laws should be made and implemented against polluting the ecosystem.
- Farmers must be taught about the harmful impact of pesticides on human life and soil.
- Improved auto fuel should be supplied.
- Most of the e-waste is not hazardous if it is stocked in safe storage or recycled by scientific methods. Safe transportation from one place to the other in parts or in totality is also important. Hence, e-waste must be recycled with care.
- Vehicles and industrial emission norms should be strictly followed.
- Promotion of cleaner technologies.
- Awareness programmes should be conducted.
- Action plans for major cities and critically polluted areas should be prepared and implemented.

Check Your LEARNING...

1. Name any two sources of domestic waste.
2. Give any one example of pollutant.
3. Mention any one impact of waste generation on terrestrial life.
4. Give an impact of waste accumulation on marine life.
5. Minamata Bay is located in which country?

Safe Disposal of Waste

All the wastes depending upon their type i.e. solid, liquid or gases, organic or inorganic wastes, toxic or non-toxic wastes, should be disposed accordingly. There are several methods of disposing the wastes are

Segregation of Waste

It is a method of dividing garbage into different categories as wet or biodegradable and dry or non-biodegradable. Wet waste is a type of biodegradable waste as it is organic in nature. For example, kitchen waste, vegetables, flowers, garden waste, etc. Dry waste is a type of waste which is non-biodegradable. For example, timber, discarded furniture, household junk, tetra packs, steel wares, etc. Segregation is important because if the waste is not separated properly, it all gets mixed up in landfills. The danger of this is that they all leak after a period of time, resulting in contamination of groundwater.

Open Dump (Dumping)

It refers to uncovered areas that are used to dump solid waste of all kinds. The waste is untreated, uncovered and not segregated. It is the breeding ground for flies, rats and other insects that spread diseases. The rainwater runoff from these dumps contaminate nearby land, water and air thereby spreading disease.

Treatment of open dumps needs to be phased out by **landfills**. These landfills are generally located in urban areas. It is a pit that is dug in the ground. The garbage is dumped and the pit is covered with soil everyday thus, preventing the breeding of flies and rats.

It is then subjected to bacterial decomposition. Different gases are generated through physical, chemical and biological reactions that takes place in these landfills. These gases can be recovered and used to generate power.

But landfills have some limitations. Water seeps through landfills and contaminate the groundwater. Methane gas is also produced in the landfills that is not good for the plants growing there as it is poisonous.

Composting

It is a biological process in which micro-organisms, mainly fungi and bacteria, decompose biodegradable or organic waste in the presence of oxygen. In this method, various wastes like leaves, grass, fruit peels and vegetable peels, etc. are dumped into a pit and then covered which helps to produce compost and biogas or gobar gas.

Compost is a rich source of organic matter. It plays an important role in sustaining soil fertility. Soil composting may be divided into two categories by the nature of the decomposition process. They are **anaerobic** and **aerobic**. In anaerobic composting, decomposition occurs where oxygen is absent or in limited supply. Aerobic composting takes place in the presence of ample oxygen. Both manual as well as mechanical methods of composting are used in India.

Benefits of Composting

- The soil becomes more resistant to stresses such as drought, diseases and toxicity.
- It helps the crop in better absorption of nutrients from the soil.
- It increases the quality of poor soils by adding humus.
- It reduces soil erosion.
- It is cost effective for farming as composting does not require excess water, fertilisers and pesticides.

Need for Waste Management

Waste management is needed due to the following reasons

- Accumulation of wastes have led to serious environmental consequences. It also possess a great health risk.
- High degree of growth in population and industrialisation has made environmental degradation a serious problem in many urban areas.
- The rapid increase in the number of vehicles on the road especially in metropolitan cities has degraded the quality of air severely. It leads to acid rain which adversely affects forests, freshwater, soil, monuments, human health, plant growth, aquatic, species, etc.
- The land gets littered by plastic bag, garbage and becomes ugly and unhygienic. Burning of plastics, especially PVC releases dioxin which is highly **carcinogenic**[5] and toxic.
- Plastic bags can also contaminate food stuffs due to **leaching**[6] of toxic dyes and transfer of pathogens. Careless disposal of plastic bags chokes drains, blocks the **porosity**[7] of the soil and causes problems for groundwater recharge. The waste must be recycled to conserve our resources and protect our environment.

Need for Reducing, Reusing and Recycling of Waste

In developing countries, waste management is turning out to be a major problem. The government and local bodies are looking for sustainable ways to dispose these wastes and reduce the harmful effects it has on the environment. The waste material could be managed by using three R's which are

(i) Reducing

The generation of unnecessary waste should be reduced in the following ways

- The harmful commodities like polythene bags should not be used as it is non-biodegradable waste. Shopping bags such as cloth bags and paper bags should be used.
- Using solar heaters and other solar products which are not harmful for the environment will help in reducing the waste generation at the source point.

5 **Carcinogenic** A substance that causes cancer.
6 **Leaching** It is extraction of minerals from a carrier to any sustance attached with it.
7 **Porosity** It is the quality of being porous or full of tiny holes.

- Vegetable peels, papers, wrappers, leftover food, etc are the household wastes which can be reduced by making compost.
- After using, various disposables such as plastic plates, plastic food containers, etc should be kept and not thrown away immediately as they can be put to many uses even after its first main purpose is served.
- Avoiding purchase of new items immediately after a slight fault in the old product as it would save money and reduce unnecessary deposition of garbage.
- Use washable table napkins instead of paper.
- Use **incineration**[8] method to get rid of inflammable wastes.

(ii) Reusing

The products which we use at home, offices, schools, etc can be put to many uses before discarding it. By changing its appearance, it can be made workable for other purposes. Various methods of reusing materials are as follows

- Allowing customers to return used packaging such as boxes, bubble wrap, so that they can be used again.
- Furnishing an office with reclaimed materials instead of purchasing new chairs, tables, etc.
- Personal computers, printers, fax machines, television, video cassette recorders, etc can be reused in business, personal and non-profit environments.
- By buying appliances, clothes, furnitures, dishes, vehicles, paint and virtually anything else, made up of reused products instead of brand new products.
- Some solid materials from industries can be used. Fly ash is one such residue which is produced whenever combustion of solid material takes place. Cement can be replaced by fly ash upto 35% thus, reducing the cost of construction of roads. Bricks are also made from it.
- Rag pickers collect the solid wastes and supply them to specialised artisans who take some useful waste materials to make different articles and earn a living from them.

For example, Rock garden is created by **Nek Chand** in Chandigarh from various waste materials like cans, bottles, broken pieces of crockery, etc.

(iii) Recycling

It is a method in which used waste materials are changed into new and useful products. This is done to reduce the use of raw materials that would have been used. Recycling also uses less energy and it is a great way of controlling air, water and land pollution. Recycling is possible only if the waste is segregated at its source and then cleaned and reprocessed into new useful products.

Recycling is beneficial in following ways

- It helps to protect the precious environment because if we burn the recyclable waste materials, these would pollute our air, land, water and soil.
- Recycling conserves natural resources. Recycling more waste means that we do not depend too much on raw resources, which are already massively depleted.
- It saves energy. It takes more energy to produce items with raw materials than from recycled materials.
- It creates jobs where people are employed to collect, sort and work in recycling companies.

Method of Waste Recycle

Several organisation and recycling centres have been established to collect recyclable waste. In these organisations, process waste is treated and made into something valuable. The methods of waste recycling are

- **Paper Recycling** In this method, the waste paper which are produced from households, offices, schools, etc are used to make new fresh paper. **Bagasse**[9] from sugarcane can be used to make paper pulp and thus, can help to save trees.
- **Plastic Recycling** It is the process of recovering scrap or waste plastics from the cities and reprocessing the material into useful products. e.g. soft drink bottles casted into plastic chairs and tables. Plastic can be used in the construction of roads. The Government of India order in November 2015 made it mandatory to use waste plastic in the construction of roads.

---

8 **Incineration** It is a waste treatment process that involves the combustion of substances contained in waste materials.

9 **Bagasse** It is a dry pulpy residue left after extraction of juice from sugarcane.

For this purpose, Chemistry Prof. **Rajagopalan Vasudevan**, in Thiagarajar college of Engineering, Madurai, developed technology for this purpose. Thus, he is known as **Plastic Man of India**. He first used this technology in 2002 for the construction of the road of college premises.

Check Your LEARNING...

1. Give an example of dry waste.
2. Gobar gas is also known by which other name?
3. State any one example of reusing materials.
4. State any one point of benefit of recycling.
5. State any one method of waste recycling.

QUiCK Revision

- Waste material is the normal term used to describe the products that has been used in any activity and now is rejected for further usage. It is generated by the natural vegetation, animals, insects and humans.
- Wastes are classified into various types such as biodegradable wastes and non-biodegradable wastes, toxic wastes and non-toxic wastes.
- The sources of waste are domestic, agriculture, industries, medical, nuclear, etc.
- The impact of waste accumulation can be seen by many ways, e.g. spoilage of landscape, causes pollution, bad impact on health and causes many diseases.
- Global warming and greenhouse effect is caused when some greenhouse gases such as carbon dioxide, methane, nitrous oxide, chlorofluorocarbons (CFCs) are released in the environment.
- Ozone present in the upper portion of the atmosphere. It prevents the harmful ultraviolet rays coming from the Sun but this layes is deplated due to air pollution.
- When acid exceeds is rain water it is known as acid rain which is the result of air pollution.
- Methyl mercury is a toxic chemical which is very harmful and cause disease of Minamata.
- Waste accumulation is dangerous for terrestrial life like for human beings, animals and plants, for fresh water aquatic life and marine water aquatic life.
- Open dumps are the uncovered areas that are used to dump solid waste of all kinds. It is usually the breeding ground for flies, rats and insects.
- Landfills are the pit that is dug in the ground and garbage is dumped before covering it with soil, preventing the breeding of flies and insects.
- Composting is a biological process in which micro-organisms, mainly fungi and bacteria decompose degradable organic waste into humus like substance in the presence of oxygen.
- To reduce waste we should focus on three R's i.e. reduce, reuse and recycle. These ways help to cut down on the amount of waste and manage the waste in a constructive way.

Chapter Practice

Section-I

Multiple Choice Questions

1. The most serious environmental effect posed by hazardous wastes is
   (a) air pollution
   (b) contamination of groundwater
   (c) more use of land area for landfills
   (d) None of the above

Ans. (b) contamination of ground water

2. How does an organic material decompose in the buried solid waste?
   (a) By the action of micro-organisms
   (b) By the action of oxidation
   (c) By the soil particles
   (d) By the flow of water

Ans. (a) By the action of micro-organisms

3. The 'Municipal Solid Waste' is the term used to describe which kind of solid waste?
   (a) Hazardous (b) Toxic
   (c) Non-hazardous (d) Non-toxic

Ans. (c) Non-hazardous

4. Which of the following methods of waste disposal is harmful ? [2023]
   (a) Composting (b) Segregation
   (c) Dumping (d) Vermicomposting

Ans. (b) Segregation

5. Why do plastics fall under a difficult material to recycle?
   (a) Because it is a very hard material.
   (b) Because plastic is very adhesive in its nature.
   (c) Because of different types of polymer resins.
   (d) Because of the different sizes of plastic.

Ans. (c) Because of different types of polymer resins.

6. What is the order of waste management hierarchy, from most to least favoured?
   (a) Prevention- Recycle-Reuse- Disposal
   (b) Prevention-Reuse-Disposal-Recycle
   (c) Prevention-Disposal -Reuse-Recycle
   (d) Prevention-Reuse-Recycle-Disposal

Ans. (d) Prevention-Reuse-Recycle-Disposal

7. Identify the following ones which can be recycled many times.
   (a) Plastic (b) Wood
   (c) Organic materials (d) Aluminium

Ans. (d) Aluminium

8. The process of burning municipal solid wastes under suitable temperature and conditions in a specific furnace is called ....
   (a) Landfill (b) Incineration
   (c) Recycling (d) Vermicomposting

Ans. (b) Incineration

9. .... is done on an individual level.
   (a) Burning (b) Disposal
   (c) Recycling (d) Source reduction

Ans. (d) Source reduction

10. When the organic matter present in the sanitary landfill decomposes, it generates ....
    (a) Methane (b) Nitrogen
    (c) Hydrogen (d) All of these

Ans. (a) Methane

11. Give reason for the following
    Biodegradable waste is not harmful.
    (a) It consists of glass, wood, polythene bags, etc.
    (b) It is decomposed by bacteria.
    (c) It creates a breeding ground of many diseases which are curable.
    (d) None of the above

Ans. (b) It is decomposed by bacteria.

12. Give reason for the following.
    Non- biodegradable waste is very harmful for the environment.
    (a) It consists of vegetable peels, paper, dead animals, plants, etc.
    (b) It cannot be broken down by the bacteria.
    (c) It can be recycled.
    (d) None of the above

Ans. (b) It cannot be broken down by the bacteria.

13. Give reason for the following
    Toxic waste is called hazardous waste.
    (a) It consists of poisonous wastes.
    (b) It can lead many diseases.
    (c) It can be biodegradable in nature.
    (d) Both (a) and (b)

Ans. (d) Both (a) and (b)

14. Give reason for the following
    Human is responsible for toxic waste generation.
    (a) Industrial activities are the main culprit for generation of toxic wastes.
    (b) Household activities are the main culprit for generation of toxic wastes.
    (c) Agricultural activities are the main culprit for generation of toxic wastes.
    (d) Both (a) and (c)

Ans. (d) Both (a) and (c)

15. Give reason for the following
Major cities are facing problem of garbage accumulation.
(a) Indiscriminate dumping of waste.
(b) Lack of space for garbage in cities.
(c) Increasing population is responsible for garbage accumulation.
(d) All of the above

Ans. (d) All of the above

16. The burning of solid waste is not recommended because
(i) it is very costly
(ii) it requires a lot of space
(iii) it requires modern technologies
(iv) it causes several environmental issues

Codes
(a) Only (i) (b) Only (ii)
(c) Only (iii) (d) All of these

Ans. (c) Only (iii)

17. Which of the following statements is correct?
(i) The waste from one process becomes the input for another process.
(ii) All the processes related to consumption and production produce some kind of waste.
(iii) There is no real waste in nature.

Codes
(a) Only (i) (b) Only (ii)
(c) Only (iii) (d) All of these

Ans. (d) All of these

18. Match the following.

	List-I		List-II
A.	Ozone layer depletion	1.	Solid waste
B.	Acid rain	2.	Carbon dioxide
C.	Global Warming	3.	Sulphur dioxide and nitrogen dioxide
D.	Non-toxic wastes	4.	Chlorofluorocarbons

Codes

	A	B	C	D		A	B	C	D
(a)	1	2	3	4	(b)	2	1	4	3
(c)	3	4	1	2	(d)	4	3	2	1

Ans. (d)

19. Match the following.

	List-I		List-II
A.	Industrial wastes	1.	Crop residue
B.	Agricultural waste	2.	Gases
C.	Domestic waste	3.	Syringes
D.	Biomedical waste	4.	Vegetable peels

Codes

	A	B	C	D		A	B	C	D
(a)	1	2	3	4	(b)	2	1	4	3
(c)	3	4	1	2	(d)	4	3	2	1

Ans. (b)

20. Match the following.

	List-I		List-II
A.	Mining waste	1.	Huge amount of dust
B.	Nuclear waste	2.	Radioactive elements
C.	Construction waste	3.	Bricks
D.	Electronic waste	4.	Discarded refrigerators

Codes

	A	B	C	D		A	B	C	D
(a)	1	2	3	4	(b)	2	1	4	3
(c)	3	4	1	2	(d)	4	3	2	1

Ans. (a)

Section-II

Short Questions

1. Answer the following questions.
(i) What do you understand by waste?
(ii) How many types of waste are there?

Ans. (i) Waste is the term used to describe the products that has been used in any activity and now is rejected for further usage.
(ii) Wastes are of three types biodegradable, non-biodegradable, toxic waste and non-toxic waste.

2. Answer the following questions.
(i) Mention two sources of waste.
(ii) What are biodegradable wastes? **[2016]**

Ans. (i) Agriculture waste and industrial waste are two sources of waste.
(ii) Biodegradable wastes are the objects which decompose through the action of bacteria, fungi and other living organisms.

3. Answer the following questions.
(i) What do you understand by toxic wastes?
(ii) What do you understand by non-toxic waste?

Ans. (i) Toxic wastes are the wastes that are poisonous such as radioactive wastes, industrial wastes, effluents, medical wastes, etc.
(ii) Non-toxic wastes are non-poisonous wastes, which are less harmful than toxic wastes. E.g. paper, plastic bags, containers, pieces of rope, etc.

4. What do you understand by industrial waste? Give examples of industrial waste.

Ans. Industrial waste is the waste produced by industrial activity which includes any material that is left useless during a manufacturing process.
Examples of Industrial wastes are chemical solvents, pigments, sludge, metals, ash, paints, sandpaper, paper products, industrial by-products, metals and radioactive wastes and effluents etc.

5. (i) What do you mean by domestic waste?
(ii) What is biomedical waste?

Ans. (i) Domestic waste refers to waste generated in household activity like vegetable peels, paper, plastic, etc.
(ii) Biomedical waste consist of used bandages, syringes, empty medicine bottles, expired medicines, etc.

6. Mention one advantage and one disadvantage of dumping of waste. **[2023]**

Ans. **Advantage** The main benefit of effective waste disposal include environmental protection from pollution or contamination.

Disadvantage Poor waste management contributes to climate change, and air pollution, and directly affects many ecosystems and species.

7. What is hazardous waste? How is it generated?

Ans. Hazardous waste is waste material, often found in chemical form that comes from agriculture, radioactive sources and industries. This can pose a long term risk to health and environment.

It is generated from chemical industries, leather industries, etc.

8. (i) Define gaseous waste.
(ii) What are the waste materials produced from mining?

Ans. (i) Gaseous waste includes fuel exhausts containing carbon dioxide, nitrogen oxides, carbon monoxide smog, etc.
(ii) Waste materials produced from mining are various suspended solid particles, chlorides, sulphuric acid, ferric hydroxide, heavy metals, etc.

9. Answer the following questions.
(i) What do you understand by the word 'Pollution'?
(ii) What is air pollution?

Ans. (i) Pollution refers to the addition of undesirable and unfavorable particles in the environment entirely or partly due to direct or indirect human actions.
(ii) Chemicals, suspended particulated matter, toxic wastes, biological wastes suspended into the atmosphere by direct or indirect human action, which degrading the quality of air is known as air pollution.

10. What impact does the waste accumulation have on the following? **[2019]**
(i) Quality of air around us.
(ii) Quality of water around us.

Ans. (i) Waste accumulation has bad impact on the quality of air around us. When we dump waste at the site and cover it with Earth then methane gas gets generated by decomposition of solid wate in landfills. This methane is not good for our atmosphere and warms up the air temperature which absorbs the Sun's heat.
(ii) The sewage waste coming from factories and industries reaches the water bodies and causes many water related diseases like diarrhea and typhoid.

11. Answer the following questions.
(i) State the main objective of the treatment of gaseous waste. **[2013]**
(ii) Name two common diseases caused as a result of gaseous pollution.

Ans. (i) The objective of treatment of gaseous waste is to minimise the generation of gaseous waste and to reduce the diseases caused due to gaseous pollution.
(ii) Asthma and bronchitis are two common diseases caused as a result of gaseous pollution.

12. (i) How does fresh water get polluted? **[2020]**
(ii) Why should sewage be treated before disposal?

Ans. (i) Sewage from municipalities and tanneries discharged into the rivers, canals and lakes, etc carry many species of bacteria and other microbes which pollutes the fresh water and cause diseases in human and animals.
(ii) Sewage should be treated before its disposal because sewage water contains harmful substances. So, when sewage is discharged untreated into the water bodies, it becomes dangerous for aquatic plants and animals.

13. Name any three source of marine pollution.

Ans. Three sources of marine pollution are
(i) Massive oil spills.
(ii) Growth of marine algae.
(iii) Discharge of harmful pesticides.

14. Why is there a need for waste management in India? **[Specimen Paper Semester-II 2022]**

Ans. There is a need for waste management in India because
- High degree of growth in population and industrialisation has made environment polluted which is a serious problem in many urban areas.
- The rapid increase in the number of vehicles on the road especially in metropolitan cities has degraded the quality of air severely. It leads to acid rain which adversely affects forests, freshwater, soil, killing insects as acid rain increases acidity in the soil, affects buldings, mouments, human health, plant growth, aquatic, species, etc.

15. Give two reasons as to why there is a need for safe waste disposal. **[2018]**

Ans. There is a need for safe waste disposal because of the following reasons
(i) It helps to prevent additional pollution which can improve public health.
(ii) Waste that is properly disposed off has a lesser chance of getting into the water supply and causing illness.

16. (i) What do you mean by segregation of waste? **[2020]**

(ii) Why is segregation of waste essential before its disposal?

Ans. (i) Segregation of waste means dividing the waste into different categories like dry and wet or biodegradable and non-biodegradable.

(ii) Segregation of waste is essential before its disposal because it reduces the volume of waste that reaches to the landfills.

17. Segregation is considered a safe method of waste disposal? Explain. **[Specimen Paper Semester- II 2022]**

Ans. Segregation is considered a safe method of waste disposal. It is due to the fact that in this method waste is segregated into different categories like dry and wet or biodegradable and non-biodegradable wastes and can dispose accordingly.

18. Mention two ways in which the decomposition of waste in open areas can effect human health. **[2019]**

Ans. Two ways is which the decomposition of waste in open areas can effect human health are

(i) In open areas, solid waste of all kinds is dumped. This waste is uncovered and not segregated. It becomes the breeding ground for flies, rats and other insects that spread disease and affect human health.

(ii) When waste water gets accumulated in open spaces it affects the soil and plant health and results in accumulation of toxic substances and infestation of mosquitoes and disease causing germs.

19. How can waste be reused? Explain with help of an example. **[2018]**

Ans. Waste can be reused by clearing or cleaning the material, repairing instead of buying new, etc.

For example, instead of using paper towels to clean the house, one can use a washable rag and instead of throwing out the clothes or toys pass them to a neighbour, charity, etc.

Long Questions

1. How does waste accumulation affect the environment? **[2014]**

Ans. Waste accumulation affects the environment such as

(i) When the waste is dumped in an improper way, the landscape of the area gives unpleasant look.

(ii) The uncontrolled dumping of urban waste damages the environment by causing air, water and land pollution.

(iii) When waste is accumulated and burnt, it leads air pollution.

2. With reference to waste accumulation, answer the following.

(i) Different types of primary pollutants.

(ii) Different types of secondary pollutants.

(iii) Formation of smog.

Ans. (i) Different types of primary pollutants are ashes from household, volcanic eruption, carbon monoxide from motor vehicle, etc.

(ii) Different types of secondary pollutants are burning of coal, vehicles on road and acid rain.

(iii) Smog is the mixture of smoke and fog in the air. It is also harmful for human health.

3. What is acid rain? Mention two of its effects. **[2014]**

Ans. Acid rain is a corrosive type of air pollution which occurs when oxides of sulphur and nitrogen combine with the moisture of atmosphere.

The effects of acid rain are

(i) Acid rain severely damages the various ecosystems in many parts of the world. Many forests and lakes have been damaged by it.

(ii) When acid rain pours on soil, it destroys the nutrients of the soil and reduces its fertility.

4. What was the cause of the following. **[2013]**

(i) The Bhopal Tragedy

(ii) The Minamata Disease

(iii) The Chernobyl Disaster

Ans. (i) Leakage of Methyl Isocyanate gas was the main cause for the Bhopal Gas Tragedy of 1984.

(ii) Methyl mercury, a toxic chemical, contaminated the water of Minamata (Japan) which caused serious health problems like Minamata disease.

(iii) The chernobyl disaster took place because of a combination of basic engineering deficiencies in the nuclear reactor and faulty actions of the operators.

5. What is water pollution?

Ans. Any addition of chemicals and waste material in the water bodies, which reduces the quality of the water by changing its colour, odour and composition and also reduces the natural cleansing process of water bodies, is known as water pollution.

Harmful waste from the surrounding area reaches the water bodies like ponds, lakes, rivers and groundwater and contaminates it. The sewage waste coming from factories and industries reaches the water bodies and causes many water related diseases like diarrhoea and typhoid. These sewage must be properly treated before releasing them into the environment.

6. 'Methane is an air pollutant that causes greenhouse effect'. Name three source of this gas. **[2017]**

Ans. Three sources of methane gas are

(i) **Fossil Fuel** The largest source of methane emission is from the production, distribution and combustion of fossil fuels.

(ii) **Landfills and Waste** Methane gets generated by the decomposition of solid waste in landfills.

(iii) **Wetlands** Wetlands are the largest natural sources of methane.

7. What is the impact on terrestrial life due to accumulation of wastes?

Ans. Terrestrial life consists of all the living beings that live on Earth such as humans, plants and animals. The impacts on terrestrial life are

Effect on Plants and Animals

- Many toxic chemicals, pesticides, other agricultural wastes released into the environment are taken up by the plants from air, water and soil. These toxins cause different types of leaf injuries premature leaf fall, decrease in transpiration, reduction in the rate of photosynthesis, reduction in biological nitrogen fixation.
- Exposure to high concentration of pollutants may cause acute injuries like chlorosis and discoloration. Sulphur dioxide is the most toxic pollutant which damages the crops.

Effect on Animal Life and Birds

- When birds eat waste materials like agricultural wastes. These cause defective egg shells and increase mortality rate.
- Several domestic animals like cow, buffalo, goat, etc. often eat polythene and plastic bags along with food material which ultimately reach to their alimentary canal causing many disorders and even death.

8. (i) What are open dumps?
(ii) How do they cause environmental degradation?
(iii) What can be done to stop it?

Ans. (i) Open dumps refers to uncovered areas that are used to dump solid waste of all kinds. The waste is untreated, uncovered and not segregated. It is the breeding ground for flies, rats and other insects that spread diseases. The rainwater runoff from these dumps contaminate nearby land, water and air thereby spreading disease.
(ii) The waste in open dump is left untreated, uncovered and not segregated. It becomes the breeding ground for flies, rats and other insects that spread diseases and causes environmental degradation.
(iii) Open dumps can be covered which are known as landfills. After dumping the garbage, the area can be sealed and used as a park or a parking lot.

9. Mention three reasons as to why the dumping of waste may be harmful.

Ans. The dumping of waste may be harmful because
(i) In open dumping, waste materials are dumped in open low lands far away from the city. This method is not environment-friendly as the open pits spoil the sight of the area and become a breeding ground for mosquitoes, flies, insects, etc.
(ii) Dumping sites can become the source region of harmful diseases and foul odour.
(iii) The burning of waste material in the open dumps pollutes the air.

10. Mention one way in which waste accumulation has an effect on the following. **[2018]**
(i) Aquatic life (ii) Terrestrial life
(iii) Landscape

Ans. (i) The life form in the aquatic ecosystem is adversely affected by accumulation of waste. This can decrease process of reproduction, which can eventually lead to extinction of animals.
(ii) Pesticides and weedicides are widely used in agricultural practices which are responsible for killing several types of terrestrial life like soil organisms, worms, etc.
(iii) The waste accumulation not only ruins the natural beauty of the land, but also provides a home to rats and other disease carrying organisms.

11. Give reason for the following.
(i) In the primary stage of treatment water is unfit for drinking.
(ii) In the secondary stage, water is allowed to settle.
(iii) Raw sludge is kept in airtight tanks.

Ans. (i) In the primary stage of treatment water is not clean because it contains sewage, toxic substances and chemicals.
(ii) In the secondary stage, water is allowed to settle as settling allows the micro-organisms to decompose the organic materials present in the water.
(iii) Raw sludge is kept in airtight tanks because anaerobic bacteria breaks down the raw sludge to form carbon dioxide, methane and water.

12. Explain briefly the meaning of the following terms. **[2016]**
(i) Composting (ii) Incineration (iii) Segregation

Ans. (i) Composting is a biological process of decomposing solid wastes by micro-organisms.
(ii) Incineration is a method of burning the waste to reduce its weight and volume so, that it can be disposed easily.
(iii) Segregation refers to separation of waste into different categories of waste. Classification of biodegradable and non-biodegradable wastes are two most popular segregation of wastes.

13. What do you mean by the following **[2017]**
(i) Sewage (ii) Eutrophication (iii) Recycling

Ans. (i) Sewage is waste water which is either domestic or industrial produced by human actions.
(ii) Eutrophication is the process of depletion or reduction of oxygen content from water bodies due to direct or indirect activities of human works.
(iii) Recycling is the process of changing the waste and non-usable materials into potentially useful materials.

14. Mention three ways that may be used in India to reduce waste. **[Specimen Paper Semester-II 2022]**

Ans. Three ways which can be used in India to reduce waste are

(i) Follow reduce, reuse and recycle methods.

(ii) Use carry bags made of paper or cloth instead of polythene to reduce polythene waste.

(iii) Repair old things rather than discards.

15. What type of products can be used again? Mention three methods of reusing a product.

Ans. The products which we use at home, offices, schools, etc can be put to many uses again before discarding it. Various methods of reusing materials are

- Allowing customers to return used packaging such as boxes, bubble wrap, so that they can be used again.
- Furnishing an office with reclaimed materials instead of purchasing new chairs, tables, etc.
- Personal computers, printers, fax machines, television, video cassette recorders, etc. can be reused in business, personal and non-profit environments.
- Some solid materials from industries can be used. Fly ash is one such residue which is produced whenever combustion of solid material takes place. Cement can be replaced by fly ash upto 35% thus, reducing the cost of construction of roads. Bricks are also made from it.

16. Briefly answer the following. **[2023]**

(i) How is segregation of the waste helpful?

(ii) Mention one way in which we can reuse waste.

(iii) Mention one benefit of composting.

Ans. (i) Segregation of waste is helpful as it facilitates the process of reuse, recycling, and recovery of waste. Segregating waste can improve the recycling process.

(ii) We can reuse the waste by donating the items that are still in a good and usable condition to charities.

(iii) Composting enhances the soil nutrients such as nitrogen and phosphorus. It enhances the water retention capacity of the soil and increases the fertility of soil by adding humus.

17. (i) "Waste segregation is important." Give a reason to support your answer. **[2015]**

(ii) Why is nuclear waste harmful?

(iii) Explain briefly how as a student, you can help in the reduction of waste generation.

Ans. (i) Waste segregation is important because under this waste is segregated into different categories like biodegradable and non-biodegradable and toxic wastes. It increases recycling process.

(ii) Nuclear waste is harmful because radiations from nuclear plants like uranium and radium when absorbed by the human body causes serious health problems.

(iii) We as a student should follow the following steps to reduce the waste generation.

- We should prefer the use of natural energy resources such as solar cooker and minimise the use of cooking gas.
- Stop using plastic bags and carry paper bags or jute bags.
- We should learn to repair rather than discard.
- We should stop using disposable plates.
- We should make minimum use of auto vehicles and maximum use of the public transport vehicles.

18. (i) Why segregation of waste must be done before disposal? **[2019]**

(ii) How has composting proven to be a great help in managing waste?

Ans. (i) Segregation is important to be done before disposal because if the waste is not separated properly, it all gets mixed up in landfills. Harmful gasses can leak after a period of time, resulting in contamination of groundwatar.

(ii) Composting is a biological process in which micro-organisms, mainly fungi and bacteria, decompose biodegradable or organic waste in the presence of oxygen. Composting is helpful in managing waste as in this process, various wastes like leaves, twigs, grass, fruit peels and vegetable peels, etc are dumped into a pit and then covered. This recyling process produces compost and biogas or gobar gas. Compost is a rich source of organic matter. It plays an important role in sustaining soil fertility.

19. Give a reason for each of the following **[2019]**

(i) Trees must be planted in the industrial areas.

(ii) Chemical fertilisers must be replaced by organic manure.

(iii) Plastic and polythene products must be banned.

Ans. (i) Trees must be planted in the industrial areas due to following reasons

- Trees help reduce the heat produced by the industries.
- Trees perform transpiration and can affect the climate of a region considerably.
- Trees filter harmful dust and pollutants such as ozone, carbon monoxide and sulfur dioxide from the air we breathe.

(ii) Chemical fertilisers are made from harmful chemicals. Whereas organic fertilisers are usually made from plant or animal waste, e.g. manure, compost bones and cotton seed meal. Organic fertilisers improve the structure of the soil and increase its ability to hold water and nutrients and overtime these fertilisers make soil and plants healthy and strong. Whereas chemical fertilisers are harmful when continuously used in farming. Thus, chemical fertilisers must be replaced by organic manure.

(iii) Plastic bags are a major contributor in plastic pollution. It is a kind of pollution which is deteriorating our environment. It is a threat to life on Earth. Plastic and polythene bags cause land, air and water pollution. Plastic and polythenes do not degrade instead plastic gets broken down into small tiny pieces which are swept down and end up in the ocean. It is then consumed by wildlife or keep on accumulating in the environment. Thus, plastic and polythene products must be banned.

20. Briefly answer each of the following. [2020]
(i) What is the effect of waste accumulation on terrestrial life?
(ii) What are the consequences of water pollution?
(iii) What is the benefit of composting?

Ans. (i) Refer to chapter theory page 215.
(ii) The consequences of water pollution are
- Destruction of ecosystem.
- It can cause many diseases like typhoid, cholera, hepatitis and so on.
- It can affect the foodchain.

(iii) The benefits of composting are
- The soil becomes more resistant to stresses such as drought, diseases and toxicity.
- It helps the crop in better absorption of nutrients from the soil.
- It increases the quality of poor soils by adding humus.

21. (i) How can recycling of waste help in reducing waste? Explain with suitable examples. [2020]
(ii) Mention one initiative taken by the Government to manage waste.

Or (i) How is recycling of waste helpful? Give an example of recycling of waste.
(ii) Mention any one initiative taken by the government to manage waste. [2023]

Ans. (i) Recycling of waste can help in reducing waste in many ways. For example, shoes, sandals and slippers can be made from old types, fly ash from power plants can be used as a substitute for cement, etc.
(ii) Initiatives taken by the government of India to manage waste is 'Swachh Bharat Mission' 'National Water Mission' and 'Waste to Energy'.

Picture Based Questions

1. Study the picture given below and answer the questions that follows.

(i) Name the activity shown in the above picture.
(ii) Give two advantages of this activity.

Ans. (i) Recycling of paper.
(ii) Two advantages of paper recycling are
(a) The waste paper which are produced from households, offices and schools are reused to make fresh paper.
(b) It creates jobs where people are employed to collect, sort and work in paper recycling process.

2. Study the picture given below and answer the following questions.

(i) Identify the logo given in the picture.
(ii) Give any two methods of waste recycling.

Ans. (i) The given logo is of three R's i.e. Reduce, Reuse and Recycle.
(ii) Two Methods of waste recycling are
(a) **Paper Recycling** In the process of paper recycling, the waste paper which are produced from households, offices, schools, etc are used to make new fresh paper.
(b) **Plastic Recycling** It is the process of recovering scrap or waste plastics from the cities and reprocessing the material into useful products. e.g. soft drink bottles casted into plastic chairs and tables.

Chapter Assessment

Section-I

Multiple Choice Questions

1. What is the most expensive component of solid waste handling?
   (a) Collection (b) Storage
   (c) Treatment (d) Separation
2. Which of the following waste is not used to generate fuel gases?
   (a) Municipal solid waste (b) Animal excreta
   (c) Farm waste (d) Plastic and metal
3. In villages, animal excreta and farm waste are used to produce ....
   (a) waste (b) polluting gas
   (c) gobar gas (d) contaminated liquid
4. The wastes burning is not an acceptable practice of solid waste management because ....
   (a) it requires a lot of space
   (b) it requires modern technologies
   (c) it causes several environmental issues
   (d) it is very costly
5. Degradation of oxygen content in water due to organic and chemical waste is known as
   (a) Decomposition (b) Eutrophication
   (c) Leaching (d) Composting

Section-II

Short Questions

1. Differentiate between biodegradable and non-biodegradable waste.
2. How does oil refineries contribute in water pollution?
3. How do textile industries contribute in pollution?
4. What is e-waste? Define.
5. How is carbon monoxide harmful to human life?

Long Questions

1. What is the effect of wastes on aquatic life?
2. What is the need of waste management to protect the environment and human life?
3. What is waste collection and its safe disposal?
4. What is the need for reducing, reusing and recycling in waste management?
5. Explain the impacts of waste accumulation.

SAMPLE QUESTION PAPER 1

A HIGHLY SIMULATED Sample Question Paper for ICSE Class X

Geography (Unsolved)

General Instructions

1. Answers to this paper must be written on the answer sheet provided separately.
2. You will not be allowed to write during the first 15 minutes. This time is to be spent in reading the question paper.
3. The time given at the head of this Paper is the time allowed for writing the answers.
4. Attempt seven questions in all. Part I is compulsory. All questions from Part I are to be attempted. A total of five questions are to be attempted from Part II.
5. The intended marks for questions or parts of questions are given in brackets ( ).

Time : 2 Hrs **Max. Marks : 80**

Part - I

(30 Marks)

Attempt all questions from this part

Question 1

Study the extract of the survey of India Map Sheet No- G43S10 (Eastings 48-58 and Northings 19-29) and answer the following questions.

(i) (a) Give the six-figure grid reference for .264 in the Northern part of the map extract. (2)

(b) What are the red rectangular patches in the North-West quarter of the map extract? **[Apply & Understanding]**

(ii) If Ram travels in a straight line from 04 Northing to 12 Northing on a bicycle at a speed of 6 km/hr, what is the estimated duration he will require to reach his destination? (2)

(iii) (a) What is the compass direction of Dhibri (4306) to Methipura (4204)? (2)

(b) Which geographical features can be observed if you move towards the South of the topographical map? **[Analyse]**

(iv) (a) Upon Meera's homecoming after a decade, what visual cues or noticeable changes in the surrounding area of Jaspuriya (8545) serve as clear indications of the region's progress and growth since her departure?

(b) What is the black vertical line between Easting 33 and 34? **[Apply & Remember]**

(v) Mention two man-made and two natural features in the grid square 3288. **[Understanding]**

Question 2

On the outline map of India provided,

(a) shade and label the Karakoram Mountain Range (1)

(b) shade and label the Konkan Plain (1)

(c) label the Ghaghara River (1)

(d) shade and label the Gulf of Kutch (1)

(e) mark the Tropic of Cancer (1)

(f) mark with arrows the direction of the winds which bring rain to West Bengal in summer (1)

(g) mark and label the Digboi oilfield (1)

(h) shade and label an area of Black soil (1)

(i) mark and label the city of Kolkata (1)

(j) mark and label the most densely populated state of India (1)

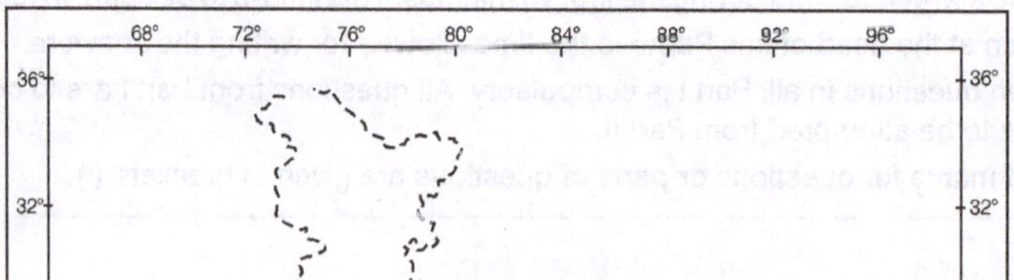

Question 3

Choose the correct option.

(i) Why has Thar developed into a desert? (1)

(a) It has no cloud cover.

(b) It is near the sea.

(c) It is on the windward side of Western Ghats.

(d) Aravalli is parallel to South-West Monsoon wind.

(ii) _______ is the most widespread soil of India. (1)

(a) Alluvial soil (b) Black soil

(c) Red soil (d) Laterite soil

(iii) Ebony: Tropical Rainforest (1)

(a) Mahogany: Furniture (b) Stilted roots: Mangrove Vegetation

(b) Teak: Tropical deciduous forest (d) Spines: Tropical Desert Vegetation

(iv) Identify the most advanced and efficient method of irrigation? (1)

(a) Canal Irrigation (b) Well Irrigation

(c) Drip Irrigation (d) Tank irrigation

(v) Select the state which is a leading producer of Manganese in India? (1)

(a) Uttar Pradesh (b) Punjab

(c) Andhra Pradesh (d) Odisha

(vi) Assertion (A) Rabi crops are sown in winter and harvested in the spring season. (1)

Reason (R) Rabi crops require a cool climate with moderate rainfall for optimal growth.

(a) Both A and R are true and R is the correct explanation of A.

(b) Both A and R are true but R does not explain A

(c) A is true but R is false

(d) A is false but R is true

(vii) Which method is not used for the sowing of rice? (1)

(a) Drilling (b) Dibbling

(c) Silting (d) Broadcasting

(viii) Which city is known as the 'Manchester of India'? (1)

(a) Mumbai (b) Surat (c) Ahmedabad (d) Kanpur

(ix) If you need to transport heavy machinery over a short distance, which mode of transport would you choose and why? (1)

(a) Road transport (b) Air transport

(c) Water transport (d) Rail transport

(x) Which type of waste management is depicted in the picture? (1)

(a) Segregation (b) Incineration (c) Composting (d) Landfilling

Part - II

(50 Marks)

Attempt any five questions from this part

4. (i) Climate change has led to extreme weather events, like storms, droughts, heavy rainfall and flooding, happening more regularly. Apart from climate change-driven events, natural global weather patterns may compound the problems further by adding to the chaos. For many in India, this climate chaos has led to a compound disaster known as Concurrent Droughts and Heatwaves or CDHW for short. *(researchmatters.in)* (2)

(a) Mention the duration of the summer season in India.

(b) What is the atmospheric pressure condition during summer season over the central part of India?

(ii) What is the source of winter rainfall in the following areas. (2)

(a) Uttar Pradesh

(b) Punjab

(iii) Give a geographical reason for each of the following. (3)

(a) Kanpur has extreme temperature conditions.

(b) Kochi is warmer than Mumbai even though both lie on the Western Coast of India.

(c) The Ganga Plain gets the monsoon rain much later than the West Coast of India.

(iv) Study the climatic data of station X and answer the following questions (3)

Month	Jan	Feb	Mar	Apr	May	Jun	Jul	Aug	Sep	Oct	Nov	Dec
Tem. (°C)	23.1	24.8	26	29.3	33	32.8	33.1	32.1	30	29.3	28.7	26.1
Rainfall (cm)	7.3	1.1	0.3	0.1	1.3	4.5	6.1	8.2	8.5	20.1	20.8	9.0

(a) What is the annual range of temperature of station X?

(b) Which is the driest month?

(c) Calculate the annual range of temperature.

5. (i) Soil conservation involves methods to prevent soil erosion and degradation that ensures the fertility of the land for sustainable farming. Techniques like afforestation, contour ploughing, terracing and the use of cover crops help in reducing the loss of topsoil, preserving soil structure and improving water retention. These practices are essential for maintaining agricultural productivity and preventing desertification. (2)

(a) What is soil conservation and why is it important for agriculture?

(b) Name two methods of soil conservation.

(ii) With reference to black soil answer the following. (2)

(a) Name one important crop which grows in this soil.

(b) Give one chemical property of this soil.

(iii) With reference to red soils in India, answer the following questions. (3)

(a) Name two states where red soil is found.

(b) State two advantages of this type of soil.

(c) Mention two important crops grown in this soil

(iv) Give a reason for the following statements. (3)

(a) Black Soil has self-ploughing properties.

(b) Laterite Soil is not suitable for cultivation.

(c) Alluvial soil is extensively found in the Northern Plains.

6. (i) Raj went for an excursion with his sister and came across an arid area with plants that had broad, flat leaves with a large surface area. (2)
   (a) Identify the type of vegetation belt he came across.
   (b) Name some areas where this kind of vegetation is found.
   (ii) (a) Why the Tropical Evergreen forests are difficult to exploit for commercial purposes. (2)
   (b) Why is tropical deciduous forest commercially the most important forest belt of India?
   (iii) Give three reasons why forests must be conserved. (3)
   (iv) (a) Name a forest conservation method that involves the local Community. (3)
   (b) Which primitive system of agriculture had led to large scale destruction of forest in the past?
   (c) Name the process which involves planting two saplings for each tree that is felled.
7. (i) Give two reasons why water scarcity occurs in India. (2)
   (ii) Distinguish between Drip irrigation and Furrow irrigation. (2)
   (iii) Explain the following types of irrigation (3)
   (a) Tank irrigation (b) Furrow irrigation
   (c) Well irrigation (3)
   (iv) (a) What is meant by rainwater harvesting? (3)
   (b) Mention any two rainwater harvesting practices popular in India.
8. (i) Energy is a critical component of the economic infrastructure, as it is the primary input required to support economic growth. Economic development and energy usage have a close relationship. The greater a country's per capita energy usage, the more developed it is and vice versa. Human civilisation is reliant on a variety of energy sources. (2)
   (a) What are some examples of non-conventional energy sources and how do they differ from conventional ones?
   (b) How does solar energy generation contribute to reducing the reliance on fossil fuels?
   (ii) With reference to Petroleum, answer the following. (2)
   (a) An off-shore oil field in the Gulf of Cambay.
   (b) An oil refinery in Bihar.
   (iii) (a) Give any two uses of Manganese (3)
   (b) Name the mineral used to strengthen steel.
   (c) Name any two indian states where iron ore is found.
   (iv)

(3)
   (a) Identity the type of energy being harnessed in the above picture
   (b) Mention any one advantage of the energy produced by this device.
   (c) How has India leveraged solar energy to meet its growing energy demands and what are the key challenges it faces in expanding solar power capacity?

9. (i) Mention any two features of Plantation farming with two examples. (2)

(ii) State one point of difference between winnowing and milling. (2)

(iii) With reference to Sugarcane, answer the following questions. (3)

(a) Mention two different ways in which it is propagated.

(b) Why is a lot of labour required for its cultivation?

(c) Why must the sugar mills be near the Sugar fields?

(iv) Sumit is talking to his friend about petrochemical industry. (3)

(a) State a reason for the growing popularity of this industry in recent times.

(b) Why is it located close to oil refineries?

10. (i) Mention two reasons, why industrial development is important for India? (2)

(ii) (a) Explain two ways by which plantation farming contribute to the economy of tropical regions. (2)

(b) What are the main crops commonly grown in plantation farming systems?

(iii) With reference to the Sugar industry, answer the following questions. (3)

(a) Why should these industries be located near sugarcane growing areas?

(b) Mention one leading sugar-producing state in India.

(c) Name any two byproducts of the Sugar Industry.

(iv) Give one reason for each of the following. (3)

(a) The largest mineral-based industry in India.

(b) Mini-steel plants cause less pollution than integrated steel plants.

(c) The electronic industry has made an impact on both entertainment and education.

11. (i) Mention two advantages of using roadways. (2)

(ii) The airways have contributed towards the growing economy of India. Explain. (2)

(iii) (a) Mention two advantages Air transport. (3)

(b) Name the authority that is responsible for monitoring Air transport in India

(iv) Give a reason for each of the following. (3)

(a) At present times, airports are being established even in smaller towns in India.

(b) Railways are less developed in the North-East states of India.

(c) Helicopter services are crucial during emergencies.

12. (i) Delhi and several northern Indian cities get enveloped in a thick blanket of smog every winter due to smoke, dust, low wind speed, vehicular emissions and crop stubble burning. The Delhi government has also enacted its Graded Response Action Plan, known as GRAP, to tackle pollution. It bans all activities that involve the use of coal and firewood, as well as diesel generator use for non-emergency services. *(www.bbc.com)* (2)

(a) What are the main causes of air pollution in urban areas?

(b) How can industries reduce their environmental impact through sustainable practices?

(c) What role can individuals and communities play in reducing air pollution levels?

(ii) (a) Why is there a need for reusing? (2)

(b) Why is recycling important for environmental sustainability and resource conservation?

(iii) Effective waste management is crucial for maintaining environmental health and sustainability. Practices like recycling, composting and waste-to-energy technologies help reduce landfill waste, conserve resources and lower pollution. Governments and individuals are increasingly adopting these methods to ensure cleaner cities and a healthier planet for future generations.

(Source: Ministry of Environment, Forest and Climate Change, Government of India) (3)

(a) What role do individuals play in waste management?
(b) What are some common methods of waste management?
(c) How does waste-to-energy technology benefit waste management?

(iv) Explain how waste generated in the following sectors may be made useful. (Give one example for each) (3)
(a) Household
(b) Industries
(c) Tourist places

Answers

1. (i) (a) 345096 (b) Settlement

(ii) Here, R: F = 1:50,000 (means 1 cm on map is equal to 50,000 cm on ground)

The distance between 06 northing to 12 northing is 12 cm.

12 cm = 50,000 × 12 = 600,000 which is 6 km (1 km = 1,00,000 cm) If Kavita moves at a speed of 3 km/hr, it will take her 4 hr to reach her destination.

(iii) (a) North (b) Sandhills

(iv) (a) Railway power line, road and metal roads

(b) Longitude 22'30'' E

(v) Roads and power lines are man-made features and trees and sandhills are natural features.

2.

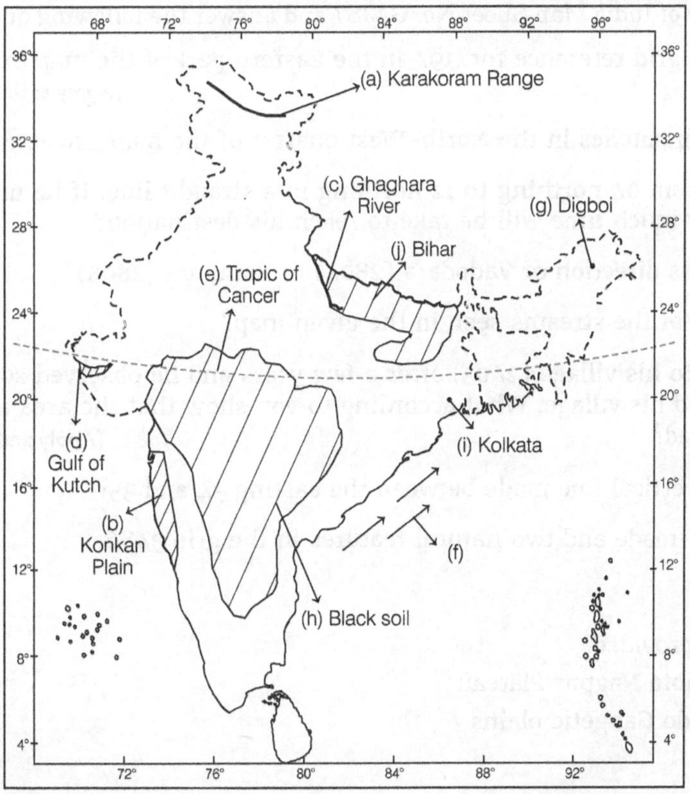

3. (i) (d), (ii) (a), (iii) (c), (iv) (c), (v) (d), (vi) (a), (vii) (c), (viii) (c), (ix) (a), (x) (a)

SAMPLE QUESTION PAPER 2

A HIGHLY SIMULATED Sample Question Paper for ICSE Class X

Geography (Unsolved)

General Instructions : See Sample Paper 1

Part - I

(30 Marks)

Attempt all questions from this part

Question 1

Study the extract of the survey of India Map Sheet No. G43S7 and answer the following questions.

(i) (a) Give the six-figure grid reference for .194 in the Eastern part of the map extract. **[Apply & Understanding] (2)**

(b) What are the brown patches in the North-West quarter of the map extract?

(ii) Ram goes on bicycle from 04 northing to 12 northing in a straight line. If he moves at a speed of 5 km/hr, how much time will he take to reach his destination? **[Apply] (2)**

(iii) (a) What is the compass direction of Vadodara (2804) to Rampura (2805)? **[Analyse] (2)**

(b) What is the nature of the streams seen in the given map?

(iv) (a) A person returned to his village (2403) after a few years and he observed some development around his village. What according to you show that the area around his village has developed? **[Apply and Remember] (2)**

(b) What is the black vertical line made between the easting 34 and 35?

(v) Mention any two man-made and two natural features in the grid 3486. **(2)**

Question 2

On the outline map of India provided,

(a) shade and label the Chota Nagpur Plateau **(1)**

(b) shade and label the Indo Gangetic plains **(1)**

(c) label the Satluj River (1)

(d) mark and label the Gulf of Khambhat (1)

(e) mark and label a densely populated state of South India (1)

(f) mark with arrows the direction of the Bay of Bengal branch of South-West monsoon (1)

(g) mark and label an offshore oilfield (1)

(h) shade an area of alluvial soil in North-East India (1)

(i) mark and label the city of Delhi (1)

(j) label the Narmada River (1)

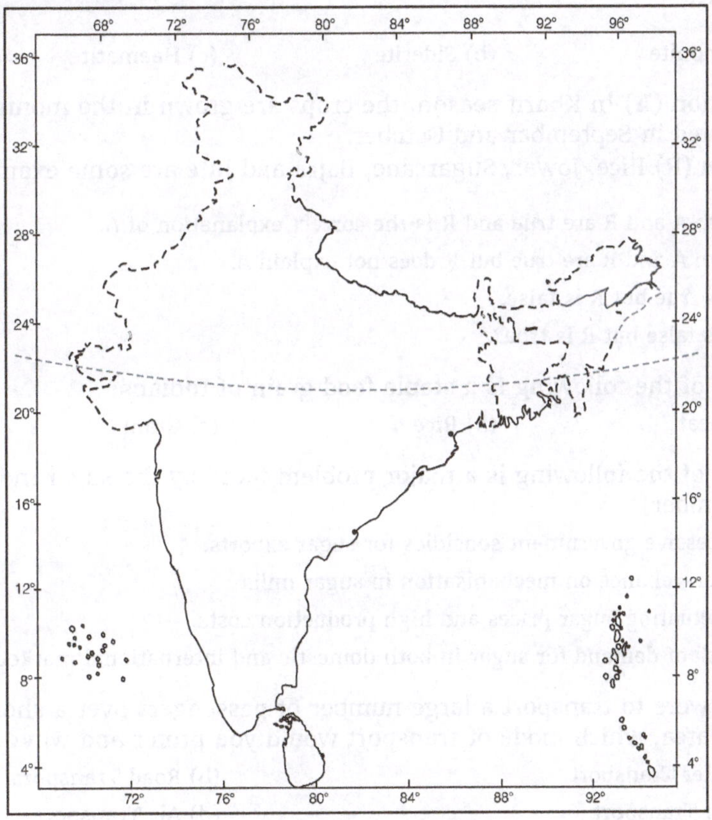

Question 3

Choose the correct answers to the questions from the given options. (10)

(Do not copy the question, write the correct answers only.)

(i) The pre-monsoon mango showers occur predominantly in: [Apply]

(a) West Bengal and Assam

(b) Deccan Plateau

(c) Gujarat and Maharashtra

(d) Kerala and Karnataka

(ii) Khadar and Bhangar are the two types of ________ soil in India. [Remember]

(a) Alluvial Soil (b) Red Soil

(c) Laterite Soil (d) Black Soil

(iii) Evergreen Forests: Assam [Remember]

(a) Deciduous Forests: Jammu and Kashmir
(b) Montane Forests: Madhya Pradesh
(c) Deciduous Forests: Uttar Pradesh
(d) Littoral Forests: Haryana

(iv) Which of the following is a groundwater source? [Understanding]

(a) Pond
(b) Lake
(c) Spring
(d) River

(v) Which of the following is the best quality iron ore and contains around 70% of iron content? [Remember]

(a) Limonite
(b) Siderite
(c) Haematite
(d) Magnetite

(vi) **Assertion (A)** In Kharif season, the crops are grown in the months of June and July and harvested in September and October.
Reason (R) Rice, Jowar, Sugarcane, Bajra and Jute are some examples of Kharif crops. [Analysis]

(a) Both A and R are true and R is the correct explanation of A.
(b) Both A and R are true but R does not explain A.
(c) A is true but R is false.
(d) A is false but R is true.

(vii) Which of the following is a staple food grain of Indians? [Remember]

(a) Wheat
(b) Rice
(c) Gram
(d) Arhar

(viii) Which of the following is a major problem faced by the sugar industry in India? [Remember]

(a) Excessive government subsidies for sugar exports.
(b) Over-reliance on mechanisation in sugar mills
(c) Fluctuating sugar prices and high production costs.
(d) Lack of demand for sugar in both domestic and international markets.

(ix) If you were to transport a large number of passengers over a short distance in a crowded urban area, which mode of transport would you prefer and why? [Apply]

(a) Water Transport
(b) Road Transport
(c) Rail Transport
(d) Air Transport

(x) Which type of waste management is depicted in the picture? [Apply]

(a) Segregation
(b) Incineration
(c) Composting
(d) Landfilling

Part - II

(50 Marks)

Attempt any five questions from this part

Question 4

(i) India is experiencing increasingly erratic monsoon patterns, with delayed arrivals, early withdrawals and unpredictable rainfall distribution. This disrupts agriculture, impacts food security and stresses water resources. Experts attribute these changes to climate change, urging stronger adaptation measures for farmers and improved water management.

(Source: India Meteorological Department (IMD), 2024 Report) (2)

(a) How are the changing monsoon patterns affecting agriculture in India?

(b) As a student of Geography, What action do you suggest to deal with changing monsoon patterns in India?

(ii) With reference to monsoon in India, name the following. (2)

(a) The winds bring heavy rain in Cherrapunji.

(b) The local winds that bring a light rainfall to South India and are good for Mango, tea and Coffee crops.

(iii) Give a reason for each of the following. (3)

(a) Kanyakumari experiences an equitable climate.

(b) Central Maharashtra gets less rainfall than coastal areas of Maharashtra.

(c) Jaipur has a higher annual range of temperature than Mumbai.

(iv) Study the climatic data of station X and answer the following questions (3)

Months	Jan	Feb	Mar	Apr	May	June	July	Aug	Sept	Oct	Nov	Dec
Tempera-ture (°C)	23	24.8	26	29	33	32.8	33	32.1	30.5	29.3	28.7	26.5
Rainfall (cm)	7.3	1.3	0.5	0.3	1.3	4.5	6.8	8.2	8.5	20.1	20.8	9.0

(a) Name the driest month.

(b) Calculate the annual rainfall experienced by station X.

(c) Calculate the annual range of temperature?

Question 5

(i) Hari, a farmer in Rajasthan, faced severe soil degradation due to overgrasing and improper irrigation techniques. This led to the depletion of nutrients in the soil, reducing crop yields. By adopting soil conservation methods like crop rotation and water-efficient practices, he was able to restore the fertility of his land. (2)

(a) What is the importance of soil conservation in India?

(b) How did soil degradation affect Hari's farming?

(ii) With reference to soil erosion, answer the following. (2)

(a) Mention one way in which man is responsible for soil erosion.

(b) How can deepening of the river bed help in preventing soil erosion?

(iii) With reference to Black Soil, answer the following. (3)

(a) How is it formed?

(b) Why is it good for Farming?

(c) Name any two areas where this soil is found.

(iv) Give a reason for each of the following (3)

(a) Why alluvial soil is good for growing sugarcane?

(b) Why black soil is good for cotton cultivation

(c) Why red soil is not found in northern India?

Question 6

(i) Sumit, a botanist in Uttarakhand, studied India's diverse natural vegetation, from the tropical rainforests in the southwest to the alpine vegetation in the Himalayan region. He observed how altitude climate and rainfall influence the growth of different plants which contributes to India's rich biodiversity. (2)

(a) What factors influence the growth of natural vegetation in India?

(b) How does altitude affect vegetation in India?

(ii) (a) Name the forests which grow on the windward slope of the Western Ghats. (2)

(b) Why do such forests grow in this region?

(iii) Give any three characteristics of Littoral forests. (3)

(iv) (a) Give one reason to explain why the Tropical Evergreen forests are difficult to exploit for commercial purposes. (3)

(b) Why is afforestation essential in the cities that have iron and steel industries?

(c) How do forests act as a source of income for the people?

Question 7

(i) Mention two conditions required for the construction of tube wells. (2)

(ii) Differentiate between Drip irrigation and Furrow irrigation. (2)

(iii) (a) Name a state where canals are commonly used for irrigation. (3)

(b) Give two reasons for the conservation of water resources.

(iv) (a) What is drip irrigation? (3)

(b) Mention any two advantages of sprinkler irrigation.

Question 8

(i) India is rich in mineral and energy resources, including coal, iron ore and natural gas, which are vital for its economic growth. The country also has significant renewable energy potential, with solar and wind energy resources seeing rapid development. These resources are key to India's industrialisation and energy security.

(Source: Ministry of Mines, Government of India, 2024) (2)

(a) What are some of the key mineral resources found in India and how do they contribute to the economy?

(b) How has India been advancing in the use of renewable energy resources like solar and wind power?

(ii) With reference to Bhakra Nangal Dam, answer the following questions. (2)

(a) What is the primary purpose of the Bhakra Nangal Dam and where is it located?

(b) How has the Bhakra Nangal Dam contributed to irrigation and power generation in India?

(iii) (a) Give any one use of copper. (3)

(b) Name the mineral that is used with copper to produce brass.

(c) Name two Indian states where manganese are found.

(iv)

(3)

(a) Identify the type of energy being harnessed in the above picture.

(b) How does this energy contribute to India's renewable energy goals?

(c) What are the advantages of using this energy over traditional fossil fuels? (3)

Question 9

(i) Mention any two features of Plantation farming with two examples. (2)

(ii) (a) State one point of difference between Subsistence and Commercial farming. (2)

(b) Why is Cultivation of wheat confined to the Northern part of India?

(iii) With reference to Rice crop, explain the process of (3)

(a) Threshing (b) Winnowing

(c) Milling

(iv) Suresh is discussing about 'RATOON' cropping with his friend (3)

(a) Name the crop which suresh is discussing with his friend.

(b) Mention any two features of this type of crop.

Question 10

(i) Mention any two points of difference between Basic and Consumer industries. (2)

(ii) 'Though Uttar Pradesh has the largest number of Sugar Mills yet Maharashtra is the largest Producer of Sugar.' Give any two reasons to justify the statement. (2)

(iii) With reference to industries, answer the following questions. (3)

(a) From where Tata Steel gets its supply of coal, iron ore and water supply from?

(b) What is the significance of the Electronics industry for education, entertainment and Research? Any two points.

(iv) Give one reason to explain each of the following. (3)

(a) Iron and steel industry is concentrated in the chhota nagpur plateau region in India.

(b) Silk products from India are becoming less popular in the international market these days.

(c) Cotton textile industry has developed in Mumbai.

Question 11

(i) Mention any two advantages of using airways. (2)

(ii) 'Transport is the backbone of a country's economy'. Give two reasons to support the statement. (2)

(iii) (a) Give one geographical reason why water transport is not as popular as land transport in India. (3)

(b) Which is Inland waterway that connects Prayagraj to Haldia.

(c) What is AAI and when was it formed?

(iv) Give a reason for each of the following. (3)

(a) Roadways are not well developed in North East India.

(b) Railways are under the public sector.

(c) Road transport is preferred in the northern plains? (3)

Question 12

(i) What is the impact of waste generation on the following. (2)

(a) Surface water (b) Landscape

(ii) Why is segregation considered a good method of waste disposal? (2)

(iii) As urbanisation increases, proper waste disposal has become a critical issue in India. Efficient waste management practices, such as recycling, composting and waste-to-energy technologies, are essential to reduce pollution and conserve resources. The government is encouraging sustainable solutions to tackle the waste crisis.

(Source: Ministry of Environment, Forest and Climate Change, 2024) (3)

(a) Why is waste management important for environmental sustainability?

(b) How does waste segregation promote sustainability?

(c) State one way in which domestic waste can be made useful.

(iv) (a) What is incineration? (3)

(b) Enumerate any two advantages of segregation of waste.

Answers

1. (i) (a) 261029 (b) Sandhills

(ii) Here, R: F = 1: 50,000 The distance between 04 northing to 12 northing is 16 cm.

∴ 16 cm = 50,000 × 16 = 8,00,000 which is 8 km (1 km = 1,00,000 cm)

If Ram speed is 5 km/hr then, he will take 8/5

Time = Distance/Speed = 1.6 hr

(iii) (a) South-East (b) Dry river

(iv) (a) Power lines, roads and towns in his village show that the area around his village has developed.

(b) 22°30' longitude.

(v) Well and temples are man-made features.

Sandhills and trees are natural features.

2.

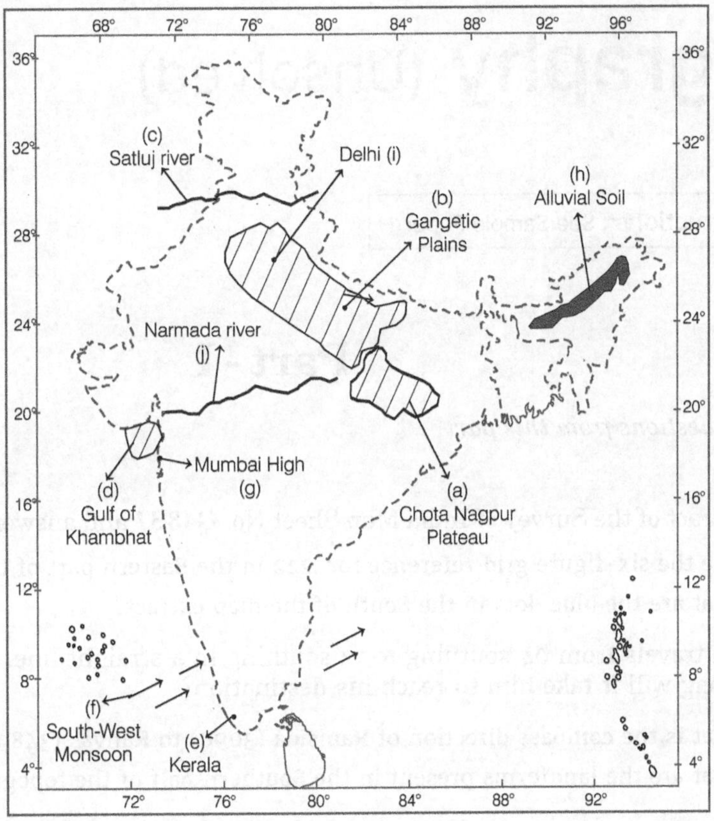

3. (i) (d), (ii) (a), (iii) (c), (iv) (c), (v) (d), (vi) (a), (vii) (c), (viii) (c), (ix) (a), (x) (a)

SAMPLE QUESTION PAPER 3

A HIGHLY SIMULATED Sample Question Paper for ICSE Class X

Geography (Unsolved)

General Instructions : See Sample Paper 1

Part - I

(30 Marks)

Attempt all questions from this part

Question 1

Study the extract of the Survey of India Map Sheet No. **G43S7** and answer the following. questions.

(i) (a) Give the six-figure grid reference for .222 in the Eastern part of the map extract. (2)

(b) What are the blue dots in the South of the map extract?

(ii) Rajesh travels from 04 southing to 12 southing in a straight line. If he travels at 4 km/hr, how long will it take him to reach his destination? (2)

(iii) (a) What is the compass direction of Ramsida (3090) to Ranvas (3489)? (2)

(b) What are the landforms present in the Southern half of the topographic map?

(iv) (a) After a gap of ten years, Meera returned to her hometown Bakodha (2600) and was delighted to witness the development in the surrounding area. What are some visible signs that indicate the progress and growth of the region? (2)

(b) What is the black vertical line made between the easting 42 and 43?

(v) Mention two man-made and two natural features in the grid square 2988. (2)

Question 2

On the outline map of India provided, mark and label

(a) Malwa Plateau (1)

(b) Konkan Coastal Plain (1)

(c) Palk Strait (1)

(d) Chilika Lake (1)

(e) Tropic of Cancer (1)

(f) Oilfield in Digboi (1)

(g) Visakhapatnam (1)

(h) State with minimum density of population (1)

(i) Garo Hills (1)

(j) Nathu-La Pass

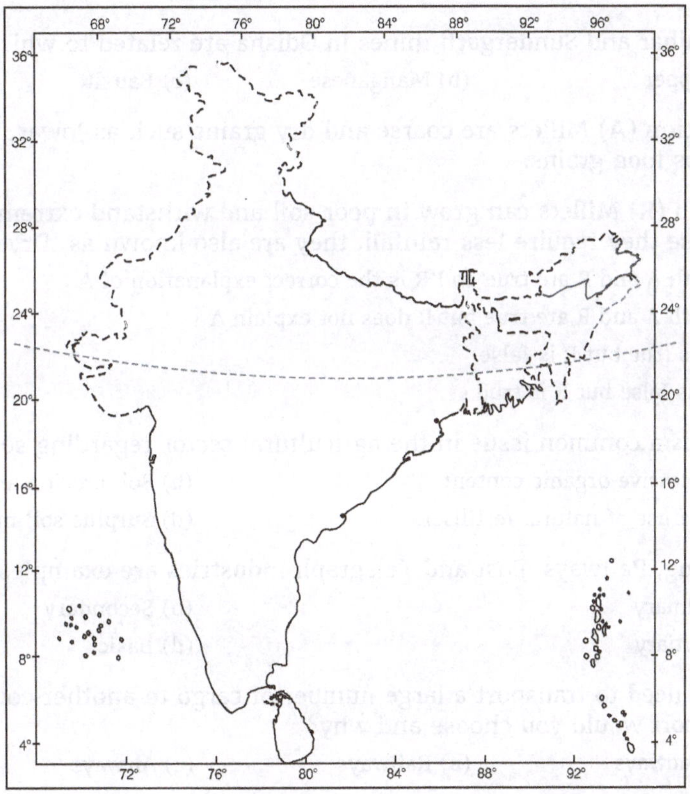

(1)

Question 3

Choose the correct answers to the questions from the given options. **(10)**

(Do not copy the question, write the correct answers only.)

(i) In May-June each year, the monsoon winds approach the Southern part of India from:

(a) North direction

(b) South-Easterly direction

(c) North-Westerly direction

(d) South-Westerly direction

(ii) ________ erosion is not a type of soil erosion?

(a) Rill erosion | (b) Plugging gullies

(c) Leaching | (d) Stream bank erosion

(iii) Littoral Forests: West Bengal

(a) Deciduous Forests: Andhra Pradesh
(b) Evergreen Forests: Kerala
(c) Montane Forests: Tamil Nadu
(d) Desert Forests: Rajasthan

(iv) Which of the following is a key objective of watershed management?

(a) To increase water consumption in urban areas.
(b) To prevent soil erosion and manage water resources effectively.
(c) To promote industrial use of water.
(d) To decrease the biodiversity in the watershed area.

(v) Kendujhar and Sundergarh mines in Odisha are related to which of the following minerals?

(a) Copper (b) Manganese (c) Bauxite (d) Iron ore

(vi) **Assertion (A)** Millets are coarse and dry grains such as Jowar, Bajra and Ragi, which are used as food grains.

Reason (R) Millets can grow in poor soil and withstand extreme weather conditions. Because they require less rainfall, they are also known as 'Dry Crops'.

(a) Both A and R are true and R is the correct explanation of A.
(b) Both A and R are true but R does not explain A
(c) A is true but R is false
(d) A is false but R is true

(vii) What is a common issue in the agricultural sector regarding soil quality?

(a) Excessive organic content
(b) Soil erosion and degradation
(c) Overuse of natural fertilisers
(d) Surplus soil moisture

(viii) Banking, Railways, Post and Telegraph industries are examples of which type of industry?

(a) Primary
(b) Secondary
(c) Tertiary
(d) Basic

(ix) If you need to transport a large number of cargo to another country, which mode of transport would you choose and why?

(a) Roadways (b) Railways (c) Airways (d) Waterways

(x) Identify the type of waste disposal depicted in the image below

(a) Segregation (b) Incineration (c) Composting (d) Landfilling

Part - II

(50 Marks)

Attempt any five questions from this part

Question 4

(i) India experiences a variety of climates, ranging from tropical in the south to temperate in the North. The country's climate significantly impacts agriculture, water resources and lifestyle, with distinct seasons like summer, monsoon and winter shaping daily life across regions. (2)

(Source: India Meteorological Department (IMD), 2024)

(a) What are the major seasons in India's climate?

(b) How does India's climate affect agriculture?

(ii) What is the source of summer rainfall in each of the following areas?

(a) Uttar Pradesh

(b) Bihar

(iii) Give reasons for the following. (3)

(a) Western Rajasthan receives no rain from the Arabian Sea branch of the South-West monsoon winds.

(b) Mangalore is not cold even in the month of December.

(c) The Coromandel coast gets most of its rain during the Winter season.

(iv) Study the climatic data of station X and answer the following questions (3)

Month	Jan.	Feb.	Mar.	Apr.	May	June	July	Aug.	Sep.	Oct.	Nov.	Dec.
Temperature (°C)	23	24.8	26	28.5	33	32.8	33	32.8	30.5	29.3	28.7	27
Rainfall (cm)	7.3	1.2	0.5	0.8	1.3	4.5	6.8	8.2	8.5	20.1	20.5	9.0

Study the climatic data given below and answer the questions that follow

(a) Identify the hottest month.

(b) Calculate the annual rainfall.

(c) Name the winds that bring the maximum rainfall to this city.

Question 5

(i) Soil conservation practices are essential to prevent soil erosion and degradation in India. Techniques like contour farming, terrace cultivation and afforestation help maintain soil fertility, improve water retention and ensure sustainable agricultural practices, securing food resources for future generations.

(Source: Ministry of Agriculture, Government of India, 2024) (2)

(a) What are some common soil conservation techniques?

(b) How does soil conservation help in water retention?

(ii) With reference to soil erosion, answer the following questions. (2)

(a) What is soil erosion, and how does it affect the fertility of the land?

(b) Suggest two methods to control soil erosion.

(iii) With reference to Laterite soil, answer the following questions. (3)

(a) Where is laterite soil commonly found in India?

(b) Give one main characteristic of laterite soil?

(c) How is laterite soil useful for agriculture?

(iv) Give a reason for the following statements. (3)

(a) Alluvial soil is found near the Ganga-Brahmaputra region.

(b) Arid Soil is not suitable for cultivation.

(c) Black soil is extensively found in the Deccan region.

Question 6

(i) Satish,an environmental researcher in Madhya Pradesh, studied India's rich natural vegetation. He observed how regions like the Western Ghats support tropical rainforests, while the Himalayan region is home to alpine vegetation. The diverse climates and altitude variations significantly influence plant growth across the country. (2)

(a) What is the impact of tropical rainforests on soil in the Western Ghats?

(b) How do different climate zones in India affect the type of soil?

(ii) (a) How does the soil in the Deccan Plateau differ from that in the Gangetic Plains? (2)

(b) What soil conservation techniques are used in the hilly areas of India?

(iii) Give three reasons why the natural vegetation in India is so diverse (3)

(iv) (a) How do desert soils in India differ from those in forested regions? (3)

(b) Mention a soil conservation method suitable for hilly areas.

(c) How can Laterite soil be made productive?

Question 7

(i) State two reasons why traditional means of irrigation are still important in most parts of India? (2)

(ii) Distinguish between tubewells and surface wells. (2)

(iii) (a) Name a state in which tank irrigation is a most important method of irrigation. (3)

(b) Give two geographical conditions that favour tank irrigation in this state.

(iv) (a) What is meant by furrow irrigation? (3)

(b) Mention any two advantages of using this irrigation. (3)

Question 8

(i) Dams play a crucial role in India's water management, irrigation and power generation. The Hirakud Dam, built across the Mahanadi River in Odisha, is one of the world's longest earthen dams. Commissioned in 1957, it helps control floods, supports irrigation and generates hydroelectric power, benefiting millions in the region. *(Source - Indiatimes.com)* (2)

(a) How do dams contribute to irrigation and agriculture in India?

(b) Explain the role of dams in India for flood control and hydroelectric power generation?

(ii) With reference to biogas, answer the following. (2)

(a) How does biogas contribute to renewable energy solutions?

(b) Mention one major advantage of using biogas over fossil fuels.

(iii) (a) Give one use of steel. (3)

(b) What are integrated steel plants?

(c) ame any one integrated steel plant of the Public sector in India.

(iv) With reference to solar energy, answer the following questions.

(3)

(a) Name one advantage of using solar energy over conventional energy sources.

(b) How does solar energy help in reducing carbon emissions?

(c) Which device is used to convert solar energy into electricity?

Question 9

(i) Mention two reasons why Poverty and Fragmentation of land are one of the biggest problems of agriculture in India. (2)

(ii) (a) State one point of difference between intensive and extensive farming. (2)

(b) Name one state that is leading producer of rice in India.

(iii) With reference to agriculture, answer the following. (3)

(a) Name a soil that is found suitable for the cultivation of jute.

(b) Name any two varieties of pulses grown in India.

(c) Explain why wheat is a popular food crop in India.

(iv) A farmer in Punjab has traditionally grown rice during the kharif season but is considering switching to wheat for the rabi season due to water scarcity and increasing input costs. The farmer has limited access to irrigation and is concerned about the timing of sowing and harvest. (3)

(a) Based on the situation of the farmer, explain the advantages and challenges of cultivating wheat as a rabi crop in comparison to rice.

(b) What factors should the farmer consider before making this switch and how can they ensure optimal growth of the wheat crop?

Question 10

(i) Mention any two points of difference between Agro based and mineral based industries. (2)

(ii) Explain two ways why iron and steel industry in important for India's economy? (2)

(iii) With reference to petrochemical industry, answer the following. (3)

(a) Name two major products of the petrochemical industry.

(b) How does the petrochemical industry contribute to the manufacturing sector?

(c) What is the environmental impact of the petrochemical industry?

(iv) Give reason to explain each of the following. (3)

(a) Kolkata is an important cotton manufacturing centre even though West Bengal is not a leading producer of cotton.

(b) The wool industry is not as well developed as compared to the cotton industry in India.

(c) Electronics industry is booming in India.

Question 11

(i) Mention two advantages of using waterways over roadways. (2)

(ii) The inland waterways has contributed towards improvement of the Indian economy - Explain. (2)

(iii) (a) Name an organisation responsible for maintaining the border roads in India. (3)

(b) Explain why a well-developed transport network is crucial for industrial growth.

(c) Mention one disadvantage of rail transport

(iv) Give a reason for each of the following. (3)

(a) Air transport is not affordable for everyone in India.

(b) Inland waterways are less developed in India compared to other countries.

(c) Metro rail systems are being expanded in Indian cities.

Question 12

(i) With reference to the pollution, explain the following terms. (2)

(a) Air pollution

(b) Water pollution

(ii) Why is composting a beneficial method of waste disposal? (2)

(iii) Effective waste management is crucial for environmental sustainability in India. With increasing urbanisation, improper disposal of waste leads to pollution and health hazards. Initiatives like waste segregation, recycling and composting help reduce landfill burden. Government policies and public participation are key to promoting sustainable waste disposal and a cleaner environment. (3)

(a) How does improper waste disposal affect the environment?

(b) How does recycling help in reducing waste pollution?

(c) What role does the government play in promoting waste management in India?

(iv) (a) What are 3Rs with reference to the waste management. (3)

(b) Enumerate any two ways in which waste accumulation affects the terrestrial life.

Answers

1. (i) (a) 343998 (b) Wells

(ii) (a) Here, R: F = 1 : 50,000 (means 1 cm on map is equal to 50,000 cm on ground)

The distance between 04 southing to 12 southing is 16 cm.

16 cm = 50,000 × 16 = 8,00,000 which is 8 km (1 km =1,00,000 cm)

If Rajesh moves at a speed of 4 km/hr, it will take him 2 hr to reach his destination.

(iiii) (a) South-East (b) Sand Hills

(iv) (a) The visible signs that indicate the progress and growth of a region are power line, wells and metalled roads.

(b) Longitudinal line 27'30''E

(v) Post office and power line are man-made features and trees and sand hills are natural features.

2.

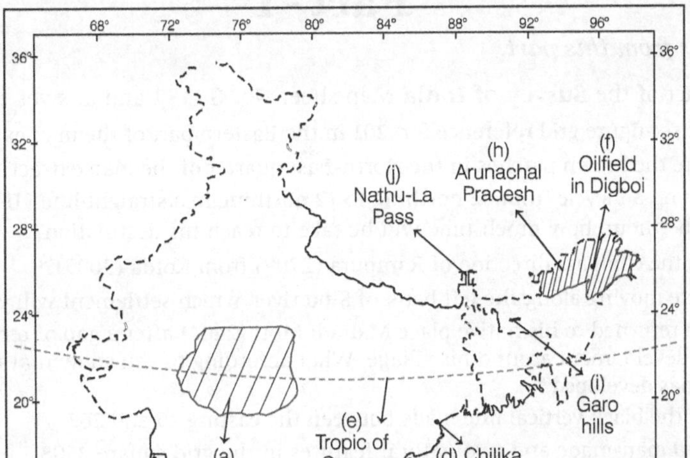

3. (i) (d), (ii) (b), (iii) (d), (iv) b, (v) (b), (vi) (a), (vii) (b), (viii) (c), (ix) (d), (x) (b)

ICSE Latest Specimen Paper

Geography (Fully Solved)

General Instructions

1. Answers to this paper must be written on the answer sheet provided separately.
2. You will not be allowed to write during the first 15 minutes. This time is to be spent in reading the question paper.
3. The time given at the head of this Paper is the time allowed for writing the answers.
4. Part I is compulsory. All questions from Part I are to be attempted. A total of five questions are to be attempted from Part II.
5. The intended marks for questions or parts of questions are given in brackets ( ).

Time : 2 Hrs **Max. Marks : 80**

Part - I

Attempt all questions from this part.

1. Study the extract of the **Survey of India** Map sheet No. **G43S7** and answer the following questions.

(i) (a) Give the six-figure grid reference for .201 in the Eastern part of the map extract. **(2)**

(b) What are the brown patches in the North-East quarter of the map extract? **[Apply & Understanding]**

(ii) Mohan goes on a bicycle from 02 northing to 12 northing in a straight line. If he moves at a speed of 10 kilometers per hour, how much time will he take to reach his destination? **[Apply] (2)**

(iii) (a) What is the compass direction of Rampura (2709) from Kotda (3005)? **(2)**

(b) If you are moving along the left bank of Sipu river, which settlement will you come across? **[Analyse]**

(iv) (a) Ramesh returned to his native place Mahudi Moti (2404) after a gap of ten years and was happy to see the development around his village. What according to you show that the area around his village has developed? **(2)**

(b) What is the black vertical line made between the easting 25 and 26? **[Apply & Remember]**

(v) Mention two man-made and two natural features in the grid square 2508. **[Understanding] (2)**

2. On the outline map of India provided **[Recall]**

(i) Shade and label an area of alluvial soil in the North-East. (1)
(ii) Mark using a dot and name the commercial capital of India. (1)
(iii) Mark and name the highest peak of Himalayas in India. (1)
(iv) Shade and label Gulf of Kutch. (1)
(v) Mark with arrows and name the wind bringing rainfall to Punjab in winter. (1)
(vi) Shade and label a sparsely populated area. (1)
(vii) Mark and label Eastern Ghats. (1)
(viii) Mark and name a tributary of an important peninsular river. (1)
(ix) Mark and label the most important latitude passing through the country. (1)
(x) Mark and label Coromandel coast. (1)

3. Choose the correct answers to the questions from the given options. (Do not copy the question, write the correct answers only). **(10)**

(i) Himalayas have a significant impact on the climate of India as they **[Apply]**
(a) block the North-East monsoon winds
(b) causes rainfall in the Gangetic plains
(c) create a rain shadow area in the Deccan plateau
(d) cause cyclonic disturbance in the Bay of Bengal

(ii) Feel and consistency of soil is called .... of the soil. **[Remember]**
(a) profile (b) parent rock (c) texture (d) density

(iii) Teak: Tropical Deciduous Forest **[Remember]**
(a) Mahogany: Furniture (b) Stilted roots: Mangrove Vegetation
(c) Ebony: Tropical Rainforest (d) Spines: Tropical Desert Vegetation

(iv) Which of the following may be used for the recharging of underground water? **[Understanding]**
(a) Planting of shelter belt (b) Plugging of gullies and ravines
(c) Percolation pit (d) Tube-well irrigation

(v) Which type of coal is referred to as industrial coal? **[Remember]**
(a) Peat (b) Lignite
(c) Bituminous (d) Anthracite

(vi) **Assertion** (A) During the late 1960s, there was a many-fold increase in the production of wheat in Punjab.
Reason (R) The Green Revolution brought about increased use of inputs like HYV seeds, fertilisers and pesticides. **[Analyse]**

Codes
(a) Both A and R are true and R is the correct explanation of A
(b) Both A and R are true, but R is not the correct explanation of A
(c) A is true but, R is false
(d) A is false, but R is true

(vii) Which crop is associated with Ratooning? **[Remember]**
(a) Sugarcane (b) Jute
(c) Rice (d) Cotton

(viii) Which steel plant amongst the following was set up with the collaboration with Germany? **[Remember]**
(a) Bhilai (b) Tata Steel
(c) Visakhapatnam (d) Rourkela

(ix) If you have to transport perishable goods over a long distance, which mode of transport will you use and why? **[Apply]**
(a) Air transport because it is the fastest.
(b) Road transport as it is economical.
(c) Rail transport as it is ecofriendly.
(d) Water transport as it can handle large amount of goods.

(x) Which of the following methods of disposal is best applicable for the waste depicted in the picture below? **[Apply]**

(a) Burning waste in open area
(b) Recycling waste
(c) Dumping
(d) Composting

Part - II

Attempt any five questions from this part.

4. (i) India Meteorological Department (IMD) brings a ray of hope for India's agricultural sector and weather patterns in the upcoming year. After grappling with 'below normal' rains and dry conditions in 2023, the forecast suggested above-normal rainfall in certain regions, including the Southernmost parts of peninsular India, North-West India and several parts of East-Central, East and North-East India. **(2)**

– Investing.com (01.11.2023)

(a) As a student of Geography, what according to you may be the possible reason for the 'below normal' rains in 2023?

(b) During which months of the year does most of India receive major amount of its rainfall? **[Analyse & Apply]**

(ii) What is the source of winter rainfall in each of the following areas? **(2)**

(a) Punjab
(b) Tamil Nadu **[Remember]**

(iii) Give a reason for each of the following. **(3)**

(a) Kerala gets rainfall from the summer monsoons much before Uttar Pradesh.
(b) Visakhapatnam records a low annual range of temperature.
(c) Winds are mostly offshore during the cold season. **[Analyse]**

(iv) Study the climatic data of station X and answer the following questions. **(3)**

Month	Temp (0°C)	Rainfall (cm)
Jan	23.1	7.3
Feb	24.8	1.1
Mar	26.5	0.3
Apr	29.3	0.1
May	32	1.3
Jun	32.8	4.5
July	33.1	6.1
Aug	32.1	8.2
Sep	30.5	8.5
Oct	29.3	20.1
Nov	28.7	20.8
Dec	26.1	9.0

(a) What is the annual range of temperature of station X? [Apply]
(b) Which is the driest month? [Understand]
(c) Name the wind that brings maximum rainfall to this station. [Analyse]

5. (i) Nathu, a farmer in Bihar, does not get good yields as the soil he tills is coarse and has fair proportion of kankars. Motilal on the other hand, has his field closer to the river and gets better yields. (2)
(a) Identify the two soils that are being discussed in the above passage.
(b) Give a possible reason why Motilal benefits from having his field along the river banks.
[Remember and Apply]

(ii) With reference to soil erosion in India answer the following questions. (2)
(a) State any two human activities that have led to soil erosion in India.
(b) Mention any two innovative agricultural techniques that can help to prevent soil erosion. **[Apply]**

(iii) With reference to red soil, answer the following. (3)
(a) How is it formed? **[Understanding]**
(b) Why is it good for dry farming? **[Apply]**
(c) Name any two areas where it is found. **[Recall]**

(iv) Give a reason for the following statements: (3)
(a) Black soil has self-ploughing property.
(b) Laterite soil is not suitable for cultivation.
(c) Alluvial soil is extensively found in the Northern Plains. **[Analyse]**

6. (i) Mahesh went for an excursion with his friend and came across a marshy area with trees that had stilt like roots. (2)
(a) Which natural vegetation belt did he come across? **[Apply]**
(b) Name an area in India where this kind of vegetation is found. **[Recall]**

(ii) (a) Why is Tropical Deciduous Forest commercially the most important forest belt of India? **[Evaluate] (2)**
(b) Why are long and deep roots a typical characteristic of desert vegetation? **[Evaluate]**

(iii) Give three reasons why forest conservation is the need of the hour. **[Analyse] (3)**

(iv) (a) Name a forest conservation method that involves the local community. (3) **[Remember]**
(b) Which primitive system of agriculture had led to large scale destruction of forest in the past? **[Remember]**
(c) Name the process which involves planting two saplings for each tree that is felled. **[Remember]**

7. (i) State two reasons why there is a need for irrigation in India. **[Understand] (2)**

(ii) Distinguish between Inundation Canals and Perennial Canals. **[Analyse] (2)**

(iii) (a) Name a state in India where tube wells are commonly used. (3)
(b) Give two geographical conditions that favour tube well irrigation in this state. **[Analyse]**

(iv) (a) What is meant by rainwater harvesting? (3)
(b) Mention any two water harvesting practices followed in India. **[Understand & Remember]**

8. (i) There is ample potential of setting up biogas plants in India. The National Bioenergy Programme has been recommended by the concerned Ministry, for implementation in two phases. The spread of biogas technology is a boon for Indian farmers with its direct and guaranteed benefits. *(https:/lbiogas.mnre.gov.in)* (2)
(a) Why do you think generation of biogas can be achieved in every household of rural India?
(b) Mention two ways in which generation of this form of energy proves to be a boon for Indian farmers.
[Analyse & Evaluate]

(ii) With reference to Hirakud project answer the following: (2)
(a) On which river is it based? **[Remember & Apply]**
(b) Name an Indian state benefitted by the project.

(iii) (a) Give anyone use of iron ore. (3)
(b) Name the mineral used to strengthen steel.

(c) Name two Indian states where copper is found. [Apply & Remember]

(iv) (3)

(a) Identify the type of energy being harnessed in the above picture.
(b) Mention why this form of energy is preferred over fossil fuels.
(c) Why does India stand at an advantage in the production of this type of energy?
[Understand, Evaluate & Apply]

9. (i) Mention two agricultural reforms done by the government for the betterment of the agricultural sector. [Understand] (2)

(ii) (a) State one point of difference between Rabi and Kharif cropping seasons. (2) [Analyse & Remember]
(b) Name the state that is the leading producer of groundnut in India.

(iii) With reference to cultivation of pulses, answer the following. (3)
(a) Name a soil found suitable for the growth of pulses. [Understand]
(b) Name any two varieties of pulses grown in India. [Remember]
(c) Give a reason, why is it a popular food crop of India? [Evaluate]

(iv) Rohan, a farmer, hired some labourers to help him with 'GINNING'. (3)
(a) Name the crop grown by Rohan. [Apply]
(b) Mention any two climatic conditions suitable for this crop. [Recall]

10. (i) Mention two points of difference between small scale and large scale industry. [Analyse] (2)

(ii) Explain two ways in which cotton textile industry is important for India's economy. (2) [Understand]

(iii) With reference to petrochemical industry, answer the following. (3)
(a) State a reason for the growing popularity of this industry in recent times. [Apply]
(b) Why is it located close to oil refineries? [Evaluate]
(c) Name any two petrochemical products. [Remember]

(iv) Give one reason to explain each of the following. (3)
(a) Sugar production is gradually gaining importance in peninsular India.
(b) Indian silk products are becoming less popular in the international market.
(c) The importance of the iron and steel industry will never decline. [Analyse]

11. (i) Mention two disadvantages of using waterways. [Understand] (2)

(ii) The Golden Quadrilateral has contributed towards improvement of the Indian economy- Explain. [Understand] (2)

(iii) (a) Which rail gauge is mostly limited to hilly areas only? (3)
(b) Name the organisation responsible for the maintenance of the National Highways of India.
(c) Which is the Inland Waterway that connects Prayagraj to Haldia? [Understand & Remember]

(iv) Give a reason for each of the following. (3)
(a) At present times, airports are being established even in smaller towns of India.
(b) Railways are well developed in the Northern states of India.
(c) Helicopter services are crucial during emergencies. [Analyse]

12. (i) What is the impact of waste generation on the following? **(2)**

(a) Surface water (b) Landscape **[Understand]**

(ii) Why is dumping considered a harmful method of waste disposal? **[Analyse] (2)**

(iii) Fire broke out at the Kochi city waste treatment plant. Thick clouds of toxic smoke engulfed the city. The waste at the plant also contained plastic and biomedical wastes, both of which on combustion are extremely harmful for the general health of people. **(3)** – *Economic Times, 10.03.2023*

(a) Which method of waste management would have helped in reducing health hazard in the above case? **[Analyse]**

(b) Mention one measure you can adopt in school to reduce waste. **[Apply]**

(c) State one way in which domestic waste can be made useful. **[Understand]**

(iv) (a) What are landfills? **(3)**

(b) Enumerate two advantages of composting as a method of waste disposal. **[Remember & Apply]**

Survey Map (G43S7)

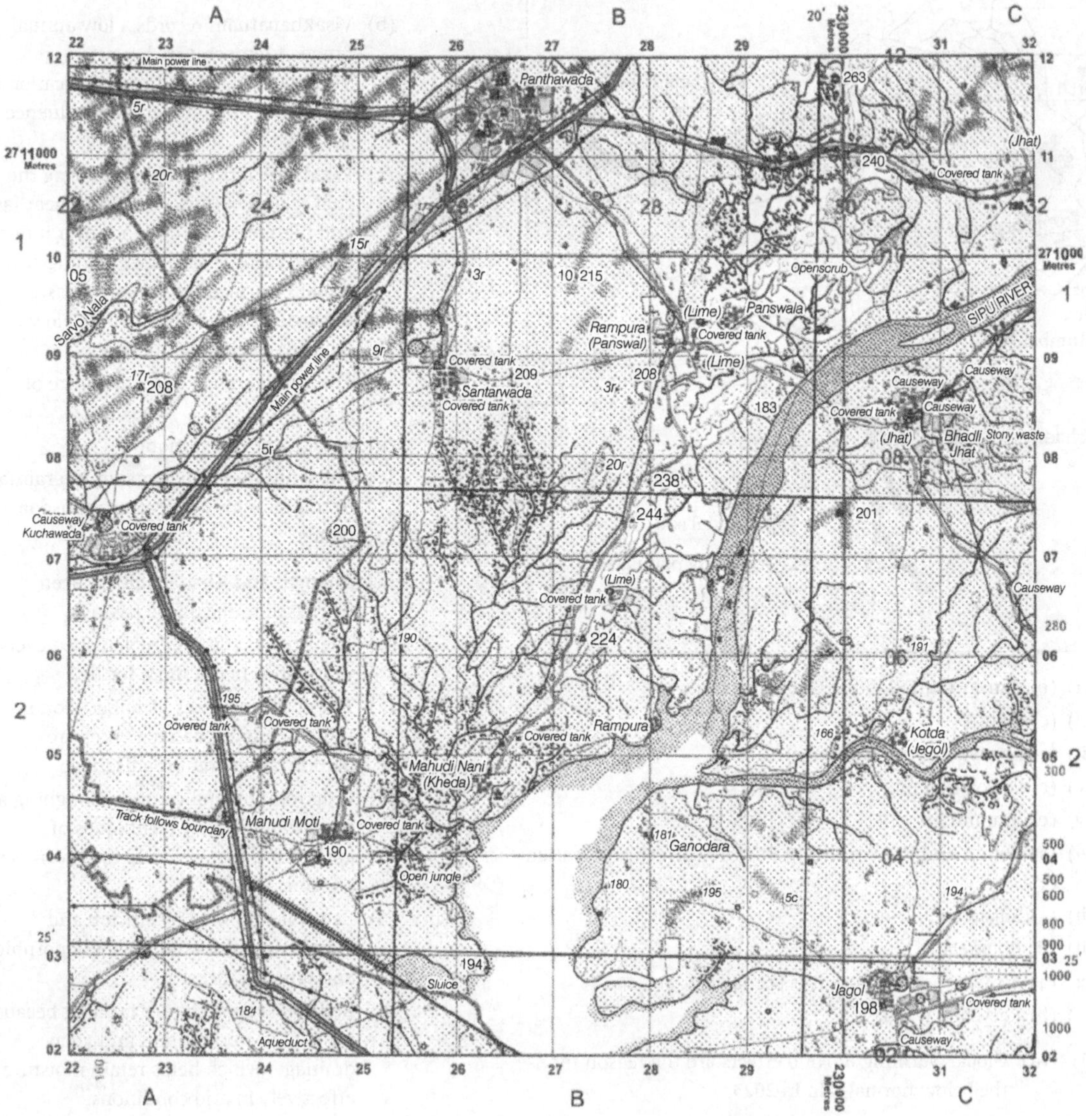

Answers

1. (i) (a) 301074 (b) Sand dunes

(ii) One hour

(iii) (a) North West (b) Jhat

(iv) (a) Powerline showing that the village now has electricity

(b) Longitude/Meridian

(v) Natural features : Sand dune, Broken Ground

Man made features : Cart track/Pack track/Permanent hut/temple

2.

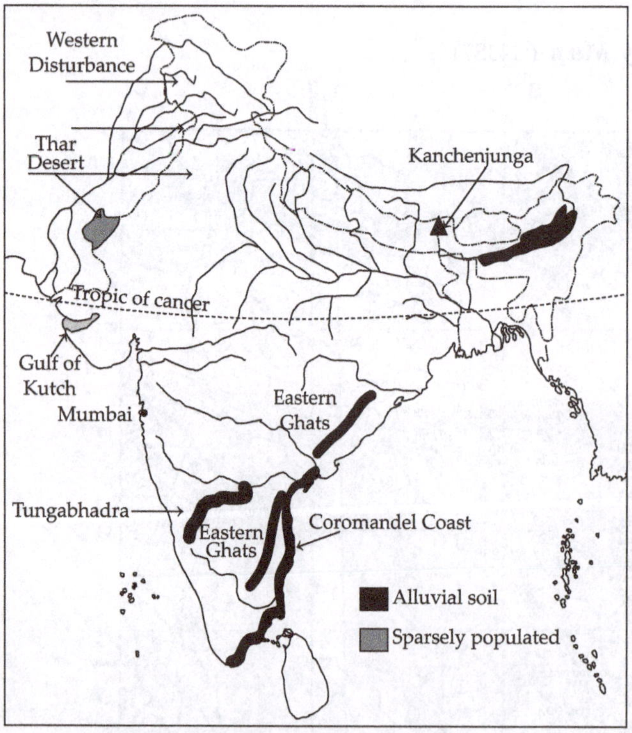

3. (i) (b) Causes rainfall in the Gangetic plains

(ii) (c) texture

(iii) (c) Ebony: Tropical Rainforest

(iv) (c) Percolation pit

(v) (c) Bituminous

(vi) (a) Both A and R are true and R is the correct explanation of A

(vii) (a) Sugarcane

(viii) (d) Rourkela

(ix) (a) Air transport because it is the fastest.

(x) (b) Recycling waste

4. (i) (a) Global warming/El Nino effects are the reason for the below normal rain in 2023.

(b) During June to September, India receives major amount of rainfall.

(ii) (a) **Punjab** Western disturbances originating in the Mediterranean region or Temperate cyclones

(b) **Tamil Nadu** North-East winter monsoon wind or retreating monsoon.

(iii) (a) Kerala gets rainfall from the summer monsoon much before Uttar Pradesh because Kerala lies in the South-West of the country where the South-West monsoon wind strikes first. The wind then advances to the North and reaches Uttar Pradesh.

(b) Visakhapatnam records a low annual range of temperature because Visakhapatnam has a coastal location and experiences the moderating influence of the sea.

(c) Winds are mostly offshore during the cold season because land loses heat fast and high pressure develops over it during the cold season. The surrounding seas remain warm and have low pressure during this time. Thus, winds blow from land to sea and are offshore.

(iv) (a) The annual range of temperature of station X is 10°C.

(b) April is the driest month.

(c) The wind that brings maximum rainfall to this station is retreating monsoon winds.

5. (i) (a) Bhangar and Khadar soil are been discussed in the above passage.

(b) The Khadar soil gets replenished every year and is hence more fertile.

(ii) (a) The possible causes of soil erosion in India due to human activities are deforestation and urbanisation.

(b) Crop rotation and contour ploughing are the two innovative techniques of agriculture that can help to prevent soil erosion.

(iii) (a) Red soil is formed by erosion and weathering of crystalline metamorphic and igneous rocks.

(b) Red soil is good for dry farming because it has a high iron content and good drainage, which helps retain moisture effectively in arid conditions.

(c) They are mostly found in parts of Odisha and Madhya Pradesh.

(iv) (a) Black soil has self-ploughing property because black soil hardens and cracks when dry which helps in aeration of the soil naturally.

(b) Laterite soil is not suitable for cultivation due to leaching, the essential minerals percolate down the soil profile making the top soil infertile.

(c) Alluvial soil is extensively found in the Northern Plains because the numerous rivers here bring large amounts of sediments and deposit them to form fertile plains.

6. (i) (a) He came across the Tidal Littoral forest.

(b) An area in India where this kind of vegetation is found is the delta of river Ganga in Sundarbans.

(ii) (a) Tropical Deciduous forests are commercially the most important forest belt in India because

(i) They supply high-quality hardwoods like teak and sal, which are crucial for furniture, construction and other industries.

(ii) They occur in pure stands making exploitation easier.

(b) Long and deep roots are typical characteristics of desert vegetation to draw water from deep underground as rainfall is scanty here.

(iii) The forest conservation is the need of the hour because

(a) **Biodiversity** Forests house 80% of terrestrial species, crucial for ecosystem balance.

(b) **Climate** Forests absorb CO_2, mitigating climate change.

(c) **Livelihoods** Forests support millions of people with food, medicine and shelter.

(iv) (a) Social forestry is the forest conservation method that involves the local community.

(b) Jhum cultivation is the primitive system of agriculture that had led to large scale destruction of the forest in the past.

(c) Reforestation is the process which involves planting two saplings for each tree that is felled.

7. (i) Irrigation is a need in India because

(a) Irrigation provides a reliable water supply, reducing reliance on unpredictable monsoon rains.

(b) It enables multiple cropping and higher crop yields, improving food security and farmers' incomes.

(ii) Inundation canals are floodwater canals that carry water only during the rainy season when the river floods.

On the other hand, perennial canals carry water all year round as they have a weir or dam at the head to regulate the flow of water.

(iii) (a) A state in India where tube wells are commonly used is Punjab.

(b) The geographical condition that favour tubewell irrigation in Punjab are

(i) **High Water Table** Punjab has a high groundwater level, making it easier and cost-effective to access water through tube wells.

(ii) **Permeable Soil** Punjab has permeable alluvial soil, which allows easy drilling and efficient water absorption for irrigation.

(iv) (a) The rainwater harvesting is collection and storage of rainwater for future use.

(b) Two water harvesting practices followed in India are

(i) **Rooftop Rainwater Harvesting** A widespread practice across India where rainwater is collected from rooftops and stored in tanks or recharge pits for various uses such as drinking, irrigation and recharging groundwater.

(ii) **Stepwells (Baolis)** These structures in Gujarat and Rajasthan designed to store rainwater and provide a water source during dry periods.

8. (i) (a) Biogas generation can be achieved in every household of rural India primarily because of the abundance of organic waste available from agricultural residues, animal dung and kitchen waste, which are essential feedstocks for biogas production.

(b) Generation of Biogas energy proves to be a boom for Indian farmers due to the following reasons

(i) **Reduced Energy Costs** Biogas generation provides a renewable and cheaper alternative to traditional fuels like firewood and LPG, saving farmers money on energy expenses.

(ii) **Improved Soil Health** The by-product of biogas production, known as bio-slurry, is a nutrient-rich organic fertiliser that enhances soil fertility and crop yields, benefiting farmers economically.

(ii) (a) River Mahanadi

(b) Odisha is benefitted by Hirakud project.

(iii) (a) Iron ore can produce steel.

(b) Manganese is used to strengthen steel.

(c) Copper is found in Madhya Pradesh and Rajasthan

(iv) (a) Solar energy is being harnessed in the above picture.

(b) It is preferred over fossil fuels because it is a clean source of energy.

(c) India stands at an advantage in the production of solar energy due to the following reasons:

- **Abundant Sunlight** India's geographical location ensures ample solar radiation.
- **Supportive Policies** Government initiatives include subsidies and incentives for solar energy.
- **Cost Efficiency** Decreasing solar technology costs make it competitive with traditional energy sources

9. (i) Two agriculture reforms done by the government for betterment of the agriculture sector are

- **Crop Diversification Policies** Introducing policies to promote diversification of crops, reducing dependency on traditional crops and enhancing resilience against climate change.
- **Integrated Watershed Management** Implementing watershed management programs to improve water efficiency in agriculture, especially in regions prone to drought or water scarcity.

(ii) (a) **Rabi Crops** is sown in October or November and harvested in February or March.

On the other hand, **Kharif crops** is sown in May or June and harvested in September or October.

(b) Gujarat is the leading producer of groundnut in India.

(iii) (a) The soil found suitable for the growth of pulses is sandy loam soil. This type of soil provides good drainage and aeration, which are beneficial for the cultivation of pulses.

(b) Moong and Masoor are the two varieties of pulses grown in India.

(c) Pulses are the most popular food crop in India because

- It is a leguminous crop
- It can help to replenish the soil naturally.

(iv) (a) Cotton is grown by Rohan.

(b) Two climatic conditions suitable for cotton cultivation are

- **Warm Climate** Cotton thrives in warm temperatures, typically between 21°C to 30°C (70°F to 86°F), which promote optimal growth and development.
- **Moderate Rainfall** Cotton requires moderate but well-distributed rainfall during its growing season. Excessive rainfall or prolonged dry spells can adversely affect cotton yields

10. (i) The differences between small scale industries and large scale industries are

Small scale industries	Large scale industries
These require less capital investment.	These require huge capital investment.
These industries employ less labour.	These industries employ more labour.

(ii) Cotton textile industries important for India's economy because:

- It gives us valuable foreign exchange
- It generates employment

(iii) (a) One reason for the growing popularity of the petrochemical industry in recent times is its durability.

(b) It is located close to oil refineries because

- To facilitates easy availability of raw materials
- To reduce transportation costs.

(c) Two petrochemical products are

- **Ethylene** Used in the production of plastics, fibers, and other industrial chemicals.
- **Propylene** Important for making plastics, synthetic fibers and various chemical products.

(iv) (a) Sugar production is gradually gaining importance in peninsular India because sugar plantations are well planned and scientifically managed.

(b) Indian silk products are becoming less popular in the international market because of the high price of Indian silk.

(c) The importance of the iron and steel industry will never decline because it is foundational to industrialisation, infrastructure development and essential sectors like construction and manufacturing.

11. (i) Two disadvantages of using waterways are

- It is a slow means of transport
- It can be affected by weather disturbances.

(ii) The Golden Quadrilateral improved India's economy in the following ways

- It has enhanced connectivity between major cities and industrial hubs.
- It has reduced transport costs and time.
- It has boosted trade and commerce across the country.

(iii) (a) The narrow gauge is mostly limited to hilly areas only.

(b) The organisation responsible for the maintenance of the National Highways of India is the National Highways Authority of India (NHAI).

(c) The inland waterway that connects Prayagraj (formerly Allahabad) to Haldia is National Waterway 1 (NW-1).

(iv) (a) At present times airports are being established even in smaller towns of India to encourage air travel for Indians as it saves time.

(b) Railways are well developed in the Northern states of India because of flat plain land.

(c) Helicopter services are crucial during emergencies because they can easily reach remote areas fast.

12. (i) (a) The impact of waste generation on surface water is that waste can contaminate surface water sources, leading to the spread of diseases and harming aquatic life.

(b) The impact of waste generation on the landscape is that waste can spoil the aesthetics of the landscape, leading to degradation of scenic beauty and potentially reducing property values.

(ii) Dumping is considered a harmful method of disposal because it leads to soil pollution and underground water pollution.

(iii) (a) Implementing proper segregation of waste and recycling would have helped in reducing health hazards in the above case.

(b) One measure that can be adopted in school to reduce waste is to promote the use of reusable water bottles and lunch boxes instead of single-use plastic items.

(c) One way in which domestic waste can be made useful is through composting organic waste to produce nutrient-rich compost for gardening and agriculture.

(iv) (a) Landfills are large areas in the outskirts of towns and cities where wastes are deposited in the ground and covered with Earth. The waste gradually decomposes, decreases in volume and gets converted to humus.

(b) Advantages of composting as a method of which disposal are

- **Reduces Landfill Waste** Composting diverts organic waste from landfills, decreasing environmental impact.
- **Produces Nutrient-rich Compost** Composting creates a valuable soil amendment that improves soil fertility and supports sustainable agriculture.

ICSE Solved Paper 2024

Geography (Fully Solved)

General Instructions

1. Answers to this Paper must be written on the answer sheet provided separately.
2. You will not be allowed to write during the first 15 minutes. This time is to be spent in reading the question paper.
3. The time given at the head of this Paper is the time allowed for writing the answers.
4. Part I is compulsory. All questions from Part I are to be attempted. A total of five questions are to be attempted from Part II.
5. The intended marks for questions or parts of questions are given in brackets ( ).

Time : 2 Hrs **Max. Marks : 80**

Part – I (30 Marks)

Attempt all questions from this Part

1. Study the extract of the Survey of India Map Sheet No. G43S7 and answer the following questions.
   - (i) (a) Give the six-figure grid reference for spot height .522. **(2)**
     (b) What is the pattern of settlement in the grid square 3591?
   - (ii) (a) Mention two man-made features seen in the grid square 3794. **(2)**
     (b) Mention two means of transport used by the people of Nani Bhatamal in the grid square 3691.
   - (iii) (a) Identify the landform marked by the contours in the grid square 3896. **(2)**
     (b) What is the pattern of drainage seen in the grid square 36977?
   - (iv) (a) What is the reason for the presence of causeway in the grid square 3695? **(2)**
     (b) What is the compass direction of Khara (4097) from Karja (3994)?
   - (v) Calculate the area in kilometre square of the region to the South of 94 Northing. **(2)**

2. On the outline map of India provided:
   - (i) Mark and label the river Krishna. **(1)**
   - (ii) Mark and label the Eastern Ghats. **(1)**
   - (iii) Shade and label a densely populated area in the Southern part of India. **(1)**
   - (iv) Shade and label the Konkan coastal plain. **(1)**
   - (v) Mark with an arrow and label the direction of Western disturbance. **(1)**
   - (vi) Shade and label the Thar Desert. **(1)**
   - (vii) Shade and label the Andaman Sea. **(1)**
   - (viii) Mark and label the city Chennai. **(1)**
   - (ix) Mark and name the highest peak of Himalayas in India. **(1)**
   - (x) Mark and label Mumbai High. **(1)**

3. Choose the correct answers to the questions from the given options. (10)

(i) What causes snowfall in Kashmir during winter?

(a) Tropical cyclone (b) North-East Monsoon wind

(c) South-West Monsoon wind (d) Temperate cyclone

(ii) Which of the following helps in soil conservation?

(a) Afforestation (b) Overgrazing

(c) Mining (d) Shifting agriculture

(iii) Which means of irrigation can be developed with minimum expenditure?

(a) Tube well (b) Canal (c) Well (d) Drip irrigation

(iv) Read the table and identify the pair that is

	Natural Vegetation Belt	Tree
P	Tropical evergreen	Babool
Q	Tropical deciduous	Teak
R	Littoral	Ebony
S	Mountain forest	Banyan

(a) P (b) Q (c) R (d) S

(v) Bauxite is the ore of

(a) Aluminium (b) Copper (c) Manganese (d) Iron

(vi) Identify the source of energy that leads to pollution.

(a) Tidal energy (b) Wind energy (c) Natural gas (d) Geo-thermal energy

(vii) Which of the following is not a centre for the iron and steel industry?

(a) Bhilai (b) Bengaluru (c) Rourkela (d) Visakhapatnam

(viii) Which of the following farming methods is used to grow tea on a large scale?

(a) Subsistence farming (b) Plantation farming

(c) Mixed farming (d) Shifting agriculture

(ix) Which of the following means of transport has best use during floods/ earthquake?

(a) Airways (b) Railways (c) Roadways (d) Waterways

(x) Which of the following is a biodegradable waste?

(a) Broken glass (b) Wastepaper (c) Polythene (d) Plastic bags

Part - II (50 Marks)

Attempt any five questions from this Part

4. (i) 'Himalayas act as a climatic divide'. Justify the statement giving two reasons. (2)

(ii) Differentiate between South-West Monsoon and Retreating Monsoon. (Any two differences) (2)

(iii) Give a geographical reason for the following. (3)

(a) Kolkata gets more rain than Delhi during rainy season.

(b) Though both are hill stations, Shimla experiences snowfall during the winters but Ooty does not.

(c) Winter monsoons bring less rain.

(iv) Study the climate data of Station X and answer the questions that follow. (3)

Month	Jan	Feb	Mar	Apr	May	Jun	Jul	Aug	Sep	Oct	Nov	Dec
Temp (C)	8.4	11.5	21.6	28.3	35.1	38.5	41.0	38.0	30.8	29.2	15.6	10.2
Rainfall (cms)	1.5	0.9	0.5	-	-	12.5	17.8	18.5	12.5	12.5	6.2	2.1

(a) Calculate the annual range of temperature of Station X.

(b) Name the rainiest month of the Station X.

(c) Is the Station X located in coastal area or in the continental interior?

5. (i) Why is Black soil found suitable for the production of cotton? (Any two points) (2)

(ii) Give one difference between each of the following. (2)

(a) Alluvial soil of Uttarakhand and alluvial soil of West Bengal.

(b) Transported soil and residual soil.

(iii) With reference to Laterite soil, answer the questions that follow. (3)

(a) How is Laterite soil formed?

(b) How can Laterite soil be made productive?

(c) Name one region where Laterite soil is found.

(iv) (a) Mention two causes of soil erosion in India. (3)

(b) Mention a soil conservation method suitable for hilly area.

6. (i) How is tropical monsoon forest useful for the Indian economy? (Any two points) (2)

(ii) Mention the climatic condition that leads to the development of tropical desert vegetation. (2)

(iii) Give a reason to explain each of the following. (3)

(a) Mountains have varied vegetation.

(b) Stilt like / aerial roots are a typical feature of littoral forest.

(c) The tropical evergreen forests do not look bare at any time of the year.

(iv) (a) How has the rising population of India resulted in the loss of forest cover? (Any one point) (3)

(b) Mention any two forest conservation methods that may be adopted to protect the forests.

7. (i) Mention one advantage and one disadvantage of using tank irrigation. (2)

(ii) (a) What is the advantage of using drip irrigation? (2)

(b) Why is drip irrigation not practiced on a large scale in India?

(iii) Give a reason to explain each of the following. (3)

(a) Sprinkler irrigation is gaining popularity in recent times.

(b) Tube well irrigation is used in Punjab.

(c) North India has more area under canal irrigation.

(iv)

(a) Name the water conservation practice shown in the above picture. (3)

(b) How does this system help to reduce floods?

(c) Why is water conservation necessary? (Any two reasons)

8. (i) (a) Name any three varieties of coal produced in India. (2)

(b) Name the variety of coal widely used in Iron and Steel Industries of India.

(ii) (a) Name the state that is the largest producer of iron ore in India. **(2)**

(b) Name any one mining area of Iron ore from the state mentioned by you.

(iii) (a) Mention two ways in which Hirakud dam has helped the people of Odisha. **(3)**

(b) Across which river is the Hirakud dam built?

(iv) Give reasons for each of the following. **(3)**

(a) Geothermal energy is not popular in India.

(b) Solar energy is gaining popularity.

(c) Petroleum is considered a harmful source of energy.

9. (i) Why is agriculture considered an important sector of Indian economy? (Any two points) **(2)**

(ii) (a) What is mixed farming?

(b) Mention any one advantage of mixed farming.

(iii) Give one reason to explain each of the following. **(3)**

(a) West Bengal is a leading producer of jute.

(b) Millets are fast becoming the popular food crops.

(c) More than two ratoon crops are not advisable for sugarcane farmers.

(iv) (a) With reference to tea cultivation, explain the term 'fine pluck'. **(3)**

(b) Name the Indian state that leads in coffee production.

(c) Why is cotton grown as a Kharif crop in India?

10. (i) (a) Based on the ownership, what type of industry is Visakhapatnam Steel Plant? **(2)**

(b) What is meant by co-operative sector industry?

(ii) Explain the following terms. **(2)**

(a) Sericulture (b) Integrated steel plant

(iii) Give one reason to explain each of the following. **(3)**

(a) Mini-Steel plants help in conservation of coal.

(b) Location of sugar industry is shifting to the Southern part of India.

(c) The electronic industry is growing at a fast rate.

(iv) (a) State two conditions that favour the location of cotton textile industry in Ahmedabad. **(3)**

(b) State any one advantage of locating iron and steel industry at Rourkela.

11. (i) Why is road transport an important means of transport in India? (Any two reasons) **(2)**

(ii) Give a reason for each of the following. **(2)**

(a) Northern plain is best suited for the development of Railways.

(b) Railways are managed completely by the Central Government.

(iii) Mention two advantages and one disadvantage of Inland water transport. **(3)**

(iv) Why has airway become more popular than other means of transport? (Any three reasons) **(3)**

12. (i) With- reference to the picture below, answer the questions that follow. **(2)**

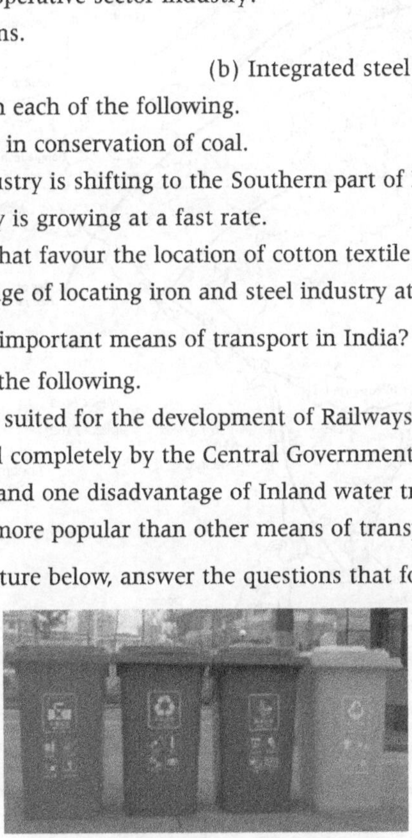

(a) Which waste management method is depicted here?

(b) State one way in which this method may be implemented at our home.

(ii) Explain how waste accumulation can be harmful. (Any two points) **(2)**

(iii) Explain how waste generated in following sectors may be made useful. (Give one example for each) **(3)**

(a) Household (b) Industry (c) Agriculture

(iv) (a) Give two uses of composting. **(3)**

(b) Why are landfills set up far away from the city? (Any two reasons)

Answers

1. (i) (a) 375966 (b) Dispersed/Scatter

(ii) (a) Chattri, Cart track, well, nets (b) Roadway and Waterways

(iii) (a) Ridge (b) Radial

(iv) (a) Cross minor stream (b) North-East

(v) 4 Northing × 9 Easting = 36 sq km

2.

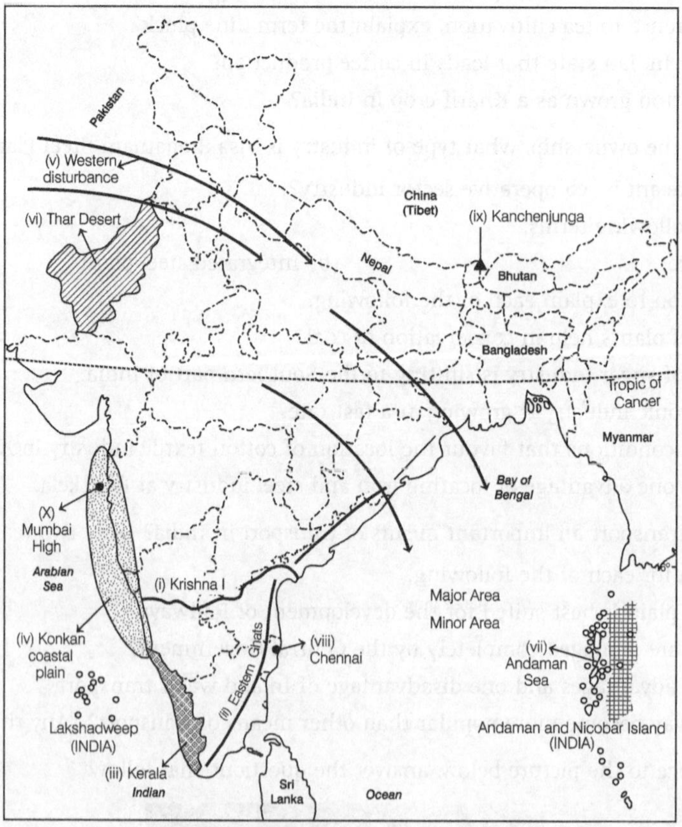

3. (i) (d) Temperate cyclone (ii) (a) Afforestation

(iii) (d) Drip irrigation (iv) (b) Q

(v) (a) Aluminium (vi) (c) Natural gas

(vii) (b) Bengaluru (viii) (b) Plantation farming

(ix) (a) Airways (x) (b) Wastepaper

4. (i) The Himalayas act as a climatic divide due to two main reasons

(a) The Himalayan mountains act as a natural barrier against the cold winds of Central Asia and Siberia to enter India thus, preventing a severe cold climate.

(b) The Himalayas trap the rain bearing winds of South-West monsoon causing them to shed their moisture in the Indian sub-continent thus, making agriculture possible on a large scale.

(ii) The differences between South-West Monsoon and Retreating Monsoon are

South-West Monsoon	Retreating Monsoon
These winds blow from June to September.	These winds blow from October to November.
This monsoon wind covers the whole India and gives heavy rainfall.	The Eastern coast of South India receives rainfall from this wind.
Wind movement is from sea to land.	Wind movement is from land to sea.

(iii) (a) Kolkata gets more rain than Delhi during rainy season because Kolkata lies in the lower Ganga plain so it receives more rainfall from the Bay of Bengal branch of South-West monsoon but by the time, monsoon wind reach Delhi, the moisture holding capacity of the wind decreases therefore it sheds less rainfall.

(b) Though both are hill stations, Shimla experiences snowfall during the winter but Ooty does not because Shimla is located in higher elevation and close to the Himalayan range, whereas Ooty is located at a lower elevation in the Nilgiri Hills of Southern India.

(c) Winter monsoons bring less rain because during winter the direction of the prevailing winds reverse. The wind starts blowing from land towards sea. As they originate from continental interiors they carry less moisture as compared to the summer monsoon winds.

(iv) (a) The annual range of temperature is calculated through the given formula
Highest temperature- lowest temperature 41.0- 8.4= 32.6

(b) Through the observation of the given table, it is clear that August receives the maximum rainfall at 18.5 cm.

(c) Through the observation, Station X seems to be the region in the continental interior. The range of temperature varies from 8 degrees Celsius in winter to 35 degrees Celsius in summer.

5. (i) Black soil is found suitable for the production of cotton because

(a) It has excellent moisture retention capacity. It can hold water for a longer duration. This property helps in maintaining adequate soil moisture levels required for cotton cultivation.

(b) Black soil is rich in calcium carbonate, magnesium carbonate, potash and lime. These nutrients are essentials for the healthy growth of cotton plants and contribute to higher yields.

(ii) (a) Alluvial soil of Uttarakhand is relatively younger and coarser.
On the other hand, alluvial soil of West Bengal is older and more finely textured.

(b) Transported soil is found at places where they got transported by agents of erosion i.e. wind and rivers.
On the other hand, residual soil is found at places where they are formed by disintegration and weathering of rocks.

(iii) (a) Laterite soil is formed through the process of intense leaching in hot and humid tropical climates. It results from the leaching of silica and other soluble materials, leaving behind a rich concentration of iron and aluminum oxides.

(b) Laterite soil can be made productive by adding adequate amounts of manure and chemical fertilisers.

(c) Laterite soil is found in the region of Eastern and Western Ghats.

(iv) (a) The two causes of soil erosion in India are

- **Overgrazing** The continuous grazing by animals on the same piece of land without sufficient recovery periods, leads to the removals of plant cover on a large scale and become open to erosion by wind and water.
- **Deforestation** The cutting down of forests on a large scale which leaves an open and exposed landscape leads to soil erosion causing leaching and flash floods.

(b) A soil conservation method suitable for hilly area is terrace farming. In this farming method, step-like terraces are built on slopes. They prevent the soil from being washed away by running water.

6. (i) Tropical monsoon forests is useful for the Indian economy in the following ways

(a) **Biodiversity Hotspot** These forests have a rich variety of flora and fauna, attracting tourism and promoting eco-tourism, which generates revenue and employment opportunities.

(b) **Natural Resources** They provide valuable resources such as timber, medicinal plants, and non-timber forest products, supporting industries and livelihoods across the country.

(ii) The climatic condition that leads to the development of trophical desert vegetation are

- Regions having annual rainfall of 50 cm.
- Regions having average temperature between 25°C to 27°C.
- Evaporation rate is higher than precipitation due to high temperature.

(iii) (a) Mountains have diverse vegetation due to variations in altitude, climate, soil and exposure to sunlight. These factors create distinct ecological niches, protecting the evolution of different plant species adapted to specific conditions, resulting in rich biodiversity.

(b) Stilt-like/ aerial roots are a typical feature of littoral forest because this type of vegetation flourishes in wet marshy areas in river deltas, saline or other swampy areas.

(c) The tropical evergreen forests do not look bare at any time of the year because these forests have a constant supply of moisture and sunlight throughout the year, allowing vegetation to remain lush and dense. Additionally, the trees in these forests shed their leaves at different times rather than all at once, ensuring they never appear bare.

(iv) (a) The rising population of India has resulted in the loss of forest covered in the following ways

- Increasing population demand for land for housing, agriculture and infrastructure development as a result, forests are often cleared to make way for these activities, leading to the loss of forest cover.
- The growing population puts pressure on natural resources, leading to unsustainable exploitation and further degradation of forests.

(b) The two forest conservation methods to protect the forests are

- **The National Forest Policy** It was introduced in 1894 which was revised in 1952 and 1988. The main aim of this policy is protection, conservation and development of forests. It led with a programme named joint forest management which involves the local communities for protection and conservation of the nearby forest.
- **Control of Deforestation** Efforts should be made to minimise the cutting of young trees and regulate commercial deforestation. Implementing strategies like selective logging and controlled harvesting can ensure forests are utilised sustainably while preserving their ecological balance.

7. (i) One advantage of tank irrigation is that it can store abundant rainwater and it reduces the wastage of the excessive flowing water.

One disadvantage of tank irrigation is that in the absence of rainwater during the dry season, the tanks become dry and fail to provide water for irrigation.

(ii) (a) The advantage of drip irrigation is that it delivers water directly to the root zone of plants, minimising evaporation and runoff. This can save significant amounts of water compared to traditional methods like sprinklers, which can lose water to the air or leave puddles on the surface.

(b) Drip irrigation is not practiced on a large scale in India because of high initial cost. Setting up a drip irrigation system can be expensive, particularly for smallholder farmers who dominate Indian agriculture. The cost of materials, design, and installation can be a significant restriction.

(iii) (a) Sprinkler irrigation is gaining popularity in recent times due to its versatility, cost-effectiveness and its efficiency to consume water.

(b) Tube well irrigation is used in Punjab due to following reasons

- The level of water table is high in Punjab due to which tubewell irrigation is favourable.
- The soil in Punjab is soft which makes it easier to dug holes required for tubewell irrigation.

(c) North India has more area under canal irrigation because it has low level relief, deep fertile soils and perennial source of water.

(iv) (a) The water consuming practice shown in the above picture is called rooftop rainwater harvesting.

(b) Rainwater harvesting systems help reduce flooding by capturing and storing rainwater that would otherwise run off surfaces like roofs, pavements and roads, leading to floods. This stored water can then be slowly released or utilised for various purposes; this reduces water volume rushing into drainage systems during heavy rains.

(c) Water conservation is necessary due to following reasons

- Rainfall is unevenly distributed over time and space as different area receive different amounts of rainfall.
- Rapid industrialisation and urbanisation are continuously reducing the availability of water and exerting a lot of pressure on the available water resources in the country.

8. (i) (a) The three varieties of coal produced in India are

- Bituminous coal (Odisha, West Bengal, Jharkhand)

- Lignite (Tamil Nadu, Rajasthan, Kerala)
- Peat (Nilgiri mountain, Kashmir valley , swampy areas of coastal plains)

(b) The iron and steel industries in India mainly use coking coal, also known as metallurgical coal.

(ii) (a) The largest producer of iron ore in India is Odisha.

(b) A mining area of iron ore from Odisha is Gorumahisani in Mayurbhanj district.

(iii) (a) Hirakud dam has helped the people of Odisha by

- controlling the flood in Mahanadi delta
- providing about 75,000 sq km of land
- helping to generate hydro electricity.

(b) Hirakud dam is built across river Mahanadi.

(iv) (a) Geothermal energy is not popular in India because geothermal power plants and systems are expensive to build and operate.

(b) Solar energy is gaining popularity because as a tropical country India receives about 5000 trillion KWh solar energy per year that can help to produce a large amount of free energy and it is renewable and an inexhaustible source of energy.

(c) Petroleum is considered a harmful source of energy because after burning it emits large amounts of carbon dioxide and greenhouse gas which leads to global warming.

9. (i) Agriculture is considered an important sector of Indian economy because

(a) Agriculture sector provides employment to vast section of the population in our country.

(b) It provides food and food products like rice, wheat milk, etc. to human population and fodder for livestock.

(ii) (a) The practise of cultivation of crops as well as raising of animals/livestock simultaneously is popularly known as mixed farming.

(b) An advantage of mixed farming is that it gives security to the farmers because even if the crops fail they can rely on their cattle rearing for income.

(iii) (a) West Bengal is a leading producer of jute because the region has a hot and humid climate which is favourable for jute production.

(b) Millets are fast becoming the popular food crops because they contain various nutrients like iron, calcium, zinc and magnesium.

(c) More than two ratoon crops are not advisable for sugarcane farmers because it degrades the quality of the crops. The sucrose content and overall quality of sugarcane may diminish with each subsequent ratoon crop, leading to lower returns for farmers.

(iv) (a) Plucking two tender leaves and a bud or shoot together is known as fine plucking.

(b) Karnataka leads in coffee production among the states of India.

(c) Cotton is grown as a kharif crop in India because it requires a long growing season with high temperatures and adequate water availability, which coincide with the monsoon season. The warm and humid conditions during the kharif season are beneficial to cotton growth, leading to better yields.

10. (i) (a) On the basis of ownership Visakhapatnam steel plant is a public sector based industry, managed by Rashtriya Ispat Nigam.

(b) Cooperative sector industries are owned and managed on cooperatives basis by those who are producers of the raw materials required for industry. Example- dairy industry (Amul).

(ii) (a) The rearing of silkworms for the production of silk is called 'sericulture'.

(b) Integrated steel plants are the plants where all the processes of making steel such as melting of iron ore, processing of steel and shaping of metals are carried out at one place.

(iii) (a) Mini steel plants help to conserve coal due to their smaller scale and more efficient processes. These plants utilise scrap steel as a primary raw material, which reduces the dependence on coal for iron ore smelting.

(b) Location of sugar industry is shifting to the Southern part of India because the cane produced in South India has higher sucrose content which is of superior quality and gives higher yield.

(c) The electronic industry is growing at a fast rate due to advancements in technology, and increased consumer demand for electronic devices.

(iv) (a) Two conditions favouring the location of the cotton textile industry in Ahmedabad are

- **Availability of Raw Materials** Ahmedabad is close to major cotton-growing regions in Gujarat, ensuring a steady and reliable supply of raw materials for textile production.
- **Availability of Skilled Labour** The city has a skilled workforce with experience in textile manufacturing, providing a ready labour pool for the industry's needs.

(b) An advantage of locating the Iron and steel industry at Rourkela is availability of iron ore from Sundergarh and Keonjhar district.

11. (i) Road transport is an important means of transport in India because of the following reasons

(a) It is more suitable for short distance travel and it connects small villages and places where other means of transport cannot reach.

(b) It saves cost of transportation from one station to another station and it also saves the time.

(ii) (a) Northern plain is best suited for the development of railways because the land is fertile and levelled in the region.

(b) Railways are managed by the central government in India to ensure uniformity, efficiency and seamless connectivity across the country.

(iii) The two advantages of inland water transport are as follows

(a) **Cost-effective** It is often cheaper than other modes of transport for bulky and non-perishable goods, as it requires less fuel and infrastructure maintenance compared to road or rail transport.

(b) **Environmentally Friendly** Inland water transport has lower carbon emissions and pollution compared to road and air transport, making it a more sustainable option for freight transportation.

A disadvantage of inland water transport is that it may not reach all areas, limiting accessibility compared to road or rail transport, especially in regions with uneven terrain or inadequate water depth.

(iv) The three reasons due to which airways are becoming a popular means of transport in modern India are

(a) It is the fastest means of movement from one place to the other for a vast country like India.

(b) It has reduced the distance by minimising the travel time.

(c) It helps to reach the large and difficult terrain places which are inaccessible through other modes of transport.

12. (i) (a) Solid waste management method is depicted here.

(b) One way to implement solid waste management at home is by segregating waste into different bins for recyclables, organic waste and non-recyclable waste. This helps in efficient disposal and promotes recycling and composting of biodegradable waste.

(ii) Waste accumulation can be harmful in the following ways

(a) Waste accumulation has bad impact on the quality of air around us. When we dump waste at the site and cover it with Earth then methane gas gets generated by decomposition of solid waste in landfills. This methane is not good for our atmosphere and warms up the air temperature which absorbs the Sun's heat.

(b) The sewage waste coming from factories and industries reaches the water bodies and causes many water related diseases like diarrhea and typhoid.

(iii) Waste generated in the following sectors may be made useful in the following ways

(a) **Household** Household waste can be made useful through composting organic waste. For example, kitchen waste can be composted to produce nutrient-rich compost, which can then be used as fertiliser for gardening or landscaping.

(b) **Industry** Industrial waste can be made useful through recycling and reuse. For example, manufacturing waste such as scrap metal or plastic can be recycled into new products or materials, reducing the need for virgin resources and minimising environmental impact.

(c) **Agriculture** Agricultural waste can be made useful through biomass conversion. For example, crop residues such as straw or husks can be converted into biofuels or used as feedstock for biogas production, providing renewable energy sources for agricultural operations or other purposes.

(iv) (a) Two uses of composting are

- **Soil Amendment** Compost improves soil structure, increases soil fertility, and enhances its water retention capacity, making it an excellent organic fertiliser for gardens, lawns and agricultural fields.
- **Waste Reduction** Composting reduces the volume of organic waste sent to landfills, thereby minimising greenhouse gas emissions and helping to alleviate environmental pollution.

(b) Landfills are setup far away from cities due to the following reasons

- **Public Health and Safety** Landfills can attract pests like rodents and insects, which can spread diseases. Additionally, decomposing waste can generate harmful gases and toxic liquid that can pollute the air and water near the landfill.
- **Odour and Aesthetics** Landfills can produce unpleasant odours, which would be undesirable for residents living nearby areas.

ICSE Solved Paper 2025

Geography (Fully Solved)

General Instructions

1. Answers to this Paper must be written on the answer sheet provided separately.
2. You will not be allowed to write during the first 15 minutes. This time is to be spent in reading the question paper.
3. The time given at the head of this Paper is the time allowed for writing the answers.
4. Part I is compulsory. All questions from Part I are to be attempted. A total of five questions are to be attempted from Part II.
5. The intended marks for questions or parts of questions are given in brackets ( ).

Time : 2 Hrs **Max. Marks : 80**

Part - I

(30 Marks)

Attempt all questions from this Part.

1 Study the extract of the Survey of India Map Sheet No. G43S10 and answer the following questions **(2)**

(i) (a) Give the six-figure grid reference for spot height. 437 in the southeastern part of the map extract.

(b) Aman, a local craftsman, wants to sell his product to a large gathering to earn money instantly.

1. Which settlement should he go to?

2. Name the month in which he should visit the settlement named by you above.

(ii) (a) On which bank of the Sukli nadi is the settlement of Pamera situated? **(2)**

(b) Identify the settlement pattern seen in the grid square 6732.

(iii) Roshan, while travelling from Sirori to Tokra, observed that the surface water sources are dry except for the reservoir near Tokra. **(2)**

(a) What according to you may be the reason for the presence of water in the reservoir in 6832 near Tokra settlement?

(b) State whether this reservoir is artificial or natural source of water.

(iv) (a) What is the direct distance between Gulabganj to Pithapura? Give your answer in kilometre. **(2)**

(b) Mention the compass direction of Pithapura from Gulabganj.

(v) (a) Name two man-made features seen in the grid square 6534. **(2)**

(b) Define contour interval.

2 On the outline map of India provided **(10)**

(i) Mark and label the Nathu-La pass.

(ii) Shade and name the coastal plain that occupies a large part of Kerala.

(iii) Mark and label Digboi.

(iv) Mark and label Chilka lake.

(v) Mark with arrows and name the wind that brings rainfall to Tamil Nadu coast during winter.

(vi) Mark and label the River Sutlej.

(vii) Mark and label the Standard Meridian of India.

(viii) Mark and label Satpura range.

(ix) Shade and label the Chota Nagpur plateau.

(x) Mark and label Visakhapatnam.

3 Choose the correct answers to the questions from the given options. **(10)**
(Do not copy the questions, write the correct answers only.)

(i) **Assertion** (A) Mumbai receives more rainfall than Pune.
Reason (R) Mumbai gets rain from Arabian Sea branch of South-West monsoon.

(a) Both (A) and (R) are true and (R) is the correct explanation for (A).
(b) Both (A) and (R) are true and (R) is not the correct explanation for (A).
(c) (A) is true and (R) is false
(d) (A) is false and (R) is true

(ii) Which of the following pairs of soils displays similar characteristics in terms of their colour and texture?

(a) Alluvial soil and laterite soil (b) Black soil and red soil
(c) Red soil and laterite soil (d) Alluvial soil and black soil

(iii) The type of natural vegetation shown in the picture given below is found on

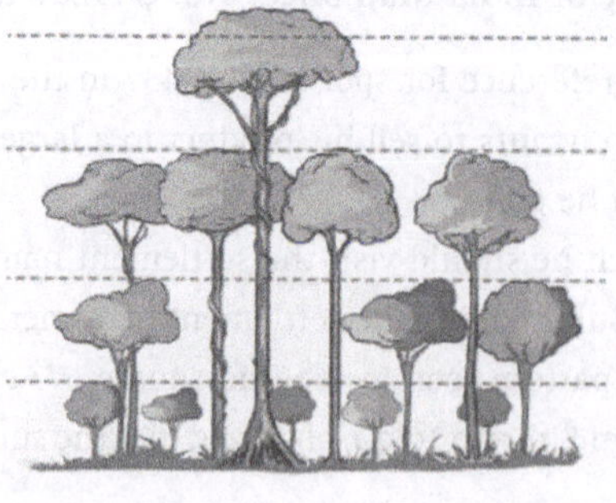

(a) Tropical desert (b) Tropical deciduous (c) Tropical evergreen (d) Littoral forest

(iv) Which of the following prevents wastage of water?

(a) Canal (b) Well (c) Sprinkler (d) Tube well

(v) Balaghat : Manganese :: Mumbai High :

(a) Copper (b) Coal (c) Iron Ore (d) Petroleum

(vi) A microbiological process that loosens the bark of a crop and facilitates removal of fibre from the stalk

(a) Rolling (b) Ratooning (c) Retting (d) Fermentation

(vii) Which industry amongst the following has revolutionised the lifestyle of the Indian masses in recent years?

(a) Cotton Textile (b) Electronic (c) Iron and Steel (d) Sugar

(vii) Which of the following household products is associated with the petrochemical industry?

(a) Glass bottle (b) Wooden chopping board
(c) Kitchen knife (d) Plastic mug

(ix) Raman, a dairy farmer in Ludhiana, supplies milk within the city on a daily basis. Which mode of transport is he most likely to use

(a) Railway (b) Roadway (c) Airway (d) Waterway

(x) The collection of discarded materials and converting them into useful products ist

(a) Recycling (b) Processing (c) Reducing (d) Composting

Part - II

(50 Marks)

Attempt any five questions from this Part.

4 (i) 'Severe cyclonic storms are often formed over the Bay of Bengal during the retreating monsoon season.' **(2)**

(a) Name two states that are affected by tropical cyclones on the eastern coast of India.

(b) The temperate cyclones cause less damage than the tropical cyclones. Give any two points to support this statement.

(ii) (a) Name the local wind that causes rainfall in the states of Assam and West Bengal in the month of April. **(2)**

(b) How is this rainfall beneficial for the states mentioned above?

(iii) With reference to Figure A and Figure B given below, answer the questions that follow. **(3)**

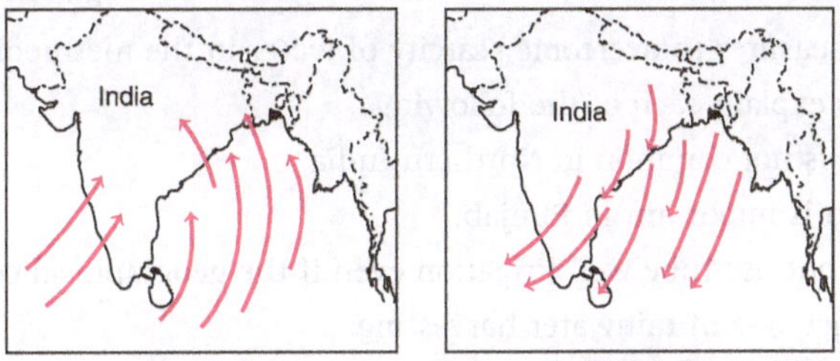

Figure A Figure B

(a) Name the winds shown by arrows in Figure A and Figure B.

(b) How is the wind shown in Figure A different from the one shown in Figure B?

(iv) Study the climate data of station X and answer the following questions **(3)**

Month	Jan	Feb	Mar	Apr	May	Jun	July	Aug	Sep	Oct	Nov	Dec
Temp (°C)	24.0	25.4	26.7	28.3	30.0	28.9	27.6	27.4	27.3	27.1	27.0	25.0
Rainfall (cm)	0.25	0.25	-	-	1.75	50.2	61.0	37.0	27.0	4.75	1.50	-

(a) What is the annual range of temperature for station X?

(b) Which is the wettest month?

(c) Name the wind which brings rainfall for station X during the rainy season.

5 (i) The Ganga Plain is known for its fertile soil, it is often referred to as the Food bowl of India. This region supports a variety of crops such as rice, wheat, pulses, jute and sugarcane. **(2)**

(a) Name the soil that is found in large parts of Ganga plain.

(b) Give two properties of this soil which helps it to produce a variety of crops.

(ii) (a) What is meant by soil erosion? **(2)**

(b) Name any two agents of soil erosion.

(iii) Give a geographical reason to explain each of the following. (3)

(a) Soil conservation is the need of the hour.

(b) Red soil has a poor water retention capacity.

(c) Laterite soils are infertile.

(iv) With reference to black soil of India, answer the following questions. (3)

(a) How is this soil formed?

(b) How is this soil able to retain moisture for a long period?

(c) Mention any two minerals present in this soil.

6 (i) India has lost 2.33 million hectares of tree cover since the year 2000. This is equivalent to a six percent decrease in tree cover during this period. *Source: The Indian Express, Date 12th April, 2024* (2)

(a) Mention any two causes of the decrease in the forest cover of India.

(b) Name a conservation method that may be used to help in increasing the forest cover.

(ii) Mention the climatic condition suitable for the development of tropical evergreen forest. (2)

(iii) State any three differences between tropical deciduous and tropical desert vegetation. (3)

(iv) (a) Give any two reasons for the great diversity of natural vegetation in India. (3)

(b) How do the forests help in maintenance of air quality?

7 (i) Mention any one advantage and any one disadvantage of well irrigation. (2)

(ii) Suggest any two measures to overcome scarcity of water in the metropolitan cities of India. (2)

(iii) Give one reason to explain each of the following (3)

(a) Tank irrigation is not common in Northern India.

(b) Canal irrigation is important in Punjab.

(c) All farmers do not use tube well irrigation even if the geographical condition is favourable.

(iv) State any three objectives of rainwater harvesting. (3)

8 (i) With the rising price of fossil fuel every passing day, it is very important to develop non-conventional energy resource. *Bulletin-Department of Non-conventional Sources of Energy* (2)

(a) Name a non-conventional energy source that can be harnessed by taking advantage of India's vast coastline.

(b) State one advantage of using geothermal energy.

(ii) (a) How is Biogas formed? (2)

(b) Mention any one advantage of Biogas over other non-conventional energy resources.

(iii) Give a reason for each of the following. (3)

(a) Iron ore is called a versatile mineral.

(b) Windmills set up on agricultural lands are beneficial to farmers.

(c) Coal is the most preferred source of energy in Indian industries.

(iv) (3)

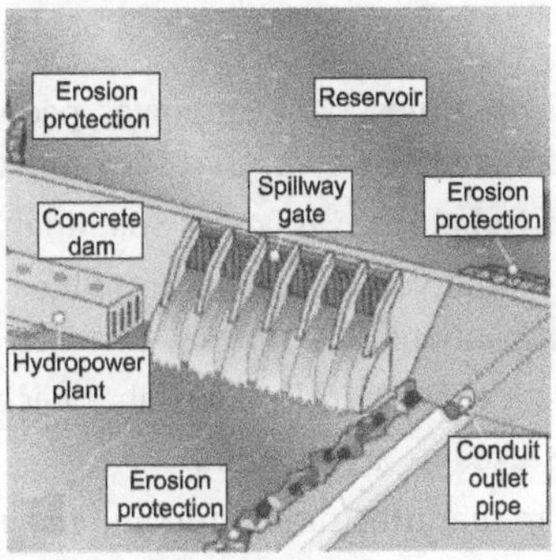

(a) Identify the type of energy being generated in the picture given above.

(b) State why this type of energy is cheaper in the long run.

(c) Name a power project associated with the generation of this energy in the Northern part of India.

9 (i) Mention two climatic conditions that favour the cultivation of groundnut. (2)

(ii) Give any two reasons why Maharashtra has emerged as an important sugarcane producing state. (2)

(iii) Give one reason to explain each of the following. (3)

(a) Trees are planted in between the rows of coffee plants.

(b) Cotton cultivation requires plenty of cheap labour.

(c) Hill slopes are best suited for tea cultivation.

(iv) Explain the following (3)

(a) Mixed farming (b) Zayad (c) Transplantation

10 (i) State any two factors that are responsible for the growth of the cotton textile industry in Kolkata. (2)

(ii) 'Karnataka is the leading state for silk production in India'. (2)

Give any two reasons to justify the above statement.

(iii) (a) Name the Iron and Steel industry located at Chhattisgarh. (3)

(b) From where does the industry named by you above get its supply of the following?

1. Iron ore 2. Coal

(iv) Raghav has been given a project by his teacher in which he has to write about the by-products of an industry that is used for preparing shoe polish, carbon paper and cardboard. (3)

(a) Which industry will he be writing about?

(b) Name any two by-products of the industry mentioned by you.

11 (i) Why is a well-developed transport network important for India? (2)

(ii) Mention any two advantages of road transport. (2)

(iii) Name the following (3)

(a) The mode of transport that ensures comfortable journey, especially for elders and children.

(b) The highway connecting Silchar in Assam to Porbandar in Gujarat.

(c) The cheapest means of transport for bulky goods.

(iv) Give a reason for each of the following. (3)

(a) Airways are the most efficient mode of transport to connect North-East India with the rest of the country.

(b) Railways are easily developed in the Northern plains of India.

(c) Rivers of peninsular India are not ideal for inland water transport.

12 (i) (a) Give a reason for a substantial rise of E-waste in India **(2)**

(b) What is dumping?

(ii) 'You cannot protect environment unless you empower people, you inform them and help them to understand that these resources are their own, that they must protect them'. **(2)**

Wangari Maathar (recipient of Nobel Prize 2004 for Sustainable Developments)

As a responsible student how would you contribute to reduce and manage the waste generated in your surroundings. Explain by giving suitable examples.

(iii) With reference to the 3Rs, give a term that best describes each of the following. **(3)**

(a) An empty soft drink can is used as a pen stand.

(b) Old scrap papers are used to manufacture handmade paper.

(c) No food is wasted in the household.

(iv) Give a reason for the following statements. **(3)**

(a) Organic manure should replace chemical fertilisers.

(b) There should be a ban on the use of polythene and plastic products.

(c) Manual handling of waste must be avoided.

Answers

1. (i) (a) 673295

(b) 1. Malgoan or Pamera both are correct.

2. March

(ii) (a) Right bank (b) Scattered

(iii) (a) Sipu Nadi (b) Artificial

(iv) (a) 2.25 km (b) North-East

(v) (a) Settlement, Roads, Well, Temple, Post-office.

(b) **Contour Interval** A contour interval refers to the vertical distance or elevation difference between adjacent contour lines.

2.

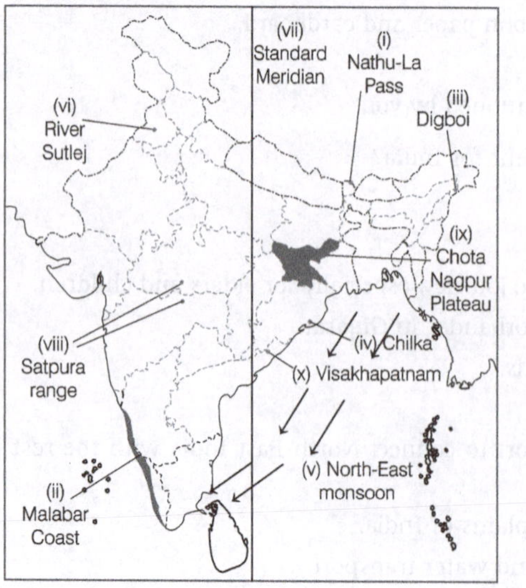

3. (i) (a) Both (A) and (R) are true and (R) is the correct explanation for (A).

(ii) (c) Red soil and laterite soil

(iii) (d) Littoral forest (iv) (c) Sprinkler

(v) (d) Petroleum (vi) (c) Retting

(vii) (b) Electronic (viii) (d) Plastic mug

(ix) (b) Roadway (x) (a) Recycling

4. (i) (a) Two states that are affected by tropical cyclones on the eastern coast of India are West Bengal and Odisha.

(b) The temperate cyclones cause less damage than the tropical cyclones due to the following reasons

- **Lower Wind Speeds** Temperate cyclones have weaker winds than tropical cyclones, causing less damage.
- **Wider Area of Influence** Temperate cyclones affect a larger area with less intensity, while tropical cyclones are more concentrated and destructive.

(ii) (a) The local wind that causes rainfall in the states of Assam and West Bengal in the month of April is the 'Norwesters' or 'Kalbaisakhi'.

(b) This rainfall benefits Assam and West Bengal by aiding crop growth and cooling down temperatures, providing relief from the heat.

(iii) (a) The winds shown by arrows in Figure A represent the South-West monsoon winds. The winds shown by arrows in Figure B represent the North-East monsoon winds.

(b) The wind shown in Figure A is different from the one shown in Figure B in the following ways

- **South-West Monsoon Winds (Figure A)** These winds blow from the Indian Ocean towards the Indian subcontinent during the summer season (June to September), bringing heavy rainfall to most parts of India.
- **North-East Monsoon Winds (Figure B)** These winds blow from the land (India) towards the Indian Ocean during the winter season (October to December), bringing rainfall mainly to the southeastern coast of India (Tamil Nadu, Andhra Pradesh, etc.).

(iv) (a) Annual range of temperature = Highest temperature – Lowest temperature

= 30.0°C (May) - 24.0°C (January)

= 6.0°C

(b) July is the wettest month.

(c) The wind that brings rainfall to station X during the rainy season is the South-West monsoon winds.

5. (i) (a) The soil found in large parts of the Ganga Plain is Alluvial soil.

(b) Two properties of alluvial soil that help in producing a variety of crops

- **High Fertility** It is rich in nutrients like potash, phosphoric acid and lime, which support the growth of crops like rice, wheat and sugarcane.
- **Good Moisture Retention** This soil has the ability to retain water, making it suitable for both rain-fed and irrigated agriculture.

(ii) (a) Soil erosion is the removal of the top fertile layer of soil by natural forces such as wind and water, leading to the loss of nutrients and reduced soil fertility.

(b) Two agents of soil erosion are wind and water.

(iii) (a) Soil conservation is the need of the hour as soil is essential for agriculture and vegetation, but erosion, deforestation, and overuse reduce its fertility. Soil conservation is necessary to prevent land degradation, maintain food security, and protect the environment.

(b) Red soil is rich in iron but has a sandy texture and lacks humus, making it less capable of retaining water. This results in quick drainage and lower moisture availability for crops.

(c) Laterite soil undergoes intense leaching due to heavy rainfall, washing away essential nutrients. As a result, it becomes acidic and lacks fertility, making it unsuitable for most crops without proper treatment.

(iv) (a) Black soil is formed from the weathering of volcanic rocks, primarily from the Deccan Plateau region.

(b) Black soil has a high clay content, which allows it to absorb and retain moisture for a long time, even during dry seasons.

(c) Two minerals present in this soil are iron and magnesium.

6. (i) (a) Two causes of the decrease in forest cover in India

- **Deforestation for agriculture and urbanisation** Large areas of forests are cleared to make space for farming, industries, and expanding cities.
- **Illegal logging and overexploitation** Excessive cutting of trees for timber, firewood and other commercial purposes leads to forest depletion.

(b) A conservation method that may be used to help in increasing the forest cover is afforestation, i.e, planting new trees in deforested areas.

(ii) (a) The climatic condition suitable for the development of tropical evergreen forest are

- **High Temperature** The temperature remains warm and humid throughout the year, typically ranging between 25°C to 27°C.
- **Heavy Rainfall** These forests require more than 200 cm of annual rainfall, which is evenly distributed throughout the year.

(iii) Three differences between tropical deciduous and tropical desert vegetation are

Tropical Deciduous Vegetation	Tropical Desert Vegetation
Found in monsoon regions with moderate rainfall (100-200 cm).	Found in areas with extremely low rainfall (less than 25 cm), hot and dry climate.
They shed leaves in dry season to conserve water.	They have small, thorny, or wax-coated leaves to reduce water loss.
Examples-Sal, teak, and neem	Examples-cactus, acacia, and date palm

(iv) (a) Two reasons for the great diversity of natural vegetation in India are

- **Varied Climate** India has diverse climatic conditions, ranging from tropical in the South to temperate and alpine in the North. Different temperatures, rainfall patterns and humidity levels support a wide range of vegetation types.
- **Diverse Landforms** India has mountains, plateaus, plains and coastal regions, each providing unique soil types and environmental conditions that influence the growth of different plant species.

(b) The forests help in maintenance of air quality in the following ways

- **Absorption of Carbon Dioxide** Trees absorb CO_2 during photosynthesis, reducing greenhouse gases and improving air quality.
- **Release of Oxygen** Forests release oxygen (O_2), which is essential for life.

7. (i) **Advantage of Well Irrigation**

- **Low Cost and Easy to Construct** Wells can be dug at a low cost and require simple technology, making them accessible for small farmers.

Disadvantage of Well Irrigation

- **Limited Water Supply** Wells depend on groundwater, which can dry up during summers or in areas with low water tables.

(ii) Two measures to overcome water scarcity in metropolitan cities of India are

- **Rainwater Harvesting** Collecting and storing rainwater from rooftops and open spaces can help in recharging groundwater and meeting daily water needs.
- **Wastewater Recycling and Reuse** Treating and recycling wastewater for non-drinking purposes like gardening, cleaning and industrial use can reduce water wastage.

(iii) (a) Tank irrigation is not common in Northern India because of flat terrain. Northern India, especially the Indo-Gangetic Plain, has a flat landscape, making it difficult to construct tanks, which require natural depressions to store water.

(b) Canal irrigation is important in Punjab because the region has a network of perennial rivers like the Satluj, Beas, and Ravi, which provide a continuous water supply for irrigation through canals.

(c) All farmers do not use tube well irrigation even if the geographical conditions are favourable because the installation and maintenance of tube wells are expensive. Small and marginal farmers may not afford the high initial cost of setting up tube wells and the electricity or diesel expenses required to operate them.

(iv) The three objectives of rainwater harvesting are

- **Conservation of Water** To collect and store rainwater for future use, reducing dependence on groundwater and other water sources.
- **Groundwater Recharge** To replenish underground water levels by allowing rainwater to seep into the soil, preventing depletion.
- **Flood and Soil Erosion Control** To reduce surface runoff, preventing floods and soil erosion, especially in urban and hilly areas.

8. (i) (a) A non-conventional energy source that can be harnessed using India's vast coastline is Tidal Energy.

(b) Geothermal energy is a clean and sustainable source of power, producing minimal pollution and reducing dependence on fossil fuels.

(ii) (a) Biogas is formed through the anaerobic decomposition of organic waste like animal dung, plant material and kitchen waste by bacteria. This process called anaerobic digestion produces methane-rich gas, which can be used as fuel.

(b) Biogas is a continuous and reliable source of energy, unlike solar and wind energy, which depend on weather conditions.

(iii) (a) Iron ore is called a versatile mineral because it is the primary raw material for making steel, which is used in various industries like construction, transportation, machinery and infrastructure development.

(b) Windmills set up on agricultural lands are beneficial to farmers because they generate additional income for farmers through land lease payments while allowing them to continue farming activities beneath the wind turbines.

(c) Coal is the most preferred source of energy in Indian industries because it is abundantly available, affordable and provides a reliable energy source for industries like steel, cement and power generation.

(iv) (a) The type of energy being generated in the picture is Hydroelectric Energy.

(b) This type of energy is cheaper in the long run because

- It uses renewable water resources, which do not require fuel costs.
- Hydroelectric power plants have low operational and maintenance costs after initial construction. (any one point)

(c) A power project associated with the generation of this energy in Northern India is the Bhakra Nangal Hydroelectric Project on the Sutlej river.

9. (i) The two climatic conditions that favour the cultivation of groundnut are

- **Warm Temperature** Groundnut requires a warm climate with temperatures between 20°C to 30°C for proper growth.
- **Moderate Rainfall** It grows best in areas with 50-100 cm of rainfall, as excessive moisture can damage the crop.

(ii) Maharashtra has emerged as an important sugarcane-producing state due to the following reasons

- **Favourable Climate** The state has a tropical climate with hot and humid conditions, which are ideal for sugarcane cultivation. Additionally, moderate rainfall and well-distributed irrigation facilities support high yields.
- **Well-Developed Irrigation Facilities** Despite having relatively low rainfall in some regions, Maharashtra has well-developed canal and well irrigation systems, ensuring a continuous water supply for sugarcane crops.

(iii) (a) Trees are planted in between the rows of coffee plants to provide shade and protect the coffee plants from direct sunlight and strong winds, which can affect their growth and quality.

(b) Cotton cultivation requires plenty of cheap labour because most of the processes, like sowing, picking and ginning are done manually, requiring a large workforce.

(c) Hill slopes are best suited for tea cultivation because they ensure proper drainage, preventing waterlogging, which is harmful to tea plants. Additionally, the cool and humid climate of hills favours tea growth.

(iv) (a) Mixed farming is a type of agriculture where both crops and livestock are raised on the same farm.

(b) Zayad is the short cropping season between the Rabi and Kharif seasons in India, from March to June.

(c) Transplantation is the process of growing seedlings in a nursery and then shifting them to the main field for better growth.

10. (i) The growth of the cotton textile industry in Kolkata is due to the following factors

- **Availability of Cheap Labour** Kolkata has a large workforce, including migrant labourers from neighbouring states like Bihar and Odisha, which helps in keeping production costs low.
- **Well-Connected Transportation System** The city has a good network of roads, railways and a major port, making it easy to transport raw materials (cotton) and finished goods both within India and internationally.

(ii) Karnataka is the leading state for silk production in India due to the following reasons

- **Favourable Climate** Karnataka has a moderate climate with suitable temperature and humidity, which is ideal for silkworm rearing and mulberry cultivation.
- **Availability of Mulberry Leaves** The state has extensive mulberry plantations, providing a steady food supply for silkworms, essential for high-quality silk production.

(iii) (a) The Iron and Steel industry located in Chhattisgarh is the Bhilai Steel Plant.

(b) Sources of raw materials for Bhilai Steel Plant

- **Iron Ore** Sourced from the Dalli-Rajhara mines in Chhattisgarh.
- **Coal** Supplied from the Korba and Jharia coalfields.

(iv) (a) Raghav will be writing about the Sugar Industry because its by-products are used in making shoe polish, carbon paper and cardboard.

(b) Two by-products of the sugar industry are bagasse and molasses.

11. (i) A well-developed transport network is important for India because

- **Boosts Trade and Economy** Efficient transport helps in the movement of goods across the country and supports industries, agriculture and exports.
- **Enhances Connectivity** It connects remote and rural areas with cities, improving access to markets, healthcare and education.

(ii) Two advantages of road transport are

- **Door-to-Door Service** Road transport provides direct delivery of goods and passengers to their destination, reducing the need for additional handling.
- **Flexibility and Accessibility** Roads can be built in remote areas, making transport possible even in hilly and rural regions where other modes may not be available.

(iii) (a) Rail transport ensures a comfortable journey, especially for elders and children, as trains provide seating, sleeping arrangements and other facilities.

(b) The highway connecting Silchar in Assam to Porbandar in Gujarat is part of the East-West Corridor.

(c) The cheapest means of transport for bulky goods is water transport, as it is cost-effective and fuel-efficient, especially for long-distance trade.

(iv) (a) Airways are the most efficient mode of transport to connect North-East India with the rest of the country because the region has rugged terrain, dense forests and frequent floods, making road and rail transport difficult.

(b) Railways are easily developed in the Northern plains of India because the region has flat and fertile land, which makes track construction and maintenance easier compared to hilly or plateau regions.

(c) Rivers of peninsular India are not ideal for inland water transport because they are seasonal, with water levels fluctuating throughout the year. Additionally, these rivers have many waterfalls, rapids and rocky beds, making navigation difficult.

12. (i) (a) The increase in the use of electronic devices such as mobile phones, computers, televisions and home appliances, along with rapid technological advancements, has led to a substantial rise in E-waste in India.

(b) Dumping is the practice of disposing of waste materials, including industrial, household and hazardous waste, in an uncontrolled manner, often in landfills, open spaces or water bodies.

(ii) As a responsible student, I can contribute to reducing and managing waste in my surroundings through the following steps

- **Reduce Waste Generation** Use reusable items like steel water bottles, cloth bags and lunch boxes instead of plastic ones.
- **Spread Awareness** Organise cleanliness drives in school and the local community.

(iii) (a) **Reuse** Using an item again for a different purpose instead of throwing it away.

(b) **Recycle** Processing waste materials into new products to prevent waste.

(c) **Reduce** Using resources wisely to minimise waste generation.

(iv) (a) Organic manure should replace chemical fertilisers because it improves soil fertility naturally without harming beneficial microbes. Unlike chemical fertilisers, which can degrade soil quality over time, organic manure enhances soil structure and retains moisture, leading to sustainable farming.

(b) There should be a ban on the use of polythene and plastic products because they are non-biodegradable and cause severe environmental pollution. Plastic waste clogs drains, harms marine and wildlife, and releases toxic chemicals when burned, contributing to climate change.

(c) Manual handling of waste must be avoided because it poses serious health risks to workers due to exposure to harmful bacteria, toxic chemicals and sharp objects. Instead, proper waste management systems, including protective gear and mechanised waste disposal, should be implemented for safety and hygiene.